T0285939

THE BOOK OF MORMON

■

THE EARLIEST TEXT

The Book of Mormon

The Earliest Text

SECOND EDITION

EDITED BY

Royal Skousen

Yale
UNIVERSITY PRESS
New Haven and London

© 2009, 2022 by Royal Skousen
First edition 2009. Second edition 2022.

Library of Congress Control Number: 2021948233

ISBN 978-0-300-26337-4 (paperback : alk. paper)

A catalogue record for this book is available from the British Library.
This paper meets the requirements of ANSI/NISO Z39.48-1992 (Permanence of Paper).

PRINTED IN THE UNITED STATES OF AMERICA

10 9 8 7 6 5 4 3 2 1

Contents

Introduction

Many readers of the Book of Mormon simply assume that the modern printed editions contain the same text that Joseph Smith originally dictated to his scribes in 1828–29, but in fact even the first edition of the Book of Mormon (published in 1830) ended up with a considerable number of changes, including many that had entered the text during its dictation. Most of the early changes were made when the scribes transcribed the printer's manuscript from the original manuscript; but there were also many changes that the 1830 typesetter, John Gilbert, introduced into the text. Subsequent editions have continued to make changes in the text, including numerous grammatical emendations in an attempt to eliminate the nonstandard English from the original text of the Book of Mormon. All these layers of change have resulted in a very complex textual history, one that has led to a massive scholarly project.

The result is the critical text of the Book of Mormon. A critical text provides, first of all, the original text for a work, to the extent it can be determined by scholarly means. Typically there is an apparatus—printed either on each page of the critical text or at the end of the work—that gives in a succinct way a description of the history of that text, namely, how the original has changed over time and when and who made the changes. Providing a list of alternative readings is what makes a text a critical text. And this Book of Mormon is a critical text: in its appendix is an apparatus that lists 724 significant changes that the text has undergone, from its original dictation to its most recent publication.

This book is the culmination of over thirty years of work on the Critical Text Project of the Book of Mormon. The ultimate goal of this project has been to restore the original English-language text of the Book of Mormon, and to provide a history of the changes the text has undergone. The first edition of *The Book of Mormon: The Earliest Text* was published in 2009 by Yale University Press in a large-size hardback format, with an introductory essay by my colleague Grant Hardy and an editor's preface by me. Now that the Critical Text Project is coming to completion, Yale University Press is publishing a second edition, but in a more compact format and with this new introduction that describes in some detail the Book of Mormon Critical Text Project and its relationship to the Yale edition.

The Two Manuscripts

The original goal of the Book of Mormon Critical Text Project was to make detailed transcripts of the two manuscripts of the Book of Mormon—the original manuscript and the printer's manuscript—and then to publish those transcripts since prior to this project there had never been any published transcripts of either manuscript.

The original manuscript (𝒪) is the manuscript the scribes wrote down as Joseph Smith dictated the Book of Mormon, initially in 1828 (including the lost 116 pages which contained the book of Lehi as well as the first chapter or so of the book of Mosiah) and then in 1829 (basically giving us the Book of Mormon as we have it today). For that second part, Oliver Cowdery was the main scribe. In October 1841, Joseph Smith placed this manuscript in the cornerstone of the Nauvoo House, a hotel being built at the time in Nauvoo, Illinois. When the manuscript was retrieved in 1882, most of it had been destroyed by water and mold. Today, only about 28 percent of 𝒪 remains, most of which is held by the Church of Jesus Christ of Latter-day Saints (the LDS Church).

The printer's manuscript (𝒫) is a copy of 𝒪 that the scribes made and then took to E. B. Grandin's print shop in Palmyra, New York, for the printing of the 1830 edition of the Book of Mormon. The scribes' copy work took over five months, from August 1829 through January 1830. Again, Oliver Cowdery was the main scribe. 𝒫 is a copy of 𝒪, but because 𝒪 is only 28 percent extant, 𝒫 is more than just a copy: for 72 percent of the text, it represents the earliest extant version of the text. Unlike the original manuscript, 𝒫 is virtually extant, with only a few lines of text missing at the bottom of the first leaf. 𝒫 was earlier owned by the Reorganized Church of Jesus Christ of Latter Day Saints (the RLDS Church, renamed the Community of Christ in 2001), but in 2017 the LDS Church purchased the manuscript from the Community of Christ.

Publishing the Transcripts

In the summer of 1988, my colleague John W. Welch arranged for the project to get on loan a set of clear photographs for both manuscripts: black-and-white ultraviolet photographs of 𝒪 (from the LDS Church) and a large photocopy of 𝒫 (from the RLDS Church). From these photographs, I was able to make my initial transcripts and then compare my work against independent transcripts made by paid research assistants.

Finally, I went through the difficult process of comparing the transcripts against the actual manuscripts, including newly discovered fragments of 𝒪 held by the Wilford Wood family (about two percent of the original text) as well as a smaller collection of fragments from two leaves of 𝒪 held by the descendants of Ada Cheney.

In 2001, after 13 years of work, my completed transcripts of 𝒪 and 𝒫 were published by the Foundation for Ancient Research and Mormon Studies (FARMS) and Brigham Young University (BYU), in two volumes. Volume 1 covers the 28 percent of 𝒪 that remains, and volume 2 covers the virtually intact printer's manuscript, in two parts.

Publishing Photographs of the Manuscripts

With each volume of transcripts, I was able to publish some photographs: from 𝒪, four intact pages and three partial pages from the LDS Church's collection, plus six large fragments from the Wilford Wood collection; and from 𝒫, a selection of eight pages.

The next step, of course, has been to publish photographs (along with their transcripts) of all the extant pages and reconstructed fragments for the two manuscripts. We are now in the middle of doing this work as part of the Joseph Smith Papers (JSP). In 2015, my transcript of 𝒫 along with color photographs of all 468 pages of 𝒫 were published by the JSP, again in two parts:

> *Printer's Manuscript of the Book of Mormon,* edited by Royal Skousen and Robin Scott Jensen. Volume 3, Revelations and Translations, Joseph Smith Papers (Salt Lake City, Utah: The Church Historian's Press, 2015)
>
> > Part 1: Title Page, 1830 Preface; 1 Nephi 1 — Alma 35
> > Part 2: Alma 36 — Moroni 10; Witness Statements

For each individual manuscript page, the JSP volume provides a two-page spread, with the photograph on the left side and my transcript on the right.

We are now doing the same for the original manuscript, but it has taken a lot more time to obtain sufficiently legible photographs of 𝒪 (the result of its 41 years in the wet and moldy cornerstone of the Nauvoo House). The damaged manuscript is being re-photographed using multispectral imaging. And for many leaves of 𝒪, all the photographs of the individual fragments ("the puzzle pieces") have to be put together to produce a composite photograph to go along with the transcript. Plans are for this volume to appear in late 2021:

> *Original Manuscript of the Book of Mormon,* edited by Royal Skousen and Robin Scott Jensen. Volume 5, Revelations and Translations, Joseph Smith Papers (Salt Lake City, Utah: The Church Historian's Press)

Changes in the Text

It turns out that the Critical Text Project has become much more than publishing transcripts and photographs of the two manuscripts. One important finding has been that the manuscripts show that the text had undergone numerous changes right from the very beginning of the transmission process. Just three months into this project, by August of 1988, I had discovered 16 different readings in the first 43 extant pages of the original manuscript (from 1 Nephi 2:2 to 2 Nephi 1:30, covering 4.3 percent of the text). These differences had never been noticed before and had subsequently never appeared in any of the standard editions of the Book of Mormon. Here are three that were published early on (in the Winter 1990 issue of *BYU Studies*); each of these three examples represents an error that Oliver Cowdery made when he copied the text from 𝒪 into 𝒫:

1 Nephi 8:31	and he also saw other multitudes **pressing** > **feeling** their way towards that great and spacious building
1 Nephi 22:8	it is likened unto the being **nursed** > **nourished** by the Gentiles
2 Nephi 1:5	the Lord hath **consecrated** > **covenanted** this land unto me

Here the standard editions of the Book of Mormon have followed the secondary readings in 𝒫 rather than the original readings in 𝒪. In a sense, these mistakes work — that's why they've remained in the text. These readings, however, are contradicted by usage found elsewhere in the Book of Mormon.

Take, for instance, the first example, the accidental misreading of *pressing* as *feeling* that occurred when Oliver Cowdery copied the text from 𝒪 into 𝒫. Similar descriptions in Lehi's dream always use the verb *press* rather than *feel* when referring to the masses of moving people:

1 Nephi 8:21
and I saw numberless concourses of people many of whom were **pressing** forward

1 Nephi 8:24
and it came to pass that I beheld others **pressing** forward . . .
and they did **press forward** through the mists of darkness

1 Nephi 8:30
behold he saw other multitudes **pressing** forwards . . .
and they did **press** their way forward

It turns out that there are no examples in the text of "feeling one's way." Thus restoring the original reading removes an exceptional — and difficult — reading.

When we compare the original text with the current LDS edition (1981), we find that the original is significantly more consistent in its phraseology and vocabulary.

Here are three striking examples that showed no variation in phraseology or word usage in the original text, but now do in the standard edition:

- □ *whatsoever,* never *whatever*

  originally   75 to 0

  current text   72 to 2

- □ "observe **to keep** the commandments", never "observe the commandments"

  originally   11 to 0

  current text   10 to 1

- □ "thus **ended** <a period of time>", never "thus **endeth** <a period of time>"

  originally   47 to 0

  current text   43 to 4

There are at least 133 instances of phraseology and word usage where the earliest readings are fully consistent but over time a few wrinkles, so to speak, have entered the text. Yet the imposition of regularity was never a goal of my editing: there are also at least 38 instances where the original text restores a unique phrase or word choice. But in examining the differences between the original Book of Mormon text and the current LDS edition, we generally find that the changes in the text have led to irregularity in the language.

By the end of 2016, I had identified 612 original readings that had never appeared in any standard printed edition of the Book of Mormon (published by either the LDS or the RLDS Church). Of these 612 new readings, 494 of them come from the two manuscripts:

216 readings found only in 𝒪 (incorrectly copied from 𝒪 into 𝒫)

188 readings found only in 𝒫 (incorrectly copied from 𝒫 into the 1830 edition, where 𝒪 is either no longer extant or it contains an impossible reading)

88 readings in both 𝒪 and 𝒫 (incorrectly copied from 𝒫 into the 1830 edition, where 𝒪 is extant and reads the same as 𝒫)

2 readings from several firsthand copies of the original title page (which is no longer extant)

Conjectural Emendations

The remaining 118 changes, the ones not based on manuscript readings, involved conjecture. Sometimes we have a passage where none of the variant readings make sense, neither the current reading nor earlier readings found either in preceding editions or in the two manuscripts. Whenever someone proposes a new reading for a questionable passage, we refer to that reading as a conjectural emendation. As part of this project, I have re-evaluated over a thousand textual changes that the text itself has undergone from its earliest transmission to now. In addition, I have considered a couple hundred proposed changes that various readers have suggested as additional emendations to the text. By the end of 2016, I had examined the evidence both for and against a total of 1,346 conjectural emendations, and ultimately I accepted 118 of them. Within the last five years, I have continued to evaluate additional proposed changes to the text, with the number of accepted conjectural emendations now having increased to 121. But the important point to keep in mind here is that I have accepted less than one tenth of all the suggested conjectural emendations.

Here is a good example where some kind of conjectural emendation is necessary. In 1 Nephi 7:5, the original manuscript reads: "the Lord did soften the heart of Ishmael and also his **hole hole**". Oliver Cowdery, when he copied the text from 𝓞 into 𝓟, interpreted *hole hole* as a mistake for *household*, thus 𝓟 reads "the Lord did soften the heart of Ishmael and also his **household**". Based on usage elsewhere in the text and considering what could have caused Christian Whitmer, the scribe here in 𝓞, to write the impossible *hole hole,* I have proposed that the original reading was "the Lord did soften the heart of Ishmael and also his **whole household**". In my conjecture, the first *hole* stands for the homophone *whole* and the second *hole* is a mishearing of the *hold* in *household*. It's important to note that my suggested change to *whole household* and Oliver Cowdery's change to *household* are both conjectural emendations. In textual criticism, the tendency is to no longer view a textual change as a conjecture once it appears in a manuscript or in a printed edition: instead of a conjecture, it becomes just a variant reading, accepted on equal footing with all other readings. Cowdery's conjecture should not be privileged over my conjecture simply because it appeared in 𝓟 in 1829 and in the 1830 edition (and in all subsequent standard editions), while mine had to wait until 2009 to appear in the first printing of the Yale edition.

Introducing 121 conjectural emendations into the Yale text seems to be quite a lot, yet it's actually quite conservative for a text of 270,012 words. Making conjectural emendations has never been that unusual. In my 2016 analysis, I discovered that Oliver Cowdery, the main scribe for Joseph Smith, made 131 conjectural emendations when he copied the text from 𝓞 into 𝓟, while John Gilbert made 167 of them when he set the type for the 1830 edition from the manuscripts. Later editors have also made numerous conjectural emendations in their editing, especially Joseph Smith for the 1837 and 1840 editions (198 in the 1837 edition, and 19 more when he did the 1840 edition). In modern times, James E. Talmage made 130 conjectural emendations in the LDS Church's 1920 edition. Taking into account the text's full history, we find that the LDS text currently has a total of 654 conjectural emendations (with only 10 of these dating from the 1981 edition itself), while the Yale text has a little more than half that many, 357. Yet both texts agree in having 187 of the same conjectures. Of the 724 readings listed in the appendix to this second edition of the Yale text, 101 of them involve conjectural emendation, and all but two of these have been accepted into the Yale text.

Name Changes

Perhaps more noticeable to lifetime readers of the Book of Mormon will be 19 changes in the spelling of various names in the book, especially these seven frequent names:

> *Amalekite > Amlicite, Gadianton > Gaddianton, Kishkumen > Kishcumen,*
> *Morianton > Morionton, Mulek > Muloch, Pahoran > Parhoron, Zenock > Zenoch*

Two of these name changes are particularly significant:

(1) the youngest son of King Zedekiah is *Muloch* rather than *Mulek;* his name appears to be a form of the Canaanite god *Moloch* (or *Molech*), the god that the Israelites sacrificed their children to (prior to the Babylonian captivity);

(2) in Alma 21–43, the apostate *Amalekites* are actually the *Amlicites* who are mentioned earlier in Alma 2–3, which means that we replace *Amalekite(s)* with *Amlicite(s)*. The name *Amalekite* is a biblical name that was accidentally introduced into the text by Oliver Cowdery when he copied from 𝓞 into 𝓟.

The Significance of the Changes

With 615 new readings restored in this second edition of the Yale text (this includes five new conjectures, but rejects two earlier conjectures), most readers will wonder just how many of these readings really make a difference in meaning. Another way to ask this question is this: How many of these readings would show up as differences when translating the Book of Mormon into a foreign language? The answer is: 251 of them would require some change in the translated wording. This would hold, for instance, for the four corrections that we have already noted: *pressing* in place of *feeling* (in 1 Nephi 8:31), *nourished* in place of *nursed* (in 1 Nephi 22:8), *consecrated* in place of *covenanted* (in 2 Nephi 1:5), and *whole household* in place of *household* (in 1 Nephi 7:5).

One could even go further and ask whether changes have ever affected the doctrine of the book or its fundamental narrative. Under this restriction, it turns out that no restoration of the original reading has ever altered doctrinal belief or the basic story line. Restoring the original reading either makes the actual doctrine come through better or it makes the historical account more accurate or consistent, as in these two examples:

(1) *Restoring the correct doctrine of repentance*

Alma 39:13 read as follows in the original manuscript:

> but rather return unto them and **acknowledge** your faults
> and **repair** that wrong which ye have done

Here Alma is telling his son Corianton to return to the Zoramites to acknowledge his moral failures as a missionary and to repair the wrong he has done. After writing the text on this page of Ơ, Oliver Cowdery accidentally spilled quite a few ink drops on the page. One dropped on the letter *p* in the word *repair,* which then led Oliver to misread the word as *retain* when he copied the text from Ơ into Ᵽ. The editors for the 1920 LDS edition removed the word *retain* here since it didn't make much sense, but the resulting text now read as if all Corianton had to do was to say he was sorry for his mistakes: "**acknowledge** your faults and that wrong which ye have done". In the Book of Mormon, repentance requires restitution—however difficult—in addition to admitting you're at fault, as can be seen in Helaman 5:17: "they came forth and **did confess their sins** and were baptized unto repentance and immediately returned to the Nephites to endeavor **to repair unto them the wrongs** which they had done".

(2) *The dissenters from the Nephites almost outnumbered the remaining Nephites*

Alma 43:13–14 reads as follows in the original manuscript:

> and thus the Nephites were compelled alone to withstand against the Lamanites . . .
> and **all those which had dissented** from the Nephites
> which were Amlicites and Zoramites and **the descendants of the priests of Noah**
> now those **dissenters** were as numerous nearly as were the Nephites

Here in Alma 43:14, when Oliver Cowdery copied the text from Ơ into Ᵽ, he misread *dissenters* as *descendants.* Cowdery was undoubtedly influenced by the word *descendants* in the immediately preceding text ("the descendants of the priests of Noah"). Thus the standard text nonsensically ends up stating that within a few generations the offspring of king Noah's priests had multiplied so rapidly that now there were almost as many of them as Nephites. An incredible population explosion! Of course, what the original text says here is much more reasonable, that there were now almost as many Nephite dissenters that had gone over to the Lamanites as there were that remained Nephites, thus leading to a very ominous situation.

Evidence for the Changes

We can get a fair idea of the changes the text has historically undergone by surveying the 724 significant textual changes listed in the appendix to this edition of the Book of Mormon. Yet by just looking at the apparatus, it is sometimes quite difficult to see the importance of any given change and figure out why we should prefer, say, an earlier reading, or a later one, or a proposed conjectural emendation. What we really need to see are the arguments both for and against any given reading. As we might expect, there is no room in the Yale edition itself for including these arguments along with the actual list of the significant textual changes. This is, in fact, a common deficiency in critical texts: they typically list only the variants and their sources, but give no reasons for why one particular variant was adopted in the text itself. It's left for the reader to figure it all out — or just accept it.

In the case of the Book of Mormon Critical Text Project, these arguments are crucial for establishing the original text; and except for one recent change, all the arguments have been published in volume 4 of the critical text, *Analysis of Textual Variants of the Book of Mormon* (referred to as ATV), a series of six large maroon books. In ATV, I discuss all the significant textual changes in the Book of Mormon, beginning with the title page, then working through each chapter of the Book of Mormon, from 1 Nephi 1 through Moroni 10. The first edition of ATV was published over a period of six years, from 2004 through 2009, and it ended up with a total of 4,060 pages. The first printing of the Yale edition of the Book of Mormon, which also came out in 2009, followed the critical text decisions made in that first edition of ATV. This first edition of ATV is now available online from the Interpreter Foundation or from Book of Mormon Central. A second, corrected edition of volume 4, again in six books but now with 4,105 pages, was published in 2017:

> *Analysis of Textual Variants of the Book of Mormon,* Royal Skousen. Volume 4 in the Book of Mormon Critical Text Project, second edition, in six parts (Provo, Utah: FARMS and BYU Studies, 2017)

This second edition of ATV includes a number of additional changes to the text as well as some revisions to my previous analyses; and all of them are found in this second edition of *The Book of Mormon: The Earliest Text.*

The History of the Text

Having established the original text of the Book of Mormon (to the extent possible), we can turn to analyzing the language itself and see how that original language has been changed through the various printed editions of the book. Volume 3 of the critical text, entitled *The History of the Text of the Book of Mormon,* is dedicated to such questions. When complete, volume 3 will have eight parts (or printed books). Thus far, the first six parts have been published, and the last two parts are now being written up and should be completed by 2023. Each part of volume 3 is bound in forest green, to distinguish these eight books from the six maroon books that make up volume 4, *Analysis of Textual Variants,* and from the three blue books that make up volumes 1 and 2, the transcripts of the two manuscripts 𝕆 and 𝕇.

Nonstandard Grammar

The first two parts of volume 3 are entitled *Grammatical Variation.* Published as two books in 2016, they form a set and comprise 1,281 pages in which I discuss, along with my colleague Stanford Carmack, all the nonstandard grammar in the original text of the Book of Mormon. This nonstandard grammar has been largely removed from the standard editions of the Book of Mormon, but restored in *The Earliest Text.* These first two parts of volume 3 describe in detail all the grammatical editing that the Book of Mormon has undergone. Here are two examples of nonstandard English in the original text of the Book of Mormon, along with the editing they have undergone:

Alma 9:31 (change made in the 1840 edition)
   they was > **they were** a hard-hearted and a stiffnecked people

Helaman 13:37 (change made in the 1837 edition)
   and this shall be your language **in them days** > **in those days**

Most readers of the first edition of the Book of Mormon (in 1830) very likely assumed that this nonstandard English was simply the result of Joseph Smith's upstate New York dialect. And from 1837 on, there have been fairly systematic attempts, led by Joseph Smith himself, to grammatically emend the text—to clean it up, so to speak. But in 2014 Stanford Carmack proposed that this "bad grammar" in the original text would have been acceptable language usage in the English of the 16th and 17th centuries (known as Early Modern English), and that it could be found in scholarly writing published in the 1500s and 1600s, as in these examples corresponding to the two cases cited above:

1657, Thomas Robins, *England's Prayers to Heaven for Mercy*
   they was a wicked and a sinful people

1598, Robert Barret, *The Theory and Practice of Modern Wars*
   the wars and weapons are now altered **from them days**

In *Grammatical Variation,* Carmack and I show that for virtually each case of Book of Mormon nonstandard English, examples of that usage can be found in Early Modern English. This analysis vindicated my decision to restore the original nonstandard English in the 2009 Yale edition of the Book of Mormon, even though at that time I had worried that the normal reader was going to misinterpret its occurrence in the text as simply bad English.

Hebraistic Constructions

A separate chapter in *Grammatical Variation* is devoted to what might be considered Hebraisms in the original text. One very interesting example of this Hebrew-like usage is the occurrence of an extra *and* between an initial subordinate clause and its following main clause. This usage is more regular in Hebrew, but in the original text of the Book of Mormon it occurs only when there is an intervening parenthetical clause between the initial subordinate clause and the following main clause. Here are five different types of subordinate constructions in the original text. In each example, the intervening clause, which triggers the need in the original text for the extra *and,* is set in italics. And in each case, the extra *and,* since its use here is totally uncharacteristic of English, was soon edited out of the text:

1 Nephi 8:13 (the *and* was removed by Oliver Cowdery when he copied Ⓞ into Ⓟ)
and **as** I cast my eyes around about
that perhaps I might discover my family also
and I beheld a river of water

Helaman 13:28 (the *and* was removed in the 1837 edition)
and **because** he speaketh flattering words unto you
and he saith that all is well
and then ye will not find no fault with him

3 Nephi 23:8 (the *and* was removed in the 1830 edition)
and **when** Nephi had brought forth the records
and laid them before him
and he cast his eyes upon them and saith . . .

Mormon 3:4 (the *and* was removed in the 1830 edition)
and it came to pass that **after** this tenth year had passed away
making in the whole three hundred and sixty years from the coming of Christ
and the king of the Lamanites sent an epistle unto me

Moroni 10:4 (the *and* was removed in the 1837 edition)
and **if** ye shall ask with a sincere heart with real intent
having faith in Christ
and he will manifest the truth of it unto you by the power of the Holy Ghost

This construction also adds strong support for the hypothesis that Joseph Smith was given the text word for word, including constructions with instances of non-English use of *and* that would not have been dictated if the text were wholly English in nature. And despite the difficulties these original readings hold for English readers, they are restored in the Yale edition since they were not the result of scribal error but were definitely intended.

Early Modern English

In the late 1990s, a research assistant of mine, Renee Bangerter, made an important discovery: a number of words, as used in the Book of Mormon, had meanings that dated from the 1500s and 1600s (and even earlier); and those meanings had since then disappeared from English, long before the early 1800s, the time period when Joseph Smith translated the book. Bangerter published her surprising findings in her BYU MA thesis in 1998, but it was only in 2003 that I started to concentrate on extending her research approach to the entire lexicon, to see how many of the word meanings had become archaic by the 1700s. And in 2014 Stanford Carmack began to assist me in this research. Our major findings were published in parts 3 and 4 of volume 3 of the critical text, entitled *The Nature of the Original Language,* with 1,383 pages dedicated to an in-depth study of the original language of the Book of Mormon, in particular its vocabulary, phrases, expressions, and syntax. These findings substantiate our work in parts 1 and 2, *Grammatical Variation,* where we found that the nonstandard usage in the original text of the Book of Mormon could just as well be assigned to Early Modern English as to Joseph Smith's dialectal English.

Our basic finding in *The Nature of the Original Language* is that, with only a few exceptions, the meanings of the Book of Mormon words agree with how they were used in English from the 1530s up through the 1730s, and that in fact a large number of these words had lost those meanings at least a hundred years or more before the Book of Mormon was translated in 1828–29. Here are some examples of archaic usage from the original text of the Book of Mormon, along with the last citation for each of these words and phrases that we have been able to find in English, as given either in the Oxford English Dictionary (OED) or in the online database Early English Books Online (EEBO). All of the Book of Mormon meanings for these words and phrases appear to have died out by the beginning of the Modern English period (that is, by the early 1700s):

(1) **Archaic Word Meanings**

counsel 'to consult'

Alma 37:37
counsel the Lord in all thy doings

OED: 1547, John Hooper, early writings
this cause of religion was not brought unto the bishop and priests to be defined, but unto Moses, who **counseled the Lord** and thereupon advised his subjects what was to be done in such a case

depart 'to divide, separate, or part'

> Helaman 8:11
>> God gave power unto one man even Moses to smite upon the waters of the Red Sea
>> and they **departed** hither and thither
>
> EEBO: 1615, Helkiah Crooke, *Microcosmographia*
>> but the auxiliary vein **departeth** into two branches

flatter 'to coax or entice'

> Alma 52:19
>> that they might by some means **flatter** them out of their strong holds
>
> EEBO: 1601, Patrick Simon (translator), Jean de Hainault, *The Estate of the Church*
>> the Turk by **flatteries** drew him out of the castle where he was

welfare 'success'

> Alma 59:1
>> he was exceedingly rejoiced because of the **welfare**—yea the exceeding success—
>> which Helaman had had in obtaining those lands
>
> OED: 1681, George Archibald, letter to refugee friends in Holland
>> and do heartily wish you all **welfare** in that place where the Lord hath cast your lot

(2) **Archaic Phrases**

but if 'unless'

> Mosiah 3:19
>> for the natural man is an enemy to God and has been from the fall of Adam
>> and will be forever and ever **but if** he yieldeth to the enticings of the Holy Spirit
>
> OED: 1580, Philip Sidney, *Arcadia*
>> he did not like that maids should once stir out of their fathers' houses
>> **but if** it were to milk a cow

do away 'to dismiss, put away'

> Moroni 10:26
>> and woe unto them which shall **do** these things **away** and die
>> for they die in their sins and they cannot be saved in the kingdom of God
>
> OED: 1596, Edmund Spenser, *The Faerie Queene*
>> **do** fear **away** and tell

harrow up 'to vex, disturb'

> Alma 29:4
>> I had not ought to **harrow up** in my desires **the firm decree** of a just God
>
> EEBO: 1604, Anthony Scoloker, *Daiphantus*
>> I'll have revenge, or **harrow up my will**

to that 'until'

> 1 Nephi 18:9
>> insomuch that they began to dance and to sing and to speak
>> with much rudeness / yea even **to that** they did forget by what power
>> they had been brought thither

> OED: 1626, James Haig, letter
>> and **to that** I be into fashion / I am ashamed to presume

Four of these Book of Mormon examples have been edited out of the text: *counsel >
counsel with* (1920 LDS edition), *departed > parted* (1830 edition), *but if > unless* (1920
LDS edition), and *to that > that* (1837 edition). But the four others have never been
altered: *flatter, welfare, do away,* and *harrow up.*

This finding of Early Modern English in the original text of the Book of Mormon
has been difficult for many scholars to accept, especially when they assume that Joseph
Smith was the author of the text. Some have proposed that Joseph Smith's upstate New
York English was a relic dialect and that the resulting archaic Book of Mormon usage
reflects older language forms that had died out elsewhere in the English-speaking
world but not in Palmyra, New York. Yet thus far we have been unable to find any evidence for such forms in dialect studies from that part of the United States (or anywhere
else), nor have we found these forms in Joseph Smith's own writing or in that of his
contemporaries. Yet the evidence is overwhelming that these indicators of non-biblical
Early Modern English are indeed in the Book of Mormon. In my opinion, our current
task is not to explain away this linguistic conundrum, but to study it out, in all of its
variety, and to accurately describe it. The resulting research is going to be a very complex endeavor, and it must be based on the original text of the Book of Mormon, not
on one of the standard editions.

Reformed Protestantism

Another aspect of the Early Modern English period that shows up in the Book of
Mormon deals with the book's themes, especially with the religious and political issues
that arose in the early 1500s during the Protestant Reformation rather than the issues
that were relevant to Christians in Joseph Smith's time (the early 1800s). The Book of
Mormon narrative is infused with practices dating from the 16th and 17th centuries,
such as (1) burning people at the stake for heresy, (2) the rise of secret combinations to
overthrow legitimate government, (3) Anabaptist arguments against infant baptism,
(4) the establishment of the church of Christ with only two sacraments, namely, baptism
and the Eucharist, and (5) public confession of sins rather than private confession to

a priest. It is not at all accurate to claim, as Alexander Campbell did in 1831, that in the Book of Mormon Joseph Smith deals with "every error and almost every truth discussed in New York for the last ten years," and that "he decides all the great controversies," to which Campbell then appends a long list of 19th-century topics, followed by his unsupported claim that in the Book of Mormon "all these topics are repeatedly alluded to."

Quotations from the King James Bible

Another striking Book of Mormon characteristic from Early Modern English is the abundance of quotations from the King James Bible. As readers start their way through the Book of Mormon, they are soon confronted by a substantial quotation from the book of Isaiah (two chapters in 1 Nephi 20–21), and this is soon followed by a whole series of quotations from Isaiah (in 2 Nephi 6–9), and finally what has been called "the great barrier" to reading the Book of Mormon, 13 chapters of Isaiah (in 2 Nephi 12–24), which some have suggested that readers should just skip. And if that isn't enough, in the latter part of the Book of Mormon, in 3 Nephi, the resurrected Jesus delivers a long, modified version of the Sermon on the Mount, after which he cites a number of passages from various Old Testament prophets (Isaiah once again, plus Micah and Malachi). In all, there are 36 Book of Mormon passages with direct quotations from the King James Bible; these passages each involve sequences of at least 16 identical words. On the other hand, when we consider shorter sequences of identical words (ones ranging from 7 to 15), we get 58 paraphrastic quotations. All 94 of these quotations are listed in part 5 of volume 3 of the critical text, *The King James Quotations in the Book of Mormon.*

One might think that there would be some limit to the paraphrastic King James quotations in the Book of Mormon, but this is not the case. There are instances of paraphrastic quotation where the sequences of identical words are as low as one. In such cases, the paraphrastic quotations are blended right into the Book of Mormon text, as in this example from Alma 40:14 which has a sequence of four identical words ("fearful looking for of") as well as one of only two identical words ("fiery indignation"):

Hebrews 10:27	Alma 40:14
but a certain **fearful looking for of** judgment and **fiery indignation** which shall devour the adversaries	and a state of awful **fearful looking for of** the **fiery indignation** of the wrath of God upon them

Or we have this even more striking paraphrastic example from Mosiah 16:11:

John 5:29	Mosiah 16:11
they that have done **good**	if **they** be **good**
unto **the resurrection**	to **the resurrection**
of life	**of** endless **life** and happiness
and they that have done **evil**	**and if they** be **evil**
unto **the resurrection**	to **the resurrection**
of damnation	**of** endless **damnation**

Here Mosiah 16:11 has two instances of the same sequence of three identical words ("the resurrection of"); but even more surprising are the numerous instances of single-word identity, yet all of these occur in the same order: *they, good, life, and, they, evil, damnation.*

Another characteristic of many paraphrastic quotations in the Book of Mormon is that they quote from multiple King James passages, one after the other, but with all of them blended into a single passage:

Mosiah 18:21	KING JAMES SOURCES	
having **one faith** and **one baptism**	Ephesians 4:5	one Lord, **one faith, one baptism**
having **their hearts knit together**	Colossians 2:2	**their hearts** might be comforted being **knit together** in love
in unity	Psalm 133:1	to dwell **together in unity**
and in love **one** towards **another**	1 Thessalonians 3:12	**and** abound **in love** **one** toward **another**

The quotations from the King James Bible also introduce anachronistic elements into the Book of Mormon, in particular words and phrases that culturally tie the Book of Mormon translation to the 1500s. For instance, Isaiah 11:15 (quoted in 1 Nephi 21:15) translates as "in sandals" in the original Hebrew (as well as in the Greek and Latin) and culturally means 'with their shoes on'. But that wouldn't have meant much to Englishmen who were used to crossing dry riverbeds with their shoes on, so in 1535 Miles Coverdale translated the phrase as *dry-shod*, meaning that while crossing they wouldn't get their shoes wet. In a similar way, various kinds of translation errors end up in the Book of Mormon, precisely those that the King James translators accepted, such as *rent* instead of the correct *rope* in quoting Isaiah 3:24: "and instead of a girdle, a rent," which is correctly translated today as "and instead of a belt, a rope." These difficulties arise because the biblical quotations in the Book of Mormon derive from the King James translation. Ultimately, this means that the Book of Mormon cannot be a literal translation dating back to biblical times, but instead is a cultural and creative translation grounded in Early Modern English, especially in its quoting from the King James Bible.

Nonstandard Spellings in the Manuscripts

There is one aspect of the Book of Mormon text that does not derive from Early Modern English, and that is the nonstandard spellings found in the Book of Mormon manuscripts. The scribes for the original and printer's manuscripts did not in any way follow the archaic spellings of the 1500s and 1600s, but at the same time they didn't always use the standardized English spellings of the early 1800s. Instead, they followed their own idiosyncratic spellings. The subject is thoroughly discussed in part 6 of volume 3 of the critical text, *Spelling in the Manuscripts and Editions.*

There is a common belief among LDS people that spelling had not yet been standardized when the 1830 edition of the Book of Mormon was published. Although in the early 1800s, individuals' spelling showed great variety in their own writing, typesetters had been using an informally agreed upon spelling standard for English, one that dated back to Samuel Johnson's 1755 *A Dictionary of the English Language.* John Gilbert, the typesetter for the 1830 edition, set the type for that edition using standardized spellings rather than the scribes' manuscript misspellings. We can see this when we measure the error rate in spelling for John Gilbert in comparison to Oliver Cowdery and the other Book of Mormon scribes. Gilbert was a first-rate speller (0.3 errors per thousand words), while Cowdery was a second-rate speller (averaging 12 errors per thousand words), and so was Martin Harris (10 errors per thousand words) and John Whitmer (27 errors per thousand words); but two others were third-rate: Hyrum Smith (66 errors per thousand words) and Christian Whitmer (73 errors per thousand words). Unlike the other scribes, however, Cowdery's spelling improved as he proofed the 1830 typeset sheets against his manuscript copy, going from 18 errors per thousand in the beginning (for 1 Nephi) down to 5 errors per thousand at the end (for the book of Moroni). In other words, Cowdery gradually learned how to spell words that he had earlier misspelled in his copy work.

The Transmission of the Text

Within the next two years, the last two parts of volume 3 will be published. The first of these will be part 7, *The Transmission of the Text: From the Manuscripts Through the Editions.* Most of part 7 will deal with the early transmission of the text and will concentrate on four specific stages: (1) Joseph Smith's dictation of the text; (2) the original manuscript (what the scribes wrote down as Joseph Smith dictated the text); (3) the printer's manuscript (the copy of the original manuscript that the scribes made to take to the printer; and (4) the typesetting of the 1830 edition of the Book of Mormon from the two manuscripts: five-sixths from the printer's manuscript, but one-sixth—from Helaman 13 through Mormon 9—from the original manuscript.

Witnesses of the Dictation

A long chapter in part 7 will deal with the witnesses who actually observed Joseph Smith dictating the text of the Book of Mormon to his scribes. We have at least eight individuals who qualify as firsthand witnesses of the translation process, and they each independently refer to Smith as using a seer stone to translate the Book of Mormon, from the beginning in the spring of 1828 in Susquehanna, Pennsylvania, to the end in June 1829 at the Peter Whitmer home in Fayette, New York; that is, from the very first book of Lehi to the small plates of Nephi at the end; or from the first scribes (Emma Smith, Reuben Hale, and Martin Harris) to the final scribes (Oliver Cowdery and the two Whitmers, John and Christian). All but Martin Harris explicitly state that the seer stone was placed in a hat. Some add that the purpose of the hat was to exclude the ambient light, which would have interfered with what Smith was trying to read using the seer stone. In these statements, there is some variety in how the seer stone is referred to: once as "the Urim and Thummim" (Joseph Knight), once as "the director" (Elizabeth Anne Whitmer), three times as simply "the stone" (Emma Smith, Elizabeth McKune, and Joseph McKune), and three times as "the seer stone" (Michael Morse, David Whitmer, and Martin Harris). By implication, there was no curtain or blanket separating Joseph Smith and his scribe. Nor did Smith have any books, manuscripts, or notes that he was consulting. The witnesses were especially clear on this last point.

When we compare the testimonies of these eight witnesses against the evidence in the original manuscript, we find that certain claims are supported by manuscript evidence:

□ When necessary, Joseph Smith would spell out the strange Book of Mormon names to his scribe. He also probably spelled out infrequent, difficult biblical names (such as those in the Isaiah quotations).

□ It is possible that Joseph Smith could have spelled out words of English to his scribe, if necessary, but the evidence for this practice is meager, at best. Smith may have once spelled out the word *genealogy* to Christian Whitmer. Otherwise, the original manuscript is full of misspellings.

□ After Joseph Smith dictated what he was viewing with his instrument, the scribe would read it back to Smith, and thus the scribe would make sure what he had written agreed with what Smith was viewing, at least to the degree that they could do this aurally.

□ In using his translation instrument, Joseph Smith was viewing at least 20 words and probably up to 30 or more words at a time.

□ Before quitting a translation session, Joseph Smith had to make sure the scribe had gotten down all the words that he had last been viewing with his instrument. As a result, when he would start up after an interruption, Smith never needed to be prompted because the instrument would simply start off with the next viewing of text and would not repeat what had last been viewed.

But there is one major claim of the witnesses of the translation that is directly contradicted by manuscript evidence, namely, the claim that no error in the transmission could ever occur, that the instrument would not go on to the next viewing unless the scribe had gotten down everything correctly. These witnesses claimed that this accuracy not only included words and word forms, but also the spelling of words. In other words, the scribe's transmission had to be letter-perfect. This claim is clearly wrong. Besides the obvious ones dealing with spelling, there are errors in the actual words of the text, as in these striking examples from the original manuscript:

Christian Whitmer
   1 Nephi 7:5   the lord did soften the hart of ishmael and also his **hole hole**
                        [error for either "whole household" or just "household"]

John Whitmer
   1 Nephi 14:27   **the name & apostle** of the Lamb was John
                        [error for "the name of the apostle"]

Oliver Cowdery
   1 Nephi 17:30   they being lead **the Lead their God** their redeemer going before them
                        [error for "the Lord their God"]

The instrument did not prevent Joseph Smith and his scribe from going on even when the reading in the original manuscript was incorrect. The witnesses believed the instrument had an ironclad control over what the scribe ended up writing. This assumption of theirs was wrong; and it seems to have been based on the witnesses seeing Smith occasionally spelling out names and on the continual reading back of the text by the scribe. Despite the joint carefulness of Joseph Smith and his scribe, errors did occur.

The last sections of part 7 will treat the transmission of the text through the editions of the Book of Mormon, from the 1830 edition up to the most recent editions, including the canonical editions: for the LDS, the 1981 edition and its very minor revision, the 2013 edition; and for the RLDS, their 1953 edition, plus their 1966 grammatical modernization of the text. I will also consider two quite different questions regarding the textual transmission of the Book of Mormon: first, how each edition has been grammatically emended; and second, how the format for the Book of Mormon has been changed and how this has affected our reading of the text.

Sense-Lines in the Yale Edition

When one first examines the Yale edition, there is something else that strikes the reader's eye much more dramatically than the occasional textual variant, the nonstandard English, or the change in a name, and that is its format: the text is printed in sense-lines. With sense-lines, each line of text forms a coherent phrase or clause. It looks like poetry to most readers, but this is not its function. To be sure, readers of the Yale edition have found the sense-line format much easier to read than the traditional formats, whether the text is set in paragraphs (as with the original 1830 edition) or in two narrow columns with numbered paragraphs for the verses (the LDS text since 1920). The latter formatting style dates all the way back to 1560 when the Geneva Bible was first published this way and then followed by the 1611 King James Bible. This last format may be helpful for citation purposes, but it is certainly awkward to read the text this way.

There is a second, more important aspect to the use of sense-lines, one that reflects more directly on restoring the earliest text of the Book of Mormon, namely, Joseph Smith would have dictated the text to his scribes in sense-lines, with him pausing at the end of phrases and short clauses to help the scribe keep up with him, but he would not have dictated full sentences unless they were sufficiently short—and he definitely would not have dictated whole paragraphs at once without breaking them up. As a result of the sense-lines, in reading the Yale edition out loud, we get a feel for how witnesses of the translation would have heard the Book of Mormon as Joseph Smith originally dictated it.

Principles of Textual Criticism

Volume 3 will end with part 8, *Book of Mormon Textual Criticism*. This last part will consider how well the principles of textual criticism have held up in the Critical Text Project. There is considerable evidence that in the early transmission of the Book of Mormon text the tendency was to create more difficult readings as well as shorter readings, which goes against what most textual critics have assumed to be the normal way a text changes over time.

Part 8 will also deal with the difficult issue of conjectural emendation, and will make explicit the conditions under which we should allow conjectures to be accepted.

Here I will also list all of the proposed conjectural emendations, including the 193 that 48 readers suggested to me over the first three decades of this project. In my mind, there are tremendous advantages when a critical text project has a public front and is open to suggestions from both scholars and lay readers. I have always endeavored to personally answer each respondent; and whenever I would write up their suggested emendation in *Analysis of Textual Variants,* I would make sure they were credited for coming up with that conjecture.

In part 8, I will discuss some of the earlier translations of the original English-language Book of Mormon into foreign languages, and will show that in many cases those translators independently came up with many of the conjectures proposed by this project. One particularly striking example is the French translation made in 1852 by Louis Bertrand, who ended up with twenty of the Yale conjectural emendations (somewhat surprisingly, five of them remain in the current French translation).

And finally, I will close this last part of volume 3 with a history of the Critical Text Project and compare it with earlier critical text work done on the Book of Mormon.

The Computerized Collation

The engine driving the Critical Text Project is a huge computerized collation that compares every difference between the two manuscripts 𝒪 and 𝒫 and 20 editions of the Book of Mormon (beginning with the 1830 edition and ending with the 1981 LDS edition). An electronic version of the collation will be made available as volume 5 of the critical text, but only after the last two parts of volume 3 have been published. The collation will be in a WordCruncher format, and the user will be able to look up any word or phrase and see all of its examples and how they've changed over time. It will be possible, for example, to look up every original instance in the text of "it came to pass" (all 1,399 of them) as well as identify the 47 that were removed by Joseph Smith in his editing for the 1837 edition of the Book of Mormon.

It is worth noting that the Yale text is not derived from a copytext (that is, from a marked-up copy of some particular edition of the Book of Mormon), but rather from the computerized collation. This led to a surprising result when we prepared the initial copy for the first printing of the Yale edition in 2009: as expected, we found typos in the original introductory materials and in the appendix to the first edition, but there were no typos in the entire canonical text of the Book of Mormon, a feat that appeared rather astounding and would have been virtually impossible had the text been actually keyed in letter by letter.

Deriving the Yale Text from the Computerized Collation

To see how the computerized collation was used to derive the Yale text, consider the collation for that portion of 1 Nephi as it transitions from chapter 3 into chapter 4:

```
{num} [ 01ABCDEFGH|30 IJLMNOQRT|76 K|96 PS]
{punctnum} [ 01ABCDEFGHKPST|. IJLMNOQR]
{&} {cap} [& 01|And ABCDEFGHIJKLMNOPQRST|and <accidentals>] after
{subst,gram,delete,subord,that>0,js} [that 0A|that >js NULL 1| BCDEFGHIJKLMNOPQRST]
{subst,anticipate,correct,$20} [he > the angel 0|the angel 1ABCDEFGHIJKLMNOPQRST] had
{subst,gram,pastpart,spake>spoken,A}[spake 01|spoken ABCDEFGHIJKLMNOPQRST] unto us
{punct} [ 01|, ABCDEFGHIJKLMNOPQRST] he departed
{punct} [ 01|. ABCDEFGHIJKLMNOPQRST]
{punct,eoln,D;correct,F} [ 01ABCGIJKLMNOPQRST|- DEH|- > NULL F]
{num} [ 01ABCDEFGH|31 IJLMNOQRT|77 K|97 PS]
{punctnum} [ 01ABCDEFGHKPST|. IJLMNOQR]
{&} {cap} [& 01|And ABCDEFGHIJKLMNOPQRST|and <accidentals>] after
{subst,gram,delete,subord,that>0,js} [that 0A|that >js NULL 1| BCDEFGHIJKLMNOPQRST]
   the angel had departed
{punct} [ 01|, ABCDEFGHIJKLMNOPQRST] Laman
{&} [& 01|and ABCDEFGHIJKLMNOPQRST]
{cap,proper,$20} [lemuel 0|Lemuel 1ABCDEFGHIJKLMNOPQRST]
{spell,space,$20} [a gain 0|again 1ABCDEFGHIJKLMNOPQRST] began to
{spell,er/ur,$20} [murmer 0|murmur 1ABCDEFGHIJKLMNOPQRST]
{punct} [ 01|, ABCDEFGHIJKLMNOPQRST] saying
{punct} [ 01EFH|, ABCDGIJKLMNOPQS|: RT]
{cap} [how 01ABCDEFG|How HIJKLMNOPQRST] is it
{spell,twin,s/ss,$20} [posible 0|possible 1ABCDEFGHIJKLMNOPQRST] that the Lord will
   deliver Laban into our hands
{punct} [ 01|? ABCDEFGHIJKLMNOPQRST]
{num} [ 01ABCDEFGHIJKLMNOQRT|98 PS]
{cap} [behold 01|Behold ABCDEFGHIJKLMNOPQRST]
{punct,correct,F} [ 01ABDEHKPS|, CGIJLMNOQRT|NULL > , F] he is a mighty man
{punct} [ 01|, ABCDEFGHIJKLMNOPQRST]
{&} [& 01|and ABCDEFGHIJKLMNOPQRST] he can command fifty
{punct} [ 01|, ABCDEFGHIJKLMNOPQRST]
{slip,h#,correct,%,$20} [yeah >% yea 0|yea 1ABCDEFGHIJKLMNOPQRST]
{punct} [ 01|, ABCDEFGHIJKLMNOPQRST] even he can slay fifty
{punct} [ 01|; ABCDEFGHIJKLMNOPQRST]
{skip,correct,0>then,$20} [NULL > then 0|then 1ABCDEFGHIJKLMNOPQRST] why not us
{punct} [ 01|? ABCDEFGHIJKLMNOPQRST]
{ref} <chapter 4>
{chpt} {allcap} [ 01ABCDEFGHKPS|CHAPTER IJLMNOQRT]
{num} [ 01ABCDEFGHKPS|4 IJLMNOQRT]
{punctnum} [ 01ABCDEFGHKPST|. IJLMNOQR]
{indent,num} [ 01T|$ ABCDEG|31 FH|1 IJLMNOQR|78 K|99 PS]
{punctnum} [ 01ABCDEGKPST|. FHIJLMNOQR]
{&} {cap} {allcap} [& 01|And ABCDEFGHKPQRS|AND IJLMNOT|and <accidentals>] it came to
{*s,$20} [pa*ss 0|pass 1ABCDEFGHIJKLMNOPQRST] that I spake unto my
{cap,$20,$1P} [Brethren 01|brethren ABCDEFGHIJKLMNOPQRST] saying
{punct} [ 01|: ART|, BCDEFGHIJKLMNOPQRST]
{cap} [let 01BCDEFG|Let AHIJKLMNOPQRST] us go up again unto Jerusalem
{punct} [ 01|, ABCDEFGHIJKLMNOPQRST]
{&} [& 01|and ABCDEFGHIJKLMNOPQRST] let us be faithful in keeping the commandments of
   the Lord
{punct} [ 01|; ABCDEFGHIJKLMNOPQRST] for behold
{punct} [ 01ABDEFHIJKLMNOPQRST|, CG] he is
{spell,e/i,$20} {slip,0/e,$20} {spell,y+er,$1P} [mighter 0|mightyer 1|
   mightier ABCDEFGHIJKLMNOPQRST]
{spell,pronunc,en/an,$20,$1P} [then 01|than ABCDEFGHIJKLMNOPQRST] all the
{cap,$20} [Earth 0|earth 1ABCDEFGHIJKLMNOPQRST]
{punct} [ 01|, ABCDEFGHIJKLMNOPQRST] then why not
{spell,e/i,$20} {spell,e/i,correct,partial,y+er,$1P} [mighteer 0|mighteer > mightyer 1|
   mightier ABCDEFGHIJKLMNOPQRST]
{spell,pronunc,en/an,$20,$1P} [then 01|than ABCDEFGHIJKLMNOPQRST] Laban
{&} [& 01|and ABCDEFGHIJKLMNOPQRST] his fifty
{punct} [ 01|, ABCDEFGHIJKLMNOPQRST] yea
{punct} [ 01|, ABCDEFGHIJKLMNOPQRST] or even
{spell,pronunc,en/an,$20,$1P} {subst,expect,loss,correct,+,$1P} [then 0|NULL >+ then 1|
   than ABCDEFGHIJKLMNOPQRST] his tens of thousands
{punct} [ 01|. ABCDEFGHIJKLMNOPQS|? GRT]
```

```
{num}     [  01ABCDEFGH|2 IJLMNOQRT|79 K|100 PS]
{punctnum} [  01ABCDEFGHKPST|. IJLMNOQR]
{cap}     [therefore  01|Therefore ABCDEFGHIJKLMNOPQRST]
{punct}   [  01ABDEFHIJKLMNOPQRST|, CG] let us go up
{punct}   [  01|; ABCDEFGHIJKLMNOPQRST]
```

At the beginning of each line in this collation, before each textual variant, there is some indication in curly brackets of the kind of variant that will follow. Then in square brackets the actual variant is specified. The very first variant in this sampling from the collation is a number—in fact, it's a verse number. The two manuscripts are represented by the symbols 0 and 1; and since the manuscripts don't have any verse numbers, there is in this case no number assigned to the original and printer's manuscripts. For the rest of the textual variant we find the capital letters A through T, which stand for the printed editions of the Book of Mormon (from the 1830 edition to the 1981 edition). In this instance, the majority of the printed editions have a verse number, but the particular number varies (here the LDS text is assigned verse 30). The user can go down through the collation and consider in the same way each variant in turn.

The underlined text in the collation represents what I am proposing is the original text (but with the spelling we expect in today's standard English). The text in bold stands for the reading of the original manuscript. In other portions of the collation (not shown here), the user won't find any bolding, which means that the original manuscript is not extant for those portions. With the help of my colleague Deryle Lonsdale, I was able to extract the underlined text. For this portion of the collation covering the transition between 1 Nephi 3 and 4, we got the following:

> and after that the angel had spake unto us he departed and after that the angel had departed Laman and Lemuel again began to murmur saying how is it possible that the Lord will deliver Laban into our hands behold he is a mighty man and he can command fifty yea even he can slay fifty then why not us and it came to pass that I spake unto my brethren saying let us go up again unto Jerusalem and let us be faithful in keeping the commandments of the Lord for behold he is mightier than all the earth then why not mightier than Laban and his fifty yea or even than his tens of thousands therefore let us go up

The resulting linear sequence of words is the proposed original text for this passage—and without any punctuation or intended line breaks. This is much like what the 1830 typesetter was confronted with when he set the type from manuscript—a long string of words with no breaks except when a new (original) chapter began.

From this long string of words, I then constructed the sense-lines and put in extra blank lines of spacing for where I thought we could add paragraph breaks to assist the reader; I also added the LDS chapter and verse numbers in the left margin, separated from the actual original text (which had no chapter or verse numbers):

30 and after that the angel had spake unto us he departed

31 and after that the angel had departed
Laman and Lemuel again began to murmur saying
how is it possible that the Lord will deliver Laban into our hands
behold he is a mighty man and he can command fifty
yea even he can slay fifty then why not us

4 | 1 and it came to pass that I spake unto my brethren saying
let us go up again unto Jerusalem
and let us be faithful in keeping the commandments of the Lord
for behold he is mightier than all the earth
then why not mightier than Laban and his fifty
yea or even than his tens of thousands

2 therefore let us go up

One of the things the reader will notice here is that the LDS chapter 4 comes in the middle of a paragraph. Reading this portion of the text, one sees that there probably shouldn't be a chapter break, not even a paragraph break, here where chapter 4 begins. (Although there are no instances in this sampling, the original text of the Book of Mormon had its own system of chapter breaks. These breaks are indicated here in the Yale edition by the special symbol ══.)

And finally, after the chapter and verse numbers had been added, I put in the punctuation (along with any necessary capitalization), but from scratch, without looking—except afterwards—at the original 1830 punctuation or the current LDS punctuation (which derives from the 1830 punctuation):

30 And after that the angel had spake unto us, he departed.

31 And after that the angel had departed,
Laman and Lemuel again began to murmur, saying:
How is it possible that the Lord will deliver Laban into our hands?
Behold, he is a mighty man and he can command fifty.
Yea, even he can slay fifty, then why not us?

4 | 1 And it came to pass that I spake unto my brethren, saying:
Let us go up again unto Jerusalem,
and let us be faithful in keeping the commandments of the Lord.
For behold, he is mightier than all the earth.
Then why not mightier than Laban and his fifty?
Yea, or even than his tens of thousands?

2 Therefore let us go up.

I found this last task of adding the punctuation to be the most difficult one in preparing the Yale edition. It is quite astounding when we recognize what John Gilbert, the

1830 typesetter, was able to do here, especially given the complex syntactic structure of the Book of Mormon. In fact, for about two-thirds of the text Gilbert added the punctuation as he set the type. And he did a fine job, although from our modern point of view he over-punctuated the text (but this was the kind of punctuation that was expected in his day). As far as I know, the Yale edition represents only the second time that the punctuation has been done completely from scratch—at least in a published edition of the Book of Mormon.

My Perspective after Three Decades

As editor of the Critical Text Project of the Book of Mormon, my original goal was to produce accurate transcripts of the two manuscripts and to establish the history of the text. In the beginning I did not expect to find the large number of textual errors that resulted when the text was copied from the original manuscript into the printer's manuscript. Over time, I have come to realize that because only 28 percent of the original manuscript is extant, we will never be able to fully recover the original text of the Book of Mormon by scholarly means. Further, textual criticism of the Book of Mormon is a continuing process, and it is doubtful, even foolish, to think that it is ever completely finished.

Over the thirty-three years that I have worked on this project, I have discovered other, even more important, aspects to this text. We now know much more about the original text of the Book of Mormon, especially its occasional Hebrew-like syntax, the archaic language dating from Early Modern English, and its systematic phraseology. And we now have a much clearer insight into how Joseph Smith translated (however one interprets the word *translate*), with strong evidence that he dictated the text word for word and that he controlled for the spelling of the strange Book of Mormon names. In my mind, the original text as given to Joseph Smith is "a marvelous work and a wonder" and not to be treated lightly. My ultimate goal has been to pay this text the respect it deserves. In preparing this edition, I have done my utmost to ensure that the Yale edition of the original text is reproduced as accurately as possible and in a format that brings the text forth in a new light.

— ROYAL SKOUSEN, *Editor*
The Book of Mormon Critical Text Project
10 August 2021

The Book of Mormon

Translated by Joseph Smith, Junior

THE BOOK OF MORMON

An account written by the hand of Mormon upon plates,
taken from the plates of Nephi.

Wherefore it is an abridgment of the record
of the people of Nephi, and also of the Lamanites,
written to the Lamanites,
which are a remnant of the house of Israel,
and also to Jew and Gentile,
written by way of commandment,
and also by the spirit of prophecy and of revelation,
written and sealed and hid up unto the Lord
that they might not be destroyed,
to come forth by the gift and power of God
unto the interpretation thereof,
sealed up by the hand of Moroni,
and hid up unto the Lord,
to come forth in due time by the way of Gentile,
the interpretation thereof by the gift of God—

an abridgment taken from the book of Ether also,
which is a record of the people of Jared,
which were scattered at the time
the Lord confounded the language of the people
when they were building a tower to get to heaven—

which is to shew unto the remnant of the house of Israel
how great things the Lord hath done for their fathers,
and that they may know the covenants of the Lord,
that they are not cast off forever,
and also to the convincing of the Jew and Gentile
that Jesus is the Christ, the Eternal God,
manifesting himself unto all nations.

And now if there be fault, it be the mistake of men.
Wherefore condemn not the things of God,
that ye may be found spotless at the judgment seat of Christ.

THE BOOK OF NEPHI,
His Reign and Ministry

An account of Lehi and his wife Sariah and his four sons,
being called, beginning at the eldest,
Laman, Lemuel, Sam, and Nephi.

The Lord warns Lehi to depart out of the land of Jerusalem
because he prophesieth unto the people concerning their iniquity
and they seek to destroy his life.

He taketh three days' journey into the wilderness with his family.

Nephi taketh his brethren and returns to the land of Jerusalem
after the record of the Jews.

The account of their sufferings.

They take the daughters of Ishmael to wife.

They take their families and depart into the wilderness.

Their sufferings and afflictions in the wilderness.

The course of their travels.

They come to the large waters.

Nephi's brethren rebelleth against him.

He confoundeth them and buildeth a ship.

They call the name of the place Bountiful.

They cross the large waters into the promised land etc.

This is according to the account of Nephi,
or in other words, I Nephi wrote this record.

1 | 1 I Nephi having been born of goodly parents,
therefore I was taught somewhat in all the learning of my father.
And having seen many afflictions in the course of my days,
nevertheless having been highly favored of the Lord in all my days,

yea, having had a great knowledge of the goodness and the mysteries of God,
therefore I make a record of my proceedings in my days.

2   Yea, I make a record in the language of my father,
which consists of the learning of the Jews and the language of the Egyptians.

3   And I know that the record which I make to be true.
And I make it with mine own hand,
and I make it according to my knowledge.

4   For it came to pass in the commencement of the first year
of the reign of Zedekiah, king of Judah
—my father Lehi having dwelt at Jerusalem in all his days—
and in that same year there came many prophets prophesying unto the people
that they must repent or the great city Jerusalem must be destroyed.

5   Wherefore it came to pass that
my father Lehi, as he went forth, prayed unto the Lord,
yea, even with all his heart, in behalf of his people.

6   And it came to pass as he prayed unto the Lord,
there came a pillar of fire and dwelt upon a rock before him,
and he saw and heard much.
And because of the things which he saw and heard,
he did quake and tremble exceedingly.

7   And it came to pass that he returned to his own house at Jerusalem.
And he cast himself upon his bed,
being overcome with the Spirit and the things which he had seen.

8   And being thus overcome with the Spirit,
he was carried away in a vision,
even that he saw the heavens open
and he thought he saw God sitting upon his throne,
surrounded with numberless concourses of angels
in the attitude of singing and praising their God.

9   And it came to pass that he saw one descending out of the midst of heaven,
and he beheld that his luster was above that of the sun at noonday.

10   And he also saw twelve others following him,
and their brightness did exceed that of the stars in the firmament.

11   And they came down and went forth upon the face of the earth.
And the first came and stood before my father
and gave unto him a book and bade him that he should read.

12   And it came to pass that as he read,
he was filled with the Spirit of the Lord.

13   And he read, saying: Woe woe unto Jerusalem,

for I have seen thine abominations.
Yea, and many things did my father read concerning Jerusalem,
that it should be destroyed and the inhabitants thereof;
many should perish by the sword
and many should be carried away captive into Babylon.

14 And it came to pass that when my father had read
and saw many great and marvelous things,
he did exclaim many things unto the Lord, such as:
Great and marvelous are thy works, O Lord God Almighty.
Thy throne is high in the heavens,
and thy power and goodness and mercy is over all the inhabitants of the earth.
And because thou art merciful,
thou wilt not suffer those who come unto thee that they shall perish.

15 And after this manner was the language of my father in the praising of his God,
for his soul did rejoice and his whole heart was filled
because of the things which he had seen,
yea, which the Lord had shewn unto him.

16 And now I Nephi do not make a full account of the things
which my father hath written,
for he hath written many things which he saw in visions and in dreams.
And he also hath written many things
which he prophesied and spake unto his children,
of which I shall not make a full account.

17 But I shall make an account of my proceedings in my days.
Behold, I make an abridgment of the record of my father
upon plates which I have made with mine own hands.
Wherefore after that I have abridged the record of my father,
then will I make an account of mine own life.

18 Therefore I would that ye should know that
after the Lord had shewn so many marvelous things unto my father Lehi,
yea, concerning the destruction of Jerusalem,
behold, he went forth among the people and began to prophesy
and to declare unto them concerning the things
which he had both seen and heard.

19 And it came to pass that the Jews did mock him
because of the things which he testified of them,
for he truly testified of their wickedness and their abominations.
And he testified that the things which he saw and heard,
and also the things which he read in the book,

manifested plainly of the coming of a Messiah
and also the redemption of the world.

20   And when the Jews heard these things, they were angry with him,
yea, even as with the prophets of old,
whom they had cast out and stoned and slain.
And they also sought his life that they might take it away.
But behold, I Nephi will shew unto you
that the tender mercies of the Lord is over all them
whom he hath chosen because of their faith
to make them mighty, even unto the power of deliverance.

2 | 1   For behold, it came to pass that the Lord spake unto my father,
yea, even in a dream, and saith unto him:
Blessed art thou Lehi because of the things which thou hast done.
And because thou hast been faithful
and declared unto this people the things which I commanded thee,
behold, they seek to take away thy life.

2   And it came to pass that the Lord commanded my father, even in a dream,
that he should take his family and depart into the wilderness.

3   And it came to pass that he was obedient unto the word of the Lord;
wherefore he did as the Lord commanded him.

4   And it came to pass that he departed into the wilderness.
And he left his house and the land of his inheritance
and his gold and his silver and his precious things
and took nothing with him save it were his family and provisions and tents,
and he departed into the wilderness.

5   And he came down by the borders near the shore of the Red Sea,
and he traveled in the wilderness in the borders which was nearer the Red Sea.
And he did travel in the wilderness with his family,
which consisted of my mother Sariah and my elder brethren,
which were Laman, Lemuel, and Sam.

6   And it came to pass that when he had traveled three days in the wilderness,
he pitched his tent in a valley beside a river of water.

7   And it came to pass that he built an altar of stones,
and he made an offering unto the Lord
and gave thanks unto the Lord our God.

8   And it came to pass that he called the name of the river Laman,
and it emptied into the Red Sea.
And the valley was in the borders near the mouth thereof.

9   And when my father saw that the waters of the river
emptied into the fountain of the Red Sea,

he spake unto Laman, saying:
O that thou mightest be like unto this river,
continually running into the fountain of all righteousness.

10 And he also spake unto Lemuel, saying:
O that thou mightest be like unto this valley,
firm and steadfast and immovable in keeping the commandments of the Lord.

11 Now this he spake because of the stiffneckedness of Laman and Lemuel.
For behold, they did murmur in many things against their father
because that he was a visionary man
and that he had led them out of the land of Jerusalem,
to leave the land of their inheritance
and their gold and their silver and their precious things,
and to perish in the wilderness.
And this they said that he had done
because of the foolish imaginations of his heart.

12 And thus Laman and Lemuel, being the eldest,
did murmur against their father.
And they did murmur because they knew not
the dealings of that God who had created them.

13 Neither did they believe that Jerusalem, that great city,
could be destroyed according to the words of the prophets.
And they were like unto the Jews which were at Jerusalem,
which sought to take away the life of my father.

14 And it came to pass that my father did speak unto them
in the valley of Lemuel with power, being filled with the Spirit,
until their frames did shake before him.
And he did confound them that they durst not utter against him;
wherefore they did do as he commanded them.

15 And my father dwelt in a tent.

16 And it came to pass that I Nephi being exceeding young,
nevertheless being large in stature,
and also having great desires to know of the mysteries of God,
wherefore I cried unto the Lord.
And behold, he did visit me and did soften my heart
that I did believe all the words which had been spoken by my father;
wherefore I did not rebel against him like unto my brothers.

17 And I spake unto Sam, making known unto him the things
which the Lord had manifested unto me by his Holy Spirit.
And it came to pass that he believed in my words.

18 But behold, Laman and Lemuel would not hearken unto my words.

And being grieved because of the hardness of their hearts,
I cried unto the Lord for them.

19 And it came to pass that the Lord spake unto me, saying:
Blessed art thou Nephi because of thy faith,
for thou hast sought me diligently with lowliness of heart.

20 And inasmuch as ye shall keep my commandments,
ye shall prosper and shall be led to a land of promise,
yea, even a land which I have prepared for you,
a land which is choice above all other lands.

21 And inasmuch as thy brethren shall rebel against thee,
they shall be cut off from the presence of the Lord.

22 And inasmuch as thou shalt keep my commandments,
thou shalt be made a ruler and a teacher over thy brethren.

23 For behold, in that day that they shall rebel against me,
I will curse them even with a sore curse,
and they shall have no power over thy seed
except they shall rebel against me also.

24 And if it so be that they rebel against me,
they shall be a scourge unto thy seed
to stir them up in the ways of remembrance.

3 | 1 And it came to pass that I Nephi returned
from speaking with the Lord to the tent of my father.

2 And it came to pass that he spake unto me, saying:
Behold, I have dreamed a dream
in the which the Lord hath commanded me
that thou and thy brethren shall return to Jerusalem.

3 For behold, Laban hath the record of the Jews
and also a genealogy of my forefathers,
and they are engraven upon plates of brass.

4 Wherefore the Lord hath commanded me
that thou and thy brothers should go unto the house of Laban
and seek the records and bring them down hither into the wilderness.

5 And now behold, thy brothers murmur,
saying it is a hard thing which I have required of them.
But behold, I have not required it of them,
but it is a commandment of the Lord.

6 Therefore go, my son,
and thou shalt be favored of the Lord
because thou hast not murmured.

7 And it came to pass that I Nephi said unto my father:

I will go and do the things which the Lord hath commanded,
for I know that the Lord giveth no commandments unto the children of men
save he shall prepare a way for them
that they may accomplish the thing which he commandeth them.

8 And it came to pass that when my father had heard these words,
he was exceeding glad,
for he knew that I had been blessed of the Lord.

9 And I Nephi and my brethren took our journey in the wilderness with our tents
to go up to the land of Jerusalem.

10 And it came to pass that when we had gone up to the land of Jerusalem,
I and my brethren did consult one with another.

11 And we cast lots which of us should go in unto the house of Laban.
And it came to pass that the lot fell upon Laman.
And Laman went in unto the house of Laban,
and he talked with him as he sat in his house.

12 And he desired of Laban the records
which were engraven upon the plates of brass,
which contained the genealogy of my father.

13 And behold, it came to pass that Laban was angry
and thrust him out from his presence,
and he would not that he should have the records.
Wherefore he said unto him:
Behold, thou art a robber and I will slay thee.

14 But Laman fled out of his presence
and told the things which Laban had done
unto us.
And we began to be exceeding sorrowful,
and my brethren were about to return unto my father in the wilderness.

15 But behold, I said unto them that
as the Lord liveth and as we live,
we will not go down unto our father in the wilderness
until we have accomplished the thing which the Lord hath commanded us.

16 Wherefore let us be faithful in keeping the commandments of the Lord.
Therefore let us go down to the land of our father's inheritance.
For behold, he left gold and silver and all manner of riches,
and all this he hath done because of the commandment.

17 For he knowing that Jerusalem must be destroyed
because of the wickedness of the people

18 —for behold, they have rejected the words of the prophets—
wherefore if my father should dwell in the land
after that he hath been commanded to flee out of the land,

behold, he would also perish;
wherefore it must needs be that he flee out of the land.

19 And behold, it is wisdom in God that we should obtain these records
that we might preserve unto our children the language of our fathers,

20 and also that we may preserve unto them the words
which have been spoken by the mouth of all the holy prophets,
which have been delivered unto them by the Spirit and power of God
since the world began, even down unto this present time.

21 And it came to pass that after this manner of language
did I persuade my brethren that they might be faithful
in keeping the commandments of God.

22 And it came to pass that we went down to the land of our inheritance,
and we did gather together our gold and our silver and our precious things.

23 And after that we had gathered these things together,
we went up again unto the house of Laban.

24 And it came to pass that we went in unto Laban and desired him
that he would give unto us the records
which were engraven upon the plates of brass,
for which we would give unto him
our gold and our silver and all our precious things.

25 And it came to pass that
when Laban saw our property that it was exceeding great,
he did lust after it,
insomuch that he thrust us out and sent his servants to slay us
that he might obtain our property.

26 And it came to pass that we did flee before the servants of Laban,
and we were obliged to leave behind our property,
and it fell into the hands of Laban.

27 And it came to pass that we fled into the wilderness,
and the servants of Laban did not overtake us,
and we hid ourselves in the cavity of a rock.

28 And it came to pass that Laman was angry with me and also with my father
—and also was Lemuel, for he hearkened unto the words of Laman—
wherefore Laman and Lemuel did speak many hard words
unto us their younger brothers,
and they did smite us, even with a rod.

29 And it came to pass as they smote us with a rod,
behold, an angel of the Lord came and stood before them,
and he spake unto them, saying:
Why do ye smite your younger brother with a rod?

Know ye not that the Lord hath chosen him to be a ruler over you?
—and this because of your iniquities.
Behold, thou shalt go up to Jerusalem again,
and the Lord will deliver Laban into your hands.

30 And after that the angel had spake unto us, he departed.

31 And after that the angel had departed,
Laman and Lemuel again began to murmur, saying:
How is it possible that the Lord will deliver Laban into our hands?
Behold, he is a mighty man and he can command fifty.
Yea, even he can slay fifty, then why not us?

4 | 1 And it came to pass that I spake unto my brethren, saying:
Let us go up again unto Jerusalem,
and let us be faithful in keeping the commandments of the Lord.
For behold, he is mightier than all the earth.
Then why not mightier than Laban and his fifty?
Yea, or even than his tens of thousands?

2 Therefore let us go up.

Let us be strong like unto Moses,
for he truly spake unto the waters of the Red Sea
and they divided hither and thither,
and our fathers came through out of captivity on dry ground,
and the armies of Pharaoh did follow
and were drownded in the waters of the Red Sea.

3 Now behold, ye know that this is true.
And ye also know that an angel hath spoken unto you.
Wherefore can ye doubt?
Let us go up.
The Lord is able to deliver us, even as our fathers,
and to destroy Laban, even as the Egyptians.

4 Now when I had spoken these words,
they was yet wroth and did still continue to murmur.
Nevertheless they did follow me up
until we came without the walls of Jerusalem.

5 And it was by night,
and I caused that they should hide themselves without the wall.

And after that they had hid themselves,
I Nephi crept into the city and went forth towards the house of Laban.

6 And I was led by the Spirit,
not knowing beforehand the things which I should do.

7   Nevertheless I went forth.
    And as I came near unto the house of Laban, I beheld a man,
    and he had fallen to the earth before me,
    for he was drunken with wine.

8   And when I came to him, I found that it was Laban.
9   And I beheld his sword, and I drew it forth from the sheath thereof.
    And the hilt thereof was of pure gold,
    and the workmanship thereof was exceeding fine.
    And I saw that the blade thereof was of the most precious steel.

10 And it came to pass that
    I was constrained by the Spirit that I should kill Laban.
    But I said in my heart:
    Never at any time have I shed the blood of man.
    And I shrunk and would that I might not slay him.
11 And the Spirit saith unto me again:
    Behold, the Lord hath delivered him into thy hands.
    Yea, and I also knew that he had sought to take away mine own life.
    Yea, and he would not hearken unto the commandments of the Lord.
    And he also had taken away our property.
12 And it came to pass that the Spirit said unto me again:
    Slay him, for the Lord hath delivered him into thy hands.
13 Behold, the Lord slayeth the wicked to bring forth his righteous purposes.
    It is better that one man should perish
    than that a nation should dwindle and perish in unbelief.

14 And now when I Nephi had heard these words,
    I remembered the words of the Lord
    which he spake unto me in the wilderness,
    saying that inasmuch as thy seed shall keep my commandments,
    they shall prosper in the land of promise.
15 Yea, and I also thought that they could not keep the commandments of the Lord
    according to the law of Moses save they should have the law.
16 And I also knew that the law was engraven upon the plates of brass.
17 And again I knew that the Lord had delivered Laban into my hands for this cause
    that I might obtain the records according to his commandments.

18 Therefore I did obey the voice of the Spirit
    and took Laban by the hair of the head,
    and I smote off his head with his own sword.
19 And after that I had smote off his head with his own sword,
    I took the garments of Laban and put them

upon mine own body, yea, even every whit.
And I did gird on his armor about my loins.

20 And after that I had done this, I went forth unto the treasury of Laban.
And as I went forth towards the treasury of Laban,
behold, I saw the servant of Laban which had the keys of the treasury,
and I commanded him in the voice of Laban
that he should go with me into the treasury.

21 And he supposing me to be his master Laban
—for he beheld the garments and also the sword girded about my loins—

22 and he spake unto me concerning the elders of the Jews,
he knowing that his master Laban had been out by night among them.

23 And I spake unto him as if it had been Laban.

24 And I also spake unto him that I should carry the engravings
which were upon the plates of brass
to my elder brethren, which were without the wall.

25 And I also bade him that he should follow me.

26 And he supposing that I spake of the brethren of the church
and that I was truly that Laban whom I had slew,
wherefore he did follow me.

27 And he spake unto me many times concerning the elders of the Jews
as I went forth unto my brethren, which were without the wall.

28 And it came to pass that when Laman saw me,
he was exceedingly frightened, and also Lemuel and Sam.
And they fled from before my presence,
for they supposed it was Laban
and that he had slain me and had sought to take away their lives also.

29 And it came to pass that I called after them and they did hear me;
wherefore they did cease to flee from my presence.

30 And it came to pass that when the servant of Laban beheld my brethren,
he began to tremble and was about to flee from before me
and return to the city of Jerusalem.

31 And now I Nephi being a man large in stature,
and also having received much strength of the Lord,
therefore I did seize upon the servant of Laban
and held him that he should not flee.

32 And it came to pass that I spake with him
that if he would hearken unto my words
—as the Lord liveth and as I live—
even so that if he would hearken unto our words, we would spare his life.

33 And I spake unto him, even with an oath, that he need not fear,
that he should be a free man like unto us
if he would go down into the wilderness with us.

34 And I also spake unto him, saying:
Surely the Lord hath commanded us to do this thing.
And shall we not be diligent in keeping the commandment of the Lord?
Therefore if thou wilt go down into the wilderness to my father,
thou shalt have place with us.

35 And it came to pass that Zoram did take courage at the words which I spake
—now Zoram was the name of the servant—
and he promised that he would go down into the wilderness unto our father;
yea, and he also made an oath unto us
that he would tarry with us from that time forth.

36 Now we were desirous that he should tarry with us for this cause
that the Jews might not know concerning our flight into the wilderness,
lest they should pursue us and destroy us.

37 And it came to pass that when Zoram had made an oath unto us,
our fears did cease concerning him.

38 And it came to pass that we took the plates of brass and the servant of Laban
and departed into the wilderness and journeyed unto the tent of our father.

5 | 1 And it came to pass that after we had came down
into the wilderness unto our father,
behold, he was filled with joy.
And also my mother Sariah was exceeding glad,
for she truly had mourned because of us,

2 for she had supposed that we had perished in the wilderness.
And she also had complained against my father,
telling him that he was a visionary man, saying:
Behold, thou hast led us forth from the land of our inheritance,
and my sons are no more, and we perish in the wilderness.

3 And after this manner of language had my mother complained against my father.

4 And it had came to pass that my father spake unto her, saying:
I know that I am a visionary man,
for if I had not seen the things of God in a vision,
I should not have known the goodness of God
but had tarried at Jerusalem and had perished with my brethren.

5 But behold, I have obtained a land of promise, in the which things I do rejoice.
Yea, and I know that the Lord will deliver my sons out of the hands of Laban
and bring them down again unto us in the wilderness.

6 And after this manner of language
did my father Lehi comfort my mother Sariah concerning us

while we journeyed in the wilderness up to the land of Jerusalem
to obtain the record of the Jews.

7   And when we had returned to the tent of my father,
    behold, their joy was full, and my mother was comforted.

8   And she spake, saying:
    Now I know of a surety that the Lord hath commanded
    my husband to flee into the wilderness;
    yea, and I also know of a surety
    that the Lord hath protected my sons
    and delivered them out of the hands of Laban
    and gave them power whereby they could accomplish the thing
    which the Lord hath commanded them.
    And after this manner of language did she speak.

9   And it came to pass that they did rejoice exceedingly
    and did offer sacrifice and burnt offerings unto the Lord,
    and they gave thanks unto the God of Israel.

10 And after that they had given thanks unto the God of Israel,
    my father Lehi took the records which were engraven upon the plates of brass
    and he did search them from the beginning.

11 And he beheld that they did contain the five books of Moses,
    which gave an account of the creation of the world
    and also of Adam and Eve, which was our first parents,

12 and also a record of the Jews from the beginning,
    even down to the commencement of the reign of Zedekiah, king of Judah,

13 and also the prophecies of the holy prophets from the beginning,
    even down to the commencement of the reign of Zedekiah,
    and also many prophecies which have been spoken by the mouth of Jeremiah.

14 And it came to pass that my father Lehi also found
    upon the plates of brass a genealogy of his fathers;
    wherefore he knew that he was a descendant of Joseph,
    yea, even that Joseph which was the son of Jacob,
    which was sold into Egypt and which was preserved by the hand of the Lord
    that he might preserve his father Jacob and all his household
    from perishing with famine.

15 And they were also led out of captivity and out of the land of Egypt
    by that same God who had preserved them.

16 And thus my father Lehi did discover the genealogy of his fathers.
    And Laban also was a descendant of Joseph;
    wherefore he and his fathers had kept the records.

17 And now when my father saw all these things,
    he was filled with the Spirit and began to prophesy concerning his seed,

18 that these plates of brass should go forth
    unto all nations, kindreds, tongues, and people which were of his seed.
19 Wherefore he said that these plates of brass should never perish,
    neither should they be dimmed any more by time.
    And he prophesied many things concerning his seed.

20 And it came to pass that thus far I and my father had kept the commandments
    wherewith the Lord had commanded us.
21 And we had obtained the record which the Lord had commanded us
    and searched them and found that they were desirable,
    yea, even of great worth unto us,
    insomuch that we could preserve
    the commandments of the Lord unto our children.
22 Wherefore it was wisdom in the Lord that we should carry them with us
    as we journeyed in the wilderness toward the land of promise.

6 | 1 And now I Nephi do not give the genealogy of my fathers
    in this part of my record,
    neither at any time shall I give it after upon these plates which I am writing,
    for it is given in the record which has been kept by my father;
    wherefore I do not write it in this work.
2 For it sufficeth me to say that we are a descendant of Joseph.
3 And it mattereth not to me that I am particular to give a full account
    of all the things of my father,
    for they cannot be written upon these plates,
    for I desire the room that I may write of the things of God.
4 For the fullness of mine intent is that I may persuade men to come
    unto the God of Abraham and the God of Isaac and the God of Jacob
    and be saved.
5 Wherefore the things which are pleasing unto the world I do not write,
    but the things which are pleasing unto God
    and unto them which are not of the world.
6 Wherefore I shall give commandment unto my seed
    that they shall not occupy these plates with things
    which are not of worth unto the children of men.

7 | 1 And now I would that ye might know that
    after my father Lehi had made an end of prophesying concerning his seed,
    it came to pass that the Lord spake unto him again
    that it was not meet for him Lehi
    that he should take his family into the wilderness alone,

but that his sons should take daughters to wife
that they might raise up seed unto the Lord in the land of promise.

2 And it came to pass that the Lord commanded him
that I Nephi and my brethren should again return into the land of Jerusalem
and bring down Ishmael and his family into the wilderness.

3 And it came to pass that I Nephi did again with my brethren
go forth into the wilderness to go up to Jerusalem.

4 And it came to pass that we went up unto the house of Ishmael,
and we did gain favor in the sight of Ishmael,
insomuch that we did speak unto him the words of the Lord.

5 And it came to pass that the Lord did soften the heart of Ishmael
and also his whole household,
insomuch that they took their journey with us
down into the wilderness to the tent of our father.

6 And it came to pass that as we journeyed in the wilderness,
behold, Laman and Lemuel and two of the daughters of Ishmael
and the two sons of Ishmael and their families did rebel against us,
yea, against I Nephi and Sam
and their father Ishmael and his wife and his three other daughters.

7 And it came to pass that in the which rebellion
they were desirous to return unto the land of Jerusalem.

8 And now I Nephi being grieved for the hardness of their hearts,
therefore I spake unto them, saying,
yea, even unto Laman and unto Lemuel:
Behold, thou art mine elder brethren,
and how is it that ye are so hard in your hearts and so blind in your minds
that ye have need that I, your younger brother, should speak unto you?
Yea, and set an example for you?

9 How is it that ye have not hearkened unto the word of the Lord?

10 How is it that ye have forgotten that ye have seen an angel of the Lord?

11 Yea, and how is it that ye have forgotten
how great things the Lord hath done for us
in delivering us out of the hands of Laban
and also that we should obtain the record?

12 Yea, and how is it that ye have forgotten
that the Lord is able to do all things
according to his will for the children of men?
—if it so be that they exercise faith in him.
Wherefore let us be faithful in him.

13 And if it so be that we are faithful in him,
we shall obtain the land of promise.

And ye shall know at some future period
that the word of the Lord shall be fulfilled
concerning the destruction of Jerusalem,
for all things which the Lord hath spoken
concerning the destruction of Jerusalem must be fulfilled.

14 For behold, the Spirit of the Lord ceaseth soon to strive with them.
For behold, they have rejected the prophets,
and Jeremiah have they cast into prison,
and they have sought to take away the life of my father,
insomuch that they have driven him out of the land.

15 Now behold, I say unto you
that if ye will return unto Jerusalem, ye shall also perish with them.
And now if ye have choice, go up to the land,
and remember the words which I speak unto you,
that if ye go, ye will also perish.
For thus the Spirit of the Lord constraineth me that I should speak.

16 And it came to pass that
when I Nephi had spoken these words unto my brethren,
they were angry with me.
And it came to pass that they did lay their hands upon me,
for behold, they were exceeding wroth.
And they did bind me with cords, for they sought to take away my life,
that they might leave me in the wilderness to be devoured by wild beasts.

17 But it came to pass that I prayed unto the Lord, saying:
O Lord, according to my faith which is in me,
wilt thou deliver me from the hands of my brethren!
Yea, even give me strength that I may burst these bands with which I am bound.

18 And it came to pass that when I had said these words,
behold, the bands were loosed from off my hands and feet,
and I stood before my brethren, and I spake unto them again.

19 And it came to pass that they were angry with me again
and sought to lay hands upon me.
But behold, one of the daughters of Ishmael,
yea, and also her mother and one of the sons of Ishmael,
did plead with my brethren,
insomuch that they did soften their hearts
and they did cease striving to take away my life.

20 And it came to pass that they were sorrowful because of their wickedness,

insomuch that they did bow down before me
and did plead with me that I would forgive them of the thing
that they had done against me.

21 And it came to pass that I did frankly forgive them all that they had done.
And I did exhort them that they would pray
unto the Lord their God for forgiveness.
And it came to pass that they did so.

And after that they had done praying unto the Lord,
we did again travel on our journey toward the tent of our father.

22 And it came to pass that we did come down unto the tent of our father.
And after that I and my brethren and all the house of Ishmael
had come down unto the tent of my father,
they did give thanks unto the Lord their God,
and they did offer sacrifice and burnt offerings unto him.

8 | 1 And it came to pass that we had gathered together
all manner of seeds of every kind,
both of grain of every kind and also of the seeds of fruits of every kind.

2 And it came to pass that while my father tarried in the wilderness,
he spake unto us, saying:
Behold, I have dreamed a dream,
or in other words, I have seen a vision.

3 And behold, because of the thing which I have seen,
I have reason to rejoice in the Lord because of Nephi and also of Sam.
For I have reason to suppose
that they and also many of their seed will be saved.

4 But behold, Laman and Lemuel, I fear exceedingly because of you.

For behold, methought I saw a dark and dreary wilderness.

5 And it came to pass that I saw a man and he was dressed in a white robe.
And he came and stood before me.

6 And it came to pass that he spake unto me and bade me follow him.

7 And it came to pass that I followed him.
And after I had followed him,
I beheld myself that I was in a dark and dreary waste.

8 And after that I had traveled for the space of many hours in darkness,
I began to pray unto the Lord that he would have mercy on me
according to the multitude of his tender mercies.

9 And it came to pass that after I had prayed unto the Lord,
I beheld a large and spacious field.

10 And it came to pass that I beheld a tree

whose fruit was desirable to make one happy.

11 And it came to pass that I did go forth and partook of the fruit thereof
and beheld that it was most sweet, above all that I ever had before tasted.
Yea, and I beheld that the fruit thereof was white
to exceed all the whiteness that I had ever seen.

12 And as I partook of the fruit thereof,
it filled my soul with exceeding great joy.

Wherefore I began to be desirous that my family should partake of it also,
for I knew that it was desirous above all other fruit.

13 And as I cast my eyes around about
that perhaps I might discover my family also,
and I beheld a river of water and it ran along,
and it was near the tree of which I was partaking the fruit.

14 And I looked to behold from whence it came,
and I saw the head thereof a little way off.
And at the head thereof I beheld your mother Sariah and Sam and Nephi,
and they stood as if they knew not whither they should go.

15 And it came to pass that I beckoned unto them.
And I also did say unto them with a loud voice
that they should come unto me and partake of the fruit,
which was desirable above all other fruit.

16 And it came to pass that they did come unto me and partake of the fruit also.

17 And it came to pass that I was desirous
that Laman and Lemuel should come and partake of the fruit also.
Wherefore I cast mine eyes toward the head of the river
that perhaps I might see them.

18 And it came to pass that I saw them,
but they would not come unto me and partake of the fruit.

19 And I beheld a rod of iron,
and it extended along the bank of the river
and led to the tree by which I stood.

20 And I also beheld a straight and narrow path
which came along by the rod of iron,
even to the tree by which I stood.
And it also led by the head of the fountain unto a large and spacious field,
as if it had been a world.

21 And I saw numberless concourses of people,
many of whom were pressing forward
that they might obtain the path

which led unto the tree by which I stood.

22 And it came to pass that they did come forth
and commenced in the path which led to the tree.

23 And it came to pass that there arose a mist of darkness,
yea, even an exceeding great mist of darkness,
insomuch that they which had commenced in the path did lose their way,
that they wandered off and were lost.

24 And it came to pass that I beheld others pressing forward.
And they came forth and caught hold of the end of the rod of iron.
And they did press forward through the mists of darkness,
clinging to the rod of iron,
even until they did come forth and partook of the fruit of the tree.

25 And after that they had partook of the fruit of the tree,
they did cast their eyes about as if they were ashamed.

26 And I also cast my eyes around about
and beheld on the other side of the river of water a great and spacious building.
And it stood as it were in the air, high above the earth.

27 And it was filled with people, both old and young, both male and female,
and their manner of dress was exceeding fine.
And they were in the attitude of mocking and pointing their fingers
towards those which had came up and were partaking of the fruit.

28 And after that they had tasted of the fruit, they were ashamed
because of those that were a scoffing at them,
and they fell away into forbidden paths and were lost.

29 And now I Nephi do not speak all the words of my father.

30 But to be short in writing, behold, he saw other multitudes pressing forwards.
And they came and caught hold of the end of the rod of iron.
And they did press their way forward,
continually holding fast to the rod of iron,
until they came forth and fell down and partook of the fruit of the tree.

31 And he also saw other multitudes pressing their way
towards that great and spacious building.

32 And it came to pass that many were drowned in the depths of the fountain,
and many were lost from his view, wandering in strange roads.

33 And great was the multitude that did enter into that strange building.
And after that they did enter into that building,
they did point the finger of scorn at me
and those that were partaking of the fruit also,
but we heeded them not.

34 Thus is the words of my father,

for as many as heeded them had fallen away.

35 And Laman and Lemuel partook not of the fruit, saith my father.

36 And it came to pass that after my father had spoken
all the words of his dream or vision, which were many,
he said unto us,
because of these things which he saw in a vision,
he exceedingly feared for Laman and Lemuel.
Yea, he feared lest they should be cast off from the presence of the Lord.

37 And he did exhort them then with all the feeling of a tender parent
that they would hearken to his words,
in that perhaps the Lord would be merciful to them and not cast them off.
Yea, my father did preach unto them.

38 And after that he had preached unto them
and also prophesied unto them of many things,
he bade them to keep the commandments of the Lord.
And he did cease speaking unto them.

9 | 1 And all these things did my father see and hear and speak
as he dwelt in a tent in the valley of Lemuel,
and also a great many more things which cannot be written upon these plates.

2 And now as I have spoken concerning these plates,
behold, they are not the plates
upon which I make a full account of the history of my people,
for the plates upon which I make a full account of my people
I have given the name of Nephi;
wherefore they are called the plates of Nephi after mine own name.
And these plates also are called the plates of Nephi.

3 Nevertheless I have received a commandment of the Lord
that I should make these plates for the special purpose
that there should be an account engraven of the ministry of my people.

4 And upon the other plates should be engraven
an account of the reigns of the kings
and the wars and contentions of my people.
Wherefore these plates are for the more part of the ministry,
and the other plates are for the more part of the reigns of the kings
and the wars and contentions of my people.

5 Wherefore the Lord hath commanded me to make these plates
for a wise purpose in him, which purpose I know not.

6 But the Lord knoweth all things from the beginning.
Wherefore he prepareth a way
to accomplish all his works among the children of men.

For behold, he hath all power unto the fulfilling of all his words.

And thus it is.

Amen.

⸺

10 | 1 And now I Nephi proceed to give an account upon these plates

of my proceedings and my reign and ministry.

Wherefore to proceed with mine account,

I must speak somewhat of the things of my father and also of my brethren.

2 For behold, it came to pass that after my father had made an end

of speaking the words of his dream and also of exhorting them to all diligence,

he spake unto them concerning the Jews,

3 how that after they were destroyed

—yea, even that great city Jerusalem—

and that many were carried away captive into Babylon,

that according to the own due time of the Lord they should return again

—yea, even be brought back out of captivity—

and after that they are brought back out of captivity,

to possess again their land of inheritance

4 —yea, even six hundred years from the time that my father left Jerusalem—

a prophet would the Lord God raise up among the Jews,

yea, even a Messiah, or in other words, a Savior of the world.

5 And he also spake concerning the prophets,

how great a number had testified of these things

concerning this Messiah of which he had spoken,

or this Redeemer of the world.

6 Wherefore all mankind was in a lost and in a fallen state and ever would be

save they should rely on this Redeemer.

7 And he spake also concerning a prophet

which should come before the Messiah to prepare the way of the Lord,

8 yea, even he should go forth and cry in the wilderness:

Prepare ye the way of the Lord and make his paths straight,

for there standeth one among you whom ye know not

—and he is mightier than I—

whose shoe's latchet I am not worthy to unloose.

And much spake my father concerning this thing.

9 And my father saith that he should baptize in Bethabara beyond Jordan.

And he also spake that he should baptize with water,

yea, even that he should baptize the Messiah with water.

10 And after that he had baptized the Messiah with water,

he should behold and bear record that he had baptized the Lamb of God,
which should take away the sin of the world.

11 And it came to pass that after my father had spoken these words,
he spake unto my brethren concerning the gospel
which should be preached among the Jews,
and also concerning the dwindling of the Jews in unbelief.
And after that they had slain the Messiah which should come—
and after that he had been slain,
he should rise from the dead
and should make himself manifest by the Holy Ghost unto the Gentiles.

12 Yea, even my father spake much concerning the Gentiles
and also concerning the house of Israel,
that they should be compared like unto an olive tree
whose branches should be broken off
and should be scattered upon all the face of the earth.

13 Wherefore he said it must needs be
that we should be led with one accord into the land of promise,
unto the fulfilling of the word of the Lord
that we should be scattered upon all the face of the earth.

14 And after that the house of Israel should be scattered,
they should be gathered together again,
or in fine, that after the Gentiles had received the fullness of the gospel,
the natural branches of the olive tree or the remnants of the house of Israel
should be grafted in or come to the knowledge of the true Messiah,
their Lord and their Redeemer.

15 And after this manner of language did my father prophesy
and speak unto my brethren,
and also many more things which I do not write in this book;
for I have written as many of them as were expedient for me in mine other book.

16 And all these things of which I have spoken was done
as my father dwelt in a tent in the valley of Lemuel.

17 And it came to pass that after I Nephi having heard all the words of my father
concerning the things which he saw in a vision
and also the things which he spake by the power of the Holy Ghost,
which power he received by faith on the Son of God
—and the Son of God was the Messiah which should come—
and it came to pass that I Nephi was desirous also
that I might see and hear and know of these things
by the power of the Holy Ghost,
which is the gift of God unto all those who diligently seek him
as well in times of old

as in the time that he should manifest himself unto the children of men,

18   for he is the same yesterday and today and forever.
And the way is prepared for all men from the foundation of the world
if it so be that they repent and come unto him.

19   For he that diligently seeketh shall find,
and the mysteries of God shall be unfolded to them
by the power of the Holy Ghost
as well in this time as in times of old
and as well in times of old as in times to come;
wherefore the course of the Lord is one eternal round.

20   Therefore remember, O man:
for all thy doings thou shalt be brought into judgment.

21   Wherefore if ye have sought to do wickedly in the days of your probation,
then ye are found unclean before the judgment seat of God.
And no unclean thing can dwell with God;
wherefore ye must be cast off forever.

22   And the Holy Ghost giveth authority
that I should speak these things and deny them not.

11 | 1   For it came to pass that after I had desired
to know the things that my father had seen,
and believing that the Lord was able to make them known unto me,
wherefore as I sat pondering in mine heart,
I was caught away in the Spirit of the Lord,
yea, into an exceeding high mountain,
a mountain which I never had before seen
and upon which I never had before sat my foot.

2   And the Spirit saith unto me:
Behold, what desirest thou?

3   And I saith:
I desire to behold the things which my father saw.

4   And the Spirit saith unto me:
Believest thou that thy father saw the tree of which he hath spoken?

5   And I said:
Yea, thou knowest that I believe all the words of my father.

6   And when I had spake these words,
the Spirit cried with a loud voice, saying:
Hosanna to the Lord, the Most High God,
for he is God over all the earth, yea, even above all.
And blessed art thou Nephi because thou believest in the Son of the Most High;
wherefore thou shalt behold the things which thou hast desired.

7 And behold, this thing shall be given unto thee for a sign,
that after thou hast beheld the tree
which bare the fruit of which thy father tasted,
thou shalt also behold a man descending out of heaven
and him shall ye witness.
And after that ye shall have witnessed him,
ye shall bear record that it is the Son of God.

8 And it came to pass that the Spirit saith unto me: Look!
And I looked and beheld a tree,
and it was like unto the tree which my father had seen.
And the beauty thereof was far beyond, yea, exceeding of all beauty,
and the whiteness thereof did exceed the whiteness of the driven snow.

9 And it came to pass that after that I had seen the tree,
I said unto the Spirit:
I behold thou hast shewn unto me the tree
which is most precious above all.

10 And he saith unto me:
What desirest thou?

11 And I said unto him:
To know the interpretation thereof.
For I spake unto him as a man speaketh,
for I beheld that he was in the form of a man,
yet nevertheless I knew that it was the Spirit of the Lord,
and he spake unto me as a man speaketh with another.

12 And it came to pass that he said unto me: Look!
And I looked as if to look upon him and I saw him not,
for he had gone from before my presence.

13 And it came to pass that I looked
and beheld the great city Jerusalem and also other cities.
And I beheld the city of Nazareth.
And in the city of Nazareth I beheld a virgin,
and she was exceeding fair and white.

14 And it came to pass that I saw the heavens open,
and an angel came down and stood before me.
And he saith unto me:
Nephi, what beholdest thou?

15 And I saith unto him:
A virgin most beautiful and fair above all other virgins.

16 And he saith unto me:

Knowest thou the condescension of God?

17 And I said unto him:
I know that he loveth his children;
nevertheless I do not know the meaning of all things.

18 And he said unto me:
Behold, the virgin which thou seest is the mother of God
after the manner of the flesh.

19 And it came to pass that I beheld that she was carried away in the spirit.
And after that she had been carried away in the spirit for the space of a time,
the angel spake unto me, saying: Look!

20 And I looked and beheld the virgin again,
bearing a child in her arms.

21 And the angel said unto me:
Behold the Lamb of God, yea, even the Eternal Father.
Knowest thou the meaning of the tree which thy father saw?

22 And I answered him, saying:
Yea, it is the love of God,
which sheddeth itself abroad in the hearts of the children of men;
wherefore it is the most desirable above all things.

23 And he spake unto me, saying:
Yea, and the most joyous to the soul.

24 And after that he had said these words,
he said unto me: Look!
And I looked and I beheld the Son of God
a going forth among the children of men.
And I saw many fall down at his feet and worship him.

25 And it came to pass that I beheld
that the rod of iron which my father had seen was the word of God,
which led to the fountain of living waters or to the tree of life,
which waters are a representation of the love of God.
And I also beheld that the tree of life was a representation of the love of God.

26 And the angel said unto me again:
Look and behold the condescension of God!

27 And I looked and beheld the Redeemer of the world,
of which my father had spoken.
And I also beheld the prophet which should prepare the way before him.
And the Lamb of God went forth and was baptized of him.
And after that he was baptized,
I beheld the heavens open

and the Holy Ghost came down out of heaven
and abode upon him in the form of a dove.

28 And I beheld that he went forth
ministering unto the people in power and great glory,
and the multitudes were gathered together to hear him.
And I beheld that they cast him out from among them.
29 And I also beheld twelve others following him.
And it came to pass that
they were carried away in the spirit from before my face,
that I saw them not.

30 And it came to pass that the angel spake unto me, saying: Look!
And I looked and I beheld the heavens open again.
And I saw angels descending upon the children of men,
and they did minister unto them.

31 And he spake unto me again, saying: Look!
And I looked and I beheld the Lamb of God
going forth among the children of men.
And I beheld multitudes of people which were sick
and which were afflicted of all manner of diseases
and with devils and unclean spirits
—and the angel spake and shewed all these things unto me—
and they were healed by the power of the Lamb of God,
and the devils and the unclean spirits were cast out.

32 And it came to pass that the angel spake unto me again, saying: Look!
And I looked and beheld the Lamb of God
that he was taken by the people,
yea, the everlasting God was judged of the world.
And I saw and bare record.
33 And I Nephi saw that he was lifted up upon the cross
and slain for the sins of the world.

34 And after that he was slain, I saw the multitudes of the earth
that they were gathered together to fight against the apostles of the Lamb,
for thus were the twelve called by the angel of the Lord.
35 And the multitude of the earth was gathered together,
and I beheld that they were in a large and spacious building,
like unto the building which my father saw.
And the angel of the Lord spake unto me, saying:
Behold the world and the wisdom thereof;
yea, behold, the house of Israel hath gathered together
to fight against the twelve apostles of the Lamb.

36 And it came to pass that I saw and bare record
 that the great and spacious building was the pride of the world;
 and the fall thereof was exceeding great.
 And the angel of the Lord spake unto me, saying:
 Thus shall be the destruction of all nations, kindreds, tongues, and people
 that shall fight against the twelve apostles of the Lamb.

12 | 1 And it came to pass that the angel said unto me:
 Look and behold thy seed and also the seed of thy brethren.
 And I looked and beheld the land of promise.
 And I beheld multitudes of people,
 yea, even as it were in number as many as the sand of the sea.
 2 And it came to pass that I beheld multitudes gathered together
 to battle one against the other.
 And I beheld wars and rumors of wars
 and great slaughters with the sword among my people.
 3 And it came to pass that I beheld many generations pass away
 after the manner of wars and contentions in the land.
 And I beheld many cities,
 yea, even that I did not number them.

 4 And it came to pass that I saw a mist of darkness
 on the face of the land of promise.
 And I saw lightnings and I heard thunderings and earthquakes
 and all manner of tumultuous noises.
 And I saw the earth that it rent the rocks,
 and I saw mountains tumbling into pieces,
 and I saw the plains of the earth that they were broken up.
 And I saw many cities that they were sunk,
 and I saw many that they were burnt with fire,
 and I saw many that they did tumble to the earth
 because of the quaking thereof.

 5 And it came to pass that after I saw these things,
 I saw the vapor of darkness
 that it passed from off the face of the earth.
 And behold, I saw the multitudes which had not fallen
 because of the great and terrible judgments of the Lord.
 6 And I saw the heavens open and the Lamb of God descending out of heaven.
 And he came down and he shewed himself unto them.

 7 And I also saw and bare record
 that the Holy Ghost fell upon twelve others,
 and they were ordained of God and chosen.

8 And the angel spake unto me, saying:
Behold the twelve disciples of the Lamb
which are chosen to minister unto thy seed.

9 And he saith unto me:
Thou rememberest the twelve apostles of the Lamb.
Behold, they are they which shall judge the twelve tribes of Israel;
wherefore the twelve ministers of thy seed shall be judged of them,
for ye are of the house of Israel.

10 And these twelve ministers which thou beholdest shall judge thy seed.
And behold, they are righteous forever,
for because of their faith in the Lamb of God,
their garments are made white in his blood.

11 And the angel saith unto me: Look!
And I looked and beheld three generations did pass away in righteousness,
and their garments were white, even like unto the Lamb of God.
And the angel said unto me:
These are made white in the blood of the Lamb
because of their faith in him.

12 And I Nephi also saw many of the fourth generation
which did pass away in righteousness.

13 And it came to pass that I saw the multitudes of the earth gathered together.

14 And the angel said unto me:
Behold thy seed and also the seed of thy brethren.

15 And it came to pass that I looked and beheld the people of my seed
gathered together in multitudes against the seed of my brethren;
and they were gathered together to battle.

16 And the angel spake unto me, saying:
Behold the fountain of filthy water which thy father saw,
yea, even the river of which he spake;
and the depths thereof are the depths of hell.

17 And the mists of darkness are the temptations of the devil,
which blindeth the eyes and hardeneth the hearts of the children of men
and leadeth them away into broad roads
that they perish and are lost.

18 And the large and spacious building which thy father saw
is vain imaginations and the pride of the children of men.
And a great and a terrible gulf divideth them,
yea, even the sword of the justice of the Eternal God and Jesus Christ,
which is the Lamb of God,

of whom the Holy Ghost beareth record
from the beginning of the world until this time
and from this time henceforth and forever.

19 And while the angel spake these words,
I beheld and saw that the seed of my brethren did contend against my seed,
according to the word of the angel.
And because of the pride of my seed and the temptations of the devil,
I beheld that the seed of my brethren did overpower the people of my seed.

20 And it came to pass that I beheld and saw the people of the seed of my brethren
that they had overcome my seed.
And they went forth in multitudes upon the face of the land;
21 and I saw them gathered together in multitudes.
And I saw wars and rumors of wars among them,
and in wars and rumors of wars I saw many generations pass away.

22 And the angel said unto me:
Behold, these shall dwindle in unbelief.
23 And it came to pass that I beheld that after they had dwindled in unbelief,
they became a dark and loathsome and a filthy people,
full of idleness and all manner of abominations.

13 | 1 And it came to pass that the angel spake unto me, saying: Look!
And I looked and beheld many nations and kingdoms.
2 And the angel saith unto me:
What beholdest thou?
And I said:
I behold many nations and kingdoms.
3 And he saith unto me:
These are the nations and kingdoms of the Gentiles.
4 And it came to pass that I saw among the nations of the Gentiles
the formation of a great church.
5 And the angel said unto me:
Behold the formation of a church
which is most abominable above all other churches,
which slayeth the saints of God,
yea, and tortureth them and bindeth them down
and yoketh them with a yoke of iron
and bringeth them down into captivity.
6 And it came to pass that I beheld this great and abominable church,
and I saw the devil that he was the founder of it.

7 And I also saw gold and silver and silks and scarlets
and fine twined linen and all manner of precious clothing,
and I saw many harlots.

8 And the angel spake unto me, saying:
Behold, the gold and the silver and the silks and the scarlets
and the fine twined linen and the precious clothing and the harlots
are the desires of this great and abominable church.

9 And also for the praise of the world do they destroy the saints of God
and bring them down into captivity.

10 And it came to pass that I looked and beheld many waters,
and they divided the Gentiles from the seed of my brethren.

11 And it came to pass that the angel saith unto me:
Behold, the wrath of God is upon the seed of thy brethren.

12 And I looked and beheld a man among the Gentiles,
which were separated from the seed of my brethren by the many waters.
And I beheld the Spirit of God
that it came down and wrought upon the man,
and he went forth upon the many waters,
even unto the seed of my brethren, which were in the promised land.

13 And it came to pass that I beheld the Spirit of God
that it wrought upon other Gentiles,
and they went forth out of captivity upon the many waters.

14 And it came to pass that I beheld
many multitudes of the Gentiles upon the land of promise.
And I beheld the wrath of God
that it was upon the seed of my brethren,
and they were scattered before the Gentiles and they were smitten.

15 And I beheld the Spirit of the Lord that it was upon the Gentiles,
that they did prosper and obtain the land for their inheritance.
And I beheld that they were white and exceeding fair and beautiful,
like unto my people before that they were slain.

16 And it came to pass that I Nephi beheld that the Gentiles
which had gone forth out of captivity
did humble themselves before the Lord,
and the power of the Lord was with them.

17 And I beheld that their mother Gentiles was gathered together
upon the waters and upon the land also,
to battle against them.

18 And I beheld that the power of God was with them,

and also that the wrath of God was upon all those
that were gathered together against them to battle.

19 And I Nephi beheld that the Gentiles which had gone out of captivity
were delivered by the power of God out of the hands of all other nations.

20 And it came to pass that I Nephi beheld that they did prosper in the land.
And I beheld a book and it was carried forth among them.

21 And the angel saith unto me:
Knowest thou the meaning of the book?

22 And I saith:
I know not.

23 And he saith:
Behold, it proceedeth out of the mouth of a Jew.
And I Nephi beheld it.
And he saith unto me:
The book which thou beholdest is a record of the Jews,
which contain the covenants of the Lord
which he hath made unto the house of Israel.
And it also containeth many of the prophecies of the holy prophets.
And it is a record like unto the engravings
which are upon the plates of brass,
save there are not so many.
Nevertheless they contain the covenants of the Lord
which he hath made unto the house of Israel;
wherefore they are of great worth unto the Gentiles.

24 And the angel of the Lord said unto me:
Thou hast beheld that the book proceeded forth from the mouth of a Jew.
And when it proceeded forth from the mouth of a Jew,
it contained the fullness of the gospel of the Lamb,
of whom the twelve apostles bare record.
And they bare record according to the truth which is in the Lamb of God.

25 Wherefore these things go forth from the Jews in purity unto the Gentiles,
according to the truth which is in God.

26 And after that they go forth by the hand of the twelve apostles of the Lamb
from the Jews unto the Gentiles,
behold, after this thou seest the formation of that great and abominable church,
which is the most abominable of all other churches.
For behold, they have taken away from the gospel of the Lamb
many parts which are plain and most precious;
and also many covenants of the Lord have they taken away.

27 And all this have they done that they might pervert the right ways of the Lord, that they might blind the eyes and harden the hearts of the children of men.

28 Wherefore thou seest that after the book hath gone forth
through the hands of the great and abominable church
that there are many plain and most precious things taken away from the book,
which is the book of the Lamb of God.

29 And after that these plain and precious things were taken away,
it goeth forth unto all the nations of the Gentiles.
And after it goeth forth unto all the nations of the Gentiles,
yea, even across the many waters—which thou hast seen—
with the Gentiles which have gone forth out of captivity,
and thou seest because of the many plain and precious things
which have been taken out of the book,
which were plain unto the understanding of the children of men
according to the plainness which is in the Lamb of God—
and because of these things which are taken away out of the gospel of the Lamb,
an exceeding great many do stumble,
yea, insomuch that Satan hath great power over them.

30 Nevertheless thou beholdest that the Gentiles
which have gone forth out of captivity
and have been lifted up by the power of God
above all other nations upon the face of the land
which is choice above all other lands,
which is the land which the Lord God hath covenanted with thy father
that his seed should have for the land of their inheritance,
wherefore thou seest that the Lord God will not suffer
that the Gentiles will utterly destroy the mixture of thy seed
which is among thy brethren.

31 Neither will he suffer that the Gentiles shall destroy the seed of thy brethren.

32 Neither will the Lord God suffer that the Gentiles shall forever remain
in that state of awful wickedness which thou beholdest that they are in
because of the plain and most precious parts of the gospel of the Lamb
which hath been kept back by that abominable church,
whose formation thou hast seen.

33 Wherefore, saith the Lamb of God,
I will be merciful unto the Gentiles,
unto the visiting of the remnant of the house of Israel in great judgment.

34 And it came to pass that the angel of the Lord spake unto me, saying:
Behold, saith the Lamb of God,
after that I have visited the remnant of the house of Israel
—and this remnant of which I speak is the seed of thy father—

wherefore after that I have visited them in judgment
and smitten them by the hand of the Gentiles,
and after that the Gentiles do stumble exceedingly
because of the most plain and precious parts of the gospel of the Lamb
which hath been kept back by that abominable church,
which is the mother of harlots, saith the Lamb,
wherefore I will be merciful unto the Gentiles in that day, saith the Lamb,
insomuch that I will bring forth unto them in mine own power
much of my gospel, which shall be plain and precious, saith the Lamb.

35 For behold, saith the Lamb, I will manifest myself unto thy seed
that they shall write many things which I shall minister unto them,
which shall be plain and precious.

And after that thy seed shall be destroyed and dwindle in unbelief,
and also the seed of thy brethren,
behold, these things shall be hid up to come forth unto the Gentiles
by the gift and power of the Lamb.

36 And in them shall be written my gospel, saith the Lamb,
and my rock and my salvation.

37 And blessed are they which shall seek to bring forth my Zion at that day,
for they shall have the gift and the power of the Holy Ghost.
And if they endure unto the end,
they shall be lifted up at the last day
and shall be saved in the everlasting kingdom of the Lamb.
Yea, whoso shall publish peace
—that shall publish tidings of great joy—
how beautiful upon the mountains shall they be!

38 And it came to pass that I beheld the remnant of the seed of my brethren
and also the book of the Lamb of God
which had proceeded forth from the mouth of the Jew.
And I beheld that it came forth from the Gentiles
unto the remnant of the seed of my brethren.

39 And after it had come forth unto them, I beheld other books
which came forth by the power of the Lamb from the Gentiles unto them,
unto the convincing of the Gentiles
and the remnant of the seed of my brethren
—and also to the Jews, which were scattered upon all the face of the earth—
that the records of the prophets and of the twelve apostles of the Lamb are true.

40 And the angel spake unto me, saying:
These last records which thou hast seen among the Gentiles
shall establish the truth of the first,
which is of the twelve apostles of the Lamb,

and shall make known the plain and precious things
which have been taken away from them
and shall make known to all kindreds, tongues, and people
that the Lamb of God is the Eternal Father and the Savior of the world
and that all men must come unto him or they cannot be saved.

41 And they must come according to the words
which shall be established by the mouth of the Lamb.
And the words of the Lamb shall be made known in the records of thy seed
as well as in the records of the twelve apostles of the Lamb.
Wherefore they both shall be established in one,
for there is one God and one Shepherd over all the earth.

42 And the time cometh that he shall manifest himself unto all nations,
both unto the Jews and also unto the Gentiles.
And after that he hath manifested himself
unto the Jews and also unto the Gentiles,
then he shall manifest himself unto the Gentiles and also unto the Jews.
And the last shall be first and the first shall be last.

14 | 1 And it shall come to pass that
if the Gentiles shall hearken unto the Lamb of God in that day,
that he shall manifest himself unto them in word and also in power, in very deed,
unto the taking away of their stumbling blocks,
if it so be that they harden not their hearts against the Lamb.

2 And if it so be that they harden not their hearts against the Lamb of God,
they shall be numbered among the seed of thy father;
yea, they shall be numbered among the house of Israel.
And they shall be a blessed people upon the promised land forever.
They shall be no more brought down into captivity,
and the house of Israel shall no more be confounded.

3 And that great pit which hath been digged for them
by that great and abominable church,
which was founded by the devil and his children
that he might lead away the souls of men down to hell—
yea, that great pit which hath been digged for the destruction of men
shall be filled by those who digged it,
unto their utter destruction, saith the Lamb of God—
not the destruction of the soul,
save it be the casting of it into that hell which hath no end.

4 For behold, this is according to the captivity of the devil,
and also according to the justice of God,
upon all those who will work wickedness and abomination before him.

5 And it came to pass that the angel spake unto me Nephi, saying:
Thou hast beheld that if the Gentiles repent, it shall be well with them.

And thou also knowest concerning the covenants of the Lord
unto the house of Israel.
And thou also hast heard that whoso repenteth not must perish.

6   Therefore woe be unto the Gentiles
if it so be that they harden their hearts against the Lamb of God.

7   For the time cometh, saith the Lamb of God,
that I will work a great and a marvelous work among the children of men,
a work which shall be everlasting,
either on the one hand or on the other,
either to the convincing of them unto peace and life eternal
or unto the deliverance of them to the hardness of their hearts
and the blindness of their minds,
unto their being brought down into captivity,
and also unto destruction both temporally and spiritually,
according to the captivity of the devil of which I have spoken.

8   And it came to pass that
when the angel had spoken these words,
he saith unto me:
Remember thou the covenants of the Father unto the house of Israel?
I saith unto him: Yea.

9   And it came to pass that he saith unto me:
Look and behold that great and abominable church,
which is the mother of abominations, whose founder is the devil.

10   And he saith unto me:
Behold, there is save it be two churches;
the one is the church of the Lamb of God
and the other is the church of the devil.
Wherefore whoso belongeth not to the church of the Lamb of God
belongeth to that great church which is the mother of abominations,
and she is the whore of all the earth.

11   And it came to pass that I looked and beheld the whore of all the earth.
And she sat upon many waters,
and she had dominion over all the earth
among all nations, kindreds, tongues, and people.

12   And it came to pass that I beheld the church of the Lamb of God;
and its numbers were few
because of the wickedness and abominations of the whore
which sat upon many waters.
Nevertheless I beheld that the church of the Lamb,
which were the saints of God,
were also upon all the face of the earth;

and their dominions upon the face of the earth were small
because of the wickedness of the great whore which I saw.

13 And it came to pass that I beheld that the great mother of abominations
did gather together in multitudes upon the face of all the earth
among all the nations of the Gentiles
to fight against the Lamb of God.

14 And it came to pass that I Nephi beheld the power of the Lamb of God
that it descended upon the saints of the church of the Lamb
and upon the covenant people of the Lord,
which were scattered upon all the face of the earth.
And they were armed with righteousness
and with the power of God in great glory.

15 And it came to pass that I beheld that
the wrath of God was poured out upon that great and abominable church,
insomuch that there were wars and rumors of wars
among all the nations and kindreds of the earth.

16 And as there began to be wars and rumors of wars
among all the nations which belonged to the mother of abominations,
the angel spake unto me, saying:
Behold, the wrath of God is upon the mother of harlots.
And behold, thou seest all these things.

17 And when the day cometh
that the wrath of God is poured out upon the mother of harlots
—which is the great and abominable church of all the earth,
whose founder is the devil—
then at that day the work of the Father shall commence
in preparing the way for the fulfilling of his covenants
which he hath made to his people which are of the house of Israel.

18 And it came to pass that the angel spake unto me, saying: Look!

19 And I looked and beheld a man, and he was dressed in a white robe.

20 And the angel said unto me:
Behold one of the twelve apostles of the Lamb.

21 Behold, he shall see and write the remainder of these things,
yea, and also many things which have been.

22 And he shall also write concerning the end of the world.

23 Wherefore the things which he shall write are just and true.
And behold, they are written in the book
which thou beheld proceeding out of the mouth of the Jew.
And at the time they proceeded out of the mouth of the Jew,
or at the time the book proceeded out of the mouth of the Jew,
the things which were written were plain and pure and most precious

and easy to the understanding of all men.

24 And behold, the things which this apostle of the Lamb shall write
are many things which thou hast seen.
And behold, the remainder shalt thou see.

25 But the things which thou shalt see hereafter
thou shalt not write,
for the Lord God hath ordained the apostle of the Lamb of God
that he should write them.

26 And also others which have been,
to them hath he shown all things,
and they have written them.
And they are sealed up to come forth in their purity,
according to the truth which is in the Lamb,
in the own due time of the Lord,
unto the house of Israel.

27 And I Nephi heard and bare record
that the name of the apostle of the Lamb was John,
according to the word of the angel.

28 And behold, I Nephi am forbidden
that I should write the remainder of the things which I saw.
Wherefore the things which I have written sufficeth me,
and I have not written but a small part of the things which I saw.

29 And I bear record that I saw the things which my father saw,
and the angel of the Lord did make them known unto me.

30 And now I make an end of speaking concerning the things
which I saw while I was carried away in the spirit.
And if all the things which I saw are not written,
the things which I have written are true.
And thus it is.
Amen.

15 | 1 And it came to pass that
after I Nephi had been carried away in the spirit and seen all these things,
I returned to the tent of my father.

2 And it came to pass that I beheld my brethren,
and they were disputing one with another
concerning the things which my father had spoken unto them.

3 For he truly spake many great things unto them
which was hard to be understood
save a man should inquire of the Lord.

And they being hard in their hearts,
therefore they did not look unto the Lord as they had ought.

4 And now I Nephi was grieved because of the hardness of their hearts,
and also because of the things which I had seen,
and knew they must unavoidably come to pass
because of the great wickedness of the children of men.
5 And it came to pass that I was overcome because of my afflictions,
for I considered that mine afflictions was great above all
because of the destruction of my people,
for I had beheld their fall.

6 And it came to pass that after I had received strength,
I spake unto my brethren,
desiring to know of them the cause of their disputations.
7 And they said:
Behold, we cannot understand the words which our father hath spoken
concerning the natural branches of the olive tree
and also concerning the Gentiles.
8 And I said unto them:
Have ye inquired of the Lord?
9 And they said unto me:
We have not,
for the Lord maketh no such thing known unto us.
10 Behold, I said unto them:
How is it that ye do not keep the commandments of the Lord?
How is it that ye will perish because of the hardness of your hearts?
11 Do ye not remember the thing which the Lord hath said?
—if ye will not harden your hearts and ask me in faith,
believing that ye shall receive,
with diligence in keeping my commandments,
surely these things shall be made known unto you.

12 Behold, I say unto you that the house of Israel was compared unto an olive tree
by the Spirit of the Lord which was in our father.
And behold, are we not broken off from the house of Israel?
And are we not a branch of the house of Israel?
13 And now the thing which our father meaneth
concerning the grafting in of the natural branches
through the fullness of the Gentiles
is that in the latter days, when our seed shall have dwindled in unbelief,
yea, for the space of many years and many generations,
after that the Messiah hath manifested himself in body unto the children of men,
then shall the fullness of the gospel of the Messiah come unto the Gentiles,

and from the Gentiles unto the remnant of our seed.

14 And at that day shall the remnant of our seed know
that they are of the house of Israel
and that they are the covenant people of the Lord.
And then shall they know and come to the knowledge of their forefathers
and also to the knowledge of the gospel of their Redeemer,
which was ministered unto their fathers by him.
Wherefore they shall come to the knowledge of their Redeemer
and the very points of his doctrine,
that they may know how to come unto him and be saved.

15 And then at that day will they not rejoice
and give praise unto their everlasting God, their rock and their salvation?
Yea, at that day will they not receive
strength and nourishment from the true vine?
Yea, will they not come unto the true fold of God?

16 Behold, I say unto you:
Yea, they shall be numbered again among the house of Israel;
they shall be grafted in, being a natural branch of the olive tree,
into the true olive tree.

17 And this is what our father meaneth.
And he meaneth that it will not come to pass
until after that they are scattered by the Gentiles.
And he meaneth that it shall come by way of the Gentiles,
that the Lord may shew his power unto the Gentiles,
for the very cause that he shall be rejected of the Jews or of the house of Israel.

18 Wherefore our father hath not spoken of our seed alone
but also of all the house of Israel,
pointing to the covenant which should be fulfilled in the latter days,
which covenant the Lord made to our father Abraham, saying:
In thy seed shall all the kindreds of the earth be blessed.

19 And it came to pass that I Nephi spake much unto them concerning these things;
yea, I spake unto them concerning the restoration of the Jews in the latter days.

20 And I did rehearse unto them the words of Isaiah,
which spake concerning the restoration of the Jews or of the house of Israel.
And after that they were restored, they should no more be confounded,
neither should they be scattered again.
And it came to pass that I did speak so many words unto my brethren
that they were pacified and did humble themselves before the Lord.

21 And it came to pass that they did speak unto me again, saying:
What meaneth the things which our father saw in a dream?

What meaneth the tree which he saw?

22 And I said unto them:
It was a representation of the tree of life.

23 And they said unto me:
What meaneth the rod of iron which our father saw that led to the tree?

24 And I said unto them that it was the word of God,
and that whoso would hearken unto the word of God
and would hold fast unto it, they would never perish,
neither could the temptations and the fiery darts of the adversary
overpower them unto blindness,
to lead them away to destruction.

25 Wherefore I Nephi did exhort them to give heed unto the word of the Lord.
Yea, I did exhort them with all the energies of my soul
and with all the faculty which I possessed
that they would give heed to the word of God
and remember to keep his commandments always in all things.

26 And they said unto me:
What meaneth the river of water which our father saw?

27 And I said unto them that the water which my father saw was filthiness.
And so much was his mind swallowed up in other things
that he beheld not the filthiness of the water.

28 And I said unto them that it was an awful gulf which separateth the wicked
from the tree of life and also from the saints of God.

29 And I said unto them that it was a representation of that awful hell
which the angel said unto me was prepared for the wicked.

30 And I said unto them that our father also saw
that the justice of God did also divide the wicked from the righteous,
and the brightness thereof was like unto the brightness of a flaming fire
which ascendeth up unto God forever and ever and hath no end.

31 And they said unto me:
Doth this thing mean the torment of the body in the days of probation,
or doth it mean the final state of the soul after the death of the temporal body,
or doth it speak of the things which are temporal?

32 And it came to pass that I said unto them
that it was a representation of things both temporal and spiritual.
For the day should come that they must be judged of their works,
yea, even the works which were done by the temporal body
in their days of probation.

33 Wherefore if they should die in their wickedness,
they must be cast off also as to the things which are spiritual,
which are pertaining unto righteousness.

Wherefore they must be brought to stand before God
to be judged of their works.
And if their works have been filthiness, they must needs be filthy.
And if they be filthy, it must needs be
that they cannot dwell in the kingdom of God;
if so, the kingdom of God must be filthy also.

34 But behold, I say unto you that the kingdom of God is not filthy,
that there cannot any unclean thing enter into the kingdom of God.
Wherefore there must needs be a place of filthiness
prepared for that which is filthy.

35 And there is a place prepared,
yea, even that awful hell of which I have spoken,
and the devil is the proprietor of it.
Wherefore the final state of the soul of man
is to dwell in the kingdom of God or to be cast out
because of that justice of which I have spoken.

36 Wherefore the wicked are separated from the righteous
and also from that tree of life,
whose fruit is most precious and most desirable of all other fruits;
yea, and it is the greatest of all the gifts of God.

And thus I spake unto my brethren.
Amen.

16 | 1 And now it came to pass that
after I Nephi had made an end of speaking to my brethren,
behold, they said unto me:
Thou hast declared unto us hard things,
more than that which we are able to bear.

2 And it came to pass that I said unto them
that I knew that I had spoken hard things against the wicked
according to the truth,
and the righteous have I justified
and testified that they should be lifted up at the last day.
Wherefore the guilty taketh the truth to be hard,
for it cutteth them to the very center.

3 And now my brethren, if ye were righteous
and were willing to hearken to the truth and give heed unto it,
that ye might walk uprightly before God,
then ye would not murmur because of the truth and say:
Thou speakest hard things against us.

4 And it came to pass that I Nephi did exhort my brethren with all diligence
   to keep the commandments of the Lord.
5 And it came to pass that they did humble themselves before the Lord,
   insomuch that I had joy and great hopes of them,
   that they would walk in the paths of righteousness.
6 Now all these things were said and done
   as my father dwelt in a tent in the valley which he called Lemuel.

7 And it came to pass that I Nephi took one of the daughters of Ishmael to wife,
   and also my brethren took of the daughters of Ishmael to wife,
   and also Zoram took the eldest daughter of Ishmael to wife.
8 And thus my father had fulfilled all the commandments of the Lord
   which had been given unto him.
   And also I Nephi had been blessed of the Lord exceedingly.

9 And it came to pass that the voice of the Lord spake unto my father by night
   and commanded him that on the morrow
   he should take his journey into the wilderness.
10 And it came to pass that as my father arose in the morning
   and went forth to the tent door,
   and to his great astonishment he beheld upon the ground
   a round ball of curious workmanship,
   and it was of fine brass.
   And within the ball was two spindles,
   and the one pointed the way whither we should go into the wilderness.
11 And it came to pass that we did gather together
   whatsoever things we should carry into the wilderness
   and all the remainder of our provisions which the Lord had given unto us.
   And we did take seed of every kind that we might carry into the wilderness.

12 And it came to pass that we did take our tents
   and departed into the wilderness across the river Laman.
13 And it came to pass that we traveled for the space of four days
   nearly a south-southeast direction.
   And we did pitch our tents again,
   and we did call the name of the place Shazer.
14 And it came to pass that we did take our bows and our arrows
   and go forth into the wilderness to slay food for our families.
   And after that we had slain food for our families,
   we did return again to our families in the wilderness to the place of Shazer.

   And we did go forth again in the wilderness, following the same direction,
   keeping in the most fertile parts of the wilderness

which was in the borders near the Red Sea.

15 And it came to pass that we did travel for the space of many days,
slaying food by the way
with our bows and our arrows and our stones and our slings.

16 And we did follow the directions of the ball,
which led us in the more fertile parts of the wilderness.

17 And after that we had traveled for the space of many days,
we did pitch our tents for the space of a time,
that we might again rest ourselves and obtain food for our families.

18 And it came to pass that as I Nephi went forth to slay food,
behold, I did break my bow, which was made of fine steel.
And after that I did break my bow,
behold, my brethren were angry with me because of the loss of my bow,
for we did obtain no food.

19 And it came to pass that we did return without food to our families;
and being much fatigued because of their journeying,
they did suffer much for the want of food.

20 And it came to pass that Laman and Lemuel and the sons of Ishmael
did begin to murmur exceedingly
because of their sufferings and afflictions in the wilderness.
And also my father began to murmur against the Lord his God;
yea, and they were all exceeding sorrowful,
even that they did murmur against the Lord.

21 Now it came to pass that
I Nephi having been afflicted with my brethren because of the loss of my bow
and their bows having lost their springs,
it began to be exceeding difficult,
yea, insomuch that we could obtain no food.

22 And it came to pass that I Nephi did speak much unto my brethren
because that they had hardened their hearts again,
even unto complaining against the Lord their God.

23 And it came to pass that I Nephi did make out of wood a bow
and out of a straight stick an arrow;
wherefore I did arm myself with a bow and an arrow,
with a sling and with stones.
And I said unto my father:
Whither shall I go to obtain food?

24 And it came to pass that he did inquire of the Lord,

for they had humbled themselves because of my words;
for I did say many things unto them in the energy of my soul.

25 And it came to pass that the voice of the Lord came unto my father,
and he was truly chastened because of his murmurings against the Lord,
insomuch that he was brought down into the depths of sorrow.

26 And it came to pass that the voice of the Lord said unto him:
Look upon the ball and behold the things which are written.

27 And it came to pass that when my father beheld the things
which were written upon the ball,
he did fear and tremble exceedingly,
and also my brethren and the sons of Ishmael and our wives.

28 And it came to pass that I Nephi beheld
that the pointers which were in the ball
that they did work according to the faith and diligence and heed
which we did give unto them.

29 And there was also written upon them
a new writing which was plain to be read,
which did give us understanding concerning the ways of the Lord.
And it was written and changed from time to time
according to the faith and diligence which we gave unto it.
And thus we see that by small means the Lord can bring about great things.

30 And it came to pass that I Nephi did go forth up into the top of the mountain
according to the directions which was given upon the ball.

31 And it came to pass that I did slay wild beasts,
insomuch that I did obtain food for our families.

32 And it came to pass that I did return to our tents,
bearing the beasts which I had slain.
And now when they beheld that I had obtained food,
how great was their joy!
And it came to pass that they did humble themselves before the Lord
and did give thanks unto him.

33 And it came to pass that we did again take our journey,
traveling nearly the same course as in the beginning.
And after that we had traveled for the space of many days,
we did pitch our tents again,
that we might tarry for the space of a time.

34 And it came to pass that Ishmael died
and was buried in the place which was called Nahom.

35 And it came to pass that the daughters of Ishmael did mourn exceedingly
because of the loss of their father

and because of their afflictions in the wilderness.
And they did murmur against my father
because that he had brought them out of the land of Jerusalem, saying:
Our father is dead.
Yea, and we have wandered much in the wilderness,
and we have suffered much afflictions, hunger, thirst, and fatigue.
And after all these sufferings we must perish in the wilderness with hunger.

36 And thus they did murmur against my father and also against me.
And they were desirous to return again to Jerusalem.

37 And Laman saith unto Lemuel and also unto the sons of Ishmael:
Behold, let us slay our father and also our brother Nephi,
who hath taken it upon him to be our ruler and our teacher,
who are his elder brethren.

38 Now he saith that the Lord hath talked with him,
and also that angels hath ministered unto him.
But behold, we know that he lieth unto us.
And he telleth us these things,
and he worketh many things by his cunning arts
that he may deceive our eyes,
thinking perhaps that he may lead us away into some strange wilderness.
And after that he hath led us away,
he hath thought to make himself a king and a ruler over us,
that he may do with us according to his will and pleasure.
And after this manner did my brother Laman stir up their hearts to anger.

39 And it came to pass that the Lord was with us,
yea, even the voice of the Lord came and did speak many words unto them
and did chasten them exceedingly.
And after that they were chastened by the voice of the Lord,
they did turn away their anger and did repent of their sins,
insomuch that the Lord did bless us again with food that we did not perish.

17 | 1 And it came to pass that we did again take our journey in the wilderness.
And we did travel nearly eastward from that time forth.
And we did travel and wade through much affliction in the wilderness,
and our women bare children in the wilderness.

2 And so great was the blessings of the Lord upon us
that while we did live upon raw meat in the wilderness,
our women did give plenty of suck for their children and were strong,
yea, even like unto the men.
And they began to bear their journeyings without murmuring.

3 And thus we see that the commandments of God must be fulfilled.
And if it so be that the children of men keep the commandments of God,
he doth nourish them and strengthen them
and provide ways and means whereby they can accomplish the thing
which he hath commanded them.
Wherefore he did provide ways and means for us
while we did sojourn in the wilderness.

4 And we did sojourn for the space of many years,
yea, even eight years in the wilderness.
5 And we did come to the land which we called Bountiful
because of its much fruit and also wild honey.
And all these things were prepared of the Lord that we might not perish.
And we beheld the sea, which we called Irreantum,
which being interpreted is many waters.
6 And it came to pass that we did pitch our tents by the seashore.
And notwithstanding we had suffered many afflictions and much difficulty,
yea, even so much that we cannot write them all,
we was exceedingly rejoiced when we came to the seashore.
And we called the place Bountiful because of its much fruit.

7 And it came to pass that after I Nephi had been in the land Bountiful
for the space of many days,
the voice of the Lord came unto me, saying:
Arise and get thee into the mountain.
And it came to pass that I arose and went up into the mountain
and cried unto the Lord.
8 And it came to pass that the Lord spake unto me, saying:
Thou shalt construct a ship after the manner which I shall shew thee
that I may carry thy people across these waters.
9 And I saith:
Lord, whither shall I go that I may find ore to molten
that I may make tools to construct the ship
after the manner which thou hast shewn unto me?
10 And it came to pass that the Lord told me
whither I should go to find ore that I might make tools.

11 And it came to pass that
I Nephi did make bellowses wherewith to blow the fire
of the skins of beasts.
And after that I had made bellowses
that I might have wherewith to blow the fire,
I did smite two stones together that I might make fire.

12 For the Lord had not hitherto suffered that we should make much fire
as we journeyed in the wilderness,
for he saith:
I will make that thy food shall become sweet,
that ye cook it not.

13 And I will also be your light in the wilderness.
And I will prepare the way before you
if it so be that ye shall keep my commandments.
Wherefore inasmuch as ye shall keep my commandments,
ye shall be led towards the promised land.
And ye shall know that it is by me that ye are led.

14 Yea, and the Lord said also that
after ye have arriven to the promised land,
ye shall know that I the Lord am God
and that I the Lord did deliver you from destruction,
yea, that I did bring you out of the land of Jerusalem.

15 Wherefore I Nephi did strive to keep the commandments of the Lord,
and I did exhort my brethren to faithfulness and diligence.

16 And it came to pass that I did make tools of the ore
which I did molten out of the rock.

17 And when my brethren saw that I was about to build a ship,
they began to murmur against me, saying:
Our brother is a fool,
for he thinketh that he can build a ship.
Yea, and he also thinketh that he can cross these great waters.

18 And thus my brethren did complain against me
and were desirous that they might not labor,
for they did not believe that I could build a ship,
neither would they believe that I were instructed of the Lord.

19 And now it came to pass that I Nephi was exceeding sorrowful
because of the hardness of their hearts.
And now when they saw that I began to be sorrowful,
they were glad in their hearts,
insomuch that they did rejoice over me, saying:
We knew that ye could not construct a ship,
for we knew that ye were lacking in judgment;
wherefore thou canst not accomplish so great a work.

20 And thou art like unto our father,
led away by the foolish imaginations of his heart.
Yea, he hath led us out of the land of Jerusalem,

and we have wandered in the wilderness for these many years.
And our women have toiled being big with child,
and they have borne children in the wilderness
and suffered all things save it were death.
And it would have been better that they had died
before they came out of Jerusalem
than to have suffered these afflictions.

21 Behold, these many years we have suffered in the wilderness,
which time we might have enjoyed our possessions
and the land of our inheritance;
yea, and we might have been happy.

22 And we know that the people which were in the land of Jerusalem
were a righteous people,
for they keep the statutes and the judgments of the Lord
and all his commandments according to the law of Moses;
wherefore we know that they are a righteous people.
And our father hath judged them
and hath led us away because we would hearken unto his word;
yea, and our brother is like unto him.
And after this manner of language
did my brethren murmur and complain against us.

23 And it came to pass that I Nephi spake unto them, saying:
Do ye believe that our fathers, which were the children of Israel,
would have been led away out of the hands of the Egyptians
if they had not hearkened unto the words of the Lord?

24 Yea, do ye suppose that they would have been led out of bondage
if the Lord had not commanded Moses
that he should lead them out of bondage?

25 Now ye know that the children of Israel were in bondage,
and ye know that they were laden with tasks
which were grievious to be borne.
Wherefore ye know that it must needs be a good thing for them
that they should be brought out of bondage.

26 Now ye know that Moses was commanded of the Lord to do that great work.
And ye know that by his word
the waters of the Red Sea was divided hither and thither,
and they passed through on dry ground.

27 But ye know that the Egyptians were drowned in the Red Sea,
which were the armies of Pharaoh.

28 And ye also know that they were fed with manna in the wilderness.
29 Yea, and ye also know that Moses by his word
   according to the power of God which was in him
   smote the rock and there came forth water,
   that the children of Israel might quench their thirst.
30 And notwithstanding they being led,
   the Lord their God, their Redeemer, going before them,
   leading them by day and giving light unto them by night,
   and doing all things for them which was expedient for man to receive,
   they hardened their hearts and blinded their minds
   and reviled against Moses and against the true and living God.
31 And it came to pass that according to his word he did destroy them,
   and according to his word he did lead them,
   and according to his word he did do all things for them.
   And there was not any thing done save it were by his word.

32 And after they had crossed the river Jordan,
   he did make them mighty unto the driving out the children of the land,
   yea, unto the scattering them to destruction.
33 And now do ye suppose that the children of this land,
   which were in the land of promise,
   which were driven out by our fathers,
   do ye suppose that they were righteous?
   Behold, I say unto you: Nay.
34 Do ye suppose that our fathers would have been more choice than they
   if they had been righteous?
   I say unto you: Nay.

35 Behold, the Lord esteemeth all flesh in one;
   he that is righteous is favored of God.
   But behold, this people had rejected every word of God,
   and they were ripe in iniquity,
   and the fullness of the wrath of God was upon them.
   And the Lord did curse the land against them
   and bless it unto our fathers.
   Yea, he did curse it against them unto their destruction,
   and he did bless it unto our fathers
   unto their obtaining power over it.

36 Behold, the Lord hath created the earth that it should be inhabited,
   and he hath created his children that they should possess it.
37 And he raiseth up a righteous nation and destroyeth the nations of the wicked.

38 And he leadeth away the righteous into precious lands,
    and the wicked he destroyeth and curseth the land unto them for their sakes.
39 He ruleth high in the heavens,
    for it is his throne,
    and this earth is his footstool.

40 And he loveth them which will have him to be their God.
    Behold, he loved our fathers;
    and he covenanted with them,
    yea, even Abraham and Isaac and Jacob,
    and he remembered the covenants which he had made;
    wherefore he did bring them out of the land of Egypt.
41 And he did straiten them in the wilderness with his rod,
    for they hardened their hearts even as ye have.
    And the Lord straitened them because of their iniquity.
    He sent flying fiery serpents among them.
    And after they were bitten,
    he prepared a way that they might be healed.
    And the labor which they had to perform were to look.
    And because of the simpleness of the way or the easiness of it,
    there were many which perished.
42 And they did harden their hearts from time to time,
    and they did revile against Moses and also against God.
    Nevertheless ye know that they were led forth
    by his matchless power into the land of promise.

43 And now after all these things,
    the time has come that they have became wicked,
    yea, nearly unto ripeness.
    And I know not but they are at this day about to be destroyed,
    for I know that the day must surely come
    that they must be destroyed save a few only
    which shall be led away into captivity.
44 Wherefore the Lord commanded my father
    that he should depart into the wilderness.

    And the Jews also sought to take away his life.
    Yea, and ye also have sought to take away his life.
    Wherefore ye are murderers in your hearts,
    and ye are like unto they.
45 Ye are swift to do iniquity
    but slow to remember the Lord your God.

Ye have seen an angel and he spake unto you.
Yea, ye have heard his voice from time to time,
and he hath spoken unto you in a still small voice;
but ye were past feeling, that ye could not feel his words.
Wherefore he hath spoken unto you like unto the voice of thunder,
which did cause the earth to shake as if it were to divide asunder.

46 And ye also know that by the power of his almighty word
he can cause the earth that it shall pass away.
Yea, and ye know that by his word he can cause
that rough places be made smooth and smooth places shall be broken up.
O then why is it that ye can be so hard in your hearts?
47 Behold, my soul is rent with anguish because of you,
and my heart is pained.
I fear lest ye shall be cast off forever.
Behold, I am full of the Spirit of God,
insomuch as if my frame had no strength.

48 And now it came to pass that when I had spoken these words,
they were angry with me and were desirous
to throw me into the depths of the sea.
And as they came forth to lay their hands upon me,
I spake unto them, saying:
In the name of the Almighty God I command you that ye touch me not,
for I am filled with the power of God,
even unto the consuming of my flesh.
And whoso shall lay their hands upon me
shall wither even as a dried reed,
and he shall be as naught before the power of God,
for God shall smite him.

49 And it came to pass that I Nephi saith unto them
that they should murmur no more against their father,
neither should they withhold their labor from me,
for God had commanded me that I should build a ship.
50 And I saith unto them:
If God had commanded me to do all things,
I could do it.
If he should command me
that I should say unto this water:
Be thou earth!
—and it shall be earth.

And if I should say it,
it would be done.

51 And now if the Lord hath such great power
and hath wrought so many miracles among the children of men,
how is it that he cannot instruct me that I should build a ship?

52 And it came to pass that I Nephi said many things unto my brethren,
insomuch that they were confounded and could not contend against me,
neither durst they lay their hands upon me nor touch me with their fingers,
even for the space of many days.
Now they durst not do this lest they should wither before me,
so powerful was the Spirit of God.
And thus it had wrought upon them.

53 And it came to pass that the Lord said unto me:
Stretch forth thine hand again unto thy brethren.
And they shall not wither before thee,
but I will shake them, saith the Lord.
And this will I do that they may know that I am the Lord their God.

54 And it came to pass that I stretched forth my hand unto my brethren.
And they did not wither before me, but the Lord did shake them,
even according to the word which he had spoken.

55 And now they said:
We know of a surety that the Lord is with thee,
for we know that it is the power of the Lord that hath shaken us.
And they fell down before me and were about to worship me,
but I would not suffer them, saying:
I am thy brother, yea, even thy younger brother.
Wherefore worship the Lord thy God
and honor thy father and thy mother,
that thy days may be long in the land
which the Lord thy God shall give thee.

18 | 1 And it came to pass that
they did worship the Lord and did go forth with me,
and we did work timbers of curious workmanship.
And the Lord did shew me from time to time
after what manner I should work the timbers of the ship.

2 Now I Nephi did not work the timbers
after the manner which was learned by men,
neither did I build the ship after the manner of men,
but I did build it after the manner which the Lord had shewn unto me;
wherefore it was not after the manner of men.

3 And I Nephi did go into the mount oft,

and I did pray oft unto the Lord;
wherefore the Lord shewed unto me great things.

4 And it came to pass that after I had finished the ship
according to the word of the Lord,
my brethren beheld that it was good
and that the workmanship thereof was exceeding fine;
wherefore they did humble themselves again before the Lord.

5 And it came to pass that the voice of the Lord came unto my father
that we should arise and go down into the ship.
6 And it came to pass that on the morrow,
after that we had prepared all things,
much fruits and meat from the wilderness
and honey in abundance and provisions,
according to that which the Lord had commanded us,
we did go down into the ship with all our loading and our seeds
and whatsoever things we had brought with us,
every one according to his age;
wherefore we did all go down into the ship with our wives and our children.
7 And now my father had begat two sons in the wilderness;
the elder was called Jacob and the younger Joseph.

8 And it came to pass that after we had all gone down into the ship
and had taken with us our provisions
and things which had been commanded us,
we did put forth into the sea and were driven forth before the wind
towards the promised land.
9 And after that we had been driven forth before the wind
for the space of many days,
behold, my brethren and the sons of Ishmael and also their wives
began to make themselves merry,
insomuch that they began to dance and to sing
and to speak with much rudeness,
yea, even to that they did forget by what power they had been brought thither;
yea, they were lifted up unto exceeding rudeness.

10 And I Nephi began to fear exceedingly lest the Lord should be angry with us
and smite us because of our iniquity,
that we should be swallowed up in the depths of the sea;
wherefore I Nephi began to speak to them with much soberness.
But behold, they were angry with me, saying:
We will not that our younger brother shall be a ruler over us.
11 And it came to pass that Laman and Lemuel did take me
and bind me with cords, and they did treat me with much harshness.

Nevertheless the Lord suffered it that he might shew forth his power
unto the fulfilling of his word which he hath spoken concerning the wicked.

12 And it came to pass that after they had bound me,
insomuch that I could not move,
the compass which had been prepared of the Lord did cease to work;
13 wherefore they knew not whither they should steer the ship,
insomuch that there arose a great storm,
yea, a great and terrible tempest,
and we were driven back upon the waters for the space of three days.
And they began to be frightened exceedingly
lest they should be drowned in the sea.
Nevertheless they did loose me not.

14 And on the fourth day which we had been driven back,
the tempest began to be exceeding sore.
15 And it came to pass that
we were about to be swallowed up in the depths of the sea.
And after that we had been driven back upon the waters
for the space of four days,
my brethren began to see that the judgments of God was upon them
and that they must perish save that they should repent of their iniquities.
Wherefore they came unto me and loosed the bands which was upon my wrists,
and behold, they had swollen exceedingly;
and also mine ankles were much swollen, and great was the soreness thereof.
16 Nevertheless I did look unto my God
and I did praise him all the day long,
and I did not murmur against the Lord because of mine afflictions.

17 Now my father Lehi had said many things unto them
and also unto the sons of Ishmael,
but behold, they did breathe out much threatenings
against any one that should speak for me.
And my parents being stricken in years
and having suffered much grief because of their children,
they were brought down, yea, even upon their sickbeds.
18 Because of their grief and much sorrow and the iniquity of my brethren,
they were brought near even to be carried out of this time to meet their God.
Yea, their gray hairs were about to be brought down to lie low in the dust;
yea, even they were near to be cast with sorrow into a watery grave.
19 And Jacob and Joseph also
—being young, having need of much nourishment—
were grieved because of the afflictions of their mother.
And also my wife with her tears and prayers and also my children

did not soften the hearts of my brethren
that they would loose me.

20 And there was nothing save it were the power of God
which threatened them with destruction
could soften their hearts.
Wherefore when they saw that
they were about to be swallowed up in the depths of the sea,
they repented of the thing which they had done,
insomuch that they loosed me.

21 And it came to pass that after they had loosed me,
behold, I took the compass and it did work whither I desired it.
And it came to pass that I prayed unto the Lord;
and after that I had prayed,
the winds did cease and the storm did cease and there was a great calm.

22 And it came to pass that I Nephi did guide the ship,
that we sailed again towards the promised land.

23 And it came to pass that after we had sailed for the space of many days,
we did arrive to the promised land.
And we went forth upon the land and did pitch our tents,
and we did call it the promised land.

24 And it came to pass that we did begin to till the earth,
and we began to plant seeds;
yea, we did put all our seeds into the earth
which we had brought from the land of Jerusalem.
And it came to pass that they did grow exceedingly;
wherefore we were blessed in abundance.

25 And it came to pass that we did find upon the land of promise
as we journeyed in the wilderness
that there was beasts in the forests of every kind,
both the cow and the ox and the ass and the horse and the goat and the wild goat
and all manner of wild animals which were for the use of man.
And we did find all manner of ore, both of gold and of silver and of copper.

19 | 1 And it came to pass that the Lord commanded me,
wherefore I did make plates of ore
that I might engraven upon them the record of my people.
And upon the plates which I made I did engraven the record of my father
and also our journeyings in the wilderness and the prophecies of my father.
And also many of mine own prophecies have I engraven upon them.

2 And I knew not at that time which I made them

that I should be commanded of the Lord to make these plates.
Wherefore the record of my father and the genealogy of his forefathers
and the more part of all our proceedings in the wilderness
are engraven upon those first plates of which I have spoken.
Wherefore the things which transpired before that I made these plates
are of a truth more particularly made mention upon the first plates.

3 And after that I made these plates by way of commandment,
   I Nephi received a commandment
   that the ministry and the prophecies
   —the more plain and precious parts of them—
   should be written upon these plates,
   and that the things which were written
   should be kept for the instruction of my people,
   which should possess the land,
   and also for other wise purposes,
   which purposes are known unto the Lord.
4 Wherefore I Nephi did make a record upon the other plates,
   which gives an account or which gives a greater account
   of the wars and contentions and destructions of my people.
   And now this have I done and commanded my people
   that they should do after that I was gone
   and that these plates should be handed down
   from one generation to another or from one prophet to another
   until further commandments of the Lord.

5 And an account of my making these plates shall be given hereafter.
   And then behold, I proceed according to that which I have spoken;
   and this I do that the more sacred things may be kept
   for the knowledge of my people.
6 Nevertheless I do not write any thing upon plates
   save it be that I think it be sacred.

   And now if I do err,
   even did they err of old—
   not that I would excuse myself because of other men,
   but because of the weakness which is in me according to the flesh,
   I would excuse myself.
7 For the things which some men esteem to be of great worth,
   both to the body and soul,
   others set at naught and trample under their feet,
   yea, even the very God of Israel do men trample under their feet.
   I say trample under their feet,

but I would speak in other words:
they do set him at naught and hearken not to the voice of his counsels.

8 And behold, he cometh according to the words of the angel
in six hundred years from the time my father left Jerusalem.
9 And the world because of their iniquity shall judge him to be a thing of naught.
Wherefore they scourge him and he suffereth it;
and they smite him and he suffereth it;
yea, they spit upon him and he suffereth it because of his loving-kindness
and his long-suffering towards the children of men.
10 And the God of our fathers, which were led out of Egypt out of bondage,
and also were preserved in the wilderness by him,
yea, the God of Abraham and of Isaac and the God of Jacob yieldeth himself
according to the words of the angel
as a man into the hands of wicked men,
to be lifted up according to the words of Zenoch,
and to be crucified according to the words of Neum,
and to be buried in a sepulchre according to the words of Zenos,
which he spake concerning the three days of darkness
which should be a sign given of his death unto them
who should inhabit the isles of the sea,
more especially given unto them which are of the house of Israel.

11 For thus spake the prophet:
The Lord God surely shall visit all the house of Israel at that day,
some with his voice because of their righteousness,
unto their great joy and salvation,
and others with the thunderings and the lightnings of his power,
by tempest, by fire, and by smoke and vapor of darkness
and by the opening of the earth
and by mountains which shall be carried up.
12 And all these things must surely come, saith the prophet Zenos,
and the rocks of the earth must rend.
And because of the groanings of the earth,
many of the kings of the isles of the sea
shall be wrought upon by the Spirit of God to exclaim:
The God of nature suffers.

13 And as for they which are at Jerusalem, saith the prophet,
they shall be scourged by all people, saith the prophet,
because they crucified the God of Israel and turned their hearts aside,
rejecting signs and wonders and power and glory of the God of Israel.
14 And because they have turned their hearts aside, saith the prophet,
and have despised the Holy One of Israel,

they shall wander in the flesh and perish
and become a hiss and a byword and be hated among all nations.

15 Nevertheless when that day cometh, saith the prophet,
   that they no more turn aside their hearts against the Holy One of Israel,
   then will he remember the covenants which he made to their fathers.
16 Yea, then will he remember the isles of the sea;
   yea, and all the people which are of the house of Israel
   will I gather in, saith the Lord,
   according to the words of the prophet Zenos,
   from the four quarters of the earth.
17 Yea, and all the earth shall see the salvation of the Lord, saith the prophet;
   every nation, kindred, tongue, and people shall be blessed.

18 And I Nephi have written these things unto my people
   that perhaps I might persuade them
   that they would remember the Lord their Redeemer.
19 Wherefore I speak unto all the house of Israel,
   if it so be that they should obtain these things.
20 For behold, I have workings in the spirit which doth weary me,
   even that all my joints are weak,
   for they which are at Jerusalem.
   For hath not the Lord been merciful
   to shew unto me concerning them
   even as he had prophets of old?
21 For he surely did shew unto prophets of old all things concerning them.
   And also he did shew unto many concerning us;
   wherefore it must needs be that we know concerning them,
   for they are written upon the plates of brass.

22 Now it came to pass that I Nephi did teach my brethren these things.
   And it came to pass that I did read many things to them
   which were engraven upon the plates of brass,
   that they might know concerning the doings of the Lord
   in other lands among people of old.
23 And I did read many things unto them which were in the books of Moses.
   But that I might more fully persuade them to believe in the Lord their Redeemer,
   wherefore I did read unto them that which was written by the prophet Isaiah;
   for I did liken all scriptures unto us,
   that it might be for our profit and learning.

24 Wherefore I spake unto them, saying:
   Hear ye the words of the prophet,

ye which are a remnant of the house of Israel,
a branch which have been broken off.
Hear ye the words of the prophet
which was written unto all the house of Israel
and liken it unto yourselves,
that ye may have hope as well as your brethren
from whom ye have been broken off.

For after this manner hath the prophet written:

20 | 1 Hearken and hear this, O house of Jacob,
which are called by the name of Israel
and are come forth out of the waters of Judah,
which swear by the name of the Lord
and make mention of the God of Israel;
yet they swear not in truth nor in righteousness.

2 Nevertheless they call themselves of the holy city,
but they do not stay themselves upon the God of Israel,
which is the Lord of Hosts;
yea, the Lord of Hosts is his name.

3 Behold, I have declared the former things from the beginning.
And they went forth out of my mouth and I shewed them.
I did shew them suddenly.

4 And I did it because I knew that thou art obstinate,
and thy neck was an iron sinew and thy brow brass.

5 And I have even from the beginning declared to thee;
before it came to pass, I shewed them thee.
And I shewed them for fear lest thou shouldest say:
Mine idol hath done them,
and my graven image and my molten image hath commanded them.

6 Thou hast heard and seen all this,
and will ye not declare them?
And that I have shewed thee new things from this time,
even hidden things,
and thou didst not know them.

7 They are created now and not from the beginning.
Even before the day when thou heardest them not,
they were declared unto thee,
lest thou shouldst say:
Behold, I knew them.

8 Yea, and thou heardest not,
yea, thou knewest not;
yea, from that time thine ear was not opened.

For I knew that thou wouldst deal very treacherously
and wast called a transgressor from the womb.

9 Nevertheless for my name's sake will I defer mine anger.
And for my praise will I refrain from thee,
that I cut thee not off.

10 For behold, I have refined thee;
I have chosen thee in the furnace of affliction.

11 For mine own sake—yea, for mine own sake—will I do this.
For how should I suffer my name to be polluted?
And I will not give my glory unto another.

12 Hearken unto me, O Jacob and Israel my called.
For I am he, and I am the first and I am also the last.

13 Mine hand hath also laid the foundation of the earth,
and my right hand hath spanned the heavens.
And I called unto them and they stand up together.

14 All ye, assemble yourselves and hear.
Which among them hath declared these things unto them?
The Lord hath loved him.
Yea, and he will fulfill his word which he hath declared by them.
And he will do his pleasure on Babylon,
and his arm shall come upon the Chaldeans.

15 Also saith the Lord:
I the Lord, yea, I have spoken.
Yea, I have called him to declare;
I have brought him,
and he shall make his way prosperous.

16 Come ye near unto me.
I have not spoken in secret from the beginning;
from the time that it was declared have I spoken.
And the Lord God and his Spirit hath sent me.

17 And thus saith the Lord thy Redeemer, the Holy One of Israel:
I have sent him.
The Lord thy God,
which teacheth thee to profit,
which leadeth thee by the way thou shouldst go,
hath done it.

18 O that thou hadst hearkened to my commandments!
Then had thy peace been as a river
and thy righteousness as the waves of the sea.

19 Thy seed also had been as the sand,
      the offspring of thy bowels like the gravel thereof.
      His name should not have been cut off,
      nor destroyed from before me.

20 Go ye forth of Babylon;
      flee ye from the Chaldeans.
      With a voice of singing declare ye, tell this;
      utter to the end of the earth, say ye:
      The Lord hath redeemed his servant Jacob.

21 And they thirsted not.
      He led them through the deserts.
      He caused the waters to flow out of the rock for them.
      He clave the rock also and the waters gushed out.

22 And notwithstanding he hath done all this and greater also,
      there is no peace, saith the Lord, unto the wicked.

21 | 1 And again, hearken, O ye house of Israel,
      all ye that are broken off and are driven out
      because of the wickedness of the pastors of my people,
      yea, all ye that are broken off,
      that are scattered abroad,
      which are of my people, O house of Israel.
      Listen, O isles, unto me,
      and hearken, ye people, from far.

      The Lord hath called me from the womb;
      from the bowels of my mother hath he made mention of my name.

2 And he hath made my mouth like a sharp sword.
      In the shadow of his hand hath he hid me
      and made me a polished shaft;
      in his quiver hath he hid me—

3 and said unto me:
      Thou art my servant, O Israel,
      in whom I will be glorified.

4 Then I said:
      I have labored in vain.
      I have spent my strength for naught and in vain.
      Surely my judgment is with the Lord
      and my work with my God.

5 And now saith the Lord that formed me from the womb
      that I should be his servant to bring Jacob again to him.

Though Israel be not gathered,
yet shall I be glorious in the eyes of the Lord,
and my God shall be my strength.

6 And he said:
It is a light thing
that thou shouldst be my servant,
to raise up the tribes of Jacob
and to restore the preserved of Israel.
I will also give thee for a light to the Gentiles,
that thou mayest be my salvation unto the ends of the earth.

7 Thus saith the Lord, the Redeemer of Israel, his Holy One,
to him whom man despiseth,
to him whom the nation abhorreth,
to a servant of rulers:
Kings shall see and arise,
princes also shall worship,
because of the Lord that is faithful.

8 Thus saith the Lord:
In an acceptable time have I heard thee, O isles of the sea;
and in a day of salvation have I helped thee.
And I will preserve thee and give thee my servant
for a covenant of the people,
to establish the earth,
to cause to inherit the desolate heritages,
9 that thou mayest say to the prisoners:
Go forth;
to them that sit in darkness:
Shew yourselves.

They shall feed in the ways,
and their pastures shall be in all high places.
10 They shall not hunger nor thirst,
neither shall the heat nor the sun smite them.
For he that hath mercy on them shall lead them;
even by the springs of water shall he guide them.
11 And I will make all my mountains a way,
and my highways shall be exalted.

12 And then, O house of Israel,
behold, these shall come from far;
and lo, these from the north and from the west,
and these from the land of Sinim.

13 Sing, O heavens, and be joyful, O earth,
for the feet of them which are in the east shall be established.
And break forth into singing, O mountains,
for they shall be smitten no more.
For the Lord hath comforted his people
and will have mercy upon his afflicted.

14 But behold, Zion hath said:
The Lord hath forsaken me,
and my Lord hath forgotten me.
But he will shew that he hath not.

15 For can a woman forget her sucking child,
that she should not have compassion on the son of her womb?
Yea, they may forget,
yet will I not forget thee, O house of Israel.

16 Behold, I have graven thee upon the palms of my hands.
Thy walls are continually before me.

17 Thy children shall make haste against thy destroyers,
and they that made thee waste shall go forth of thee.

18 Lift up thine eyes round about and behold,
all these gather themselves together
and they shall come to thee.
And as I live, saith the Lord,
thou shalt surely clothe thee with them all as with an ornament
and bind them on, even as a bride.

19 For thy waste and thy desolate places and the land of thy destruction
shall even now be too narrow by reason of the inhabitants.
And they that swallowed thee up shall be far away.

20 The children which thou shalt have after thou hast lost the other
shall say again in thine ears:
The place is too strait for me;
give place to me that I may dwell.

21 Then shalt thou say in thine heart:
Who hath begotten me these,
seeing I have lost my children
and am desolate, a captive,
and removing to and fro?
And who hath brought up these?
Behold, I was left alone.
These, where have they been?

22 Thus saith the Lord God:
Behold, I will lift up mine hand to the Gentiles

and set up my standard to the people.
And they shall bring thy sons in their arms
and thy daughters shall be carried upon their shoulders.

23 And kings shall be thy nursing fathers
and their queens thy nursing mothers.
They shall bow down to thee with their face towards the earth
and lick up the dust of thy feet.
And thou shalt know that I am the Lord,
for they shall not be ashamed that wait for me.

24 For shall the prey be taken from the mighty
or the lawful captive delivered?

25 But thus saith the Lord:
Even the captive of the mighty shall be taken away,
and the prey of the terrible shall be delivered.
For I will contend with him that contendeth with thee,
and I will save thy children.

26 And I will feed them that oppress thee with their own flesh.
They shall be drunken with their own blood as with sweet wine.
And all flesh shall know that
I the Lord am thy Savior and thy Redeemer, the Mighty One of Jacob.

22 | 1 And now it came to pass that after I Nephi—
after that I had read these things which were engraven upon the plates of brass,
my brethren came unto me and said unto me:
What mean these things which ye have read?
Behold, are they to be understood according to things which are spiritual
which shall come to pass according to the Spirit and not the flesh?

2 And I Nephi saith unto them:
Behold, they were made manifest unto the prophet by the voice of the Spirit,
for by the Spirit are all things made known unto the prophets
which shall come upon the children of men according to the flesh.

3 Wherefore the things of which I have read
are things pertaining to things both temporal and spiritual.

For it appears that the house of Israel sooner or later will be scattered
upon all the face of the earth and also among all nations.

4 And behold, there are many which are already lost
from the knowledge of they which are at Jerusalem;
yea, the more part of all the tribes have been led away,
and they are scattered to and fro upon the isles of the sea.

And whither they are none of us knoweth,
save that we know that they have been led away.

5 And since that they have been led away,
these things have been prophesied concerning them,
and also concerning all they
which shall hereafter be scattered and be confounded
because of the Holy One of Israel,
for against him will they harden their hearts.
Wherefore they shall be scattered among all nations
and shall be hated by all men.

6 Nevertheless, after that they have been nursed by the Gentiles,
and the Lord hath lifted up his hand upon the Gentiles
and set them up for a standard,
and their children shall be carried in their arms
and their daughters shall be carried upon their shoulders—
behold, these things of which are spoken are temporal,
for thus is the covenants of the Lord with our fathers.
And it meaneth us in the days to come
and also all our brethren which are of the house of Israel.

7 And it meaneth that the time cometh that
after all the house of Israel have been scattered and confounded
that the Lord God will raise up a mighty nation among the Gentiles,
yea, even upon the face of this land,
and by them shall our seed be scattered.

8 And after that our seed is scattered,
the Lord God will proceed to do a marvelous work among the Gentiles
which shall be of great worth unto our seed.
Wherefore it is likened unto the being nursed by the Gentiles
and being carried in their arms and upon their shoulders.

9 And it shall also be of worth unto the Gentiles
—and not only unto the Gentiles but unto all the house of Israel—
unto the making known of the covenants of the Father of heaven
unto Abraham, saying:
In thy seed shall all the kindreds of the earth be blessed.

10 And I would, my brethren, that ye should know
that all the kindreds of the earth cannot be blessed
unless he shall make bare his arm in the eyes of the nations.

11 Wherefore the Lord God will proceed to make bare his arm
in the eyes of all the nations,
in bringing about his covenants and his gospel unto they

which are of the house of Israel.

12 Wherefore he will bring them again out of captivity,
and they shall be gathered together to the lands of their first inheritance.
And they shall be brought out of obscurity and out of darkness,
and they shall know that
the Lord is their Savior and their Redeemer, the Mighty One of Israel.

13 And the blood of that great and abominable church,
which is the whore of all the earth,
shall turn upon their own heads,
for they shall war among themselves.
And the sword of their own hands shall fall upon their own heads,
and they shall be drunken with their own blood.

14 And every nation which shall war against thee, O house of Israel,
shall be turned one against another.
And they shall fall into the pit
which they digged to ensnare the people of the Lord.
And all they which fight against Zion shall be destroyed.
And that great whore which hath perverted the right ways of the Lord,
yea, that great and abominable church,
shall tumble to the dust,
and great shall be the fall of it.

15 For behold, saith the prophet, that the time cometh speedily
that Satan shall have no more power over the hearts of the children of men.
For the day soon cometh
that all the proud and they which do wickedly shall be as stubble.
And the day cometh that they must be burned.

16 For the time soon cometh that the fullness of the wrath of God
shall be poured out upon all the children of men,
for he will not suffer that the wicked shall destroy the righteous.

17 Wherefore he will preserve the righteous by his power,
even if it so be that the fullness of his wrath must come
and the righteous be preserved,
even unto the destruction of their enemies by fire.
Wherefore the righteous need not fear,
for thus, saith the prophet, they shall be saved,
even if it so be as by fire.

18 Behold, my brethren, I say unto you
that these things must shortly come;
yea, even blood and fire and vapor of smoke must come,
and it must needs be upon the face of this earth.

And it cometh unto men according to the flesh
if it so be that they will harden their hearts against the Holy One of Israel.

19 For behold, the righteous shall not perish,
for the time surely must come
that all they which fight against Zion shall be cut off.

20 And the Lord will surely prepare a way for his people
unto the fulfilling of the words of Moses,
which he spake, saying:
A prophet shall the Lord your God raise up unto you like unto me;
him shall ye hear in all things whatsoever he shall say unto you.
And it shall come to pass that all they which will not hear that prophet
shall be cut off from among the people.

21 And now I Nephi declare unto you that
this prophet of whom Moses spake was the Holy One of Israel.
Wherefore he shall execute judgment in righteousness.

22 And the righteous need not fear.
For it is they which shall not be confounded,
but it is the kingdom of the devil
which shall be built up among the children of men,
which kingdom is established among them which are in the flesh.

23 For the time speedily shall come that all churches
which are built up to get gain
and all they which are built up to get power over the flesh
and they which are built up to become popular in the eyes of the world
and they which seek the lusts of the flesh and the things of the world
and to do all manner of iniquity,
yea, in fine, all they which belong to the kingdom of the devil,
it is they which need fear and tremble and quake;
it is they which must be brought low in the dust;
it is they which must be consumed as stubble.
And this is according to the words of the prophet.

24 And the time cometh speedily
that the righteous must be led up as calves of the stall,
and the Holy One of Israel must reign
in dominion and might and power and great glory.

25 And he gathereth his children from the four quarters of the earth,
and he numbereth his sheep and they know him.
And there shall be one fold and one shepherd;
and he shall feed his sheep
and in him they shall find pasture.

26   And because of the righteousness of his people, Satan hath no power;
     wherefore he cannot be loosed for the space of many years,
     for he hath no power over the hearts of the people,
     for they dwell in righteousness
     and the Holy One of Israel reigneth.

27   And now behold, I Nephi say unto you
     that all these things must come according to the flesh.
28   But behold, all nations, kindreds, tongues, and people
     shall dwell safely in the Holy One of Israel
     if it so be that they will repent.

29   And now I Nephi make an end,
     for I durst not speak further as yet concerning these things.
30   Wherefore, my brethren, I would that ye should consider
     that the things which have been written upon the plates of brass are true,
     and they testify that a man must be obedient to the commandments of God.
31   Wherefore ye need not suppose that I and my father are the only ones
     which have testified and also taught them.
     Wherefore if ye shall be obedient to the commandments and endure to the end,
     ye shall be saved at the last day.
     And thus it is.
     Amen.

The Book of Nephi

An account of the death of Lehi.
Nephi's brethren rebelleth against him.
The Lord warns Nephi to depart into the wilderness etc.
His journeyings in the wilderness etc.

1 | 1   And now it came to pass
        after I Nephi had made an end of teaching my brethren,
        our father Lehi also spake many things unto them
        and rehearsed unto them how great things the Lord had done for them
        in bringing them out of the land of Jerusalem.
    2   And he spake unto them concerning their rebellions upon the waters

and the mercies of God in sparing their lives,
that they were not swallowed up in the sea.

3 And he also spake unto them concerning the land of promise,
   which they had obtained:
   How merciful the Lord had been in warning us
   that we should flee out of the land of Jerusalem.
4 For behold, saith he, I have seen a vision,
   in the which I know that Jerusalem is destroyed;
   and had we remained in Jerusalem, we should also have perished.
5 But, said he, notwithstanding our afflictions,
   we have obtained a land of promise,
   a land which is choice above all other lands,
   a land which the Lord God hath covenanted with me
   should be a land for the inheritance of my seed.
   Yea, the Lord hath consecrated this land unto me and to my children forever,
   and also all they which should be led out of other countries
   by the hand of the Lord.

6 Wherefore I Lehi prophesy
   according to the workings of the Spirit which is in me
   that there shall be none come into this land
   save they should be brought by the hand of the Lord.
7 Wherefore this land is consecrated unto him whom he shall bring.
   And if it so be that they shall serve him
   according to the commandments which he hath given,
   it shall be a land of liberty unto them;
   wherefore they shall never be brought down into captivity.
   If so, it shall be because of iniquity;
   for if iniquity shall abound,
   cursed shall be the land for their sakes.
   But unto the righteous it shall be blessed forever.

8 And behold, it is wisdom that this land should be kept
   as yet from the knowledge of other nations.
   For behold, many nations would overrun this land,
   that there would be no place for an inheritance.
9 Wherefore I Lehi have obtained a promise that
   inasmuch as they which the Lord God shall bring out of the land of Jerusalem
   shall keep his commandments,
   they shall prosper upon the face of this land.
   And they shall be kept from all other nations,

that they may possess this land unto themselves.
And if it so be that they shall keep his commandments,
they shall be blessed upon the face of this land.
And there shall be none to molest them
nor to take away the land of their inheritance,
and they shall dwell safely forever.

10 But behold, when the time cometh
that they shall dwindle in unbelief,
after that they have received so great blessings from the hand of the Lord,
having a knowledge of the creation of the earth and all men,
knowing the great and marvelous works of the Lord
from the creation of the world,
having power given them to do all things by faith,
having all the commandments from the beginning,
and having been brought by his infinite goodness
into this precious land of promise,
behold, I say, if the day shall come
that they will reject the Holy One of Israel,
the true Messiah, their Redeemer and their God,
behold, the judgments of him that is just shall rest upon them.
11 Yea, he will bring other nations unto them,
and he will give unto them power,
and he will take away from them the lands of their possessions,
and he will cause them to be scattered and smitten.
12 Yea, as one generation passeth to another,
there shall be bloodsheds and great visitations among them.

Wherefore, my sons, I would that ye would remember;
yea, I would that ye would hearken unto my words.
13 O that ye would awake, awake from a deep sleep
—yea, even from the sleep of hell—
and shake off the awful chains by which ye are bound,
which are the chains which bind the children of men,
that they are carried away captive down to the eternal gulf of misery and woe.
14 Awake and arise from the dust
and hear the words of a trembling parent,
whose limbs ye must soon lay down in the cold and silent grave,
from whence no traveler can return.
A few more days and I go the way of all the earth.
15 But behold, the Lord hath redeemed my soul from hell.

I have beheld his glory,
and I am encircled about eternally in the arms of his love.

16 And I desire that ye should remember
to observe the statutes and the judgments of the Lord.
Behold, this hath been the anxiety of my soul from the beginning.
17 My heart hath been weighed down with sorrow from time to time,
for I have feared, lest for the hardness of your hearts,
lest the Lord your God should come out
in the fullness of his wrath upon you,
that ye be cut off and destroyed forever,
18 or that a cursing should come upon you for the space of many generations
and ye are visited by sword and by famine and are hated
and are led according to the will and captivity of the devil.

19 O my sons, that these things might not come upon you,
but that ye might be a choice and a favored people of the Lord.
But behold, his will be done,
for his ways are righteousness forever.
20 And he hath said that
inasmuch as ye shall keep my commandments,
ye shall prosper in the land.
But inasmuch as ye will not keep his commandments,
ye shall be cut off from his presence.

21 And now that my soul might have joy in you
and that my heart might leave this world with gladness because of you,
that I might not be brought down with grief and sorrow to the grave—
arise from the dust, my sons, and be men,
and be determined in one mind and in one heart, united in all things,
that ye may not come down into captivity,
22 that ye may not be cursed with a sore cursing;
and also that ye may not incur the displeasure of a just God upon you
unto the destruction—yea, the eternal destruction—of both soul and body.
23 Awake, my sons, put on the armor of righteousness,
shake off the chains with which ye are bound,
and come forth out of obscurity and arise from the dust.

24 Rebel no more against your brother,
whose views have been glorious,
and who hath kept the commandments from the time we left Jerusalem,
and who hath been an instrument in the hands of God
in bringing us forth into the land of promise.

For were it not for him, we must have perished with hunger in the wilderness.
Nevertheless ye sought to take away his life.
Yea, and he hath suffered much sorrow because of you.

25 And I exceedingly fear and tremble because of you,
lest he shall suffer again.

For behold, ye have accused him
that he sought power and authority over you.
But I know that he hath not sought for power nor authority over you,
but he hath sought the glory of God and your own eternal welfare.

26 And ye have murmured because he hath been plain unto you.
Ye say that he hath used sharpness;
ye say that he hath been angry with you.
But behold, his sharpness was the sharpness of the power
of the word of God which was in him.
And that which ye call anger was the truth
according to that which is in God,
which he could not constrain,
manifesting boldly concerning your iniquities.

27 And it must needs be that the power of God must be with him,
even unto his commanding you that ye must obey.
But behold, it was not him,
but it was the Spirit of the Lord which was in him
which opened his mouth to utterance, that he could not shut it.

28 And now my son Laman, and also Lemuel and Sam,
and also my sons which are the sons of Ishmael,
behold, if ye will hearken unto the voice of Nephi,
ye shall not perish.
And if ye will hearken unto him,
I leave unto you a blessing, yea, even my first blessing.

29 But if ye will not hearken unto him, I take away my first blessing
—yea, even my blessing—and it shall rest upon him.

30 And now Zoram, I speak unto you:
Behold, thou art the servant of Laban;
nevertheless thou hast been brought out of the land of Jerusalem.
And I know that thou art a true friend unto my son Nephi forever.

31 Wherefore because thou hast been faithful,
thy seed shall be blessed with his seed,
that they dwell in prosperity long upon the face of this land.
And nothing save it shall be iniquity among them
shall harm or disturb their prosperity upon the face of this land forever.

32 Wherefore if ye shall keep the commandments of the Lord,
the Lord hath consecrated this land for the security of thy seed
with the seed of my son.

2 | 1 And now Jacob, I speak unto you:
Thou art my first born in the days of my tribulation in the wilderness.
And behold, in thy childhood thou hast suffered afflictions and much sorrow
because of the rudeness of thy brethren.

2 Nevertheless, Jacob my first born in the wilderness,
thou knowest the greatness of God.
And he shall consecrate thine afflictions for thy gain.

3 Wherefore thy soul shall be blessed,
and thou shalt dwell safely with thy brother Nephi,
and thy days shall be spent in the service of thy God.
Wherefore I know that thou art redeemed
because of the righteousness of thy Redeemer,
for thou hast beheld that in the fullness of time
he cometh to bring salvation unto men.

4 And thou hast beheld in thy youth his glory,
wherefore thou art blessed
even as they unto whom he shall minister in the flesh.
For the Spirit is the same yesterday, today, and forever,
and the way is prepared from the fall of man,
and salvation is free.

5 And men are instructed sufficiently that they know good from evil,
and the law is given unto men.
And by the law no flesh is justified;
or by the law men are cut off,
yea, by the temporal law they were cut off.
And also by the spiritual law they perish from that which is good
and become miserable forever.

6 Wherefore redemption cometh in and through the Holy Messiah,
for he is full of grace and truth.

7 Behold, he offereth himself a sacrifice for sin,
to answer the ends of the law unto all those
which have a broken heart and a contrite spirit.
And unto none else can the ends of the law be answered.

8 Wherefore how great the importance
to make these things known unto the inhabitants of the earth,
that they may know that there is no flesh
that can dwell in the presence of God

save it be through the merits and mercy and grace of the Holy Messiah,
which layeth down his life according to the flesh
and taketh it again by the power of the Spirit,
that he may bring to pass the resurrection of the dead,
being the first that should rise.

9 Wherefore he is the firstfruits unto God,
inasmuch as he shall make intercession for all the children of men,
and they that believe in him shall be saved.

10 And because of the intercession for all,
all men cometh unto God.
Wherefore they stand in the presence of him to be judged of him
according to the truth and holiness which is in him;
wherefore the ends of the law which the Holy One hath given
unto the inflicting of the punishment which is affixed,
which punishment that is affixed is in opposition
to that of the happiness which is affixed,
to answer the ends of the atonement —

11 for it must needs be that there is an opposition in all things.
If not so, my first born in the wilderness,
righteousness could not be brought to pass,
neither wickedness, neither happiness nor misery, neither good nor bad;
wherefore all things must needs be a compound in one.
Wherefore if it should be one body,
it must needs remain as dead,
having no life neither death, nor corruption nor incorruption,
happiness nor misery, neither sense nor insensibility.

12 Wherefore it must needs have been created for a thing of naught;
wherefore there would have been no purpose in the end of its creation.
Wherefore this thing must needs destroy
the wisdom of God and his eternal purposes,
and also the power and the mercy and the justice of God.

13 And if ye shall say there is no law,
ye shall also say there is no sin.
And if ye shall say there is no sin,
ye shall also say there is no righteousness.
And if there be no righteousness,
there be no happiness.
And if there be no righteousness nor happiness,
there be no punishment nor misery.
And if these things are not,
there is no God.

And if there is no God,
we are not, neither the earth.
For there could have been no creation of things,
neither to act nor to be acted upon;
wherefore all things must have vanished away.

14 And now my sons,
I speak unto you these things for your profit and learning.
For there is a God and he hath created all things,
both the heavens and the earth and all things that in them is,
both things to act and things to be acted upon.
15 And to bring about his eternal purposes in the end of man
—after that he had created our first parents
and the beasts of the field and the fowls of the air
and, in fine, all things which are created—
it must needs be that there was an opposition,
even the forbidden fruit in opposition to the tree of life,
the one being sweet and the other bitter.

16 Wherefore the Lord God gave unto man that he should act for himself;
wherefore man could not act for himself
save it should be that he were enticed by the one or the other.
17 And I Lehi, according to the things which I have read,
must needs suppose that an angel of God,
according to that which is written,
had fallen from heaven;
wherefore he became a devil,
having sought that which was evil before God.
18 And because that he had fallen from heaven
and had became miserable forever,
he sought also the misery of all mankind;
wherefore he saith unto Eve
—yea, even that old serpent which is the devil,
which is the father of all lies—
wherefore he saith:
Partake of the forbidden fruit and ye shall not die,
but ye shall be as God, knowing good and evil.

19 And after that Adam and Eve had partaken of the forbidden fruit,
they were driven out from the garden of Eden to till the earth.
20 And they have brought forth children,
yea, even the family of all the earth.
21 And the days of the children of men were prolonged,
according to the will of God,

that they might repent while in the flesh.
Wherefore their state became a state of probation,
and their time was lengthened according to the commandments
which the Lord God gave unto the children of men.
For he gave commandment that all men must repent,
for he shewed unto all men that they were lost
because of the transgression of their parents.

22 And now behold, if Adam had not transgressed,
he would not have fallen,
but he would have remained in the garden of Eden;
and all things which were created must have remained
in the same state which they were
after that they were created.
And they must have remained forever and had no end,
23 and they would have had no children.
Wherefore they would have remained in a state of innocence,
having no joy, for they knew no misery,
doing no good, for they knew no sin.

24 But behold, all things have been done
in the wisdom of him who knoweth all things.
25 Adam fell that men might be,
and men are that they might have joy.
26 And the Messiah cometh in the fullness of time
that he might redeem the children of men from the fall.
And because that they are redeemed from the fall,
they have become free forever,
knowing good from evil,
to act for themselves and not to be acted upon,
save it be by the punishment of the law at the great and last day,
according to the commandments which God hath given.

27 Wherefore men are free according to the flesh,
and all things are given them which is expedient unto man.
And they are free to choose liberty and eternal life
through the great Mediator of all men,
or to choose captivity and death
according to the captivity and power of the devil,
for he seeketh that all men might be miserable like unto himself.

28 And now my sons,
I would that ye should look to the great Mediator
and hearken unto his great commandments

and be faithful unto his words
and choose eternal life according to the will of his Holy Spirit,

29 and not choose eternal death according to the will of the flesh
and the evil which is therein,
which giveth the spirit of the devil power to captivate,
to bring you down to hell,
that he may reign over you in his own kingdom.

30 I have spoken these few words unto you all, my sons,
in the last days of my probation.
And I have chosen the good part, according to the words of the prophet.
And I have none other object save it be the everlasting welfare of your souls.
Amen.

3 | 1 And now I speak unto you Joseph, my last born:
Thou wast born in the wilderness of mine afflictions;
yea, in the days of my greatest sorrow did thy mother bear thee.

2 And may the Lord consecrate also unto thee this land,
which is a most precious land,
for thine inheritance and the inheritance of thy seed with thy brethren,
for thy security forever,
if it so be that ye shall keep the commandments of the Holy One of Israel.

3 And now Joseph, my last born,
whom I have brought out of the wilderness of mine afflictions,
may the Lord bless thee forever,
for thy seed shall not utterly be destroyed.

4 For behold, thou art the fruit of my loins,
and I am a descendant of Joseph, which was carried captive into Egypt.

And great was the covenants of the Lord which he made unto Joseph.

5 Wherefore Joseph truly saw our day,
and he obtained a promise of the Lord
that out of the fruit of his loins
the Lord God would raise up a righteous branch unto the house of Israel,
not the Messiah, but a branch which was to be broken off,
nevertheless to be remembered in the covenants of the Lord,
that the Messiah should be made manifest unto them in the latter days
in the spirit of power unto the bringing of them out of darkness unto light,
yea, out of hidden darkness and out of captivity unto freedom.

6 For Joseph truly testified, saying:
A seer shall the Lord my God raise up,

which shall be a choice seer unto the fruit of my loins.
7 Yea, Joseph truly said:
Thus saith the Lord unto me:
A choice seer will I raise up out of the fruit of thy loins,
and he shall be esteemed highly among the fruit of thy loins.
And unto him will I give commandment
that he shall do a work for the fruit of thy loins, his brethren,
which shall be of great worth unto them,
even to the bringing of them to the knowledge of the covenants
which I have made with thy fathers.
8 And I will give unto him a commandment
that he shall do none other work
save the work which I shall command him.
And I will make him great in mine eyes,
for he shall do my work.

9 And he shall be great like unto Moses,
whom I have said I would raise up unto you
to deliver my people, O house of Israel.
10 And Moses will I raise up to deliver thy people out of the land of Egypt,
11 but a seer will I raise up out of the fruit of thy loins.
And unto him will I give power
to bring forth my word unto the seed of thy loins —
and not to the bringing forth my word only, saith the Lord,
but to the convincing them of my word
which shall have already gone forth among them.

12 Wherefore the fruit of thy loins shall write,
and the fruit of the loins of Judah shall write.
And that which shall be written by the fruit of thy loins,
and also that which shall be written by the fruit of the loins of Judah,
shall grow together unto the confounding of false doctrines
and laying down of contentions
and establishing peace among the fruit of thy loins
and bringing them to the knowledge of their fathers in the latter days
and also to the knowledge of my covenants, saith the Lord.

13 And out of weakness he shall be made strong in that day
when my work shall commence among all my people,
unto the restoring thee, O house of Israel, saith the Lord.
14 And thus prophesied Joseph, saying:
Behold, that seer will the Lord bless.
And they that seek to destroy him shall be confounded,
for this promise, of which I have obtained of the Lord,

of the fruit of my loins shall be fulfilled.
Behold, I am sure of the fulfilling of this promise.

15 And his name shall be called after me,
and it shall be after the name of his father.
And he shall be like unto me,
for the thing which the Lord shall bring forth by his hand
by the power of the Lord
shall bring my people unto salvation.

16 Yea, thus prophesied Joseph:
I am sure of this thing,
even as I am sure of the promise of Moses.
For the Lord hath said unto me:
I will preserve thy seed forever.

17 And the Lord hath said:
I will raise up Moses,
and I will give power unto him in a rod.
And I will give judgment unto him in writing,
yet I will not loose his tongue that he shall speak much,
for I will not make him mighty in speaking.
But I will write unto him my law by the finger of mine own hand,
and I will make one a spokesman for him.

18 And the Lord said unto me also:
I will raise up one unto the fruit of thy loins,
and I will make for him a spokesman.
And I, behold, I will give unto him
that he shall write the writing of the fruit of thy loins
unto the fruit of thy loins.
And the spokesman of thy loins shall declare it.

19 And the words which he shall write shall be the words
which is expedient in my wisdom should go forth unto the fruit of thy loins.
And it shall be as if the fruit of thy loins had cried unto them from the dust,
for I know their faith.

20 And they shall cry from the dust,
yea, even repentance unto their brethren,
even that after many generations have gone by them.
And it shall come to pass that their cry shall go forth,
even according to the simpleness of their words.

21 Because of their faith their words shall proceed forth out of my mouth
unto their brethren which are the fruit of thy loins.

And the weakness of their words will I make strong in their faith
unto the remembering of my covenant which I made unto thy fathers.

22 And now behold, my son Joseph,
after this manner did my father of old prophesy.
23 Wherefore because of this covenant thou art blessed,
for thy seed shall not be destroyed,
for they shall hearken unto the words of the book.
24 And there shall raise up one mighty among them
which shall do much good, both in word and in deed,
being an instrument in the hands of God
with exceeding faith to work mighty wonders
and do that thing which is great in the sight of God,
unto the bringing to pass much restoration
unto the house of Israel and unto the seed of thy brethren.

25 And now, blessed art thou Joseph.
Behold, thou art little;
wherefore hearken unto the words of thy brother Nephi.
And it shall be done unto thee
even according to the words which I have spoken.
Remember the words of thy dying father.
Amen.

⟶

4 | 1 And now I Nephi speak concerning the prophecies
of which my father hath spoken concerning Joseph,
who was carried into Egypt.
2 For behold, he truly prophesied concerning all his seed.
And the prophecies which he wrote,
there are not many greater.
And he prophesied concerning us and our future generations,
and they are written upon the plates of brass.

3 Wherefore after my father had made an end of speaking
concerning the prophecies of Joseph,
he called the children of Laman, his sons and his daughters,
and saith unto them:
Behold, my sons and my daughters
which are the sons and the daughters of my first born,
I would that ye should give ear unto my words.
4 For the Lord God hath said that
inasmuch as ye shall keep my commandments,

ye shall prosper in the land.
And inasmuch as ye will not keep my commandments,
ye shall be cut off from my presence.

5 But behold, my sons and my daughters,
I cannot go down to my grave save I should leave a blessing upon you.
For behold, I know that if ye are brought up in the right way that ye should go,
ye will not depart from it.
6 Wherefore if ye are cursed,
behold, I leave my blessing upon you,
that the cursing may be taken from you
and be answered upon the heads of your parents.
7 Wherefore because of my blessing
the Lord God will not suffer that ye shall perish;
wherefore he will be merciful unto you and unto your seed forever.

8 And it came to pass that after my father had made an end of speaking
to the sons and daughters of Laman,
he caused the sons and daughters of Lemuel to be brought before him,
9 and he spake unto them, saying:
Behold, my sons and my daughters
which are the sons and the daughters of my second son,
behold, I leave unto you the same blessing
which I left unto the sons and daughters of Laman;
wherefore thou shalt not utterly be destroyed,
but in the end thy seed shall be blessed.

10 And it came to pass that
when my father had made an end of speaking unto them,
behold, it came to pass that he spake unto the sons of Ishmael,
yea, and even all his household.

11 And after that he had made an end of speaking unto them,
he spake unto Sam, saying:
Blessed art thou and thy seed,
for thou shalt inherit the land like unto thy brother Nephi,
and thy seed shall be numbered with his seed.
And thou shalt be even like unto thy brother,
and thy seed like unto his seed.
And thou shalt be blessed in all thy days.

12 And it came to pass that
after Lehi had spake unto all his household
according to the feelings of his heart

and the Spirit of the Lord which was in him,
he waxed old.
And it came to pass that he died and was buried.

13　And it came to pass that not many days after his death,
Laman and Lemuel and the sons of Ishmael were angry with me
because of the admonitions of the Lord.

14　For I Nephi was constrained to speak unto them according to the word,
for I had spake many things unto them,
and also my father before his death,
many of which sayings are written upon mine other plates,
for a more history part are written upon mine other plates.

15　And upon these I write the things of my soul
and many of the scriptures which are engraven upon the plates of brass.

For my soul delighteth in the scriptures,
and my heart pondereth them
and writeth them for the learning and the profit of my children.

16　Behold, my soul delighteth in the things of the Lord,
and my heart pondereth continually
upon the things which I have seen and heard.

17　Nevertheless—notwithstanding the great goodness of the Lord
in shewing me his great and marvelous works—
my heart exclaimeth:
O wretched man that I am!
Yea, my heart sorroweth because of my flesh.
My soul grieveth because of mine iniquities.

18　I am encompassed about
because of the temptations and the sins which doth so easily beset me.

19　And when I desire to rejoice,
my heart groaneth because of my sins.

Nevertheless I know in whom I have trusted.

20　My God hath been my support.
He hath led me through mine afflictions in the wilderness,
and he hath preserved me upon the waters of the great deep.

21　He hath filled me with his love,
even unto the consuming of my flesh.

22　He hath confounded mine enemies,
unto the causing of them to quake before me.

23　Behold, he hath heard my cry by day,
and he hath given me knowledge by visions in the nighttime.

24　And by day have I waxed bold in mighty prayer before him.

Yea, my voice have I sent up on high,
and angels came down and ministered unto me.
25 And upon the wings of his Spirit hath my body been carried
away up on exceeding high mountains;
and mine eyes hath beheld great things
—yea, even too great for man—
therefore I was bidden that I should not write them.

26 O then if I have seen so great things,
if the Lord in his condescension unto the children of men
hath visited me in so much mercy,
why should my heart weep
and my soul linger in the valley of sorrow
and my flesh waste away
and my strength slacken because of mine afflictions?
27 And why should I yield to sin because of my flesh?
Yea, why should I give way to temptations,
that the evil one have place in my heart
to destroy my peace and afflict my soul?
Why am I angry because of mine enemy?

28 Awake, my soul!
No longer droop in sin!
Rejoice, O my heart,
and give place no more for the enemy of my soul.
29 Do not anger again because of mine enemies.
Do not slacken my strength because of mine afflictions.
30 Rejoice, O my heart,
and cry unto the Lord and say:
O Lord, I will praise thee forever.
Yea, my soul will rejoice in thee, my God and the rock of my salvation.

31 O Lord, wilt thou redeem my soul!
Wilt thou deliver me out of the hands of mine enemies!
Wilt thou make me that I may shake at the appearance of sin!
32 May the gates of hell be shut continually before me
because that my heart is broken and my spirit is contrite.
O Lord, wilt thou not shut the gates of thy righteousness before me,
that I may walk in the path of the low valley,
that I may be strict in the plain road.
33 O Lord, wilt thou encircle me around in the robe of thy righteousness!
O Lord, wilt thou make a way for mine escape before mine enemies!
Wilt thou make my path straight before me!
Wilt thou not place a stumbling block in my way,

but that thou wouldst clear my way before me
and hedge not up my way but the ways of mine enemy.

34 O Lord, I have trusted in thee,
and I will trust in thee forever.
I will not put my trust in the arm of flesh,
for I know that cursed is he that putteth his trust in the arm of flesh.
Yea, cursed is he that putteth his trust in man or maketh flesh his arm.

35 Yea, I know that God will give liberally to him that asketh;
yea, my God will give me if I ask not amiss.
Therefore I will lift up my voice unto thee,
yea, I will cry unto thee, my God, the rock of my righteousness.
Behold, my voice shall forever ascend up unto thee,
my rock and mine everlasting God.
Amen.

5 | 1 Behold, it came to pass that I Nephi did cry much unto the Lord my God
because of the anger of my brethren.

2 But behold, their anger did increase against me,
insomuch that they did seek to take away my life.

3 Yea, they did murmur against me, saying:
Our younger brother thinketh to rule over us,
and we have had much trial because of him.
Wherefore now let us slay him,
that we may not be afflicted more because of his words.
For behold, we will not that he shall be our ruler,
for it belongeth unto us which are the elder brethren to rule over this people.

4 Now I do not write upon these plates all the words
which they murmured against me,
but it sufficeth me to say that they did seek to take away my life.

5 And it came to pass that the Lord did warn me
that I Nephi should depart from them and flee into the wilderness,
and all they which would go with me.

6 Wherefore it came to pass that I Nephi did take my family,
and also Zoram and his family,
and Sam mine elder brother and his family,
and Jacob and Joseph, my younger brethren,
and also my sisters,
and all they which would go with me.
And all they which would go with me were they

which believed in the warnings and the revelations of God;
wherefore they did hearken unto my words.

7   And we did take our tents and whatsoever things were possible for us
and did journey in the wilderness for the space of many days.
And after that we had journeyed for the space of many days,
we did pitch our tents.

8   And my people would that we should call the name of the place Nephi;
wherefore we did call it Nephi.

9   And all they which were with me did take it upon them
to call themselves the people of Nephi.

10 And we did observe to keep the judgments and the statutes
and the commandments of the Lord,
in all things according to the law of Moses.

11 And the Lord was with us and we did prosper exceedingly,
for we did sow seed and we did reap again in abundance.
And we began to raise flocks and herds and animals of every kind.

12 And I Nephi had also brought the records
which were engraven upon the plates of brass,
and also the ball or the compass
which was prepared for my father by the hand of the Lord,
according to that which is written.

13 And it came to pass that we began to prosper exceedingly
and to multiply in the land.

14 And I Nephi did take the sword of Laban
and after the manner of it did make many swords,
lest by any means the people which were now called Lamanites
should come upon us and destroy us.
For I knew their hatred towards me and my children
and they which were called my people.

15 And I did teach my people that they should build buildings
and that they should work in all manner of wood
and of iron and of copper and of brass and of steel
and of gold and of silver and of precious ores,
which were in great abundance.

16 And I Nephi did build a temple.
And I did construct it after the manner of the temple of Solomon,
save it were not built of so many precious things
—for they were not to be found upon the land—
wherefore it could not be built like unto Solomon's temple.

But the manner of the construction was like unto the temple of Solomon,
and the workmanship thereof was exceeding fine.

17 And it came to pass that I Nephi did cause my people
that they should be industrious
and that they should labor with their hands.

18 And it came to pass that they would that I should be their king,
but I Nephi was desirous that they should have no king.
Nevertheless I did do for them according to that which was in my power.

19 And behold, the words of the Lord had been fulfilled unto my brethren
which he spake concerning them, that I should be their ruler and their teacher.
Wherefore I had been their ruler and their teacher
according to the commandments of the Lord
until the time that they sought to take away my life.

20 Wherefore the word of the Lord was fulfilled
which he spake unto me,
saying that inasmuch as they will not hearken unto thy words,
they shall be cut off from the presence of the Lord.
And behold, they were cut off from his presence.

21 And he had caused the cursing to come upon them,
yea, even a sore cursing because of their iniquity.
For behold, they had hardened their hearts against him,
that they had become like unto a flint.
Wherefore as they were white and exceeding fair and delightsome,
that they might not be enticing unto my people,
therefore the Lord God did cause a skin of blackness to come upon them.

22 And thus saith the Lord God:
I will cause that they shall be loathsome unto thy people
save they shall repent of their iniquities.

23 And cursed shall be the seed of him that mixeth with their seed,
for they shall be cursed even with the same cursing.
And the Lord spake it, and it was done.

24 And because of their cursing which was upon them,
they did become an idle people, full of mischief and subtlety,
and did seek in the wilderness for beasts of prey.

25 And the Lord God said unto me:
They shall be a scourge unto thy seed to stir them up in remembrance of me.
And inasmuch as they will not remember me and hearken unto my words,
they shall scourge them even unto destruction.

26 And it came to pass that I Nephi did consecrate Jacob and Joseph,
that they should be priests and teachers over the land of my people.

27 And it came to pass that we lived after the manner of happiness.

28 And thirty years had passed away from the time we left Jerusalem.

29 And I Nephi had kept the records
upon my plates which I had made
of my people thus far.

30 And it came to pass that the Lord God said unto me:
Make other plates;
and thou shalt engraven many things upon them
which are good in my sight for the profit of thy people.

31 Wherefore I Nephi, to be obedient to the commandments of the Lord,
went and made these plates upon which I have engraven these things.

32 And I engravened that which is pleasing unto God.
And if my people be pleased with the things of God,
they be pleased with mine engravings which are upon these plates.

33 And if my people desire to know the more particular part
of the history of my people,
they must search mine other plates.

34 And it sufficeth me to say that forty years had passed away,
and we had already had wars and contentions with our brethren.

6 | 1 The words of Jacob the brother of Nephi
which he spake unto the people of Nephi:

2 Behold, my beloved brethren,
that I Jacob having been called of God
and ordained after the manner of his holy order
and having been consecrated by my brother Nephi,
unto whom ye look as a king or a protector
and on whom ye depend for safety,
behold, ye know that I have spoken unto you exceeding many things.

3 Nevertheless I speak unto you again,
for I am desirous for the welfare of your souls.
Yea, mine anxiety is great for you.
And ye yourselves know that it ever has been,
for I have exhorted you with all diligence.
And I have taught you the words of my father,
and I have spoken unto you concerning all things
which are written from the creation of the world.

4 And now behold, I would speak unto you
concerning things which are and which are to come.

Wherefore I will read you the words of Isaiah,
and they are the words which my brother hath desired me
that I should speak unto you.
And I speak them unto you for your sakes,
that ye may learn and glorify the name of your God.

5 And now the words which I shall read are they
which Isaiah spake concerning all the house of Israel.
Wherefore they may be likened unto you,
for ye are of the house of Israel.
And there are many things which have been spoken by Isaiah
which may be likened unto you
because that ye are of the house of Israel.

6 And now these are the words:
Thus saith the Lord God:
Behold, I will lift up mine hand to the Gentiles
and set up my standard to the people.
And they shall bring thy sons in their arms,
and thy daughters shall be carried upon their shoulders.

7 And kings shall be thy nursing fathers,
and their queens thy nursing mothers.
They shall bow down to thee with their faces towards the earth
and lick up the dust of thy feet.
And thou shalt know that I am the Lord,
for they shall not be ashamed that wait for me.

8 And now I Jacob would speak somewhat concerning these words.
For behold, the Lord hath shewn me
that they which were at Jerusalem, from whence we came,
have been slain and carried away captive.

9 Nevertheless the Lord hath shewn unto me
that they should return again.
And he also hath shewn unto me
that the Lord God, the Holy One of Israel,
should manifest himself unto them in the flesh.
And after that he should manifest himself,
they should scourge him and crucify him,
according to the words of the angel which spake it unto me.

10 And after that they have hardened their hearts
and stiffened their necks against the Holy One of Israel,
behold, the judgments of the Holy One of Israel shall come upon them.
And the day cometh that they shall be smitten and afflicted.

11 Wherefore after they are driven to and fro
—for thus saith the angel:
Many shall be afflicted in the flesh
and shall not be suffered to perish because of the prayers of the faithful—
wherefore they shall be scattered and smitten and hated.
Nevertheless the Lord will be merciful unto them,
that when they shall come to the knowledge of their Redeemer,
they shall be gathered together again to the lands of their inheritance.

12 And blessed are the Gentiles,
they of whom the prophet hath written.
For behold, if it so be that they shall repent and fight not against Zion
and do not unite themselves to that great and abominable church,
they shall be saved,
for the Lord God will fulfill his covenants
which he hath made unto his children.
And for this cause the prophet hath written these things.

13 Wherefore they that fight against Zion and the covenant people of the Lord
shall lick up the dust of their feet.
And the people of the Lord shall not be ashamed,
for the people of the Lord are they which wait for him,
for they still wait for the coming of the Messiah.

14 And behold, according to the words of the prophet,
the Messiah will set himself again the second time to recover them.
Wherefore he will manifest himself unto them in power and great glory
unto the destruction of their enemies,
when that day cometh when they shall believe in him.
And none will he destroy that believeth in him.
15 And they that believe not in him shall be destroyed,
both by fire and by tempest and by earthquakes
and by bloodsheds and by pestilence and by famine.
And they shall know that the Lord is God, the Holy One of Israel.
16 For shall the prey be taken from the mighty
or the lawful captive delivered?

17 But thus saith the Lord:
Even the captives of the mighty shall be taken away,
and the prey of the terrible shall be delivered,
for the mighty God shall deliver his covenant people.
For thus saith the Lord:
I will contend with them that contendeth with thee.

18 And I will feed them that oppress thee with their own flesh.
And they shall be drunken with their own blood as with sweet wine.
And all flesh shall know that
I the Lord am thy Savior and thy Redeemer, the Mighty One of Jacob.

7 | 1 Yea, for thus saith the Lord:
Have I put thee away or have I cast thee off forever?
For thus saith the Lord:
Where is the bill of your mother's divorcement?
To whom have I put thee away?
Or to which of my creditors have I sold you?
Yea, to whom have I sold you?
Behold, for your iniquities have ye sold yourselves,
and for your transgressions is your mother put away.

2 Wherefore when I came, there was no man;
when I called, yea, there was none to answer.
O house of Israel, is my hand shortened at all that it cannot redeem?
Or have I no power to deliver?
Behold, at my rebuke I dry up the sea.
I make the rivers a wilderness and their fish to stink
because the waters are dried up and they dieth because of thirst.
3 I clothe the heavens with blackness,
and I make sackcloth their covering.

4 The Lord God hath given me the tongue of the learned,
that I should know how to speak a word in season
unto thee, O house of Israel, when ye are weary.
He wakeneth morning by morning;
he wakeneth mine ear to hear as the learned.
5 The Lord God hath opened mine ear,
and I was not rebellious, neither turned away back.
6 I gave my back to the smiters
and my cheeks to them that plucked off the hair.
I hid not my face from shame and spitting.

7 For the Lord God will help me,
therefore shall I not be confounded.
Therefore have I set my face like a flint,
and I know that I shall not be ashamed.
8 And the Lord is near and he justifieth me.
Who will contend with me?
Let us stand together.
Who is mine adversary?

Let him come near me,
and I will smite him with the strength of my mouth.

9   For the Lord God will help me.

And all they which shall condemn me,
behold, all they shall wax old as a garment
and the moth shall eat them up.

10   Who is among you that feareth the Lord,
that obeyeth the voice of his servant,
that walketh in darkness and hath no light?

11   Behold, all ye that kindle a fire,
that compass yourselves about with sparks,
walk in the light of your fire and in the sparks which ye have kindled.
This shall ye have of mine hand:
ye shall lie down in sorrow.

8 | 1   Hearken to me, ye that follow after righteousness.
Look unto the rock from whence ye are hewn
and to the hole of the pit from whence ye are digged.

2   Look unto Abraham, your father,
and unto Sarah, she that bare you.
For I called him alone and blessed him.

3   For the Lord shall comfort Zion.
He will comfort all her waste places,
and he will make her wilderness like Eden
and her desert like the garden of the Lord.
Joy and gladness shall be found therein,
thanksgiving and the voice of melody.

4   Hearken unto me, my people,
and give ear unto me, O my nation.
For a law shall proceed from me,
and I will make my judgment to rest for a light of the people.

5   My righteousness is near.
My salvation is gone forth,
and mine arm shall judge the people.
The isles shall wait upon me,
and on mine arm shall they trust.

6   Lift up your eyes to the heavens
and look upon the earth beneath,
for the heavens shall vanish away like smoke
and the earth shall wax old like a garment.
And they that dwell therein shall die in like manner.

But my salvation shall be forever,
and my righteousness shall not be abolished.

7 Hearken unto me, ye that know righteousness,
the people in whose heart I have written my law.
Fear ye not the reproach of men,
neither be ye afraid of their revilings.
8 For the moth shall eat them up like a garment,
and the worm shall eat them like wool.
But my righteousness shall be forever,
and my salvation from generation to generation.

9 Awake, awake, put on strength, O arm of the Lord.
Awake as in the ancient days.
Art thou not it that hath cut Rahab and wounded the dragon?
10 Art thou not it which hath dried the sea,
the waters of the great deep,
that hath made the depths of the sea a way
for the ransomed to pass over?

11 Therefore the redeemed of the Lord shall return
and come with singing unto Zion.
And everlasting joy and holiness shall be upon their heads,
and they shall obtain gladness and joy.
Sorrow and mourning shall flee away.
12 I am he, yea, I am he that comforteth you.
Behold, who art thou that thou shouldst be afraid of man, which shall die,
and of the son of man, which shall be made like unto grass,
13 and forgettest the Lord thy maker
that hath stretched forth the heavens and laid the foundations of the earth
and hast feared continually every day because of the fury of the oppressor,
as if he were ready to destroy?
And where is the fury of the oppressor?

14 The captive exile hasteneth that he may be loosed,
and that he should not die in the pit, nor that his bread should fail.
15 But I am the Lord thy God whose waves roared.
The Lord of Hosts is my name.
16 And I have put my words in thy mouth
and hath covered thee in the shadow of mine hand,
that I may plant the heavens and lay the foundations of the earth,
and say unto Zion:
Behold, thou art my people.

17 Awake, awake, stand up, O Jerusalem,

which hast drunk at the hand of the Lord the cup of his fury;
thou hast drunken the dregs of the cup of trembling wrung out—

18 and none to guide her among all the sons she hath brought forth,
neither that taketh her by the hand of all the sons she hath brought up.

19 These two sons are come unto thee.
Who shall be sorry for thee,
thy desolation and destruction and the famine and the sword?
And by whom shall I comfort thee?

20 Thy sons have fainted save these two.
They lie at the head of all the streets as a wild bull in a net.
They are full of the fury of the Lord, the rebuke of thy God.

21 Therefore hear now this,
thou afflicted and drunken, and not with wine:

22 Thus saith thy Lord the Lord,
and thy God pleadeth the cause of his people:
Behold, I have taken out of thine hand the cup of trembling,
the dregs of the cup of my fury;
thou shalt no more drink it again.

23 But I will put it into the hand of them that afflict thee,
which have said to thy soul:
Bow down that we may go over.
And thou hast laid thy body as the ground and as the street
to them that went over.

24 Awake, awake, put on thy strength, O Zion!
Put on thy beautiful garments, O Jerusalem the holy city!
For henceforth there shall no more come into thee
the uncircumcised and the unclean.

25 Shake thyself from the dust! Arise!
Sit down, O Jerusalem!
Loose thyself from the bands of thy neck,
O captive daughter of Zion!

9 | 1 And now my beloved brethren, I have read these things
that ye might know concerning the covenants of the Lord,
that he hath covenanted with all the house of Israel,

2 that he hath spoken unto the Jews by the mouth of his holy prophets,
even from the beginning down from generation to generation
until the time cometh that they shall be restored
to the true church and fold of God,

when they shall be gathered home to the lands of their inheritance
and shall be established in all their lands of promise.

3 Behold, my beloved brethren,
I speak unto you these things
that ye may rejoice and lift up your heads forever
because of the blessings which the Lord God shall bestow upon your children.

4 For I know that thou hast searched much, many of you,
to know of things to come.
Wherefore I know that ye know that our flesh must waste away and die;
nevertheless in our bodies we shall see God.

5 Yea, and I know that ye know that in the body he shall shew himself
unto they at Jerusalem, from whence we came,
for it is expedient that it should be among them.
For it behooveth the great Creator that he suffereth himself
to become subject unto man in the flesh and die for all men,
that all men might become subject unto him.

6 For as death hath passed upon all men
to fulfill the merciful plan of the great Creator,
there must needs be a power of resurrection.
And the resurrection must needs come unto man by reason of the fall,
and the fall came by reason of transgression.
And because man became fallen,
they were cut off from the presence of the Lord.

7 Wherefore it must needs be an infinite atonement;
save it should be an infinite atonement,
this corruption could not put on incorruption.
Wherefore the first judgment which came upon man
must needs have remained to an endless duration.
And if so, this flesh must have laid down to rot
and to crumble to its mother earth, to rise no more.

8 O the wisdom of God, his mercy and grace!
For behold, if the flesh should rise no more,
our spirits must become subject to that angel
which fell from before the presence of the Eternal God
and became the devil,
to rise no more.

9 And our spirits must have become like unto him,
and we become devils, angels to a devil
—to be shut out from the presence of our God
and to remain with the father of lies,
in misery like unto himself—

yea, to that being who beguiled our first parents,
who transformeth himself nigh unto an angel of light
and stirreth up the children of men unto secret combinations of murder
and all manner of secret works of darkness.

10 O how great the goodness of our God
who prepareth a way for our escape from the grasp of this awful monster!
Yea, that monster death and hell
which I call the death of the body and also the death of the spirit.
11 And because of the way of deliverance of our God, the Holy One of Israel,
this death of which I have spoken, which is the temporal,
shall deliver up its dead, which death is the grave.
12 And this death of which I have spoken, which is the spiritual death,
shall deliver up its dead, which spiritual death is hell.
Wherefore death and hell must deliver up its dead,
and hell must deliver up its captive spirits
and the grave must deliver up its captive bodies.
And the bodies and the spirits of men will be restored one to the other;
and it is by the power of the resurrection of the Holy One of Israel.

13 O how great the plan of our God!
For on the other hand,
the paradise of God must deliver up the spirits of the righteous,
and the grave deliver up the bodies of the righteous.
And the spirit and the body is restored to itself again,
and all men become incorruptible and immortal,
and they are living souls—having a perfect knowledge—
like unto us in the flesh
save it be that our knowledge shall be perfect.
14 Wherefore we shall have a perfect knowledge of all our guilt
and our uncleanness and our nakedness.
And the righteous shall have a perfect knowledge
of their enjoyment and their righteousness,
being clothed with purity,
yea, even with the robe of righteousness.

15 And it shall come to pass that
when all men shall have passed from this first death unto life,
insomuch as they have become immortal,
they must appear before the judgment seat of the Holy One of Israel.
And then cometh the judgment,
and then must they be judged according to the holy judgment of God.
16 And assuredly as the Lord liveth
—for the Lord God hath spoken it

and it is his eternal word which cannot pass away—
that they which are righteous shall be righteous still
and they which are filthy shall be filthy still.
Wherefore they which are filthy are the devil and his angels,
and they shall go away into everlasting fire prepared for them;
and their torment is a lake of fire and brimstone,
whose flames ascendeth up forever and ever and hath no end.

17 O the greatness and the justice of our God!
For he executeth all his words;
and they have gone forth out of his mouth,
and his law must be fulfilled.

18 But behold, the righteous, the saints of the Holy One of Israel,
they which have believed in the Holy One of Israel,
they which have endured the crosses of the world and despised the shame of it,
they shall inherit the kingdom of God,
which was prepared for them from the foundation of the world;
and their joy shall be full forever.

19 O the greatness of the mercy of our God, the Holy One of Israel!
For he delivereth his saints from that awful monster,
the devil and death and hell
and that lake of fire and brimstone which is endless torment.

20 O how great the holiness of our God!
For he knoweth all things, and there is not any thing save he know it.

21 And he cometh into the world that he may save all men,
if they will hearken unto his voice.
For behold, he suffereth the pains of all men,
yea, the pains of every living creature, both men women and children,
which belong to the family of Adam.

22 And he suffereth this that the resurrection might pass upon all men,
that all might stand before him at the great and judgment day.

23 And he commandeth all men that they must repent
and be baptized in his name,
having perfect faith in the Holy One of Israel,
or they cannot be saved in the kingdom of God.

24 And if they will not repent and believe in his name
and be baptized in his name and endure to the end,
they must be damned,
for the Lord God, the Holy One of Israel, hath spoken it.

25 Wherefore he hath given a law.
And where there is no law given there is no punishment,

and where there is no punishment there is no condemnation,
and where there is no condemnation
the mercies of the Holy One of Israel hath claim upon them
because of the atonement,
for they are delivered by the power of him.

26 For the atonement satisfieth the demands of his justice
upon all those who hath not the law given to them,
that they are delivered from that awful monster, death and hell and the devil
and the lake of fire and brimstone which is endless torment;
and they are restored to that God who gave them breath,
which is the Holy One of Israel.

27 But woe unto him that hath the law given,
yea, that hath all the commandments of God, like unto us,
and that transgresseth them and that wasteth the days of his probation,
for awful is his state.

28 O that cunning plan of the evil one!
O the vainness and the frailties and the foolishness of men!
When they are learned they think they are wise,
and they hearken not unto the counsel of God,
for they set it aside, supposing they know of themselves.
Wherefore their wisdom is foolishness and it profiteth them not;
wherefore they shall perish.

29 But to be learned is good
if it so be that they hearken unto the counsels of God.

30 But woe unto the rich which are rich as to the things of the world,
for because that they are rich, they despise the poor and they persecute the meek.
And their hearts are upon their treasures;
wherefore their treasure is their god.
And behold, their treasure shall perish with them also.

31 And woe unto the deaf that will not hear,
for they shall perish.

32 Woe unto the blind that will not see,
for they shall perish also.

33 Woe unto the uncircumcised of heart,
for a knowledge of their iniquities shall smite them at the last day.

34 Woe unto the liar,
for he shall be thrust down to hell.

35 Woe unto the murderer who deliberately killeth,
for he shall die.

36 Woe unto them who commit whoredoms,
for they shall be thrust down to hell.

37 Yea, woe unto they that worship idols,
   for the devil of all devils delighteth in them.
38 And in fine, woe unto all they that die in their sins,
   for they shall return to God and behold his face and remain in their sins.

39 O my beloved brethren,
   remember the awfulness in transgressing against that holy God,
   and also the awfulness of yielding to the enticings of that cunning one.
   Remember, to be carnally minded is death
   and to be spiritually minded is life eternal.

40 O my beloved brethren, give ear to my words.
   Remember the greatness of the Holy One of Israel.
   Do not say that I have spoken hard things against you;
   for if ye do, ye will revile against the truth;
   for I have spoken the words of your Maker.
   I know that the words of truth are hard against all uncleanness,
   but the righteous fear it not,
   for they love the truth and are not shaken.

41 O then, my beloved brethren, come unto the Lord, the Holy One.
   Remember that his paths are righteousness.
   Behold, the way for man is narrow,
   but it lieth in a straight course before him.
   And the keeper of the gate is the Holy One of Israel,
   and he employeth no servant there.
   And there is none other way save it be by the gate,
   for he cannot be deceived,
   for the Lord God is his name.
42 And whoso knocketh to him will he open.
   And the wise and the learned and they that are rich
   which are puffed up because of their learning
   and their wisdom and their riches,
   yea, they are they whom he despiseth.
   And save they shall cast these things away
   and consider themselves fools before God
   and come down in the depths of humility,
   he will not open unto them.
43 But the things of the wise and the prudent shall be hid from them forever,
   yea, that happiness which is prepared for the saints.

44 O my beloved brethren, remember my words.
   Behold, I take off my garments and I shake them before you.
   I pray the God of my salvation that he view me with his all-searching eye.

Wherefore ye shall know at the last day,
when all men shall be judged of their works,
that the God of Israel did witness
that I shook your iniquities from my soul
and that I stand with brightness before him
and am rid of your blood.

45 O my beloved brethren, turn away from your sins.
Shake off the chains of him that would bind you fast.
Come unto that God who is the rock of your salvation.

46 Prepare your souls for that glorious day
when justice shall be administered unto the righteous,
even the day of judgment,
that ye may not shrink with awful fear,
that ye may not remember your awful guilt in perfectness,
and be constrained to exclaim:
Holy holy are thy judgments, O Lord God Almighty,
but I know my guilt.
I transgressed thy law and my transgressions are mine;
and the devil hath obtained me,
that I am a prey to his awful misery.

47 But behold, my brethren,
is it expedient that I should awake you to an awful reality of these things?
Would I harrow up your souls if your minds were pure?
Would I be plain unto you according to the plainness of the truth
if ye were freed from sin?

48 Behold, if ye were holy, I would speak unto you of holiness.
But as ye are not holy and ye look upon me as a teacher,
it must needs be expedient that I teach you the consequences of sin.

49 Behold, my soul abhorreth sin,
and my heart delighteth in righteousness.
And I will praise the holy name of my God.

50 Come, my brethren, every one that thirsteth, come ye to the waters.
And he that hath no money, come, buy and eat,
yea, come, buy wine and milk without money and without price.

51 Wherefore do not spend money for that which is of no worth,
nor your labor for that which cannot satisfy.
Hearken diligently unto me
and remember the words which I have spoken,
and come unto the Holy One of Israel,

and feast upon that which perisheth not, neither can be corrupted,
and let your soul delight in fatness.

52 Behold, my beloved brethren, remember the words of your God.
Pray unto him continually by day
and give thanks unto his holy name by night.
Let your hearts rejoice!

53 And behold, how great the covenants of the Lord!
And how great his condescensions unto the children of men!
And because of his greatness and his grace and mercy,
he hath promised unto us
that our seed shall not utterly be destroyed according to the flesh,
but that he would preserve them.
And in future generations they shall become
a righteous branch unto the house of Israel.

54 And now my brethren, I would speak unto you more;
but on the morrow I will declare unto you the remainder of my words.
Amen.

10 | 1 And now I Jacob speak unto you again, my beloved brethren,
concerning this righteous branch of which I have spoken.

2 For behold, the promises which we have obtained
are promises unto us according to the flesh.
Wherefore as it hath been shewn unto me
that many of our children shall perish in the flesh because of unbelief,
nevertheless God will be merciful unto many,
and our children shall be restored,
that they may come to that which will give them
the true knowledge of their Redeemer.

3 Wherefore as I said unto you,
it must needs be expedient that Christ
—for in the last night the angel spake unto me
that this should be his name—
that he should come among the Jews,
among they which are the more wicked part of the world.
And they shall crucify him
—for it behooveth our God—
and there is none other nation on earth
that would crucify their God.

4 For should the mighty miracles be wrought among other nations,
   they would repent and know that he be their God.
5 But because of priestcrafts and iniquities
   they at Jerusalem will stiffen their necks against him,
   that he be crucified.

6 Wherefore because of their iniquities,
   destructions, famines, pestilences, and bloodsheds shall come upon them.
   And they which shall not be destroyed shall be scattered among all nations.
7 But behold, thus saith the Lord God:
   When the day cometh that they shall believe in me, that I am Christ,
   then have I covenanted with their fathers
   that they shall be restored in the flesh upon the earth
   unto the lands of their inheritance.
8 And it shall come to pass that they shall be gathered in
   from their long dispersion from the isles of the sea
   and from the four parts of the earth.

   And the nations of the Gentiles shall be great in the eyes of me, saith God,
   in carrying them forth to the lands of their inheritance.
9 Yea, the kings of the Gentiles shall be nursing fathers unto them,
   and their queens shall become nursing mothers.
   Wherefore the promises of the Lord is great unto the Gentiles,
   for he hath spoken it, and who can dispute?

10 But behold, this land, saith God, shall be a land of thine inheritance;
    and the Gentiles shall be blessed upon the land.
11 And this land shall be a land of liberty unto the Gentiles,
    and there shall be no kings upon the land
    which shall raise up unto the Gentiles.
12 And I will fortify this land against all other nations.
13 And he that fighteth against Zion shall perish, saith God.
14 For he that raiseth up a king against me shall perish,
    for I the Lord, the king of heaven, will be their king,
    and I will be a light unto them forever that hear my words.

15 Wherefore for this cause that my covenants may be fulfilled
    which I have made unto the children of men
    that I will do unto them while they are in the flesh,
    I must needs destroy the secret works of darkness
    and of murders and of abominations.
16 Wherefore he that fighteth against Zion,
    both Jew and Gentile, both bond and free, both male and female, shall perish.

For they are they which are the whore of all the earth,
for they which are not for me are against me, saith our God.

17 For I will fulfill my promises which I have made unto the children of men
that I will do unto them while they are in the flesh.

18 Wherefore, my beloved brethren, thus saith our God,
I will afflict thy seed by the hand of the Gentiles.
Nevertheless I will soften the hearts of the Gentiles,
that they shall be like unto a father to them.
Wherefore the Gentiles shall be blessed
and numbered among the house of Israel.

19 Wherefore I will consecrate this land unto thy seed
—and they which shall be numbered among thy seed—
forever, for the land of their inheritance;
for it is a choice land, saith God, unto me,
above all other lands.
Wherefore I will have all men that dwell thereon
that they shall worship me, saith God.

20 And now my beloved brethren,
seeing that our merciful God hath given us
so great knowledge concerning these things,
let us remember him and lay aside our sins and not hang down our heads,
for we are not cast off.
Nevertheless we have been driven out of the land of our inheritance,
but we have been led to a better land,
for the Lord hath made the sea our path
and we are upon an isle of the sea.

21 But great is the promises of the Lord unto they
which are upon the isles of the sea.
Wherefore as it saith isles, there must needs be more than this,
and they are inhabited also by our brethren.

22 For behold, the Lord God hath led away from time to time
from the house of Israel according to his will and pleasure.
And now behold, the Lord remembereth all they which have been broken off;
wherefore he remembereth us also.

23 Therefore cheer up your hearts
and remember that ye are free to act for yourselves,
to choose the way of everlasting death or the way of eternal life.

24 Wherefore, my beloved brethren, reconcile yourselves to the will of God
and not to the will of the devil and the flesh.
And remember that after ye are reconciled unto God
that it is only in and through the grace of God that ye are saved.

25 Wherefore may God raise you from death by the power of the resurrection,
and also from everlasting death by the power of the atonement,
that ye may be received into the eternal kingdom of God,
that ye may praise him through grace divine.
Amen.

        ━━

11 | 1 And now Jacob spake many more things to my people at that time.
Nevertheless only these things have I caused to be written,
for the things which I have written sufficeth me.

2 And now I Nephi write more of the words of Isaiah,
for my soul delighteth in his words.
For I will liken his words unto my people.
And I will send them forth unto all my children,
for he verily saw my Redeemer, even as I have seen him.
3 And my brother Jacob also hath seen him, as I have seen him.
Wherefore I will send their words forth unto my children
to prove unto them that my words are true.
Wherefore by the words of three, God hath said, I will establish my word.
Nevertheless God sendeth more witnesses, and he proveth all his words.

4 Behold, my soul delighteth in proving unto my people
the truth of the coming of Christ,
for for this end hath the law of Moses been given.
And all things which have been given of God
from the beginning of the world unto man
are the typifying of him.
5 And also my soul delighteth in the covenants of the Lord
which he hath made to our fathers.
Yea, my soul delighteth in his grace and his justice and power and mercy,
in the great and eternal plan of deliverance from death.
6 And my soul delighteth in proving unto my people
that save Christ should come all men must perish.
7 For if there be no Christ there be no God.
And if there be no God we are not,
for there could have been no creation.
But there is a God and he is Christ,
and he cometh in the fullness of his own time.

8 And now I write some of the words of Isaiah,
that whoso of my people which shall see these words

may lift up their hearts and rejoice for all men.

Now these are the words, and ye may liken them unto you and unto all men.

12 | 1 The word that Isaiah the son of Amoz saw concerning Judah and Jerusalem:

2 And it shall come to pass in the last days,
when the mountain of the Lord's house
shall be established in the top of the mountains
and shall be exalted above the hills,
and all nations shall flow unto it.

3 And many people shall go and say:
Come ye and let us go up to the mountain of the Lord,
to the house of the God of Jacob,
and he will teach us of his ways and we will walk in his paths.
For out of Zion shall go forth the law
and the word of the Lord from Jerusalem.

4 And he shall judge among the nations and shall rebuke many people.
And they shall beat their swords into plowshares
and their spears into pruning hooks.
Nation shall not lift up sword against nation,
neither shall they learn war any more.

5 O house of Jacob, come ye and let us walk in the light of the Lord,
yea, come, for ye have all gone astray, every one to his wicked ways.

6 Therefore, O Lord, thou hast forsaken thy people, the house of Jacob,
because they be replenished from the east
and hearken unto soothsayers like the Philistines,
and they please themselves in the children of strangers.

7 Their land also is full of silver and gold,
neither is there any end of their treasures.
Their land is also full of horses,
neither is there any end of their chariots.

8 Their land also is full of idols;
they worship the work of their own hands,
that which their own fingers have made.

9 And the mean man boweth down
and the great man humbleth himself;
therefore forgive them not.

10 O ye wicked ones, enter into the rock and hide thee in the dust,
for the fear of the Lord and the glory of his majesty shall smite thee.

11 And it shall come to pass that the lofty looks of man shall be humbled
and the haughtiness of men shall be bowed down.
And the Lord alone shall be exalted in that day.

12 For the day of the Lord of Hosts soon cometh upon all nations,
    yea, upon every one, yea, upon the proud and lofty,
    and upon every one which is lifted up;
    and he shall be brought low.
13 Yea, and the day of the Lord shall come upon all the cedars of Lebanon,
    for they are high and lifted up,
    and upon all the oaks of Bashan,
14 and upon all the high mountains and upon all the hills,
    and upon all the nations which are lifted up and upon every people,
15 and upon every high tower and upon every fenced wall,
16 and upon all the ships of the sea and upon all the ships of Tarshish,
    and upon all the pleasant pictures.

17 And the loftiness of man shall be bowed down
    and the haughtiness of men shall be made low.
    And the Lord alone shall be exalted in that day.
18 And the idols he shall utterly abolish.
19 And they shall go into the holes of the rocks and into the caves of the earth,
    for the fear of the Lord shall come upon them.
    And the glory of his majesty shall smite them
    when he ariseth to shake terribly the earth.
20 In that day a man shall cast his idols of silver and his idols of gold
    which he hath made for himself to worship,
    to the moles and to the bats,
21 to go into the clefts of the rocks and into the tops of the ragged rocks.
    For the fear of the Lord shall come upon them,
    and the majesty of his glory shall smite them
    when he ariseth to shake terribly the earth.
22 Cease ye from man, whose breath is in his nostrils,
    for wherein is he to be accounted of?

13 | 1 For behold, the Lord, the Lord of Hosts, doth take away
    from Jerusalem and from Judah
    the stay and the staff,
    the whole staff of bread and the whole stay of water,
2 the mighty man and the man of war,
    the judge and the prophet and the prudent and the ancient,
3 the captain of fifty and the honorable man and the counselor
    and the cunning artificer and the eloquent orator.

4 And I will give children unto them to be their princes,
    and babes shall rule over them.
5 And the people shall be oppressed,

every one by another and every one by his neighbor.
The child shall behave himself proudly against the ancient,
and the base against the honorable.

6 When a man shall take hold of his brother of the house of his father
and shall say:
Thou hast clothing, be thou our ruler,
and let not this ruin come under thy hand—

7 in that day shall he swear, saying:
I will not be a healer,
for in my house there is neither bread nor clothing.
Make me not a ruler of the people.

8 For Jerusalem is ruined and Judah is fallen
because their tongues and their doings have been against the Lord,
to provoke the eyes of his glory.

9 The shew of their countenance doth witness against them
and doth declare their sin to be even as Sodom,
and they cannot hide it.

Woe unto their souls, for they have rewarded evil unto themselves.

10 Say unto the righteous that it is well with them,
for they shall eat the fruit of their doings.

11 Woe unto the wicked, for they shall perish.
For the reward of their hands shall be upon them.

12 And my people, children are their oppressors,
and women rule over them.
O my people, they which lead thee cause thee to err
and destroy the way of thy paths.

13 The Lord standeth up to plead and standeth to judge the people.

14 The Lord will enter into judgment
with the ancients of his people and the princes thereof.
For ye have eaten up the vineyard and the spoil of the poor in your houses.

15 What mean ye?
Ye beat my people to pieces
and grind the faces of the poor,
saith the Lord God of Hosts.

16 Moreover the Lord saith:
Because the daughters of Zion are haughty
and walk with stretched forth necks and wanton eyes,
walking and mincing as they go,
and making a tinkling with their feet,

17 therefore the Lord will smite with a scab
the crown of the head of the daughters of Zion.
And the Lord will discover their secret parts.

18 In that day the Lord will take away the bravery of tinkling ornaments
and cauls and round tires like the moon,

19 the chains and the bracelets and the mufflers,

20 the bonnets and the ornaments of the legs
and the headbands and the tablets and the earrings,

21 the rings and nose jewels,

22 the changeable suits of apparel
and the mantles and the wimples and the crisping pins,

23 the glasses and the fine linen and hoods and the veils.

24 And it shall all come to pass:
instead of sweet smell there shall be stink,
and instead of a girdle a rent,
and instead of well-set hair baldness,
and instead of a stomacher a girding of sackcloth,
burning instead of beauty.

25 Thy men shall fall by the sword and thy mighty in the war.

26 And her gates shall lament and mourn,
and she shall be desolate and shall sit upon the ground.

14 | 1 And in that day seven women shall take hold of one man, saying:
We will eat our own bread and wear our own apparel,
only let us be called by thy name to take away our reproach.

2 In that day shall the branch of the Lord be beautiful and glorious—
the fruit of the earth, excellent and comely to them that are escaped of Israel.

3 And it shall come to pass:
them that are left in Zion and remaineth in Jerusalem shall be called holy,
every one that is written among the living in Jerusalem,

4 when the Lord shall have washed away the filth of the daughters of Zion
and shall have purged the blood of Jerusalem from the midst thereof
by the spirit of judgment and by the spirit of burning.

5 And the Lord will create
upon every dwelling place of mount Zion
and upon her assemblies
a cloud and smoke by day
and the shining of a flaming fire by night,
for upon all the glory of Zion shall be a defense.

6 And there shall be a tabernacle

for a shadow in the daytime from the heat,
and for a place of refuge and a covert from storm and from rain.

15 | 1 And then will I sing to my well beloved
a song of my beloved touching his vineyard.
My well beloved hath a vineyard in a very fruitful hill.

2 And he fenced it and gathered out the stones thereof
and planted it with the choicest vine
and built a tower in the midst of it
and also made a winepress therein.
And he looked that it should bring forth grapes,
and it brought forth wild grapes.

3 And now O inhabitants of Jerusalem and men of Judah,
judge I pray you betwixt me and my vineyard.

4 What could have been done more to my vineyard that I have not done in it?
Wherefore when I looked that it should bring forth grapes,
it brought forth wild grapes.

5 And now go to;
I will tell you what I will do to my vineyard.
I will take away the hedge thereof and it shall be eaten up.
And I will break down the wall thereof and it shall be trodden down.

6 And I will lay it waste.
It shall not be pruned nor digged,
but there shall come up briars and thorns.
I will also command the clouds that they rain no rain upon it.

7 For the vineyard of the Lord of Hosts is the house of Israel,
and the men of Judah his pleasant plant.
And he looked for judgment — and behold, oppression;
for righteousness — but behold, a cry.

8 Woe unto them that join house to house till there can be no place,
that they may be placed alone in the midst of the earth.

9 In mine ears saith the Lord of Hosts:
Of a truth many houses shall be desolate,
and great and fair cities without inhabitant.

10 Yea, ten acres of vineyard shall yield one bath,
and the seed of a homer shall yield an ephah.

11 Woe unto them that rise up early in the morning
that they may follow strong drink,
that continue until night and wine inflame them.

12 And the harp and the viol,

the tabret and pipe and wine are in their feasts,
but they regard not the work of the Lord,
neither consider the operation of his hands.

13 Therefore my people are gone into captivity
because they have no knowledge.
And their honorable men are famished,
and their multitude dried up with thirst.

14 Therefore hell hath enlarged herself and opened her mouth without measure,
and their glory and their multitude and their pomp and he that rejoiceth
shall descend into it.

15 And the mean man shall be brought down,
and the mighty man shall be humbled,
and the eyes of the lofty shall be humbled.

16 But the Lord of Hosts shall be exalted in judgment,
and God that is holy shall be sanctified in righteousness.

17 Then shall the lambs feed after their manner,
and the waste places of the fat ones shall strangers eat.

18 Woe unto them that draw iniquity with cords of vanity
and sin as it were with a cart rope,

19 that say:
Let him make speed,
hasten his work that we may see it.
And let the counsel of the Holy One of Israel draw nigh and come,
that we may know it.

20 Woe unto them that call evil good and good evil,
that put darkness for light and light for darkness,
that put bitter for sweet and sweet for bitter.

21 Woe unto the wise in their own eyes and prudent in their own sight.

22 Woe unto the mighty to drink wine
and men of strength to mingle strong drink,

23 which justify the wicked for reward
and take away the righteousness of the righteous from him.

24 Therefore as the fire devoureth the stubble and the flame consumeth the chaff,
their root shall be rottenness and their blossom shall go up as dust
because they have cast away the law of the Lord of Hosts
and despised the word of the Holy One of Israel.

25 Therefore is the anger of the Lord kindled against his people,
and he hath stretched forth his hand against them and hath smitten them.
And the hills did tremble

and their carcasses were torn in the midst of the streets.
For all this his anger is not turned away, but his hand stretched out still.

26 And he will lift up an ensign to the nations from far
and will hiss unto them from the end of the earth.
And behold, they shall come with speed swiftly.

27 None shall be weary nor stumble among them.
None shall slumber nor sleep,
neither shall the girdle of their loins be loosed,
nor the latchet of their shoes be broken,

28 whose arrows shall be sharp,
and all their bows bent.
And their horses' hoofs shall be counted like flint,
and their wheels like a whirlwind,
their roaring like a lion.

29 They shall roar like young lions;
yea, they shall roar and lay hold of the prey
and shall carry away safe, and none shall deliver.

30 And in that day they shall roar against them like the roaring of the sea.
And if they look unto the land, behold, darkness and sorrow,
and the light is darkened in the heavens thereof.

⸻

16 | 1 In the year that king Uzziah died,
I saw also the Lord sitting upon a throne, high and lifted up,
and his train filled the temple.

2 Above it stood the seraphims;
each one had six wings:
with twain he covered his face,
and with twain he covered his feet,
and with twain he did fly.

3 And one cried unto another and said:
Holy holy holy is the Lord of Hosts;
the whole earth is full of his glory.

4 And the posts of the door moved at the voice of him that cried,
and the house was filled with smoke.

5 Then said I:
Woe me, for I am undone
because I a man of unclean lips,
and I dwell in the midst of a people of unclean lips.
For mine eyes have seen the King, the Lord of Hosts.

6 Then flew one of the seraphims unto me,
having a live coal in his hand,

which he had taken with the tongs from off the altar.

7 And he laid upon my mouth and said:
Lo, this hath touched thy lips,
and thine iniquity is taken away and thy sin purged.

8 Also I heard the voice of the Lord, saying:
Whom shall I send?
And who will go for us?
Then I said:
Here I, send me.

9 And he said:
Go and tell this people:
Hear ye indeed, but they understand not;
and see ye indeed, but they perceive not.

10 Make the heart of this people fat
and make their ears heavy and shut their eyes,
lest they see with their eyes and hear with their ears
and understand with their heart and convert and be healed.

11 Then said I:
Lord, how long?
And he said:
Until the cities be wasted without inhabitant,
and the houses without man,
and the land be utterly desolate,

12 and the Lord have removed men far away,
for there shall be a great forsaking in the midst of the land.

13 But yet in it there shall be a tenth,
and they shall return and shall be eaten;
as a teil tree and as an oak
whose substance is in them when they cast their leaves,
so the holy seed shall be the substance thereof.

17 | 1 And it came to pass
—in the days of Ahaz the son of Jotham the son of Uzziah, king of Judah—
Rezin, king of Syria, and Pekah the son of Remaliah, king of Israel, went up
towards Jerusalem to war against it but could not prevail against it.

2 And it was told the house of David, saying:
Syria is confederate with Ephraim.
And his heart was moved and the heart of his people,
as the trees of the wood are moved with the wind.

3 Then said the Lord unto Isaiah:
Go forth now to meet Ahaz,
thou and Shear-jashub thy son,

at the end of the conduit of the upper pool
in the highway of the fuller's field,

4 and say unto him:
Take heed and be quiet.
Fear not, neither be fainthearted
for the two tails of these smoking firebrands,
for the fierce anger of Rezin with Syria and of the son of Remaliah,

5 because Syria, Ephraim, and the son of Remaliah have taken evil counsel
against thee, saying:

6 Let us go up against Judah and vex it.
And let us make a breach therein for us
and set a king in the midst of it,
yea, the son of Tabeal.

7 Thus saith the Lord God:
It shall not stand, neither shall it come to pass.

8 For the head of Syria is Damascus and the head of Damascus Rezin,
and within threescore and five years shall Ephraim be broken,
that it be not a people.

9 And the head of Ephraim is Samaria
and the head of Samaria is Remaliah's son.
If ye will not believe, surely ye shall not be established.

10 Moreover the Lord spake again unto Ahaz, saying:

11 Ask thee a sign of the Lord thy God;
ask either in the depths or in the heights above.

12 But Ahaz said:
I will not ask, neither will I tempt the Lord.

13 And he said:
Hear ye now, O house of David:
Is it a small thing for you to weary men,
but will ye weary my God also?

14 Therefore the Lord himself shall give you a sign:
behold, a virgin shall conceive and shall bear a son
and shall call his name Immanuel.

15 Butter and honey shall he eat,
that he may know to refuse the evil and to choose the good.

16 For before the child shall know to refuse the evil and choose the good,
the land that thou abhorrest shall be forsaken of both her kings.

17 The Lord shall bring upon thee
and upon thy people and upon thy father's house
days that have not come from the day that Ephraim departed from Judah,
the king of Assyria.

18 And it shall come to pass in that day
    that the Lord shall hiss for the fly that is in the uttermost part of Egypt
    and for the bee that is in the land of Assyria.

19 And they shall come and shall rest, all of them,
    in the desolate valleys and in the holes of the rocks
    and upon all thorns and upon all bushes.

20 In the same day shall the Lord shave with a razor
    that is hired by them beyond the river, by the king of Assyria,
    the head and the hair of the feet;
    and it shall also consume the beard.

21 And it shall come to pass that in that day
    a man shall nourish a young cow and two sheep.

22 And it shall come to pass,
    for the abundance of milk they shall give, he shall eat butter,
    for butter and honey shall every one eat that is left in the land.

23 And it shall come to pass in that day every place shall be
    where there were a thousand vines at a thousand silverlings,
    which shall be for briars and thorns.

24 With arrows and with bows shall men come thither
    because all the land shall become briars and thorns.

25 And all hills that shall be digged with the mattock,
    there shall not come thither the fear of briars and thorns,
    but it shall be for the sending forth of oxen and the treading of lesser cattle.

18 | 1 Moreover the word of the Lord said unto me:
    Take thee a great roll and write in it with a man's pen
    concerning Maher-shalal-hash-baz.

2 And I took unto me faithful witnesses to record,
    Uriah the priest and Zechariah the son of Jeberechiah.

3 And I went unto the prophetess,
    and she conceived and bare a son.
    Then said the Lord to me:
    Call his name Maher-shalal-hash-baz.

4 For behold, the child shall not have knowledge to cry my father and my mother
    before the riches of Damascus and the spoil of Samaria
    shall be taken away before the king of Assyria.

5 The Lord spake also unto me again, saying:

6 Forasmuch as this people refuseth the waters of Shiloah that go softly
    and rejoice in Rezin and Remaliah's son,

7 now therefore behold, the Lord bringeth up upon them the waters of the river,
    strong and many, even the king of Assyria and all his glory.
    And he shall come up over all his channels and go over all his banks,

8 and he shall pass through Judah.
   He shall overflow and go over;
   he shall reach even to the neck,
   and the stretching out of his wings
   shall fill the breadth of thy land, O Immanuel.

9 Associate yourselves, O ye people, and ye shall be broken in pieces.
   And give ear, all ye of far countries:
   Gird yourselves and ye shall be broken in pieces;
   gird yourselves and ye shall be broken in pieces.
10 Take counsel together and it shall come to naught.
   Speak the word and it shall not stand,
   for God is with us.

11 For the Lord spake thus to me with a strong hand
   and instructed me that I should not walk in the way of this people, saying:
12 Say ye not a confederacy
   to all to whom this people shall say a confederacy,
   neither fear ye their fear nor be afraid.
13 Sanctify the Lord of Hosts himself,
   and let him be your fear and let him be your dread.
14 And he shall be for a sanctuary,
   but for a stone of stumbling and for a rock of offense
   to both the houses of Israel,
   for a gin and a snare to the inhabitants of Jerusalem.
15 And many among them shall stumble and fall
   and be broken and be snared and be taken.

16 Bind up the testimony,
   seal the law among my disciples.
17 And I will wait upon the Lord,
   that hideth his face from the house of Jacob,
   and I will look for him.
18 Behold, I and the children whom the Lord hath given me
   are for signs and for wonders in Israel
   from the Lord of Hosts, which dwelleth in mount Zion.

19 And when they shall say unto you:
   Seek unto them that have familiar spirits
   and unto wizards that peep and mutter—
   Should not a people seek unto their God,
   for the living to hear from the dead,
20 to the law and to the testimony?
   And if they speak not according to this word,

it is because there is no light in them.

21 And they shall pass through it hardly bestead and hungry.
And it shall come to pass that when they shall be hungry,
they shall fret themselves and curse their king and their God and look upward.

22 And they shall look unto the earth
—and behold, trouble and darkness, dimness of anguish—
and shall be driven to darkness.

19 | 1 Nevertheless the dimness shall not be such as was in her vexation,
when at the first he lightly afflicted the land of Zebulun and the land of Naphtali,
and afterward did more grievously afflict by the way of the Red Sea,
beyond Jordan in Galilee of the nations.

2 The people that walked in darkness have seen a great light.
They that dwell in the land of the shadow of death,
upon them hath the light shined.

3 Thou hast multiplied the nation and increased the joy.
They joy before thee according to the joy in harvest
and as men rejoice when they divide the spoil.

4 For thou hast broken the yoke of his burden
and the staff of his shoulder, the rod of his oppressor.

5 For every battle of the warrior with confused noise and garments rolled in blood—
but this shall be with burning and fuel of fire.

6 For unto us a child is born,
unto us a son is given.
And the government shall be upon his shoulder,
and his name shall be called Wonderful Counselor,
the Mighty God, the Everlasting Father, the Prince of Peace.

7 Of the increase of government and peace there is no end,
upon the throne of David and upon his kingdom,
to order it and to establish it,
with judgment and with justice
from henceforth, even forever.
The zeal of the Lord of Hosts will perform this.

8 The Lord sent his word unto Jacob,
and it hath lighted upon Israel.

9 And all the people shall know,
even Ephraim and the inhabitants of Samaria,
that say in the pride and the stoutness of heart:

10 The bricks are fallen down, but we will build with hewn stones;
the sycamores are cut down, but we will change them into cedars.

11 Therefore the Lord shall set up the adversaries of Rezin against him

and join his enemies together,

12 the Syrians before and the Philistines behind,
and they shall devour Israel with open mouth.
For all this his anger is not turned away, but his hand stretched out still.

13 For the people turneth not unto him that smiteth them,
neither do they seek the Lord of Hosts.

14 Therefore will the Lord cut off from Israel head and tail,
branch and rush in one day.

15 The ancient, he is the head;
and the prophet that teacheth lies, he is the tail.

16 For the leaders of this people cause them to err,
and they that are led of them are destroyed.

17 Therefore the Lord shall have no joy in their young men,
neither shall have mercy on their fatherless and widows.
For every one of them is a hypocrite and an evildoer,
and every mouth speaketh folly.
For all this his anger is not turned away, but his hand stretched out still.

18 For wickedness burneth as the fire.
It shall devour the briars and thorns
and shall kindle in the thickets of the forests,
and they shall mount up like the lifting up of smoke.

19 Through the wrath of the Lord of Hosts is the land darkened,
and the people shall be as the fuel of the fire.
No man shall spare his brother.

20 And he shall snatch on the right hand and be hungry;
and he shall eat on the left hand, and they shall not be satisfied.
They shall eat every man the flesh of his own arm:

21 Manasseh, Ephraim; and Ephraim, Manasseh.
They together shall be against Judah.
For all this his anger is not turned away, but his hand stretched out still.

20 | 1 Woe unto them that decree unrighteous decrees
and that write grievousness which they have prescribed,

2 to turn aside the needy from judgment
and to take away the right from the poor of my people,
that widows may be their prey and that they may rob the fatherless.

3 And what will ye do in the day of visitation
and in the desolation which shall come from far?
To whom will ye flee for help?
And where will ye leave your glory?

4 Without me they shall bow down under the prisoners,

and they shall fall under the slain.
For all this his anger is not turned away, but his hand stretched out still.

5 O Assyrian, the rod of mine anger;
and the staff in their hand is their indignation.
6 I will send him against a hypocritical nation,
and against the people of my wrath will I give him a charge
to take the spoil and to take the prey
and to tread them down like the mire of the streets.

7 Howbeit he meaneth not so,
neither doth his heart think so;
but in his heart it is to destroy and cut off nations not a few.
8 For he saith:
Are not my princes altogether kings?
9 Is not Calno as Carchemish?
Is not Hamath as Arpad?
Is not Samaria as Damascus?
10 As my hand hath found the kingdoms of the idols
and whose graven images did excel them of Jerusalem and of Samaria,
11 shall I not as I have done unto Samaria and her idols
so do to Jerusalem and to her idols?

12 Wherefore it shall come to pass that
when the Lord hath performed his whole work
upon mount Zion and upon Jerusalem,
I will punish the fruit of the stout heart of the king of Assyria
and the glory of his high looks.
13 For he saith:
By the strength of my hand and by my wisdom
I have done these things,
for I am prudent.
And I have removed the borders of the people and have robbed their treasures,
and I have put down the inhabitants like a valiant man.
14 And my hand hath found as a nest the riches of the people,
and as one gathereth eggs that are left have I gathered all the earth.
And there was none that moved the wing or opened the mouth or peeped.
15 Shall the ax boast itself against him that heweth therewith?
Shall the saw magnify itself against him that shaketh it?
As if the rod should shake itself against them that lift it up?
Or as if the staff should lift up itself as if it were no wood?

16 Therefore shall the Lord, the Lord of Hosts, send among his fat ones leanness,
and under his glory he shall kindle a burning like the burning of a fire.

17 And the light of Israel shall be for a fire and his Holy One for a flame,
   and shall burn and shall devour his thorns and his briars in one day,
18 and shall consume the glory of his forest and of his fruitful field,
   both soul and body.
   And they shall be as when a standard-bearer fainteth.
19 And the rest of the trees of his forest shall be few,
   that a child may write them.

20 And it shall come to pass in that day
   that the remnant of Israel and such as are escaped of the house of Jacob
   shall no more again stay upon him that smote them,
   but shall stay upon the Lord, the Holy One of Israel, in truth.
21 The remnant shall return,
   yea, even the remnant of Jacob, unto the mighty God.
22 For though thy people Israel be as the sand of the sea,
   yet a remnant of them shall return.
   The consumption decreed shall overflow with righteousness;
23 for the Lord God of Hosts shall make a consumption,
   even determined in all the land.

24 Therefore thus saith the Lord God of Hosts:
   O my people that dwellest in Zion,
   be not afraid of the Assyrian.
   He shall smite thee with a rod
   and shall lift up his staff against thee after the manner of Egypt.
25 For yet a very little while and the indignation shall cease
   and mine anger in their destruction.
26 And the Lord of Hosts shall stir up a scourge for him
   according to the slaughter of Midian at the rock of Oreb.
   And as his rod was upon the sea,
   so shall he lift it up after the manner of Egypt.
27 And it shall come to pass in that day
   that his burden shall be taken away from off thy shoulder
   and his yoke from off thy neck,
   and the yoke shall be destroyed because of the anointing.

28 He is come to Aiath.
   He is passed to Migron.
   At Michmash he hath laid up his carriages.
29 They are gone over the passage.
   They have taken up their lodging at Geba.
   Ramah is afraid.
   Gibeah of Saul is fled.
30 Lift up the voice, O daughter of Gallim.

Cause it to be heard unto Laish,
O poor Anathoth.

31 Madmenah is removed.
The inhabitants of Gebim gather themselves to flee.

32 As yet shall he remain at Nob that day.
He shall shake his hand against the mount of the daughter of Zion,
the hill of Jerusalem.

33 Behold, the Lord, the Lord of Hosts, shall lop the bough with terror;
and the high ones of stature shall be hewn down,
and the haughty shall be humbled.

34 And he shall cut down the thickets of the forests with iron,
and Lebanon shall fall by a mighty one.

21 | 1 And there shall come forth a rod out of the stem of Jesse,
and a branch shall grow out of his roots.

2 And the Spirit of the Lord shall rest upon him,
the spirit of wisdom and understanding,
the spirit of counsel and might,
the spirit of knowledge and of the fear of the Lord,

3 and shall make him of quick understanding in the fear of the Lord.
And he shall not judge after the sight of his eyes,
neither reprove after the hearing of his ears,

4 but with righteousness shall he judge the poor
and reprove with equity for the meek of the earth.
And he shall smite the earth with the rod of his mouth,
and with the breath of his lips shall he slay the wicked.

5 And righteousness shall be the girdle of his loins,
and faithfulness the girdle of his reins.

6 The wolf also shall dwell with the lamb,
and the leopard shall lie down with the kid,
and the calf and the young lion and the fatling together;
and a little child shall lead them.

7 And the cow and the bear shall feed;
their young ones shall lie down together.
And the lion shall eat straw like the ox.

8 And the sucking child shall play on the hole of the asp,
and the weaned child shall put his hand on the cockatrice's den.

9 They shall not hurt nor destroy in all my holy mountain,
for the earth shall be full of the knowledge of the Lord
as the waters cover the sea.

10 And in that day there shall be a root of Jesse
which shall stand for an ensign of the people;

to it shall the Gentiles seek, and his rest shall be glorious.
11 And it shall come to pass in that day
that the Lord shall set his hand again the second time
to recover the remnant of his people
which shall be left from Assyria and from Egypt
and from Pathros and from Cush and from Elam
and from Shinar and from Hamath and from the islands of the sea.
12 And he shall set up an ensign for the nations
and shall assemble the outcasts of Israel
and gather together the dispersed of Judah
from the four corners of the earth.

13 The envy of Ephraim also shall depart,
and the adversaries of Judah shall be cut off.
Ephraim shall not envy Judah,
and Judah shall not vex Ephraim.
14 But they shall fly upon the shoulders of the Philistines toward the west;
they shall spoil them of the east together.
They shall lay their hand upon Edom and Moab,
and the children of Ammon shall obey them.

15 And the Lord shall utterly destroy the tongue of the Egyptian sea.
And with his mighty wind he shall shake his hand over the river
and shall smite it in the seven streams
and make men go over dry-shod.
16 And there shall be a highway for the remnant of his people
which shall be left from Assyria,
like as it was to Israel in the day that he came up out of the land of Egypt.

22 | 1 And in that day thou shalt say:
O Lord, I will praise thee.
Though thou wast angry with me,
thine anger is turned away and thou comfortedst me.
2 Behold, God is my salvation.
I will trust and not be afraid,
for the Lord Jehovah is my strength and my song;
he also is become my salvation.

3 Therefore with joy shall ye draw water out of the wells of salvation.
4 And in that day shall ye say:
Praise the Lord,
call upon his name,
declare his doings among the people,
make mention that his name is exalted.

5 Sing unto the Lord,
  for he hath done excellent things.
  This is known in all the earth.

6 Cry out and shout, thou inhabitant of Zion,
  for great is the Holy One of Israel in the midst of thee.

23 | 1 The burden of Babylon which Isaiah the son of Amoz did see.

2 Lift ye up a banner upon the high mountain,
  exalt the voice unto them,
  shake the hand that they may go into the gates of the nobles.

3 I have commanded my sanctified ones;
  I have also called my mighty ones.
  For mine anger is not upon them that rejoice in my highness.

4 The noise of the multitude in the mountains like as of a great people,
  a tumultuous noise of the kingdoms of nations gathered together—
  the Lord of Hosts mustereth the host of the battle.

5 They come from a far country, from the end of heaven,
  yea, the Lord and the weapons of his indignation,
  to destroy the whole land.

6 Howl ye, for the day of the Lord is at hand.
  It shall come as a destruction from the Almighty.

7 Therefore shall all hands be faint.
  Every man's heart shall melt,

8 and they shall be afraid.
  Pangs and sorrows shall take hold of them.
  They shall be amazed one at another.
  Their faces shall be as flames.

9 Behold, the day of the Lord cometh,
  cruel both with wrath and fierce anger,
  to lay the land desolate.
  And he shall destroy the sinners thereof out of it.

10 For the stars of heaven and the constellations thereof shall not give their light.
  The sun shall be darkened in his going forth,
  and the moon shall not cause her light to shine.

11 And I will punish the world for evil and the wicked for their iniquity.
  I will cause the arrogancy of the proud to cease
  and will lay down the haughtiness of the terrible.

12 I will make a man more precious than fine gold,
  even a man than the golden wedge of Ophir.

13 Therefore I will shake the heavens,

and the earth shall remove out of her place,
in the wrath of the Lord of Hosts and in the day of his fierce anger.

14 And it shall be as the chased roe and as a sheep that no man taketh up.
They shall every man turn to his own people
and flee every one into his own land.
15 Every one that is proud shall be thrust through.
Yea, and every one that is joined to the wicked shall fall by the sword.
16 Their children also shall be dashed to pieces before their eyes.
Their houses shall be spoiled and their wives ravished.
17 Behold, I will stir up the Medes against them,
which shall not regard silver and gold,
nor they s9hall not delight in it.
18 Their bows shall also dash the young men to pieces.
And they shall have no pity on the fruit of the womb;
their eyes shall not spare children.

19 And Babylon, the glory of kingdoms, the beauty of the Chaldees' excellency,
shall be as when God overthrew Sodom and Gomorrah.
20 It shall never be inhabited, neither shall it be dwelt in,
from generation to generation.
Neither shall the Arabian pitch tent there,
neither shall the shepherds make their fold there.
21 But wild beasts of the desert shall lie there,
and their houses shall be full of doleful creatures.
And owls shall dwell there,
and satyrs shall dance there.
22 And the wild beasts of the islands shall cry in their desolate houses,
and dragons in their pleasant palaces.
And her time is near to come
and her day shall not be prolonged,
for I will destroy her speedily.
Yea, for I will be merciful unto my people,
but the wicked shall perish.

24 | 1 For the Lord will have mercy on Jacob
and will yet choose Israel and set them in their own land.
And the strangers shall be joined with them,
and they shall cleave to the house of Jacob.
2 And the people shall take them and bring them to their place,
yea, from far unto the ends of the earth.
And they shall return to their lands of promise,
and the house of Israel shall possess them.
And the land of the Lord shall be for servants and handmaids.

And they shall take them captives unto whom they were captives,
and they shall rule over their oppressors.

3 And it shall come to pass that in that day
that the Lord shall give thee rest from thy sorrow and from thy fear
and from the hard bondage wherein thou wast made to serve.

4 And it shall come to pass in that day
that thou shalt take up this proverb against the king of Babylon and say:
How hath the oppressor ceased,
the golden city ceased!

5 The Lord hath broken the staff of the wicked,
the scepters of the rulers.

6 He who smote the people in wrath with a continual stroke,
he that ruled the nations in anger, is persecuted and none hindereth.

7 The whole earth is at rest and is quiet.
They break forth into singing.

8 Yea, the fir trees rejoice at thee,
and also the cedars of Lebanon, saying:
Since thou art laid down,
no feller is come up against us.

9 Hell from beneath is moved for thee,
to meet thee at thy coming.
It stirreth up the dead for thee,
even all the chief ones of the earth.
It hath raised up from their thrones all the kings of the nations.

10 All they shall speak and say unto thee:
Art thou also become weak as we?
Art thou become like unto us?

11 Thy pomp is brought down to the grave.
The noise of thy viols is not heard.
The worm is spread under thee and the worms cover thee.

12 How art thou fallen from heaven, O Lucifer, son of the morning,
art thou cut down to the ground which did weaken the nations!

13 For thou hast said in thy heart:
I will ascend into heaven.
I will exalt my throne above the stars of God.
I will sit also upon the mount of the congregation in the sides of the north.

14 I will ascend above the heights of the clouds.
I will be like the Most High.

15 Yet thou shalt be brought down to hell, to the sides of the pit.

16 They that see thee shall narrowly look upon thee
and shall consider thee and shall say:

Is this the man that made the earth to tremble,
that did shake kingdoms

17 and made the world as a wilderness
and destroyed the cities thereof
and opened not the house of his prisoners?

18 All the kings of the nations, yea, all of them, lie in glory,
every one of them in his own house.

19 But thou art cast out of thy grave
like an abominable branch
and the raiment of those that are slain,
thrust through with a sword,
that go down to the stones of the pit,
as a carcass trodden under feet.

20 Thou shalt not be joined with them in burial
because thou hast destroyed thy land and slain thy people.
The seed of evildoers shall never be renowned.

21 Prepare slaughter for his children
for the iniquities of their fathers,
that they do not rise nor possess the land
nor fill the face of the world with cities.

22 For I will rise up against them, saith the Lord of Hosts,
and cut off from Babylon the name and remnant,
and son and nephew, saith the Lord.

23 I will also make it a possession for the bittern and pools of water.
And I will sweep it with the besom of destruction, saith the Lord of Hosts.

24 The Lord of Hosts hath sworn, saying:
Surely as I have thought, so shall it come to pass;
and as I have purposed, so shall it stand,

25 that I will break the Assyrian in my land
and upon my mountains tread him under foot.
Then shall his yoke depart from off them,
and his burden depart from off their shoulders.

26 This is the purpose that is purposed upon the whole earth.
And this is the hand that is stretched out upon all nations.

27 For the Lord of Hosts hath purposed,
and who shall disannul?
And his hand stretched out,
and who shall turn it back?

28 In the year that king Ahaz died was this burden.

29 Rejoice not thou, whole Palestina,
because the rod of him that smote thee is broken.

For out of the serpent's root shall come forth a cockatrice,
and his fruit shall be a fiery flying serpent.

30 And the first born of the poor shall feed,
and the needy shall lie down in safety.
And I will kill thy root with famine,
and he shall slay thy remnant.

31 Howl, O gate; cry, O city!
Thou whole Palestina art dissolved.
For there shall come from the north a smoke.
And none shall be alone in his appointed times.

32 What shall then answer the messengers of the nations?
That the Lord hath founded Zion,
and the poor of his people shall trust in it.

—

25 | 1 Now I Nephi do speak somewhat
concerning the words which I have written,
which have been spoken by the mouth of Isaiah.
For behold, Isaiah spake many things which were hard
for many of my people to understand,
for they know not concerning the manner of prophesying among the Jews.

2 For I Nephi have not taught them many things
concerning the manner of the Jews,
for their works were works of darkness
and their doings were doings of abomination.

3 Wherefore I write unto my people,
unto all they that shall receive hereafter these things which I write,
that they may know the judgments of God,
that they come upon all nations according to the word which he hath spoken.

4 Wherefore hearken, O my people which are of the house of Israel,
and give ear unto my words,
for because that the words of Isaiah are not plain unto you
—nevertheless they are plain unto all they
that are filled with the spirit of prophecy,
but I give unto you a prophecy according to the Spirit which is in me—
wherefore I shall prophesy according to the plainness
which hath been with me from the time
that I came out from Jerusalem with my father.
For behold, my soul delighteth in plainness unto my people, that they may learn.

5 Yea, and my soul delighteth in the words of Isaiah,
for I came out from Jerusalem
and mine eyes hath beheld the things of the Jews.

And I know that the Jews do understand the things of the prophets.
And there is none other people
that understand the things which were spoken unto the Jews
like unto them,
save it be that they are taught after the manner of the things of the Jews.
6 But behold, I Nephi have not taught my children after the manner of the Jews;
but behold, I of myself have dwelt at Jerusalem,
wherefore I know concerning the regions round about.
And I have made mention concerning the judgments of God
which hath come to pass among the Jews
unto my children
according to all that which Isaiah hath spoken,
and I do not write them.

7 But behold, I proceed with mine own prophecy according to my plainness,
in the which I know that no man can err.
Nevertheless in the days that the prophecies of Isaiah shall be fulfilled,
men shall know of a surety at the times when they shall come to pass.
8 Wherefore they are of worth unto the children of men.
And he that supposeth that they are not,
unto them will I speak particularly
and confine the words unto mine own people,
for I know that they shall be of great worth unto them in the last days,
for in that day shall they understand them.
Wherefore for their good have I written them.
9 And as one generation hath been destroyed among the Jews because of iniquity,
even so have they been destroyed
from generation to generation according to their iniquities.
And never hath any of them been destroyed
save it were foretold them by the prophets of the Lord.
10 Wherefore it hath been told them concerning the destruction
which should come upon them immediately after my father left Jerusalem.
Nevertheless they hardened their hearts;
and according to my prophecy they have been destroyed,
save it be those which are carried away captive into Babylon.

11 And now this I speak because of the Spirit which is in me.
And notwithstanding that they have been carried away,
they shall return again and possess the land of Jerusalem.
Wherefore they shall be restored again to the lands of their inheritance.
12 But behold, they shall have wars and rumors of wars.
And when the day cometh that the Only Begotten of the Father
—yea, even the Father of heaven and of earth—

shall manifest himself unto them in the flesh,
behold, they will reject him because of their iniquities
and the hardness of their hearts and the stiffness of their necks.
13 Behold, they will crucify him.
And after that he is laid in a sepulchre for the space of three days,
he shall rise from the dead with healing in his wings,
and all they that shall believe on his name
shall be saved in the kingdom of God.
Wherefore my soul delighteth to prophesy concerning him,
for I have seen his day, and my heart doth magnify his holy name.

14 And behold, it shall come to pass that
after the Messiah hath risen from the dead
and hath manifested himself unto his people,
unto as many as will believe on his name,
behold, Jerusalem shall be destroyed again;
for woe unto them that fight against God and the people of his church.
15 Wherefore the Jews shall be scattered among all nations;
yea, and also Babylon shall be destroyed.
Wherefore the Jews shall be scattered by other nations.

16 And after that they have been scattered
and the Lord God hath scourged them
by other nations for the space of many generations
—yea, even down from generation to generation
until they shall be persuaded to believe in Christ the Son of God
and the atonement, which is infinite for all mankind—
and when that day shall come that they shall believe in Christ
and worship the Father in his name with pure hearts and clean hands
and look not forward any more for another Messiah
—and then at that time the day will come
that it must needs be expedient that they should believe these things—
17 the Lord will set his hand again the second time
to restore his people from their lost and fallen state.
Wherefore he will proceed to do a marvelous work and a wonder
among the children of men.

18 Wherefore he shall bring forth his words unto them,
which words shall judge them at the last day;
for they shall be given them for the purpose of convincing them
of the true Messiah, who was rejected by them,
and unto the convincing of them
that they need not look forward any more for a Messiah to come;
for there should not any come save it should be a false Messiah

which should deceive the people.
For there is save one Messiah spoken of by the prophets,
and that Messiah is he which should be rejected of the Jews.

19 For according to the words of the prophets,
the Messiah cometh in six hundred years
from the time that my father left Jerusalem.
And according to the words of the prophets
and also the word of the angel of God,
his name should be Jesus Christ the Son of God.

20 And now my brethren, I have spoken plain that ye cannot err.
And as the Lord God liveth that brought Israel up out of the land of Egypt
and gave unto Moses power that he should heal the nations
after that they had been bitten by the poisonous serpents,
if they would cast their eyes unto the serpent
which he did raise up before them,
and also gave him power that he should smite the rock
and the water should come forth,
yea, behold I say unto you that as these things are true
and as the Lord God liveth,
there is none other name given under heaven
save it be this Jesus Christ of which I have spoken
whereby man can be saved.

21 Wherefore for this cause hath the Lord God promised unto me
that these things which I write shall be kept and preserved
and handed down unto my seed from generation to generation,
that the promise may be fulfilled unto Joseph
that his seed should never perish as long as the earth should stand.

22 Wherefore these things shall go from generation to generation
as long as the earth shall stand;
and they shall go according to the will and pleasure of God.
And the nations which shall possess them shall be judged of them
according to the words which are written.

23 For we labor diligently to write,
to persuade our children and also our brethren
to believe in Christ and to be reconciled to God,
for we know that it is by grace that we are saved
after all that we can do.

24 And notwithstanding we believe in Christ,
we keep the law of Moses
and look forward with steadfastness unto Christ
until the law shall be fulfilled,

25 for for this end was the law given.
Wherefore the law hath become dead unto us,
and we are made alive in Christ because of our faith,
yet we keep the law because of the commandments.

26 And we talk of Christ,
we rejoice in Christ,
we preach of Christ,
we prophesy of Christ;
and we write according to our prophecies
that our children may know to what source they may look
for a remission of their sins.

27 Wherefore we speak concerning the law,
that our children may know the deadness of the law.
And they, by knowing the deadness of the law,
may look forward unto that life which is in Christ
and know for what end the law was given—
and after that the law is fulfilled in Christ,
that they need not harden their hearts against him
when the law had ought to be done away.

28 And now behold, my people, ye are a stiffnecked people.
Wherefore I have spoken plain unto you,
that ye cannot misunderstand.
And the words which I have spoken shall stand as a testimony against you,
for they are sufficient to teach any man the right way.
For the right way is to believe in Christ and deny him not,
for by denying him ye also deny the prophets and the law.

29 And now behold, I say unto you
that the right way is to believe in Christ and deny him not.
And Christ is the Holy One of Israel;
wherefore ye must bow down before him
and worship him with all your might, mind, and strength, and your whole soul.
And if ye do this, ye shall in no wise be cast out.

30 And inasmuch as it shall be expedient,
ye must keep the performances and ordinances of God
until the law shall be fulfilled which was given unto Moses.

26 | 1 And after that Christ shall have risen from the dead,
he shall shew himself unto you, my children and my beloved brethren,
and the words which he shall speak unto you shall be the law which ye shall do.

2 For behold, I say unto you that I have beheld
that many generations shall pass away
and there shall be great wars and contentions among my people.

3 And after that the Messiah shall come,
   there shall be signs given unto my people of his birth
   and also of his death and resurrection.
   And great and terrible shall that day be unto the wicked,
   for they shall perish;
   and they perish because they cast out the prophets and the saints
   and stone them and slay them.
   Wherefore the cry of the blood of the saints
   shall ascend up to God from the ground against them.

4 Wherefore all they that are proud and that do wickedly,
   the day that cometh shall burn them up, saith the Lord of Hosts,
   for they shall be as stubble.
5 And they that kill the prophets and the saints,
   the depths of the earth shall swallow them up, saith the Lord of Hosts,
   and mountains shall cover them,
   and whirlwinds shall carry them away,
   and buildings shall fall upon them
   and crush them to pieces and grind them to powder.
6 And they shall be visited with thunderings and lightnings
   and earthquakes and all manner of destructions,
   for the fire of the anger of the Lord shall be kindled against them,
   and they shall be as stubble.
   And the day that cometh shall consume them, saith the Lord of Hosts.

7 O the pain and the anguish of my soul for the loss of the slain of my people!
   For I Nephi hath seen it,
   and it well nigh consumeth me before the presence of the Lord.
   But I must cry unto my God:
   Thy ways are just!
8 But behold, the righteous that hearken unto the words of the prophets
   and destroy them not but look forward unto Christ
   with steadfastness for the signs which are given,
   notwithstanding all persecutions,
   behold, they are they which shall not perish.
9 But the Sun of righteousness shall appear unto them and he shall heal them.
   And they shall have peace with him
   until three generations shall have passed away,
   and many of the fourth generation shall have passed away in righteousness.

10 And when these things shall have passed away,
    a speedy destruction cometh unto my people.
    For notwithstanding the pains of my soul, I have seen it;
    wherefore I know that it shall come to pass.

And they sell themselves for naught,
for for the reward of their pride and their foolishness they shall reap destruction;
for because they yieldeth unto the devil
and choose works of darkness rather than light,
therefore they must go down to hell.

11 For the Spirit of the Lord will not always strive with man.
And when the Spirit ceaseth to strive with man, then cometh speedy destruction,
and this grieveth my soul.

12 And as I spake concerning the convincing of the Jews
that Jesus is the very Christ,
it must needs be that the Gentiles be convinced also
that Jesus is the Christ, the Eternal God,

13 and that he manifesteth himself unto all they that believe in him
by the power of the Holy Ghost,
yea, unto every nation, kindred, tongue, and people,
working mighty miracles, signs, and wonders
among the children of men according to their faith.

14 But behold, I prophesy unto you concerning the last days,
concerning the days when the Lord God shall bring these things forth
unto the children of men.

15 After that my seed and the seed of my brethren shall have dwindled in unbelief
and shall have been smitten by the Gentiles
—yea, after that the Lord God shall have camped against them round about
and shall have laid siege against them with a mount
and raised forts against them,
and after that they shall have been brought down low in the dust,
even that they are not—
yet the words of the righteous shall be written
and the prayers of the faithful shall be heard,
and all they which have dwindled in unbelief shall not be forgotten.

16 For they which shall be destroyed shall speak unto them out of the ground,
and their speech shall be low out of the dust,
and their voice shall be as one that hath a familiar spirit.
For the Lord God will give unto him power
that he may whisper concerning them,
even as it were out of the ground;
and their speech shall whisper out of the dust.

17 For thus saith the Lord God:
They shall write the things which shall be done among them,
and they shall be written and sealed up in a book.
And they that have dwindled in unbelief shall not have them,

for they seek to destroy the things of God.

18 Wherefore as they which have been destroyed have been destroyed speedily
and the multitude of their terrible ones shall be as chaff that passeth away,
yea, thus saith the Lord God:
It shall be at an instant, suddenly.

19 And it shall come to pass that they which have dwindled in unbelief
shall be smitten by the hand of the Gentiles.

20 And the Gentiles are lifted up in the pride of their eyes
and have stumbled because of the greatness of their stumbling block,
that they have built up many churches.
Nevertheless they put down the power and the miracles of God
and preach up unto themselves their own wisdom and their own learning,
that they may get gain and grind upon the face of the poor.

21 And there are many churches built up
which causeth envyings and strifes and malice.

22 And there are also secret combinations, even as in times of old,
according to the combinations of the devil,
for he is the founder of all these things
—yea, the founder of murder and works of darkness—
yea, and he leadeth them by the neck with a flaxen cord
until he bindeth them with his strong cords forever.

23 For behold, my beloved brethren, I say unto you
that the Lord God worketh not in darkness.

24 He doeth not any thing save it be for the benefit of the world,
for he loveth the world, even that he layeth down his own life
that he may draw all men unto him;
wherefore he commandeth none that they shall not partake of his salvation.

25 Behold, doth he cry unto any, saying:
Depart from me!
Behold, I say unto you: Nay.
But he saith:
Come unto me, all ye ends of the earth;
buy milk and honey without money and without price.

26 Behold, hath he commanded any that they should depart
out of the synagogues or out of the houses of worship?
Behold, I say unto you: Nay.

27 Hath he commanded any that they should not partake of his salvation?
Behold, I say unto you: Nay.
But he hath given it free for all men.
And he hath commanded his people
that they should persuade all men unto repentance.

28 Behold, hath the Lord commanded any
   that they should not partake of his goodness?
   Behold, I say unto you: Nay.
   But all men are privileged the one like unto the other,
   and none are forbidden.

29 He commandeth that there shall be no priestcrafts.
   For behold, priestcrafts are that men preach and set themselves up
   for a light unto the world,
   that they may get gain and praise of the world,
   but they seek not the welfare of Zion.

30 Behold, the Lord hath forbidden this thing.

   Wherefore the Lord God hath given a commandment
   that all men should have charity, which charity is love.
   And except they should have charity, they were nothing.
   Wherefore if they should have charity,
   they would not suffer the laborer in Zion to perish.

31 But the laborer in Zion shall labor for Zion;
   for if they labor for money, they shall perish.

32 And again the Lord God hath commanded
   that men should not murder,
   that they should not lie,
   that they should not steal,
   that they should not take the name of the Lord their God in vain,
   that they should not envy,
   that they should not have malice,
   that they should not contend one with another,
   that they should not commit whoredoms,
   and that they should not do none of these things.
   For whoso doeth them shall perish,

33 for none of these iniquities come of the Lord.

   For he doeth that which is good among the children of men.
   And he doeth nothing save it be plain unto the children of men.
   And he inviteth them all to come unto him and partake of his goodness.
   And he denieth none that come unto him,
   black and white, bond and free, male and female;
   and he remembereth the heathen.
   And all are alike unto God, both Jew and Gentile.

27 | 1 But behold, in the last days or in the days of the Gentiles
   —yea, behold all the nations of the Gentiles and also the Jews,

both they which shall come upon this land
and they which shall be upon other lands,
yea, even upon all the lands of the earth —
behold, they will be drunken with iniquity and all manner of abominations.

2 And when that day shall come,
they shall be visited of the Lord of Hosts
with thunder and with earthquake and with a great noise
and with storm and tempest and with the flame of devouring fire.

3 And all the nations that fight against Zion and that distress her
shall be as a dream of a night vision.
Yea, it shall be unto them
even as unto a hungry man which dreameth:
and behold, he eateth,
but he awaketh and his soul is empty;
or like unto a thirsty man which dreameth:
and behold, he drinketh,
but he awaketh and behold, he is faint and his soul hath appetite.
Yea, even so shall the multitude of all the nations be
that fight against mount Zion.

4 For behold, all ye that do iniquity, stay yourselves and wonder,
for ye shall cry out and cry.
Yea, ye shall be drunken but not with wine;
ye shall stagger but not with strong drink.

5 For behold, the Lord hath poured out upon you the spirit of deep sleep.
For behold, ye have closed your eyes;
and ye have rejected the prophets,
and your rulers and the seers hath he covered because of your iniquity.

6 And it shall come to pass that
the Lord God shall bring forth unto you the words of a book.
And they shall be the words of them which have slumbered.

7 And behold, the book shall be sealed.
And in the book shall be a revelation from God
from the beginning of the world to the ending thereof.

8 Wherefore because of the things which are sealed up,
the things which are sealed shall not be delivered
in the day of the wickedness and abominations of the people.
Wherefore the book shall be kept from them.

9 But the book shall be delivered unto a man,
and he shall deliver the words of the book,
which are the words of they which have slumbered in the dust,
and he shall deliver these words unto another.

10 But the words which are sealed he shall not deliver,
       neither shall he deliver the book,
       for the book shall be sealed by the power of God;
       and the revelation which was sealed shall be kept in the book
       until the own due time of the Lord,
       that they may come forth.
       For behold, they reveal all things,
       from the foundation of the world unto the end thereof.
11 And the day cometh that the words of the book which were sealed
       shall be read upon the housetops;
       and they shall be read by the power of Christ.
       And all things shall be revealed unto the children of men
       which ever hath been among the children of men
       and which ever will be, even unto the end of the earth.

12 Wherefore at that day when the book shall be delivered
       unto the man of whom I have spoken,
       the book shall be hid from the eyes of the world,
       that the eyes of none shall behold it
       save it be that three witnesses shall behold it by the power of God,
       besides him to whom the book shall be delivered.
       And they shall testify to the truth of the book and the things therein.
13 And there is none other which shall view it,
       save it be a few according to the will of God,
       to bear testimony of his word unto the children of men.
       For the Lord God hath said
       that the words of the faithful should speak as if it were from the dead.
14 Wherefore the Lord God will proceed to bring forth the words of the book.
       And in the mouth of as many witnesses as seemeth him good
       will he establish his word.
       And woe be unto him that rejecteth the word of God.

15 But behold, it shall come to pass that
       the Lord God shall say unto him to whom he shall deliver the book:
       Take these words which are not sealed and deliver them to another,
       that he may shew them unto the learned, saying:
       Read this, I pray thee.
       And the learned shall say:
       Bring hither the book and I will read them.
16 And now because of the glory of the world and to get gain will they say this,
       and not for the glory of God.
17 And the man shall say:

I cannot bring the book, for it is sealed.

18 Then shall the learned say:
I cannot read it.

19 Wherefore it shall come to pass that
the Lord God will deliver again the book and the words thereof
to him that is not learned.
And the man that is not learned shall say:
I am not learned.

20 Then shall the Lord God say unto him:
The learned shall not read them,
for they have rejected them.
And I am able to do mine own work;
wherefore thou shalt read the words which I shall give unto thee.

21 Touch not the things which are sealed,
for I will bring them forth in mine own due time.
For I will shew unto the children of men that I am able to do mine own work.

22 Wherefore when thou hast read the words which I have commanded thee
and obtained the witnesses which I have promised unto thee,
then shalt thou seal up the book again and hide it up unto me,
that I may preserve the words which thou hast not read
until I shall see fit in mine own wisdom
to reveal all things unto the children of men.

23 For behold, I am God, and I am a God of miracles.
And I will shew unto the world
that I am the same yesterday, today, and forever,
and I work not among the children of men save it be according to their faith.

24 And again it shall come to pass that the Lord shall say unto him
that shall read the words that shall be delivered him:

25 Forasmuch as this people draw near unto me with their mouth
and with their lips do honor me
but have removed their heart far from me
and their fear towards me is taught by the precept of men,

26 therefore I will proceed to do a marvelous work among this people
—yea, a marvelous work and a wonder—
for the wisdom of their wise and learned shall perish,
and the understanding of their prudent shall be hid.

27 And woe unto them that seek deep to hide their counsel from the Lord,
and their works are in the dark.
And they say:
Who seeth us and who knoweth us?

And they also say:
Surely your turning of things upside down
shall be esteemed as the potter's clay!
But behold, I will shew unto them, saith the Lord of Hosts,
that I know all their works.
For shall the work say of him that made it:
He made me not!
Or shall the thing framed say of him that framed it:
He had no understanding!

28 But behold, saith the Lord of Hosts,
I will shew unto the children of men
that it is not yet a very little while
and Lebanon shall be turned into a fruitful field
and the fruitful field shall be esteemed as a forest.

29 And in that day shall the deaf hear the words of the book,
and the eyes of the blind shall see out of obscurity and out of darkness.

30 And the meek also shall increase and their joy shall be in the Lord,
and the poor among men shall rejoice in the Holy One of Israel.

31 For assuredly as the Lord liveth,
they shall see that the terrible one is brought to naught
and the scorner is consumed.
And all that watch for iniquity are cut off,

32 and they that make a man an offender for a word
and lay a snare for him that reproveth in the gate
and turn aside the just for a thing of naught.

33 Therefore thus saith the Lord, who redeemed Abraham,
concerning the house of Jacob:
Jacob shall not now be ashamed,
neither shall his face now wax pale.

34 But when he seeth his children,
the work of my hands, in the midst of him,
they shall sanctify my name and sanctify the Holy One of Jacob
and shall fear the God of Israel.

35 They also that erred in spirit shall come to understanding,
and they that murmured shall learn doctrine.

28 | 1 And now behold, my brethren, I have spoken unto you
according as the Spirit hath constrained me;
wherefore I know that they must surely come to pass.

2 And the things which shall be written out of the book
shall be of great worth unto the children of men
and especially unto our seed, which are a remnant of the house of Israel.

3 For it shall come to pass in that day
that the churches which are built up and not unto the Lord,
when the one shall say unto the other:
Behold I, I am the Lord's!
And the other shall say:
I, I am the Lord's!
—and thus shall every one say
that hath built up churches and not unto the Lord.

4 And they shall contend one with another,
and their priests shall contend one with another.
And they shall teach with their learning
and deny the Holy Ghost, which giveth utterance.

5 And they deny the power of God, the Holy One of Israel.

And they say unto the people:
Hearken unto us and hear ye our precept.
For behold, there is no God today;
for the Lord and the Redeemer hath done his work,
and he hath given his power unto men.

6 Behold, hearken ye unto my precept.
If they shall say there is a miracle wrought by the hand of the Lord,
believe it not!
For this day he is not a God of miracles;
he hath done his work.

7 Yea, and there shall be many which shall say:
Eat, drink, and be merry,
for tomorrow we die and it shall be well with us.

8 And there shall also be many which shall say:
Eat, drink, and be merry,
nevertheless fear God.
He will justify in committing a little sin.
Yea, lie a little,
take the advantage of one because of his words,
dig a pit for thy neighbor;
there is no harm in this.
And do all these things, for tomorrow we die.
And if it so be that we are guilty,

God will beat us with a few stripes,
and at last we shall be saved in the kingdom of God.

9 Yea, and there shall be many
which shall teach after this manner false and vain and foolish doctrines
and shall be puffed up in their hearts
and shall seek deep to hide their counsels from the Lord,
and their works shall be in the dark.

10 And the blood of the saints shall cry from the ground against them.

11 Yea, they have all gone out of the way.
They have become corrupted because of pride.

12 And because of false teachers and false doctrines,
their churches have become corrupted and their churches are lifted up;
because of pride they are puffed up.

13 They rob the poor because of their fine sanctuaries;
they rob the poor because of their fine clothing.
And they persecute the meek and the poor in heart
because in their pride they are puffed up.

14 They wear stiff necks and high heads;
yea, and because of pride and wickedness and abominations and whoredoms,
they have all gone astray
save it be a few which are the humble followers of Christ.
Nevertheless they are led that in many instances they do err
because they are taught by the precepts of men.

15 O the wise and the learned and the rich
that are puffed up in the pride of their hearts,
and all they that preach false doctrines,
and all they that commit whoredoms and pervert the right way of the Lord,
woe woe woe be unto them, saith the Lord God Almighty,
for they shall be thrust down to hell.

16 Woe unto them that turn aside the just for a thing of naught
and revile against that which is good
and say that it is of no worth,
for the day shall come
that the Lord God will speedily visit the inhabitants of the earth.
And in that day that they are fully ripe in iniquity they shall perish.

17 But behold, if the inhabitants of the earth shall repent
of their wickedness and abominations,
they shall not be destroyed, saith the Lord of Hosts.

18 But behold, that great and abominable church,
the whore of all the earth,

must tumble to the earth;
and great must be the fall thereof.

19 For the kingdom of the devil must shake.
And they which belong to it must needs be stirred up unto repentance,
or the devil will grasp them with his everlasting chains
and they be stirred up to anger and perish.

20 For behold, at that day shall he rage in the hearts of the children of men
and stir them up to anger against that which is good.

21 And others will he pacify and lull them away into carnal security,
that they will say:
All is well in Zion;
yea, Zion prospereth.
All is well!
And thus the devil cheateth their souls
and leadeth them away carefully down to hell.

22 And behold, others he flattereth away and telleth them:
There is no hell.
And he saith unto them:
I am no devil,
for there is none.
And thus he whispereth in their ears
until he grasps them with his awful chains,
from whence there is no deliverance.

23 Yea, they are grasped with death and hell and the devil;
and all that have been seized therewith must stand before the throne of God
and be judged according to their works,
from whence they must go into the place prepared for them,
even a lake of fire and brimstone, which is endless torment.

24 Therefore woe be unto him that is at ease in Zion!

25 Woe be unto him that crieth:
All is well!

26 Yea, woe be unto him that hearkeneth unto the precepts of men
and denieth the power of God and the gift of the Holy Ghost.

27 Yea, woe be unto him that saith:
We have received and we need no more.

28 And in fine, woe unto all they
that tremble and are angry because of the truth of God.
For behold, he that is built upon the rock receiveth it with gladness.
And he that is built upon a sandy foundation trembleth lest he shall fall.

29 Woe be unto him that shall say:

We have received the word of God,
and we need no more of the word of God,
for we have enough.

30 For behold, thus saith the Lord God:
I will give unto the children of men line upon line and precept upon precept,
here a little and there a little.
And blessed are they that hearken unto my precepts
and lend an ear unto my counsel,
for they shall learn wisdom.
For unto him that receiveth I will give more;
and them that shall say we have enough,
from them shall be taken away even that which they have.

31 Cursed is he that putteth his trust in man or maketh flesh his arm,
or shall hearken unto the precepts of men,
save their precepts shall be given by the power of the Holy Ghost.
32 Woe be unto the Gentiles, saith the Lord God of Hosts;
for notwithstanding I shall lengthen out mine arm unto them from day to day,
they will deny me.
Nevertheless I will be merciful unto them, saith the Lord God,
if they will repent and come unto me.
For mine arm is lengthened out all the day long, saith the Lord God of Hosts.

29 | 1 But behold, there shall be many at that day
when I shall proceed to do a marvelous work among them,
that I may remember my covenants
which I have made unto the children of men,
that I may set my hand again the second time
to recover my people which are of the house of Israel
2 —and also that I may remember the promises
which I have made unto thee Nephi and also unto thy father,
that I would remember your seed,
and that the words of your seed should proceed forth
out of my mouth unto your seed,
and my words shall hiss forth unto the ends of the earth
for a standard unto my people which are of the house of Israel—
3 and because my words shall hiss forth,
many of the Gentiles shall say:
A Bible, a Bible, we have got a Bible!
And there cannot be any more Bible!

4 But thus saith the Lord God:
O fools, they shall have a Bible,

and it shall proceed forth from the Jews, mine ancient covenant people.
And what thank they the Jews for the Bible which they receive from them?
Yea, what do the Gentiles mean?
Do they remember the travails and the labors and the pains of the Jews
and their diligence unto me in bringing forth salvation unto the Gentiles?

5 O ye Gentiles, have ye remembered the Jews, mine ancient covenant people?
Nay, but ye have cursed them and have hated them
and have not sought to recover them.
But behold, I will return all these things upon your own heads,
for I the Lord hath not forgotten my people.

6 Thou fool that shall say:
A Bible, we have got a Bible, and we need no more Bible!
Have ye obtained a Bible save it were by the Jews?

7 Know ye not that there are more nations than one?
Know ye not that I the Lord your God have created all men
and that I remember they which are upon the isles of the sea
and that I rule in the heavens above and in the earth beneath
and I bring forth my word unto the children of men,
yea, even unto all the nations of the earth?

8 Wherefore murmur ye because that ye shall receive more of my word?
Know ye not that the testimony of two nations
is a witness unto you that I am God,
that I remember one nation like unto another?

Wherefore I speak the same words unto one nation like unto another;
and when the two nations shall run together,
the testimony of the two nations shall run together also.

9 And I do this that I may prove unto many
that I am the same yesterday, today, and forever
and that I speak forth my words according to mine own pleasure.
And because that I have spoken one word,
ye need not suppose that I cannot speak another.
For my work is not yet finished,
neither shall it be until the end of man,
neither from that time henceforth and forever.

10 Wherefore because that ye have a Bible,
ye need not suppose that it contains all my words;
neither need ye suppose that I have not caused more to be written.

11 For I command all men,
both in the east and in the west and in the north and in the south
and in the islands of the sea,
that they shall write the words which I speak unto them,

for out of the books which shall be written I will judge the world,
every man according to their works,
according to that which is written.

12 For behold, I shall speak unto the Jews, and they shall write it;
and I shall also speak unto the Nephites, and they shall write it;
and I shall also speak unto the other tribes of the house of Israel
which I have led away,
and they shall write it;
and I shall also speak unto all the nations of the earth,
and they shall write it.

13 And it shall come to pass that the Jews shall have the words of the Nephites;
and the Nephites shall have the words of the Jews;
and the Nephites and the Jews shall have the words of the lost tribes of Israel;
and the lost tribes of Israel shall have the words of the Nephites and the Jews.

14 And it shall come to pass that
my people which are of the house of Israel shall be gathered home
unto the lands of their possessions.
And my word also shall be gathered in one,
and I will show unto them that fight against my word
and against my people which are of the house of Israel
that I am God and that I covenanted with Abraham
that I would remember his seed forever.

30 | 1 And now behold, my beloved brethren, I would speak unto you,
for I Nephi would not suffer that ye should suppose
that ye are more righteous than the Gentiles shall be.
For behold, except ye shall keep the commandments of God,
ye shall all likewise perish.
And because of the words which have been spoken,
ye need not suppose that the Gentiles are utterly destroyed.

2 For behold, I say unto you:
As many of the Gentiles as will repent are the covenant people of the Lord;
and as many of the Jews as will not repent shall be cast off.
For the Lord covenanteth with none
save it be with them that repent
and believe in his Son, which is the Holy One of Israel.

3 And now I would prophesy somewhat more
concerning the Jews and the Gentiles.
For after the book of which I have spoken shall come forth
and be written unto the Gentiles
and sealed up again unto the Lord,
there shall be many which shall believe the words which are written,

and they shall carry them forth unto the remnant of our seed.

4 And then shall the remnant of our seed know concerning us,
   how that we came out from Jerusalem
   and that they are a descendant of the Jews.

5 And the gospel of Jesus Christ shall be declared among them;
   wherefore they shall be restored unto the knowledge of their fathers
   and also to the knowledge of Jesus Christ, which was had among their fathers.

6 And then shall they rejoice,
   for they shall know that it is a blessing unto them from the hand of God.
   And their scales of darkness shall begin to fall from their eyes.
   And many generations shall not pass away among them
   save they shall be a white and a delightsome people.

7 And it shall come to pass that the Jews which are scattered
   also shall begin to believe in Christ,
   and they shall begin to gather in upon the face of the land.
   And as many as shall believe in Christ shall also become a delightsome people.

8 And it shall come to pass that
   the Lord God shall commence his work
   among all nations, kindreds, tongues, and people
   to bring about the restoration of his people upon the earth.

9 And with righteousness shall the Lord God judge the poor
   and reprove with equity for the meek of the earth.
   And he shall smite the earth with the rod of his mouth,
   and with the breath of his lips shall he slay the wicked.

10 For the time speedily cometh
   that the Lord God shall cause a great division among the people;
   and the wicked will he destroy and he will spare his people,
   yea, even if it so be that he must destroy the wicked by fire.

11 And righteousness shall be the girdle of his loins,
   and faithfulness the girdle of his reins.

12 And then shall the wolf dwell with the lamb,
   and the leopard shall lie down with the kid,
   and the calf and the young lion and the fatling together;
   and a little child shall lead them.

13 And the cow and the bear shall feed;
   their young ones shall lie down together.
   And the lion shall eat straw like the ox.

14 And the sucking child shall play on the hole of the asp,
   and the weaned child shall put his hand on the cockatrice's den.

15 They shall not hurt nor destroy in all my holy mountain,

for the earth shall be full of the knowledge of the Lord
as the waters cover the sea.

16 Wherefore the things of all nations shall be made known;
yea, all things shall be made known unto the children of men.
17 There is nothing which is secret save it shall be revealed;
there is no work of darkness save it shall be made manifest in the light.
And there is nothing which is sealed upon earth save it shall be loosed.
18 Wherefore all things which have been revealed unto the children of men
shall at that day be revealed.
And Satan shall have power over the hearts of the children of men no more
for a long time.

And now my beloved brethren, I must make an end of my sayings.

31 | 1 And now I Nephi make an end of my prophesying
unto you, my beloved brethren.
And I cannot write but a few things which I know must surely come to pass,
neither can I write but a few of the words of my brother Jacob.
2 Wherefore the things which I have written sufficeth me,
save it be a few words which I must speak concerning the doctrine of Christ.
Wherefore I shall speak unto you plainly
according to the plainness of my prophesying.
3 For my soul delighteth in plainness,
for after this manner doth the Lord God work among the children of men.
For the Lord God giveth light unto the understanding,
for he speaketh unto men according to their language unto their understanding.

4 Wherefore I would that ye should remember that I have spoken unto you
concerning that prophet which the Lord shewed unto me
that should baptize the Lamb of God,
which should take away the sin of the world.
5 And now if the Lamb of God, he being holy, should have need
to be baptized by water to fulfill all righteousness,
O then how much more need have we, being unholy,
to be baptized, yea, even by water!
6 And now I would ask of you, my beloved brethren,
wherein the Lamb of God did fulfill all righteousness in being baptized by water?
7 Know ye not that he was holy?
But notwithstanding he being holy,
he showeth unto the children of men
that according to the flesh he humbleth himself before the Father
and witnesseth unto the Father

that he would be obedient unto him in keeping his commandments.

8 Wherefore after that he was baptized with water,
the Holy Ghost descended upon him in the form of a dove.

9 And again it sheweth unto the children of men
the straitness of the path and the narrowness of the gate
by which they should enter,
he having set the example before them.

10 And he saith unto the children of men:
Follow thou me.
Wherefore, my beloved brethren, can we follow Jesus
save we shall be willing to keep the commandments of the Father?

11 And the Father saith:
Repent ye, repent ye, and be baptized in the name of my Beloved Son.

12 And also the voice of the Son came unto me, saying:
He that is baptized in my name,
to him will the Father give the Holy Ghost like unto me.
Wherefore follow me and do the things which ye have seen me do.

13 Wherefore, my beloved brethren,
I know that if ye shall follow the Son with full purpose of heart,
acting no hypocrisy and no deception before God but with real intent,
repenting of your sins,
witnessing unto the Father that ye are willing
to take upon you the name of Christ by baptism,
yea, by following your Lord and Savior down into the water
according to his word,
behold, then shall ye receive the Holy Ghost.
Yea, then cometh the baptism of fire and of the Holy Ghost,
and then can ye speak with the tongue of angels
and shout praises unto the Holy One of Israel.

14 But behold, my beloved brethren,
thus came the voice of the Son unto me, saying:
After that ye have repented of your sins and witnessed unto the Father
that ye are willing to keep my commandments by the baptism of water
and have received the baptism of fire and of the Holy Ghost
and can speak with a new tongue
—yea, even with the tongue of angels—
and after this should deny me,
it would have been better for you that ye had not known me.

15 And I heard a voice from the Father, saying:
Yea, the words of my Beloved are true and faithful;
he that endureth to the end, the same shall be saved.

16 And now my beloved brethren,
    I know by this that unless a man shall endure to the end
    in following the example of the Son of the living God,
    he cannot be saved.

17 Wherefore do the things which I have told you that I have seen,
    that your Lord and your Redeemer should do.
    For for this cause have they been shewn unto me,
    that ye might know the gate by which ye should enter.
    For the gate by which ye should enter is repentance and baptism by water,
    and then cometh a remission of your sins by fire and by the Holy Ghost.
18 And then are ye in this straight and narrow path which leads to eternal life,
    yea, ye have entered in by the gate.
    Ye have done according to the commandments of the Father and the Son,
    and ye have received the Holy Ghost, which witness of the Father and the Son
    unto the fulfilling of the promise which he hath made,
    that if ye entered in by the way,
    ye should receive.

19 And now my beloved brethren,
    after that ye have got into this straight and narrow path,
    I would ask if all is done.
    Behold, I say unto you: Nay.
    For ye have not come thus far
    save it were by the word of Christ with unshaken faith in him,
    relying wholly upon the merits of him who is mighty to save.
20 Wherefore ye must press forward with a steadfastness in Christ,
    having a perfect brightness of hope and a love of God and of all men;
    wherefore if ye shall press forward,
    feasting upon the word of Christ
    and endure to the end,
    behold, thus saith the Father,
    ye shall have eternal life.

21 And now behold, my beloved brethren, this is the way.
    And there is none other way nor name given under heaven
    whereby man can be saved in the kingdom of God.
    And now behold, this is the doctrine of Christ,
    and the only and true doctrine
    of the Father and of the Son and of the Holy Ghost,
    which is one God without end.
    Amen.

32 | 1 And now behold, my beloved brethren,
I suppose that ye ponder somewhat in your hearts
concerning that which ye should do
after that ye have entered in by the way.
But behold, why do ye ponder these things in your hearts?

2 Do ye not remember that I said unto you
that after ye had received the Holy Ghost,
ye could speak with the tongue of angels?
And now, how could ye speak with the tongue of angels
save it were by the Holy Ghost?

3 Angels speak by the power of the Holy Ghost;
wherefore they speak the words of Christ.
Wherefore I said unto you:
Feast upon the words of Christ;
for behold, the words of Christ will tell you all things what ye should do.

4 Wherefore now after that I have spoken these words,
if ye cannot understand them,
it will be because ye ask not, neither do ye knock.
Wherefore ye are not brought into the light
but must perish in the dark.

5 For behold, again I say unto you
that if ye will enter in by the way and receive the Holy Ghost,
it will shew unto you all things what ye should do.

6 Behold, this is the doctrine of Christ.
And there will be no more doctrine given
until after that he shall manifest himself unto you in the flesh.
And when he shall manifest himself unto you in the flesh,
the things which he shall say unto you shall ye observe to do.

7 And now I Nephi cannot say more.
The Spirit stoppeth mine utterance,
and I am left to mourn because of the unbelief and the wickedness
and the ignorance and the stiffneckedness of men.
For they will not search knowledge
nor understand great knowledge when it is given unto them in plainness,
even as plain as word can be.

8 And now my beloved brethren,
I perceive that ye ponder still in your hearts.
And it grieveth me that I must speak concerning this thing.
For if ye would hearken unto the Spirit which teacheth a man to pray,
ye would know that ye must pray;
for the evil spirit teacheth not a man to pray,

but teacheth him that he must not pray.

9 But behold, I say unto you that ye must pray always and not faint,
that ye must not perform any thing unto the Lord
save in the first place ye shall pray unto the Father in the name of Christ
that he will consecrate thy performance unto thee,
that thy performance may be for the welfare of thy soul.

33 | 1 And now I Nephi cannot write all the things
which were taught among my people,
neither am I mighty in writing like unto speaking.
For when a man speaketh by the power of the Holy Ghost,
the power of the Holy Ghost carrieth it unto the hearts of the children of men.

2 But behold, there are many that harden their hearts against the Holy Spirit,
that it hath no place in them.
Wherefore they cast many things away which are written
and esteem them as things of naught.

3 But I Nephi have written what I have written,
and I esteem it as of great worth and especially unto my people.
For I pray continually for them by day,
and mine eyes water my pillow by night because of them.
And I cry unto my God in faith,
and I know that he will hear my cry.

4 And I know that the Lord God will consecrate my prayers
for the gain of my people.
And the things which I have written in weakness
will he make strong unto them,
for it persuadeth them to do good.
It maketh known unto them of their fathers.
And it speaketh of Jesus and persuadeth men
to believe in him and to endure to the end, which is life eternal.

5 And it speaketh harsh against sin according to the plainness of the truth.
Wherefore no man will be angry at the words which I have written
save he shall be of the spirit of the devil.

6 I glory in plainness;
I glory in truth;
I glory in my Jesus,
for he hath redeemed my soul from hell.

7 I have charity for my people and great faith in Christ
that I shall meet many souls spotless at his judgment seat;

8 I have charity for the Jew—

I say Jew because I mean them from whence I came;

9 I also have charity for the Gentiles.
But behold, for none of these I cannot hope
except they shall be reconciled unto Christ
and enter into the narrow gate
and walk in the strait path which leads to life
and continue in the path until the end of the day of probation.

10 And now my beloved brethren and also Jew and all ye ends of the earth,
hearken unto these words and believe in Christ.
And if ye believe not in these words,
believe in Christ;
and if ye shall believe in Christ,
ye will believe in these words,
for they are the words of Christ.
And he hath given them unto me,
and they teach all men that they should do good.

11 And if they are not the words of Christ, judge ye.
For Christ will shew unto you with power and great glory
that they are his words
at the last day.
And you and I shall stand face to face before his bar,
and ye shall know that I have been commanded of him
to write these things, notwithstanding my weakness.

12 And I pray the Father in the name of Christ
that many of us, if not all, may be saved in his kingdom
at that great and last day.

13 And now my beloved brethren,
all they which are of the house of Israel and all ye ends of the earth,
I speak unto you as the voice of one crying from the dust.
Farewell until that great day shall come.

14 And you that will not partake of the goodness of God
and respect the words of the Jews and also my words
and the words which shall proceed forth out of the mouth of the Lamb of God,
behold, I bid you an everlasting farewell,
for these words shall condemn you at the last day.

15 For what I seal on earth shall be brought against you at the judgment bar.
For thus hath the Lord commanded me,
and I must obey.
Amen.

The Book of Jacob
the brother of Nephi

The words of his preaching unto his brethren.
He confoundeth a man who seeketh to overthrow the doctrine of Christ.
A few words concerning the history of the people of Nephi.

1 | 1 For behold, it came to pass that fifty and five years had passed away
from the time that Lehi left Jerusalem;
wherefore Nephi gave me Jacob a commandment
concerning these small plates upon which these things are engraven.

2 And he gave me Jacob a commandment that I should write upon these plates
a few of the things which I considered to be most precious,
that I should not touch save it were lightly
concerning the history of this people, which are called the people of Nephi.

3 For he said that the history of his people
should be engraven upon his other plates
and that I should preserve these plates and hand them down
unto my seed from generation to generation.

4 And if there were preaching which was sacred,
or revelation which was great, or prophesying,
that I should engraven the heads of them upon these plates
and touch upon them as much as it were possible,
for Christ's sake and for the sake of our people.

5 For because of faith and great anxiety,
it truly had been made manifest unto us concerning our people
what things should happen unto them.

6 And we also had many revelations and the spirit of much prophecy;
wherefore we knew of Christ and his kingdom, which should come.

7 Wherefore we labored diligently among our people
that we might persuade them to come unto Christ
and partake of the goodness of God,
that they might enter into his rest,
lest by any means he should swear in his wrath they should not enter in,
as in the provocation in the days of temptation
while the children of Israel were in the wilderness.

8 Wherefore we would to God that we could persuade all men
not to rebel against God, to provoke him to anger,

but that all men would believe in Christ
and view his death and suffer his cross and bear the shame of the world.
Wherefore I Jacob take it upon me
to fulfill the commandment of my brother Nephi.

9 Now Nephi began to be old and he saw that he must soon die.
Wherefore he anointed a man to be a king and a ruler over his people.

10 Now according to the reigns of the kings
—the people having loved Nephi exceedingly,
he having been a great protector for them,
having wielded the sword of Laban in their defense
and having labored in all his days for their welfare—

11 wherefore the people were desirous to retain in remembrance his name,
and whoso should reign in his stead were called by the people
second Nephi and third Nephi etc.,
according to the reigns of the kings;
and thus they were called by the people,
let them be of whatsoever name they would.

12 And it came to pass that Nephi died.

13 Now the people which were not Lamanites were Nephites;
nevertheless they were called Nephites, Jacobites, Josephites, Zoramites,
Lamanites, Lemuelites, and Ishmaelites.

14 But I Jacob shall not hereafter distinguish them by these names,
but I shall call them Lamanites, they that seek to destroy the people of Nephi,
and they which are friendly to Nephi I shall call Nephites or the people of Nephi,
according to the reigns of the kings.

15 And now it came to pass that
the people of Nephi under the reign of the second king
began to grow hard in their hearts
and indulge themselves somewhat in wicked practices,
such as like unto David of old,
desiring many wives and concubines,
and also Solomon his son.

16 Yea, and they also began to search much gold and silver
and began to be lifted up somewhat in pride.

17 Wherefore I Jacob gave unto them these words as I taught them in the temple,
having firstly obtained mine errand from the Lord,

18 for I Jacob and my brother Joseph had been consecrated
priests and teachers of this people by the hand of Nephi.

19 And we did magnify our office unto the Lord,
taking upon us the responsibility,

answering the sins of the people upon our own heads
if we did not teach them the word of God with all diligence;
wherefore by laboring with our mights,
their blood might not come upon our garments;
otherwise their blood would come upon our garments
and we would not be found spotless at the last day.

2 | 1 The words which Jacob the brother of Nephi spake
unto the people of Nephi after the death of Nephi:

2 Now my beloved brethren, I Jacob,
according to the responsibility which I am under to God
to magnify mine office with soberness
and that I might rid my garments of your sins,
I come up into the temple this day
that I might declare unto you the word of God.

3 And ye yourselves know that I have hitherto been diligent
in the office of my calling,
but I this day am weighed down
with much more desire and anxiety for the welfare of your souls
than I have hitherto been.

4 For behold, as yet ye have been obedient
unto the word of the Lord which I have given unto you.

5 But behold, hearken ye unto me and know
that by the help of the all-powerful Creator of heaven and earth
I can tell you concerning your thoughts,
how that ye are beginning to labor in sin,
which sin appeareth very abominable unto me,
yea, and abominable unto God.

6 Yea, and it grieveth my soul and causeth me to shrink with shame
before the presence of my Maker
that I must testify unto you concerning the wickedness of your hearts.

7 And also it grieveth me that I must use so much boldness of speech
concerning you before your wives and your children,
many of whose feelings are exceeding tender and chaste and delicate before God,
which thing is pleasing unto God.

8 And it supposeth me that they have come up hither
to hear the pleasing word of God,
yea, the word which healeth the wounded soul.

9 Wherefore it burdeneth my soul that I should be constrained
because of the strict commandment which I have received from God

to admonish you according to your crimes,
to enlarge the wounds of those which are already wounded,
instead of consoling and healing their wounds.
And those which have not been wounded,
instead of feasting upon the pleasing word of God,
have daggers placed to pierce their souls and wound their delicate minds.

10 But notwithstanding the greatness of the task,
I must do according to the strict commands of God
and tell you concerning your wickedness and abominations
in the presence of the pure in heart and the broken heart
and under the glance of the piercing eye of the Almighty God.

11 Wherefore I must tell you the truth
according to the plainness of the word of God.
For behold, as I inquired of the Lord,
thus came the word unto me, saying:
Jacob, get thou up into the temple on the morrow
and declare the word which I shall give thee
unto this people.

12 And now behold, my brethren, this is the word which I declare unto you,
that many of you have begun to search for gold and for silver
and for all manner of precious ores
in the which this land,
which is a land of promise unto you and to your seed,
doth abound most plentifully.

13 And the hand of Providence hath smiled upon you most pleasingly,
that ye have obtained many riches.
And because that some of you have obtained more abundantly
than that of your brethren,
ye are lifted up in the pride of your hearts and wear stiff necks and high heads
because of the costliness of your apparel
and persecute your brethren
because that ye suppose that ye are better than they.

14 And now my brethren, do ye suppose
that God justifieth you in this thing?
Behold, I say unto you: Nay.
But he condemneth you;
and if ye persist in these things,
his judgments must speedily come unto you.

15 O that he would show you that he can pierce you
and with one glance of his eye he can smite you to the dust!

16 O that he would rid you from this iniquity and abomination!
And O that ye would listen unto the word of his commands
and let not this pride of your hearts destroy your souls!

17 Think of your brethren like to yourselves,
and be familiar with all and free with your substance,
that they may be rich like unto you.
18 But before that ye seek for riches,
seek ye for the kingdom of God.
19 And after that ye have obtained a hope in Christ,
ye shall obtain riches if ye seek them;
and ye will seek them for the intent to do good,
to clothe the naked and to feed the hungry
and to liberate the captive and administer relief to the sick and the afflicted.

20 And now my brethren, I have spoken unto you concerning pride.
And those of you which have afflicted your neighbor and persecuted him
because that ye were proud in your hearts
of the things which God hath given you,
what say ye of it?
21 Do ye not suppose that such things are abominable
unto him who created all flesh?
And the one being is as precious in his sight as the other.
And all flesh is of the dust;
and for the selfsame end hath he created them,
that they should keep his commandments and glorify him forever.

22 And now I make an end of speaking unto you concerning this pride.
And were it not that I must speak unto you concerning a grosser crime,
my heart would rejoice exceedingly because of you.
23 But the word of God burthens me because of your grosser crimes.
For behold, thus saith the Lord:
This people beginneth to wax in iniquity;
they understand not the scriptures,
for they seek to excuse themselves in committing whoredoms
because of the things which are written concerning David and Solomon his son.
24 Behold, David and Solomon truly had many wives and concubines,
which thing was abominable before me, saith the Lord.

25 Wherefore thus saith the Lord:
I have led this people forth out of the land of Jerusalem
by the power of mine arm,
that I might raise up unto me a righteous branch
from the fruit of the loins of Joseph.

26 Wherefore I the Lord God will not suffer
    that this people shall do like unto them of old.
27 Wherefore, my brethren, hear me and hearken to the word of the Lord,
    for there shall not any man among you have save it be one wife,
    and concubines he shall have none.
28 For I the Lord God delighteth in the chastity of women;
    and whoredoms is abomination before me, thus saith the Lord of Hosts.
29 Wherefore this people shall keep my commandments, saith the Lord of Hosts,
    or cursed be the land for their sakes.
30 For if I will, saith the Lord of Hosts, raise up seed unto me,
    I will command my people;
    otherwise, they shall hearken unto these things.

31 For behold, I the Lord have seen the sorrow and heard the mourning
    of the daughters of my people in the land of Jerusalem,
    yea, and in all the lands of my people,
    because of the wickedness and abominations of their husbands.
32 And I will not suffer, saith the Lord of Hosts,
    that the cries of the fair daughters of this people,
    which I have led out of the land of Jerusalem,
    shall come up unto me against the men of my people, saith the Lord of Hosts,
33 for they shall not lead away captive the daughters of my people
    because of their tenderness,
    save I shall visit them with a sore curse, even unto destruction,
    for they shall not commit whoredoms
    like unto they of old, saith the Lord of Hosts.

34 And now behold, my brethren, ye know
    that these commandments was given to our father Lehi;
    wherefore ye have known them before.
    And ye have come unto great condemnation,
    for ye have done these things which ye ought not to have done.
35 Behold, ye have done greater iniquity than the Lamanites our brethren.
    Ye have broken the hearts of your tender wives
    and lost the confidence of your children
    because of your bad examples before them.
    And the sobbings of their hearts ascendeth up to God against you.
    And because of the strictness of the word of God
    which cometh down against you,
    many hearts died, pierced with deep wounds.

3 | 1 But behold, I Jacob would speak unto you that are pure in heart.

Look unto God with firmness of mind
and pray unto him with exceeding faith,
and he will console you in your afflictions,
and he will plead your cause
and send down justice upon those who seek your destruction.
2 O all ye that are pure in heart,
lift up your heads and receive the pleasing word of God
and feast upon his love,
for ye may — if your minds are firm — forever.

3 But woe woe unto you that are not pure in heart,
that are filthy this day before God,
for except ye shall repent, the land is cursed for your sakes;
and the Lamanites, which are not filthy like unto you
— nevertheless they are cursed with a sore cursing —
shall scourge you even unto destruction.
4 And the time speedily cometh that except ye repent,
they shall possess the land of your inheritance
and the Lord God will lead away the righteous out from among you.

5 Behold, the Lamanites your brethren, whom ye hate
because of their filthiness and the cursing which hath come upon their skins,
are more righteous than you.
For they have not forgotten the commandment of the Lord
which was given unto our father,
that they should have save it were one wife,
and concubines they should have none,
and there should not be whoredoms committed among them.
6 And now this commandment they observe to keep;
wherefore because of this observance in keeping this commandment,
the Lord God will not destroy them but will be merciful unto them,
and one day they shall become a blessed people.

7 Behold, their husbands love their wives
and their wives love their husbands,
and their husbands and their wives love their children.
And their unbelief and their hatred towards you
is because of the iniquity of their fathers;
wherefore how much better are you than they
in the sight of your great Creator?
8 O my brethren, I fear that unless ye shall repent of your sins

that their skins will be whiter than yours
when ye shall be brought with them before the throne of God.

9   Wherefore a commandment I give unto you, which is the word of God,
     that ye revile no more against them because of the darkness of their skin.
     Neither shall ye revile against them because of their filthiness,
     but ye shall remember your own filthiness
     and remember that their filthiness came because of their fathers.
10   Wherefore ye shall remember your children,
     how that ye have grieved their hearts
     because of the example that ye have sat before them;
     and also remember that ye may because of your filthiness
     bring your children unto destruction
     and their sins be heaped upon your heads at the last day.

11   O my brethren, hearken unto my words.
     Arouse the faculties of your souls,
     shake yourselves that ye may awake from the slumber of death,
     and loose yourselves from the pains of hell,
     that ye may not become angels to the devil,
     to be cast into that lake of fire and brimstone, which is the second death.

12   And now I Jacob spake many more things unto the people of Nephi,
     warning them against fornication and lasciviousness and every kind of sin,
     telling them the awful consequences of them.
13   And a hundredth part of the proceedings of this people,
     which now began to be numerous,
     cannot be written upon these plates;
     but many of their proceedings are written upon the larger plates,
     and their wars and their contentions and the reigns of their kings.
14   These plates are called the plates of Jacob,
     and they were made by the hand of Nephi.
     And I make an end of speaking these words.

4 | 1   Now behold, it came to pass that
        I Jacob having ministered much unto my people in word
        —and I cannot write but a little of my words
        because of the difficulty of engraving our words upon plates—
        and we know that the things which we write upon plates must remain,
   2   but whatsoever things we write upon any thing save it be upon plates
        must perish and vanish away;

but we can write a few words upon plates,
which will give our children and also our beloved brethren
a small degree of knowledge concerning us or concerning their fathers.

3 Now in this thing we do rejoice,
and we labor diligently to engraven these words upon plates,
hoping that our beloved brethren and our children
will receive them with thankful hearts
and look upon them that they may learn with joy
and not with sorrow, neither with contempt,
concerning their first parents.

4 For for this intent have we written these things
that they may know that we knew of Christ,
and we had a hope of his glory many hundred years before his coming.
And not only we ourselves had a hope of his glory,
but also all the holy prophets which were before us.

5 Behold, they believed in Christ and worshipped the Father in his name;
and also we worship the Father in his name.
And for this intent we keep the law of Moses,
it pointing our souls to him.
And for this cause it is sanctified unto us for righteousness,
even as it was accounted unto Abraham in the wilderness to be obedient
unto the commands of God in offering up his son Isaac,
which was a similitude of God and his Only Begotten Son.

6 Wherefore we search the prophets,
and we have many revelations and the spirit of prophecy.
And having all these witnesses,
we obtain a hope and our faith becometh unshaken,
insomuch that we truly can command in the name of Jesus
and the very trees obey us or the mountains or the waves of the sea.

7 Nevertheless the Lord God sheweth us our weakness that we may know
that it is by his grace and his great condescensions unto the children of men
that we have power to do these things.

8 Behold, great and marvelous are the works of the Lord!
How unsearchable are the depths of the mysteries of him!
And it is impossible that man should find out all his ways.
And no man knoweth of his ways save it be revealed unto him;
wherefore, brethren, despise not the revelations of God.

9 For behold, by the power of his word
man came upon the face of the earth,

which earth was created by the power of his word.
Wherefore if God being able to speak and the world was
and to speak and man was created,
O then why not able to command the earth,
or the workmanship of his hands upon the face of it,
according to his will and pleasure?

10 Wherefore, brethren, seek not to counsel the Lord,
but to take counsel from his hand.
For behold, ye yourselves know that he counseleth
in wisdom and in justice and in great mercy over all his works.
11 Wherefore, beloved, be reconciled unto him
through the atonement of Christ his Only Begotten Son,
that ye may obtain a resurrection
according to the power of the resurrection which is in Christ
and be presented as the firstfruits of Christ unto God,
having faith and having obtained a good hope of glory in him
before he manifesteth himself in the flesh.

12 And now beloved, marvel not that I tell you these things;
for why not speak of the atonement of Christ
and attain to a perfect knowledge of him
as to attain to the knowledge of a resurrection and the world to come?
13 Behold, my brethren, he that prophesieth,
let him prophesy to the understanding of men,
for the Spirit speaketh the truth and lieth not.
Wherefore it speaketh of things as they really are
and of things as they really will be.
Wherefore these things are manifested unto us plainly
for the salvation of our souls.

But behold, we are not witnesses alone in these things;
for God also spake them unto prophets of old.
14 But behold, the Jews were a stiffnecked people,
and they despised the words of plainness and killed the prophets
and sought for things that they could not understand.
Wherefore because of their blindness,
which blindness came by looking beyond the mark,
they must needs fall;
for God hath taken away his plainness from them
and delivered unto them many things which they cannot understand
because they desired it.

And because they desired it,
God hath done it that they may stumble.

15 And now I Jacob am led on by the Spirit unto prophesying,
for I perceive by the workings of the Spirit which is in me
that by the stumbling of the Jews they will reject the stone
upon which they might build and have safe foundation.
16 But behold, according to the scriptures,
this stone shall become the great and the last and the only sure foundation
upon which the Jews can build.
17 And now my beloved, how is it possible
that these, after having rejected the sure foundation, can ever build upon it
that it may become the head of their corner?
18 Behold, my beloved brethren, I will unfold this mystery unto you
if I do not by any means get shaken from my firmness in the Spirit
and stumble because of my overanxiety for you.

5 | 1 Behold, my brethren, do ye not remember
to have read the words of the prophet Zenos
which he spake unto the house of Israel, saying:
2 Hearken, O ye house of Israel,
and hear the words of me, a prophet of the Lord.
3 For behold, thus saith the Lord,
I will liken thee, O house of Israel, like unto a tame olive tree
which a man took and nourished in his vineyard,
and it grew and waxed old and began to decay.
4 And it came to pass that the master of the vineyard went forth
and he saw that his olive tree began to decay, and he saith:
I will prune it and dig about it and nourish it,
that perhaps it may shoot forth young and tender branches and it perish not.
5 And it came to pass that he pruned it and digged about it and nourished it
according to his word.

6 And it came to pass that after many days
it began to put forth somewhat a little young and tender branches,
but behold the main top thereof began to perish.
7 And it came to pass that the master of the vineyard saw it,
and he saith unto his servant:
It grieveth me that I should lose this tree.
Wherefore go and pluck the branches from a wild olive tree
and bring them hither unto me;
and we will pluck off those main branches,

which are beginning to wither away,
and we will cast them into the fire that they may be burned.

8 And behold, saith the Lord of the vineyard,
I will take away many of these young and tender branches,
and I will graft them whithersoever I will—and it mattereth not—
that if it so be that the root of this tree will perish,
I may preserve the fruit thereof unto myself.
Wherefore I will take these young and tender branches,
and I will graft them whithersoever I will.

9 Take thou the branches of the wild olive tree
and graft them in in the stead thereof.
And these which I have plucked off,
I will cast into the fire and burn them,
that they may not cumber the ground of my vineyard.

10 And it came to pass that the servant of the Lord of the vineyard
done according to the word of the Lord of the vineyard
and grafted in the branches of the wild olive tree.

11 And the Lord of the vineyard caused
that it should be digged about and pruned and nourished,
saying unto his servant:
It grieveth me that I should lose this tree;
wherefore that perhaps I might preserve the roots thereof,
that they perish not, that I might preserve them unto myself,
I have done this thing.

12 Wherefore go thy way;
watch the tree and nourish it according to my words.

13 And these will I place in the nithermost parts of my vineyard,
whithersoever I will, it mattereth not unto thee.
And I do it that I may preserve unto myself the natural branches of the tree,
and also that I may lay up fruit thereof against the season unto myself.
For it grieveth me that I should lose this tree and the fruit thereof.

14 And it came to pass that the Lord of the vineyard went his way
and hid the natural branches of the tame olive tree
in the nithermost parts of the vineyard, some in one and some in another,
according to his will and pleasure.

15 And it came to pass that a long time passed away,
and the Lord of the vineyard saith unto his servant:
Come, let us go down into the vineyard
that we may labor in the vineyard.

16 And it came to pass that the Lord of the vineyard and also the servant
    went down into the vineyard to labor.

    And it came to pass that the servant saith unto his master:
    Behold, look here; behold the tree.
17 And it came to pass that the Lord of the vineyard looked
    and beheld the tree in the which the wild olive branches had been grafted,
    and it had sprang forth and began to bear fruit.
    And he beheld that it was good,
    and the fruit thereof was like unto the natural fruit.
18 And he saith unto the servant:
    Behold, the branches of the wild tree
    hath taken hold of the moisture of the root thereof,
    that the root thereof hath brought forth much strength.
    And because of the much strength of the root thereof,
    the wild branches hath brought forth tame fruit.
    Now if we had not grafted in these branches,
    the tree thereof would have perished.
    And now behold, I shall lay up much fruit,
    which the tree thereof hath brought forth.
    And the fruit thereof I shall lay up against the season unto mine own self.

19 And it came to pass that the Lord of the vineyard saith unto the servant:
    Come, let us go to the nithermost parts of the vineyard,
    and behold if the natural branches of the tree
    hath not brought forth much fruit also,
    that I may lay up of the fruit thereof against the season unto mine own self.
20 And it came to pass that they went forth
    whither the master of the vineyard had hid the natural branches of the tree,
    and he saith unto the servant:
    Behold these!
    And he beheld the first that it had brought forth much fruit,
    and he beheld also that it was good.
    And he saith unto the servant:
    Take of the fruit thereof and lay it up against the season,
    that I may preserve it unto mine own self.
    For behold, saith he, this long time have I nourished it,
    and it hath brought forth much fruit.

21 And it came to pass that the servant saith unto his master:
    How camest thou hither to plant this tree or this branch of the tree?
    For behold, it was the poorest spot in all the land of thy vineyard.

22 And the Lord of the vineyard saith unto him:
Counsel me not.
I knew that it was a poor spot of ground.
Wherefore I said unto thee I have nourished it this long time,
and thou beholdest that it hath brought forth much fruit.

23 And it came to pass that the Lord of the vineyard saith unto his servant:
Look hither! Behold, I have planted another branch of the tree also,
and thou knowest that this spot of ground was poorer than the first.
But behold the tree!
I have nourished it this long time,
and it hath brought forth much fruit.
Therefore gather it and lay it up against the season,
that I may preserve it unto mine own self.

24 And it came to pass that the Lord of the vineyard saith again unto his servant:
Look hither and behold another branch also which I have planted.
Behold that I have nourished it also,
and it hath brought forth fruit.

25 And he saith unto the servant:
Look hither and behold the last!
Behold, this have I planted in a good spot of ground,
and I have nourished it this long time.
And only a part of the tree hath brought forth tame fruit,
and the other part of the tree hath brought forth wild fruit.
Behold, I have nourished this tree like unto the others.

26 And it came to pass that the Lord of the vineyard saith unto the servant:
Pluck off the branches that have not brought forth good fruit,
and cast them into the fire.

27 But behold, the servant saith unto him:
Let us prune it and dig about it and nourish it a little longer,
that perhaps it may bring forth good fruit unto thee,
that thou canst lay it up against the season.

28 And it came to pass that
the Lord of the vineyard and the servant of the Lord of the vineyard
did nourish all the fruit of the vineyard.

29 And it came to pass that a long time had passed away,
and the Lord of the vineyard saith unto his servant:
Come, let us go down into the vineyard,
that we may labor again in the vineyard.

For behold, the time draweth near and the end soon cometh;
wherefore I must lay up fruit against the season unto mine own self.

30 And it came to pass that
the Lord of the vineyard and the servant went down into the vineyard,
and they came to the tree whose natural branches had been broken off
and the wild branches had been grafted in;
and behold, all sorts of fruit did cumber the tree.

31 And it came to pass that the Lord of the vineyard
did taste of the fruit, every sort according to its number.

And the Lord of the vineyard saith:
Behold, this long time have we nourished this tree,
and I have laid up unto myself against the season much fruit.

32 But behold, this time it hath brought forth much fruit,
and there is none of it which is good;
and behold, there are all kinds of bad fruit,
and it profiteth me nothing, notwithstanding all our labor.
And now it grieveth me that I should lose this tree.

33 And the Lord of the vineyard saith unto the servant:
What shall we do unto the tree
that I may preserve again good fruit thereof unto mine own self?

34 And the servant saith unto his master:
Behold, because thou didst graft in the branches of the wild olive tree,
they have nourished the roots,
that they are alive and they have not perished;
wherefore thou beholdest that they are yet good.

35 And it came to pass that the Lord of the vineyard saith unto his servant:
The tree profiteth me nothing
and the roots thereof profiteth me nothing
so long as it shall bring forth evil fruit.

36 Nevertheless I know that the roots are good,
and for mine own purpose I have preserved them.
And because of their much strength
they have hitherto brought forth from the wild branches good fruit.

37 But behold, the wild branches have grew and have overran the roots thereof.
And because that the wild branches have overcome the roots thereof,
it hath brought forth much evil fruit.
And because that it hath brought forth so much evil fruit,
thou beholdest that it beginneth to perish.

And it will soon become ripened that it may be cast into the fire
except we should do something for it to preserve it.

38 And it came to pass that the Lord of the vineyard saith unto his servant:
Let us go down into the nithermost parts of the vineyard,
and behold if the natural branches have also brought forth evil fruit.

39 And it came to pass that they went down
into the nithermost parts of the vineyard.
And it came to pass that they beheld
that the fruit of the natural branches had become corrupt also
—yea, the first and the second and also the last—
and they had all become corrupt.

40 And the wild fruit of the last had overcome
that part of the tree which brought forth good fruit,
even that the branch had withered away and died.

41 And it came to pass that the Lord of the vineyard wept
and saith unto the servant:
What could I have done more for my vineyard?

42 Behold, I knew that all the fruit of the vineyard,
save it were these, had become corrupted.
And now these which have once brought forth good fruit
have also become corrupted.
And now all the trees of my vineyard are good for nothing,
save it be to be hewn down and cast into the fire.

43 And behold, this last whose branch hath withered away
I did plant in a good spot of ground,
yea, even that which was choice unto me
above all other parts of the land of my vineyard.

44 And thou beholdest that I also cut down
that which cumbered this spot of ground
that I might plant this tree in the stead thereof.

45 And thou beholdest that a part thereof brought forth good fruit
and the other part thereof brought forth wild fruit.
And because that I plucked not the branches thereof and cast them into the fire,
behold, they have overcome the good branch, that it hath withered away.

46 And now behold, notwithstanding all the care
which we have taken of my vineyard,
the trees thereof hath become corrupted,
that they bring forth no good fruit.
And these I had hope to preserve,
to have laid up fruit thereof against the season unto mine own self.
But behold, they have become like unto the wild olive tree,

and they are of no worth but to be hewn down and cast into the fire.
And it grieveth me that I should lose them.

47 But what could I have done more in my vineyard?
Have I slackened mine hand that I have not nourished it?
Nay, I have nourished it and I have digged it
and I have pruned it and I have dunged it,
and I have stretched forth mine hand almost all the day long;
and the end draweth nigh.
And it grieveth me that I should hew down all the trees of my vineyard
and cast them into the fire that they should be burned.
Who is it that hath corrupted my vineyard?

48 And it came to pass that the servant saith unto his master:
Is it not the loftiness of thy vineyard?
Hath not the branches thereof overcame the roots which are good?
And because that the branches have overcame the roots thereof
—for behold, they grew faster than the strength of the roots thereof,
taking strength unto themselves—
behold, I say:
Is not this the cause
that the trees of thy vineyard hath become corrupted?

49 And it came to pass that the Lord of the vineyard saith unto the servant:
Let us go to and hew down the trees of the vineyard and cast them into the fire,
that they shall not cumber the ground of my vineyard,
for I have done all.
What could I have done more for my vineyard?

50 But behold, the servant saith unto the Lord of the vineyard:
Spare it a little longer.

51 And the Lord saith:
Yea, I will spare it a little longer,
for it grieveth me that I should lose the trees of my vineyard.

52 Wherefore let us take of the branches of these
which I have planted in the nithermost parts of my vineyard
and let us graft them into the tree from whence they came.
And let us pluck from the tree those branches whose fruit is most bitter
and graft in the natural branches of the tree in the stead thereof.

53 And this will I do that the tree may not perish,
that perhaps I may preserve unto myself the roots thereof
for mine own purpose.

54 And behold, the roots of the natural branches of the tree,
which I planted whithersoever I would, are yet alive;
wherefore that I may preserve them also for mine own purpose,

I will take of the branches of this tree and I will graft them in unto them.
Yea, I will graft in unto them the branches of their mother tree,
that I may preserve the roots also unto mine own self,
that when they shall be sufficiently strong
that perhaps they may bring forth good fruit unto me,
and I may yet have glory in the fruit of my vineyard.

55 And it came to pass that they took from the natural tree which had become wild
and grafted in unto the natural trees which also had become wild.
56 And they also took of the natural trees which had become wild
and grafted into their mother tree.
57 And the Lord of the vineyard saith unto the servant:
Pluck not the wild branches from the trees save it be those which are most bitter.
And in them ye shall graft according to that which I have said.
58 And we will nourish again the trees of the vineyard.
And we will trim up the branches thereof,
and we will pluck from the trees those branches
which are ripened, that must perish,
and cast them into the fire.
59 And this I do that perhaps the roots thereof may take strength
because of their goodness and because of the change of the branches,
that the good may overcome the evil.

60 And because that I have preserved the natural branches and the roots thereof,
and that I have grafted in the natural branches again into their mother tree
and have preserved the roots of their mother tree,
that perhaps the trees of my vineyard may bring forth again good fruit,
and that I may have joy again in the fruit of my vineyard,
and perhaps that I may rejoice exceedingly
that I have preserved the roots and the branches of the first fruit,
61 wherefore go to and call servants,
that we may labor diligently with our mights in the vineyard,
that we may prepare the way that I may bring forth again the natural fruit,
which natural fruit is good and the most precious above all other fruit.

62 Wherefore let us go to and labor with our mights this last time;
for behold, the end draweth nigh,
and this is for the last time that I shall prune my vineyard.
63 Graft in the branches
—begin at the last, that they may be first and that the first may be last—
and dig about the trees, both old and young
—the first and the last, and the last and the first—
that all may be nourished once again for the last time.

64 Wherefore dig about them and prune them
and dung them once more for the last time;
for the end draweth nigh.
And if it so be that these last grafts shall grow and bring forth the natural fruit,
then shall ye prepare the way for them that they may grow.

65 And as they begin to grow,
ye shall clear away the branches which bring forth bitter fruit,
according to the strength of the good and the size thereof.
And ye shall not clear away the bad thereof all at once,
lest the roots thereof should be too strong for the graft
and the graft thereof shall perish and I lose the trees of my vineyard,
66 for it grieveth me that I should lose the trees of my vineyard.
Wherefore ye shall clear away the bad according as the good shall grow,
that the root and the top may be equal in strength
until the good shall overcome the bad
and the bad be hewn down and cast into the fire,
that they cumber not the ground of my vineyard;
and thus will I sweep away the bad out of my vineyard.

67 And the branches of the natural tree will I graft in again
into the natural tree,
68 and the branches of the natural tree will I graft
into the natural branches of the tree.
And thus will I bring them together again,
that they shall bring forth the natural fruit,
and they shall be one.
69 And the bad shall be cast away,
yea, even out of all the land of my vineyard.
For behold, only this once will I prune my vineyard.

70 And it came to pass that the Lord of the vineyard sent his servant,
and the servant went and did as the Lord had commanded him
and brought other servants, and they were few.
71 And the Lord of the vineyard saith unto them:
Go to and labor in the vineyard with your mights.
For behold, this is the last time that I shall nourish my vineyard;
for the end is nigh at hand and the season speedily cometh.
And if ye labor with your mights with me, ye shall have joy in the fruit
which I shall lay up unto myself against the time which will soon come.

72 And it came to pass that the servants did go to it and labor with their mights,
and the Lord of the vineyard labored also with them.
And they did obey the commandments of the Lord of the vineyard in all things.

73 And there began to be the natural fruit again in the vineyard,
and the natural branches began to grow and thrive exceedingly;
and the wild branches began to be plucked off and to be cast away.
And they did keep the root and the top thereof equal
according to the strength thereof.

74 And thus they labored with all diligence
according to the commandments of the Lord of the vineyard,
even until the bad had been cast away out of the vineyard
and the good the Lord had preserved unto himself,
that the trees had brought again the natural fruit.
And they became like unto one body and the fruit were equal;
and the Lord of the vineyard had preserved unto himself the natural fruit,
which was most precious unto him from the beginning.

75 And it came to pass that when the Lord of the vineyard saw
that his fruit was good and that his vineyard was no more corrupt,
he calleth up his servants and saith unto them:
Behold, for this last time have we nourished my vineyard.
And thou beholdest that I have done according to my will;
and I have preserved the natural fruit,
that it is good even like as it was in the beginning.
And blessed art thou,
for because that ye have been diligent in laboring with me in my vineyard
and have kept my commandments
—and it hath brought unto me again the natural fruit,
that my vineyard is no more corrupted and the bad is cast away—
behold, ye shall have joy with me because of the fruit of my vineyard.

76 For behold, for a long time will I lay up of the fruit of my vineyard
unto mine own self against the season, which speedily cometh.
And for the last time have I nourished my vineyard
and pruned it and dug about it and dunged it.
Wherefore I will lay up unto mine own self of the fruit for a long time,
according to that which I have spoken.

77 And when the time cometh that evil fruit shall again come into my vineyard,
then will I cause the good and the bad to be gathered;
and the good will I preserve unto myself,
and the bad will I cast away into its own place.
And then cometh the season and the end,
and my vineyard will I cause to be burned with fire.

6 | 1 And now behold, my brethren,
as I said unto you that I would prophesy,
behold, this is my prophecy,
that the things which this prophet Zenos spake concerning the house of Israel,
in the which he likened them unto a tame olive tree,
must surely come to pass.
2 And in the day that he shall set his hand again the second time
to recover his people is the day—yea, even the last time—
that the servants of the Lord shall go forth
in his power to nourish and prune his vineyard;
and after that the end soon cometh.

3 And how blessed are they who have labored diligently in his vineyard!
And how cursed are they which shall be cast out into their own place!
And the world shall be burned with fire.
4 And how merciful is our God unto us!
For he remembereth the house of Israel, both roots and branches.
And he stretches forth his hands unto them all the day long.
And they are a stiffnecked and a gainsaying people,
but as many as will not harden their hearts
shall be saved in the kingdom of God.

5 Wherefore, my beloved brethren, I beseech of you in words of soberness
that ye would repent and come with full purpose of heart
and cleave unto God as he cleaveth unto you.
And while his arm of mercy is extended towards you in the light of the day,
harden not your hearts;
6 yea, today—if ye will hear his voice—
harden not your hearts.
For why will ye die?
7 For behold, after that ye have been nourished
by the good word of God all the day long,
will ye bring forth evil fruit,
that ye must be hewn down and cast into the fire?
8 Behold, will ye reject these words?
Will ye reject the words of the prophets?
And will ye reject all the words
which have been spoken concerning Christ
after that so many have spoken concerning him,
and deny the good word of Christ and the power of God
and the gift of the Holy Ghost
and quench the Holy Spirit

and make a mock of the great plan of redemption
which hath been laid for you?

9 Know ye not that if ye will do these things
that the power of the redemption and the resurrection which is in Christ
will bring you to stand with shame and awful guilt before the bar of God,

10 and according to the power of justice
—for justice cannot be denied—
that ye must go away into that lake of fire and brimstone?
—whose flames are unquenchable
and whose smoke ascendeth up forever and ever,
which lake of fire and brimstone is endless torment.

11 O then, my beloved brethren, repent ye
and enter ye in at the strait gate
and continue in the way which is narrow
until ye shall obtain eternal life.

12 O be wise!
What can I say more?

13 Finally, I bid you farewell
until I shall meet you before the pleading bar of God,
which bar striketh the wicked with awful dread and fear.
Amen.

7 | 1 And now it came to pass that some years had passed away
and there came a man among the people of Nephi whose name was Sherem.

2 And it came to pass that he began to preach among the people
and to declare unto them that there should be no Christ.
And he preached many things which were flattering unto the people,
and this he done that he might overthrow the doctrine of Christ.

3 And he labored diligently that he might lead away the hearts of the people,
insomuch that he did lead away many hearts.

And he knowing that I Jacob had faith in Christ, which should come,
wherefore he sought much opportunity that he might come unto me.

4 And he was learned,
that he had a perfect knowledge of the language of the people;
wherefore he could use much flattery
and much power of speech according to the power of the devil.

5 And he had hope to shake me from the faith,
notwithstanding the many revelations
and the many things which I had seen concerning these things.
For I truly had seen angels and they had ministered unto me.

And also I had heard the voice of the Lord speaking unto me
in very word from time to time;
wherefore I could not be shaken.

6 And it came to pass that he came unto me
and on this wise did he speak unto me, saying:
Brother Jacob, I have sought much opportunity that I might speak unto you,
for I have heard and also know that thou goest about much,
preaching that which ye call the gospel or the doctrine of Christ.

7 And ye have led away much of this people,
that they pervert the right way of God
and keep not the law of Moses, which is the right way,
and convert the law of Moses into the worship of a being
which ye say shall come many hundred years hence.
And now behold, I Sherem declare unto you that this is blasphemy,
for no man knoweth of such things;
for he cannot tell of things to come.
And after this manner did Sherem contend against me.

8 But behold, the Lord God poured in his Spirit into my soul,
insomuch that I did confound him in all his words.

9 And I saith unto him:
Deniest thou the Christ, which should come?
And he saith:
If there should be a Christ,
I would not deny him;
but I know that there is no Christ,
neither hath been nor never will be.

10 And I saith unto him:
Believest thou the scriptures?
And he saith: Yea.

11 And I saith unto him:
Then ye do not understand them,
for they truly testify of Christ.
Behold, I say unto you
that none of the prophets have written nor prophesied
save they have spoken concerning this Christ.

12 And this is not all.
It hath been made manifest unto me
—for I have heard and seen
and it also hath been made manifest unto me
by the power of the Holy Ghost—

wherefore I know if there should be no atonement made,
all mankind must be lost.

13 And it came to pass that he saith unto me:
Shew me a sign by this power of the Holy Ghost,
in the which ye know so much.
14 And I said unto him:
What am I that I should tempt God to shew unto thee a sign
in the thing which thou knowest to be true?
Yet thou wilt deny it because thou art of the devil.
Nevertheless not my will be done;
but if God shall smite thee, let that be a sign unto thee
that he hath power both in heaven and in earth
and also that Christ shall come.
And thy will, O Lord, be done and not mine.

15 And it came to pass that when I Jacob had spoken these words,
the power of the Lord came upon him,
insomuch that he fell to the earth.
And it came to pass that he was nourished for the space of many days.
16 And it came to pass that he saith unto the people:
Gather together on the morrow, for I shall die;
wherefore I desire to speak unto the people before that I shall die.

17 And it came to pass that on the morrow
that the multitude were gathered together,
and he spake plainly unto them
and denied the things which he had taught them,
and confessed the Christ and the power of the Holy Ghost
and the ministering of angels.
18 And he spake plainly unto them
that he had been deceived by the power of the devil.
And he spake of hell and of eternity and of eternal punishment.
19 And he saith:
I fear lest I have committed the unpardonable sin,
for I have lied unto God.
For I denied the Christ and said that I believed the scriptures—
and they truly testify of him.
And because that I have thus lied unto God,
I greatly fear lest my case shall be awful but I confess unto God.

20 And it came to pass that when he had said these words,
he could say no more and he gave up the ghost.

21 And when the multitude had witnessed
that he spake these things as he was about to give up the ghost,
they were astonished exceedingly,
insomuch that the power of God came down upon them
and they were overcome, that they fell to the earth.

22 Now this thing was pleasing unto me Jacob,
for I had requested it of my Father which was in heaven,
for he had heard my cry and answered my prayer.

23 And it came to pass that
peace and the love of God was restored again among the people.
And they searched the scriptures
and hearkened no more to the words of this wicked man.

24 And it came to pass that many means were devised
to reclaim and restore the Lamanites to the knowledge of the truth;
but it all were vain,
for they delighted in wars and bloodsheds,
and they had an eternal hatred against us their brethren,
and they sought by the power of their arms to destroy us continually.

25 Wherefore the people of Nephi did fortify against them
with their arms and with all their might,
trusting in the God and the rock of their salvation;
wherefore they became as yet conquerors of their enemies.

26 And it came to pass that I Jacob began to be old.
And the record of this people being kept on the other plates of Nephi,
wherefore I conclude this record,
declaring that I have written according to the best of my knowledge,
by saying that the time passed away with us,
and also our lives passed away like as it were unto us a dream,
we being a lonesome and a solemn people,
wanderers cast out from Jerusalem,
born in tribulation in a wild wilderness,
and hated of our brethren, which caused wars and contentions;
wherefore we did mourn out our days.

27 And I Jacob saw that I must soon go down to my grave;
wherefore I said unto my son Enos:
Take these plates.
And I told him the things which my brother Nephi had commanded me,
and he promised obedience unto the commands.

And I make an end of my writing upon these plates,
which writing hath been small.
And to the reader I bid farewell,
hoping that many of my brethren may read my words.
Brethren, adieu.

THE BOOK OF ENOS

1 | 1   Behold, it came to pass that
I Enos knowing my father that he was a just man,
for he taught me in his language
and also in the nurture and admonition of the Lord
—and blessed be the name of my God for it—
2   and I will tell you of the wrestle which I had before God
before that I received a remission of my sins.
3   Behold, I went to hunt beasts in the forest,
and I remembered the words which I had often heard my father speak
concerning eternal life and the joy of the saints;
and the words of my father sunk deep into my heart,
4   and my soul hungered,
and I kneeled down before my Maker,
and I cried unto him in mighty prayer and supplication for mine own soul.
And all the day long did I cry unto him;
yea, and when the night came, I did still raise my voice high,
that it reached the heavens.

5   And there came a voice unto me, saying:
Enos, thy sins are forgiven thee, and thou shalt be blessed.
6   And I Enos knew that God could not lie;
wherefore my guilt was swept away.
7   And I saith:
Lord, how is it done?
8   And he saith unto me:
Because of thy faith in Christ,
whom thou hast not heard nor seen
—and many years passeth away
before that he shall manifest himself in the flesh—

    wherefore go to it;
    thy faith hath made thee whole.

9 Now it came to pass that when I had heard these words,
    I began to feel a desire for the welfare of my brethren the Nephites;
    wherefore I did pour out my whole soul unto God for them.

10 And while I was thus struggling in the spirit,
    behold, the voice of the Lord came into my mind again, saying:
    I will visit thy brethren
    according to their diligence in keeping my commandments.
    I have given unto them this land,
    and it is a holy land;
    and I curse it not save it be for the cause of iniquity.
    Wherefore I will visit thy brethren according as I have said,
    and their transgressions will I bring down with sorrow upon their own heads.

11 And after that I Enos had heard these words,
    my faith began to be unshaken in the Lord.
    And I prayed unto him with many long strugglings
    for my brethren the Lamanites.

12 And it came to pass that
    after I had prayed and labored with all diligence,
    the Lord said unto me:
    I will grant unto thee according to thy desires because of thy faith.

13 And now behold, this was the desire which I desired of him,
    that if it should so be that my people the Nephites should fall into transgression
    and by any means be destroyed and the Lamanites should not be destroyed
    that the Lord God would preserve a record of my people the Nephites,
    even if it so be by the power of his holy arm,
    that it might be brought forth some future day unto the Lamanites,
    that perhaps they might be brought unto salvation.

14 For at the present our strugglings were vain
    in restoring them to the true faith.
    And they swore in their wrath
    that if it were possible,
    they would destroy our records and us
    and also all the traditions of our fathers.

15 Wherefore I knowing
    that the Lord God was able to preserve our records,
    I cried unto him continually,
    for he had said unto me:

Whatsoever thing ye shall ask in faith
—believing that ye shall receive—
in the name of Christ,
ye shall receive it.

16 And I had faith and I did cry unto God
that he would preserve the records.
And he covenanted with me
that he would bring them forth unto the Lamanites in his own due time.

17 And I Enos knew that it would be according to the covenant which he had made;
wherefore my soul did rest.

18 And the Lord said unto me:
Thy fathers have also required of me this thing.
And it shall be done unto them according to their faith,
for their faith was like unto thine.

19 And now it came to pass that
I Enos went about among the people of Nephi,
prophesying of things to come
and testifying of the things which I had heard and seen.

20 And I bear record that the people of Nephi did seek diligently
to restore the Lamanites unto the true faith in God,
but our labors were vain.
Their hatred was fixed;
and they were led by their evil nature,
that they became wild and ferocious
and a bloodthirsty people full of idolatry and filthiness,
feeding upon beasts of prey,
dwelling in tents and wandering about in the wilderness,
with a short skin girded about their loins and their heads shaven.
And their skill was in the bow and the scimitar and the ax;
and many of them did eat nothing save it was raw meat.
And they were continually seeking to destroy us.

21 And it came to pass that the people of Nephi did till the land
and raise all manner of grain and of fruit
and flocks of herds and flocks of all manner of cattle of every kind
and goats and wild goats and also much horses.

22 And there were exceeding many prophets among us;
and the people were a stiffnecked people,
hard to understand.

23 And there was nothing save it was exceeding harshness,
preaching and prophesying of wars and contentions and destructions,
and continually reminding them of death

and of the duration of eternity and the judgments and the power of God,
and all these things stirring them up continually
to keep them in the fear of the Lord—
I say, there was nothing short of these things
and exceeding great plainness of speech
would keep them from going down speedily to destruction.
And after this manner do I write concerning them.

24 And I saw wars between the Nephites and the Lamanites in the course of my days.

25 And it came to pass that I began to be old.
And an hundred and seventy and nine years had passed away
from the time that our father Lehi left Jerusalem.

26 And as I saw that I must soon go down to my grave,
having been wrought upon by the power of God
that I must preach and prophesy unto this people
and declare the word according to the truth which is in Christ—
and I have declared it in all my days
and have rejoiced in it above that of the world.

27 And I soon go to the place of my rest,
which is with my Redeemer;
for I know that in him I shall rest.
And I rejoice in the day
when my mortal shall put on immortality
and shall stand before him.
Then shall I see his face with pleasure,
and he will say unto me:
Come unto me, ye blessed;
there is a place prepared for you in the mansions of my Father.
Amen.

The Book of Jarom

1 | 1 Now behold, I Jarom write a few words
according to the commandment of my father Enos,
that our genealogy may be kept.

2 And as these plates are small
and as these things are written
for the intent of the benefit of our brethren the Lamanites,

wherefore it must needs be that I write a little.
But I shall not write the things of my prophesying nor of my revelations.
For what could I write more than my fathers have written,
for have not they revealed the plan of salvation?
I say unto you: Yea;
and this sufficeth me.

3 Behold, it is expedient that much should be done among this people
because of the hardness of their hearts and the deafness of their ears
and the blindness of their minds and the stiffness of their necks.
Nevertheless God is exceeding merciful unto them
and hath not as yet swept them off from the face of the land.
4 And there are many among us which have many revelations,
for they are not all stiffnecked.
And as many as are not stiffnecked and have faith
have communion with the Holy Spirit,
which maketh manifest unto the children of men according to their faith.

5 And now behold, two hundred years had passed away,
and the people of Nephi had waxed strong in the land.
They observed to keep the law of Moses
and the sabbath day holy unto the Lord,
and they profaned not, neither did they blaspheme.
And the laws of the land were exceeding strict.
6 And they were scattered upon much of the face of the land,
and the Lamanites also.
And they were exceeding more numerous than were they of the Nephites.
And they loved murder and would drink the blood of beasts.
7 And it came to pass that they came many times against us the Nephites to battle.
But our kings and our leaders were mighty men in the faith of the Lord,
and they taught the people the ways of the Lord.
Wherefore we withstood the Lamanites
and swept them away out of our lands
and began to fortify our cities or whatsoever place of our inheritance.

8 And we multiplied exceedingly and spread upon the face of the land
and became exceeding rich in gold and in silver and in precious things
and in fine workmanship of wood, in buildings and in machinery,
and also in iron and copper and brass and steel,
making all manner of tools of every kind to till the ground,
and weapons of war
—yea, the sharp pointed arrow and the quiver and the dart and the javelin—
and all preparations for war.

9 And thus being prepared to meet the Lamanites,
they did not prosper against us.
But the word of the Lord was verified which he spake unto our fathers,
saying that inasmuch as ye will keep my commandments,
ye shall prosper in the land.

10 And it came to pass that the prophets of the Lord
did threaten the people of Nephi according to the word of God
that if they did not keep the commandments but should fall into transgression,
they should be destroyed from off the face of the land.

11 Wherefore the prophets and the priests and the teachers did labor diligently,
exhorting with all long-suffering the people to diligence,
teaching the law of Moses and the intent for which it was given,
persuading them to look forward unto the Messiah
and believe in him to come as though he already was.
And after this manner did they teach them.

12 And it came to pass that by so doing
they kept them from being destroyed upon the face of the land;
for they did prick their hearts with the word,
continually stirring them up unto repentance.

13 And it came to pass that
two hundred and thirty and eight years had passed away,
after the manner of wars and contentions and dissensions
for the space of much of the time.

14 And I Jarom do not write more,
for the plates are small.
But behold, my brethren, ye can go to the other plates of Nephi.
For behold, upon them the record of our wars are engraven
according to the writings of the kings,
or that which they caused to be written.

15 And I deliver these plates into the hands of my son Omni,
that they may be kept according to the commandments of my fathers.

The Book of Omni

1 | 1 Behold, it came to pass that
I Omni being commanded by my father Jarom
that I should write somewhat upon these plates to preserve our genealogy,

2 wherefore in my days I would that ye should know

that I fought much with the sword to preserve my people the Nephites
from falling into the hands of their enemies the Lamanites.
But behold, I of myself am a wicked man,
and I have not kept the statutes and the commandments of the Lord
as I ought to have done.

3 And it came to pass that
two hundred and seventy and six years had passed away;
and we had many seasons of peace,
and we had many seasons of serious war and bloodshed.
Yea, and in fine, two hundred and eighty and two years had passed away;
and I had kept these plates according to the commandments of my fathers,
and I conferred them upon my son Amaron.
And I make an end.

4 And now I Amaron write the things whatsoever I write,
which are few, in the book of my father.
5 Behold, it came to pass that three hundred and twenty years had passed away;
and the more wicked part of the Nephites were destroyed.
6 For the Lord would not suffer
after he had led them out of the land of Jerusalem
and kept and preserved them from falling into the hands of their enemies,
yea, he would not suffer that the words should not be verified
which he spake unto our fathers,
saying that inasmuch as ye will not keep my commandments,
ye shall not prosper in the land.
7 Wherefore the Lord did visit them in great judgment.
Nevertheless he did spare the righteous, that they should not perish,
but did deliver them out of the hands of their enemies.
8 And it came to pass that I did deliver the plates unto my brother Chemish.

9 Now I Chemish write what few things I write in the same book with my brother.
For behold, I saw the last which he wrote,
that he wrote it with his own hand;
and he wrote it in the day that he delivered them unto me.
And after this manner we keep the record,
for it is according to the commandments of our fathers.
And I make an end.

10 Behold, I Abinadom I am the son of Chemish.
Behold, it came to pass that I saw much war and contention
between my people the Nephites and the Lamanites.
And I with mine own sword have taken the lives of many of the Lamanites
in the defense of my brethren.

11 And behold, the record of this people is engraven upon plates,
which is had by the kings according to the generations.
And I know of no revelation save that which has been written, neither prophecy.
Wherefore that which is sufficient is written.
And I make an end.

12 Behold, I am Amaleki the son of Abinadom.
Behold, I will speak unto you somewhat concerning Mosiah,
which was made king over the land of Zarahemla.
For behold, he being warned of the Lord
that he should flee out of the land of Nephi
—and as many as would hearken unto the voice of the Lord
should also depart out of the land with him into the wilderness—

13 and it came to pass that he did according as the Lord had commanded him.
And they departed out of the land into the wilderness,
as many as would hearken unto the voice of the Lord.
And they were led by many preachings and prophesyings,
and they were admonished continually by the word of God,
and they were led by the power of his arm through the wilderness,
until they came down into the land which is called the land of Zarahemla.

14 And they discovered a people which was called the people of Zarahemla.

Now there was great rejoicing among the people of Zarahemla,
and also Zarahemla did rejoice exceedingly
because that the Lord had sent the people of Mosiah
with the plates of brass, which contained the record of the Jews.

15 Behold, it came to pass that Mosiah discovered
that the people of Zarahemla came out from Jerusalem at the time
that Zedekiah, king of Judah, was carried away captive into Babylon;

16 and they journeyed in the wilderness
and was brought by the hand of the Lord across the great waters
into the land where Mosiah discovered them;
and they had dwelt there from that time forth.

17 And at the time that Mosiah discovered them,
they had became exceeding numerous.
Nevertheless they had had many wars and serious contentions
and had fallen by the sword from time to time.
And their language had become corrupted;
and they had brought no records with them.
And they denied the being of their Creator.
And Mosiah—nor the people of Mosiah—could not understand them.

18 But it came to pass that Mosiah caused
that they should be taught in his language.

And it came to pass that after they were taught in the language of Mosiah,
Zarahemla gave a genealogy of his fathers according to his memory;
and they are written but not in these plates.

19 And it came to pass that
the people of Zarahemla and of Mosiah did unite together,
and Mosiah was appointed to be their king.

20 And it came to pass in the days of Mosiah
there was a large stone brought unto him with engravings on it,
and he did interpret the engravings by the gift and power of God.

21 And they gave an account of one Coriantumr and the slain of his people.
And Coriantumr was discovered by the people of Zarahemla,
and he dwelt with them for the space of nine moons.

22 It also spake a few words concerning his fathers;
and his first parents came out from the tower
at the time the Lord confounded the language of the people.
And the severity of the Lord fell upon them
according to his judgments, which is just,
and their bones lay scattered in the land northward.

23 Behold, I Amaleki was born in the days of Mosiah;
and I have lived to see his death and Benjamin his son reigneth in his stead.

24 And behold, I have seen in the days of king Benjamin
a serious war and much bloodshed between the Nephites and the Lamanites.
But behold, the Nephites did obtain much advantage over them,
yea, insomuch that king Benjamin did drive them out of the land of Zarahemla.

25 And it came to pass that I began to be old;
and having no seed
and knowing king Benjamin to be a just man before the Lord,
wherefore I shall deliver up these plates unto him,
exhorting all men to come unto God, the Holy One of Israel,
and believe in prophesying and in revelations
and in the ministering of angels
and in the gift of speaking with tongues
and in the gift of interpreting languages
and in all things which is good,
for there is nothing which is good save it comes from the Lord;
and that which is evil cometh from the devil.

26 And now my beloved brethren,
I would that ye should come unto Christ, which is the Holy One of Israel,
and partake of his salvation and the power of his redemption;
yea, come unto him and offer your whole souls as an offering unto him

and continue in fasting and praying and endure to the end;
and as the Lord liveth, ye will be saved.

27 And now I would speak somewhat concerning a certain number
which went up into the wilderness to return to the land of Nephi,
for there was a large number which were desirous
to possess the land of their inheritance;

28 wherefore they went up into the wilderness.
And their leader being a strong and a mighty man and a stiffnecked man,
wherefore he caused a contention among them.
And they were all slain save fifty in the wilderness,
and they returned again to the land of Zarahemla.

29 And it came to pass that they also took others to a considerable number
and took their journey again into the wilderness.

30 And I Amaleki had a brother which also went with them;
and I have not since known concerning them.
And I am about to lay down in my grave;
and these plates are full,
and I make an end of my speaking.

The Words of Mormon

1 | 1 And now I Mormon being about to deliver up the record
which I have been making
into the hands of my son Moroni,
behold, I have witnessed almost all the destruction of my people the Nephites.

2 And it is many hundred years after the coming of Christ
that I deliver these records into the hands of my son.
And it supposeth me that he will witness the entire destruction of my people.
But may God grant that he may survive them,
that he may write somewhat concerning them
and somewhat concerning Christ,
that perhaps some day it may profit them.

3 And now I speak somewhat concerning that which I have written.
For after that I had made an abridgment from the plates of Nephi
down to the reign of this king Benjamin of which Amaleki spake,
I searched among the records which had been delivered into my hands,

and I found these plates which contained this small account of the prophets
from Jacob down to the reign of this king Benjamin,
and also many of the words of Nephi.

4 And the things which are upon these plates pleasing me
because of the prophecies of the coming of Christ,
and my fathers knowing that many of them have been fulfilled
—yea, and I also know that as many things as have been prophesied
concerning us down to this day has been fulfilled,
and as many as go beyond this day must surely come to pass—

5 wherefore I choose these things to finish my record upon them,
which remainder of my record I shall take from the plates of Nephi.
And I cannot write a hundredth part of the things of my people.

6 But behold, I shall take these plates
which contain these prophesyings and revelations
and put them with the remainder of my record,
for they are choice unto me;
and I know they will be choice unto my brethren.

7 And I do this for a wise purpose,
for thus it whispereth me
according to the workings of the Spirit of the Lord which is in me.
And now I do not know all things,
but the Lord knoweth all things which is to come;
wherefore he worketh in me to do according to his will.

8 And my prayer to God is concerning my brethren,
that they may once again come to the knowledge of God,
yea, the redemption of Christ,
that they may once again be a delightsome people.

9 And now I Mormon proceed to finish out my record
which I take from the plates of Nephi;
and I make it according to the knowledge and the understanding
which God hath given me.

10 Wherefore it came to pass that
after Amaleki had delivered up these plates into the hands of king Benjamin,
he took them and put them with the other plates,
which contained records which had been handed down
by the kings from generation to generation until the days of king Benjamin.

11 And they were handed down from king Benjamin from generation to generation
until they have fallen into my hands.
And I Mormon pray to God
that they may be preserved from this time henceforth.

And I know that they will be preserved,
for there are great things written upon them
out of which my people and their brethren
shall be judged at the great and last day,
according to the word of God which is written.

12 And now concerning this king Benjamin:
he had somewhat contentions among his own people.
13 And it came to pass also that the armies of the Lamanites came down
out of the land of Nephi to battle against his people.
But behold, king Benjamin gathered together his armies,
and he did stand against them,
and he did fight with the strength of his own arm with the sword of Laban.
14 And in the strength of the Lord they did contend against their enemies
until they had slain many thousands of the Lamanites.
And it came to pass that they did contend against the Lamanites
until they had driven them out of all the lands of their inheritance.

15 And it came to pass that after there had been false Christs
and their mouths had been shut
—and they punished according to their crimes—
16 and after there had been false prophets
and false preachers and teachers among the people
—and all these having been punished according to their crimes—
and after there having been much contentions
and many dissensions away unto the Lamanites,
behold, it came to pass that king Benjamin
with the assistance of the holy prophets which were among his people
17 —for behold, king Benjamin was a holy man,
and he did reign over his people in righteousness;
and there were many holy men in the land,
and they did speak the word of God with power and with authority,
and they did use much sharpness because of the stiffneckedness of the people—
18 wherefore with the help of these,
king Benjamin by laboring with all the might of his body
and the faculty of his whole soul
—and also the prophets—
wherefore they did once more establish peace in the land.

THE BOOK OF MOSIAH

1 | 1 And now there was no more contention in all the land of Zarahemla
among all the people which belonged to king Benjamin,
so that king Benjamin had continual peace all the remainder of his days.

2 And it came to pass that he had three sons,
and he called their names Mosiah and Helorum and Helaman.
And he caused that they should be taught in all the language of his fathers,
that thereby they might become men of understanding
and that they might know concerning the prophecies
which had been spoken by the mouths of their fathers,
which was delivered them by the hand of the Lord.

3 And he also taught them concerning the records
which were engraven on the plates of brass, saying:
My sons, I would that ye should remember
that were it not for these plates
which contain these records and these commandments,
we must have suffered in ignorance, even at this present time,
not knowing the mysteries of God.

4 For it were not possible
that our father Lehi could have remembered all these things,
to have taught them to his children,
except it were for the help of these plates;
for he having been taught in the language of the Egyptians,
therefore he could read these engravings and teach them to his children,
that thereby they could teach them to their children,
and so fulfilling the commandments of God,
even down to this present time.

5 I say unto you my sons:
Were it not for these things
which have been kept and preserved by the hand of God,
that we might read and understand of his mysteries
and have his commandments always before our eyes,
that even our fathers would have dwindled in unbelief,
and we should have been like unto our brethren the Lamanites,
which know nothing concerning these things,

or even do not believe them when they are taught them
because of the traditions of their fathers, which are not correct.

6 O my sons, I would that ye should remember
that these sayings are true,
and also that these records are true.
And behold also the plates of Nephi
which contain the records and the sayings of our fathers
from the time they left Jerusalem until now,
and they are true;
and we can know of their surety
because we have them before our eyes.
7 And now my sons, I would that ye should remember to search them diligently,
that ye may profit thereby.
And I would that ye should keep the commandments of God,
that ye may prosper in the land
according to the promises which the Lord made unto our fathers.
8 And many more things did king Benjamin teach his sons
which are not written in this book.

9 And it came to pass that
after king Benjamin had made an end of teaching his sons
that he waxed old,
and he saw that he must very soon go the way of all the earth.
Therefore he thought it expedient
that he should confer the kingdom upon one of his sons;
10 therefore he had Mosiah brought before him,
and these are the words which he spake unto him, saying:
My son, I would that ye should make a proclamation
throughout all this land among all this people,
or the people of Zarahemla and the people of Mosiah which dwell in this land,
that thereby they may be gathered together,
for on the morrow I shall proclaim unto this my people out of mine own mouth
that thou art a king and a ruler over this people,
which the Lord our God hath given us.

11 And moreover I shall give this people a name
that thereby they may be distinguished above all the people
which the Lord God hath brought out of the land of Jerusalem.
And this I do because they have been a diligent people
in keeping the commandments of the Lord.
12 And I give unto them a name that never shall be blotted out
except it be through transgression.

13 Yea, and moreover I say unto you that
    if this highly favored people of the Lord should fall into transgression
    and become a wicked and an adulterous people
    that the Lord will deliver them up,
    that thereby they become weak like unto their brethren,
    and he will no more preserve them by his matchless and marvelous power
    as he hath hitherto preserved our fathers.

14 For I say unto you that
    if he had not extended his arm in the preservation of our fathers,
    they must have fallen into the hands of the Lamanites
    and become victims to their hatred.

15 And it came to pass that
    after king Benjamin had made an end of these sayings to his son
    that he gave him charge concerning all the affairs of the kingdom.

16 And moreover he also gave him charge concerning the records
    which were engraven on the plates of brass,
    and also the plates of Nephi,
    and also the sword of Laban,
    and the ball or director which led our fathers through the wilderness,
    which was prepared by the hand of the Lord
    that thereby they might be led, every one,
    according to the heed and diligence which they gave unto him.

17 Therefore as they were unfaithful,
    they did not prosper nor progress in their journey,
    but were driven back and incurred the displeasure of God upon them;
    and therefore they were smitten with famine and sore afflictions,
    to stir them up in remembrance of their duty.

18 And now it came to pass that
    Mosiah went and did as his father had commanded him
    and proclaimed unto all the people which were in the land of Zarahemla
    that thereby they might gather themselves together to go up to the temple
    to hear the words which his father should speak unto them.

2 | 1 And it came to pass that
    after Mosiah had done as his father had commanded him
    and had made a proclamation throughout all the land
    that the people gathered themselves together throughout all the land,
    that they might go up to the temple to hear the words
    which king Benjamin should speak unto them.

2 And there were a great number,
    even so many that they did not number them,

for they had multiplied exceedingly and waxed great in the land.

3 And they also took of the firstlings of their flocks,
that they might offer sacrifice and burnt offerings according to the law of Moses

4 and also that they might give thanks to the Lord their God,
who had brought them out of the land of Jerusalem,
and who had delivered them out of the hands of their enemies
and had appointed just men to be their teachers
and also a just man to be their king,
who had established peace in the land of Zarahemla,
and who had taught them to keep the commandments of God,
that thereby they might rejoice and be filled with love towards God and all men.

5 And it came to pass that when they came up to the temple,
they pitched their tents round about,
every man according to his family,
consisting of his wife and his sons and his daughters
and their sons and their daughters,
from the eldest down to the youngest,
every family being separate one from another.

6 And they pitched their tents round about the temple,
every man having his tent with the door thereof towards the temple,
that thereby they might remain in their tents
and hear the words which king Benjamin should speak unto them;

7 for the multitude being so great
that king Benjamin could not teach them all within the walls of the temple,
therefore he caused a tower to be erected,
that thereby his people might hear the words
which he should speak unto them.

8 And it came to pass that
he began to speak to his people from the tower,
and they could not all hear his words because of the greatness of the multitude.
Therefore he caused that the words which he spake should be written
and sent forth among those that were not under the sound of his voice,
that they might also receive his words.

9 And these are the words which he spake and caused to be written, saying:
My brethren, all ye that have assembled yourselves together,
you that can hear my words which I shall speak unto you this day,
for I have not commanded you to come up hither
to trifle with the words which I shall speak,
but that you should hearken unto me
and open your ears that ye may hear

and your hearts that ye may understand
and your minds that the mysteries of God may be unfolded to your view.

10 I have not commanded you to come up hither that ye should fear me,
or that ye should think that I of myself am more than a mortal man.

11 But I am like as yourselves,
subject to all manner of infirmities in body and mind.
Yet as I have been chosen by this people
and was consecrated by my father
and was suffered by the hand of the Lord
that I should be a ruler and a king over this people
and have been kept and preserved by his matchless power,
to serve thee with all the might, mind, and strength
which the Lord hath granted unto me—

12 I say unto you that as I have been suffered
to spend my days in your service, even up to this time,
and have not sought gold nor silver
nor no manner of riches of you,

13 neither have I suffered that ye should be confined in dungeons
nor that ye should make slaves one of another
or that ye should murder or plunder or steal or commit adultery,
or even I have not suffered that ye should commit any manner of wickedness,
and have taught you that ye should keep the commandments of the Lord
in all things which he hath commanded you—

14 and even I myself have labored with mine own hands that I might serve you
and that ye should not be laden with taxes
and that there should nothing come upon you which was grievous to be borne—
and of all these things which I have spoken,
ye yourselves are witnesses this day.

15 Yet my brethren, I have not done these things that I might boast,
neither do I tell these things that thereby I might accuse you.
But I tell you these things that ye may know
that I can answer a clear conscience before God this day.

16 Behold, I say unto you that
because I said unto you that I had spent my days in your service,
I do not desire to boast,
for I have only been in the service of God.

17 And behold, I tell you these things that ye may learn wisdom,
that ye may learn that when ye are in the service of your fellow beings,
ye are only in the service of your God.

18 Behold, ye have called me your king.
And if I, whom ye call your king, do labor to serve you,

then had not ye ought to labor to serve one another?
19 And behold also, if I, who ye call your king,
    who has spent his days in your service
    and yet hath been in the service of God,
    doth merit any thanks from you,
    O how had you ought to thank your heavenly King!

20 I say unto you my brethren
    that if you should render all the thanks and praise
    which your whole souls hath power to possess
    to that God who hath created you
    and hath kept and preserved you
    and hath caused that ye should rejoice
    and hath granted that ye should live in peace one with another—
21 I say unto you that
    if ye should serve him who hath created you from the beginning
    and art preserving you from day to day by lending you breath
    that ye may live and move and do according to your own will,
    and even supporting you from one moment to another
    —I say if ye should serve him with all your whole soul—
    and yet ye would be unprofitable servants.

22 And behold, all that he requires of you is to keep his commandments.
    And he hath promised you that if ye would keep his commandments,
    ye should prosper in the land.
    And he never doth vary from that which he hath said;
    therefore if ye do keep his commandments,
    he doth bless you and prosper you.

23 And now in the first place, he hath created you
    and granted unto you your lives,
    for which ye are indebted unto him.
24 And secondly, he doth require
    that ye should do as he hath commanded you,
    for which if ye do,
    he doth immediately bless you,
    and therefore he hath paid you.
    And ye are still indebted unto him
    and are and will be forever and ever.
    Therefore of what have ye to boast?

25 And now I ask:
    Can ye say aught of yourselves?
    I answer you: Nay.

Ye cannot say that thou art even as much as the dust of the earth,
yet thou wast created of the dust of the earth;
but behold, it belongeth to him who created you.

26 And I, even I, whom ye call your king, am no better than ye yourselves are,
for I am also of the dust.
And thou beholdest that I am old
and am about to yield up this mortal frame to its mother earth.

27 Therefore as I said unto you
that I had served you, walking with a clear conscience before God,
even so I at this time have caused that ye should assemble yourselves together,
that I might be found blameless
and that your blood should not come upon me
when I shall stand to be judged of God of the things
whereof he hath commanded me concerning you.

28 I say unto you that I have caused that ye should assemble yourselves together
that I might rid my garments of your blood,
at this period of time when I am about to go down to my grave,
that I might go down in peace
and my immortal spirit may join the choirs above
in singing the praises of a just God.

29 And moreover I say unto you
that I have caused that ye should assemble yourselves together
that I might declare unto you
that I can no longer be your teacher nor your king.

30 For even at this time my whole frame doth tremble exceedingly
while attempting to speak unto you,
but the Lord God doth support me
and hath suffered me that I should speak unto you
and hath commanded me that I should declare unto you this day
that my son Mosiah is a king and a ruler over you.

31 And now my brethren, I would that ye should do as ye hath hitherto done;
as ye have kept my commandments,
and also the commandments of my father,
and have prospered and have been kept
from falling into the hands of your enemies,
even so if ye shall keep the commandments of my son,
or the commandments of God which shall be delivered unto you by him,
ye shall prosper in the land,
and your enemies shall have no power over you.

32 But O my people, beware lest there shall arise contentions among you,

and ye list to obey the evil spirit which was spoken of by my father Mosiah.

33 For behold, there is a woe pronounced upon him who listeth to obey that spirit;
   for if he listeth to obey him and remaineth and dieth in his sins,
   the same drinketh damnation to his own soul,
   for he receiveth for his wages an everlasting punishment,
   having transgressed the law of God contrary to his own knowledge.

34 I say unto you that there are not one among you
   —except it be your little children—
   that have not been taught concerning these things
   but what knoweth that ye are eternally indebted to your heavenly Father,
   to render to him all that you have and are,
   and also have been taught concerning the records,
   which contain the prophecies which hath been spoken by the holy prophets,
   even down to the time our father Lehi left Jerusalem,

35 and also all that hath been spoken by our fathers until now.
   And behold also, they spake that which was commanded them of the Lord;
   therefore they are just and true.

36 And now I say unto you my brethren that
   after ye have known and have been taught all these things,
   if ye should transgress and go contrary to that which hath been spoken,
   that ye do withdraw yourselves from the Spirit of the Lord,
   that it may have no place in you to guide you in wisdom's paths
   that ye may be blessed, prospered, and preserved—

37 I say unto you that the man that doeth this,
   the same cometh out in open rebellion against God;
   therefore he listeth to obey the evil spirit
   and becometh an enemy to all righteousness.
   Therefore the Lord hath no place in him,
   for he dwelleth not in unholy temples.

38 Therefore if that man repenteth not
   and remaineth and dieth an enemy to God,
   the demands of divine justice doth awaken his immortal soul
   to a lively sense of his own guilt,
   which doth cause him to shrink from the presence of the Lord
   and doth fill his breast with guilt and pain and anguish,
   which is like an unquenchable fire whose flames ascendeth up forever and ever.

39 And now I say unto you that mercy hath no claim on that man;
   therefore his final doom is to endure a never-ending torment.

40 O all ye old men and also ye young men
   and you little children which can understand my words

—for I have spoken plain unto you that ye might understand—
I pray that ye should awake to a remembrance of the awful situation
of those that have fallen into transgression.

41 And moreover I would desire
that ye should consider on the blessed and happy state
of those that keep the commandments of God;
for behold, they are blessed in all things, both temporal and spiritual.
And if they hold out faithful to the end,
they are received into heaven,
that thereby they may dwell with God in a state of never-ending happiness.
O remember, remember that these things are true,
for the Lord God hath spoken it.

3 | 1 And again my brethren, I would call your attention,
for I have somewhat more to speak unto you;
for behold, I have things to tell you concerning that which is to come.

2 And the things which I shall tell you
are made known unto me by an angel from God.
And he said unto me:
Awake!
And I awoke;
and behold, he stood before me.

3 And he said unto me:
Awake and hear the words which I shall tell thee;
for behold, I am come to declare unto thee glad tidings of great joy.

4 For the Lord hath heard thy prayers and hath judged of thy righteousness
and hath sent me to declare unto thee,
that thou mayest rejoice,
and that thou mayest declare unto thy people,
that they may also be filled with joy.

5 For behold, the time cometh and is not far distant
that with power the Lord Omnipotent who reigneth,
which was and is from all eternity to all eternity,
shall come down from heaven among the children of men
and shall dwell in a tabernacle of clay
and shall go forth amongst men, working mighty miracles,
such as healing the sick,
raising the dead,
causing the lame to walk,
the blind to receive their sight,
and the deaf to hear,
and curing all manner of diseases.

6 And he shall cast out devils,
or the evil spirits which dwelleth in the hearts of the children of men.

7 And lo, he shall suffer temptations
and pain of body, hunger, thirst, and fatigue,
even more than man can suffer except it be unto death;
for behold, blood cometh from every pore,
so great shall be his anguish for the wickedness
and the abominations of his people.

8 And he shall be called Jesus Christ the Son of God,
the Father of heaven and of earth,
the Creator of all things from the beginning;
and his mother shall be called Mary.

9 And lo, he cometh unto his own
that salvation might come unto the children of men,
even through faith on his name.
And even after all this,
they shall consider him as a man and say that he hath a devil,
and shall scourge him and shall crucify him.

10 And he shall rise the third day from the dead;
and behold, he standeth to judge the world.
And behold, all these things are done
that a righteous judgment might come upon the children of men.

11 For behold, and also his blood atoneth for the sins of those
who have fallen by the transgression of Adam
who hath died not knowing the will of God concerning them
or who have ignorantly sinned.

12 But woe woe unto him who knoweth that he rebelleth against God;
for salvation cometh to none such
except it be through repentance and faith on the Lord Jesus Christ.

13 And the Lord God hath sent his holy prophets among all the children of men
to declare these things to every kindred, nation, and tongue,
that thereby whosoever should believe that Christ should come,
the same might receive remission of their sins
and rejoice with exceeding great joy,
even as though he had already come among them.

14 Yet the Lord God saw that his people were a stiffnecked people,
and he appointed unto them a law, even the law of Moses.

15 And many signs and wonders and types and shadows
shewed he unto them concerning his coming;
and also holy prophets spake unto them concerning his coming.

And yet they hardened their hearts and understood not
that the law of Moses availeth nothing
except it were through the atonement of his blood.

16 And even if it were possible that little children could sin,
they could not be saved.
But I say unto you:
They are blessed;
for behold, as in Adam or by nature they fall,
even so the blood of Christ atoneth for their sins.

17 And moreover I say unto you
that there shall be no other name given nor no other way nor means
whereby salvation can come unto the children of men,
only in and through the name of Christ the Lord Omnipotent.

18 For behold, he judgeth and his judgment is just.
And the infant perisheth not that dieth in his infancy,
but men drinketh damnation to their own souls
except they humble themselves and become as little children
and believeth that salvation was and is and is to come
in and through the atoning blood of Christ the Lord Omnipotent.

19 For the natural man is an enemy to God
and has been from the fall of Adam and will be forever and ever
but if he yieldeth to the enticings of the Holy Spirit
and putteth off the natural man
and becometh a saint through the atonement of Christ the Lord
and becometh as a child,
submissive, meek, humble, patient, full of love,
willing to submit to all things which the Lord seeth fit to inflict upon him,
even as a child doth submit to his father.

20 And moreover I say unto you
that the time shall come when the knowledge of a Savior shall spread
throughout every nation, kindred, tongue, and people.

21 And behold, when that time cometh,
none shall be found blameless before God,
except it be little children,
only through repentance and faith on the name of the Lord God Omnipotent.

22 And even at this time when thou shalt have taught thy people the things
which the Lord thy God hath commanded thee,
even then are they found no more blameless in the sight of God,
only according to the words which I have spoken unto thee.

23 And now I have spoken the words

which the Lord God hath commanded me.

24 And thus saith the Lord:
   They shall stand as a bright testimony against this people at the judgment day;
   whereof they shall be judged every man according to his works,
   whether they be good or whether they be evil.

25 And if they be evil,
   they are consigned to an awful view of their own guilt and abominations,
   which doth cause them to shrink from the presence of the Lord
   into a state of misery and endless torment,
   from whence they can no more return;
   therefore they have drunk damnation to their own souls.

26 Therefore they have drunk out of the cup of the wrath of God,
   which justice could no more deny unto them than it could deny
   that Adam should fall because of his partaking of the forbidden fruit;
   therefore mercy could have claim on them no more forever.

27 And their torment is as a lake of fire and brimstone
   whose flames are unquenchable
   and whose smoke ascendeth up forever and ever.
   Thus hath the Lord commanded me.
   Amen.

4 | 1 And now it came to pass that
   when king Benjamin had made an end of speaking the words
   which had been delivered unto him by the angel of the Lord
   that he cast his eyes round about on the multitude,
   and behold, they had fell to the earth,
   for the fear of the Lord had come upon them.

2 And they had viewed themselves in their own carnal state,
   even less than the dust of the earth,
   and they all cried aloud with one voice, saying:
   O have mercy and apply the atoning blood of Christ
   that we may receive forgiveness of our sins
   and our hearts may be purified,
   for we believe in Jesus Christ the Son of God,
   who created heaven and earth and all things,
   who shall come down among the children of men.

3 And it came to pass that after they had spoken these words,
   the Spirit of the Lord came upon them,
   and they were filled with joy,

having received a remission of their sins
and having peace of conscience because of the exceeding faith
which they had in Jesus Christ, which should come,
according to the words which king Benjamin had spoken unto them.

4 And king Benjamin again opened his mouth
and began to speak unto them, saying:
My friends and my brethren, my kindred and my people,
I would again call your attention,
that ye may hear and understand the remainder of my words
which I shall speak unto you.
5 For behold that if the knowledge of the goodness of God
at this time hath awakened you
to a sense of your nothingness and your worthless and fallen state—
6 I say unto you that
if ye have come to a knowledge of the goodness of God
and his matchless power and his wisdom and his patience
and his long-suffering towards the children of men,
and also the atonement which hath been prepared
from the foundation of the world,
that thereby salvation might come to him
that should put his trust in the Lord
and should be diligent in keeping his commandments
and continue in the faith, even unto the end of his life
—I mean the life of the mortal body—
7 I say that this is the man that receiveth salvation
through the atonement which was prepared from the foundation of the world
for all mankind which ever was, ever since the fall of Adam,
or which is or which ever shall be, even unto the end of the world.
8 And this is the means whereby salvation cometh.
And there is none other salvation save this which hath been spoken of;
neither is there any conditions whereby man can be saved
except the conditions which I have told you.

9 Believe in God!
Believe that he is and that he created all things, both in heaven and in earth;
believe that he hath all wisdom and all power, both in heaven and in earth;
believe that man doth not comprehend all the things
which the Lord can comprehend.
10 And again, believe that ye must repent of your sins and forsake them
and humble yourselves before God and ask in sincerity of heart
that he would forgive you.

And now if you believe all these things,
see that ye do them.

11   And again I say unto you, as I have said before,
that as ye have come to the knowledge of the glory of God
or if ye have known of his goodness and have tasted of his love
and have received a remission of your sins,
which causeth such exceeding great joy in your souls,
even so I would that ye should remember and always retain in remembrance
the greatness of God and your own nothingness
and his goodness and long-suffering towards you unworthy creatures,
and humble yourselves even in the depths of humility,
calling on the name of the Lord daily
and standing steadfastly in the faith of that which is to come,
which was spoken by the mouth of the angel.

12   And behold, I say unto you that if ye do this,
ye shall always rejoice and be filled with the love of God
and always retain a remission of your sins;
and ye shall grow in the knowledge of the glory of him that created you,
or in the knowledge of that which is just and true.

13   And ye will not have a mind to injure one another but to live peaceably,
and to render to every man according to that which is his due.

14   And ye will not suffer your children that they go hungry or naked,
neither will you suffer that they transgress the laws of God
and fight and quarrel one with another
and serve the devil, which is the master of sin,
or which is the evil spirit, which hath been spoken of by our fathers,
he being an enemy to all righteousness.

15   But ye will teach them to walk in the ways of truth and soberness;
ye will teach them to love one another and to serve one another.

16   And also, ye yourselves will succor those that stand in need of your succor;
ye will administer of your substance unto him that standeth in need,
and ye will not suffer that the beggar putteth up his petition to you in vain
and turn him out to perish.

17   Perhaps thou shalt say:
The man hath brought upon himself his misery;
therefore I will stay my hand and will not give unto him of my food,
nor impart unto him of my substance that he may not suffer,
for his punishments are just.

18   But I say unto you, O man:
Whosoever doeth this, the same hath great cause to repent;
and except he repenteth of that which he hath done,

he perisheth forever and hath no interest in the kingdom of God.

19 For behold, are we not all beggars?
Do we not all depend upon the same Being, even God,
for all the substance which we have,
for both food and raiment and for gold and for silver
and for all the riches which we have, of every kind?

20 And behold, even at this time ye have been calling on his name
and begging for a remission of your sins.
And hath he suffered that ye have begged in vain?
Nay, he hath poured out his Spirit upon you
and hath caused that your hearts should be filled with joy
and hath caused that your mouths should be stopped,
that ye could not find utterance,
so exceeding great was your joy.

21 And now if God, who hath created you,
on whom you are dependent for your lives and for all that ye have and are,
doth grant unto you whatsoever ye ask that is right,
in faith believing that ye shall receive,
O then how had ye ought to impart of the substance
that ye have one to another!

22 And if ye judge the man who putteth up his petition to you
for your substance that he perish not,
and condemn him,
how much more just will be your condemnation
for withholding your substance, which doth not belong to you but to God,
to whom also your life belongeth,
and yet ye put up no petition
or repenteth not of the thing which thou hast done.

23 I say unto you:
Woe be unto that man,
for his substance shall perish with him.
And now I say these things unto those which are rich
as pertaining to the things of this world.

24 And again I say unto the poor, ye that have not
and yet hath sufficient that ye remain from day to day
—I mean all you that deny the beggar because ye have not—
I would that ye say in your hearts
that I give not because I have not,
but if I had, I would give.

25 And now if ye say this in your hearts,
ye remain guiltless;

otherwise ye are condemned,
and your condemnation is just,
for ye covet that which ye have not received.

26 And now for the sake of these things which I have spoken unto you
— that is, for the sake of retaining a remission of your sins from day to day,
that ye may walk guiltless before God —
I would that ye should impart of your substance to the poor,
every man according to that which he hath,
such as feeding the hungry,
clothing the naked,
visiting the sick and administering to their relief,
both spiritually and temporally according to their wants.

27 And see that all these things are done in wisdom and order,
for it is not requisite that a man should run faster than what he hath strength.
And again, it is expedient that he should be diligent,
that thereby he might win the prize.
Therefore all things must be done in order.

28 And I would that ye should remember
that whosoever among you that borroweth of his neighbor
should return the thing that he borroweth,
according as he doth agree;
or else thou shalt commit sin,
and perhaps thou shalt cause thy neighbor to commit sin also.

29 And finally, I cannot tell you all the things whereby ye may commit sin;
for there are divers ways and means,
even so many that I cannot number them.

30 But this much I can tell you,
that if ye do not watch yourselves
and your thoughts and your words and your deeds
and observe to keep the commandments of God
and continue in the faith of what ye have heard
concerning the coming of our Lord,
even unto the end of your lives,
ye must perish.
And now O man, remember and perish not!

5 | 1 And now it came to pass that
when king Benjamin had thus spoken to his people,
he sent among them, desiring to know of his people

if they believed the words which he had spoken unto them.

2 And they all cried with one voice, saying:
    Yea, we believe all the words which thou hast spoken unto us.
    And also we know of their surety and truth
    because of the Spirit of the Lord Omnipotent,
    which hath wrought a mighty change in us or in our hearts,
    that we have no more disposition to do evil but to do good continually.

3 And we ourselves also through the infinite goodness of God
    and the manifestations of his Spirit
    have great views of that which is to come.
    And were it expedient, we could prophesy of all things.

4 And it is the faith which we have had on the things
    which our king hath spoken unto us
    and hath brought us to this great knowledge,
    whereby we do rejoice with such exceeding great joy.

5 And we are willing to enter into a covenant with our God
    to do his will and to be obedient to his commandments
    in all things that he shall command us
    all the remainder of our days,
    that we may not bring upon ourselves a never-ending torment
    as has been spoken by the angel,
    that we may not drink out of the cup of the wrath of God.

6 And now these are the words which king Benjamin desired of them.
    And therefore he said unto them:
    Ye have spoken the words that I desired,
    and the covenant which ye have made is a righteous covenant.

7 And now because of the covenant which ye have made,
    ye shall be called the children of Christ, his sons and his daughters;
    for behold, this day he hath spiritually begotten you,
    for ye say that your hearts are changed through faith on his name;
    therefore ye are born of him and have become his sons and his daughters.

8 And under this head ye are made free,
    and there is no other head whereby ye can be made free;
    there is no other name given whereby salvation cometh.
    Therefore I would that ye should take upon you the name of Christ,
    all you that have entered into the covenant with God
    that ye should be obedient unto the end of your lives.

9 And it shall come to pass that
    whosoever doeth this shall be found at the right hand of God,
    for he shall know the name by which he is called;
    for he shall be called by the name of Christ.

10 And now it shall come to pass that
    whosoever shall not take upon them the name of Christ
    must be called by some other name;
    therefore he findeth himself on the left hand of God.

11 And I would that ye should remember also
    that this is the name that I said I should give unto you
    that never should be blotted out except it be through transgression;
    therefore take heed that ye do not transgress,
    that the name be not blotted out of your hearts.

12 I say unto you:
    I would that ye should remember
    to retain the name written
    always in your hearts,
    that ye are not found on the left hand of God,
    but that ye hear and know the voice by which ye shall be called,
    and also the name by which he shall call you.

13 For how knoweth a man the master which he hath not served
    and which is a stranger unto him
    and is far from the thoughts and intents of his heart?

14 And again, doth a man take an ass
    which belongeth to his neighbor and keep him?
    I say unto you: Nay.
    He will not even suffer that he shall feed among his flocks,
    but will drive him away and cast him out.
    I say unto you that even so shall it be among you
    if ye know not the name by which ye are called.

15 Therefore I would that ye should be steadfast and immovable,
    always abounding in good works,
    that Christ the Lord God Omnipotent may seal you his,
    that you may be brought to heaven,
    that ye may have everlasting salvation and eternal life
    through the wisdom and power and justice and mercy of him
    who created all things in heaven and in earth,
    who is God above all.
    Amen.

6 | 1 And now king Benjamin thought it was expedient,
       after having finished speaking to the people,
       that he should take the names of all those
       who had entered into a covenant with God to keep his commandments.

2 And it came to pass that there was not one soul, except it were little children,
but what had entered into the covenant
and had taken upon them the name of Christ.

3 And again it came to pass that
when king Benjamin had made an end of all these things
and had consecrated his son Mosiah to be a ruler and a king over his people
and had given him all the charges concerning the kingdom
and also had appointed priests to teach the people,
that thereby they might hear and know the commandments of God,
and to stir them up in remembrance of the oath which they had made,
he dismissed the multitude,
and they returned every one according to their families to their own houses.

4 And Mosiah began to reign in his father's stead,
and he began to reign in the thirtieth year of his age,
making in the whole about four hundred and seventy six years
from the time that Lehi left Jerusalem.
5 And king Benjamin lived three years and he died.

6 And it came to pass that king Mosiah did walk in the ways of the Lord
and did observe his judgments and his statutes
and did keep his commandments in all things whatsoever he commanded him.
7 And king Mosiah did cause his people that they should till the earth,
and he also himself did till the earth,
that thereby he might not become burthensome to his people,
that he might do according to that which his father had done in all things.
And there was no contention among all his people for the space of three years.

7 | 1 And now it came to pass that
after king Mosiah had had continual peace for the space of three years,
he was desirous to know concerning the people
which went up to dwell in the land of Lehi-Nephi, or in the city of Lehi-Nephi,
for his people had heard nothing from them
from the time they left the land of Zarahemla;
therefore they wearied him with their teasings.
2 And it came to pass that king Mosiah granted
that sixteen of their strong men might go up to the land of Lehi-Nephi
to inquire concerning their brethren.

3 And it came to pass that on the morrow they started to go up,
having with them one Ammon,
he being a strong and mighty man and a descendant of Zarahemla;

and he was also their leader.

4 And now they knew not the course they should travel in the wilderness
to go up to the land of Lehi-Nephi;
therefore they wandered many days in the wilderness,
even forty days did they wander.

5 And when they had wandered forty days,
they came to a hill which is north of the land of Shilom,
and there they pitched their tents.

6 And Ammon took three of his brethren
—and their names were Amaleki, Helem, and Hem—
and they went down into the land of Nephi.

7 And behold, they met the king of the people
which was in the land of Nephi and in the land of Shilom;
and they were surrounded by the king's guard
and was taken and was bound and was committed to prison.

8 And it came to pass when they had been in prison two days,
they were again brought before the king
and their bands were loosed;
and they stood before the king
and was permitted—or rather commanded—
that they should answer the questions which he should ask them.

9 And he saith unto them:
Behold, I am Limhi the son of Noah, which was the son of Zeniff,
which came up out of the land of Zarahemla
to inherit this land which was the land of their fathers,
which was made a king by the voice of the people.

10 And now I desire to know the cause whereby ye were so bold
as to come near the walls of the city
when I myself was with my guards without the gate.

11 And now for this cause have I suffered that ye should be preserved,
that I might inquire of you;
or else I should have caused that my guards should have put you to death.
Ye are permitted to speak.

12 And now when Ammon saw that he was permitted to speak,
he went forth and bowed himself before the king;
and rising again, he said:
O king, I am very thankful before God this day
that I am yet alive and am permitted to speak.
And I will endeavor to speak with boldness;

13 for I am assured that if ye had known me,
ye would not have suffered that I should have wore these bands;

for I am Ammon and am a descendant of Zarahemla
and have come up out of the land of Zarahemla
to inquire concerning our brethren which Zeniff brought up out of that land.

14 And now it came to pass that
after Limhi had heard the words of Ammon,
he was exceeding glad and said:
Now I know of a surety
that my brethren which was in the land of Zarahemla are yet alive.
And now I will rejoice,
and on the morrow I will cause that my people shall rejoice also.
15 For behold, we are in bondage to the Lamanites
and are taxed with a tax which is grievous to be borne.
And now behold, our brethren will deliver us out of our bondage,
or out of the hands of the Lamanites.
And we will be their slaves,
for it is better that we be slaves to the Nephites
than to pay tribute to the king of the Lamanites.

16 And now king Limhi commanded his guards
that they should no more bind Ammon nor his brethren,
but caused that they should go to the hill which was north of Shilom
and bring their brethren into the city,
that thereby they might eat and drink
and rest themselves from the labors of their journey,
for they had suffered many things;
they had suffered hunger, thirst, and fatigue.

17 And now it came to pass on the morrow
that king Limhi sent a proclamation among all his people,
that thereby they might gather themselves together to the temple
to hear the words which he should speak unto them.
18 And it came to pass that when they had gathered themselves together
that he spake unto them in this wise, saying:
O ye my people, lift up your heads and be comforted;
for behold, the time is at hand—or is not far distant—
when we shall no longer be in subjection to our enemies;
notwithstanding our many strugglings which have been in vain,
yet I trust there remaineth an effectual struggle to be made.

19 Therefore lift up your heads and rejoice and put your trust in God,
in that God who was the God of Abraham and Isaac and Jacob,
and also that God who brought the children of Israel out of the land of Egypt
and caused that they should walk through the Red Sea on dry ground

and fed them with manna that they might not perish in the wilderness;
and many more things did he do for them.

20 And again, that same God hath brought our fathers
out of the land of Jerusalem
and hath kept and preserved his people even until now.
And behold, it is because of our iniquities and abominations
that has brought us into bondage.

21 And ye all are witnesses this day
that Zeniff, who was made king over this people,
he being overzealous to inherit the land of his fathers,
therefore being deceived by the cunning and craftiness of king Laman,
who having entered into a treaty with king Zeniff
and having yielded up into his hands the possessions of a part of the land,
or even the city of Lehi-Nephi and the city of Shilom
and the land round about—

22 and all this he done for the sole purpose
of bringing this people into subjection or into bondage.
And behold, we at this time do pay tribute to the king of the Lamanites
to the amount of one half of our corn and our barley,
and even all our grain of every kind,
and one half of the increase of our flocks and our herds;
and even one half of all we have or possess
the king of the Lamanites doth exact of us—or our lives.

23 And now, is not this grievious to be borne?
And is not this our afflictions great?

Now behold, how great reason have we to mourn!

24 Yea, I say unto you:
Great are the reasons which we have to mourn;
for behold, how many of our brethren have been slain
and their blood hath been spilt in vain—
and all because of iniquity!

25 For if this people had not fallen into transgression,
the Lord would not have suffered that this great evil should come upon them.
But behold, they would not hearken unto his words,
but there arose contentions among them,
even so much that they did shed blood among themselves.

26 And a prophet of the Lord have they slain—
yea, a chosen man of God
who told them of their wickedness and abominations
and prophesied of many things which is to come,
yea, even the coming of Christ.

27 And because he saith unto them
that Christ was the God the Father of all things
and saith that he should take upon him the image of man
and it should be the image after which man was created in the beginning
—or in other words, he said that man was created after the image of God
and that God should come down among the children of men
and take upon him flesh and blood
and go forth upon the face of the earth—
28 and now because he said this, they did put him to death.
And many more things did they do
which brought down the wrath of God upon them.

Therefore who wondereth that they are in bondage
and that they are smitten with sore afflictions!
29 For behold, the Lord hath said:
I will not succor my people in the day of their transgression,
but I will hedge up their ways, that they prosper not;
and their doings shall be as a stumbling block before them.
30 And again he saith:
If my people shall sow filthiness,
they shall reap the chaff thereof in the whirlwind;
and the effects thereof is poison.
31 And again he saith:
If my people shall sow filthiness,
they shall reap the east wind, which bringeth immediate destruction.

32 And now behold, the promise of the Lord is fulfilled,
and ye are smitten and afflicted.
33 But if ye will turn to the Lord with full purpose of heart
and put your trust in him and serve him with all diligence of mind—
and if ye do this,
he will, according to his own will and pleasure, deliver you out of bondage.

8 | 1 And it came to pass that
after king Limhi had made an end of speaking to his people
—for he spake many things unto them,
and only a few of them have I written in this book—
he told his people all the things concerning their brethren
which were in the land of Zarahemla.
2 And he caused that Ammon should stand up before the multitude
and rehearse unto them all that had happened unto their brethren
from the time that Zeniff went up out of the land
even until the time that he himself came up out of the land.
3 And he also rehearsed unto them the last words

which king Benjamin had taught them,
and explained them to the people of king Limhi,
so that they might understand all the words which he spake.

4 And it came to pass that after he had done all this
that king Limhi dismissed the multitude
and caused that they should return every one unto his own house.

5 And it came to pass that he caused that the plates
which contained the record of his people
from the time that they left the land of Zarahemla
should be brought before Ammon, that he might read them.

6 Now as soon as Ammon had read the record,
the king inquired of him to know if he could interpret languages.
And Ammon told him that he could not.

7 And the king saith unto him:
I being grieved for the afflictions of my people,
I caused that forty and three of my people
should take a journey into the wilderness,
that thereby they might find the land of Zarahemla,
that we might appeal unto our brethren to deliver us out of bondage.

8 And they were lost in the wilderness for the space of many days,
yet they were diligent and found not the land of Zarahemla
but returned to this land,
having traveled in a land among many waters,
having discovered a land which was covered with bones
of men and of beasts etc.,
and was also covered with ruins of buildings of every kind,
having discovered a land which had been peopled with a people
which were as numerous as the hosts of Israel.

9 And for a testimony that the things that they have said is true,
they have brought twenty four plates which are filled with engravings;
and they are of pure gold.

10 And behold also, they have brought breastplates which are large,
and they are of brass and of copper and are perfectly sound.

11 And again, they have brought swords;
the hilts thereof hath perished
and the blades thereof were cankered with rust.

And there is no one in the land that is able to interpret the language
or the engravings that are on the plates.
Therefore I said unto thee:
Canst thou translate?

12 And I say unto thee again:

Knowest thou of any one that can translate?
For I am desirous that these records should be translated into our language,
for perhaps they will give us a knowledge of a remnant of the people
which have been destroyed,
from whence these records came.
Or perhaps they will give us a knowledge of this very people
which hath been destroyed.
And I am desirous to know the cause of their destruction.

13 Now Ammon saith unto him:
I can assuredly tell thee, O king, of a man that can translate the records;
for he hath wherewith that he can look
and translate all records that are of ancient date,
and it is a gift from God.
And the things are called interpreters,
and no man can look in them except he be commanded,
lest he should look for that he had not ought and he should perish.
And whosoever is commanded to look in them, the same is called seer.
14 And behold, the king of the people which is in the land of Zarahemla
is the man that is commanded to do these things
and which hath this high gift from God.

15 And the king saith that a seer is greater than a prophet.
16 And Ammon saith that a seer is a revelator and a prophet also.
And a gift which is greater can no man have
except he should possess the power of God, which no man can;
yet a man may have great power given him from God.
17 But a seer can know of things which has passed,
and also of things which is to come;
and by them shall all things be revealed
—or rather shall secret things be made manifest—
and hidden things shall come to light,
and things which is not known shall be made known by them,
and also things shall be made known by them
which otherwise could not be known.
18 Thus God hath provided a means
that man through faith might work mighty miracles;
therefore he becometh a great benefit to his fellow beings.

19 And now when Ammon had made an end of speaking these words,
the king rejoiced exceedingly and gave thanks to God, saying:
Doubtless a great mystery is contained within these plates;
and these interpreters was doubtless prepared

for the purpose of unfolding all such mysteries to the children of men.
20 O how marvelous are the works of the Lord!
And how long doth he suffer with his people!
Yea, and how blind and impenetrable
are the understandings of the children of men,
for they will not seek wisdom,
neither do they desire that she should rule over them.
21 Yea, they are as a wild flock which fleeth from the shepherd and scattereth,
and are driven and are devoured by the beasts of the forest.

The Record of Zeniff

An account of his people from the time they left the land of Zarahemla
until the time that they were delivered out of the hands of the Lamanites.

9 | 1 I Zeniff having been taught in all the language of the Nephites
and having had a knowledge of the land of Nephi,
or of the land of our fathers' first inheritance,
and I having been sent as a spy among the Lamanites
that I might spy out their forces,
that our army might come upon them and destroy them —
but when I saw that which was good among them,
I was desirous that they should not be destroyed.
2 Therefore I contended with my brethren in the wilderness,
for I would that our ruler should make a treaty with them,
but he being an austere and a bloodthirsty man
commanded that I should be slain.
But I was rescued by the shedding of much blood,
for father fought against father and brother against brother
until the greatest number of our army was destroyed in the wilderness;
and we returned — those of us that were spared — to the land of Zarahemla
to relate that tale to their wives and their children.

3 And yet I being overzealous to inherit the land of our fathers
collected as many as were desirous to go up to possess the land
and started again on our journey into the wilderness to go up to the land;
but we were smitten with famine and sore affliction,
for we were slow to remember the Lord our God.
4 Nevertheless, after many days wandering in the wilderness,

we pitched our tents in the place where our brethren were slain,
which was near to the land of our fathers.

5 And it came to pass that
I went again with four of my men into the city in unto the king
that I might know of the disposition of the king
and that I might know if I might go in with my people
and possess the land in peace.
6 And I went in unto the king and he covenanted with me
that I might possess the land of Lehi-Nephi and the land of Shilom.
7 And he also commanded that his people should depart out of that land,
and I and my people went into the land that we might possess it.
8 And we began to build buildings and to repair the walls of the city,
yea, even the walls of the city of Lehi-Nephi and the city of Shilom.
9 And we began to till the ground,
yea, even with all manner of seeds:
with seeds of corn and of wheat and of barley
and with neas and with sheum
and with seeds of all manner of fruits.
And we did begin to multiply and prosper in the land.

10 Now it was the cunning and the craftiness of king Laman
to bring my people into bondage
that he yielded up the land that we might possess it.
11 Therefore it came to pass that
after we had dwelt in the land for the space of twelve years
that king Laman began to grow uneasy
lest by any means my people should wax strong in the land
and that they could not overpower them and bring them into bondage.
12 Now they were a lazy and an idolatrous people.
Therefore they were desirous to bring us into bondage
that they might glut themselves with the labors of our hands,
yea, that they might feast themselves upon the flocks of our fields.

13 Therefore it came to pass that king Laman began to stir up his people
that they should contend with my people;
therefore there began to be wars and contentions in the land.
14 For in the thirteenth year of my reign
in the land of Nephi, away on the south of the land of Shilom,
when my people were watering and feeding their flocks and tilling their lands,
a numerous host of Lamanites came upon them and began to slay them
and to take of their flocks and the corn of their fields.
15 Yea, and it came to pass that

they fled—all that were not overtaken—even into the city of Nephi
and did call upon me for protection.

16 And it came to pass that I did arm them with bows and with arrows,
with swords and with scimitars and with clubs and with slings,
and with all manner of weapons which we could invent.
And I and my people did go forth against the Lamanites to battle;

17 yea, in the strength of the Lord did we go forth to battle against the Lamanites.
For I and my people did cry mightily to the Lord
that he would deliver us out of the hands of our enemies,
for we were awakened to a remembrance of the deliverance of our fathers.

18 And God did hear our cries and did answer our prayers,
and we did go forth in his might;
yea, we did go forth against the Lamanites.
And in one day and a night we did slay three thousand and forty three;
we did slay them even until we had driven them out of our land.

19 And I myself with mine own hands did help bury their dead.
And behold, to our great sorrow and lamentation,
two hundred and seventy nine of our brethren were slain.

10 | 1 And it came to pass that we again began to establish the kingdom,
and we again began to possess the land in peace.
And I caused that there should be weapons of war made of every kind,
that thereby I might have weapons for my people
against the time the Lamanites should come up again to war against my people.

2 And I sat guards round about the land
that the Lamanites might not come upon us again unawares and destroy us.
And thus I did guard my people and my flocks
and keep them from falling into the hands of our enemies.

3 And it came to pass that we did inherit the land of our fathers for many years,
yea, for the space of twenty and two years.

4 And I did cause that the men should till the ground
and raise all manner of grain and all manner of fruit of every kind.

5 And I did cause that the women should spin and toil
and work all manner of fine linen,
yea, and cloth of every kind,
that we might clothe our nakedness.
And thus we did prosper in the land;
thus we did have continual peace in the land
for the space of twenty and two years.

6 And it came to pass that king Laman died,
and his son began to reign in his stead.

And he began to stir his people up in rebellion against my people.
Therefore they began to prepare for war
and to come up to battle against my people,

7 but I having sent my spies out round about the land of Shemlon
that I might discover their preparations, that I might guard against them,
that they might not come upon my people and destroy them.

8 And it came to pass that they came up
upon the north of the land of Shilom with their numerous hosts,
men armed with bows and with arrows
and with swords and with scimitars and with stones and with slings.
And they had their heads shaved that they were naked,
and they were girded about with a leathern girdle about their loins.

9 And it came to pass that I caused
that the women and children of my people should be hid in the wilderness.
And I also caused that all my old men that could bear arms
and also all my young men that were able to bear arms
should gather themselves together to go to battle against the Lamanites,
and I did place them in their ranks every man according to his age.

10 And it came to pass that we did go up to battle against the Lamanites;
and I, even I in my old age, did go up to battle against the Lamanites.
And it came to pass that we did go up in the strength of the Lord to battle.

11 Now the Lamanites knew nothing
concerning the Lord nor the strength of the Lord;
therefore they depended upon their own strength,
yet they were a strong people as to the strength of men.

12 They were a wild and ferocious and a bloodthirsty people,
believing in the tradition of their fathers, which is this:
believing that they were driven out of the land of Jerusalem
because of the iniquities of their fathers,
and that they were wronged in the wilderness by their brethren,
and they were also wronged while crossing the sea,

13 and again, that they were wronged while in the land of their first inheritance
after they had crossed the sea—
and all this because that Nephi was more faithful
in keeping the commandments of the Lord;
therefore he was favored of the Lord,
for the Lord heard his prayers and answered them;
and he took the lead of their journey in the wilderness.

14 And his brethren were wroth with him
because they understood not the dealings of the Lord.
They were also wroth with him upon the waters

because they hardened their hearts against the Lord.

15 And again, they were wroth with him
when they had arriven to the promised land
because they said that he had taken the ruling of the people out of their hands;
and they sought to kill him.

16 And again, they were wroth with him
because he departed into the wilderness as the Lord had commanded him
and took the records which were engraven on the plates of brass,
for they said that he robbed them.

17 And thus they have taught their children that they should hate them,
and that they should murder them,
and that they should rob and plunder them
and do all they could to destroy them.
Therefore they have an eternal hatred towards the children of Nephi.

18 For this very cause hath king Laman
by his cunning and lying craftiness and his fair promises hath deceived me,
that I have brought this my people up into this land,
that they may destroy them;
yea, and we have suffered this many years in the land.

19 And now I Zeniff,
after having told all these things unto my people concerning the Lamanites,
I did stimulate them to go to battle with their might,
putting their trust in the Lord.
Therefore we did contend with them face to face.

20 And it came to pass that we did drive them again out of our land;
and we slew them with a great slaughter,
even so many that we did not number them.

21 And it came to pass that we returned again to our own land,
and my people again began to tend their flocks and to till their ground.

22 And now I being old did confer the kingdom upon one of my sons;
therefore I say no more.
And may the Lord bless my people!
Amen.

⌒

11 | 1 And now it came to pass that
Zeniff conferred the kingdom upon Noah, one of his sons;
therefore Noah began to reign in his stead.
And he did not walk in the ways of his father;

2 for behold, he did not keep the commandments of God,
but he did walk after the desires of his own heart.
And he had many wives and concubines.

And he did cause his people to commit sin
and do that which was abominable in the sight of the Lord;
yea, and they did commit whoredoms and all manner of wickedness.

3 And he laid a tax of one fifth part of all they possessed:
a fifth part of their gold and of their silver,
and a fifth part of their ziff and of their copper and of their brass and their iron,
and a fifth part of their fatlings,
and also a fifth part of all their grain.

4 And all this did he take to support himself and his wives and his concubines,
and also his priests and their wives and their concubines.

Thus he had changed the affairs of the kingdom,
5 for he put down all the priests that had been consecrated by his father
and consecrated new ones in their stead
such as were lifted up in the pride of their hearts.

6 Yea, and thus were they supported in their laziness
and in their idolatry and in their whoredoms
by the taxes which king Noah had put upon his people.
Thus did the people labor exceedingly to support iniquity.

7 Yea, and they also became idolatrous
because they were deceived
by the vain and flattering words of the king and priests,
for they did speak flattering things unto them.

8 And it came to pass that
king Noah built many elegant and spacious buildings,
and he ornamented them with fine work of wood
and of all manner of precious things,
of gold and of silver and of iron and of brass and of ziff and of copper.

9 And he also built him a spacious palace and a throne in the midst thereof,
all of which was of fine wood
and was ornamented with gold and silver and with precious things.

10 And he also caused that his workmen should work
all manner of fine work within the walls of the temple,
of fine wood and of copper and of brass.

11 And the seats which was sat apart for the high priests,
which was above all the other seats,
he did ornament with pure gold.
And he caused a breastwork to be built before them
that they might rest their bodies and their arms upon
while they should speak lying and vain words to his people.

12 And it came to pass that he built a tower near the temple,
yea, a very high tower,

even so high that he could stand upon the top thereof
and overlook the land of Shilom
and also the land of Shemlon, which was possessed by the Lamanites;
and he could even look over all the land round about.

13 And it came to pass that he caused
many buildings to be built in the land Shilom.
And he caused a great tower to be built on the hill north of the land Shilom,
which had been a resort for the children of Nephi
at the time they fled out of the land.
And thus he did do with the riches
which he obtained by the taxation of his people.

14 And it came to pass that he placed his heart upon his riches,
and he spent his time in riotous living with his wives and his concubines;
and so did also his priests spend their time with harlots.

15 And it came to pass that he planted vineyards round about in the land,
and he built winepresses and made wine in abundance;
and therefore he became a winebibber, and also his people.

16 And it came to pass that the Lamanites began
to come in upon his people, upon small numbers,
and to slay them in their fields and while they were tending their flocks.

17 And king Noah sent guards round about the land to keep them off,
but he did not send a sufficient number;
and the Lamanites came upon them and killed them
and drove many of their flocks out of the land.
Thus the Lamanites began to destroy them
and to exercise their hatred upon them.

18 And it came to pass that king Noah sent his armies against them;
and they were driven back, or they drove them back for a time.
Therefore they returned rejoicing in their spoil.

19 And now because of this great victory
they were lifted up in the pride of their hearts;
they did boast in their own strength,
saying that their fifty could stand against thousands of the Lamanites.
And thus they did boast and did delight
in blood and the shedding of the blood of their brethren—
and this because of the wickedness of their king and priests.

20 And it came to pass that there was a man among them whose name was Abinadi;
and he went forth among them and began to prophesy, saying:
Behold, thus saith the Lord and thus hath he commanded me, saying:
Go forth and say unto this people:

Thus saith the Lord:
Woe be unto this people,
for I have seen their abominations and their wickedness and their whoredoms;
and except they repent, I will visit them in mine anger.

21 And except they repent and turn to the Lord their God,
behold, I will deliver them into the hands of their enemies;
yea, and they shall be brought into bondage,
and they shall be afflicted by the hand of their enemies.

22 And it shall come to pass that they shall know
that I am the Lord their God and am a jealous God,
visiting the iniquities of my people.

23 And it shall come to pass that
except this people repent and turn to the Lord their God,
they shall be brought into bondage;
and none shall deliver them except it be the Lord the Almighty God.

24 Yea, and it shall come to pass that
when they shall cry unto me,
I will be slow to hear their cries.
Yea, and I will suffer them that they be smitten by their enemies.

25 And except they repent in sackcloth and ashes
and cry mightily to the Lord their God,
I will not hear their prayers,
neither will I deliver them out of their afflictions.
And thus saith the Lord and thus hath he commanded me.

26 Now it came to pass that when Abinadi had spake these words unto them,
they were wroth with him and sought to take away his life;
but the Lord delivered him out of their hands.

27 Now when king Noah had heard of the words
which Abinadi had spake unto the people,
he was also wroth and he saith:
Who is Abinadi, that I and my people should be judged of him?
Or who is the Lord that shall bring upon my people such great affliction?

28 I command you to bring Abinadi hither that I may slay him,
for he hath said these things
that he might stir up my people to anger one with another
and to raise contentions among my people;
therefore I will slay him.

29 Now the eyes of the people were blinded;
therefore they hardened their hearts against the words of Abinadi,
and they sought from that time forward to take him.

And king Noah hardened his heart against the word of the Lord,
and he did not repent of his evil doings.

12 | 1 And it came to pass that after the space of two years
that Abinadi came among them in disguise,
that they knew him not,
and began again to prophesy among them, saying:
Thus hath the Lord commanded me, saying:
Abinadi, go and prophesy unto this my people,
for they have hardened their hearts against my words;
they have repented not of their evil doings.
Therefore I will visit them in my anger;
yea, in my fierce anger will I visit them in their iniquities and abominations;
2 yea, woe be unto this generation.
And the Lord said unto me:
Stretch forth thy hand and prophesy, saying:
Thus saith the Lord:
It shall come to pass that this generation because of their iniquities
shall be brought into bondage and shall be smitten on the cheek,
yea, and shall be driven by men and shall be slain.
And the vultures of the air and the dogs
—yea, and the wild beasts—
shall devour their flesh.
3 And it shall come to pass that
the life of king Noah shall be valued even as a garment in a hot furnace,
for he shall know that I am the Lord.

4 And it shall come to pass that
I will smite this my people with sore afflictions,
yea, with famine and with pestilence.
And I will cause that they shall howl all the day long.
5 Yea, and I will cause that they shall have burdens lashed upon their backs,
and they shall be driven before like a dumb ass.
6 And it shall come to pass that I will send forth hail among them,
and it shall smite them;
and they shall also be smitten with the east wind;
and insects shall pester their land also and devour their grain;
7 and they shall be smitten with a great pestilence.
And all this will I do because of their iniquities and abominations.

8 And it shall come to pass that except they repent,
I will utterly destroy them from off the face of the earth.
Yet they shall leave a record behind them,

and I will preserve them for other nations which shall possess the land.
Yea, even this will I do
that I may discover the abominations of this people to other nations.
And many things did Abinadi prophesy against this people.

9 And it came to pass that they were angry with him;
and they took him and carried him bound before the king
and saith unto the king:
Behold, we have brought a man before thee
which has prophesied evil concerning thy people
and saith that God will destroy them.
10 And he also prophesieth evil concerning thy life
and saith that thy life shall be as a garment in a furnace of fire.
11 And again, he saith that thou shall be as a stalk,
even as a dry stalk of the field,
which is ran over by the beasts and trodden under foot.
12 And again, he saith thou shalt be as the blossoms of a thistle,
which when it is fully ripe, if the wind bloweth,
it is driven forth upon the face of the land.
And he pretendeth the Lord hath spoken it.
And he saith all this shall come upon thee except thou repent—
and this because of thine iniquities.

13 And now, O king, what great evil hast thou done?
Or what great sins has thy people committed
that we should be condemned of God or judged of this man?
14 And now, O king, behold, we are guiltless.
And thou, O king, hast not sinned.
Therefore this man hath lied concerning you,
and he hath prophesied in vain.
15 And behold, we are strong;
we shall not come into bondage or be taken captive by our enemies.
Yea, and thou hast prospered in the land, and thou shalt also prosper.
16 Behold, here is the man.
We deliver him into thy hands.
Thou mayest do with him as seemeth thee good.

17 And it came to pass that king Noah caused
that Abinadi should be cast into prison.
And he commanded that the priests should gather themselves together
that he might hold a council with them what he should do with him.
18 And it came to pass that they saith unto the king:
Bring him hither that we may question him.
And the king commanded that he should be brought before them.

19 And they began to question him, that they might cross him,
   that thereby they might have wherewith to accuse him.
   But he answered them boldly and withstood all their questions
   —yea, to their astonishment—
   for he did withstand them in all their questions
   and did confound them in all their words.

20 And it came to pass that one of them saith unto him:
   What meaneth the words which are written
   and which have been taught by our fathers, saying:
21 How beautiful upon the mountains are the feet of him
   that bringeth good tidings,
   that publisheth peace,
   that bringeth good tidings of good,
   that publisheth salvation,
   that saith unto Zion:
   Thy God reigneth!
22 Thy watchmen shall lift up the voice;
   with the voice together shall they sing.
   For they shall see eye to eye when the Lord shall bring again Zion.
23 Break forth into joy!
   Sing together, ye waste places of Jerusalem!
   For the Lord hath comforted his people;
   he hath redeemed Jerusalem.
24 The Lord hath made bare his holy arm in the eyes of all the nations,
   and all the ends of the earth shall see the salvation of our God.

25 And now Abinadi saith unto them:
   Are you priests and pretend to teach this people
   and to understand the spirit of prophesying,
   and yet desireth to know of me what these things mean?
26 I say unto you:
   Woe be unto you for perverting the ways of the Lord!
   For if ye understand these things, ye have not taught them.
   Therefore ye have perverted the ways of the Lord.
27 Ye have not applied your hearts to understanding;
   therefore ye have not been wise.
   Therefore what teachest thou this people?
28 And they said:
   We teach the law of Moses.

29 And again he saith unto them:
   If ye teach the law of Moses,
   why do ye not keep it?

Why do ye set your hearts upon riches?
Why do ye commit whoredoms and spend your strength with harlots,
yea, and cause this people to commit sin,
that the Lord hath cause to send me to prophesy against this people?
—yea, even a great evil against this people.

30 Knowest thou not that I speak the truth?
Yea, thou knowest that I speak the truth;
and you had ought to tremble before God.

31 And it shall come to pass that ye shall be smitten for thine iniquities,
for ye have said that ye teach the law of Moses.
And what knowest thou concerning the law of Moses?
Doth salvation come by the law of Moses?
What sayest thou?

32 And they answered and said
that salvation did come by the law of Moses.

33 But now Abinadi saith unto them:
I know if ye keep the commandments of God, ye shall be saved—
yea, if ye keep the commandments
which the Lord delivered unto Moses in the mount of Sinai, saying:

34 I am the Lord thy God,
which have brought thee out of the land of Egypt,
out of the house of bondage.

35 Thou shalt have no other God before me.

36 Thou shalt not make unto thee any graven image,
or any likeness of any thing in the heaven above,
or things which is in the earth beneath.

37 Now Abinadi saith unto them:
Have ye done all this?
I say unto you:
Nay, ye have not.
And have ye taught this people that they should do all these things?
I say unto you:
Nay, ye have not.

13 | 1 And now when the king had heard these words,
he said unto his priests:
Away with this fellow and slay him!
For what have we to do with him?
—for he is mad!

2 And they stood forth and attempted to lay their hands on him,
but he withstood them and said unto them:

3 Touch me not!
  For God shall smite you if ye lay your hands upon me,
  for I have not delivered the message which the Lord sent me to deliver,
  neither have I told you that which ye requested that I should tell.
  Therefore God will not suffer that I shall be destroyed at this time.
4 But I must fulfill the commandments wherewith God hath commanded me.
  And because I have told you the truth, ye are angry with me.
  And again, because I have spoken the word of God,
  ye have judged me that I am mad.

5 Now it came to pass after Abinadi had spoken these words
  that the people of king Noah durst not lay their hands on him,
  for the Spirit of the Lord was upon him.
  And his face shone with exceeding luster even as Moses' did
  while in the mount of Sinai while speaking with the Lord.
6 And he spake with power and authority from God.
  And he continued his words, saying:
7 Ye see that ye have not power to slay me.
  Therefore I finish my message.
  Yea, and I perceive that it cuts you to your hearts
  because I tell you the truth concerning your iniquities.
8 Yea, and my words fill you with wonder and amazement and with anger.
9 But I finish my message,
  and then it matters not whither I go,
  if it so be that I am saved.
10 But this much I tell you:
  What you do with me after this
  shall be as a type and a shadow of things which is to come.

11 And now I read unto you the remainder of the commandments of God,
  for I perceive that they are not written in your hearts.
  I perceive that ye have studied and taught iniquity the most part of your lives.
12 And now ye remember that I said unto you:
  Thou shalt not make unto thee any graven image,
  or any likeness of things which is in heaven above,
  or which is in the earth beneath,
  or which is in the water under the earth.
13 And again, thou shalt not bow down thyself unto them nor serve them,
  for I the Lord thy God am a jealous God,
  visiting the iniquities of the fathers upon the children
  unto the third and fourth generation of them that hate me,
14 and shewing mercy unto thousands of them

that love me and keep my commandments.

15 Thou shalt not take the name of the Lord thy God in vain,
for the Lord will not hold him guiltless that taketh his name in vain.

16 Remember the sabbath day, to keep it holy.
17 Six days shalt thou labor and do all thy work;
18 but the seventh day, the sabbath of the Lord thy God,
thou shalt not do any work, thou nor thy son nor thy daughter,
thy manservant nor thy maidservant nor thy cattle
nor thy stranger that is within thy gates.
19 For in six days the Lord made heaven and earth and the sea
and all that in them is;
wherefore the Lord blessed the sabbath day and hallowed it.

20 Honor thy father and thy mother,
that thy days may be long upon the land
which the Lord thy God giveth thee.

21 Thou shalt not kill.
22 Thou shalt not commit adultery.
Thou shalt not steal.
23 Thou shalt not bear false witness against thy neighbor.
24 Thou shalt not covet thy neighbor's house;
thou shalt not covet thy neighbor's wife,
nor his manservant nor his maidservant nor his ox nor his ass,
nor any thing that is thy neighbor's.

25 And it came to pass that
after Abinadi had made an end of these sayings
that he said unto them:
Have ye taught this people that they should observe to do all these things,
for to keep these commandments?
26 I say unto you: Nay.
For if ye had,
the Lord would not have caused me to come forth
and to prophesy evil concerning this people.

27 And now ye have said that salvation cometh by the law of Moses.
I say unto you that it is expedient that ye should keep the law of Moses as yet;
but I say unto you that the time shall come
when it shall no more be expedient to keep the law of Moses.
28 And moreover I say unto you

that salvation doth not come by the law alone.
And were it not for the atonement
which God himself shall make for the sins and iniquities of his people
that they must unavoidably perish,
notwithstanding the law of Moses.

29 And now I say unto you that it was expedient
that there should be a law given to the children of Israel,
yea, even a very strict law.
For they were a stiffnecked people,
quick to do iniquity and slow to remember the Lord their God.

30 Therefore there was a law given them,
yea, a law of performances and of ordinances,
a law which they were to observe strictly from day to day
to keep them in remembrance of God and their duty towards him.

31 But behold, I say unto you that all these things were types of things to come.

32 And now, did they understand the law?
I say unto you:
Nay, they did not all understand the law —
and this because of the hardness of their hearts.
For they understood not that there could not any man be saved
except it were through the redemption of God.

33 For behold, did not Moses prophesy unto them
concerning the coming of the Messiah
and that God should redeem his people?
Yea, and even all the prophets
which have prophesied ever since the world began,
have they not spoken more or less concerning these things?

34 Have they not said
that God himself should come down among the children of men
and take upon him the form of man
and go forth in mighty power upon the face of the earth?

35 Yea, and have they not said also
that he should bring to pass the resurrection of the dead
and that he himself should be oppressed and afflicted?

14 | 1 Yea, even doth not Isaiah say:
Who hath believed our report?
And to whom is the arm of the Lord revealed?

2 For he shall grow up before him
as a tender plant and as a root out of dry ground.
He hath no form nor comeliness.

And when we shall see him,
there is no beauty that we should desire him.

3 He is despised and rejected of men,
a man of sorrows and acquainted with grief.
And we hid, as it were, our faces from him.
He was despised and we esteemed him not.

4 Surely he hath borne our griefs and carried our sorrows.
Yet we did esteem him stricken,
smitten of God and afflicted.

5 But he was wounded for our transgressions.
He was bruised for our iniquities.
The chastisement of our peace was upon him,
and with his stripes we are healed.

6 All we like sheep have gone astray.
We have turned every one to his own way.
And the Lord hath laid on him the iniquities of us all.

7 He was oppressed and he was afflicted,
yet he opened not his mouth.
He is brought as a lamb to the slaughter;
and as a sheep before her shearers is dumb,
so he opened not his mouth.

8 He was taken from prison and from judgment.
And who shall declare his generation?
For he was cut off out of the land of the living.
For the transgressions of my people was he stricken.

9 And he made his grave with the wicked,
and with the rich in his death —
because he had done no evil,
neither was any deceit in his mouth.

10 Yet it pleased the Lord to bruise him.
He hath put him to grief.

When thou shalt make his soul an offering for sin,
he shall see his seed.
He shall prolong his days,
and the pleasure of the Lord shall prosper in his hand.

11 He shall see of the travail of his soul and shall be satisfied.
By his knowledge shall my righteous servant justify many,
for he shall bear their iniquities.

12 Therefore will I divide him a portion with the great,
and he shall divide the spoil with the strong —
because he hath poured out his soul unto death
and he was numbered with the transgressors.

And he bare the sins of many
and made intercession for the transgressors.

15 | 1 And now Abinadi saith unto them:
I would that ye should understand
that God himself shall come down among the children of men
and shall redeem his people.

2 And because he dwelleth in flesh,
he shall be called the Son of God;
and having subjected the flesh to the will of the Father,
being the Father and the Son,

3 the Father because he was conceived by the power of God
and the Son because of the flesh,
thus becoming the Father and Son

4 —and they are one God,
yea, the very Eternal Father of heaven and of earth—

5 and thus the flesh becoming subject to the spirit,
or the Son to the Father, being one God,
suffereth temptation and yieldeth not to the temptation,
but suffereth himself to be mocked and scourged
and cast out and disowned by his people.

6 And after all this
and after working many mighty miracles among the children of men,
he shall be led
—yea, even as Isaiah said,
as a sheep before the shearer is dumb,
so he opened not his mouth—

7 yea, even so he shall be led, crucified, and slain,
the flesh becoming subject even unto death,
the will of the Son being swallowed up in the will of the Father.

8 And thus God breaketh the bands of death,
having gained the victory over death,
giving the Son power to make intercession for the children of men,

9 having ascended into heaven,
having the bowels of mercy,
being filled with compassion toward the children of men,
standing betwixt them and justice,
having broken the bands of death,
having taken upon himself their iniquity and their transgressions,
having redeemed them and satisfied the demands of justice.

10 And now I say unto you:
Who shall declare his generation?

Behold, I say unto you that
when his soul has been made an offering for sin,
he shall see his seed.
And now, what say ye?
And who shall be his seed?

11 Behold, I say unto you that
whosoever hath heard the words of the prophets,
yea, all the holy prophets which have prophesied
concerning the coming of the Lord,
I say unto you that all those who hath hearkened unto their words
and believed that the Lord would redeem his people
and have looked forward to that day for a remission of their sins,
I say unto you that these are his seed —
or they are heirs of the kingdom of God.

12 For these are they whose sins he hath borne;
these are they for whom he hath died,
to redeem them from their transgressions.
And now, are they not his seed?

13 Yea, and are not the prophets,
every one that has opened his mouth to prophesy
that has not fallen into transgression
—I mean all the holy prophets ever since the world began—
I say unto you that they are his seed.

14 And these are they which hath published peace,
that hath brought good tidings of good,
that hath published salvation,
that saith unto Zion:
Thy God reigneth!

15 And O how beautiful upon the mountains were their feet!

16 And again, how beautiful upon the mountains are the feet of those
that are still publishing peace!

17 And again, how beautiful upon the mountains are the feet of those
who shall hereafter publish peace,
yea, from this time henceforth and forever!

18 And behold, I say unto you:
This is not all,
for O how beautiful upon the mountains are the feet of him
that bringeth good tidings,
that is the founder of peace,
yea, even the Lord who hath redeemed his people,
yea, him who hath granted salvation unto his people.

19 For were it not for the redemption which he hath made for his people,
which was prepared from the foundation of the world,
I say unto you
—were it not for this—
that all mankind must have perished.

20 But behold, the bands of death shall be broken.
And the Son reigneth and hath power over the dead;
therefore he bringeth to pass the resurrection of the dead.

21 And there cometh a resurrection,
even a first resurrection,
yea, even a resurrection of those
that have been and which are and which shall be,
even until the resurrection of Christ,
for so shall he be called.

22 And now the resurrection of all the prophets
and all those that have believed in their words
—or all those that have kept the commandments of God—
these shall come forth in the first resurrection;
therefore they are the first resurrection.

23 They are raised to dwell with God, who hath redeemed them.
Thus they have eternal life through Christ,
who hath broken the bands of death.

24 And there are those who have part in the first resurrection,
and these are they that have died before Christ came,
in their ignorance,
not having salvation declared unto them.
And thus the Lord bringeth about the restoration of these,
and they have a part in the first resurrection or hath eternal life,
being redeemed by the Lord.

25 And little children also hath eternal life.

26 But behold and fear and tremble before God
—for ye had ought to tremble—
for the Lord redeemeth none such
that rebelleth against him and dieth in their sins
—yea, even all those that have perished in their sins,
ever since the world began—
that have willfully rebelled against God,
that have known the commandments of God and would not keep them.
These are they that have no part in the first resurrection.

27 Therefore had ye not ought to tremble?

For salvation cometh to none such,
for the Lord hath redeemed none such.
Yea, neither can the Lord redeem such,
for he cannot deny himself;
for he cannot deny justice when it hath its claim.

28 And now I say unto you that the time shall come
that the salvation of the Lord shall be declared
to every nation, kindred, tongue, and people.

29 Yea, Lord, thy watchmen shall lift up their voice;
with the voice together shall they sing.
For they shall see eye to eye when the Lord shall bring again Zion.

30 Break forth into joy!
Sing together, ye waste places of Jerusalem!
For the Lord hath comforted his people;
he hath redeemed Jerusalem.

31 The Lord hath made bare his holy arm in the eyes of all the nations,
and all the ends of the earth shall see the salvation of our God.

16 | 1 And now it came to pass that after Abinadi had spoken these words,
he stretched forth his hands and said:
The time shall come when all shall see the salvation of the Lord,
when every nation, kindred, tongue, and people shall see eye to eye
and shall confess before God that his judgments are just.

2 And then shall the wicked be cast out,
and they shall have cause to howl and weep and wail and gnash their teeth—
and this because they would not hearken unto the voice of the Lord.
Therefore the Lord redeemeth them not.

3 For they are carnal and devilish;
and the devil hath power over them,
yea, even that old serpent that did beguile our first parents,
which was the cause of their fall,
which was the cause of all mankind's becoming carnal, sensual, devilish,
knowing evil from good,
subjecting themselves to the devil.

4 Thus all mankind were lost.
And behold, they would have been endlessly lost
were it not that God redeemed his people from their lost and fallen state.

5 But remember that he that persists in his own carnal nature
and goes on in the ways of sin and rebellion against God,
he remaineth in his fallen state,
and the devil hath all power over him.
Therefore he is as though there was no redemption made,

being an enemy to God;
and also is the devil an enemy to God.

6 And now if Christ had not come into the world
—speaking of things to come as though they had already come—
there could have been no redemption.

7 And if Christ had not risen from the dead
or broken the bands of death
—that the grave should have no victory
and that death should have no sting—
there could have been no resurrection.

8 But there is a resurrection.
Therefore the grave hath no victory,
and the sting of death is swallowed up in Christ.

9 He is the light and the life of the world,
yea, a light that is endless that can never be darkened;
yea, and also a life which is endless, that there can be no more death.

10 Even this mortal shall put on immortality,
and this corruption shall put on incorruption
and shall be brought to stand before the bar of God
to be judged of him according to their works,
whether they be good or whether they be evil:

11 if they be good, to the resurrection of endless life and happiness;
and if they be evil, to the resurrection of endless damnation,
being delivered up to the devil,
who hath subjected them—which is damnation—

12 having gone according to their own carnal wills and desires,
having never called upon the Lord
while the arms of mercy was extended towards them
—for the arms of mercy was extended towards them and they would not—
they being warned of their iniquities,
and yet they would not depart from them.
And they were commanded to repent,
and yet they would not repent.

13 And now had ye not ought to tremble and repent of your sins?
—and remember, only in and through Christ ye can be saved.

14 Therefore if ye teach the law of Moses,
also teach that it is a shadow of those things which are to come.

15 Teach them that redemption cometh through Christ the Lord,
which is the very Eternal Father.
Amen.

17 | 1 And now it came to pass that when Abinadi had finished these sayings
that the king commanded that the priests should take him
and cause that he should be put to death.

2 But there was one among them whose name was Alma,
he also being a descendant of Nephi,
and he was a young man.
And he believed the words which Abinadi had spoken,
for he knew concerning the iniquity which Abinadi had testified against them.
Therefore he began to plead with the king
that he would not be angry with Abinadi
but suffer that he might depart in peace.

3 But the king was more wroth and caused
that Alma should be cast out from among them
and sent his servants after him that they might slay him.

4 But he fled from before them and hid himself that they found him not.
And he being concealed for many days
did write all the words which Abinadi had spoken.

5 And it came to pass that the king caused
that his guards should surround Abinadi and take him;
and they bound him and cast him into prison.

6 And after three days, having counseled with his priests,
he caused that he should again be brought before him.

7 And he said unto him:
Abinadi, we have found an accusation against thee,
and thou art worthy of death.

8 For thou hast said that
God himself should come down among the children of men.
And now for this cause thou shalt be put to death
unless thou wilt recall all the words
which thou hast spoken evil concerning me and my people.

9 Now Abinadi saith unto him:
I say unto you:
I will not recall the words
which I have spoken unto you concerning this people,
for they are true.
And that ye may know of their surety,
I have suffered myself that I have fallen into your hands.

10 Yea, and I will suffer even unto death.
And I will not recall my words,
and they shall stand as a testimony against you.

And if ye slay me, ye will shed innocent blood.
And this shall also stand as a testimony against you at the last day.

11 And now king Noah was about to release him, for he feared his word;
for he feared that the judgments of God would come upon him.
12 But the priests lifted up their voices against him
and began to accuse him, saying:
He hath reviled the king!
Therefore the king was stirred up in anger against him,
and he delivered him up that he might be slain.

13 And it came to pass that they took him and bound him
and scorched his skin with fagots,
yea, even unto death.
14 And now when the flames began to scorch him,
he cried unto them, saying:
15 Behold, even as ye have done unto me,
so shall it come to pass that
thy seed shall cause that many shall suffer the pains that I do suffer,
even the pains of death by fire—
and this because they believe in the salvation of the Lord their God.
16 And it will come to pass that
ye shall be afflicted with all manner of diseases because of your iniquities.
17 Yea, and ye shall be smitten on every hand
and shall be driven and scattered to and fro,
even as a wild flock is driven by wild and ferocious beasts.
18 And in that day ye shall be hunted,
and ye shall be taken by the hand of your enemies.
And then ye shall suffer as I suffer the pains of death by fire.
19 Thus God executeth vengeance upon those that destroy his people.
O God, receive my soul!

20 And now when Abinadi had said these words,
he fell, having suffered death by fire,
yea, having been put to death
because he would not deny the commandments of God,
having sealed the truth of his words by his death.

18 | 1 And now it came to pass that
Alma, who had fled from the servants of king Noah,
repented of his sins and iniquities
and went about privately among the people
and began to teach the words of Abinadi,

2 yea, concerning that which was to come,
and also concerning the resurrection of the dead,
and the redemption of the people which was to be brought to pass
through the power and sufferings and death of Christ
and his resurrection and ascension into heaven.

3 And as many as would hear his word he did teach;
and he taught them privately,
that it might not come to the knowledge of the king.
And many did believe his words.

4 And it came to pass that
as many as did believe him did go forth to a place which was called Mormon,
having received its name from the king,
being in the borders of the land,
having been infested by times or at seasons by wild beasts.

5 Now there was in Mormon a fountain of pure water;
and Alma resorted thither,
there being near the water a thicket of small trees
where he did hide himself in the daytime from the searches of the king.

6 And it came to pass that
as many as believed him went thither to hear his words.

7 And it came to pass after many days
there were a goodly number gathered together
to the place of Mormon to hear the words of Alma;
yea, all were gathered together that believed on his word to hear him.
And he did teach them and did preach unto them
repentance and redemption and faith on the Lord.

8 And it came to pass that he said unto them:
Behold, here is the waters of Mormon,
for thus were they called.
And now as ye are desirous to come into the fold of God
and to be called his people
and are willing to bear one another's burdens,
that they may be light,

9 yea, and are willing to mourn with those that mourn,
yea, and comfort those that stand in need of comfort,
and to stand as witnesses of God at all times and in all things
and in all places that ye may be in,
even until death,
that ye may be redeemed of God
and be numbered with those of the first resurrection,
that ye may have eternal life—

10 now I say unto you,
  if this be the desires of your hearts,
  what have you against being baptized in the name of the Lord,
  as a witness before him
  that ye have entered into a covenant with him,
  that ye will serve him and keep his commandments,
  that he may pour out his Spirit more abundantly upon you?

11 And now when the people had heard these words,
  they clapped their hands for joy and exclaimed:
  This is the desires of our hearts!
12 And now it came to pass that Alma took Helam,
  he being one of the first,
  and went and stood forth in the water and cried, saying:
  O Lord, pour out thy Spirit upon thy servant,
  that he may do this work with holiness of heart.
13 And when he had said these words,
  the Spirit of the Lord was upon him and he said:
  Helam, I baptize thee,
  having authority from the Almighty God,
  as a testimony that ye have entered into a covenant to serve him
  until you are dead as to the mortal body;
  and may the Spirit of the Lord be poured out upon you,
  and may he grant unto you eternal life through the redemption of Christ,
  which he hath prepared from the foundation of the world.

14 And after Alma had said these words,
  both Alma and Helam was buried in the water.
  And they arose and came forth out of the water rejoicing,
  being filled with the Spirit.
15 And again Alma took another
  and went forth a second time into the water
  and baptized him according to the first,
  only he did not bury himself again in the water.
16 And after this manner he did baptize every one
  that went forth to the place of Mormon
  —and they were in number about two hundred and four souls—
  yea, and they were baptized in the waters of Mormon
  and were filled with the grace of God.
17 And they were called the church of God, or the church of Christ,
  from that time forward.
  And it came to pass that

whosoever was baptized by the power and authority of God,
they was added to his church.

18 And it came to pass that Alma having authority from God ordained priests,
even one priest to every fifty of their number
did he ordain to preach unto them
and to teach them concerning the things pertaining to the kingdom of God.
19 And he commanded them that they should teach nothing
save it were the things which he had taught
and which had been spoken by the mouth of the holy prophets.
20 Yea, even he commanded them that they should preach nothing
save it were repentance and faith on the Lord, who hath redeemed his people.
21 And he commanded them that there should be no contention one with another,
but that they should look forward with one eye,
having one faith and one baptism,
having their hearts knit together in unity and in love one towards another.
22 And thus he commanded them to preach.
And thus they became the children of God.

23 And he commanded them
that they should observe the sabbath day and keep it holy,
and also every day they should give thanks to the Lord their God.
24 And he also commanded them that the priests which he had ordained
should labor with their own hands for their support.
25 And there was one day in every week that was set apart
that they should gather themselves together to teach the people
and to worship the Lord their God,
and also as often as it was in their power to assemble themselves together.
26 And the priests was not to depend upon the people for their support,
but for their labor they were to receive the grace of God,
that they might wax strong in the Spirit,
having the knowledge of God,
that they might teach with power and authority from God.

27 And again Alma commanded
that the people of the church should impart of their substance,
every one according to that which he hath:
if he have more abundantly, he should impart more abundantly;
and he that hath but little, but little should be required;
and to him that hath not should be given.
28 And thus they should impart of their substance
of their own free will and good desires towards God
to those priests that stood in need,
yea, and to every needy, naked soul.

29 And this he said unto them,
    having been commanded of God.
    And they did walk uprightly before God,
    imparting to one another both temporally and spiritually
    according to their needs and their wants.

30 And now it came to pass that all this was done in Mormon,
    yea, by the waters of Mormon,
    in the forest that was near the waters of Mormon,
    yea, the place of Mormon, the waters of Mormon, the forest of Mormon.
    How beautiful are they to the eyes of them
    who there came to the knowledge of their Redeemer!
    Yea, and how blessed are they, for they shall sing to his praise forever.

31 And these things were done in the borders of the land
    that they might not come to the knowledge of the king.
32 But behold, it came to pass that
    the king having discovered a movement among the people
    sent his servants to watch them.
    Therefore on the day that they were assembling themselves together
    to hear the word of the Lord,
    they were discovered unto the king.

33 And now the king saith
    that Alma was a stirring up the people to a rebellion against him.
    Therefore he sent his army to destroy them.
34 And it came to pass that Alma and the people of the Lord
    were apprised of the coming of the king's army.
    Therefore they took their tents and their families
    and departed into the wilderness.
35 And they were in number about four hundred and fifty souls.
19 | 1 And it came to pass that the army of the king returned,
    having searched in vain for the people of the Lord.

2 And now behold, the forces of the king were small, having been reduced.
   And there began to be a division among the remainder of the people.
3 And the lesser part began to breathe out threatenings against the king,
   and there began to be a great contention among them.
4 And now there was a man among them whose name was Gideon.
   And he being a strong man and an enemy to the king,
   therefore he drew his sword and swore in his wrath
   that he would slay the king.
5 And it came to pass that he fought with the king.
   And when the king saw that he was about to overpower him,

he fled and ran and got upon the tower which was near the temple.

6 And Gideon pursued after him
and was about to get upon the tower to slay the king.
And the king cast his eyes round about towards the land of Shemlon —
and behold, the army of the Lamanites were within the borders of the land!

7 And now the king cried out in the anguish of his soul, saying:
Gideon, spare me!
For the Lamanites are upon us and they will destroy them —
yea, they will destroy my people.
8 And now the king was not so much concerned about his people
as he was about his own life.
Nevertheless Gideon did spare his life.

9 And the king commanded the people
that they should flee before the Lamanites,
and he himself did go before them.
And they did flee into the wilderness with their women and their children.
10 And it came to pass that the Lamanites did pursue them
and did overtake them and began to slay them.
11 Now it came to pass that the king commanded them
that all the men should leave their wives and their children
and flee before the Lamanites.
12 Now there were many that would not leave them
but had rather stay and perish with them.
And the rest left their wives and their children and fled.

13 And it came to pass that
those that tarried with their wives and their children caused
that their fair daughters should stand forth and plead with the Lamanites
that they would not slay them.
14 And it came to pass that the Lamanites had compassion on them,
for they were charmed with the beauty of their women.
15 Therefore the Lamanites did spare their lives and took them captives
and carried them back to the land of Nephi and granted unto them
that they might possess the land under the conditions
that they would deliver up the king Noah into the hands of the Lamanites
and deliver up their property,
even one half of all they possessed:
one half of their gold and their silver and all their precious things.
And thus they should pay tribute to the king of the Lamanites from year to year.

16 And now there was one of the sons of the king
among those that was taken captive

whose name was Limhi.

17 And now Limhi was desirous that his father should not be destroyed.
Nevertheless Limhi was not ignorant of the iniquities of his father,
he himself being a just man.

18 And it came to pass that Gideon sent men into the wilderness secretly
to search for the king and those that was with him.
And it came to pass that they met the people in the wilderness,
all save the king and his priests.

19 Now they had sworn in their hearts
that they would return to the land of Nephi;
and if their wives and their children were slain,
and also those that had tarried with them,
that they would seek revenge and also perish with them.

20 And the king commanded them that they should not return,
and they were angry with the king
and caused that he should suffer even unto death by fire.

21 And they were about to take the priests also to put them to death,
and they fled before them.

22 And it came to pass that
they were about to return to the land of Nephi,
and they met the men of Gideon.
And the men of Gideon told them
of all that had happened to their wives and their children
and that the Lamanites had granted unto them
that they might possess the land
by paying a tribute to the Lamanites of one half of all they possessed.

23 And the people told the men of Gideon that they had slain the king,
and his priests had fled from them farther into the wilderness.

24 And it came to pass that after they had ended the sermon
that they returned to the land of Nephi,
rejoicing because their wives and their children were not slain;
and they told Gideon what they had done to the king.

25 And it came to pass that the king of the Lamanites made an oath unto them
that his people should not slay them.

26 And also Limhi, being the son of the king,
having the kingdom conferred upon him by the people,
made oath unto the king of the Lamanites
that his people should pay tribute unto him,
even one half of all they possessed.

27 And it came to pass that Limhi began to establish the kingdom

and to establish peace among his people.

28 And the king of the Lamanites set guards round about the land,
that he might keep the people of Limhi in the land,
that they might not depart into the wilderness.
And he did support his guards out of the tribute
which he did receive from the Nephites.

29 And now king Limhi did have continual peace
in his kingdom for the space of two years,
that the Lamanites did not molest them nor seek to destroy them.

20 | 1 Now there was a place in Shemlon
where the daughters of the Lamanites did gather themselves together
for to sing and to dance and to make themselves merry.

2 And it came to pass that there was one day
a small number of them gathered together to sing and to dance.

3 And now the priests of king Noah
being ashamed to return to the city of Nephi,
yea, and also fearing that the people would slay them,
therefore they durst not return to their wives and their children.

4 And having tarried in the wilderness
and having discovered the daughters of the Lamanites,
they laid and watched them.

5 And when there were but few of them gathered together to dance,
they came forth out of their secret places
and took them and carried them into the wilderness,
yea, twenty and four of the daughters of the Lamanites
they carried into the wilderness.

6 And it came to pass that when the Lamanites found
that their daughters had been missing,
they were angry with the people of Limhi;
for they thought it was the people of Limhi.

7 Therefore they sent their armies forth
— yea, even the king himself went before his people —
and they went up to the land of Nephi to destroy the people of Limhi.

8 And now Limhi had discovered them from the tower,
even all their preparations for war did he discover.
Therefore he gathered his people together
and laid wait for them in the fields and in the forests.

9 And it came to pass that when the Lamanites had come up
that the people of Limhi began to fall upon them from their waiting places
and began to slay them.

10 And it came to pass that the battle became exceeding sore,
for they fought like lions for their prey.
11 And it came to pass that
the people of Limhi began to drive the Lamanites before them.
Yet they were not half so numerous as the Lamanites,
but they fought for their lives and for their wives and for their children.
Therefore they exerted themselves and like dragons did they fight.

12 And it came to pass that they found the king of the Lamanites
among the number of their dead,
yet he was not dead,
having been wounded and left upon the ground,
so speedy was the flight of his people.
13 And they took him and bound up his wounds
and brought him before Limhi and said:
Behold, here is the king of the Lamanites;
he having received a wound hath fallen among their dead,
and they have left him.
And behold, we have brought him before you.
And now let us slay him!
14 But Limhi saith unto them:
Ye shall not slay him but bring him hither that I may see him.
And they brought him, and Limhi saith unto him:
What cause have ye to come up to war against my people?
Behold, my people have not broken the oath that I made unto you.
Therefore why should ye break the oath which ye made unto my people?
15 And now the king said:
I have broken the oath
because thy people did carry away the daughters of my people.
Therefore in my anger I did cause my people
to come up to war against thy people.
16 Now Limhi had heard nothing concerning this matter.
Therefore he saith:
I will search among my people;
and whosoever hath done this thing shall perish.
Therefore he caused a search to be made among his people.

17 Now when Gideon had heard these things,
he being the king's captain,
he went forth and said unto the king:
I pray thee forbear and do not search this people;
and lay not this thing to their charge.

18 For do ye not remember the priests of thy father,
which this people sought to destroy?
And are they not in the wilderness?
And is it not they which have stolen the daughters of the Lamanites?

19 And now behold and tell the king of these things,
that he may tell his people, that they may be pacified towards us.
For behold, they are already preparing to come against us.
And behold also, there are but few of us.

20 And behold, they come with their numerous hosts;
and except the king doth pacify them towards us, we must perish.

21 For are not the words of Abinadi fulfilled which he prophesied against us—
and all this because we would not hearken unto the word of the Lord
and turn from our iniquities?

22 And now let us pacify the king,
and we fulfill the oath which we have made unto him.
For it is better that we should be in bondage
than that we should lose our lives.
Therefore let us put a stop to the shedding of so much blood.

23 And now Limhi told the king all the things
concerning his father and the priests that had fled into the wilderness
and attributed the carrying away of their daughters to them.

24 And it came to pass that the king was pacified towards his people,
and he said unto them:
Let us go forth to meet my people without arms;
and I swear unto you with an oath
that my people shall not slay thy people.

25 And it came to pass that they followed the king
and went forth without arms to meet the Lamanites.
And it came to pass that they did meet the Lamanites,
and the king of the Lamanites did bow himself down before them
and did plead in behalf of the people of Limhi.

26 And when the Lamanites saw the people of Limhi
that they were without arms,
that they had compassion on them and were pacified towards them
and returned with their king in peace to their own land.

21 | 1 And it came to pass that Limhi and his people returned to the city of Nephi
and began to dwell in the land again in peace.

2 And it came to pass that after many days
the Lamanites began again to be stirred up in anger against the Nephites,
and they began to come into the borders of the land round about.

3 Now they durst not slay them because of the oath
   which their king had made unto Limhi,
   but they would smite them on their cheeks
   and exercise authority over them
   and began to put heavy burdens upon their backs
   and drive them as they would a dumb ass.
4 Yea, all this was done that the word of the Lord might be fulfilled.
5 And now the afflictions of the Nephites was great.
   And there was no way that they could deliver themselves out of their hands,
   for the Lamanites had surrounded them on every side.

6 And it came to pass that
   the people began to murmur with the king because of their afflictions.
   And they began to be desirous to go against them to battle,
   and they did afflict the king sorely with their complaints.
   Therefore he granted unto them that they should do according to their desires.
7 And they gathered themselves together again and put on their armor
   and went forth against the Lamanites to drive them out of their land.
8 And it came to pass that the Lamanites did beat them
   and drove them back and slew many of them.
9 And now there was a great mourning and lamentation
   among the people of Limhi,
   the widow a mourning for her husband,
   the son and the daughter a mourning for their father,
   and the brothers for their brethren.
10 Now there were a great many widows in the land,
   and they did cry mightily from day to day,
   for a great fear of the Lamanites had come upon them.

11 And it came to pass that
   their continual cries did stir up the remainder of the people of Limhi
   to anger against the Lamanites.
   And they went again to battle,
   but they were driven back again,
   suffering much loss.
12 Yea, they went again, even the third time,
   and suffered in the like manner.
   And those that were not slain returned again to the city of Nephi.
13 And they did humble themselves even to the dust,
   subjecting themselves to the yoke of bondage,
   submitting themselves to be smitten
   and to be driven to and fro and burdened
   according to the desires of their enemies.

14 And they did humble themselves even in the depths of humility.
And they did cry mightily to God,
yea, even all the day long did they cry unto their God
that he would deliver them out of their afflictions.

15 And now the Lord was slow to hear their cry because of their iniquities.
Nevertheless the Lord did hear their cries
and began to soften the hearts of the Lamanites,
that they began to ease their burdens.
Yet the Lord did not see fit to deliver them out of bondage.

16 And it came to pass that they began to prosper by degrees in the land
and began to raise grain more abundantly and flocks and herds,
that they did not suffer with hunger.

17 Now there was a great number of women, more than there was of men.
Therefore king Limhi commanded
that every man should impart to the support of the widows and their children,
that they might not perish with hunger.
And this they did because of the greatness of their number that had been slain.

18 Now the people of Limhi kept together in a body
as much as it was possible
to secure their grain and their flocks.

19 And the king himself did not trust his person without the walls of the city
unless he took his guards with him,
fearing that he might by some means fall into the hands of the Lamanites.

20 And he caused that his people should watch the land round about,
that by some means they might take those priests that fled into the wilderness,
which had stolen the daughters of the Lamanites,
and that had caused such a great destruction to come upon them.

21 For they were desirous to take them that they might punish them,
for they had come into the land of Nephi by night
and carried off of their grain and many of their precious things.
Therefore they laid wait for them.

22 And it came to pass that there was no more disturbance
between the Lamanites and the people of Limhi,
even until the time that Ammon and his brethren came into the land.

23 And the king having been without the gates of the city with his guard,
he discovered Ammon and his brethren;
and supposing them to be priests of Noah,
therefore he caused that they should be taken and bound and cast into prison.
And had they been the priests of Noah,
he would have caused that they should be put to death.

24 But when he found that they were not,

but that they were his brethren and had come from the land of Zarahemla,
he was filled with exceeding great joy.

25 Now king Limhi had sent previous to the coming of Ammon
a small number of men to search for the land of Zarahemla,
but they could not find it;
and they were lost in the wilderness.

26 Nevertheless they did find a land which had been peopled,
yea, a land which was covered with dry bones,
yea, a land which had been peopled and which had been destroyed.
And they having supposed it to be the land of Zarahemla
returned to the land of Nephi,
having arrived in the borders of the land
not many days before the coming of Ammon.

27 And they brought a record with them,
even a record of the people whose bones they had found;
and they were engraven on plates of ore.

28 And now Limhi was again filled with joy
on learning from the mouth of Ammon
that king Benjamin had a gift from God
whereby he could interpret such engravings
yea, and Ammon also did rejoice.

29 Yet Ammon and his brethren were filled with sorrow
because so many of his brethren had been slain,

30 and also that king Noah and his priests had caused the people
to commit so many sins and iniquities against God.
And they also did mourn for the death of Abinadi
and also for the departure of Alma and the people that went with him,
who had formed a church of God
through the strength and power of God
and faith on the words which had been spoken by Abinadi.

31 Yea, they did mourn for their departure,
for they knew not whither they had fled.
Now they would have gladly joined with them,
for they themselves had entered into a covenant with God
to serve him and keep his commandments.

32 And now since the coming of Ammon,
king Limhi had also entered into a covenant with God,
and also many of his people,
to serve him and keep his commandments.

33 And it came to pass that
king Limhi and many of his people was desirous to be baptized,

but there was none in the land that had authority from God.
And Ammon declined doing this thing,
considering himself an unworthy servant.

34 Therefore they did not at that time form themselves into a church,
waiting upon the Spirit of the Lord.
Now they were desirous to become even as Alma and his brethren,
which had fled into the wilderness.

35 They were desirous to be baptized as a witness and a testimony
that they were willing to serve God with all their hearts.
Nevertheless they did prolong the time;
and an account of their baptism shall be given hereafter.

36 And now all the study of Ammon and his people and king Limhi and his people
was to deliver themselves out of the hands of the Lamanites and from bondage.

22 | 1 And now it came to pass that
Ammon and king Limhi began to consult with the people
how they should deliver themselves out of bondage.
And even they did cause that all the people should gather themselves together;
and this they did that they might have
the voice of the people concerning the matter.

2 And it came to pass that they could find no way
to deliver themselves out of bondage
except it were to take their women and children
and their flocks and their herds and their tents
and depart into the wilderness,
for the Lamanites being so numerous
that it was impossible for the people of Limhi to contend with them,
thinking to deliver themselves out of bondage by the sword.

3 Now it came to pass that
Gideon went forth and stood before the king and said unto him:
Now, O king, thou hast hitherto hearkened unto my words many times
when we have been contending with our brethren the Lamanites.

4 And now, O king, if thou hast not found me to be an unprofitable servant,
or if thou hast hitherto listened to my words in any degree
and they have been of service to thee,
even so I desire that thou wouldst listen to my words at this time;
and I will be thy servant and deliver this people out of bondage.

5 And the king granted unto him that he might speak,
and Gideon saith unto him:

6 Behold the back pass through the back wall on the back side of the city.
The Lamanites, or the guards of the Lamanites, by night are drunken.
Therefore let us send a proclamation among all this people
that they gather together their flocks and herds,
that they may drive them into the wilderness by night.

7 And I will go according to thy command
and pay the last tribute of wine to the Lamanites,
and they will be drunken;
and we will pass through the secret pass on the left of their camp
when they are drunken and asleep.

8 Thus we will depart
with our women and our children, our flocks and our herds,
into the wilderness;
and we will travel around the land of Shilom.

9 And it came to pass that the king hearkened unto the words of Gideon.

10 And it came to pass that king Limhi caused
that his people should gather their flocks together.
And he sent the tribute of wine to the Lamanites;
and he also sent more wine as a present unto them,
and they did drink freely of the wine
which king Limhi did send unto them.

11 And it came to pass that the people of king Limhi did depart by night
into the wilderness with their flocks and their herds.
And they went round about the land of Shilom in the wilderness
and bent their course towards the land of Zarahemla,
being led by Ammon and his brethren.

12 And they had taken all their gold and silver
and their precious things which they could carry,
and also their provisions,
with them into the wilderness,
and they pursued their journey.

13 And after being many days in the wilderness,
they arrived in the land of Zarahemla,
and joined his people and became his subjects.

14 And it came to pass that Mosiah received them with joy,
and he also received their records and also the records
which had been found by the people of Limhi.

15 And now it came to pass when the Lamanites had found
that the people of Limhi had departed out of the land by night
that they sent an army into the wilderness to pursue them.

16 And after they had pursued them two days,
    they could no longer follow their tracks;
    therefore they were lost in the wilderness.

―――

An account of Alma and the people of the Lord,
which was driven into the wilderness by the people of king Noah.

23 | 1 Now Alma having been warned of the Lord
       that the armies of king Noah would come upon them
       and had made it known to his people,
       therefore they gathered together their flocks and took of their grain
       and departed into the wilderness before the armies of king Noah.
    2 And the Lord did strengthen them,
       that the people of king Noah could not overtake them to destroy them.
    3 And it came to pass that
       they fled eight days' journey into the wilderness;
    4 and they came to a land,
       yea, even a very beautiful and pleasant land,
       a land of pure water.
    5 And it came to pass that they pitched their tents
       and began to till the ground and began to build buildings etc.;
       yea, they were industrious and did labor exceedingly.

    6 And it came to pass that the people were desirous
       that Alma should be their king,
       for he was beloved by his people.
    7 But he saith unto them:
       Behold, it is not expedient that we should have a king,
       for thus saith the Lord:
       Ye shall not esteem one flesh above another,
       or one man shall not think himself above another.
       Therefore I say unto you:
       It is not expedient that ye should have a king;
    8 nevertheless, if it were possible
       that ye could always have just men to be your kings,
       it would be well for you to have a king—
    9 but remember the iniquity of king Noah and his priests.
       And I myself was caught in a snare
       and did many things which was abominable in the sight of the Lord,
       which caused me sore repentance.

10 Nevertheless, after much tribulation the Lord did hear my cries
and did answer my prayers
and hath made me an instrument in his hands
in bringing so many of you to a knowledge of his truth.
11 Nevertheless in this I do not glory,
for I am unworthy to glory of myself.

12 And now I say unto you:
As you have been oppressed by king Noah
and have been in bondage to him and his priests
and have been brought into iniquity by them,
therefore ye were bound with the bands of iniquity.
13 And now as ye have been delivered by the power of God out of these bonds,
yea, even out of the hands of king Noah and his people,
and also from the bonds of iniquity,
even so I desire that ye should stand fast in this liberty
wherewith ye have been made free
and that ye trust no man to be a king over you —
14 and also trusting no one to be your teachers nor your ministers
except he be a man of God,
walking in his ways and keeping his commandments.
15 Thus did Alma teach his people,
that every man should love his neighbor as himself,
that there should be no contention among them.

16 And now Alma was their high priest,
he being the founder of their church.
17 And it came to pass that
none received authority to preach or to teach
except it were by him from God;
therefore he consecrated all their priests and all their teachers,
and none were consecrated except it were just men.
18 Therefore they did watch over their people
and did nourish them with things pertaining to righteousness.

19 And it came to pass that
they began to prosper exceedingly in the land,
and they called the land Helam.
20 And it came to pass that
they did multiply and prosper exceedingly in the land of Helam.
And they built a city which they called the city of Helam.
21 Nevertheless the Lord seeth fit to chasten his people;
yea, he trieth their patience and their faith.

22 Nevertheless, whosoever putteth his trust in him,
    the same shall be lifted up at the last day;
    yea, and thus it was with this people.
23 For behold, I will shew unto you
    that they were brought into bondage,
    and none could deliver them but the Lord their God,
    yea, even the God of Abraham and of Isaac and of Jacob.
24 And it came to pass that he did deliver them;
    and he did shew forth his mighty power unto them,
    and great was their rejoicings.

25 For behold, it came to pass that
    while they were in the land of Helam,
    yea, in the city of Helam,
    while tilling the land round about,
    behold, an army of the Lamanites were in the borders of the land.
26 Now it came to pass that the brethren of Alma fled from their fields
    and gathered themselves together into the city of Helam,
    and they were much frightened because of the appearance of the Lamanites.
27 But Alma went forth and stood among them
    and exhorted them that they should not be frightened,
    but that they should remember the Lord their God
    and he would deliver them.
28 Therefore they hushed their fears
    and began to cry unto the Lord
    that he would soften the hearts of the Lamanites,
    that they would spare them and their wives and children.
29 And it came to pass that the Lord did soften the hearts of the Lamanites.
    And Alma and his brethren went forth
    and delivered themselves up into their hands,
    and the Lamanites took possession of the land of Helam.

30 Now the armies of the Lamanites,
    which had followed after the people of king Limhi,
    had been lost in the wilderness for many days.
31 And behold, they had found those priests of king Noah
    in a place which they called Amulon,
    and they had began to possess the land of Amulon
    and had began to till the ground.
32 Now the name of the leader of those priests was Amulon.
33 And it came to pass that Amulon did plead with the Lamanites,
    and he also sent forth their wives,
    which was the daughters of the Lamanites,

to plead with their brethren
that they should not destroy their husbands.

34 And it came to pass that
the Lamanites had compassion on Amulon and his brethren
and did not destroy them because of their wives.

35 And Amulon and his brethren did join the Lamanites,
and they were traveling in the wilderness in search of the land of Nephi
when they discovered the land of Helam,
which was possessed by Alma and his brethren.

36 And it came to pass that the Lamanites promised unto Alma and his brethren
that if they would shew them the way which led to the land of Nephi
that they would grant unto them their lives and their liberty.

37 But it came to pass that
after Alma had shewn them the way that led to the land of Nephi,
the Lamanites would not keep their promise,
but they set guards round about the land of Helam over Alma and his brethren.

38 And the remainder of them went to the land of Nephi;
and a part of them returned to the land of Helam
and also brought with them the wives and the children of the guards
which had been left in the land.

39 And the king of the Lamanites had granted unto Amulon
that he should be a king and a ruler over his people
which was in the land of Helam;
nevertheless he should have no power to do any thing
contrary to the will of the king of the Lamanites.

24 | 1 And it came to pass that Amulon did gain favor
in the eyes of the king of the Lamanites;
therefore the king of the Lamanites granted unto him and his brethren
that they should be appointed teachers over his people,
yea, even over the people
which was in the land of Shemlon and the land of Shilom,
and in the land of Amulon.

2 For the Lamanites had taken possession of all these lands;
therefore the king of the Lamanites had appointed kings over all these lands.

3 And now the name of the king of the Lamanites was Laman,
being called after the name of his father;
and therefore he was called king Laman.
And he was king over a numerous people.

4 And he appointed teachers of the brethren of Amulon
in every land which was possessed by his people.

And thus the language of Nephi began to be taught
among all the people of the Lamanites.

5 And they were a people friendly one with another.
Nevertheless they knew not God;
neither did the brethren of Amulon teach them any thing
concerning the Lord their God,
neither the law of Moses,
nor did they teach them the words of Abinadi.

6 But they taught them that they should keep their record
and that they might write one to another.

7 And thus the Lamanites began to increase in riches
and began to trade one with another and wax great
and began to be a cunning and a wise people as to the wisdom of the world,
yea, a very cunning people,
delighting in all manner of wickedness and plunder,
except it were among their own brethren.

8 And now it came to pass that
Amulon began to exercise authority over Alma and his brethren
and began to persecute him
and cause that his children should persecute their children.

9 For Amulon knew Alma,
that he had been one of the king's priests
and that it was he that believed the words of Abinadi
and was driven out before the king,
and therefore he was wroth with him;
for he was subject to king Laman,
yet he exercised authority over them
and put tasks upon them and put taskmasters over them.

10 And it came to pass that so great was their afflictions
that they began to cry mightily to God.

11 And it came to pass that Amulon commanded them
that they should stop their cries
and put guards over them to watch them,
that whosoever should be found calling upon God should be put to death.

12 And it came to pass that
Alma and his people did not raise their voices to the Lord their God
but did pour out their hearts to him;
and he did know the thoughts of their hearts.

13 And it came to pass that
the voice of the Lord came to them in their afflictions, saying:

Lift up your heads and be of good comfort,
for I know of the covenant which ye have made unto me.
And I will covenant with this my people and deliver them out of bondage.

14 And I will also ease the burdens which is put upon your shoulders,
that even you cannot feel them upon your backs,
even while you are in bondage.
And this will I do that ye may stand as witnesses for me hereafter,
and that ye may know of a surety
that I the Lord God do visit my people in their afflictions.

15 And now it came to pass that
the burdens which was laid upon Alma and his brethren were made light;
yea, the Lord did strengthen them
that they could bear up their burdens with ease,
and they did submit cheerfully and with patience to all the will of the Lord.

16 And it came to pass that so great was their faith and their patience
that the voice of the Lord came unto them again, saying:
Be of good comfort,
for on the morrow I will deliver thee out of bondage.

17 And he saith unto Alma:
Thou shalt go before this people,
and I will go with thee and deliver this people out of bondage.

18 Now it came to pass that
Alma and his people in the nighttime gathered their flocks together
and also of their grain,
yea, even all the nighttime were they gathering their flocks together.

19 And in the morning the Lord caused a deep sleep to come upon the Lamanites;
yea, and all their taskmasters were in a profound sleep.

20 And it came to pass that Alma and his people departed into the wilderness.
And when they had traveled all day, they pitched their tents in a valley;
and they called the name of the valley Alma
because he led their way in the wilderness.

21 Yea, and in the valley of Alma they poured out their thanks to God
because he had been merciful unto them
and eased their burdens and had delivered them out of bondage;
for they were in bondage and none could deliver them
except it were the Lord their God.

22 And they gave thanks to God;
yea, all their men and all their women and all their children that could speak
lifted their voices in the praises of their God.

23 And now the Lord said unto Alma:
Haste thee and get thou and this people out of this land,

for the Lamanites have awoke and doth pursue thee.
Therefore get thee out of this land;
and I will stop the Lamanites in this valley,
that they come no further in pursuit of this people.

24 And it came to pass that they departed out of the valley
and took their journey into the wilderness.

25 And it came to pass that after they had been in the wilderness twelve days,
they arrived to the land of Zarahemla;
and king Mosiah did also receive them with joy.

25 | 1 And now king Mosiah caused that all the people should be gathered together.

2 Now there were not so many of the children of Nephi,
or so many of those which were descendants of Nephi,
as there were of the people of Zarahemla,
which was a descendant of Muloch
and those which came with him into the wilderness.

3 And there were not so many
of the people of Nephi and of the people of Zarahemla
as there was of the Lamanites;
yea, they were not half so numerous.

4 And now all the people of Nephi was assembled together,
and also all the people of Zarahemla;
and they were gathered together in two bodies.

5 And it came to pass that Mosiah did read
and caused to be read the records of Zeniff to his people;
yea, he read the records of the people of Zeniff
from the time they left the land of Zarahemla until the time they returned again.

6 And he also read the account of Alma and his brethren and all their afflictions.
And he also read the account of Ammon and his brethren and all their afflictions
from the time they left the land of Zarahemla until the time they returned again.

7 And now when Mosiah had made an end of reading the records,
his people which tarried in the land was struck with wonder and amazement,

8 for they knew not what to think.
For when they beheld those that had been delivered out of bondage,
they were filled with exceeding great joy.

9 And again, when they thought of their brethren
which had been slain by the Lamanites,
they were filled with sorrow and even shed many tears of sorrow.

10 And again, when they thought of the immediate goodness of God
and his power in delivering Alma and his brethren
out of the hands of the Lamanites and of bondage,
they did raise their voices and gave thanks to God.

11 And again, when they thought upon the Lamanites,
    which was their brethren,
    of their sinful and polluted state,
    they were filled with pain and anguish for the welfare of their souls.

12 And it came to pass that
    when those which were the children of Amulon and his brethren,
    which had taken to wife the daughters of the Lamanites
    —they were displeased with the conduct of their fathers
    and they would no longer be called by the names of their fathers—
    therefore they took upon themselves the name of Nephi,
    that they might be called the children of Nephi
    and be numbered among those which were called Nephites.
13 And now all the people of Zarahemla were numbered with the Nephites—
    and this because the kingdom had been conferred upon none
    but those which were descendants of Nephi.

14 And now it came to pass that
    when Mosiah had made an end of speaking and reading to the people,
    he desired that Alma should also speak to the people.
15 And it came to pass that Alma did speak unto them
    when they were assembled together in large bodies;
    and he went from one body to another,
    preaching unto the people repentance and faith on the Lord.
16 And he did exhort the people of Limhi and his brethren
    —all those that had been delivered out of bondage—
    that they should remember that it was the Lord that did deliver them.

17 And it came to pass that
    after Alma had taught the people many things
    and had made an end of speaking to them
    that king Limhi was desirous that he might be baptized.
    And all his people were desirous that they might be baptized also.
18 Therefore Alma did go forth into the water and did baptize them;
    yea, he did baptize them
    after the manner he did his brethren in the waters of Mormon.
    Yea, and as many as he did baptize did belong to the church of God—
    and this because of their belief on the words of Alma.

19 And it came to pass that king Mosiah granted unto Alma
    that he might establish churches throughout all the land of Zarahemla,
    and gave him power to ordain priests and teachers over every church.
20 Now this was done because there was so many people
    that they could not be all governed by one teacher,

neither could they all hear the word of God in one assembly.

21 Therefore they did assemble themselves together in different bodies,
being called churches,
every church having their priests and their teachers,
and every priest preaching the word
according as it was delivered to him by the mouth of Alma.

22 And thus notwithstanding there being many churches,
they were all one church,
yea, even the church of God;
for there was nothing preached in all the churches
except it were repentance and faith in God.

23 And now there was seven churches in the land of Zarahemla.
And it came to pass that
whosoever was desirous to take upon them the name of Christ or of God,
they did join the churches of God;

24 and they were called the people of God.
And the Lord did pour out his Spirit upon them,
and they were blessed and prospered in the land.

26 | 1 Now it came to pass that there was many of the rising generation
that could not understand the words of king Benjamin,
being little children at the time he spake unto his people;
and they did not believe the tradition of their fathers.

2 They did not believe what had been said
concerning the resurrection of the dead,
neither did they believe concerning the coming of Christ.

3 And now because of their unbelief
they could not understand the word of God;
and their hearts were hardened.

4 And they would not be baptized,
neither would they join the church.
And they were a separate people as to their faith and remained so ever after,
even in their carnal and sinful state,
for they would not call upon the Lord their God.

5 And now in the reign of Mosiah
they were not half so numerous as the people of God,
but because of the dissensions among the brethren
they became more numerous.

6 For it came to pass that
they did deceive many with their flattering words
which were in the church
and did cause them to commit many sins.
Therefore it became expedient

that those who committed sin that was in the church
should be admonished by the church.

7 And it came to pass that they were brought before the priests
and delivered up unto the priests by the teachers;
and the priests brought them before Alma, which was the high priest

8 —now king Mosiah had given Alma the authority over the church—

9 and it came to pass that Alma did know concerning them,
for there were many witnesses against them;
yea, the people stood and testified of their iniquity in abundance.

10 Now there had not any such thing happened before in the church.
Therefore Alma was troubled in his spirit,
and he caused that they should be brought before the king.

11 And he saith unto the king:
Behold, here are many which we have brought before thee
which are accused of their brethren.
Yea, and they have been taken in divers iniquities,
and they do not repent of their iniquities.
Therefore we have brought them before thee,
that thou may judge them according to their crimes.

12 But king Mosiah saith unto Alma:
Behold, I judge them not.
Therefore I deliver them into thy hands to be judged.

13 And now the spirit of Alma was again troubled.
And he went and inquired of the Lord what he should do concerning this matter,
for he feared that he should do wrong in the sight of God.

14 And it came to pass that after he had poured out his whole soul to God,
the voice of the Lord came to him, saying:

15 Blessed art thou Alma.
And blessed are they which were baptized in the waters of Mormon.
Thou art blessed because of thy exceeding faith
in the words alone of my servant Abinadi.

16 And blessed are they because of their exceeding faith
in the words alone which thou hast spoken unto them.

17 And blessed art thou because thou hast established a church among this people.
And they shall be established, and they shall be my people.

18 Yea, blessed is this people, which is willing to bear my name;
for in my name shall they be called, and they are mine.

19 And because thou hast inquired of me concerning the transgressor,
thou art blessed.

20 Thou art my servant,
and I covenant with thee that thou shalt have eternal life.

And thou shalt serve me and go forth in my name
and shall gather together my sheep.

21 And he that will hear my voice shall be my sheep;
and him shall ye receive into the church,
and him will I also receive.

22 For behold, this is my church.
Whosoever that is baptized shall be baptized unto repentance;
and whosoever ye receive shall believe in my name,
and him will I freely forgive.

23 For it is I that taketh upon me the sins of the world,
for it is I that hath created them.
And it is I that granteth unto him that believeth
in the end a place at my right hand.

24 For behold, in my name are they called;
and if they know me,
they shall come forth and shall have a place eternally at my right hand.

25 And it shall come to pass that when the second trump shall sound,
then shall they that never knew me come forth
and shall stand before me.

26 And then shall they know that I am the Lord their God,
that I am their Redeemer,
but they would not be redeemed.

27 And then will I confess unto them that I never knew them,
and they shall depart into everlasting fire prepared for the devil and his angels.

28 Therefore I say unto you
that he that will not hear my voice,
the same shall ye not receive into my church,
for him I will not receive at the last day.

29 Therefore I say unto you: Go;
and whosoever transgresseth against me,
him shall ye judge according to the sins which he hath committed.
And if he confess his sins before thee and me
and repenteth in the sincerity of his heart,
him shall ye forgive;
and I will forgive him also.

30 Yea, and as often as my people repent
will I forgive them their trespasses against me.

31 And ye shall also forgive one another your trespasses.
For verily I say unto you:
He that forgiveth not his neighbor's trespasses when he saith that he repenteth,
the same hath brought himself under condemnation.

32 Now I say unto you: Go;
and whosoever will not repent of his sins,
the same shall not be numbered among my people.
And this shall be observed from this time forward.

33 And it came to pass,
when Alma had heard these words,
he wrote them down
that he might have them
and that he might judge the people of that church
according to the commandments of God.
34 And it came to pass that Alma went
and judged those that had been taken in iniquity,
according to the word of the Lord.
35 And whosoever repented of their sins and did confess them,
them he did number among the people of the church.
36 And them that would not confess their sins and repent of their iniquity,
the same were not numbered among the people of the church;
and their names were blotted out.

37 And it came to pass that Alma did regulate all the affairs of the church.
And they began again to have peace
and to prosper exceedingly in the affairs of the church,
walking circumspectly before God,
receiving many and baptizing many.
38 And now all these things did Alma and his fellow laborers do
which were over the church,
walking in all diligence,
teaching the word of God in all things,
suffering all manner of afflictions,
being persecuted by all those who did not belong to the church of God.
39 And they did admonish their brethren;
and they were also admonished every one by the word of God
according to his sins or to the sins which he had committed,
being commanded of God to pray without ceasing
and to give thanks in all things.

27 | 1 And now it came to pass that
the persecutions which was inflicted on the church by the unbelievers
became so great
that the church began to murmur
and complain to their leaders concerning the matter;
and they did complain to Alma.

And Alma laid the case before their king Mosiah,
and Mosiah consulted with his priests.

2 And it came to pass that
king Mosiah sent a proclamation throughout the land round about
that there should not any unbeliever persecute any of those
which belonged to the church of God.

3 And there was a strict command throughout all the churches
that there should be no persecutions among them,
that there should be an equality among all men,

4 that they should let no pride nor haughtiness disturb their peace,
that every man should esteem his neighbor as himself,
laboring with their own hands for their support.

5 Yea, and all their priests and teachers should labor with their own hands
for their support in all cases save it were in sickness or in much want;
and doing these things, they did abound in the grace of God.

6 And there began to be much peace again in the land.
And the people began to be very numerous
and began to scatter abroad upon the face of the earth,
yea, on the north and on the south, on the east and on the west,
building large cities and villages in all quarters of the land.

7 And the Lord did visit them and prosper them,
and they became a large and a wealthy people.

8 Now the sons of Mosiah was numbered among the unbelievers;
and also one of the sons of Alma was numbered among them,
he being called Alma after his father.
Nevertheless he became a very wicked and an idolatrous man;
and he was a man of many words and did speak much flattery to the people.
Therefore he led many of the people to do after the manner of his iniquities.

9 And he became a great hinderment to the prosperity of the church of God,
stealing away the hearts of the people,
causing much dissension among the people,
giving a chance for the enemy of God to exercise his power over them.

10 And now it came to pass that
while he was going about to destroy the church of God
—for he did go about secretly with the sons of Mosiah,
seeking to destroy the church
and to lead astray the people of the Lord
contrary to the commandments of God or even the king—

11 and as I said unto you,
as they were going about rebelling against God,

behold, the angel of the Lord appeared unto them,
and he descended as it were in a cloud.
And he spake as it were with a voice of thunder,
which caused the earth to shake upon which they stood.

12 And so great was their astonishment that they fell to the earth
and understood not the words which he spake unto them.

13 Nevertheless he cried again, saying:
Alma, arise and stand forth.
For why persecutest thou the church of God?
For the Lord hath said:
This is my church and I will establish it;
and nothing shall overthrow it save it is the transgression of my people.

14 And again the angel saith:
Behold, the Lord hath heard the prayers of his people
and also the prayers of his servant Alma, which is thy father.
For he hath prayed with much faith concerning thee,
that thou mightest be brought to the knowledge of the truth.
Therefore for this purpose have I come
to convince thee of the power and authority of God,
that the prayers of his servants might be answered according to their faith.

15 And now behold, can ye dispute the power of God?
For behold, doth not my voice shake the earth?
And can ye not also behold me before you?
And I am sent from God.

16 Now I say unto thee: Go;
and remember the captivity of thy fathers
in the land of Helam and in the land of Nephi,
and remember how great things he hath done for them.
For they were in bondage and he hath delivered them.
And now I say unto thee Alma:
Go thy way and seek to destroy the church no more,
that their prayers may be answered.
And this even if thou wilt of thyself be cast off!

17 And now it came to pass that
these were the last words which the angel spake unto Alma,
and he departed.

18 And now Alma and those that were with him fell again to the earth,
for great was their astonishment.
For with their own eyes they had beheld an angel of the Lord,
and his voice was as thunder which shook the earth.

And they knew that there was nothing save the power of God
that could shake the earth and cause it to tremble
as though it would part asunder.

19 And now the astonishment of Alma was so great
that he became dumb,
that he could not open his mouth;
yea, and he became weak,
even that he could not move his hands.
Therefore he was taken by those that were with him and carried helpless,
even until he was laid before his father.

20 And they rehearsed unto his father all that had happened unto them.
And his father rejoiced,
for he knew that it was the power of God.

21 And he caused that a multitude should be gathered together,
that they might witness what the Lord had done for his son,
and also for those that were with him.

22 And he caused that the priests should assemble themselves together.
And they began to fast and to pray to the Lord their God
that he would open the mouth of Alma, that he might speak,
and also that his limbs might receive their strength,
that the eyes of the people might be opened,
to see and know of the goodness and glory of God.

23 And it came to pass
after they had fasted and prayed for the space of two days and two nights,
the limbs of Alma received their strength.
And he stood up and began to speak unto them,
bidding them to be of good comfort;

24 for, said he, I have repented of my sins
and have been redeemed of the Lord.
Behold, I am born of the Spirit.

25 And the Lord said unto me:
Marvel not that all mankind,
yea, men and women
— all nations, kindreds, tongues, and people —
must be born again, yea, born of God,
changed from their carnal and fallen state to a state of righteousness,
being redeemed of God,
becoming his sons and daughters.

26 And thus they become new creatures;
and unless they do this, they can in no wise inherit the kingdom of God.

27 I say unto you:

Unless this be the case, they must be cast off.
And this I know because I was like to be cast off.

28 Nevertheless, after wading through much tribulation,
repenting nigh unto death,
the Lord in mercy hath seen fit to snatch me out of an everlasting burning;
and I am born of God.
29 My soul hath been redeemed from the gall of bitterness and bonds of iniquity.
I was in the darkest abyss,
but now I behold the marvelous light of God.
My soul was racked with eternal torment,
but I am snatched and my soul is pained no more.
30 I rejected my Redeemer
and denied that which had been spoken of by our fathers.
But now I know that they may foresee that he will come
and that he remembereth every creature of his creating
and he will make himself manifest unto all.
31 Yea, every knee shall bow and every tongue confess before him.
Yea, even at the last day when all men shall stand to be judged of him,
then shall they confess that he is God;
then shall they confess who live without God in the world
that the judgment of an everlasting punishment is just upon them.
And they shall quake and tremble and shrink
beneath the glance of his all-searching eye.

32 And now it came to pass that
Alma began from this time forward to teach the people,
and those which were with Alma at the time the angel appeared unto them,
traveling round about through all the land,
publishing to all the people the things which they had heard and seen,
and preaching the word of God,
in much tribulation,
being greatly persecuted by those which were unbelievers,
being smitten by many of them.
33 But notwithstanding all this, they did impart much consolation to the church,
confirming their faith and exhorting them with long-suffering and much travail
to keep the commandments of God.
34 And four of them were the sons of Mosiah.
And their names were Ammon and Aaron and Omner and Himni;
these were the names of the sons of Mosiah.

35 And after they had traveled throughout all the land of Zarahemla
and among all the people which was under the reign of king Mosiah,

zealously striving to repair all the injuries which they had done to the church,
confessing all their sins and publishing all the things which they had seen,
and explaining the prophecies and the scriptures
to all who desired to hear them—

36 and thus they were instruments in the hands of God
in bringing many to the knowledge of the truth,
yea, to the knowledge of their Redeemer.

37 And how blessed are they!
For they did publish peace;
they did publish good tidings of good,
and they did declare unto the people that the Lord reigneth.

28 | 1 Now it came to pass that after the sons of Mosiah had done all these things,
they took a small number with them and returned to their father the king
and desired of him that he would grant unto them
that they might with those whom they had selected go up to the land of Nephi,
that they might preach the things which they had heard,
and that they might impart the word of God to their brethren the Lamanites,

2 that perhaps they might bring them to the knowledge of the Lord their God
and convince them of the iniquity of their fathers,
and that perhaps they might cure them of their hatred towards the Nephites,
that they might also be brought to rejoice in the Lord their God,
that they might become friendly to one another,
and that there should be no more contentions
in all the land which the Lord their God hath given them.

3 Now they were desirous that salvation should be declared to every creature,
for they could not bear that any human soul should perish;
yea, even the very thoughts that any soul should endure endless torment
did cause them to quake and tremble.

4 And thus did the Spirit of the Lord work upon them.
For they were the very vilest of sinners,
and the Lord saw fit in his infinite mercy to spare them.
Nevertheless they suffered much anguish of soul because of their iniquities—
and suffering much fearing that they should be cast off forever.

5 And it came to pass that they did plead with their father many days
that they might go up to the land of Nephi.

6 And it came to pass that king Mosiah went and inquired of the Lord
if he should let his sons go up among the Lamanites to preach the word.

7 And the Lord said unto Mosiah:
Let them go up, for many shall believe on their words;

and they shall have eternal life.
And I will deliver thy sons out of the hands of the Lamanites.

8 And it came to pass that Mosiah granted
that they might go and do according to their request.

9 And they took their journey into the wilderness
to go up to preach the word among the Lamanites.
And I shall give an account of their proceedings hereafter.

10 Now king Mosiah had no one to confer the kingdom upon,
for there was not any of his sons which would accept of the kingdom.

11 Therefore he took the records which were engraven upon the plates of brass,
and also the plates of Nephi,
and all the things which he had kept and preserved
according to the commandments of God,
and after having translated and caused to be written the records
which were on the plates of gold
which had been found by the people of Limhi,
which was delivered to him by the hand of Limhi—

12 and this he done because of the great anxiety of his people,
for they were desirous beyond measure
to know concerning those people which had been destroyed.

13 And now he translated them by the means of those two stones
which was fastened into the two rims of a bow.

14 Now these things was prepared from the beginning
and was handed down from generation to generation
for the purpose of interpreting languages.

15 And they have been kept and preserved by the hand of the Lord,
that he should discover to every creature which should possess the land
the iniquities and abominations of his people.

16 And whosoever has the things is called seer, after the manner of old times.

17 Now after Mosiah had finished translating these records,
behold, it gave an account of the people which was destroyed
from the time that they were destroyed
back to the building of the great tower,
at the time the Lord confounded the language of the people,
and they were scattered abroad upon the face of all the earth,
yea, and even from that time until the creation of Adam.

18 Now this account did cause the people of Mosiah to mourn exceedingly;
yea, they were filled with sorrow.
Nevertheless it gave them much knowledge,
in the which they did rejoice.

19 And this account shall be written hereafter;
 for behold, it is expedient
 that all people should know the things which are written in this account.

20 And now as I said unto you that
 after king Mosiah had done these things,
 he took the plates of brass and all the things which he had kept
 and conferred them upon Alma, which was the son of Alma
 —yea, all the records and also the interpreters—
 and conferred them upon him,
 and commanding him that he should keep and preserve them
 and also keep a record of the people,
 handing them down from one generation to another,
 even as they had been handed down from the time that Lehi left Jerusalem.

29 | 1 Now when Mosiah had done this,
 he sent out through all the land among all the people,
 desiring to know their will concerning who should be their king.
 2 And it came to pass that the voice of the people came, saying:
 We are desirous that Aaron thy son should be our king and our ruler.
 3 Now Aaron had gone up to the land of Nephi;
 therefore the king could not confer the kingdom upon him.
 Neither would Aaron take upon him the kingdom,
 neither was any of the sons of Mosiah willing to take upon them the kingdom.

 4 Therefore king Mosiah sent again among the people;
 yea, even a written word sent he among the people.
 And these were the words that were written, saying:
 5 Behold, O ye my people or my brethren
 —for I esteem you as such—
 for I desire that ye should consider the cause which ye are called to consider,
 for ye are desirous to have a king.
 6 Now I declare unto you that he to whom that the kingdom doth rightly belong
 hath declined and will not take upon him the kingdom.
 7 And now if there should be another appointed in his stead,
 behold, I fear there would rise contentions among you.
 And who knoweth but what my son to whom the kingdom doth belong
 should turn to be angry and draw away a part of this people after him
 —which will cause wars and contentions among you,
 which would be the cause of shedding much blood

and perverting the way of the Lord—
yea, and destroy the souls of much people.

8 Now I say unto you:
Let us be wise and consider these things.
For we have no right to destroy my son,
neither should we have any right to destroy another
if he should be appointed in his stead.

9 And if my son should turn again to his pride and vain things,
he would recall the things which he had said
and claim his right to the kingdom,
which would cause him and also this people to commit much sin.

10 And now let us be wise and look forward to these things
and do that which will make for the peace of this people.

11 Therefore I will be your king the remainder of my days.
Nevertheless let us appoint judges to judge this people according to our law,
and we will newly arrange the affairs of this people.
For we will appoint wise men to be judges
that will judge this people according to the commandments of God.

12 Now it is better that a man should be judged of God than of man;
for the judgments of God are always just,
but the judgments of man are not always just.

13 Therefore if it were possible that ye could have just men to be your kings
which would establish the laws of God
and judge this people according to his commandments,
yea, if ye could have men for your kings
which would do even as my father Benjamin did for this people,
I say unto you,
if this could always be the case,
then it would be expedient
that ye should always have kings to rule over you.

14 And even I myself have labored
with all the power and faculties which I have possessed
to teach you the commandments of God
and to establish peace throughout the land,
that there should be no wars nor contentions,
no stealing nor plundering nor murdering nor no manner of iniquity.

15 And whosoever hath committed iniquity,

him have I punished according to the crime which he hath committed
according to the law which hath been given to us by our fathers.

16 Now I say unto you that because all men are not just,
   it is not expedient that ye should have a king or kings to rule over you.
17 For behold, how much iniquity doth one wicked king cause to be committed!
   Yea, and what great destruction!
18 Yea, remember king Noah, his wickedness and his abominations,
   and also the wickedness and abominations of his people.
   Behold, what great destruction did come upon them!
   And also because of their iniquities they were brought into bondage.
19 And were it not for the interposition of their all-wise Creator
   —and this because of their sincere repentance—
   they must have unavoidably remained in bondage until now.
20 But behold, he did deliver them
   because they did humble themselves before him;
   and because they cried mightily unto him,
   he did deliver them out of bondage.
   And thus doth the Lord work with his power
   in all cases among the children of men,
   extending the arm of mercy towards them that put their trust in him.

21 And behold, now I say unto you:
   Ye cannot dethrone an iniquitous king
   save it be through much contention and the shedding of much blood.
22 For behold, he hath his friends in iniquity,
   and he keepeth his guards about him,
   and he teareth up the laws of those
   which have reigned in righteousness before him,
   and he trampleth under his feet the commandments of God.
23 And he enacteth laws and sendeth them forth among his people,
   yea, laws after the manner of his own wickedness;
   and whosoever doth not obey his laws,
   he causeth to be destroyed.
   And whosoever doth rebel against him,
   he will send his armies against them to war;
   and if he can, he will destroy them.
   And thus an unrighteous king doth pervert the ways of all righteousness.

24 And now behold, I say unto you:
   It is not expedient that such abominations should come upon you.
25 Therefore choose you by the voice of this people judges,
   that ye may be judged according to the laws

which hath been given you by our fathers,
which are correct
and which was given them by the hand of the Lord.

26 Now it is not common that the voice of the people desireth any thing
contrary to that which is right,
but it is common for the lesser part of the people
to desire that which is not right.
Therefore this shall ye observe and make it your law,
to do your business by the voice of the people.

27 And if the time cometh that the voice of the people doth choose iniquity,
then is the time that the judgments of God will come upon you.
Yea, then is the time he will visit you with great destruction,
even as he hath hitherto visited this land.

28 And now if ye have judges
and they do not judge you according to the law which has been given,
ye can cause that he may be judged of a higher judge.

29 If your higher judges doth not judge righteous judgments,
ye shall cause that a small number of your lower judges
should be gathered together
and they shall judge your higher judges
according to the voice of the people.

30 And I commanded you to do these things in the fear of the Lord;
and I commanded you to do these things and that ye have no king,
that if these people commit sins and iniquities,
they shall be answered upon their own heads.

31 For behold, I say unto you:
The sins of many people have been caused by the iniquities of their kings;
therefore their iniquities are answered upon the heads of their kings.

32 And now I desire that this unequality should be no more in this land,
especially among this my people.
But I desire that this land be a land of liberty
and every man may enjoy his rights and privileges alike
so long as the Lord sees fit that we may live and inherit the land,
yea, even as long as any of our posterity remaineth upon the face of the land.

33 And many more things did king Mosiah write unto them,
unfolding unto them all the trials and troubles of a righteous king,
yea, all the travails of soul for their people,
and also all the murmurings of the people to their king;
and he explained it all unto them.

34 And he told them that these things had not ought to be,

but that the burden should come upon all the people,
that every man might bear his part.

35 And he also unfolded unto them all the disadvantages they labored under
by having an unrighteous king to rule over them,
36 yea, all his iniquities and abominations
and all the wars and contentions and bloodshed
and the stealing and the plundering
and the committing of whoredoms
and all manner of iniquities which cannot be enumerated,
telling them that these things ought not to be,
that they was expressly repugnant to the commandments of God.

37 And now it came to pass
after king Mosiah had sent these things forth among the people,
they were convinced of the truth of his words.
38 Therefore they relinquished their desires for a king
and became exceedingly anxious
that every man should have an equal chance throughout all the land;
yea, and every man expressed a willingness to answer for his own sins.
39 Therefore it came to pass that
they assembled themselves together in bodies throughout the land
to cast in their voices concerning who should be their judges
to judge them according to the law which had been given them.
And they were exceedingly rejoiced
because of the liberty which had been granted unto them.

40 And they did wax strong in love towards Mosiah;
yea, they did esteem him more than any other man.
For they did not look upon him as a tyrant who was seeking for gain,
yea, for that lucre which doth corrupt the soul;
for he had not exacted riches of them,
neither had he delighted in the shedding of blood,
but he had established peace in the land.
And he had granted unto his people
that they should be delivered from all manner of bondage.
Therefore they did esteem him,
yea, exceedingly beyond measure.

41 And it came to pass that they did appoint judges to rule over them,
or to judge them according to the law;
and this they done throughout all the land.
42 And it came to pass that Alma was appointed to be the chief judge,
he being also the high priest,

his father having conferred the office upon him
and had given him the charge concerning all the affairs of the church.

43 And now it came to pass that Alma did walk in the ways of the Lord,
and he did keep his commandments,
and he did judge righteous judgments.
And there was continual peace through the land.

44 And thus commenced the reign of the judges
throughout all the land of Zarahemla
among all the people which was called the Nephites;
and Alma was the first and chief judge.

45 And now it came to pass that his father died,
being eighty and two years old,
having lived to fulfill the commandments of God.

46 And it came to pass that
Mosiah died also, in the thirty and third year of his reign,
being sixty and three years old,
making in the whole five hundred and nine years
from the time Lehi left Jerusalem.

47 And thus ended the reign of the kings over the people of Nephi;
and thus ended the days of Alma,
who was the founder of their church.

THE BOOK OF ALMA
the son of Alma

The account of Alma, who was the son of Alma,
the first and chief judge over the people of Nephi,
and also the high priest over the church.

An account of the reign of the judges
and the wars and contentions among the people.

And also an account of a war between the Nephites and the Lamanites
according to the record of Alma, the first and chief judge.

1 | 1 Now it came to pass that
in the first year of the reign of the judges over the people of Nephi,
from this time forward,

king Mosiah having gone the way of all the earth,
having warred a good warfare,
walking uprightly before God,
leaving none to reign in his stead
—nevertheless he established laws,
and they were acknowledged by the people—
therefore they were obliged to abide by the laws which he had made.

2 And it came to pass that
in the first year of the reign of Alma in the judgment seat,
there was a man brought before him to be judged,
a man which was large and was noted for his much strength.

3 And he had gone about among the people,
preaching to them that which he termed to be the word of God,
bearing down against the church,
declaring unto the people
that every priest and teacher had ought to become popular
and they ought not to labor with their own hands,
but that they had ought to be supported by the people.

4 And he also testified unto the people
that all mankind should be saved at the last day
and that they need not fear nor tremble,
but that they might lift up their heads and rejoice,
for the Lord had created all men and had also redeemed all men;
and in the end all men should have eternal life.

5 And it came to pass that he did teach these things so much
that many did believe on his words,
even so many that they began to support him and give him money.

6 And he began to be lifted up in the pride of his heart
and to wear very costly apparel,
yea, and even began to establish a church after the manner of his preaching.

7 And it came to pass
as he was going to preach to those who believed on his word,
he met a man which belonged to the church of God,
yea, even one of their teachers;
and he began to contend with him sharply,
that he might lead away the people of the church;
but the man withstood him,
admonishing him with the words of God.

8 Now the name of the man was Gideon,
and it was him that was an instrument in the hands of God
in delivering the people of Limhi out of bondage.

9 Now because Gideon withstood him with the words of God,

he was wroth with Gideon and drew his sword and began to smite him.
Now Gideon being stricken with many years,
therefore he was not able to withstand his blows;
therefore he was slain by the sword.

10 And the man who slew him was taken by the people of the church
and was brought before Alma to be judged
according to the crime which he had committed.

11 And it came to pass that
he stood before Alma and pled for himself with much boldness.

12 But Alma said unto him:
Behold, this is the first time
that priestcraft has been introduced among this people.
And behold, thou art not only guilty of priestcraft
but hast endeavored to enforce it by the sword.
And were priestcraft to be enforced among this people,
it would prove their entire destruction.

13 And thou hast shed the blood of a righteous man,
yea, a man which has done much good among this people.
And were we to spare thee,
his blood would come upon us for vengeance.

14 Therefore thou art condemned to die
according to the law which has been given us by Mosiah, our last king.
And they have been acknowledged by this people;
therefore this people must abide by the law.

15 And it came to pass that they took him
—and his name was Nehor—
and they carried him up on the top of the hill Manti,
and there he was caused
or rather did acknowledge between the heavens and the earth
that what he had taught to the people was contrary to the word of God;
and there he suffered an ignominious death.

16 Nevertheless this did not put an end
to the spreading of priestcraft through the land,
for there was many which loved the vain things of the world.
And they went forth preaching false doctrines,
and this they did for the sake of riches and honor.

17 Nevertheless they durst not lie—if it were known—for fear of the law,
for liars were punished.
Therefore they pretended to preach according to their belief.
And now the law could have no power on any man for their belief.

18 And they durst not steal for fear of the law,
for such were punished.

Neither durst they rob nor murder,
for he that murdereth was punished unto death.

19 But it came to pass that
whosoever did not belong to the church of God began to persecute those
that did belong to the church of God
and had taken upon them the name of Christ.

20 Yea, they did persecute them and afflict them with all manner of words —
and this because of their humility,
because they were not proud in their own eyes,
and because they did impart the word of God one with another
without money and without price.

21 Now there was a strict law among the people of the church
that there should not any man belonging to the church
arise and persecute those that did not belong to the church,
and that there should be no persecution among themselves.

22 Nevertheless there were many among them who began to be proud
and began to contend warmly with their adversaries, even unto blows;
yea, they would smite one another with their fists.

23 Now this was in the second year of the reign of Alma,
and it was a cause of much affliction to the church;
yea, it was the cause of much trial with the church.

24 For the hearts of many were hardened,
and their names were blotted out,
that they were numbered no more among the people of God;
and also many withdrew themselves from among them.

25 Now this was a great trial to those that did stand fast in the faith;
nevertheless they were steadfast and immovable
in keeping the commandments of God,
and they bore with patience the persecution which was heaped upon them.

26 And when their priests left their labor
to impart the word of God unto the people,
the people also left their labors to hear the word of God.
And when the priest had imparted unto them the word of God,
they all returned again diligently unto their labors, and the priest,
not esteeming himself above his hearers,
for the preacher was no better than the hearer,
neither was the teacher any better than the learner.
And thus they were all equal;
and they did all labor, every man according to his strength.

27 And they did impart of their substance,
every man according to that which he had,

to the poor and the needy and the sick and the afflicted.
And they did not wear costly apparel, yet they were neat and comely.

28 And thus they did establish the affairs of the church;
and thus they began to have continual peace again,
notwithstanding all their persecutions.

29 And now because of the steadiness of the church
they began to be exceeding rich,
having abundance of all things whatsoever they stood in need:
abundance of flocks and herds and fatlings of every kind,
and also abundance of grain and of gold and of silver and of precious things,
and abundance of silk and fine twined linen
and all manner of good homely cloth.

30 And thus in their prosperous circumstances
they did not send away any which was naked or that was hungry
or that was athirst or that was sick or that had not been nourished.
And they did not set their hearts upon riches.
Therefore they were liberal to all,
both old and young, both bond and free, both male and female,
whether out of the church or in the church,
having no respects to persons as to those who stood in need.

31 And thus they did prosper and become far more wealthy
than those who did not belong to their church.

32 For those who did not belong to their church
did indulge themselves in sorceries and in idolatry or idleness
and in babblings and in envyings and strife and wearing costly apparel,
being lifted up in the pride of their own eyes,
persecuting, lying, thieving, robbing,
committing whoredoms and murdering and all manner of wickedness.
Nevertheless the law was put in force upon all those who did transgress it,
inasmuch as it were possible.

33 And it came to pass that by thus exercising the law upon them,
every man suffering according to that which he had done,
they became more still
and durst not commit any wickedness, if it were known.
Therefore there was much peace among the people of Nephi
until the fifth year of the reign of the judges.

2 | 1 And it came to pass in the commencement of the fifth year of their reign
there began to be a contention among the people;
for a certain man being called Amlici,
he being a very cunning man,
yea, a wise man as to the wisdom of the world,

he being after the order of the man that slew Gideon by the sword,
who was executed according to the law—

2 now this Amlici had by his cunning drawn away much people after him,
even so much that they began to be very powerful;
and they began to endeavor to establish Amlici to be a king over the people.

3 Now this was alarming to the people of the church,
and also to all those who had not been drawn away
after the persuasions of Amlici;
for they knew that according to their law
that such things must be established by the voice of the people.

4 Therefore, if it were possible that Amlici should gain the voice of the people,
he being a wicked man would deprive them
of their rights and the privileges of the church etc.,
for it was his intent to destroy the church of God.

5 And it came to pass that
the people assembled themselves together throughout all the land
—every man according to his mind,
whether it were for or against Amlici—
in separate bodies,
having much dispute and wonderful contentions one with another.

6 And thus they did assemble themselves together
to cast in their voices concerning the matter,
and they were laid before the judges.

7 And it came to pass that the voice of the people came against Amlici,
that he was not made king over the people.

8 Now this did cause much joy in the hearts of those which were against him,
but Amlici did stir up those which were in his favor
to anger against those which were not in his favor.

9 And it came to pass that they gathered themselves together
and did consecrate Amlici to be their king.

10 Now when Amlici was made king over them,
he commanded them that they should take up arms against their brethren;
and this he done that he might subject them to him.

11 Now the people of Amlici were distinguished by the name of Amlici,
being called Amlicites;
and the remainder were called Nephites, or the people of God.

12 Therefore the people of the Nephites was aware of the intent of the Amlicites.
And therefore they did prepare for to meet them;
yea, they did arm themselves with swords and with scimitars
and with bows and with arrows

and with stones and with slings
and with all manner of weapons of war of every kind.

13 And thus they were prepared to meet the Amlicites at the time of their coming.
And there was appointed captains and higher captains and chief captains
according to their numbers.

14 And it came to pass that Amlici did arm his men
with all manner of weapons of war of every kind;
and he also appointed rulers and leaders over his people
to lead them to war against their brethren.

15 And it came to pass that the Amlicites came up upon the hill Amnihu,
which was east of the river Sidon,
which ran by the land of Zarahemla;
and there they began to make war with the Nephites.

16 Now Alma, he being the chief judge and the governor of the people of Nephi,
therefore he went up with his people,
yea, with his captains and chief captains,
yea, at the head of his armies,
against the Amlicites to battle.

17 And they began to slay the Amlicites upon the hill east of Sidon;
and the Amlicites did contend with the Nephites with great strength,
insomuch that many of the Nephites did fall before the Amlicites.

18 Nevertheless the Lord did strengthen the hand of the Nephites,
that they slew the Amlicites with a great slaughter,
that they began to flee before them.

19 And it came to pass that the Nephites did pursue the Amlicites all that day
and did slay them with much slaughter,
insomuch that there was slain of the Amlicites
twelve thousand five hundred thirty and two souls;
and there was slain of the Nephites
six thousand five hundred sixty and two souls.

20 And it came to pass that when Alma could pursue the Amlicites no longer,
he caused that his people should pitch their tents in the valley of Gideon,
the valley being called after that Gideon
which was slain by the hand of Nehor with the sword;
and in this valley the Nephites did pitch their tents for the night.

21 And Alma sent spies to follow the remnant of the Amlicites,
that he might know of their plans and their plots,
whereby he might guard himself against them,
that he might preserve his people from being destroyed.

22 Now those which he had sent out to watch the camp of the Amlicites
were called Zeram and Amnor and Manti and Limher;

these were they which went out with their men
to watch the camp of the Amlicites.

23 And it came to pass that on the morrow
they returned into the camp of the Nephites in great haste,
being greatly astonished and struck with much fear, saying:

24 Behold, we followed the camp of the Amlicites.
And to our great astonishment,
in the land of Minon, above the land of Zarahemla,
in the course of the land of Nephi,
we saw a numerous host of the Lamanites;
and behold, the Amlicites have joined them.

25 And they are upon our brethren in that land,
and they are fleeing before them,
with their flocks and their wives and their children,
towards our city.
And except we make haste,
they obtain possession of our city,
and our fathers and our wives and our children be slain.

26 And it came to pass that the people of Nephi took their tents
and departed out of the valley of Gideon
towards their city, which was the city of Zarahemla.

27 And behold, as they were crossing the river Sidon,
the Lamanites and the Amlicites,
being as numerous almost, as it were, as the sands of the sea,
came upon them to destroy them.

28 Nevertheless, the Nephites being strengthened by the hand of the Lord,
having prayed mightily to him
that he would deliver them out of the hands of their enemies,
therefore the Lord did hear their cries and did strengthen them;
and the Lamanites and the Amlicites did fall before them.

29 And it came to pass that Alma fought with Amlici with the sword face to face,
and they did contend mightily one with another.

30 And it came to pass that Alma, he being a man of God,
being exercised with much faith,
and he cried, saying:
O Lord, have mercy and spare my life
that I may be an instrument in thy hands to save and protect this people!

31 Now when Alma had said these words,
he contended again with Amlici;
and he was strengthened,

insomuch that he slew Amlici with the sword.

32 And he also contended with the king of the Lamanites,
but the king of the Lamanites fled back from before Alma
and sent his guards to contend with Alma.

33 But Alma with his guards contended
with the guards of the king of the Lamanites
until he slew and drave them back.

34 And thus he cleared the ground,
or rather the bank which was on the west of the river Sidon,
throwing the bodies of the Lamanites which had been slain
into the waters of Sidon,
that thereby his people might have room to cross
and contend with the Lamanites and the Amlicites
on the west side of the river Sidon.

35 And it came to pass that when they had all crossed the river Sidon
that the Lamanites and the Amlicites began to flee before them,
notwithstanding they were so numerous that they could not be numbered.

36 And they fled before the Nephites
towards the wilderness which was west and north,
away beyond the borders of the land.
And the Nephites did pursue them with their might and did slay them;

37 yea, they were met on every hand and slain and driven
until they were scattered on the west and on the north,
until they had reached the wilderness which was called Hermounts;
and it was that part of the wilderness
which was infested by wild and ravenous beasts.

38 And it came to pass that many died in the wilderness of their wounds
and were devoured by those beasts and also the vultures of the air.
And their bones have been found and have been heaped up on the earth.

3 | 1 And it came to pass that
the Nephites which were not slain by the weapons of war,
after having buried those which had been slain
— now the number of the slain were not numbered
because of the greatness of their number—
and after they had finished burying their dead,
they all returned to their lands
and to their houses and their wives and their children.

2 Now many women and children had been slain with the sword,
and also many of their flocks and their herds;
and also many of their fields of grain were destroyed,
for they were trodden down by the hosts of men.

3 And now as many of the Lamanites and the Amlicites
  which had been slain upon the bank of the river Sidon
  were cast into the waters of Sidon.
  And behold, their bones are in the depths of the sea,
  and they are many.

4 And the Amlicites were distinguished from the Nephites,
  for they had marked themselves with red in their foreheads
  after the manner of the Lamanites;
  nevertheless they had not shorn their heads like unto the Lamanites.
5 Now the heads of the Lamanites were shorn;
  and they were naked save it were a skin which was girded about their loins —
  and also their armor which was girded about them,
  and their bows and their arrows and their stones and their slings etc.

6 And the skins of the Lamanites were dark,
  according to the mark which was set upon their fathers,
  which was a curse upon them
  because of their transgression and their rebellion against their brethren,
  which consisted of Nephi, Jacob, and Joseph, and Sam,
  which were just and holy men;
7 and their brethren sought to destroy them.
  Therefore they were cursed,
  and the Lord God set a mark upon them,
  yea, upon Laman and Lemuel,
  and also the sons of Ishmael and the Ishmaelitish women.
8 And this was done
  that their seed might be distinguished from the seed of their brethren,
  that thereby the Lord God might preserve his people,
  that they might not mix and believe in incorrect traditions,
  which would prove their destruction.
9 And it came to pass that
  whosoever did mingle his seed with that of the Lamanites
  did bring the same curse upon his seed.
10 Therefore whomsoever suffered himself to be led away by the Lamanites
  were called under that head,
  and there was a mark set upon him.

11 And it came to pass that
  whosoever would not believe in the tradition of the Lamanites,
  but believed those records which were brought out of the land of Jerusalem,
  and also in the tradition of their fathers, which were correct,
  which believed in the commandments of God and kept them,
  were called the Nephites or the people of Nephi

from that time forth.

12 And it is they which have kept the records, which are true,
of their people and also of the people of the Lamanites.

13 Now we will return again to the Amlicites,
for they also had a mark set upon them;
yea, they set the mark upon themselves,
yea, even a mark of red upon their foreheads.

14 Thus the word of God is fulfilled,
for these are the words which he saith to Nephi:
Behold, the Lamanites have I cursed;
and I will set a mark upon them,
that they and their seed may be separated from thee and thy seed
from this time henceforth and forever
except they repent of their wickedness and turn to me,
that I may have mercy upon them.

15 And again, I will set a mark upon him that mingleth his seed with thy brethren,
that they may be cursed also.

16 And again, I will set a mark upon him that fighteth against thee and thy seed.

17 And again I say:
He that departeth from thee shall no more be called thy seed;
and I will bless thee—etc.—
and whomsoever shall be called thy seed, henceforth and forever.
And these were the promises of the Lord unto Nephi and to his seed.

18 Now the Amlicites knew not that they were fulfilling the words of God
when they began to mark themselves in their foreheads.
Nevertheless as they had come out in open rebellion against God,
therefore it was expedient that the curse should fall upon them.

19 Now I would that ye should see that they brought upon themselves the curse.
And even so doeth every man that is cursed
bringeth upon himself his own condemnation.

20 Now it came to pass that not many days after the battle
which was fought in the land of Zarahemla
by the Lamanites and the Amlicites
that there was another army of the Lamanites
came in upon the people of Nephi
in the same place where the first army met the Amlicites.

21 And it came to pass that there was an army sent to drive them out of their land.

22 Now Alma himself, being afflicted with a wound,
did not go up to battle at this time against the Lamanites,

23 but he sent up a numerous army against them.
And they went up and slew many of the Lamanites

and drove the remainder of them out of the borders of their land.

24 And then they returned again
and began to establish peace in the land,
being troubled no more for a time with their enemies.

25 Now all these things were done,
yea, all these wars and contentions
was commenced and ended in the fifth year of the reign of the judges.

26 And in one year was thousands and tens of thousands of souls
sent to the eternal world,
that they might reap their rewards according to their works,
whether they were good or whether they were bad,
to reap eternal happiness or eternal misery,
according to the spirit which he listed to obey,
whether it be a good spirit or a bad one.

27 For every man receiveth wages of him who he listeth to obey —
and this according to the words of the spirit of prophecy;
therefore let it be according to the truth.
And thus ended the fifth year of the reign of the judges.

4 | 1 Now it came to pass
in the sixth year of the reign of the judges over the people of Nephi,
there was no contentions nor wars in the land of Zarahemla.

2 And the people being afflicted,
yea, greatly afflicted, for the loss of their brethren,
and also for the loss of their flocks and herds,
and also for the loss of their fields of grain,
which was trodden under foot and destroyed by the Lamanites

3 —and so great was their afflictions that every soul had cause to mourn,
and they believed that it was the judgments of God sent upon them
because of their wickedness and their abominations —
therefore they were awakened to a remembrance of their duty,

4 and they began to establish the church more fully.
Yea, and many were baptized in the waters of Sidon
and were joined to the church of God;
yea, they were baptized by the hand of Alma,
who had been consecrated the high priest over the people of the church
by the hand of his father Alma.

5 And it came to pass in the seventh year of the reign of the judges
there was about three thousand five hundred souls
that united themselves to the church of God and were baptized.

And thus ended the seventh year
of the reign of the judges over the people of Nephi;
and there was continual peace in all that time.

6 And it came to pass in the eighth year of the reign of the judges
that the people of the church began to wax proud
because of their exceeding riches and their fine silks and their fine twined linen
and because of their many flocks and herds
and their gold and their silver and all manner of precious things
which they had obtained by their industry.
And in all these things were they lifted up in the pride of their eyes,
for they began to wear very costly apparel.

7 Now this was the cause of much affliction to Alma,
yea, and to many of the people which Alma had consecrated
to be teachers and priests and elders over the church.
Yea, many of them were sorely grieved for the wickedness
which they saw had begun to be among their people.

8 For they saw and beheld with great sorrow
that the people of the church began to be lifted up in the pride of their eyes
and to set their hearts upon riches and upon the vain things of the world,
that they began to be scornful one towards another.
And they began to persecute those that did not believe
according to their own wills and pleasure.

9 And thus in this eighth year of the reign of the judges
there began to be great contentions among the people of the church;
yea, there was envyings and strifes and malice and persecutions and pride,
even to exceed the pride of those who did not belong to the church of God.

10 And thus ended the eighth year of the reign of the judges.
And the wickedness of the church was a great stumbling block
to those who did not belong to the church;
and thus the church began to fail in its progress.

11 And it came to pass in the commencement of the ninth year,
Alma seeing the wickedness of the church
and seeing also that the example of the church
began to lead those who were unbelievers on
from one piece of iniquity to another,
thus bringing on the destruction of the people,

12 yea, seeing great unequality among the people,
some lifting themselves up with their pride, despising others,
turning their backs upon the needy and the naked
and those which were hungry and those which were athirst
and those which were sick and afflicted

13 —now this was a great cause for lamentations among the people—
while others were abasing themselves,
succoring those who stood in need of their succor,
such as imparting their substance to the poor and the needy,
feeding the hungry and suffering all manner of afflictions for Christ's sake,
which should come according to the spirit of prophecy,

14 looking forward to that day,
thus retaining a remission of their sins,
being filled with great joy
because of the resurrection of the dead,
according to the will and power and deliverance of Jesus Christ
from the bands of death—

15 and now it came to pass that
Alma having seen the afflictions of the humble followers of God
and the persecutions which was heaped upon them
by the remainder of his people
and seeing all their unequality,
he began to be very sorrowful.

Nevertheless the Spirit of the Lord did not fail him;

16 and he selected a wise man which was among the elders of the church
and gave him power according to the voice of the people,
that he might have power to enact laws
according to the laws which had been given
and to put them in force
according to the wickedness and the crimes of the people.

17 Now this man's name was Nephihah and he was appointed chief judge;
and he sat in the judgment seat to judge and to govern the people.

18 Now Alma did not grant unto him
the office of being high priest over the church,
but he retained the office of high priest unto himself—
but he delivered the judgment seat unto Nephihah.

19 And this he did that he himself might go forth among his people,
or among the people of Nephi,
that he might preach the word of God unto them,
to stir them up in remembrance of their duty,
and that he might pull down by the word of God
all the pride and craftiness and all the contentions which was among his people,
seeing no way that he might reclaim them
save it were in bearing down in pure testimony against them.

20 And thus in the commencement of the ninth year
of the reign of the judges over the people of Nephi,

Alma delivered up the judgment seat to Nephihah
and confined himself wholly to the high priesthood of the holy order of God,
to the testimony of the word according to the spirit of revelation and prophecy.

⸺

The words which Alma,
the high priest according to the holy order of God,
delivered to the people in their cities and villages throughout the land.

5 | 1   Now it came to pass that
Alma began to declare the word of God unto the people,
first in the land of Zarahemla and from thence throughout all the land.
   2   And these are the words which he spake to the people in the church
which was established in the city of Zarahemla,
according to his own record, saying:
   3   I Alma having been consecrated by my father Alma
to be a high priest over the church of God,
he having power and authority from God to do these things,
behold, I say unto you
that he began to establish a church in the land
which was in the borders of Nephi
—yea, the land was called the land of Mormon—
yea, and he did baptize his brethren in the waters of Mormon.
   4   And behold, I say unto you:
They were delivered out of the hand of the people of king Noah
by the mercy and power of God.
   5   And behold, after that they were brought into bondage
by the hands of the Lamanites in the wilderness
—yea, I say unto you, they were in captivity—
and again the Lord did deliver them out of bondage
by the power of his word.
And we were brought into this land,
and here we began to establish the church of God throughout this land also.

   6   And now behold, I say unto you my brethren,
you that belong to this church:
Have you sufficiently retained in remembrance the captivity of your fathers?
Yea, and have you sufficiently retained in remembrance
his mercy and long-suffering towards them?
And moreover, have ye sufficiently retained in remembrance
that he hath delivered their souls from hell?

7 Behold, he changed their hearts;
yea, he awaked them out of a deep sleep
and they awoke unto God.
Behold, they were in the midst of darkness;
nevertheless their souls were illuminated by the light of the everlasting word.
Yea, they were encircled about by the bands of death and the chains of hell,
and an everlasting destruction did await them.

8 And now I ask of you my brethren:
Were they destroyed?
Behold, I say unto you:
Nay, they were not.

9 And again I ask:
Was the bands of death broken?
And the chains of hell which encircled them about, were they loosed?
I say unto you:
Yea, they were loosed.
And their souls did expand,
and they did sing redeeming love.
And I say unto you that they are saved.

10 And now I ask of you:
On what conditions are they saved?
Yea, what grounds had they to hope for salvation?
What is the cause of their being loosed from the bands of death,
yea, and also the chains of hell?

11 Behold, I can tell you:
Did not my father Alma believe in the words
which was delivered by the mouth of Abinadi?
And was he not a holy prophet?
Did he not speak the word of God and my father Alma believed them?

12 And according to his faith there was a mighty change wrought in his heart.
Behold, I say unto you that this is all true.

13 And behold, he preached the word unto your fathers;
and a mighty change was also wrought in their hearts,
and they humbled themselves and put their trust in the true and living God.
And behold, they were faithful until the end;
therefore they were saved.

14 And now behold, I ask of you, my brethren of the church:
Have ye spiritually been born of God?
Have ye received his image in your own countenances?
Have ye experienced this mighty change in your hearts?

15 Do ye exercise faith in the redemption of him who created you?
   Do you look forward with an eye of faith
   and view this mortal body raised in immortality
   and this corruption raised in incorruption,
   to stand before God to be judged according to the deeds
   which hath been done in the mortal body?

16 I say unto you:
   Can you imagine to yourselves
   that ye hear the voice of the Lord saying unto you in that day:
   Come unto me, ye blessed;
   for behold, your works have been the works of righteousness
   upon the face of the earth;

17 or do ye imagine to yourselves
   that ye can lie unto the Lord at that day and say:
   Lord, our works have been righteous works upon the face of the earth —
   and that he will save you?

18 Or otherwise, can ye imagine yourselves brought before the tribunal of God
   with your souls filled with guilt and remorse,
   having a remembrance of all your guilt,
   yea, a perfect remembrance of all your wickedness,
   yea, a remembrance that ye have set at defiance the commandments of God?

19 I say unto you:
   Can ye look up to God at that day
   with a pure heart and clean hands?
   I say unto you:
   Can you look up,
   having the image of God engraven upon your countenances?

20 I say unto you:
   Can ye think of being saved
   when you have yielded yourselves to become subjects to the devil?

21 I say unto you:
   Ye will know at that day that ye cannot be saved;
   for there can no man be saved except his garments are washed white;
   yea, his garments must be purified until it is cleansed from all stain
   through the blood of him of whom it hath been spoken by our fathers
   which should come to redeem his people from their sins.

22 And now I ask of you my brethren:
   How will any of you feel if ye shall stand before the bar of God,
   having your garments stained with blood and all manner of filthiness?
   Behold, what will these things testify against you?

23 Behold, will they not testify that ye are murderers?
Yea, and also that ye are guilty of all manner of wickedness?

24 Behold, my brethren, do ye suppose
that such an one can have a place to sit down in the kingdom of God
with Abraham, with Isaac, and with Jacob, and also all the holy prophets,
whose garments are cleansed and are spotless, pure, and white?

25 I say unto you:
Nay, except ye make our Creator a liar from the beginning,
or suppose that he is a liar from the beginning.
Or also, ye cannot suppose
that such an one can have place in the kingdom of heaven,
but they shall be cast out;
for they are the children of the kingdom of the devil.

26 And now behold, I say unto you my brethren:
If ye have experienced a change of heart
and if ye have felt to sing the song of redeeming love,
I would ask:
Can ye feel so now?

27 Have ye walked keeping yourselves blameless before God?
Could ye say—if ye were called to die at this time—within yourselves
that ye have been sufficiently humble,
that your garments have been cleansed
and made white through the blood of Christ?
—which will come to redeem his people from their sins.

28 Behold, are ye stripped of pride?
I say unto you:
If ye are not, ye are not prepared to meet God.
Behold, ye must prepare quickly;
for the kingdom of heaven is soon at hand,
and such an one hath not eternal life.

29 Behold, I say:
Is there one among you who is not stripped of envy?
I say unto you that such an one is not prepared.
And I would that he should prepare quickly,
for the hour is close at hand;
and he knoweth not when the time shall come,
for such an one is not found guiltless.

30 And again I say unto you:
Is there one among you that doth make a mock of his brother
or that heapeth upon him persecutions?

31 Woe unto such an one,
    for he is not prepared;
    and the time is at hand that he must repent or he cannot be saved.

32 Yea, even woe unto all ye workers of iniquity.
    Repent, repent, for the Lord God hath spoken it.

33 Behold, he sendeth an invitation unto all men;
    for the arms of mercy is extended towards them,
    and he saith:
    Repent and I will receive you.

34 Yea, he saith:
    Come unto me and ye shall partake of the fruit of the tree of life;
    yea, ye shall eat and drink of the bread and the waters of life freely.

35 Yea, come unto me and bring forth works of righteousness,
    and ye shall not be cut down and cast into the fire.

36 For behold, the time is at hand
    that whosoever bringeth forth not good fruit,
    or whosoever doeth not the works of righteousness,
    the same hath cause to wail and mourn.

37 O ye workers of iniquity,
    ye that are puffed up in the vain things of the world,
    ye that have professed to have known the ways of righteousness!
    Nevertheless ye have gone astray as sheep having no shepherd,
    notwithstanding a shepherd hath called after you
    and art still calling after you,
    but ye will not hearken unto his voice.

38 Behold, I say unto you that the good shepherd doth call you;
    yea, and in his own name he doth call you,
    which is the name of Christ.
    And if ye will not hearken unto the voice of the good shepherd,
    to the name by which ye are called,
    behold, ye are not the sheep of the good shepherd.

39 And now if ye are not the sheep of the good shepherd,
    of what fold are ye?
    Behold, I say unto you
    that the devil is your shepherd,
    and ye are of his fold.
    And now, who can deny this?
    Behold, I say unto you:
    Whosoever denieth this is a liar and a child of the devil.

40 For I say unto you
    that whatsoever is good cometh from God

and whatsoever is evil cometh from the devil.

41 Therefore if a man bringeth forth good works,
he hearkeneth unto the voice of the good shepherd
and he doth follow him.
But whosoever bringeth forth evil works,
the same becometh a child of the devil,
for he hearkeneth unto his voice and doth follow him.

42 And whosoever doeth this must receive his wages of him.
Therefore for his wages he receiveth death
as to things pertaining unto righteousness,
being dead unto all good works.

43 And now my brethren, I would that ye should hear me,
for I speak in the energy of my soul.
For behold, I have spoken unto you plain,
that ye cannot err,
or have spoken according to the commandments of God.

44 For I am called to speak after this manner
according to the holy order of God, which is in Christ Jesus.
Yea, I am commanded to stand and testify unto this people
the things which have been spoken by our fathers
concerning the things which is to come.

45 And this is not all.
Do ye suppose that I know not of these things myself?
Behold, I testify unto you
that I do know that these things whereof I have spoken are true.
And how do ye suppose that I know of their surety?

46 Behold, I say unto you:
They are made known unto me by the Holy Spirit of God.
Behold, I have fasted and prayed many days
that I might know these things of myself.
And now I do know of myself that they are true,
for the Lord God hath made them manifest unto me by his Holy Spirit;
and this is the spirit of revelation which is in me.

47 And moreover I say unto you that
as it has thus been revealed unto me
that the words which have been spoken by our fathers are true,
even so according to the spirit of prophecy which is in me,
which is also by the manifestation of the Spirit of God,

48 I say unto you that I know of myself
that whatsoever I shall say unto you concerning that which is to come is true.

And I say unto you
that I know that Jesus Christ shall come,
yea, the Son, the Only Begotten of the Father,
full of grace and mercy and truth.
And behold, it is he that cometh to take away the sins of the world,
yea, the sins of every man which steadfastly believeth on his name.

49 And now I say unto you
that this is the order after which I am called,
yea, to preach unto my beloved brethren
—yea, and every one that dwelleth in the land—
yea, to preach unto all,
both old and young, both bond and free;
yea, I say unto you,
the aged and also the middle aged and the rising generation,
yea, to cry unto them
that they must repent and be born again.
50 Yea, thus saith the Spirit:
Repent, all ye ends of the earth,
for the kingdom of heaven is soon at hand.
Yea, the Son of God cometh in his glory,
in his might, majesty, power, and dominion.
Yea, my beloved brethren, I say unto you that the Spirit saith:
Behold, the glory of the King of all the earth and also the King of heaven
shall very soon shine forth among all the children of men.

51 And also the Spirit saith unto me,
yea, crieth unto me with a mighty voice, saying:
Go forth and say unto this people: Repent!
For except ye repent, ye can in no wise inherit the kingdom of heaven.
52 And again I say unto you:
The Spirit saith:
Behold, the ax is laid at the root of the tree.
Therefore every tree that bringeth not forth good fruit
shall be hewn down and cast into the fire,
yea, a fire which cannot be consumed,
even an unquenchable fire.
Behold and remember, the Holy One hath spoken it!

53 And now my beloved brethren, I say unto you:
Can ye withstand these sayings?
Yea, can ye lay aside these things
and trample the Holy One under your feet?

Yea, can ye be puffed up in the pride of your hearts?
Yea, will ye still persist in the wearing of costly apparel
and setting your hearts upon the vain things of the world, upon your riches?

54 Yea, will ye persist in supposing that ye are better one than another?
Yea, will ye persist in the persecutions of your brethren
who humble themselves and do walk after the holy order of God
wherewith they have been brought into this church,
having been sanctified by the Holy Spirit?
—and they do bring forth works which is meet for repentance.

55 Yea, and will you persist in turning your backs upon the poor and the needy
and in withholding your substance from them?

56 And finally, all ye that will persist in your wickedness,
I say unto you that these are they
which shall be hewn down and cast into the fire
except they speedily repent.

57 And now I say unto you,
all you that are desirous to follow the voice of the good shepherd:
Come ye out from the wicked
and be ye separate and touch not their unclean things.
And behold, their names shall be blotted out,
that the names of the wicked shall not be numbered
among the names of the righteous,
that the word of God may be fulfilled which saith:
The names of the wicked shall not be mingled with the names of my people;

58 for the names of the righteous shall be written in the book of life,
and unto them will I grant an inheritance at my right hand.

And now my brethren, what have ye to say against this?
I say unto you:
If ye speak against it, it matters not,
for the word of God must be fulfilled.

59 For what shepherd is there among you, having many sheep,
doth not watch over them
that the wolves enter not and devour his flock?
And behold, if a wolf enter his flock,
doth he not drive him out?
Yea, and at the last, if he can, he will destroy him.

60 And now I say unto you
that the good shepherd doth call after you.
And if you will hearken unto his voice,
he will bring you into his fold and ye are his sheep.

And he commandeth you that ye suffer no ravenous wolf to enter among you,
that ye may not be destroyed.

61 And now I Alma do command you
in the language of him who hath commanded me
that ye observe to do the words which I have spoken unto you.
62 I speak by way of command unto you that belong to the church.
And unto those which do not belong to the church,
I speak by way of invitation, saying:
Come and be baptized unto repentance,
that ye also may be partakers of the fruit of the tree of life.

6 | 1 And now it came to pass that
after Alma had made an end of speaking unto the people of the church
which was established in the city of Zarahemla,
he ordained priests and elders by laying on his hands,
according to the order of God,
to preside and watch over the church.
2 And it came to pass that
whomsoever did not belong to the church who repented of their sins
was baptized unto repentance and was received into the church.
3 And it also came to pass that whomsoever did belong to the church
that did not repent of their wickedness and humble themselves before God
—I mean those which were lifted up in the pride of their hearts—
the same were rejected
and their names were blotted out,
that their names were not numbered among those of the righteous.
4 And thus they began to establish
the order of the church in the city of Zarahemla.

5 Now I would that ye should understand
that the word of God was liberal unto all,
that no one was deprived of the privilege of assembling themselves together
to hear the word of God.
6 Nevertheless the children of God were commanded
that they should gather themselves together oft
and join in fasting and mighty prayer
in behalf of the welfare of the souls of those who knew not God.

7 And now it came to pass that
when Alma had made these regulations,
he departed from them,

yea, from the church which was in the city of Zarahemla,
and went over upon the east of the river Sidon into the valley of Gideon,
there having been a city built which was called the city of Gideon,
which was in the valley that was called Gideon,
being called after the man which was slain by the hand of Nehor with the sword.

8 And Alma went and began to declare the word of God
unto the church which was established in the valley of Gideon,
according to the revelation of the truth of the word
which had been spake by his fathers
and according to the spirit of prophecy which was in him
—according to the testimony of Jesus Christ the Son of God,
which should come for to redeem his people from their sins—
and the holy order by which he was called.
And thus it is written.
Amen.

*The words of Alma which he delivered to the people in Gideon,
according to his own record.*

7 | 1 Behold, my beloved brethren,
seeing that I have been permitted to come unto you,
therefore I attempt to address you in my language,
yea, by my own mouth,
seeing that it is the first time
that I have spoken unto you by the words of my mouth,
I having been wholly confined to the judgment seat,
having had much business that I could not come unto you.

2 And even I could not have come now at this time
were it not that the judgment seat hath been given to another
to reign in my stead.

And the Lord in much mercy hath granted that I should come unto you;

3 and behold, I have come having great hopes and much desire
that I should find that ye had humbled yourselves before God
and that ye had continued in the supplicating of his grace,
that I should find that ye were blameless before him,
that I should find that ye were not in the awful dilemma
that our brethren were in at Zarahemla.

4 But blessed be the name of God that he hath given unto me to know,

yea, hath given unto me the exceeding great joy of knowing
that they are established again in the way of his righteousness.

5 And I trust according to the Spirit of God which is in me
that I shall also have joy over you.
Nevertheless I do not desire
that my joy over you should come
by the cause of so much afflictions and sorrow
which I have had for the brethren at Zarahemla.
For behold, my joy cometh over them
after wading through much afflictions and sorrow.

6 But behold, I trust that ye are not in a state of so much unbelief
as were your brethren.
I trust that ye are not lifted up in the pride of your hearts.
Yea, I trust that ye have not set your hearts
upon riches and the vain things of the world.
Yea, I trust that you do not worship idols,
but that ye do worship the true and the living God
and that ye look forward for the remission of your sins
—with an everlasting faith—
which is to come.

7 For behold, I say unto you, there be many things to come.
And behold, there is one thing which is of more importance than they all:
for behold, the time is not far distant
that the Redeemer liveth and cometh among his people.

8 Behold, I do not say that he will come among us
at the time of his dwelling in his mortal tabernacle;
for behold, the Spirit hath not said unto me that this should be the case.
Now as to this thing I do not know;
but this much I do know,
that the Lord God hath power to do all things
which is according to his word.

9 But behold, the Spirit hath said this much unto me, saying:
Cry unto this people, saying:
Repent ye, repent ye,
and prepare the way of the Lord
and walk in his paths, which are straight;
for behold, the kingdom of heaven is at hand,
and the Son of God cometh upon the face of the earth.

10 And behold, he shall be born of Mary at Jerusalem,
which is the land of our forefathers,

she being a virgin, a precious and chosen vessel,
who shall be overshadowed
and conceive by the power of the Holy Ghost
and bring forth a son,
yea, even the Son of God.

11 And he shall go forth,
suffering pains and afflictions and temptations of every kind—
and this that the word might be fulfilled which saith:
He will take upon him the pains and the sicknesses of his people.

12 And he will take upon him death,
that he may loose the bands of death which binds his people.
And he will take upon him their infirmities,
that his bowels may be filled with mercy according to the flesh,
that he may know according to the flesh
how to succor his people according to their infirmities.

13 Now the Spirit knoweth all things;
nevertheless the Son of God suffereth according to the flesh,
that he might take upon him the sins of his people,
that he might blot out their transgressions
according to the power of his deliverance.
And now behold, this is the testimony which is in me.

14 Now I say unto you
that ye must repent and be born again,
for the Spirit saith:
If ye are not born again, ye cannot inherit the kingdom of heaven.
Therefore come and be baptized unto repentance,
that ye may be washed from your sins,
that ye may have faith on the Lamb of God,
which taketh away the sins of the world,
which is mighty to save and to cleanse from all unrighteousness.

15 Yea, I say unto you:
Come and fear not, and lay aside every sin which easily doth beset you,
which doth bind you down to destruction.
Yea, come and go forth, and show unto your God
that ye are willing to repent of your sins
and enter into a covenant with him to keep his commandments,
and witness it unto him this day by going into the waters of baptism.

16 And whosoever doeth this
and keepeth the commandments of God from thenceforth,
the same will remember that I say unto him,
yea, he will remember that I have said unto him:

He shall have eternal life—
according to the testimony of the Holy Spirit which testifieth in me.

17 And now my beloved brethren, do you believe these things?
Behold, I say unto you:
Yea, I know that you believe them.
And the way that I know that ye believe them
is by the manifestations of the Spirit which is in me.
And now because your faith is strong concerning that,
yea, concerning the things which I have spoken,
great is my joy.

18 For as I said unto you from the beginning,
that I had much desire
that ye was not in the state of dilemma like your brethren,
even so I have found that my desires have been gratified.

19 For I perceive that ye are in the paths of righteousness.
I perceive that ye are in the path which leads to the kingdom of God.
Yea, I perceive that ye are making his paths straight.

20 I perceive that it hath been made known unto you by the testimony of his word
that he cannot walk in crooked paths,
neither doth he vary from that which he hath said,
neither hath he a shadow of turning from the right to the left,
or from that which is right to that which is wrong.
Therefore his course is one eternal round.

21 And he doth not dwell in unholy temples,
neither can filthiness or any thing which is unclean
be received into the kingdom of God.
Therefore I say unto you:
The time shall come
—yea, and it shall be at the last day—
that he which is filthy shall remain in his filthiness.

22 And now my beloved brethren, I have said these things unto you
that I might awaken you to a sense of your duty to God,
that ye may walk blameless before him,
that ye may walk after the holy order of God
after which ye have been received.

23 And now I would that ye should be humble and be submissive and gentle,
easy to be entreated,
full of patience and long-suffering,
being temperate in all things,
being diligent in keeping the commandments of God at all times,

asking for whatsoever things ye stand in need, both spiritual and temporal,
always returning thanks unto God for whatsoever things ye do receive.

24 And see that ye have faith, hope, and charity,
and then ye will always abound in good works.

25 And may the Lord bless you and keep your garments spotless,
that ye may at last be brought to sit down with Abraham, Isaac, and Jacob,
and the holy prophets which have been ever since the world began,
having your garments spotless
—even as their garments are spotless—
in the kingdom of heaven, to go no more out.

26 And now my beloved brethren, I have spoken these words unto you
according to the Spirit which testifieth in me.
And my soul doth exceedingly rejoice
because of the exceeding diligence and heed
which ye have given unto my word.

27 And now may the peace of God rest upon you
and upon your houses and lands
and upon your flocks and herds and all that you possess,
your women and your children,
according to your faith and good works from this time forth and forever.
And thus I have spoken.
Amen.

8 | 1 And now it came to pass that Alma returned from the land of Gideon,
after having taught the people of Gideon many things which cannot be written,
having established the order of the church
according as he had before done in the land of Zarahemla,
yea, he returned to his own house at Zarahemla
to rest himself from the labors which he had performed.

2 And thus ended the ninth year
of the reign of the judges over the people of Nephi.

3 And it came to pass in the commencement of the tenth year
of the reign of the judges over the people of Nephi
that Alma departed from thence and took his journey
over into the land of Melek,
on the west of the river Sidon,
on the west by the borders of the wilderness.

4 And he began to teach the people in the land of Melek
according to the holy order of God by which he had been called,
and he began to teach the people throughout all the land of Melek.

5 And it came to pass that the people came to him
   throughout all the borders of the land which was by the wilderness side.
   And it came to pass that they were baptized throughout all the land.
6 So that when he had finished his work at Melek,
   he departed thence and traveled three days' journey
   on the north of the land of Melek,
   and he came to a city which was called Ammonihah.

7 Now it was the custom of the people of Nephi
   to call their lands and their cities and their villages,
   yea, even all their small villages,
   after the name of him who first possessed them;
   and thus it was with the land of Ammonihah.

8 And it came to pass that when Alma had came to the city of Ammonihah,
   he began to preach the word of God unto them.
9 Now Satan had got great hold
   upon the hearts of the people of the city of Ammonihah;
   therefore they would not hearken unto the words of Alma.
10 Nevertheless Alma labored much in the spirit,
   wrestling with God in mighty prayer,
   that he would pour out his Spirit upon the people which was in the city,
   that he would also grant that he might baptize them unto repentance.
11 Nevertheless they hardened their hearts, saying unto him:
   Behold, we know that thou art Alma;
   and we know that thou art high priest over the church
   which thou hast established in many parts of the land
   according to your tradition.
   And we are not of thy church,
   and we do not believe in such foolish traditions.
12 And now we know that because we are not of thy church,
   we know that thou hast no power over us.
   And thou hast delivered up the judgment seat unto Nephihah;
   therefore thou art not the chief judge over us.

13 Now when the people had said this
   and had withstood all his words and reviled him and spit upon him
   and caused that he should be cast out of their city,
   and he departed thence and took his journey
   towards the city which was called Aaron.
14 And it came to pass that while he was journeying thither,
   being weighed down with sorrow,
   wading through much tribulation and anguish of soul
   because of the wickedness of the people which was in the city of Ammonihah,

and it came to pass that while Alma was thus weighed down with sorrow,
behold, an angel of the Lord appeared unto him, saying:

15 Blessed art thou Alma.
Therefore lift up thy head and rejoice,
for thou hast great cause to rejoice.
For thou hast been faithful in keeping the commandments of God
from the time which thou received thy first message from him.
Behold, I am he that delivered it unto thee.

16 And behold, I am sent to command thee
that thou return to the city of Ammonihah
and preach again unto the people of the city,
yea, preach unto them,
yea, say unto them,
except they repent the Lord God will destroy them.

17 For behold, they do study at this time
that they may destroy the liberty of thy people
—for thus saith the Lord—
which is contrary to the statutes and judgments and commandments
which he hath given unto his people.

18 Now it came to pass that
after Alma had received his message from the angel of the Lord,
he returned speedily to the land of Ammonihah.
And it came to pass that he entered the city by another way,
yea, by the way which was on the south of the city Ammonihah.

19 And it came to pass that as he entered the city,
he was an hungered;
and he saith to a man:
Will ye give to an humble servant of God something to eat?

20 And the man saith unto him:
I am a Nephite and I know that thou art a holy prophet of God,
for thou art the man which an angel saith in a vision
thou shalt receive.
Therefore go with me into my house,
and I will impart unto thee of my food.
And I know that thou will be a blessing unto me and my house.

21 And it came to pass that the man received him into his house.
And the man was called Amulek;
and he brought forth bread and meat and sat before Alma.

22 And it came to pass that Alma ate bread and he was filled;
and he blessed Amulek and his house, and he gave thanks unto God.

23 And after he had eat and was filled, he saith unto Amulek:
   I am Alma and am the high priest
   over the churches of God throughout the land.
24 And behold, I have been called
   to preach the word of God among all this people
   according to the spirit of revelation and prophecy.
   And I was in this land;
   and they would not receive me, but they cast me out.
   And I was about to set my back towards this land forever.
25 But behold, I have been commanded
   that I should turn again and prophesy unto this people,
   yea, and to testify against them concerning their iniquities.
26 And now Amulek,
   because thou hast fed me and took me in,
   thou art blessed,
   for I was an hungered,
   for I had fasted many days.

27 And it came to pass that Alma tarried many days with Amulek
   before he began to preach unto the people.
28 And it came to pass that the people did wax more gross in their iniquities.
29 And the word came to Alma, saying: Go.
   And also say unto my servant Amulek:
   Go forth and prophesy unto this people, saying:
   Repent ye,
   for thus saith the Lord:
   Except ye repent, I will visit this people in mine anger;
   yea, and I will not turn my fierce anger away.

30 And it came to pass that
   Alma went forth—and also Amulek—among the people
   to declare the words of God unto them.
   And they were filled with the Holy Ghost;
31 and they had power given unto them,
   insomuch that they could not be confined in dungeons,
   neither were it possible that any man could slay them.
   Nevertheless they did not exercise their power
   until they were bound in bands and cast into prison.
   Now this was done that the Lord might show forth his power in them.
32 And it came to pass that they went forth
   and began to preach and to prophesy unto the people
   according to the spirit and power which the Lord had given them.

The words of Alma and also the words of Amulek
which was declared unto the people which was in the land of Ammonihah.

And also they are cast into prison
and delivered by the miraculous power of God which was in them,
according to the record of Alma.

9 | 1 And again, I Alma having been commanded of God
that I should take Amulek and go forth and preach again unto this people
— or the people which was in the city of Ammonihah —
and it came to pass as I began to preach unto them,
they began to contend with me, saying:

2 Who art thou?
Suppose ye that we shall believe the testimony of one man,
although he should preach unto us that the earth should pass away?

3 Now they understood not the words which they spake,
for they knew not that the earth should pass away.

4 And they saith also:
We will not believe thy words
if thou shouldst prophesy that this great city should be destroyed in one day.

5 Now they knew not that God could do such marvelous works,
for they were a hard-hearted and a stiffnecked people.

6 And they saith:
Who is God that sendeth no more authority than one man among this people
to declare unto them the truth of such great and marvelous things?

7 And they stood forth to lay their hands on me;
but behold, they did not.
And I stood with boldness to declare unto them;
yea, I did boldly testify unto them, saying:

8 Behold, O ye wicked and perverse generation,
how have ye forgotten the tradition of your fathers?
Yea, how soon ye have forgotten the commandments of God!

9 Do ye not remember
that our father Lehi was brought out of Jerusalem by the hand of God?
Do ye not remember
that they were all led by him through the wilderness?

10 And have ye forgotten so soon
how many times he delivered our fathers out of the hands of their enemies
and preserved them from being destroyed,
even by the hands of their own brethren?

11   Yea, and if it had not been for his matchless power
and his mercy and his long-suffering towards us,
we should unavoidably have been cut off from the face of the earth
long before this period of time,
and perhaps been consigned to a state of endless misery and woe.

12   Behold, now I say unto you that he commandeth you to repent.
And except ye repent, ye can in no wise inherit the kingdom of God.
But behold, this is not all.
He hath commanded you to repent,
or he will utterly destroy you from off the face of the earth.
Yea, he will visit you in his anger;
and in his fierce anger he will not turn away.

13   Behold, do ye not remember the words which he spake unto Lehi,
saying that inasmuch as ye shall keep my commandments,
ye shall prosper in the land.
And again it is said that inasmuch as ye will not keep my commandments,
ye shall be cut off from the presence of the Lord.

14   Now I would that ye should remember
that inasmuch as the Lamanites have not kept the commandments of God,
they have been cut off from the presence of the Lord.
Now we see that the word of the Lord hath been verified in this thing,
and the Lamanites have been cut off from his presence
from the beginning of their transgressions in the land.

15   Nevertheless I say unto you
that it shall be more tolerable for them in the day of judgment than for you
if ye remain in your sins,
yea, and even more tolerable for them in this life than for you,
except ye repent.

16   For there are many promises which is extended to the Lamanites,
for it is because of the traditions of their fathers
that causeth them to remain in their state of ignorance.
Therefore the Lord will be merciful unto them
and prolong their existence in the land.

17   And at some period of time they will be brought to believe in his word
and to know of the incorrectness of the traditions of their fathers;
and many of them will be saved,
for the Lord will be merciful unto all who call on his name.

18   But behold, I say unto you that
if ye persist in your wickedness
that your days shall not be prolonged in the land,

for the Lamanites shall be sent upon you.
And if ye repent not,
they shall come in a time when you know not,
and ye shall be visited with utter destruction.
And it shall be according to the fierce anger of the Lord,

19 for he will not suffer you that ye shall live in your iniquities,
to destroy his people.
I say unto you:
Nay, he would rather suffer that the Lamanites might destroy all this people,
which is called the people of Nephi,
if it were possible that they could fall into sins and transgressions
after having had so much light and so much knowledge
given unto them of the Lord their God;

20 yea, after having been such a highly favored people of the Lord;
yea, after having been favored
above every other nation, kindred, tongue, or people;
after having had all things made known unto them,
according to their desires and their faith and prayers,
of that which has been and which is and which is to come;

21 having been visited by the Spirit of God,
having conversed with angels,
and having been spoken unto by the voice of the Lord,
and having the spirit of prophecy and the spirit of revelation;
and also many gifts:
the gift of speaking with tongues
and the gift of preaching
and the gift of the Holy Ghost
and the gift of translation;

22 yea, and after having been delivered of God
out of the land of Jerusalem by the hand of the Lord,
having been saved from famine
and from sicknesses and all manner of diseases of every kind;
and they having been waxed strong in battle that they might not be destroyed;
having been brought out of bondage time after time
and having been kept and preserved until now;
and they have been prospered until they are rich in all manner of things—

23 and now behold, I say unto you that
if this people, who have received so many blessings from the hand of the Lord,
should transgress contrary to the light and knowledge which they do have,
I say unto you that if this be the case,
that if they should fall into transgression,
that it would be far more tolerable for the Lamanites than for them.

24 For behold, the promises of the Lord are extended to the Lamanites,
but they are not unto you if ye transgress.
For hath not the Lord expressly promised and firmly decreed
that if ye will rebel against him
that ye shall utterly be destroyed from off the face of the earth?

25 And now for this cause that ye may not be destroyed,
the Lord hath sent his angel to visit many of his people,
declaring unto them that they must go forth
and cry mightily unto this people, saying:
Repent ye, repent ye,
for the kingdom of heaven is nigh at hand.

26 And not many days hence the Son of God shall come in his glory,
and his glory shall be the glory of the Only Begotten of the Father,
full of grace, equity, and truth,
full of patience, mercy, and long-suffering,
quick to hear the cries of his people and to answer their prayers.

27 And behold, he cometh to redeem those who will be baptized
unto repentance through faith on his name.

28 Therefore prepare ye the way of the Lord,
for the time is at hand that every man shall reap a reward of their works
according to that which they have been:
if they have been righteous,
they shall reap the salvation of their souls
according to the power and deliverance of Jesus Christ;
and if they have been evil,
they shall reap the damnation of their souls
according to the power and captivation of the devil.

29 Now behold, this is the voice of the angel crying unto the people.

30 And now my beloved brethren
—for ye are my brethren
and ye had ought to be beloved—
and ye had ought to bring forth works which is meet for repentance,
seeing that your hearts have been grossly hardened against the word of God
and seeing that ye are a lost and a fallen people.

31 Now it came to pass that when I Alma had spoken these words,
behold, the people were wroth with me
because I said unto them
that they was a hard-hearted and a stiffnecked people.

32 And also because I said unto them that they were a lost and a fallen people,
they was angry with me and sought to lay their hands upon me,
that they might cast me into prison.

33 But it came to pass that the Lord did not suffer them
that they should take me at that time and cast me into prison.

34 And it came to pass that Amulek went and stood forth
and began to preach unto them also.
And now the words of Amulek are not all written;
nevertheless a part of his words are written in this book.

10 | 1 Now these are the words which Amulek preached unto the people
which was in the land of Ammonihah, saying:
2 I am Amulek.
I am the son of Gidanah,
who was the son of Ishmael,
who was a descendant of Aminadi;
and it was that same Aminadi
which interpreted the writing which was upon the wall of the temple,
which was written by the finger of God.
3 And Aminadi was a descendant of Nephi,
who was the son of Lehi,
who came out of the land of Jerusalem,
who was a descendant of Manasseh,
who was the son of Joseph,
which was sold into Egypt by the hands of his brethren.

4 And behold, I am also a man of no small reputation
among all those who know me;
yea, and behold, I have many kindred and friends.
And I have also acquired much riches by the hand of my industry.
5 Nevertheless, after all this, I never have known much of the ways of the Lord
and his mysteries and marvelous power.
I said I never had known much of these things—
but behold, I mistake,
for I have seen much of his mysteries and his miraculous power,
yea, even in the preservation of the lives of this people.
6 Nevertheless I did harden my heart,
for I was called many times and I would not hear.
Therefore I knew concerning these things,
yet I would not know.

Therefore I went on rebelling against God in the wickedness of my heart,
even until the fourth day of this seventh month,
which is in the tenth year of the reign of our judges.

7 As I was a journeying to see a very near kindred,
behold, an angel of the Lord appeared unto me and said:
Amulek, return to thine own house,
for thou shalt feed a prophet of the Lord,
yea, a holy man which art a chosen man of God;
for he hath fasted many days because of the sins of this people,
and he is an hungered.
And thou shall receive him into thy house and feed him.
And he shall bless thee and thy house,
and the blessing of the Lord shall rest upon thee and thy house.

8 And it came to pass that I obeyed the voice of the angel
and returned towards my house.
And as I was a going thither,
I found the man which the angel said unto me
thou shalt receive into thy house;
and behold, it was this same man
which hath been speaking unto you concerning the things of God.

9 And the angel said unto me:
He is a holy man.
Wherefore I know he is a holy man
because it was said by an angel of God.

10 And again I know that the things whereof he hath testified are true.
For behold, I say unto you that as the Lord liveth,
even so he hath sent his angel to make these things manifest unto me;
and this he hath done while this Alma hath dwelt at my house.

11 For behold, he hath blessed mine house;
he hath blessed me and my women and my children
and my father and my kinsfolks
—yea, even all my kindred hath he blessed—
and the blessing of the Lord hath rested upon us
according to the words which he spake.

12 And now when Amulek had spoken these words,
the people began to be astonished,
seeing there was more than one witness
which testified of the things whereof they were accused,
and also of the things which was to come,
according to the spirit of prophecy which was in them.

13 Nevertheless there were some among them which thought to question them,
that by their cunning devices they might catch them in their words,
that they might find witness against them,
that they might deliver them to the judges,

that they might be judged according to the law,
and that they might be slain or cast into prison —
according to the crime which they could make appear or witness against them.

14 Now it was those men which sought to destroy them,
which were lawyers which were hired or appointed by the people
to administer the law at their times of trial,
or at the trials of the crimes of the people before the judges
15 —now these lawyers were learned in all the arts and cunning of the people,
and this was to enable them that they might be skillful in their profession —
16 and it came to pass that they began to question Amulek,
that thereby they might make him cross his words
or contradict the words which he should speak.

17 Now they knew not that Amulek could know of their design.
But it came to pass as they began to question him,
he perceived their thoughts,
and he saith unto them:
O ye wicked and perverse generation,
ye lawyers and hypocrites,
for ye are laying the foundations of the devil,
for ye are laying traps and snares to catch the holy ones of God.
18 Ye are laying plans to pervert the ways of the righteous
and to bring down the wrath of God upon your heads,
even to the utter destruction of this people.
19 Yea, well did Mosiah say, who was our last king,
when he was about to deliver up the kingdom
—having no one to confer it upon,
causing that this people should be governed by their own voices —
yea, well did he say that
if the time should come that the voice of this people should choose iniquity
—that is, if the time should come that this people should fall into transgression —
they would be ripe for destruction.

20 And now I say unto you
that well doth the Lord judge of your iniquities;
well doth he cry unto this people by the voice of his angels:
Repent ye, repent, for the kingdom of heaven is at hand.
21 Yea, well doth he cry by the voice of his angels
that I will come down among my people with equity and justice in my hands.
22 Yea, and I say unto you that
if it were not for the prayers of the righteous which are now in the land
that ye would even now be visited with utter destruction.
Yet it would not be by flood as were the people in the days of Noah,

but it would be by famine and by pestilence and the sword.
23 But it is by the prayers of the righteous that ye are spared.
   Now therefore if ye will cast out the righteous from among you,
   then will not the Lord stay his hand,
   but in his fierce anger he will come out against you;
   then ye shall be smitten by famine and by pestilence and by the sword.
   And the time is soon at hand except ye repent.

24 And now it came to pass that the people were more angry with Amulek,
   and they cried out, saying:
   This man doth revile against our laws, which are just,
   and our wise lawyers, which we have selected.
25 But Amulek stretched forth his hand and cried the mightier unto them, saying:
   O ye wicked and perverse generation,
   why hath Satan got such great hold upon your hearts?
   Why will ye yield yourselves unto him,
   that he may have power over you to blind your eyes,
   that ye will not understand the words
   which are spoken according to their truth?
26 For behold, have I testified against your law?
   Ye do not understand.
   Ye say that I have spoken against your law,
   but I have not;
   but I have spoken in favor of your law,
   to your condemnation.
27 And now behold, I say unto you
   that the foundation of the destruction of this people is a beginning to be laid
   by the unrighteousness of your lawyers and your judges.

28 And now it came to pass that when Amulek had spoken these words,
   the people cried out against him:
   Now we know that this man is a child of the devil,
   for he hath lied unto us;
   for he hath spoken against our law.
   And now he saith that he hath not spoken against it.
29 And again, he hath reviled against our lawyers and our judges etc.

30 And it came to pass that the lawyers put it into their hearts
   that they should remember these things against him.
31 And it came to pass that
   there was one among them whose name was Zeezrom—
   now he being the foremost to accuse Amulek and Alma,
   he being one of the most expert among them,
   having much business to do among the people.

32 Now the object of these lawyers were to get gain,
and they gat gain according to their employ.

11 | 1 Now it was in the law of Mosiah
that every man which was a judge of the law,
or which was appointed to be judges,
should receive his wages according to the time
which they labored to judge those
which were brought before them to be judged.
2 Now if a man oweth another
and he would not pay that which he did owe,
he was complained of to the judge;
and the judge executed authority and sent forth officers
that the man should be brought before him.
And he judgeth the man according to the law
and the evidences which are brought against him;
and thus the man is compelled to pay that which he oweth,
or be striped or be cast out from among the people as a thief and a robber.
3 And the judge receiveth for his wages according to his time:
a senine of gold for a day,
or a senum of silver, which is equal to a senine of gold.
And this is according to the law which was given.

4 Now these are the names of the different pieces
of their gold and of their silver, according to their value;
and the names are given by the Nephites.
For they did not reckon after the manner of the Jews which were at Jerusalem,
neither did they measure after the manner of the Jews;
but they altered their reckoning and their measure
according to the minds and the circumstances of the people,
in every generation until the reign of the judges —
they having been established by king Mosiah.

5 Now the reckoning is thus:
a senine of gold,
a seon of gold,
a shum of gold,
and a limnah of gold;
6 a senum of silver,
an amnor of silver,
an ezrum of silver,
and an onti of silver.

7 A senum of silver was equal to a senine of gold,

and either for a measure of barley,
and also for a measure of every kind of grain.
8 Now the amount of a seon of gold was twice the value of a senine.
9 And a shum of gold was twice the value of a seon.
10 And a limnah of gold was the value of them all.
11 And an amnor of silver was as great as two senums.
12 And an ezrum of silver was as great as four senums.
13 And an onti was as great as them all.

14 Now this is the value of the lesser numbers of their reckoning:
15 a shiblon is half of a senum;
therefore a shiblon for a half a measure of barley.
16 And a shilum is a half of a shiblon.
17 And a leah is the half of a shilum.
18 Now an antion of gold is equal to three shiblons.
19 Now this is their number according to their reckoning.

20 Now it was for the sole purpose for to get gain,
because they received their wages according to their employ,
therefore they did stir up the people to riotings
and all manner of disturbances and wickedness,
that they might have more employ,
that they might get money according to the suits
which was brought before them;
therefore they did stir up the people against Alma and Amulek.

21 And thus Zeezrom began to question Amulek, saying:
Will ye answer me a few questions which I shall ask you?
Now Zeezrom was a man which was expert in the devices of the devil,
that he might destroy that which was good;
therefore he saith unto Amulek:
Will ye answer the questions which I shall put unto you?
22 And Amulek saith unto him:
Yea, I will if it be according to the Spirit of the Lord which is in me,
for I shall say nothing which is contrary to the Spirit of the Lord.

And Zeezrom saith unto him:
Behold, here is six onties of silver;
and all these will I give unto thee
if thou wilt deny the existence of a Supreme Being.
23 Now Amulek saith:
O thou child of hell, why tempt ye me?
Knowest thou that the righteous yieldeth to no such temptations?
24 Believest thou that there is no God?

I say unto you:
Nay, thou knowest that there is a God;
but thou lovest that lucre more than him.

25 And now thou hast lied before God unto me,
for thou saidest unto me:
Behold, these six onties—which are of great worth—
I will give unto thee—
when thou had it in thy heart to retain them from me.
And it was only thy desires that I should deny the true and living God,
that thou mightest have cause to destroy me.
And now behold, for this great evil thou shalt have thy reward.

26 And Zeezrom saith unto him:
Thou sayest there is a true and a living God?
27 And Amulek saith:
Yea, there is a true and a living God.
28 Now Zeezrom saith:
Is there more than one God?
29 And he answereth: No.
30 Now Zeezrom saith unto him again:
How knowest thou these things?
31 And he saith:
An angel hath made them known unto me.
32 And Zeezrom saith again:
Who is he that shall come?
Is it the Son of God?
33 And he saith unto him: Yea.
34 And Zeezrom saith again:
Shall he save his people in their sins?
And Amulek answered and said unto him:
I say unto you, he shall not—
for it is impossible for him to deny his word.

35 Now Zeezrom saith unto the people:
See that ye remember these things,
for he saith there is but one God,
yet he saith that the Son of God shall come
but he shall not save his people,
as though he had authority to command God.
36 Now Amulek said again unto him:
Behold, thou hast lied;
for thou sayest that I speak
as though I had authority to command God

because I said he shall not save his people in their sins.

37 And I say unto you again
that he cannot save them in their sins,
for I cannot deny his word.
And he hath said that no unclean thing can inherit the kingdom of heaven.
Therefore, how can ye be saved except ye inherit the kingdom of heaven?
Therefore ye cannot be saved in your sins.

38 Now Zeezrom saith again unto him:
Is the Son of God the very Eternal Father?

39 And Amulek saith unto him:
Yea, he is the very Eternal Father of heaven and earth
and all things which in them is.
He is the beginning and the end,
the first and the last.

40 And he shall come into the world to redeem his people.
And he shall take upon him
the transgressions of those who believe on his name;
and these are they that shall have eternal life,
and salvation cometh to none else.

41 Therefore the wicked remain as though there had been no redemption made,
except it be the loosing of the bands of death.
For behold, the day cometh that all shall rise from the dead
and stand before God and be judged according to his works.

42 Now there is a death which is called temporal death.
And the death of Christ shall loose the bands of this temporal death,
that all shall be raised from this temporal death.

43 The spirit and the body shall be reunited again in its perfect form.
Both limb and joint shall be restored to its proper frame,
even as we now are at this time;
and we shall be brought to stand before God,
knowing even as we know now,
and have a bright recollection of all our guilt.

44 Now this restoration shall come to all,
both old and young, both bond and free, both male and female,
both the wicked and the righteous.
And even there shall not so much as a hair of their heads be lost;
but all things shall be restored to its perfect frame,
as it is now, or in the body,
and all shall be brought and be raigned
before the bar of Christ the Son and God the Father and the Holy Spirit
—which is one Eternal God—

to be judged according to their works,
whether they be good or whether they be evil.

45 Now behold, I have spoken unto you concerning the death of the mortal body,
and also concerning the resurrection of the mortal body.
I say unto you that this mortal body is raised to an immortal body
—that is, from death, even from the first death unto life—
that they can die no more,
their spirits uniting with their bodies, never to be divided,
thus the whole becoming spiritual and immortal,
that they can no more see corruption.

46 Now when Amulek had finished these words,
the people began again to be astonished;
and also Zeezrom began to tremble.
And thus ended the words of Amulek,
or this is all that I have written.

12 | 1 Now Alma seeing that the words of Amulek had silenced Zeezrom
—for he beheld that Amulek had caught him
in his lying and deceiving to destroy him—
and seeing that he began to tremble under a consciousness of his guilt,
he opened his mouth and began to speak unto him
and to establish the words of Amulek and to explain things beyond,
or to unfold the scriptures beyond that which Amulek had done.
2 Now the words that Alma spake unto Zeezrom was heard
by the people round about
—for the multitude was great—
and he spake on this wise:
3 Now Zeezrom seeing that thou hast been taken in thy lyings and craftiness
—for thou hast not lied unto men only, but thou hast lied unto God,
for behold, he knows all thy thoughts—
and thou seest that thy thoughts are made known unto us by his Spirit.
4 And thou seest that we know that thy plan was a very subtle plan,
as to the subtlety of the devil, for to lie and to deceive this people,
that thou mightest set them against us,
to revile us and to cast us out.
5 Now this was a plan of thine adversary,
and he hath exercised his power in thee.

Now I would that ye should remember
that what I say unto thee I say unto all.

6 And behold, I say unto you all
that this was a snare of the adversary
which he hath laid to catch this people,
that he might bring you into subjection unto him,
that he might encircle you about with his chains,
that he might chain you down to everlasting destruction
according to the power of his captivity.

7 Now when Alma had spoken these words,
Zeezrom began to tremble more exceedingly;
for he was convinced more and more of the power of God.
And he was also convinced that Alma and Amulek had a knowledge of him;
for he was convinced that they knew the thoughts and intents of his heart,
for power was given unto them
that they might know of these things according to the spirit of prophecy.

8 And Zeezrom began to inquire of them diligently,
that he might know more concerning the kingdom of God.
And he saith unto Alma:
What does this mean which Amulek hath spoken
concerning the resurrection of the dead,
that all shall rise from the dead,
both the just and the unjust,
and are brought to stand before God
to be judged according to their works?

9 And now Alma began to expound these things unto him, saying:
It is given unto many to know the mysteries of God;
nevertheless they are laid under a strict command
that they shall not impart,
only according to the portion of his word
which he doth grant unto the children of men,
according to the heed and diligence which they give unto him.

10 And therefore he that will harden his heart,
the same receiveth the lesser portion of the word.
And he that will not harden his heart,
to him is given the greater portion of the word
until it is given unto him to know the mysteries of God,
until they know them in full.

11 And he that will harden his heart,
to him is given the lesser portion of the word
until they know nothing concerning his mysteries;
and then they are taken captive by the devil

and led by his will down to destruction.
Now this is what is meant by the chains of hell.

12 And Amulek hath spoken plainly concerning death
and being raised from this mortality to a state of immortality
and being brought before the bar of God
to be judged according to our works.
13 Then if our hearts have been hardened
—yea, if we have hardened our hearts against the word
insomuch that it hath not been found in us—
then will our state be awful,
for then we shall be condemned.
14 For our works will condemn us,
yea, all our works will condemn us;
we shall not be found spotless
—and our thoughts will also condemn us—
and in this awful state we shall not durst look up to our God.
And we would fain be glad
if we could command the rocks and the mountains to fall upon us,
to hide us from his presence.
15 But this cannot be.
We must come forth and stand before him
in his glory and in his power and in his might, majesty, and dominion,
and acknowledge to their everlasting shame that all his judgments are just,
that he is just in all his works
and that he is merciful unto the children of men
and that he hath all power to save every man
that believeth on his name and bringeth forth fruit meet for repentance.

16 And now behold, I say unto you:
Then cometh a death, even a second death, which is a spiritual death.
Then is a time that whosoever dieth in his sins as to the temporal death
shall also die a spiritual death;
yea, he shall die as to things pertaining unto righteousness.
17 Then is the time when their torments shall be as a lake of fire and brimstone
whose flames ascendeth up forever and ever.
And then is the time that
they shall be chained down to an everlasting destruction
according to the power and captivity of Satan,
having subjected them according to his will.
18 Then I say unto you:
They shall be as though there had been no redemption made,
for they cannot be redeemed according to God's justice;

and they cannot die,
seeing there is no more corruption.

19 Now it came to pass that
when Alma had made an end of speaking these words,
the people began to be more astonished.
20 But there was one Antionah, who was a chief ruler among them,
came forth and said unto him:
What is this that thou hast said,
that man should rise from the dead
and be changed from this mortal to an immortal state,
that the soul can never die?
21 What does this scripture mean which saith
that God placed cherubims and a flaming sword
on the east of the garden of Eden
lest our first parents should enter
and partake of the fruit of the tree of life and live forever?
And thus we see that there was no possible chance
that they should live forever.

22 Now Alma saith unto him:
This is the thing which I was about to explain.
Now we see that Adam did fall by partaking of the forbidden fruit,
according to the word of God.
And thus we see that by his fall
that all mankind became a lost and a fallen people.
23 And now behold, I say unto you that
if it had been possible for Adam
for to have partaken of the fruit of the tree of life at that time
that there would have been no death
and the word would have been void,
making God a liar,
for he said:
If thou eat, thou shalt surely die.
24 And we see that death comes upon mankind,
yea, the death which has been spoken of by Amulek,
which is the temporal death.

Nevertheless there was a space granted unto man in which he might repent.
Therefore this life became a probationary state,
a time to prepare to meet God,
a time to prepare for that endless state
which has been spoken of by us,
which is after the resurrection of the dead.

25 Now if it had not been for the plan of redemption
which was laid from the foundation of the world,
there could have been no resurrection of the dead.
But there was a plan of redemption laid
which shall bring to pass the resurrection of the dead,
of which has been spoken.

26 And now behold, if it were possible
that our first parents could have went forth and partaken of the tree of life,
they would have been forever miserable,
having no preparatory state.
And thus the plan of redemption would have been frustrated,
and the word of God would have been void,
taking none effect.

27 But behold, it was not so,
but it was appointed unto man that they must die.
And after death they must come to judgment,
even that same judgment of which we have spoken,
which is the end.

28 And after God had appointed that these things should come unto man,
behold, then he saw that it was expedient
that man should know concerning the things
whereof he had appointed unto them.

29 Therefore he sent angels to converse with them,
which caused men to behold of his glory.

30 And they began from that time forth to call on his name;
therefore God conversed with men
and made known unto them the plan of redemption
which had been prepared from the foundation of the world.
And this he made known unto them
according to their faith and repentance and their holy works.

31 Wherefore he gave commandments unto men,
they having first transgressed the first commandments
as to things which were temporal
and becoming as Gods,
knowing good from evil,
placing themselves in a state to act,
or being placed in a state to act according to their wills and pleasures,
whether to do evil or to do good.

32 Therefore God gave unto them commandments
after having made known unto them the plan of redemption,
that they should not do evil,

the penalty thereof being a second death,
which was an everlasting death as to things pertaining unto righteousness;
for on such the plan of redemption could have no power,
for the works of justice could not be destroyed,
according to the supreme goodness of God.

33 But God did call on men in the name of his Son,
this being the plan of redemption which was laid, saying:
If ye will repent and harden not your hearts,
then will I have mercy upon you through mine Only Begotten Son.

34 Therefore whosoever repenteth and hardeneth not his heart,
he shall have claim on mercy through mine Only Begotten Son
unto a remission of their sins;
and these shall enter into my rest.

35 And whosoever will harden his heart and will do iniquity,
behold, I swear in my wrath that they shall not enter into my rest.

36 And now my brethren, behold, I say unto you that
if ye will harden your hearts,
ye shall not enter into the rest of the Lord.
Therefore your iniquity provoketh him
that he sendeth down his wrath upon you as in the first provocation
—yea, according to his word in the last provocation as well as in the first—
to the everlasting destruction of your souls,
therefore according to his word unto the last death as well as the first.

37 And now my brethren, seeing we know these things and they are true,
let us repent and harden not our hearts,
that we provoke not the Lord our God to pull down his wrath upon us
in these his second commandments which he hath given unto us;
but let us enter into the rest of God,
which is prepared according to his word.

13 | 1 And again my brethren, I would cite your minds forward to the time
which the Lord God gave these commandments unto his children.
And I would that ye should remember
that the Lord God ordained priests after his holy order,
which was after the order of his Son,
to teach these things unto the people.

2 And those priests were ordained after the order of his Son
in a manner that thereby the people might know
in what manner to look forward to his Son for redemption.

3 And this is the manner after which they were ordained:
being called and prepared from the foundation of the world

according to the foreknowledge of God,
on account of their exceeding faith and good works—
in the first place being left to choose good or evil,
therefore they having chosen good and exercising exceeding great faith
are called with a holy calling,
yea, with that holy calling which was prepared
with and according to a preparatory redemption for such—

4 and thus they having been called to this holy calling on account of their faith,
while others would reject the Spirit of God
on account of the hardness of their hearts and blindness of their minds—
while if it had not been for this,
they might had as great privilege as their brethren—

5 or in fine, in the first place they were on the same standing with their brethren—
thus this holy calling being prepared from the foundation of the world
for such as would not harden their hearts,
being in and through the atonement of the Only Begotten Son
which was prepared—

6 and thus being called by this holy calling
and ordained unto the high priesthood of the holy order of God
to teach his commandments unto the children of men,
that they also might enter into his rest—

7 this high priesthood being after the order of his Son,
which order was from the foundation of the world,
or in other words, being without beginning of days or end of years,
being prepared from eternity to all eternity
according to his foreknowledge of all things—

8 now they were ordained after this manner:
being called with a holy calling and ordained with a holy ordinance
and taking upon them the high priesthood of the holy order—
which calling and ordinance and high priesthood is without beginning or end—

9 thus they become high priests forever
after the order of the Son, the Only Begotten of the Father,
which is without beginning of days or end of years,
which is full of grace, equity, and truth.
And thus it is.
Amen.

10 Now as I said concerning the holy order, or this high priesthood:
there were many which were ordained and became high priests of God.
And it was on account of their exceeding faith and repentance
and their righteousness before God,

they choosing to repent and work righteousness rather than to perish,

11 therefore they were called after this holy order and were sanctified;
and their garments were washed white through the blood of the Lamb.

12 Now they, after being sanctified by the Holy Ghost,
having their garments made white,
being pure and spotless before God,
could not look upon sin save it were with abhorrence.
And there were many—an exceeding great many—which were made pure
and entered into the rest of the Lord their God.

13 And now my brethren, I would that ye should humble yourselves before God
and bring forth fruit meet for repentance,
that ye may also enter into that rest.

14 Yea, humble yourselves even as the people in the days of Melchizedek,
who was also a high priest after this same order of which I have spoken,
who also took upon him the high priesthood forever.

15 And it was this same Melchizedek to whom Abraham paid tithes;
yea, even our father Abraham paid tithes of one tenth part of all he possessed.

16 Now these ordinances were given after this manner,
that thereby the people might look forward on the Son of God,
it being a type of his order or it being his order—
and this that they might look forward to him for a remission of their sins,
that they might enter into the rest of the Lord.

17 Now this Melchizedek was a king over the land of Salem.
And his people had waxed strong in iniquity and abominations;
yea, they had all gone astray;
they were full of all manner of wickedness.

18 But Melchizedek, having exercised mighty faith
and received the office of the high priesthood
according to the holy order of God,
did preach repentance unto his people.
And behold, they did repent.
And Melchizedek did establish peace in the land in his days;
therefore he was called the prince of peace,
for he was the king of Salem;
and he did reign under his father.

19 Now there were many before him,
and also there were many afterwards,
but none were greater.
Therefore of him they have more particularly made mention.

20 Now I need not rehearse the matter;
what I have said may suffice.

Behold, the scriptures are before you;
if ye will wrest them, it shall be to your own destruction.

21 And now it came to pass that when Alma had said these words unto them,
he stretched forth his hand unto them and cried with a mighty voice, saying:
Now is the time to repent,
for the day of salvation draweth nigh.

22 Yea, and the voice of the Lord by the mouth of angels
doth declare it unto all nations,
yea, doth declare it that they may have glad tidings of great joy.
Yea, and he doth sound these glad tidings among all his people,
yea, even to them that are scattered abroad upon the face of the earth;
wherefore they have come unto us.

23 And they are made known unto us in plain terms
that we may understand, that we cannot err—
and this because of our being wanderers in a strange land.
Therefore we are thus highly favored,
for we have these glad tidings declared unto us in all parts of our vineyard.

24 For behold, angels are declaring it unto many at this time in our land;
and this is for the purpose of preparing the hearts of the children of men
for to receive his word at the time of his coming in his glory.

25 And now we only wait to hear the joyful news,
declared unto us by the mouth of angels,
of his coming;
for the time cometh,
we know not how soon.
Would to God that it might be in my day;
but let it be sooner or later,
in it I will rejoice.

26 And it shall be made known unto just and holy men
by the mouth of angels at the time of his coming,
that the words of our fathers might be fulfilled,
according to that which they have spoken concerning him,
which was according to the spirit of prophecy which was in them.

27 And now my brethren, I wish from the inmost part of my heart
—yea, with great anxiety even unto pain—
that ye would hearken unto my words and cast off your sins
and not procrastinate the day of your repentance,

28 but that ye would humble yourselves before the Lord
and call on his holy name and watch and pray continually,
that ye may not be tempted above that which ye can bear,

and thus be led by the Holy Spirit,
becoming humble, meek, submissive, patient, full of love and all long-suffering,
29 having faith on the Lord,
having a hope that ye shall receive eternal life,
having the love of God always in your hearts,
that ye may be lifted up at the last day and enter into his rest.
30 And may the Lord grant unto you repentance,
that ye may not bring down his wrath upon you,
that ye may not be bound down by the chains of hell,
that ye may not suffer the second death.

31 And it came to pass that
Alma spake many more words unto the people
which are not written in this book.
14 | 1 And it came to pass that
after he had made an end of speaking unto the people,
many of them did believe on his words
and began to repent and to search the scriptures.
2 But the more part of them were desirous
that they might destroy Alma and Amulek,
for they were angry with Alma
because of the plainness of his words unto Zeezrom.
And they also said that Amulek had lied unto them
and had reviled against their law and also against their lawyers and judges.
3 And they were also angry with Alma and Amulek.
And because they had testified so plainly against their wickedness,
they sought to put them away privily.
4 But it came to pass that they did not,
but they took them and bound them with strong cords
and took them before the chief judge of the land.
5 And the people went forth and witnessed against them,
testifying that they had reviled against the law
and their lawyers and the judges of the land
and also all the people that were in the land,
and also testified that there was but one God
and that he should send his Son among the people,
but he should not save them;
and many such things did the people testify against Alma and Amulek.
And it came to pass that it was done before the chief judge of the land.

6 And it also came to pass that
Zeezrom was astonished at the words which had been spoken.
And he also knew concerning the blindness of the minds

which he had caused among the people by his lying words.

And his soul began to be harrowed up under a consciousness of his own guilt;
yea, he began to be encircled about by the pains of hell.

7 And it came to pass that he began to cry unto the people, saying:

Behold, I am guilty, and these men are spotless before God.

And it came to pass that he began to plead for them from that time forth,
but they reviled him, saying:

Art thou also possessed with the devil?

And it came to pass that they spit upon him

and cast him out from among them

and also all those who believed in the words

which had been spoken by Alma and Amulek.

And they cast them out and sent men to cast stones at them.

8 And they brought their wives and children together;

and whosoever believed or had been taught to believe in the word of God,
they caused that they should be cast into the fire.

And they also brought forth their records,

which contained the holy scriptures, and cast them into the fire also,
that they might be burned and destroyed by fire.

9 And it came to pass that they took Alma and Amulek

and carried them forth to the place of martyrdom,

that they might witness the destruction of those which were consumed by fire.

10 And it came to pass that

when Amulek saw the pains of the women and children

which were consuming in the fire,

he was also pained,

and he saith unto Alma:

How can we witness this awful scene?

Therefore let us stretch forth our hands

and exercise the power of God which is in us

and save them from the flames.

11 But Alma saith unto him:

The Spirit constraineth me that I must not stretch forth mine hand.

For behold, the Lord receiveth them up unto himself in glory.

And he doth suffer that they may do this thing

—or that the people may do this thing unto them—

according to the hardness of their hearts,

that the judgments which he shall exercise upon them in his wrath may be just.

And the blood of the innocent shall stand as a witness against them,

yea, and cry mightily against them at the last day.

12 Now Amulek saith unto Alma:

Behold, perhaps they will burn us also.

13 And Alma saith:
Be it according to the will of the Lord.
But behold, our work is not finished;
therefore they burn us not.

14 Now it came to pass that when the bodies of those
which had been cast into the fire were consumed,
and also the records which were cast in with them,
the chief judge of the land came
and stood before Alma and Amulek as they were bound,
and he smote them with his hand upon their cheeks
and saith unto them:
After what ye have seen, will ye preach again unto this people
that they shall be cast into a lake of fire and brimstone?

15 Behold, ye see that ye had not power to save these
which had been cast into the fire,
neither hath God saved them because they were of thy faith.
And the judge smote them again upon their cheeks and asked:
What say ye for yourselves?

16 Now this judge was after the order and faith of Nehor, which slew Gideon.

17 And it came to pass that Alma and Amulek answered him nothing.
And he smote them again
and delivered them to the officers to be cast into prison.

18 And it came to pass that when they had been cast into prison three days,
there came many lawyers and judges and priests and teachers
which were of the profession of Nehor,
and they came in unto the prison to see them.
And they questioned them about many words,
but they answered them nothing.

19 And it came to pass that the judge stood before them and saith:
Why do ye not answer the words of this people?
Know ye not that I have power to deliver ye up unto the flames?
And he commanded them to speak, but they answered nothing.

20 And it came to pass that they departed and went their ways,
but came again on the morrow.
And the judge also smote them again on their cheeks;
and many came forth also and smote them, saying:
Will ye stand again and judge this people and condemn our law?
If ye have such great power,
why do ye not deliver yourselves?

21 And many such things did they say unto them,

gnashing their teeth upon them and spitting upon them and saying:
How shall we look when we are damned?

22 And many such things,
yea, all manner of such things,
did they say unto them.
And thus they did mock them for many days.
And they did withhold food from them that they might hunger,
and water that they might thirst.
And they also did take from them their clothes that they were naked,
and thus they were bound with strong cords and confined in prison.

23 And it came to pass after they had thus suffered for many days
—and it was on the twelfth day in the tenth month in the tenth year
of the reign of the judges over the people of Nephi—
that the chief judge over the land of Ammonihah
and many of their teachers and their lawyers went in unto the prison
where Alma and Amulek was bound with cords.

24 And the chief judge stood before them and smote them again
and saith unto them:
If ye have the power of God,
deliver yourselves from these bands,
and then we will believe
that the Lord will destroy this people according to your words.

25 And it came to pass that they all went forth and smote them,
saying the same words, even until the last.
And when the last had spoken unto them,
the power of God was upon Alma and Amulek,
and they arose and stood upon their feet.

26 And Alma cried, saying:
How long shall we suffer these great afflictions, O Lord?
O Lord, give us strength
according to our faith which is in Christ,
even unto deliverance.
And they brake the cords with which they were bound.

And when the people saw this, they began to flee,
for the fear of destruction had come upon them.

27 And it came to pass that so great was their fear
that they fell to the earth and did not obtain the outer door of the prison.
And the earth shook mightily and the walls of the prison were rent in twain,
so that they fell to the earth;
and the chief judge and the lawyers and priests and teachers
which smote upon Alma and Amulek

were slain by the fall thereof.

28 And Alma and Amulek came forth out of the prison
and they were not hurt,
for the Lord had granted unto them power
according to their faith which was in Christ.
And they straightway came forth out of the prison,
and they were loosed from their bands;
and the prison had fallen to the earth,
and every soul which was within the walls thereof,
save it were Alma and Amulek, were slain;
and they straightway came forth into the city.

29 Now the people, having heard a great noise,
came running together by multitudes to know the cause of it.
And when they saw Alma and Amulek coming forth out of the prison
and the walls thereof had fallen to the earth,
they were struck with great fear
and fled from the presence of Alma and Amulek,
even as a goat fleeth with her young from two lions;
and thus they did flee from the presence of Alma and Amulek.

15 | 1 And it came to pass that
Alma and Amulek were commanded to depart out of that city.
And they departed and came out even into the land of Sidom.
And behold, there they found all the people
which had departed out of the land of Ammonihah,
who had been cast out and stoned
because they believed in the words of Alma.

2 And they related unto them
all that had happened unto their wives and children,
and also concerning themselves and of their power of deliverance.

3 And also Zeezrom lay sick at Sidom with a burning fever
which was caused by the great tribulations of his mind
on account of his wickedness,
for he supposed that Alma and Amulek was no more.
And he supposed that they had been slain by the cause of his iniquity.
And this great sin, and his many other sins, did harrow up his mind
until it did become exceeding sore, having no deliverance;
therefore he began to be scorched with a burning heat.

4 Now when he heard that Alma and Amulek was in the land of Sidom,
his heart began to take courage.
And he sent a message immediately unto them,
desiring them to come unto him.

5 And it came to pass that they went immediately,
obeying the message which he had sent unto them,
and they went in unto the house unto Zeezrom.
And they found him upon his bed, sick,
being very low with a burning fever;
and his mind also was exceeding sore because of his iniquities.
And when he saw them, he stretched forth his hand
and besought them that they would heal him.

6 And it came to pass that Alma said unto him, taking him by the hand:
Believest thou in the power of Christ unto salvation?

7 And he answered and said:
Yea, I believe all the words that thou hast taught.

8 And Alma saith:
If thou believest in the redemption of Christ,
thou canst be healed.

9 And he saith:
Yea, I believe according to thy words.

10 And then Alma cried unto the Lord, saying:
O Lord our God, have mercy on this man and heal him
according to his faith which is in Christ.

11 And it came to pass that when Alma had said these words
that Zeezrom leaped upon his feet and began to walk.
And this was done to the great astonishment of all the people,
and the knowledge of this went forth throughout all the land of Sidom.

12 And Alma baptized Zeezrom unto the Lord,
and he began from that time forth to preach unto the people.

13 And Alma established a church in the land of Sidom
and consecrated priests and teachers in the land,
to baptize unto the Lord whosoever were desirous to be baptized.

14 And it came to pass that they were many,
for they did flock in from all the region round about Sidom and were baptized.

15 But as to the people that were in the land of Ammonihah,
they yet remained a hard-hearted and a stiffnecked people.
And they repented not of their sins,
ascribing all the power of Alma and Amulek to the devil,
for they were of the profession of Nehor
and did not believe in the repentance of their sins.

16 And it came to pass that Alma and Amulek—
Amulek having forsaken all his gold and his silver
and his precious things which was in the land of Ammonihah
for the word of God,

he being rejected by those which were once his friends,
and also by his father and his kindred—
17 therefore after Alma having established the church at Sidom,
seeing a great check,
yea, seeing that the people were checked as to the pride of their hearts
and began to humble themselves before God
and began to assemble themselves together at their sanctuaries
to worship God before the altar,
watching and praying continually,
that they might be delivered from Satan and from death and from destruction—
18 now as I said, Alma having seen all these things,
therefore he took Amulek and came over to the land of Zarahemla
and took him to his own house
and did administer unto him in his tribulations
and strengthened him in the Lord.
19 And thus ended the tenth year
of the reign of the judges over the people of Nephi.

16 | 1 And it came to pass
in the eleventh year of the reign of the judges over the people of Nephi
on the fifth day of the second month,
there having been much peace in the land of Zarahemla,
there having been no wars nor contentions for a certain number of years,
even until the fifth day of the second month in the eleventh year,
there was a cry of war heard throughout the land.
2 For behold, the armies of the Lamanites had come in on the wilderness side
into the borders of the land, even into the city of Ammonihah,
and began to slay the people and to destroy the city.
3 And now it came to pass,
before the Nephites could raise a sufficient army to drive them out of the land,
they had destroyed the people which were in the city of Ammonihah,
and also some around the borders of Noah,
and taking others captive into the wilderness.

4 Now it came to pass that the Nephites were desirous to obtain those
which had been carried away captive into the wilderness.
5 Therefore he that had been appointed chief captain
over the armies of the Nephites
—and his name was Zoram, and he had two sons, Lehi and Aha—
now Zoram and his two sons
knowing that Alma was high priest over the church
and having heard that he had the spirit of prophecy,

therefore they went unto him and desired of him
to know whither the Lord would that they should go into the wilderness
in search of their brethren who had been taken captive by the Lamanites.

6 And it came to pass that Alma inquired of the Lord concerning the matter;
and Alma returned and said unto them:
Behold, the Lamanites will cross the river Sidon in the south wilderness,
away up beyond the borders of the land of Manti.
And behold, there shall ye meet them, on the east of the river Sidon,
and there the Lord will deliver unto thee thy brethren
which have been taken captive by the Lamanites.

7 And it came to pass that
Zoram and his sons crossed over the river Sidon with their armies
and marched away beyond the borders of Manti into the south wilderness,
which was on the east side of the river Sidon.
8 And they came upon the armies of the Lamanites,
and the Lamanites were scattered and driven into the wilderness.
And they took their brethren which had been taken captive by the Lamanites;
and there was not one soul of them which had been lost that were taken captive.
And they were brought by their brethren to possess their own lands.
9 And thus ended the eleventh year of the judges,
the Lamanites having been driven out of the land.

And the people of Ammonihah were destroyed;
yea, every living soul of the Ammonihahites were destroyed,
and also their great city,
which they said God could not destroy because of its greatness.
10 But behold, in one day it was left desolate,
and their carcasses were mangled by dogs and by wild beasts of the wilderness.
11 Nevertheless after many days
their dead bodies were heaped up upon the face of the earth,
and they were covered with a shallow covering.
And now so great was the scent thereof
that the people did not go in to possess the land of Ammonihah for many years.
And it was called Desolation of Nehors,
for they were of the profession of Nehor which were slain;
and their lands remained desolate.

12 And it came to pass that
the Lamanites did not come again to war against the Nephites
until the fourteenth year of the reign of the judges over the people of Nephi.
And thus for three years did the people of Nephi
have continual peace in all the land.

13 And Alma and Amulek went forth preaching repentance unto the people
   in their temples and in their sanctuaries and also in their synagogues,
   which was built after the manner of the Jews.

14 And as many as would hear their words,
   unto them they did impart the word of God
   without any respects of persons, continually.

15 And thus did Alma and Amulek go forth,
   and also many more which had been chosen for the work,
   to preach the word throughout all the land.
   And the establishment of the church became general throughout the land,
   in all the region round about, among all the people of the Nephites.

16 And there was no unequality among them,
   for the Lord did pour out his Spirit on all the face of the land
   for to prepare the minds of the children of men,
   or to prepare their hearts to receive the word
   which should be taught among them at the time of his coming,

17 that they might not be hardened against the word,
   that they might not be unbelieving and go on to destruction,
   but that they might receive the word with joy
   and as a branch be grafted into the true vine,
   that they might enter into the rest of the Lord their God.

18 Now those priests which did go forth among the people
   did preach against all lyings and deceivings and envyings and strifes
   and malice and revilings and stealing, robbing, plundering, murdering,
   committing adultery, and all manner of lasciviousness,
   crying that these things ought not so to be,

19 holding forth things which must shortly come,
   yea, holding forth the coming of the Son of God, his sufferings and death,
   and the resurrection of the dead.

20 And many of the people did inquire
   concerning the place where the Son of God should come.
   And they were taught that he would appear unto them after his resurrection,
   and this the people did hear with great joy and gladness.

21 And now after the church having been established throughout all the land,
   having got the victory over the devil,
   and the word of God being preached in its purity in all the land,
   and the Lord pouring out his blessings upon the people,
   and thus ended the fourteenth year
   of the reign of the judges over the people of Nephi.

An account of the sons of Mosiah,
which rejected their rights to the kingdom for the word of God
and went up to the land of Nephi to preach to the Lamanites.

Their sufferings and deliverance according to the record of Alma.

17 | 1 And now it came to pass that as Alma was journeying
from the land of Gideon southward, away to the land of Manti,
behold, to his astonishment he met the sons of Mosiah
a journeying towards the land of Zarahemla.

2 Now these sons of Mosiah were with Alma
at the time the angel first appeared unto him;
therefore Alma did rejoice exceedingly to see his brethren.
And what added more to his joy,
they were still his brethren in the Lord.
Yea, and they had waxed strong in the knowledge of the truth,
for they were men of a sound understanding;
and they had searched the scriptures diligently
that they might know the word of God.

3 But this is not all.
They had given themselves to much prayer and fasting;
therefore they had the spirit of prophecy and the spirit of revelation;
and when they taught, they taught with power and authority,
even as with the power and authority of God.

4 And they had been teaching the word of God
for the space of fourteen years among the Lamanites,
having had much success in bringing many to the knowledge of the truth;
yea, by the power of their words many were brought before the altar of God
to call on his name and confess their sins before him.

5 Now these are the circumstances which attended them in their journeyings,
for they had many afflictions:
they did suffer much, both in body and in mind,
such as hunger, thirst, and fatigue, and also much labor in the spirit.

6 Now these were their journeyings:
having taken leave of their father Mosiah
in the first year of the reign of the judges
—having refused the kingdom
which their father was desirous to confer upon them,
and also this was the minds of the people—

7 nevertheless they departed out of the land of Zarahemla
and took their swords and their spears

and their bows and their arrows and their slings;
and this they done that they might provide food for themselves
while in the wilderness.

8 And thus they departed into the wilderness
with their numbers which they had selected
to go up to the land of Nephi to preach the word unto the Lamanites.

9 And it came to pass that they journeyed many days in the wilderness.
And they fasted much and prayed much
that the Lord would grant unto them a portion of his Spirit
to go with them and abide with them,
that they might be an instrument in the hands of God
to bring, if it were possible, their brethren the Lamanites
to the knowledge of the truth,
to the knowledge of the baseness of the traditions of their fathers,
which were not correct.

10 And it came to pass that
the Lord did visit them with his Spirit
and said unto them: Be comforted.
And they were comforted.

11 And the Lord said unto them also:
Go forth among the Lamanites thy brethren and establish my word.
Yet ye shall be patient in long-suffering and afflictions,
that ye may shew forth good examples unto them in me.
And I will make an instrument of thee in my hands
unto the salvation of many souls.

12 And it came to pass that the hearts of the sons of Mosiah,
and also those which were with them,
took courage to go forth unto the Lamanites
to declare unto them the word of God.

13 And it came to pass
when they had arriven in the borders of the land of the Lamanites
that they separated themselves and departed one from another,
trusting in the Lord that they should meet again at the close of their harvest,
for they supposed that great was the work which they had undertaken.

14 And assuredly it was great,
for they had undertaken to preach the word of God
to a wild and a hardened and a ferocious people,
a people which delighted in the murdering the Nephites,
and robbing and plundering them.
And their hearts were set upon riches,

or upon gold and silver and precious stones,
yet they sought to obtain these things by murdering and plundering,
that they might not labor for them with their own hands.

15 Thus they were a very indolent people,
many of whom did worship idols.
And the curse of God had fell upon them
because of the traditions of their fathers,
notwithstanding the promises of the Lord were extended unto them
on the conditions of repentance.

16 Therefore this was the cause
for which the sons of Mosiah had undertaken the work,
that perhaps they might bring them unto repentance,
that perhaps they might bring them to know of the plan of redemption.

17 Therefore they separated themselves one from another
and went forth among them, every man alone,
according to the word and power of God which was given unto him.

18 Now Ammon being the chief among them,
or rather he did administer unto them,
he departed from them,
after having blessed them according to their several stations,
having imparted the word of God unto them,
or administered unto them before his departure.
And thus they took their several journeys throughout the land.

19 And Ammon went to the land of Ishmael,
the land being called after the sons of Ishmael, which also became Lamanites.

20 And as Ammon entered the land of Ishmael,
the Lamanites took him and bound him,
as was their custom to bind all the Nephites which fell into their hands
and carry them before the king.
And thus it was left to the pleasure of the king to slay them
or to retain them in captivity
or to cast them into prison
or to cast them out of his land,
according to his will and pleasure.

21 And thus Ammon was carried before the king
which was over the land of Ishmael
—and his name was Lamoni and he was a descendant of Ishmael—

22 and the king inquired of Ammon
if it were his desires to dwell in the land
among the Lamanites, or among his people.

23 And Ammon said unto him:

Yea, I desire to dwell among this people for a time,
yea, and perhaps until the day I die.

24 And it came to pass that king Lamoni was much pleased with Ammon
and caused that his bands should be loosed;
and he would that Ammon should take one of his daughters to wife.

25 But Ammon saith unto him:
Nay, but I will be thy servant.
Therefore Ammon became a servant to king Lamoni.

And it came to pass that he was set among other servants
to watch the flocks of Lamoni, according to the custom of the Lamanites.

26 And it came to pass that after he had been in the service of the king three days
that as he was with the Lamanitish servants
a going forth with their flocks to the place of water,
which was called the waters of Sebus
—and all the Lamanites drive their flocks hither that they might have water—

27 therefore as Ammon and the servants of the king
were driving forth their flocks to this place of water,
behold, a certain number of the Lamanites,
who had been with their flocks to water,
stood and scattered the flocks of Ammon and the servants of the king.
And they scattered them insomuch that they fled many ways.

28 Now the servants of the king began to murmur, saying:
Now the king will slay us as he has our brethren
because their flocks were scattered by the wickedness of these men.
And they began to weep exceedingly, saying:
Behold, our flocks are scattered already.

29 Now they wept because of the fear of being slain.
Now when Ammon saw this, his heart was swollen within him with joy,
for, said he, I will shew forth my power unto these my fellow servants,
or the power which is in me,
in restoring these flocks unto the king,
that I may win the hearts of these my fellow servants,
that I may lead them to believe in my words.

30 Now these were the thoughts of Ammon
when he saw the affliction of those which he termed to be his brethren.

31 And it came to pass that he flattered them by his words, saying:
My brethren, be of good cheer,
and let us go in search of the flocks;
and we will gather them together
and bring them back unto the place of water.

And thus we will reserve the flocks unto the king
and he will not slay us.

32 And it came to pass that they went in search of the flocks;
and they did follow Ammon,
and they rushed forth with much swiftness
and did head the flocks of the king
and did gather them together again to the place of water.

33 And those men again stood to scatter their flocks,
but Ammon saith unto his brethren:
Encircle the flocks round about that they flee not,
and I go and contend with these men which do scatter our flocks.

34 Therefore they did as Ammon had commanded them.

And he went forth and stood to contend with those
which stood by the waters of Sebus,
and they were not in number a very few.

35 Therefore they did not fear Ammon,
for they supposed that one of their men could slay him
according to their pleasure,
for they knew not that the Lord had promised Mosiah
that he would deliver his sons out of their hands,
neither did they know any thing concerning the Lord;
therefore they delighted in the destruction of their brethren,
and for this cause they stood to scatter the flocks of the king.

36 But Ammon stood forth and began to cast stones at them with his sling;
yea, with mighty power he did sling stones amongst them.
And thus he slew a certain number of them,
insomuch that they began to be astonished at his power.
Nevertheless they were angry because of the slain of their brethren,
and they were determined that he should fall.
Therefore seeing that they could not hit him with their stones,
they came forth with clubs to slay him.

37 But behold, every man that lifted his club to smite Ammon,
he smote off their arms with his sword,
for he did withstand their blows
by smiting their arms with the edge of his sword,
insomuch that they began to be astonished and began to flee before him;
yea, and they were not few in number.
And he caused them to flee by the strength of his arm.

38 Now six of them had fallen by the sling,
but he slew none with the sword save it were their leader.

And he smote off as many of their arms as was lifted against him,
and they were not a few.

39   And when he had driven them afar off, he returned.
And they watered their flocks and returned them to the pasture of the king
and then went in unto the king,
bearing the arms which had been smote off by the sword of Ammon
of those who sought to slay him.
And they were carried in unto the king
for a testimony of the things which they had done.

18 | 1   And it came to pass that king Lamoni caused
that his servants should stand forth and testify to all the things
which they had seen concerning the matter.

2   And when they had all testified to the things which they had seen
and he had learned of the faithfulness of Ammon in preserving his flocks
and also of his great power in contending against those who sought to slay him,
he was astonished exceedingly and saith:
Surely this is more than a man.
Behold, is not this the Great Spirit
which doth send such great punishments upon this people
because of their murders?

3   And they answered the king and said:
Whether he be the Great Spirit or a man, we know not.
But this much we do know,
that he cannot be slain by the enemies of the king,
neither can they scatter the king's flocks when he is with us
because of his expertness and great strength.
Therefore we know that he is a friend to the king.
And now, O king, we do not believe that a man hath such great power,
for we know that he cannot be slain.

4   And now when the king heard these words,
he said unto them:
Now I know that it is the Great Spirit;
and he hath come down at this time to preserve your lives,
that I might not slay you as I did your brethren.
Now this is the Great Spirit of which our fathers have spoken.

5   Now this was the tradition of Lamoni which he had received from his father,
that there was a Great Spirit;
notwithstanding they believed in a Great Spirit,
they supposed that whatsoever they did was right.
Nevertheless Lamoni began to fear exceedingly,

with fear lest he had done wrong in slaying his servants.

6 For he had slew many of them
because their brethren had scattered their flocks at the place of water;
and thus because they had had their flocks scattered,
they were slain.

7 Now it was the practice of these Lamanites
to stand by the waters of Sebus to scatter the flocks of the people
that thereby they might drive away many that were scattered
unto their own land,
it being a practice of plunder among them.

8 And it came to pass that king Lamoni inquired of his servants, saying:
Where is this man that hath such great power?

9 And they saith unto him:
Behold, he is a feeding thy horses.
Now the king had commanded his servants
previous to the time of the watering of their flocks
that they should prepare his horses and his chariots
and conduct him forth to the land of Nephi,
for there had been a great feast appointed at the land of Nephi
by the father of Lamoni, who was king over all the land.

10 Now when king Lamoni heard
that Ammon was preparing his horses and his chariots,
he was more astonished because of the faithfulness of Ammon, saying:
Surely there has not been any servant among all my servants
that has been so faithful as this man,
for even he doth remember all my commandments to execute them.

11 Now I surely know that this is the Great Spirit.
And I would desire him that he come in unto me,
but I durst not.

12 And it came to pass that
when Ammon had made ready the horses and the chariots
for the king and his servants,
he went in unto the king.
And he saw that the countenance of the king was changed;
therefore he was about to return out of his presence.

13 And one of the king's servants said unto him:
Rabbanah, which is being interpreted powerful or great king
—considering their kings to be powerful—
and thus he said unto him:
Rabbanah, the king desireth thee to stay.

14 Therefore Ammon turned himself unto the king and saith unto him:

What wilt thou that I should do for thee, O king?
And the king answered him not for the space of an hour
according to their time,
for he knew not what he should say unto him.

15 And it came to pass that Ammon said unto him again:
What desirest thou of me?
But the king answered him not.

16 And it came to pass that Ammon being filled with the Spirit of God,
therefore he perceived the thoughts of the king,
and he saith unto him:
Is it because that thou hast heard
that I defended thy servants and thy flocks
and slew seven of their brethren with the sling and with the sword
and smote off the arms of others
in order to defend thy flocks and thy servants?
Behold, is it this that causeth thy marvelings?

17 I say unto you:
What is it that thy marvelings are so great?
Behold, I am a man and am thy servant.
Therefore whatsoever thou desirest which is right, that will I do.

18 Now when the king had heard these words, he marveled again;
for he beheld that Ammon could discern his thoughts.
But notwithstanding this, king Lamoni did open his mouth and said unto him:
Who art thou?
Art thou that Great Spirit which knows all things?

19 Ammon answered and said unto him:
I am not.

20 And the king saith:
How knowest thou the thoughts of my heart?
Thou mayest speak boldly and tell me concerning these things.
And also tell me by what power
ye slew and smote off the arms of my brethren that scattered my flocks.

21 And now if thou wilt tell me concerning these things,
whatsoever thou desirest I will give unto thee.
And if it were needed, I would guard thee with my armies.
But I know that thou art more powerful than all they.
Nevertheless, whatsoever thou desirest of me,
I will grant it unto thee.

22 Now Ammon being wise yet harmless,
he saith unto Lamoni:
Wilt thou hearken unto my words

if I tell thee by what power I do these things?
And this is the thing that I desire of thee.

23 And the king answered him and said:
Yea, I will believe all thy words.
And thus he was caught with guile.

24 And Ammon began to speak unto him with boldness and said unto him:
Believest thou that there is a God?

25 And he answered unto him:
I do not know what that meaneth.

26 And then Ammon saith:
Believest thou that there is a Great Spirit?

27 And he saith: Yea.

28 And Ammon saith:
This is God.

And Ammon saith unto him again:
Believest thou that this Great Spirit, which is God,
created all things which is in heaven and in the earth?

29 And he saith:
Yea, I believe that he created all things which is in the earth.
But I do not know the heavens.

30 And Ammon saith unto him:
The heavens is a place where God dwells and all his holy angels.

31 And king Lamoni saith:
Is it above the earth?

32 And Ammon saith:
Yea, and he looketh down upon all the children of men;
and he knows all the thoughts and intents of the heart,
for by his hand were they all created from the beginning.

33 And king Lamoni saith:
I believe all these things which thou hast spoken.
Art thou sent from God?

34 Ammon saith unto him:
I am a man
—and man in the beginning was created after the image of God—
and I am called by his Holy Spirit to teach these things unto this people,
that they may be brought to a knowledge of that which is just and true.

35 And a portion of that Spirit dwelleth in me,
which giveth me knowledge and also power
according to my faith and desires which is in God.

36 Now when Ammon had said these words,
he began to the creation of the world,

and also to the creation of Adam,
and told him all the things concerning the fall of man
and rehearsed and laid before him
the records and the holy scriptures of the people,
which had been spoken by the prophets
even down to the time that their father Lehi left Jerusalem.

37 And he also rehearsed unto them
— for it was unto the king and to his servants —
all the journeyings of their fathers in the wilderness
and all their sufferings with hunger and thirst and their travail etc.

38 And he also rehearsed unto them
concerning the rebellions of Laman and Lemuel and the sons of Ishmael;
yea, all their rebellions did he relate unto them.
And he expounded unto them all the records and scriptures
from the time that Lehi left Jerusalem down to the present time.

39 But this is not all,
for he expounded unto them the plan of redemption,
which was prepared from the foundation of the world.
And he also made known unto them concerning the coming of Christ.
And all the works of the Lord did he make known unto them.

40 And it came to pass that
after he had said all these things and expounded them to the king
that the king believed all his words.

41 And he began to cry unto the Lord, saying:
O Lord, have mercy!
According to thy abundant mercy
which thou hast had upon the people of Nephi,
have upon me and my people!

42 And now when he had said this,
he fell unto the earth as if he were dead.

43 And it came to pass that his servants took him
and carried him in unto his wife and laid him upon a bed.
And he lay as if he were dead
for the space of two days and two nights.
And his wife and his sons and his daughters mourned over him
after the manner of the Lamanites, greatly lamenting his loss.

19 | 1 And it came to pass that after two days and two nights
they were about to take his body and lay it into a sepulchre
which they had made for the purpose of burying their dead.

2 Now the queen having heard of the fame of Ammon,
therefore she sent and desired that he should come in unto her.

3 And it came to pass that Ammon did as he was commanded
and went in unto the queen and desired to know
what she would that he should do.
4 And she saith unto him:
The servants of my husband have made it known unto me
that thou art a prophet of a holy God
and that thou hast power to do many mighty works in his name.
5 Therefore if this is the case,
I would that ye should go in and see my husband,
for he has been laid upon his bed for the space of two days and two nights.
And some say that he is not dead;
but others say that he is dead and that he stinketh
and that he ought to be placed in the sepulchre.
But as for myself, to me he doth not stink.

6 Now this was what Ammon desired,
for he knew that king Lamoni was under the power of God.
He knew that the dark veil of unbelief being cast away from his mind
and the light which did light up his mind,
which was the light of the glory of God,
which was a marvelous light of his goodness
—yea, this light had infused such joy into his soul,
the cloud of darkness having been dispelled,
and the light of everlasting life was lit up in his soul—
yea, he knew that this had overcame his natural frame
and he was carried away in God.
7 Therefore what the queen desired of him was his only desire.

Therefore he went in to see the king
according as the queen had desired him.
And he saw the king,
and he knew that he was not dead.
8 And he saith unto the queen:
He is not dead, but he sleepeth in God;
and on the morrow he shall rise again.
Therefore bury him not.
9 And Ammon saith unto her:
Believest thou this?
And she said unto him:
I have had no witness save thy word and the word of our servants.
Nevertheless I believe that it shall be according as thou hast said.
10 And Ammon said unto her:

Blessed art thou because of thy exceeding faith.
I say unto thee, woman,
there has not been such great faith among all the people of the Nephites.

11 And it came to pass that she watched over the bed of her husband
from that time even until that time on the morrow
which Ammon had appointed that he should rise.

12 And it came to pass that he arose according to the words of Ammon.
And as he arose, he stretched forth his hand unto the woman and said:
Blessed be the name of God!
And blessed art thou!

13 For as sure as thou livest,
behold, I have seen my Redeemer,
and he shall come forth and be born of a woman,
and he shall redeem all mankind who believe on his name.

Now when he had said these words, his heart was swollen within him.
And he sunk again with joy;
and the queen also sunk down,
being overpowered by the Spirit.

14 Now Ammon seeing the Spirit of the Lord poured out
according to his prayers
upon the Lamanites his brethren
—which had been the cause of so much mourning among the Nephites,
or among all the people of God,
because of their iniquities and their traditions—
and Ammon fell upon his knees
and began to pour out his soul
in prayer and thanksgiving to God for what he had done for his brethren;
and he also was overpowered with joy.
And thus they all three had sunk to the earth.

15 Now when the servants of the king had saw that they had fallen,
they also began to cry unto God,
for the fear of the Lord had come upon them also,
for it was they which had stood before the king
and testified unto him concerning the great power of Ammon.

16 And it came to pass that they did call on the name of the Lord in their might
even until they had all fallen to the earth,
save it were one of the Lamanitish women whose name was Abish,
she having been converted unto the Lord for many years
on account of a remarkable vision of her father

17 —thus having been converted to the Lord—
  never had made it known.

  Therefore when she saw
  that all the servants of Lamoni had fallen to the earth,
  and also her mistress the queen and the king,
  and Ammon lay prostrate upon the earth,
  she knew that it was the power of God.
  And supposing that this opportunity,
  by making known unto the people what had happened among them,
  that by beholding this scene
  it would cause them to believe in the power of God,
  therefore she ran forth from house to house making it known unto the people.

18 And they began to assemble themselves together unto the house of the king;
  and there came a multitude.
  And to their astonishment they beheld
  the king and the queen and their servants prostrate upon the earth;
  and they all lay there as though they were dead.
  And they also saw Ammon—
  and behold, he was a Nephite.

19 And now the people began to murmur among themselves,
  some saying that it was a great evil that had come upon them
  —or upon the king and his house—
  because he had suffered that the Nephite should remain in the land.

20 But others rebuked them, saying:
  The king hath brought this evil upon his house
  because he slew his servants
  who had had their flocks scattered at the waters of Sebus.

21 And they were also rebuked by those men
  which had stood at the waters of Sebus and scattered the flocks
  which belonged to the king,
  for they were angry with Ammon because of the number
  which he had slain of their brethren at the waters of Sebus
  while defending the flocks of the king.

22 Now one of them whose brother had been slain with the sword of Ammon,
  being exceeding angry with Ammon,
  drew his sword and went forth
  that he might let it fall upon Ammon to slay him.
  And as he lifted the sword to smite him,
  behold, he fell dead.

23 Now we see that Ammon could not be slain,
  for the Lord had said unto Mosiah his father:

I will spare him, and it shall be unto him according to thy faith.
Therefore Mosiah trusted him unto the Lord.

24 And it came to pass that when the multitude beheld
that the man had fell dead who lifted the sword to slay Ammon,
fear came upon them all.
And they durst not put forth their hands to touch him
or any of those which had fallen.
And they began to marvel again among themselves
what could be the cause of this great power
or what all these things could mean.
25 And it came to pass that there was many among them
who said that Ammon was the Great Spirit.
And others said he was sent by the Great Spirit.
26 But others rebuked them all,
saying that he was a monster
which hath been sent from the Nephites to torment us.
27 And there were some which said
that Ammon was sent by the Great Spirit
to afflict them because of their iniquities
and that it was the Great Spirit that had always attended the Nephites,
which had ever delivered them out of their hands.
And they said that it was this Great Spirit
which had destroyed so many of their brethren the Lamanites.
28 And thus the contention began to be exceeding sharp among them.

And while they were thus contending,
the woman servant which had caused the multitude to be gathered together came.
And when she saw the contention which was among the multitude,
she was exceeding sorrowful, even unto tears.
29 And it came to pass that she went and took the queen by the hand,
that perhaps she might raise her from the ground.
And as soon as she touched her hand,
she arose and stood upon her feet
and cried with a loud voice, saying:
O blessed Jesus who has saved me from an awful hell!
O blessed God, have mercy on this people!
30 And when she had said this, she clapped her hands,
being filled with joy,
speaking many words which were not understood.

And when she had done this,
she took the king Lamoni by the hand;
and behold, he arose and stood upon his feet.

31 And he immediately,
seeing the contention among his people,
went forth and began to rebuke them
and to teach them the words which he had heard from the mouth of Ammon.
And as many as heard his words believed and were converted unto the Lord.
32 But there was many among them who would not hear his words;
therefore they went their way.

33 And it came to pass that when Ammon arose,
he also administered unto them,
and also did all the servants of Lamoni.
And they did all declare unto the people the selfsame thing,
that their hearts had been changed,
that they had no more desire to do evil.
34 And behold, many did declare unto the people
that they had seen angels and had conversed with them.
And thus they had told them things of God and of his righteousness.

35 And it came to pass that there was many that did believe in their words.
And as many as did believe were baptized,
and they became a righteous people;
and they did establish a church among them.
36 And thus the work of the Lord did commence among the Lamanites.
Thus the Lord did begin to pour out his Spirit upon them.
And we see that his arm is extended to all people
who will repent and believe on his name.

20 | 1 And it came to pass that when they had established a church in that land
that king Lamoni desired that
Ammon should go with him to the land of Nephi,
that he might shew him unto his father.
2 And it came to pass that the voice of the Lord came to Ammon, saying:
Thou shalt not go up to the land of Nephi,
for behold, the king will seek thy life;
but thou shalt go to the land of Middoni,
for behold, thy brother Aaron and also Muloki and Ammah are in prison.

3 Now it came to pass that when Ammon had heard this,
he saith unto Lamoni:
Behold, my brother and brethren are in prison at Middoni;
and I go that I may deliver them.
4 Now Lamoni saith unto Ammon:
I know in the strength of the Lord thou canst do all things.
But behold, I will go with thee to the land of Middoni,

for the king of the land of Middoni,
whose name is Antiomno,
is a friend unto me.
Therefore I go to the land of Middoni
that I may flatter the king of the land
and he will cast thy brethren out of prison.
Now Lamoni saith unto him:
Who told thee that thy brethren were in prison?

5 And Ammon saith unto him:
No one hath told me save it be God;
and he said unto me:
Go and deliver thy brethren, for they are in prison in the land of Middoni.

6 Now when Lamoni had heard this,
he caused that his servants should make ready his horses and his chariots.

7 And he saith unto Ammon:
Come, I will go with thee down to the land of Middoni,
and there I will plead with the king that he will cast thy brethren out of prison.

8 And it came to pass that as Ammon and Lamoni was a journeying thither
that they met the father of Lamoni, who was king over all the land.

9 And behold, the father of Lamoni saith unto him:
Why did ye not come to the feast on that great day
when I made a feast unto my sons and unto my people?

10 And he also saith:
Whither art thou going with this Nephite,
which is one of the children of a liar?

11 And it came to pass that
Lamoni rehearsed unto him whither he was going,
for he feared to offend him.

12 And he also told him all the cause of his tarrying in his own kingdom,
that he did not go unto his father to the feast which he had prepared.

13 And now when Lamoni had rehearsed unto him all these things,
behold, to his astonishment his father was angry with him and saith:
Lamoni, thou art going to deliver these Nephites, which are sons of a liar;
behold, he robbed our fathers.
And now his children also are come amongst us
that they may by their cunning and their lyings deceive us,
that they again may rob us of our property.

14 Now the father of Lamoni commanded him
that he should slay Ammon with the sword;
and he also commanded him
that he should not go to the land of Middoni,

but that he should return with him to the land of Ishmael.

15 But Lamoni saith unto him:
I will not slay Ammon,
neither will I return to the land of Ishmael;
but I go to the land of Middoni that I may release the brethren of Ammon,
for I know that they are just men and holy prophets of the true God.

16 Now when his father heard these words,
he was angry with him,
and he drew his sword that he might smite him to the earth.

17 But Ammon stood forth and saith unto him:
Behold, thou shalt not slay thy son.
Nevertheless it were better that he should fall than thee,
for behold, he hath repented of his sins;
but if thou shouldst fall at this time in thine anger,
thy soul could not be saved.

18 And again, it is expedient that thou shouldst forbear,
for if thou shouldst slay thy son, he being an innocent man,
his blood would cry from the ground to the Lord his God
for vengeance to come upon thee,
and perhaps thou wouldst lose thy soul.

19 Now when Ammon had said these words unto him,
he answered him, saying:
I know that if I should slay my son that I should shed innocent blood,
for it is thou that hast sought to destroy him.

20 And he stretched forth his hand to slay Ammon,
but Ammon withstood his blows
and also smote his arm that he could not use it.

21 Now when the king saw that Ammon could slay him,
he began to plead with Ammon that he would spare his life.

22 But Ammon raised his sword and said unto him:
Behold, I will smite thee except thou wilt grant unto me
that my brethren may be cast out of prison.

23 Now the king fearing that he should lose his life said:
If thou wilt spare me,
I will grant unto thee whatsoever thou wilt ask,
even to the half of the kingdom.

24 Now when Ammon saw
that he had wrought upon the old king according to his desire,
he saith unto him:
If thou wilt grant that my brethren may be cast out of prison,
and also that Lamoni may retain his kingdom,

and that ye be not displeased with him
but grant that he may do according to his own desires
in whatsoever thing he thinketh,
and then will I spare thee;
otherwise, I will smite thee to the earth.

25 Now when Ammon had said these words,
the king began to rejoice because of his life.
26 And when he saw that Ammon had no desires to destroy him,
and when he also saw the great love he had for his son Lamoni,
he was astonished exceedingly and saith:
Because this is all that thou hast desired,
that I would release thy brethren
and suffer that my son Lamoni should retain his kingdom,
behold, I will grant unto you
that my son may retain his kingdom from this time and forever,
and I will govern him no more.
27 And I will also grant unto thee that thy brethren may be cast out of prison.
And thou and thy brethren may come unto me in my kingdom,
for I shall greatly desire to see thee.
For the king was greatly astonished at the words which he had spoken,
and also at the words which had been spoken by his son Lamoni,
therefore he was desirous to learn them.

28 And it came to pass that
Ammon and Lamoni proceeded on their journey towards the land of Middoni.
And it came to pass that Lamoni found favor in the eyes of the king of the land;
therefore the brethren of Ammon was brought forth out of prison.
29 And when Ammon did meet them, he was exceeding sorrowful;
for behold, they were naked and their skins were worn exceedingly
because of being bound with strong cords.
And they also had suffered hunger, thirst, and all kind of afflictions.
Nevertheless they were patient in all their sufferings.
30 And as it happened, it was their lot
to have fallen into the hands of a more hardened and a more stiffnecked people.
Therefore they would not hearken unto their words,
and they had cast them out and had smote them
and had driven them from house to house and from place to place
even until they had arriven to the land of Middoni.
And there they were taken and cast into prison
and bound with strong cords and kept in prison for many days
and were delivered by Lamoni and Ammon.

An account of the preaching of Aaron and Muloki and their brethren to the Lamanites.

21 | 1 Now when Ammon and his brethren separated themselves
in the borders of the land of the Lamanites,
behold, Aaron took his journey towards the land
which was called by the Lamanites Jerusalem,
calling it after the land of their fathers' nativity;
and it was away joining the borders of Mormon.

2 Now the Lamanites and the Amlicites and the people of Amulon
had built a great city which was called Jerusalem.

3 Now the Lamanites of themselves were sufficiently hardened,
but the Amlicites and the Amulonites were still harder.
Therefore they did cause the Lamanites that they should harden their hearts,
that they should wax stronger in wickedness and their abominations.

4 And it came to pass that Aaron came to the city of Jerusalem
and firstly began to preach to the Amlicites.
And he began to preach to them in their synagogues,
for they had built synagogues after the order of the Nehors,
for many of the Amlicites and the Amulonites
were after the order of the Nehors.

5 Therefore as Aaron entered into one of their synagogues
to preach unto the people,
and as he was speaking unto them,
behold, there arose an Amlicite and began to contend with him, saying:
What is that that thou hast testified?
Hast thou seen an angel?
Why do not angels appear unto us?
Behold, are not this people as good as thy people?

6 Thou also sayest:
Except we repent, we shall perish.
How knowest thou the thought and intent of our heart?
How knowest thou that we have cause to repent?
How knowest thou that we are not a righteous people?
Behold, we have built sanctuaries,
and we do assemble ourselves together to worship God.
We do believe that God will save all men.

7 Now Aaron said unto him:
Believest thou that the Son of God shall come
to redeem mankind from their sins?

8 And the man saith unto him:
　We do not believe that thou knowest any such thing.
　We do not believe in these foolish traditions.
　We do not believe that thou knowest of things to come,
　neither do we believe that thy fathers and also that our fathers did know
　concerning the things which they spake of,
　that which is to come.

9 Now Aaron began to open the scriptures unto them
　concerning the coming of Christ
　and also concerning the resurrection of the dead
　and that there could be no redemption for mankind
　save it were through the death and sufferings of Christ
　and the atonement of his blood.

10 And it came to pass that as he began to expound these things unto them,
　they were angry with him and began to mock him;
　and they would not hear the words which he spake.

11 Therefore when he saw that they would not hear his words,
　he departed out of the synagogue
　and came over to a village which was called Ani-Anti.
　And there he found Muloki a preaching the word unto them,
　and also Ammah and his brethren;
　and they contended with many about the word.

12 And it came to pass that they saw that the people would harden their hearts;
　therefore they departed and came over into the land of Middoni.
　And they did preach the word unto many,
　and few believed on the words which they taught.

13 Nevertheless Aaron and a certain number of his brethren
　were taken and cast into prison;
　and the remainder of them fled out of the land of Middoni
　unto the regions round about.

14 And those which were cast into prison suffered many things;
　and they were delivered by the hand of Lamoni and Ammon,
　and they were fed and clothed.

15 And they went forth again to declare the word.
　And thus they were delivered for the first time out of prison,
　and thus they had suffered.

16 And they went forth whithersoever they were led by the Spirit of the Lord,
　preaching the word of God in every synagogue of the Amlicites,
　or in every assembly of the Lamanites where they could be admitted.

17 And it came to pass that the Lord began to bless them,
　insomuch that they brought many to the knowledge of the truth.

Yea, they did convince many of their sins
and of the tradition of their fathers, which were not correct.

18 And it came to pass that Ammon and Lamoni returned
from the land of Middoni to the land of Ishmael,
which was the land of their inheritance.

19 And king Lamoni would not suffer
that Ammon should serve him or be his servant.

20 But he caused that there should be synagogues built in the land of Ishmael.
And he caused that his people — or the people which was under his reign —
should assemble themselves together.

21 And he did rejoice over them,
and he did teach them many things.
And he did also declare unto them
that they were a people which was under him
and that they were a free people,
that they were free from the oppressions of the king, his father,
for that his father had granted unto him that he might reign over the people
which were in the land of Ishmael and in all the land round about.

22 And he also declared unto them
that they might have the liberty of worshipping the Lord their God
according to their desires in whatsoever place they were in,
if it were in the land which was under the reign of king Lamoni.

23 And Ammon did preach unto the people of king Lamoni.
And it came to pass that he did teach them all things
concerning things pertaining to righteousness.
And he did exhort them daily with all diligence;
and they gave heed unto his word,
and they were zealous for keeping the commandments of God.

22 | 1 Now as Ammon was thus teaching the people of Lamoni continually,
we will return to the account of Aaron and his other brethren.
For after he departed from the land of Middoni,
he was led by the Spirit to the land of Nephi,
even to the house of the king which was over all the land
save it were the land of Ishmael,
and he was the father of Lamoni.

2 And it came to pass that he went in unto him,
into the king's palace, with his brethren
and bowed himself before the king and said unto him:
Behold, O king, we are the brethren of Ammon
whom thou hast delivered out of prison.

3 And now, O king, if thou wilt spare our lives, we will be thy servants.
And the king saith unto them:

Arise, for I will grant unto you your lives.
And I will not suffer that ye shall be my servants,
but I will insist that ye shall administer unto me.
For I have been somewhat troubled in mind
because of the generosity and the greatness of the words of thy brother Ammon.
And I desire to know the cause
why he has not come up out of Middoni with thee.

4 And Aaron saith unto the king:
Behold, the Spirit of the Lord hath called him another way;
he hath gone to the land of Ishmael to teach the people of Lamoni.

5 Now the king saith unto them:
What is this that ye have said concerning the Spirit of the Lord?
Behold, this is the thing which doth trouble me.

6 And also, what is this that Ammon said?
—if ye will repent, ye shall be saved;
and if ye will not repent, ye shall be cast off at the last day.

7 And Aaron answered him and said unto him:
Believest thou that there is a God?
And the king saith:
I know that the Amlicites say that there is a God.
And I have granted unto them that they should build sanctuaries,
that they might assemble themselves together to worship him.
And if now thou sayest there is a God,
behold, I will believe.

8 And now when Aaron heard this, his heart began to rejoice and he saith:
Behold, assuredly as thou livest, O king, there is a God.

9 And the king saith:
Is God that Great Spirit that brought our fathers out of the land of Jerusalem?

10 And Aaron said unto him:
Yea, he is that Great Spirit.
And he created all things, both in heaven and in earth.
Believest thou this?

11 And he saith:
Yea, I believe that the Great Spirit created all things.
And I desire that ye should tell me concerning all these things,
and I will believe thy words.

12 And it came to pass that when Aaron saw that the king would believe his words,
he began from the creation of Adam,
reading the scriptures unto the king,
how God created man after his own image
and that God gave him commandments

and that because of transgression man had fallen.

13 And Aaron did expound unto him the scriptures from the creation of Adam,
laying the fall of man before him and their carnal state,
and also the plan of redemption
which was prepared from the foundation of the world through Christ
for all whosoever would believe on his name.

14 And since man had fallen, he could not merit any thing of himself;
but the sufferings and death of Christ atoneth for their sins
through faith and repentance — etc. —
and that he breaketh the bands of death,
that the grave shall have no victory
and that the sting of death should be swallowed up in the hopes of glory.
And Aaron did expound all these things unto the king.

15 And it came to pass that
after Aaron had expounded these things unto him,
the king saith:
What shall I do that I may have this eternal life of which thou hast spoken?
Yea, what shall I do that I may be born of God,
having this wicked spirit rooted out of my breast,
and receive his Spirit, that I may be filled with joy,
that I may not be cast off at the last day?
Behold, saith he, I will give up all that I possess;
yea, I will forsake my kingdom that I may receive this great joy.

16 But Aaron saith unto him:
If thou desirest this thing,
if thou will bow down before God
—yea, if thou repent of all thy sins
and will bow down before God and call on his name in faith,
believing that ye shall receive—
then shalt thou receive the hope which thou desirest.

17 And it came to pass that when Aaron had said these words,
the king did bow down before the Lord upon his knees
—yea, even he did prostrate himself upon the earth—
and cried mightily, saying:

18 O God, Aaron hath told me that there is a God.
And if there is a God and if thou art God,
wilt thou make thyself known unto me?
And I will give away all my sins to know thee,
and that I may be raised from the dead and be saved at the last day.

And now when the king had said these words,
he was struck as if he were dead.

19 And it came to pass that his servants ran and told the queen
   all that had happened unto the king,
   and she came in unto the king.
   And when she saw him lay as if he were dead,
   and also Aaron and his brethren standing
   as though they had been the cause of his fall,
   she was angry with them
   and commanded that her servants—or the servants of the king—
   should take them and slay them.

20 Now the servants had seen the cause of the king's fall.
   Therefore they durst not lay their hands on Aaron and his brethren;
   and they pled with the queen, saying:
   Why commandest thou that we should slay these men
   when, behold, one of them is mightier than us all?
   Therefore we shall fall before them.

21 Now when the queen saw the fear of the servants,
   she also began to fear exceedingly
   lest there should some evil come upon her.
   And she commanded her servants that they should go and call the people,
   that they might slay Aaron and his brethren.

22 Now when Aaron saw the determination of the queen
   —and he also knowing the hardness of the hearts of the people
   feared lest that a multitude should assemble themselves together
   and there should be a great contention and a disturbance among them—
   therefore he put forth his hand and raised the king from the earth
   and said unto him: Stand!
   And he stood upon his feet, receiving his strength.

23 Now this was done in the presence of the queen and many of his servants.
   And when they saw it, they greatly marveled and began to fear.
   And the king stood forth and began to minister unto them;
   and he did minister unto them
   insomuch that his whole household were converted unto the Lord.

24 Now there was a multitude gathered together
   because of the commandment of the queen;
   and there began to be great murmurings among them
   because of Aaron and his brethren.

25 But the king stood forth among them and administered unto them.
   And it came to pass that they were pacified towards Aaron
   and those which were with him.

26 And it came to pass that when the king saw that the people were pacified,
   he caused that Aaron and his brethren should stand forth

in the midst of the multitude
and that they should preach the word unto them.

27 And it came to pass that the king sent a proclamation throughout all the land
amongst all his people which was in all his land,
which was in all the regions round about,
which was bordering even to the sea on the east and on the west,
and which was divided from the land of Zarahemla
by a narrow strip of wilderness which ran from the sea east even to the sea west,
and round about on the borders of the seashore
and the borders of the wilderness which was on the north
by the land of Zarahemla through the borders of Manti,
by the head of the river Sidon, running from the east towards the west;
and thus were the Lamanites and the Nephites divided.

28 Now the more idle part of the Lamanites lived in the wilderness and lived in tents.
And they were spread through the wilderness on the west in the land of Nephi,
yea, and also on the west of the land of Zarahemla in the borders by the seashore,
and on the west in the land of Nephi
in the place of their fathers' first inheritance,
and thus bordering along by the seashore.

29 And also there was many Lamanites on the east by the seashore
whither the Nephites had driven them.
And thus the Nephites were nearly surrounded by the Lamanites.

Nevertheless the Nephites had taken possession of all the northern parts
of the land bordering on the wilderness at the head of the river Sidon,
from the east to the west, round about on the wilderness side on the north,
even until they came to the land which they called Bountiful.

30 And it bordered upon the land which they called Desolation,
it being so far northward that it came into the land
which had been peopled and had been destroyed,
of whose bones we have spoken,
which was discovered by the people of Zarahemla,
it being the place of their first landing.

31 And they came from there up into the south wilderness.
Thus the land on the northward was called Desolation;
and the land on the southward was called Bountiful,
it being the wilderness which was filled
with all manner of wild animals of every kind,
a part of which had come from the land northward for food.

32 And now it was only the distance of a day and a half's journey for a Nephite
on the line between the land Bountiful and the land Desolation,

from the east to the west sea;
and thus the land of Nephi and the land of Zarahemla
was nearly surrounded by water,
there being a small neck of land
between the land northward and the land southward.

33 And it came to pass that the Nephites had inhabited the land Bountiful,
even from the east unto the west sea.

And thus the Nephites in their wisdom, with their guards and their armies,
had hemmed in the Lamanites on the south,
that thereby they should have no more possession on the north,
that they might not overrun the land northward.

34 Therefore the Lamanites could have no more possessions,
only in the land of Nephi and the wilderness round about.
Now this was wisdom in the Nephites, as the Lamanites were an enemy to them;
they would not suffer their afflictions on every hand —
and also that they might have a country
whither they might flee according to their desires.

35 And now I after having said this return again
to the account of Ammon, and Aaron, Omner, and Himni, and their brethren.

23 | 1 Behold, now it came to pass that
the king of the Lamanites sent a proclamation among all his people
that they should not lay their hands on Ammon or Aaron or Omner or Himni,
nor neither of their brethren which should go forth preaching the word of God,
in whatsoever place they should be in, in any part of their land.

2 Yea, he sent a decree among them
that they should not lay their hands on them
to bind them or to cast them into prison,
neither should they spit upon them nor smite them
nor cast them out of their synagogues nor scourge them,
neither should they cast stones at them,
but that they should have free access to their houses
and also their temples and their sanctuaries.

3 And thus they might go forth and preach the word according to their desires,
for the king had been converted unto the Lord, and all his household.
Therefore he sent this proclamation throughout the land unto his people,
that the word of God might have no obstruction
but that it might go forth throughout all the land,
that his people might be convinced
concerning the wicked traditions of their fathers,
and that they might be convinced that they were all brethren

and that they had not ought to murder nor to plunder nor to steal
nor to commit adultery nor to commit any manner of wickedness.

4 And now it came to pass that when the king had sent forth this proclamation
that Aaron and his brethren went forth from city to city
and from one house of worship to another,
establishing churches and consecrating priests and teachers
throughout the land among the Lamanites
to preach and to teach the word of God among them.
And thus they began to have great success.

5 And thousands were brought to the knowledge of the Lord;
yea, thousands were brought to believe in the traditions of the Nephites.
And they were taught the records and the prophecies
which were handed down even to the present time.

6 And as sure as the Lord liveth,
so sure as many as believed,
or as many as were brought to the knowledge of the truth
through the preaching of Ammon and his brethren
according to the spirit of revelation and of prophecy
and the power of God working miracles in them—
yea, I say unto you, as the Lord liveth,
as many of the Lamanites as believed in their preaching
and were converted unto the Lord
never did fall away.

7 For they became a righteous people;
they did lay down the weapons of their rebellion,
that they did not fight against God no more,
neither against any of their brethren.

8 Now these are they which were converted unto the Lord:

9 the people of the Lamanites which were in the land of Ishmael,

10 and also of the people of the Lamanites which were in the land of Middoni,

11 and also of the people of the Lamanites which were in the city of Nephi,

12 and also of the people of the Lamanites which were in the land of Shilom
and which were in the land of Shemlon
and in the city of Lemuel and in the city of Shimnilom.

13 And these are the names of the cities of the Lamanites
which were converted unto the Lord.
And these are they that laid down the weapons of their rebellion
—yea, all their weapons of war—
and they were all Lamanites.

14 And the Amlicites were not converted, save only one,
neither was any of the Amulonites;

but they did harden their hearts
and also the hearts of the Lamanites in that part of the land
whithersoever they dwelt,
yea, and all their villages and all their cities.

15 Therefore we have named all the cities of the Lamanites
in which they did repent
and come to the knowledge of the truth
and were converted.

16 And now it came to pass that
the king and those people which were converted were desirous
that they might have a name,
that thereby they might be distinguished from their brethren.
Therefore the king consulted with Aaron and many of their priests
concerning the name that they should take upon them,
that they might be distinguished.

17 And it came to pass that they called their name Anti-Nephi-Lehies,
and they were called by this name and were no more called Lamanites.

18 And they began to be a very industrious people;
yea, and they were friendly with the Nephites.
Therefore they did open a correspondence with them,
and the curse of God did no more follow them.

24 | 1 And it came to pass that the Amlicites and the Amulonites and the Lamanites
which were in the land of Amulon and also in the land of Helam
and which was in the land of Jerusalem
—and, in fine, in all the land round about—
which had not been converted
and had not taken upon them the name of Anti-Nephi-Lehi
were stirred up by the Amlicites and by the Amulonites
to anger against their brethren.

2 And their hatred became exceeding sore against them,
even insomuch that they began to rebel against their king,
insomuch that they would not that he should be their king.
Therefore they took up arms against the people of Anti-Nephi-Lehi.

3 Now the king conferred the kingdom upon his son,
and he called his name Anti-Nephi-Lehi.

4 And the king died in that selfsame year
that the Lamanites began to make preparations for war against the people of God.

5 Now when Ammon and his brethren and all those which had come up with them
saw the preparations of the Lamanites to destroy their brethren,
they came forth to the land of Middoni.
And there Ammon met all his brethren;

and from thence they came to the land of Ishmael
that they might hold a council with Lamoni,
and also with his brother Anti-Nephi-Lehi,
what they should do to defend themselves against the Lamanites.

6 Now there was not one soul among all the people
which had been converted unto the Lord
that would take up arms against their brethren.
Nay, they would not even make any preparations for war;
yea, and also their king commanded them that they should not.

7 Now these are the words which he said unto the people concerning the matter:
I thank my God, my beloved people, that our great God
has in goodness sent these our brethren, the Nephites, unto us,
to preach unto us and to convince us of the traditions of our wicked fathers.

8 And behold, I thank my great God
that he has given us a portion of his Spirit to soften our hearts,
that we have opened a correspondence with these brethren, the Nephites.

9 And behold, I also thank my God that by opening this correspondence
we have been convinced of our sins
and of the many murders which we have committed.

10 And I also thank my God, yea, my great God,
that he hath granted unto us that we might repent of these things,
and also that he hath forgiven us
of these our many sins and murders which we have committed
and took away the guilt from our hearts through the merits of his Son.

11 And now behold, my brethren,
since it has been all that we could do,
as we were the most lost of all mankind,
to repent of all our sins and the many murders which we have committed
and to get God to take them away from our hearts
—for it was all we could do to repent sufficiently before God
that he would take away our stains—

12 now my best beloved brethren,
since God hath taken away our stains and our swords have become bright,
then let us stain our swords no more with the blood of our brethren.

13 Behold, I say unto you:
Nay, let us retain our swords
that they be not stained with the blood of our brethren.
For perhaps if we should stain our swords again,
they can no more be washed bright
through the blood of the Son of our great God,
which shall be shed for the atonement of our sins.

14 And the great God has had mercy on us

and made these things known unto us that we might not perish.
Yea, and he hath made these things known unto us beforehand
because he loveth our souls as well as he loveth our children.
Therefore in his mercy he doth visit us by his angels,
that the plan of salvation might be made known unto us
as well as unto future generations.

15 O how merciful is our God!

And now behold, since it has been as much as we could do
to get our stains taken away from us and our swords are made bright,
let us hide them away that they may be kept bright
as a testimony to our God at the last day
—or at the day that we shall be brought to stand before him to be judged—
that we have not stained our swords in the blood of our brethren
since he imparted his word unto us and has made us clean thereby.

16 And now my brethren, if our brethren seek to destroy us,
behold, we will hide away our swords;
yea, even we will bury them deep in the earth,
that they may be kept bright
as a testimony that we have never used them,
at the last day.
And if our brethren destroy us,
behold, we shall go to our God and shall be saved.

17 And now it came to pass that
when the king had made an end of these sayings,
and all the people were assembled together,
they took their swords and all the weapons
which were used for the shedding of man's blood
and they did bury them up deep in the earth.

18 And thus they did,
it being in their view a testimony to God and also to men
that they never would use weapons again for the shedding of man's blood.

And this they did, vouching and covenanting with God that
rather than to shed the blood of their brethren,
they would give up their own lives;
and rather than to take away from a brother,
they would give unto him;
and rather than to spend their days in idleness,
they would labor abundantly with their hands.

19 And thus we see that
when these Lamanites were brought to believe and to know the truth
that they were firm and would suffer even unto death

rather than to commit sin.
And thus we see that they buried the weapons of peace —
or they buried the weapons of war for peace.

20 And it came to pass that their brethren the Lamanites
made preparations for war and came up to the land of Nephi
for the purpose of dethroning the king and to place another in his stead,
and also of destroying the people of Anti-Nephi-Lehi out of the land.

21 And it came to pass that when the people saw
that they were coming against them,
they went out to meet them and prostrated themselves before them to the earth
and began to call on the name of the Lord.
And thus they were in this attitude
when the Lamanites began to fall upon them
and began to slay them with the sword.

22 And thus without meeting any resistance
they did slay a thousand and five of them.
And we know that they are blessed,
for they have gone to dwell with their God.

23 Now when the Lamanites saw that their brethren would not flee from the sword,
neither would they turn aside to the right hand or to the left,
but that they would lay down and perish
and praised God even in the very act of perishing under the sword —

24 now when the Lamanites saw this, they did forbear from slaying them.
And there were many whose hearts had swollen in them
for those of their brethren who had fallen under the sword,
for they repented of the thing which they had done.

25 And it came to pass that they threw down their weapons of war
and they would not take them again,
for they were stung for the murders which they had committed.
And they came down, even as their brethren,
relying upon the mercies of those whose arms were lifted to slay them.

26 And it came to pass that the people of God were joined that day
by more than the number which had been slain.
And those which had been slain were righteous people;
therefore we have no reason to doubt but what they are saved.

27 And there was not a wicked man slain among them,
but there were more than a thousand brought to the knowledge of the truth.
Thus we see that the Lord worketh in many ways to the salvation of his people.

28 Now the greatest number of those of the Lamanites
which slew so many of their brethren
were Amlicites and Amulonites,

the greatest number of whom were after the order of the Nehors.

29 Now among those which joined the people of the Lord,
there were none which were Amlicites or Amulonites,
or which were after the order of Nehor,
but they were actual descendants of Laman and Lemuel.

30 And thus we can plainly discern that
after a people has been once enlightened by the Spirit of God
and hath had great knowledge of things pertaining to righteousness
and then have fallen away into sin and transgression,
they become more hardened;
and thus their state becometh worse
than as though they had never known these things.

25 | 1 And behold, now it came to pass that
these Lamanites were more angry because they had slain their brethren.
Therefore they sware vengeance upon the Nephites.
And they did no more attempt to slay the people of Anti-Nephi-Lehi at that time,

2 but they took their armies and went over
into the borders of the land of Zarahemla
and fell upon the people which were in the land of Ammonihah
and destroyed them.

3 And after that, they had many battles with the Nephites,
in the which they were driven and slain.

4 And among the Lamanites which were slain
were almost all the seed of Amulon and his brethren,
which were the priests of Noah;
and they were slain by the hands of the Nephites.

5 And the remainder having fled into the east wilderness
and having usurped the power and authority over the Lamanites
caused that many of the Lamanites should perish by fire because of their belief.

6 For many of them, after having suffered much loss and so many afflictions,
they began to be stirred up in remembrance of the words
which Aaron and his brethren had preached to them in their land.
Therefore they began to disbelieve the traditions of their fathers
and to believe in the Lord
and that he gave great power unto the Nephites;
and thus there were many of them converted in the wilderness.

7 And it came to pass that those rulers
which were the remnant of the children of Amulon
caused that they should be put to death,
yea, all those that believed in these things.

8 Now this martyrdom caused

that many of their brethren should be stirred up to anger.
And there began to be contention in the wilderness,
and the Lamanites began to hunt the seed of Amulon and his brethren
and began to slay them;
and they fled into the east wilderness.

9 And behold, they are hunted at this day by the Lamanites.

Thus the words of Abinadi was brought to pass
which he said concerning the seed of the priests,
which caused that he should suffer death by fire.

10 For he said unto them:
What ye shall do unto me shall be a type of things to come.

11 And now Abinadi was the first
that suffered death by fire because of his belief in God.
Now this is what he meant,
that many should suffer death by fire according as he had suffered.

12 And he said unto the priests of Noah
that their seed should cause many to be put to death in the like manner as he was,
and that they should be scattered abroad and slain,
even as a sheep having no shepherd is driven and slain by wild beasts.
And now behold, these words were verified,
for they were driven by the Lamanites,
and they were hunted and they were smitten.

13 And it came to pass that
when the Lamanites saw that they could not overpower the Nephites,
they returned again to their own land;
and many of them came over to dwell
in the land of Ishmael and the land of Nephi
and did join themselves to the people of God,
which was the people of Anti-Nephi-Lehi.

14 And they did also bury their weapons of war according as their brethren had.
And they began to be a righteous people,
and they did walk in the ways of the Lord
and did observe to keep his commandments and his statutes.

15 Yea, and they did keep the law of Moses,
for it was expedient that they should keep the law of Moses as yet,
for it was not all fulfilled.
But notwithstanding the law of Moses,
they did look forward to the coming of Christ,
considering that the law of Moses was a type of his coming
and believing that they must keep those outward performances
until the time that he should be revealed unto them.

16 Now they did not suppose that salvation came by the law of Moses,

but the law of Moses did serve to strengthen their faith in Christ.
And thus they did retain a hope through faith unto eternal salvation,
relying upon the spirit of prophecy, which spake of those things to come.

17 And now behold, Ammon and Aaron and Omner and Himni and their brethren
did rejoice exceedingly for the success which they had had among the Lamanites,
seeing that the Lord had granted unto them according to their prayers
and that he had also verified his word unto them in every particular.

26 | 1 And now these are the words of Ammon to his brethren, which saith thus:
My brothers and my brethren, behold, I say unto you:
How great reason have we to rejoice!
For could we have supposed when we started from the land of Zarahemla
that God would have granted unto us such great blessings?

2 And now I ask:
What great blessings hath he bestowed upon us?
Can ye tell?

3 Behold, I answer for you:
For our brethren the Lamanites were in darkness,
yea, even in the darkest abyss.
But behold, how many of them are brought
to behold the marvelous light of God!
And this is the blessing which hath been bestowed upon us,
that we have been made instruments in the hands of God
to bring about this great work.

4 Behold, thousands of them do rejoice
and have been brought into the fold of God.

5 Behold, the field was ripe.
And blessed are ye,
for ye did thrust in the sickle and did reap with your mights;
yea, all the day long did ye labor —
and behold the number of your sheaves!
And they shall be gathered into the garners, that they are not wasted.

6 Yea, they shall not be beaten down by the storm at the last day.
Yea, neither shall they be harrowed up by the whirlwinds;
but when the storm cometh, they shall be gathered together in their place,
that the storm cannot penetrate to them.
Yea, neither shall they be driven with fierce winds
whithersoever the enemy listeth to carry them.

7 But behold, they are in the hands of the Lord of the harvest.
And they are his, and he will raise them up at the last day.

8 Blessed be the name of our God!
Let us sing to his praise;

yea, let us give thanks to his holy name,
for he doth work righteousness forever.

9 For if we had not come up out of the land of Zarahemla,
these our dearly beloved brethren, which have so dearly beloved us,
would still have been racked with hatred against us.
Yea, and they would also have been strangers to God.

10 And it came to pass that when Ammon had said these words,
his brother Aaron rebuked him, saying:
Ammon, I fear that thy joy doth carry thee away unto boasting.

11 But Ammon saith unto him:
I do not boast in my own strength or in my own wisdom;
but behold, my joy is full.
Yea, my heart is brim with joy,
and I will rejoice in my God.

12 Yea, I know that I am nothing;
as to my strength, I am weak.
Therefore I will not boast of myself, but I will boast of my God;
for in his strength I can do all things.

Yea, behold, many mighty miracles we have wrought in this land,
for which we will praise his name forever.

13 Behold how many thousands of our brethren
hath he loosed from the pains of hell!
And they are brought to sing redeeming love—
and this because of the power of his word which is in us.
Therefore have we not great reason to rejoice?

14 Yea, we have reason to praise him forever,
for he is the Most High God
and has loosed these our brethren from the chains of hell.

15 Yea, they were encircled about with everlasting darkness and destruction;
but behold, he hath brought them into his everlasting light,
yea, into everlasting salvation.
And they are encircled about with the matchless bounty of his love.
Yea, and we have been instruments in his hands
of doing this great and marvelous work.

16 Therefore let us glory.
Yea, we will glory in the Lord;
yea, we will rejoice, for our joy is full;
yea, we will praise our God forever.
Behold, who can glory too much in the Lord?
Yea, who can say too much of his great power and of his mercy
and of his long-suffering towards the children of men?

Behold, I say unto you:
I cannot say the smallest part which I feel.

17 Who could have supposed that our God would have been so merciful
as to have snatched us from our awful, sinful, and polluted state?

18 Behold, we went forth even in wrath
with mighty threatenings to destroy his church.

19 O then why did he not consign us to an awful destruction?
Yea, why did he not let the sword of his justice fall upon us
and doom us to eternal despair?

20 O my soul almost, as it were, fleeth at the thought.
Behold, he did not exercise his justice upon us,
but in his great mercy hath brought us
over that everlasting gulf of death and misery,
even to the salvation of our souls.

21 And now behold, my brethren,
what natural man is there that knoweth these things?
I say unto you:
There is none that knoweth these things save it be the penitent.

22 Yea, he that repenteth and exerciseth faith
and bringeth forth good works and prayeth continually without ceasing,
unto such it is given to know the mysteries of God.
Yea, unto such it shall be given to reveal things which never have been revealed.
Yea, and it shall be given unto such to bring thousands of souls to repentance,
even as it hath been given unto us to bring these our brethren to repentance.

23 Now, do ye remember, my brethren,
that we said unto our brethren in the land of Zarahemla:
We go up to the land of Nephi to preach unto our brethren the Lamanites.
And they laughed us to scorn,

24 for they said unto us:
Do ye suppose that ye can bring the Lamanites to the knowledge of the truth?
Do ye suppose that ye can convince the Lamanites
of the incorrectness of the traditions of their fathers,
as stiffnecked a people as they are,
whose hearts delighteth in the shedding of blood,
whose days have been spent in the grossest iniquity,
whose ways have been the ways of a transgressor from the beginning?
Now my brethren, ye remember that this was their language.

25 And moreover they did say:
Let us take up arms against them,
that we destroy them and their iniquity out of the land,
lest they overrun us and destroy us.

26 But behold, my beloved brethren, we came into the wilderness,
not with the intent to destroy our brethren,
but with the intent that perhaps we might save some few of their souls.

27 Now when our hearts were depressed and we were about to turn back,
behold, the Lord comforted us and said:
Go amongst thy brethren, the Lamanites,
and bear with patience thine afflictions;
and I will give unto thee success.

28 And now behold, we have come and been forth amongst them;
and we have been patient in our sufferings.
And we have suffered every privation;
yea, we have traveled from house to house,
relying upon the mercies of the world—
not upon the mercies of the world alone,
but upon the mercies of God.

29 And we have entered into their houses and taught them;
and we have taught them in their streets;
yea, and we have taught them upon their hills;
and we have also entered into their temples
and their synagogues and taught them.
And we have been cast out and mocked
and spit upon and smote upon our cheeks.
And we have been stoned
and taken and bound with strong cords and cast into prison;
and through the power and wisdom of God we have been delivered again.

30 And we have suffered all manner of afflictions—
and all this that perhaps we might be the means of saving some soul.
And we supposed that our joy would be full
if perhaps we could be the means of saving some.

31 Now behold, we can look forth and see the fruits of our labors.
And are they few?
I say unto you:
Nay, they are many.
Yea, and we can witness of their sincerity
because of their love towards their brethren and also towards us.

32 For behold, they had rather sacrifice their lives
than even to take the life of their enemy.
And they have buried their weapons of war deep in the earth
because of their love towards their brethren.

33 And now behold, I say unto you:
Has there been so great love in all the land?

Behold, I say unto you: Nay.
There has not, even among the Nephites.

34 For behold, they would take up arms against their brethren;
they would not suffer themselves to be slain.
But behold, how many of these have laid down their lives!
And we know that they have gone to their God
because of their love and of their hatred to sin.

35 Now, have we not reason to rejoice?
Yea, I say unto you:
There never was men that had so great reason to rejoice as we
since the world began.
Yea, and my joy is carried away, even unto boasting in my God.
For he has all power, all wisdom, and all understanding;
he comprehendeth all things, and he is a merciful Being,
even unto salvation to those who will repent and believe on his name.

36 Now if this is boasting, even so will I boast.
For this is my life and my light,
my joy and my salvation and my redemption from everlasting woe.
Yea, blessed is the name of my God,
who hath been mindful of this people,
which are a branch of the tree of Israel
and hath been lost from its body in a strange land.
Yea, I say:
Blessed be the name of my God,
who hath been mindful of us, wanderers in a strange land.

37 Now my brethren, we see that God is mindful of every people
in whatsoever land they may be in;
yea, he numbereth his people.
And his bowels of mercy is over all the earth.
Now this is my joy and my great thanksgiving.
Yea, and I will give thanks unto my God forever.
Amen.

27 | 1 Now it came to pass that
when those Lamanites which had gone to war against the Nephites had found
after their many struggles for to destroy them
that it was in vain to seek their destruction,
they returned again to the land of Nephi.

2 And it came to pass that
the Amlicites, because of their loss, were exceeding angry.

And when they saw they could not seek revenge from the Nephites,
they began to stir up the people in anger
against their brethren, the people of Anti-Nephi-Lehi.
Therefore they began again to destroy them.

3 Now this people again refused to take their arms;
and they suffered themselves to be slain according to the desires of their enemy.

4 Now when Ammon and his brethren saw this work of destruction
among those who they so dearly beloved
and among those who had so dearly beloved them
—for they were treated as though they were angels sent from God
to save them from an everlasting destruction—
therefore when Ammon and his brethren saw this great work of destruction,
they were moved with compassion,
and they said unto the king:

5 Let us gather together this people of the Lord,
and let us go down to the land of Zarahemla to our brethren the Nephites
and flee out of the hands of our enemies, that we be not destroyed.

6 But the king saith unto them:
Behold, the Nephites will destroy us
because of the many murders and sins we have committed against them.

7 And Ammon saith:
I will go and inquire of the Lord.
And if he saith unto us, go down unto our brethren, will ye go?

8 And the king saith unto him:
Yea, if the Lord saith unto us, go, we will go down unto our brethren;
and we will be their slaves
until we repair unto them the many murders and sins
which we have committed against them.

9 But Ammon saith unto him:
It is against the law of our brethren which was established by my father
that there should be any slaves among them.
Therefore let us go down and rely upon the mercies of our brethren.

10 But the king saith unto him:
Inquire of the Lord,
and if he saith unto us, go, we will go.
Otherwise, we will perish in the land.

11 And it came to pass that Ammon went and inquired of the Lord,
and the Lord said unto him:

12 Get this people out of this land, that they perish not,
for Satan hath great hold on the hearts of the Amlicites,

which do stir up the Lamanites to anger against their brethren to slay them;
therefore get thee out of this land.
And blessed are this people in this generation,
for I will preserve them.

13 And now it came to pass that Ammon went and told the king
all the words which the Lord had said unto him.

14 And it came to pass that they gathered together all their people
—yea, all the people of the Lord—
and did gather together all their flocks and herds
and departed out of the land and came into the wilderness
which divided the land of Nephi from the land of Zarahemla
and came over near the borders of the land.

15 And it came to pass that Ammon saith unto them:
Behold, I and my brethren will go forth into the land of Zarahemla,
and ye shall remain here until we return;
and we will try the hearts of our brethren,
whether they will that ye shall come into their land.

16 And it came to pass that as Ammon was going forth into the land
that he and his brethren met Alma over in the place of which has been spoken.
And behold, this was a joyful meeting.

17 Now the joy of Ammon was so great even that he was full.
Yea, he was swallowed up in the joy of his God,
even to the exhausting of his strength.
And he fell again to the earth.

18 Now, was not this exceeding joy?
Behold, this is joy which none receiveth
save it be the truly penitent and humble seeker of happiness.

19 Now the joy of Alma in meeting his brethren was truly great,
and also the joy of Aaron, of Omner and Himni;
but behold, their joy was not that to exceed their strength.

20 And now it came to pass that Alma conducted his brethren
back to the land of Zarahemla, even to his own house.
And it came to pass that they went and told the chief judge
all the things which had happened unto them
in the land of Nephi among their brethren the Lamanites.

21 And it came to pass that the chief judge
sent a proclamation throughout all the land,
desiring the voice of the people concerning the admitting their brethren,
which were the people of Anti-Nephi-Lehi.

22 And it came to pass that the voice of the people came, saying:
Behold, we will give up the land of Jershon,

which is on the east by the sea,
which joins the land Bountiful,
which is on the south of the land Bountiful.
And this land Jershon is the land
which we will give unto our brethren for an inheritance.

23 And behold, we will set our armies between the land Jershon and the land Nephi,
that we may protect our brethren in the land of Jershon.
And this we do for our brethren
on account of their fear to take up arms against their brethren
lest they should commit sin;
and this their great fear came because of their sore repentance
which they had on account of their many murders and their awful wickedness.

24 And now behold, this will we do unto our brethren
that they may inherit the land Jershon.
And we will guard them from their enemies by our armies
on conditions that they will give us a portion of their substance
to assist us that we may maintain our armies.

25 Now it came to pass that when Ammon had heard this,
he returned to the people of Anti-Nephi-Lehi, and also Alma with him,
into the wilderness where they had pitched their tents
and made known unto them all these things.
And Alma also related unto them his conversion
with Ammon and Aaron and his brethren.

26 And it came to pass that it did cause great joy among them.

And it came to pass that they went down into the land of Jershon
and took possession of the land of Jershon.
And they were called by the Nephites the people of Ammon;
therefore they were distinguished by that name ever after.

27 And they were numbered among the people of Nephi,
and also numbered among the people which were of the church of God.
And they were also distinguished for their zeal
towards God and also towards men,
for they were perfectly honest and upright in all things.
And they were firm in the faith of Christ, even unto the end.

28 And they did look upon shedding the blood of their brethren
with the greatest abhorrence.
And they never could be prevailed upon to take up arms against their brethren.
And they never did look upon death with any degree of terror
for their hope and views of Christ and the resurrection.
Therefore death was swallowed up to them by the victory of Christ over it.

29 Therefore they would suffer death
in the most aggravating and distressing manner

which could be inflicted by their brethren
before they would take the sword or the scimitar to smite them.

30　And thus they were a zealous and beloved people,
a highly favored people of the Lord.

28 | 1　And now it came to pass that
after the people of Ammon were established in the land of Jershon
— and a church also established in the land —
and the armies of the Nephites were set round about the land of Jershon
— yea, in all the borders round about the land of Zarahemla —
behold, the armies of the Lamanites
had followed their brethren into the wilderness.

2　And thus there was a tremendious battle,
yea, even such an one as never had been known among all the people in the land
from the time Lehi left Jerusalem.
Yea, and tens of thousands of the Lamanites were slain and scattered abroad.

3　Yea, and also there was a tremendious slaughter among the people of Nephi;
nevertheless the Lamanites were driven and scattered,
and the people of Nephi returned again to their lands.

4　And now this was a time that there was a great mourning and lamentation
heard throughout all the land among all the people of Nephi—

5　yea, the cry of widows mourning for their husbands,
and also of fathers a mourning for their sons,
and the daughter for the brother,
yea, and the brother for the father.
And thus the cry of mourning was heard among every one of them,
a mourning for their kindred which had been slain.

6　And now surely this was a sorrowful day,
yea, a time of solemnity and a time of much fasting and prayer.

7　And thus ended the fifteenth year
of the reign of the judges over the people of Nephi.

8　And this is the account of Ammon and his brethren,
their journeyings into the land of Nephi,
their sufferings in the land,
their sorrows and their afflictions,
and their incomprehensible joy,
and the reception and safety of the brethren in the land of Jershon.
And now may the Lord, the Redeemer of all men, bless their souls forever.

9　And this is the account of the wars and contentions among the Nephites,
and also the wars between the Nephites and the Lamanites;
and the fifteenth year of the reign of the judges is ended.

10　And from the first year to the fifteenth has brought to pass

the destruction of many thousand lives;
yea, it has brought to pass an awful scene of bloodshed.

11 And the bodies of many thousands are laid low in the earth,
while the bodies of many thousands are moldering
in heaps upon the face of the earth.
Yea, and many thousands are mourning for the loss of their kindred
because they have reason to fear, according to the promises of the Lord,
that they are consigned to a state of endless woe,

12 while many thousands of others truly mourn for the loss of their kindred,
yet they rejoice and exult in the hope
—yea, and even know according to the promises of the Lord—
that they are raised to dwell at the right hand of God
in a state of never-ending happiness.

13 And thus we see how great the unequality of man is
because of sin and transgression and the power of the devil,
which comes by the cunning plans which he hath devised
to ensnare the hearts of men.

14 And thus we see the great call of the diligence of men
to labor in the vineyards of the Lord.
And thus we see the great reason of sorrow and also of rejoicing—
sorrow because of death and destruction among men,
and joy because of the light of Christ unto life.

29 | 1 O that I were an angel and could have the wish of mine heart,
that I might go forth and speak with the trump of God,
with a voice to shake the earth
and cry repentance unto every people!

2 Yea, I would declare unto every soul as with the voice of thunder
repentance and the plan of redemption,
that they should repent and come unto our God,
that there might be no more sorrow upon all the face of the earth.

3 But behold, I am a man and do sin in my wish,
for I had ought to be content with the things
which the Lord hath allotted unto me.

4 I had not ought to harrow up in my desires the firm decree of a just God,
for I know that he granteth unto men according to their desires,
whether it be unto death or unto life.
Yea, I know that he allotteth unto man,
yea, decreeth unto them decrees which are unalterable according to their wills,
whether it be unto salvation or unto destruction.

5 Yea, and I know that good and evil hath come before all men
—or he that knoweth not good from evil is blameless—

but he that knoweth good and evil,
to him it is given according to his desires,
whether he desireth good or evil, life or death, joy or remorse of conscience.

6 Now seeing that I know these things,
why should I desire more
than to perform the work to which I have been called?
7 Why should I desire that I was an angel,
that I could speak unto all the ends of the earth?
8 For behold, the Lord doth grant
unto all nations of their own nation and tongue
to teach his word,
yea, in wisdom all that he seeth fit that they should have.
Therefore we see that the Lord doth counsel in his wisdom
according to that which is just and true.
9 I know that which the Lord hath commanded me,
and I glory in it.
I do not glory of myself,
but I glory in that which the Lord hath commanded me.
Yea, and this is my glory,
that perhaps I may be an instrument in the hands of God
to bring some soul to repentance;
and this is my joy.

10 And behold, when I see many of my brethren truly penitent
and coming to the Lord their God,
then is my soul filled with joy;
then do I remember what the Lord has done for me,
yea, even that he hath heard my prayer.
Yea, then do I remember his merciful arm which he extended towards me.
11 Yea, and I also remember the captivity of my fathers,
for I surely do know that the Lord did deliver them out of bondage
and by them did establish his church.
Yea, the Lord God, the God of Abraham and the God of Isaac
and the God of Jacob, did deliver them out of bondage.
12 Yea, I have always remembered the captivity of my fathers.
And that same God who delivered them out of the hands of the Egyptians
did deliver them out of bondage.
13 Yea, and that same God did establish his church among them.
Yea, and that same God hath called me by a holy calling
to preach the word unto this people
and hath given me much success, in the which my joy is full.
14 But I do not joy in my own success alone,

but my joy is more full because of the success of my brethren
which have been up to the land of Nephi.

15 Behold, they have labored exceedingly and have brought forth much fruit.
And how great shall be their reward!

16 Now when I think of the success of these my brethren,
my soul is carried away,
even to the separation of it from the body, as it were,
so great is my joy.

17 And now may God grant unto these my brethren
that they may sit down in the kingdom of God,
yea, and also all those which are the fruit of their labor,
that they may go no more out
but that they may praise him forever.
And may God grant that it may be done according to my words,
even as I have spoken.
Amen.

⸺

30 | 1 Behold, now it came to pass that
after the people of Ammon were established in the land of Jershon,
yea, and also after the Lamanites were driven out of the land
and their dead were buried by the people of the land

2 —now their dead were not numbered because of the greatness of their numbers,
neither were the dead of the Nephites numbered—
but it came to pass that after they had buried their dead
and also after the days of fasting and mourning and prayer
—and it was in the sixteenth year
of the reign of the judges over the people of Nephi—
there began to be continual peace throughout all the land.

3 Yea, and the people did observe to keep the commandments of the Lord;
and they were strict in observing the ordinances of God
according to the law of Moses,
for they were taught to keep the law of Moses until it should be fulfilled.

4 And thus the people did have no disturbance
in all the sixteenth year of the reign of the judges over the people of Nephi.

5 And it came to pass in the commencement
of the seventeenth year of the reign of the judges,
there was continual peace.

6 But it came to pass in the latter end of the seventeenth year
there came a man into the land of Zarahemla and he was anti-Christ,
for he began to preach unto the people against the prophecies

which had been spoken by the prophets concerning the coming of Christ.

7 Now there was no law against a man's belief,
for it was strictly contrary to the commandments of God
that there should be a law which should bring men onto unequal grounds.

8 For thus saith the scripture:
Choose ye this day whom ye will serve.

9 Now if a man desired to serve God, it was his privilege
—or rather, if he believed in God, it was his privilege to serve him—
but if he did not believe in him, there was no law to punish him.

10 But if he murdered, he was punished unto death;
and if he robbed, he was also punished;
and if he stole, he was also punished;
and if he committed adultery, he was also punished;
yea, for all this wickedness they were punished.

11 For there was a law that men should be judged according to their crimes.
Nevertheless there was no law against a man's belief.
Therefore a man was punished only for the crimes which he had done;
therefore all men were on equal grounds.

12 And this anti-Christ, whose name was Korihor
—and the law could have no hold upon him—
and he began to preach unto the people that there should be no Christ.
And after this manner did he preach, saying:

13 O ye that are bound down under a foolish and a vain hope,
why do ye yoke yourselves with such foolish things?
Why do ye look for a Christ?
For no man can know of any thing which is to come.

14 Behold, these things which ye call prophecies,
which ye say are handed down by holy prophets,
behold, they are foolish traditions of your fathers.

15 How do ye know of their surety?
Behold, ye cannot know of things which ye do not see;
therefore ye cannot know that there shall be a Christ.

16 Ye look forward and say that ye see a remission of your sins,
but behold, it is the effects of a frenzied mind.
And this derangement of your minds comes
because of the tradition of your fathers,
which leads you away into a belief of things which are not so.

17 And many more such things did he say unto them,
telling them that there could be no atonement made for the sins of men,
but every man fared in this life according to the management of the creature
—therefore every man prospered according to his genius—

and that every man conquered according to his strength,
and whatsoever a man did was no crime.

18 And thus he did preach unto them,
leading away the hearts of many,
causing them to lift up their heads in their wickedness,
yea, leading away many women and also men to commit whoredoms,
telling them that when a man was dead, that was the end thereof.

19 Now this man went over to the land of Jershon also
to preach these things among the people of Ammon,
which were once the people of the Lamanites.

20 But behold, they were more wise than many of the Nephites,
for they took him and bound him and carried him before Ammon,
which was a high priest over that people.

21 And it came to pass that he caused that he should be carried out of the land.

And it came to pass that he came over into the land of Gideon
and began to preach unto them also.
And here he did not have much success,
for he was taken and bound and carried before the high priest
and also the chief judge over the land.

22 And it came to pass that the high priest saith unto him:
Why do ye go about perverting the ways of the Lord?
Why do ye teach this people that there shall be no Christ,
to interrupt their rejoicings?
Why do ye speak against all the prophecies of the holy prophets?

23 Now the high priest's name was Giddonah,
and Korihor saith unto him:
Because I do not teach the foolish traditions of your fathers
and because I do not teach this people to bind themselves down
under the foolish ordinances and performances
which are laid down by ancient priests,
to usurp power and authority over them,
to keep them in ignorance,
that they may not lift up their heads
but be brought down according to thy words.

24 Ye say that this people is a free people.
Behold, I say: These are in bondage.
Ye say that those ancient prophecies are true.
Behold, I say that ye do not know that they are true.

25 Ye say that this people is a guilty and a fallen people
because of the transgression of a parent.
Behold, I say that a child is not guilty because of its parents.

26 And ye also say that Christ shall come.
But behold, I say that ye do not know that there shall be a Christ.
And ye say also that he shall be slain for the sins of the world.

27 And thus ye lead away this people after the foolish traditions of your fathers,
and according to your own desires;
and ye keep them down, even as it were in bondage,
that ye may glut yourselves with the labors of their hands,
that they durst not look up with boldness,
and that they durst not enjoy their rights and privileges.

28 Yea, they durst not make use of that which is their own
lest they should offend their priests,
which do yoke them according to their desires
and hath brought them to believe by their traditions and their dreams
and their whims and their visions and their pretended mysteries
that they should, if they did not do according to their words,
offend some unknown being, which they say is God,
a being which never hath been seen nor known,
which never was, nor never will be.

29 Now when the high priest and the chief judge saw the hardness of his heart,
yea, when they saw that he would revile even against God,
they would not make any reply to his words,
but they caused that he should be bound;
and they delivered him up into the hands of the officers
and sent him to the land of Zarahemla,
that he might be brought before Alma and the chief judge
which was governor over all the land.

30 And it came to pass that when he was brought before Alma and the chief judge
that he did go on in the same manner as he did in the land of Gideon;
yea, he went on to blasphemy.

31 And he did rise up in great swelling words before Alma
and did revile against the priests and teachers,
accusing them of leading away the people after the silly traditions of their fathers
for the sake of glutting in the labors of the people.

32 Now Alma saith unto him:
Thou knowest that we do not glut ourselves upon the labors of this people.
For behold, I have labored
even from the commencement of the reign of the judges until now
with mine own hands for my support,
notwithstanding my many travels round about the land
to declare the word of God unto my people.

33 And notwithstanding the many labors which I have performed in the church,
I have never received so much as even one senine for my labor,
neither hath any of my brethren,
save it were in the judgment seat;
and then we have received only according to law for our time.

34 And now if we do not receive any thing for our labors in the church,
what doth it profit us to labor in the church?
— save it were to declare the truth,
that we may have rejoicings in the joy of our brethren.

35 Then why sayest thou that we preach unto this people to get gain
when thou of thyself knowest that we receive no gain?

And now, believest thou that we deceive this people
and that causeth such joy in their hearts?

36 And Korihor answered him: Yea.

37 Then Alma saith unto him:
Believest thou that there is a God?

38 And he answered: Nay.

39 Now Alma saith unto him:
If ye deny again that there is a God and also deny the Christ —
for behold, I say unto you:
I know there is a God,
and also that Christ shall come.

40 And now, what evidence have ye that there is no God or that Christ cometh not?
I say unto you that ye have none save it be your word only.

41 But behold, I have all things as a testimony that these things are true.
And ye also have all things as a testimony unto you that they are true.
And will ye deny them?
Believest thou that these things are true?

42 Behold, I know that thou believest.
But thou art possessed with a lying spirit,
and ye have put off the Spirit of God that it may have no place in you;
but the devil hath power over you,
and he doth carry you about,
working devices that he may destroy the children of God.

43 And now Korihor saith unto Alma:
If thou wilt shew me a sign that I may be convinced that there is a God,
yea, shew unto me that he hath power,
and then will I be convinced of the truth of thy words.

44 But Alma saith unto him:
Thou hast had signs enough.

Will ye tempt your God?
Will ye say,
shew unto me a sign,
when ye have the testimony of all these thy brethren
and also all the holy prophets?
The scriptures are laid before thee.
Yea, and all things denote there is a God;
yea, even the earth and all things that is upon the face of it,
yea, and its motion,
yea, and also all the planets, which move in their regular form,
doth witness that there is a Supreme Creator.

45 And yet do ye go about leading away the hearts of this people,
testifying unto them there is no God?
And yet will ye deny against all these witnesses?
And he said:
Yea, I will deny except ye shall shew me a sign.

46 And now it came to pass that Alma said unto him:
Behold, I am grieved because of the hardness of your heart,
yea, that ye will still resist the spirit of the truth,
that thy soul may be destroyed.

47 But behold, it is better that thy soul should be lost
than that thou shouldst be the means
of bringing many souls down to destruction
by thy lying and by thy flattering words.
Therefore if thou shalt deny again,
behold, God shall smite thee that thou shalt become dumb,
that thou shalt never open thy mouth any more,
that thou shalt not deceive this people any more.

48 Now Korihor saith unto him:
I do not deny the existence of a God,
but I do not believe that there is a God.
And I say also that ye do not know that there is a God;
and except ye shew me a sign, I will not believe.

49 Now Alma saith unto him:
This will I give unto thee for a sign,
that thou shalt be struck dumb according to my words.
And I say that in the name of God that ye shall be struck dumb,
that ye shall no more have utterance.

50 Now when Alma had said these words, Korihor was struck dumb,
that he could not have utterance, according to the words of Alma.

51 And now when the chief judge saw this,
he put forth his hand and wrote unto Korihor, saying:
Art thou convinced of the power of God?
In whom did ye desire that Alma should shew forth his sign?
Would ye that he should afflict others to shew unto thee a sign?
Now behold, he hath shewed unto you a sign.
And now will ye dispute more?

52 And Korihor put forth his hand and wrote, saying:
I know that I am dumb, for I cannot speak.
And I know that nothing save it were the power of God
could bring this upon me.
Yea, and I always knew that there was a God.

53 But behold, the devil hath deceived me,
for he appeared unto me in the form of an angel and said unto me:
Go and reclaim this people,
for they have all gone astray after an unknown God.
And he saith unto me:
There is no God.
Yea, and he taught me that which I should say,
and I have taught his words.
And I taught them because they were pleasing unto the carnal mind.
And I taught them even until I had much success,
insomuch that I verily believed that they were true.
And for this cause I withstood the truth,
even until I have brought this great curse upon me.

54 Now when he had said this,
he besought that Alma should pray unto God
that the curse might be taken from him.

55 But Alma said unto him:
If this curse should be taken from thee,
thou wouldst again lead away the hearts of this people.
Therefore it shall be unto thee even as the Lord will.

56 And it came to pass that the curse was not taken off of Korihor,
but he was cast out and went about from house to house a begging for his food.

57 Now the knowledge of what had happened unto Korihor
was immediately published throughout all the land;
yea, the proclamation was sent forth by the chief judge
to all the people in the land,
declaring unto those who had believed in the words of Korihor
that they must speedily repent lest the same judgments would come unto them.

58 And it came to pass that they were all convinced of the wickedness of Korihor.

Therefore they were all converted again unto the Lord.
And this put an end to the iniquity after the manner of Korihor.

And Korihor did go about from house to house a begging food for his support.
59 And it came to pass that as he went forth among the people
—yea, among a people which had separated themselves from the Nephites
and called themselves Zoramites, being led by a man whose name was Zoram—
and as he went forth amongst them,
behold, he was ran upon and trodden down, even until he was dead.
60 And thus we see the end of him who perverteth the ways of the Lord.
And thus we see that the devil will not support his children at the last day,
but doth speedily drag them down to hell.

31 | 1 Now it came to pass that after the end of Korihor,
Alma having received tidings
that the Zoramites were perverting the ways of the Lord
and that Zoram, which was their leader, was leading the hearts of the people
to bow down to dumb idols etc.,
his heart again began to sicken because of the iniquity of the people.
2 For it was the cause of great sorrow to Alma
to know of iniquity among his people;
therefore his heart was exceeding sorrowful
because of the separation of the Zoramites from the Nephites.

3 Now the Zoramites had gathered themselves together in a land
which they called Antionum, which was east of the land of Zarahemla,
which lay nearly bordering upon the seashore
which was south of the land Jershon,
which also bordered upon the wilderness south,
which wilderness was full of the Lamanites.
4 Now the Nephites greatly feared
that the Zoramites would enter into a correspondence with the Lamanites
and that it would be the means of great loss on the part of the Nephites.

5 And now as the preaching of the word had had a greater tendency
to lead the people to do that which was just
—yea, it had had more powerful effect upon the minds of the people
than the sword or any thing else which had happened unto them—
therefore Alma thought it was expedient
that they should try the virtue of the word of God.
6 Therefore he took Ammon and Aaron and Omner
—and Himni he did leave in the church in Zarahemla,
but the former three he took with him—
and also Amulek and Zeezrom, which were at Melek;

and he also took two of his sons.

7 Now the eldest of his sons he took not with him, and his name was Helaman;
but the names of those which he took with him were Shiblon and Corianton.
And these are the names of those which went with him among the Zoramites
to preach unto them the word.

8 Now the Zoramites were dissenters from the Nephites.
Therefore they had the word of God preached unto them;

9 but they had fell into great errors,
for they would not observe to keep the commandments of God and his statutes
according to the law of Moses,

10 neither would they observe the performances of the church,
to continue in prayer and supplication to God daily
that they might not enter into temptation.

11 Yea, in fine, they did pervert the ways of the Lord in very many instances.
Therefore for this cause Alma and his brethren went into the land
to preach the word unto them.

12 Now when they had came into the land,
behold, to their astonishment they found
that the Zoramites had built synagogues
and that they did gather themselves together on one day of the week,
which day they did call the day of the Lord,
and they did worship after a manner
which Alma and his brethren had never beheld.

13 For they had a place built up in the center of their synagogue,
a place of standing which was high above the head;
and the top thereof would only admit one person.

14 Therefore whosoever desired to worship
must go forth and stand upon the top thereof
and stretch forth his hands towards the heavens
and cry with a loud voice, saying:

15 Holy holy God, we believe that thou art God.
And we believe that thou art holy,
and that thou wast a spirit
and that thou art a spirit
and that thou wilt be a spirit forever.

16 Holy God, we believe that thou hast separated us from our brethren.
And we do not believe in the tradition of our brethren
which was handed down to them by the childishness of their fathers,
but we believe that thou hast elected us to be thy holy children,
and also thou hast made it known unto us that there shall be no Christ.

17 But thou art the same yesterday, today, and forever.

And thou hast elected us that we shall be saved,
whilst all around us are elected to be cast by thy wrath down to hell,
for the which holiness, O God, we thank thee.
And we also thank thee that thou hast elected us
that we may not be led away after the foolish traditions of our brethren,
which doth bind them down to a belief of Christ,
which doth lead their hearts to wander far from thee, our God.

18 And again we thank thee, O God,
that we are a chosen and a holy people.
Amen.

19 Now it came to pass that
after Alma and his brethren and his sons had heard these prayers,
they were astonished beyond all measure;

20 for behold, every man did go forth and offer up these same prayers.

21 Now the place was called by them Rameumptom,
which being interpreted is the holy stand.

22 Now from this stand they did offer up every man the selfsame prayer unto God,
thanking their God that they were chosen of him
and that he had not led them away after the tradition of their brethren
and that their hearts were not stolen away
to believe in things to come, which they knew nothing about.

23 Now when the people had all offered up thanks after their manner,
they returned to their homes, never speaking of their God again
until they had assembled themselves together again to the holy stand
to offer up thanks after their manner.

24 Now when Alma saw this, his heart was grieved;
for he saw that they were a wicked and a perverse people.
Yea, he saw that their hearts were set upon gold and upon silver
and upon all manner of fine goods.

25 Yea, and he also saw
that their hearts were lifted up unto great boasting in their pride.

26 And he lifted up his voice to heaven and cried, saying:
O how long, O Lord, wilt thou suffer
that thy servants shall dwell here below in the flesh
to behold such gross wickedness among the children of men?

27 Behold, O God, they cry unto thee,
and yet their hearts are swallowed up in their pride.
Behold, O God, they cry unto thee with their mouths
while they are puffed up, even to greatness, with the vain things of the world.

28 Behold, O my God, their costly apparel

and their ringlets and their bracelets and their ornaments of gold
and all their precious things which they are ornamented with —
and behold, their hearts are set upon them.
And yet they cry unto thee and say:
We thank thee, O God,
for we are a chosen people unto thee while others shall perish.

29 Yea, and they say that thou hast made it known unto them
that there shall be no Christ.

30 O Lord God, how long wilt thou suffer
that such wickedness and infidelity shall be among this people?
O Lord, wilt thou give me strength that I may bear with mine infirmities!
For I am infirm, and such wickedness among this people doth pain my soul.

31 O Lord, my heart is exceeding sorrowful.
Wilt thou comfort my soul in Christ!
O Lord, wilt thou grant unto me that I may have strength
that I may suffer with patience these afflictions which shall come upon me
because of the iniquity of this people!

32 O Lord, wilt thou comfort my soul and give unto me success!
And also my fellow laborers which are with me
—yea, Ammon and Aaron and Omner,
and also Amulek and Zeezrom, and also my two sons—
yea, even all these wilt thou comfort, O Lord!
Yea, wilt thou comfort their souls in Christ!

33 Wilt thou grant unto them that they may have strength,
that they may bear their afflictions which shall come upon them
because of the iniquities of this people!

34 O Lord, wilt thou grant unto us
that we may have success in bringing them again unto thee in Christ!

35 Behold, O Lord, their souls are precious;
and many of them are our near brethren.
Therefore give unto us, O Lord, power and wisdom
that we may bring these our brethren again unto thee.

36 Now it came to pass that when Alma had said these words
that he clapped his hands upon all they which were with him.
And behold, as he clapped his hands upon them,
they were filled with the Holy Spirit.

37 And after that, they did separate themselves one from another,
taking no thought for themselves what they should eat
or what they should drink or what they should put on.

38 And the Lord provided for them
that they should hunger not, neither should they thirst.

Yea, and he also gave them strength
that they should suffer no manner of afflictions
save it were swallowed up in the joy of Christ.
Now this was according to the prayer of Alma—
and this because he prayed in faith.

32 | 1 And it came to pass that they did go forth
and began to preach the word of God unto the people,
entering into their synagogues and into their houses;
yea, and even they did preach the word in their streets.
2 And it came to pass that after much labor among them,
they began to have success among the poorer class of the people;
for behold, they were cast out of the synagogues
because of the coarseness of their apparel.
3 Therefore they were not permitted
to enter into their synagogues to worship God,
being esteemed as filthiness.
Therefore they were poor;
yea, they were esteemed by their brethren as dross.
Therefore they were poor as to things of the world;
and also they were poor in heart.

4 Now as Alma was teaching and speaking unto the people upon the hill Onidah,
there came a great multitude unto him,
which were those of which we have been speaking,
which were poor in heart because of their poverty as to things of the world;
5 and they came unto Alma.
And the one which was the most foremost among them saith unto him:
Behold, what shall these my brethren do?
For they are despised of all men because of their poverty,
yea, and more especially by our priests.
For they have cast us out of our synagogues,
which we have labored abundantly to build with our own hands.
And they have cast us out because of this our exceeding poverty,
that we have no place to worship our God.
And now behold, what shall we do?

6 And now when Alma heard this,
he turned him about, his face immediately towards him.
And he beheld with great joy,
for he beheld that their afflictions had truly humbled them
and that they were in a preparation to hear the word.
7 Therefore he did say no more to the other multitude,
but he stretched forth his hand

and cried unto those which he beheld, which were truly penitent,
and saith unto them:

8 I behold that ye are lowly in heart;
and if so, blessed are ye.

9 Behold, thy brother hath said:
What shall we do?
For we are cast out of our synagogues that we cannot worship our God.

10 Behold, I say unto you:
Do ye suppose that ye cannot worship God save it be in your synagogues only?

11 And moreover, I would ask:
Do ye suppose that ye must not worship God only once in a week?

12 I say unto you:
It is well that ye are cast out of your synagogues,
that ye may be humble and that ye may learn wisdom;
for it is necessary that ye should learn wisdom.
For it is because that ye are cast out
that ye are despised of your brethren because of your exceeding poverty,
that ye are brought to a lowliness of heart;
for ye are necessarily brought to be humble.

13 And now because ye are compelled to be humble, blessed are ye;
for a man sometimes, if he is compelled to be humble, seeketh repentance.
And now surely, whosoever repenteth shall find mercy.
And he that findeth mercy and endureth to the end,
the same shall be saved.

14 And now as I said unto you
that because ye were compelled to be humble ye were blessed,
do ye not suppose that they are more blessed
who truly humble themselves because of the word?

15 Yea, he that truly humbleth himself
and repenteth of his sins and endureth to the end,
the same shall be blessed—
yea, much more blessed than they who art compelled to be humble
because of their exceeding poverty.

16 Therefore blessed are they who humbleth themselves
without being compelled to be humble.
Or rather, in other words, blessed is he that believeth in the word of God
and is baptized without stubbornness of heart,
yea, without being brought to know the word—or even compelled to know—
before they will believe.

17 Yea, there are many which do say:
If thou wilt show unto us a sign from heaven,

    then we shall know of a surety;
    then we shall believe.
18 Now I ask:
    Is this faith?
    Behold, I say unto you: Nay.
    For if a man knoweth a thing, he hath no cause to believe,
    for he knoweth it.
19 And now, how much more cursed is he
    that knoweth the will of God and doeth it not
    than he that only believeth, or only hath cause to believe,
    and falleth into transgression?
20 Now of this thing ye must judge.
    Behold, I say unto you that it is on the one hand even as it is on the other;
    and it shall be unto every man according to his work.

21 And now as I said concerning faith:
    faith is not to have a perfect knowledge of things;
    therefore if ye have faith, ye hope for things which is not seen, which are true.
22 And now behold, I say unto you—and I would that ye should remember—
    that God is merciful unto all who believe on his name.
    Therefore he desireth in the first place
    that ye should believe, yea, even on his word.
23 And now he imparteth his word by angels unto men,
    yea, not only men but women also.
    Now this is not all.
    Little children doth have words given unto them many times
    which doth confound the wise and the learned.

24 And now my beloved brethren, as ye have desired to know of me
    what ye shall do because ye are afflicted and cast out
    —now I do not desire that ye should suppose that I mean to judge you,
    only according to that which is true—
25 for I do not mean that ye, all of you, have been compelled to humble yourselves.
    For I verily believe there are some among you which would humble themselves,
    let him be in whatsoever circumstances he might.

26 Now as I said concerning faith, that it was not a perfect knowledge,
    even so it is with my words.
    Ye cannot know of their surety at first unto perfection,
    any more than faith is a perfect knowledge.
27 But behold, if ye will awake and arouse your faculties,
    even to an experiment upon my words,
    and exercise a particle of faith
    —yea, even if ye can no more than desire to believe—

let this desire work in you, even until ye believe in a manner
that ye can give place for a portion of my words.

28 Now we will compare the word unto a seed.
Now if ye give place that a seed may be planted in your heart,
behold, if it be a true seed or a good seed,
if ye do not cast it out by your unbelief
—that ye will resist the Spirit of the Lord—
behold, it will begin to swell within your breasts.
And when you feel these swelling motions,
ye will begin to say within yourselves:
It must needs be that this is a good seed, or that the word is good,
for it beginneth to enlarge my soul.
Yea, it beginneth to enlighten my understanding;
yea, and it beginneth to be delicious to me.

29 Now behold, would not this increase your faith?
I say unto you: Yea.
Nevertheless it hath not grown up to a perfect knowledge.

30 But behold, as the seed swelleth and sprouteth and beginneth to grow
and then ye must needs say that the seed is good,
for behold, it swelleth and sprouteth and beginneth to grow.
And now behold, will not this strengthen your faith?
Yea, it will strengthen your faith.
For ye will say:
I know that this is a good seed,
for behold, it sprouteth and beginneth to grow.

31 And now behold, are ye sure that this is a good seed?
I say unto you: Yea.
For every seed bringeth forth unto its own likeness.

32 Therefore if a seed groweth, it is good.
But if it groweth not, behold, it is not good;
therefore it is cast away.

33 And now behold, because ye have tried the experiment and planted the seed
and it swelleth and sprouteth and beginneth to grow,
ye must needs know that the seed is good.

34 And now behold, is your knowledge perfect?
Yea, your knowledge is perfect in that thing and your faith is dormant—
and this because you know.
For ye know that the word hath swelled your souls.
And ye also know that it hath sprouted up,
that your understanding doth begin to be enlightened
and your mind doth begin to expand.

35 O then is not this real?
    I say unto you:
    Yea, because it is light.
    And whatsoever is light is good because it is discernible;
    therefore ye must know that it is good.

    And now behold, after ye have tasted this light, is your knowledge perfect?
36 Behold, I say unto you: Nay.
    Neither must ye lay aside your faith,
    for ye have only exercised your faith to plant the seed
    that ye might try the experiment to know if the seed was good.
37 And behold, as the tree beginneth to grow, ye will say:
    Let us nourish it with great care that it may get root,
    that it may grow up and bring forth fruit unto us.
    And now behold, if ye nourish it with much care,
    it will get root and grow up and bring forth fruit.
38 But if ye neglect the tree and take no thought for its nourishment,
    behold, it will not get any root.
    And when the heat of the sun cometh and scorcheth it,
    and because it hath no root, it withereth away;
    and ye pluck it up and cast it out.
39 Now this is not because the seed was not good,
    neither is it because the fruit thereof would not be desirable.
    But it is because your ground is barren and ye will not nourish the tree;
    therefore ye cannot have the fruit thereof.
40 And thus it is: if ye will not nourish the word,
    looking forward with an eye of faith to the fruit thereof,
    ye can never pluck of the fruit of the tree of life.

41 But if ye will nourish the word,
    yea, nourish the tree as it beginneth to grow by your faith
    with great diligence and with patience,
    looking forward to the fruit thereof,
    and it shall take root.
    And behold, it shall be a tree springing up unto everlasting life.
42 And because of your diligence and your faith and your patience with the word
    in nourishing it that it may take root in you,
    behold, by and by ye shall pluck the fruit thereof, which is most precious,
    which is sweet above all that is sweet,
    and which is white above all that is white,
    yea, and pure above all that is pure;
    and ye shall feast upon this fruit even until ye are filled,
    that ye hunger not, neither shall ye thirst.

43 Then, my brethren, ye shall reap the rewards of your faith
and your diligence and patience and long-suffering,
waiting for the tree to bring forth fruit unto you.

33 | 1 Now after Alma had spoken these words,
they sent forth unto him, desiring to know
whether they should believe in one God,
that they might obtain this fruit of which he had spoken;
or how they should plant the seed, or the word of which he had spoken,
which he said must be planted in their hearts;
or in what manner they should begin to exercise their faith.

2 And Alma saith unto them:
Behold, ye have said that ye could not worship your God
because ye are cast out of your synagogues.
But behold, I say unto you:
If ye suppose that ye cannot worship your God, ye do greatly err,
and ye had ought to search the scriptures;
for if ye suppose that they have taught you this,
ye do not understand them.
3 Do ye remember to have read
what Zenos the prophet of old hath said concerning prayer or worship?
4 For he saith:
Thou art merciful, O God,
for thou hast heard my prayer,
even when I was in the wilderness.
Yea, thou wast merciful
when I prayed concerning those which were mine enemies,
and thou didst turn them to me.
5 Yea, O God, and thou wast merciful unto me
when I did cry unto thee in my field,
when I did cry unto thee in my prayer,
and thou didst hear me.
6 And again, O God, when I did turn to my house,
thou didst hear me in my prayer.
7 And when I did turn unto my closet, O Lord,
and prayed unto thee, thou didst hear me.
8 Yea, thou art merciful unto thy children;
when they cry unto thee to be heard of thee and not of men,
and thou wilt hear them.

9 Yea, O God, thou hast been merciful unto me
and heard my cries in the midst of thy congregations.

10 Yea, and thou hast also heard me
   when I have been cast out and have been despised by mine enemies.
   Yea, thou didst hear my cries and wast angry with mine enemies,
   and thou didst visit them in thine anger with speedy destruction.
11 And thou didst hear me because of mine afflictions and my sincerity.
   And it is because of thy Son that thou hast been thus merciful unto me.
   Therefore I will cry unto thee in all mine afflictions,
   for in thee is my joy;
   for thou hast turned thy judgments away from me because of thy Son.

12 And now Alma saith unto them:
   Do ye believe those scriptures which have been written by them of old?
13 Behold, if ye do, ye must believe what Zenos saith,
   for behold, he saith:
   Thou hast turned away thy judgments because of thy Son.
14 Now behold, my brethren, I would ask if ye have read these scriptures?
   If ye have, how can ye disbelieve on the Son of God?
15 For it is not written that Zenos alone spake of these things,
   but Zenoch also spake of these things,
16 for behold, he saith:
   Thou art angry, O Lord, with this people
   because they will not understand of thy mercies
   which thou hast bestowed upon them because of thy Son.

17 And now my brethren, ye see
   that a second prophet of old has testified of the Son of God.
   And because the people would not understand his words,
   they stoned him to death.
18 But behold, this is not all.
   These are not the only ones which have spoken concerning the Son of God.
19 Behold, he was spoken of by Moses.
   Yea, and behold, a type was raised up in the wilderness,
   that whosoever would look upon it might live;
   and many did look and live.
20 But few understood the meaning of those things—
   and this because of the hardness of their hearts.
   But there were many which were so hardened that they would not look;
   therefore they perished.

   Now the reason that they would not look
   is because they did not believe that it would heal them.
21 O my brethren, if ye could be healed

by merely casting about your eyes that ye might behold,
would ye not behold quickly?
Or would ye rather harden your hearts in unbelief and be slothful,
that ye would not cast about your eyes, that ye might perish?

22 If so, woe shall come upon you.
But if not so, then cast about your eyes
and begin to believe in the Son of God,
that he will come to redeem his people
and that he shall suffer and die to atone for their sins
and that he shall rise again from the dead,
which shall bring to pass the resurrection,
that all men shall stand before him
to be judged at the last and judgment day according to their works.

23 And now my brethren, I desire that ye should plant this word in your hearts.
And as it beginneth to swell, even so nourish it by your faith.
And behold, it will become a tree springing up in you unto everlasting life.
And then may God grant unto you
that your burdens may be light through the joy of his Son.
And even all this can ye do if ye will.
Amen.

34 | 1 And now it came to pass that
after Alma had spoken these words unto them,
he sat down upon the ground.
And Amulek arose and began to teach them, saying:

2 My brethren, I think that it is impossible
that ye should be ignorant of the things
which have been spoken concerning the coming of Christ,
who is taught by us to be the Son of God.
Yea, I know that these things were taught unto you bountifully
before your dissension from among us.

3 And as ye have desired of my beloved brother
that he should make known unto you
what ye should do because of your afflictions,
and he hath spoken somewhat unto you to prepare your minds,
yea, and he hath exhorted you unto faith and to patience,

4 yea, even that ye would have so much faith
as even to plant the word in your heart,
that ye may try the experiment of its goodness.

5 And we have beheld that the great question which is in your minds
is whether the word be in the Son of God or whether there shall be no Christ.

6 And ye also behold that my brother hath proven unto you in many instances
that the word is in Christ unto salvation.

7 My brother hath called upon the words of Zenos,
that redemption cometh through the Son of God,
and also upon the words of Zenoch.
And also he hath appealed unto Moses to prove that these things are true.

8 And now behold, I will testify unto you of myself that these things are true.
Behold, I say unto you that I do know
that Christ shall come among the children of men
to take upon him the transgressions of his people
and that he shall atone for the sins of the world,
for the Lord God hath spoken it.

9 For it is expedient that an atonement should be made,
for according to the great plans of the Eternal God
there must be an atonement made or else all mankind must unavoidably perish.
Yea, all are hardened;
yea, all are fallen and are lost and must perish
except it be through the atonement, which it is expedient should be made.

10 For it is expedient that there should be a great and last sacrifice
—yea, not a sacrifice of man,
neither of beasts, neither of any manner of fowl—
for it shall not be a human sacrifice,
but it must be an infinite and an eternal sacrifice.

11 Now there is not any man that can sacrifice his own blood
which will atone for the sins of another.
Now if a man murdereth,
behold, will our law, which is just, take the life of his brother?
I say unto you: Nay.

12 But the law requireth the life of him who hath murdered.
Therefore there can be nothing which is short of an infinite atonement
which will suffice for the sins of the world.

13 Therefore it is expedient that there should be a great and last sacrifice.
And then shall there be—or it is expedient there should be—
a stop to the shedding of blood;
then shall the law of Moses be fulfilled.
Yea, it shall all be fulfilled, every jot and tittle,
and none shall have passed away.

14 And behold, this is the whole meaning of the law,
every whit a pointing to that great and last sacrifice;

and that great and last sacrifice will be the Son of God,
yea, infinite and eternal.

15 And thus he shall bring salvation to all those who shall believe on his name,
this being the intent of this last sacrifice,
to bring about the bowels of mercy, which overpowereth justice
and bringeth about means unto men that they may have faith unto repentance.

16 And thus mercy can satisfy the demands of justice
and encircle them in the arms of safety,
while he that exerciseth no faith unto repentance
is exposed to the whole law of the demands of justice.
Therefore only unto him that hath faith unto repentance
is brought about the great and eternal plan of redemption.

17 Therefore may God grant unto you, my brethren,
that ye might begin to exercise your faith unto repentance,
that ye begin to call upon his holy name
that he would have mercy upon you.

18 Yea, cry unto him for mercy, for he is mighty to save.

19 Yea, humble yourselves and continue in prayer unto him.

20 Cry unto him when ye are in your fields,
yea, over all your flocks.

21 Cry unto him in your houses, yea, over all your household,
both morning, midday, and evening.

22 Yea, cry unto him against the power of your enemies.

23 Yea, cry unto him against the devil, which is an enemy to all righteousness.

24 Cry unto him over the crops of your fields, that ye may prosper in them.

25 Cry over the flocks of your fields, that they may increase.

26 But this is not all.
Ye must pour out your souls in your closets and your secret places
and in your wilderness.

27 Yea, and when you do not cry unto the Lord,
let your hearts be full,
drawn out in prayer unto him continually for your welfare
and also for the welfare of those which are around you.

28 And now behold, my brethren, I say unto you:
Do not suppose that this is all.
For after ye have done all these things,
if ye turn away the needy and the naked
and visit not the sick and afflicted
and impart of your substance, if ye have,
to those which stand in need—

I say unto you,
if ye do not any of these things,
behold, your prayer is vain and availeth you nothing,
and ye are as hypocrites which do deny the faith.

29 Therefore if ye do not remember to be charitable,
ye are as dross which the refiners do cast out
—it being of no worth—
and is trodden under foot of men.

30 And now my brethren, I would that after ye have received so many witnesses,
seeing that the holy scriptures testifies of these things,
come forth and bring fruit unto repentance.

31 Yea, I would that ye would come forth and harden not your hearts any longer.
For behold, now is the time and the day of your salvation.
And therefore, if ye will repent and harden not your hearts,
immediately shall the great plan of redemption be brought about unto you.

32 For behold, this life is the time for men to prepare to meet God.
Yea, behold, the day of this life is the day for men to perform their labors.

33 And now as I said unto you before,
as ye have had so many witnesses,
therefore I beseech of you
that ye do not procrastinate the day of your repentance until the end.
For after this day of life which is given us to prepare for eternity,
behold, if we do not improve our time while in this life,
then cometh the night of darkness wherein there can be no labor performed.

34 Ye cannot say when ye are brought to that awful crisis
that I will repent,
that I will return to my God.
Nay, ye cannot say this.
For that same spirit which doth possess your bodies
at the time that ye go out of this life,
that same spirit will have power to possess your body in that eternal world.

35 For behold, if ye have procrastinated
the day of your repentance even until death,
behold, ye have become subjected to the spirit of the devil,
and he doth seal you his.
Therefore the Spirit of the Lord hath withdrawn from you
and hath no place in you,
and the devil hath all power over you.
And this is the final state of the wicked.

36 And this I know because the Lord hath said
he dwelleth not in unholy temples,
but in the hearts of the righteous doth he dwell.

Yea, and he hath also said
that the righteous should sit down in his kingdom to go no more out,
but their garments should be made white through the blood of the Lamb.

37 And now my beloved brethren, I desire that ye should remember these things
and that ye should work out your salvation with fear before God
and that ye should no more deny the coming of Christ,
38 that ye contend no more against the Holy Ghost,
but that ye receive it and take upon you the name of Christ,
that ye humble yourselves even to the dust
and worship God in whatsoever place ye may be in,
in spirit and in truth,
and that ye live in thanksgiving daily
for the many mercies and blessings which he doth bestow upon you.
39 Yea, and I also exhort you, my brethren,
that ye be watchful unto prayer continually,
that ye may not be led away by the temptations of the devil,
that he may not overpower you,
that ye may not become his subjects at the last day.
For behold, he rewardeth you no good thing.

40 And now my beloved brethren, I would exhort you to have patience
and that ye bear with all manner of afflictions,
that ye do not revile against those
who do cast you out because of your exceeding poverty,
lest ye become sinners like unto them,
41 but that ye have patience and bear with those afflictions
with a firm hope that ye shall one day rest from all your afflictions.

35 | 1 Now it came to pass that after Amulek had made an end of these words,
they withdrew themselves from the multitude
and came over into the land of Jershon.
2 Yea, and the rest of the brethren,
after they had preached the word unto the Zoramites,
also came over into the land of Jershon.

3 And it came to pass that
after the more popular part of the Zoramites had consulted together
concerning the words which had been preached unto them,
they were angry because of the word,
for it did destroy their craft;
therefore they would not hearken unto the words.
4 And they sent and gathered together throughout all the land all the people

and consulted with them concerning the words which had been spoken.

5 Now their rulers and their priests and their teachers
did not let the people know concerning their desires.
Therefore they found out privily the minds of all the people.

6 And it came to pass that after they had found out the minds of all the people,
those which were in favor of the words
which had been spoken by Alma and his brethren
were cast out of the land—and they were many—
and they came over also into the land of Jershon.

7 And it came to pass that Alma and his brethren did minister unto them.

8 Now the people of the Zoramites were angry
with the people of Ammon, which were in Jershon.
And the chief ruler of the Zoramites being a very wicked man
sent over unto the people of Ammon,
desiring them that they should cast out of their land
all those which came over from them into their land.

9 And he breathed out many threatenings against them.
And now the people of Ammon did not fear their words.
Therefore they did not cast them out,
but they did receive all the poor of the Zoramites that came over unto them.
And they did nourish them and did clothe them
and did give unto them lands for their inheritance.
And they did administer unto them according to their wants.

10 Now this did stir up the Zoramites to anger against the people of Ammon.
And they began to mix with the Lamanites
and to stir them up also to anger against them.

11 And thus the Zoramites and the Lamanites began to make preparations for war
against the people of Ammon and also against the Nephites.

12 And thus ended the seventeenth year
of the reign of the judges over the people of Nephi.

13 And the people of Ammon departed out of the land of Jershon
and came over into the land of Melek
and gave place in the land of Jershon for the armies of the Nephites,
that they might contend with the armies of the Lamanites
and the armies of the Zoramites.
And thus commenced a war betwixt the Lamanites and the Nephites
in the eighteenth year of the reign of the judges.
And an account shall be given of their wars hereafter.

14 And Alma and Ammon and their brethren and also the two sons of Alma
returned to the land of Zarahemla,

after having been instruments in the hands of God
of bringing many of the Zoramites to repentance.
And as many as were brought to repentance were driven out of their land;
but they have lands for their inheritance in the land of Jershon.
And they have taken up arms to defend themselves
and their wives and their children and their lands.

15 Now Alma being grieved for the iniquity of his people,
yea, for the wars and the bloodsheds
and the contentions which were among them,
and having been to declare the word—or sent to declare the word—
among all the people in every city,
and seeing that the hearts of the people began to wax hard
and that they began to be offended because of the strictness of the word,
his heart was exceeding sorrowful.
16 Therefore he caused that his sons should be gathered together
that he might give unto them every one his charge separately
concerning the things pertaining unto righteousness.
And we have an account of his commandments which he gave unto them
according to his own record.

The commandments of Alma to his son Helaman.

36 | 1 My son, give ear to my words,
for I swear unto you
that inasmuch as ye shall keep the commandments of God,
ye shall prosper in the land.
2 I would that ye should do as I have done
in remembering the captivity of our fathers,
for they were in bondage and none could deliver them
except it were the God of Abraham and the God of Isaac and the God of Jacob;
and he surely did deliver them in their afflictions.

3 And now, O my son Helaman,
behold, thou art in thy youth,
and therefore I beseech of thee
that thou wilt hear my words and learn of me,
for I do know that whomsoever shall put his trust in God
shall be supported in their trials and their troubles and their afflictions
and shall be lifted up at the last day.
4 And I would not that ye think that I know of myself—

not of the temporal but of the spiritual,
not of the carnal mind but of God.

5 Now behold, I say unto you:
   If I had not been born of God, I should not have known these things.
   But God hath by the mouth of his holy angel made these things known unto me,
   not of any worthiness of myself.
6 For I went about with the sons of Mosiah seeking to destroy the church of God.
   But behold, God sent his holy angel to stop us by the way.
7 And behold, he spake unto us as it were the voice of thunder,
   and the whole earth did tremble beneath our feet.
   And we all fell to the earth,
   for the fear of the Lord came upon us.
8 But behold, the voice said unto me: Arise.
   And I arose and stood up and beheld the angel.
9 And he said unto me:
   If thou wilt of thyself be destroyed,
   seek no more to destroy the church of God.

10 And it came to pass that I fell to the earth;
   and it was for the space of three days and three nights
   that I could not open my mouth,
   neither had I the use of my limbs.
11 And the angel spake more things unto me,
   which were heard by my brethren,
   but I did not hear them.
   For when I heard the words,
   if thou wilt be destroyed of thyself,
   seek no more to destroy the church of God,
   I was struck with such great fear and amazement
   lest perhaps that I should be destroyed
   that I fell to the earth and I did hear no more.
12 But I was racked with eternal torment,
   for my soul was harrowed up to the greatest degree
   and racked with all my sins.
13 Yea, I did remember all my sins and iniquities,
   for which I was tormented with the pains of hell.
   Yea, I saw that I had rebelled against my God
   and that I had not kept his holy commandments.
14 Yea, and I had murdered many of his children
   —or rather led them away unto destruction—
   yea, and in fine, so great had been my iniquities
   that the very thoughts of coming into the presence of my God

did rack my soul with inexpressible horror.

15 O, thought I, that I could be banished and become extinct, both soul and body,
that I might not be brought to stand in the presence of my God
to be judged of my deeds.

16 And now for three days and for three nights was I racked,
even with the pains of a damned soul.

17 And it came to pass that as I was thus racked with torment,
while I was harrowed up by the memory of my many sins,
behold, I remembered also to have heard my father prophesy unto the people
concerning the coming of one Jesus Christ, a Son of God,
to atone for the sins of the world.

18 Now as my mind catched hold upon this thought,
I cried within my heart:
O Jesus, thou Son of God, have mercy on me,
who art in the gall of bitterness
and art encircled about by the everlasting chains of death.

19 And now behold, when I thought this,
I could remember my pains no more.
Yea, I was harrowed up by the memory of my sins no more.

20 And O what joy and what marvelous light I did behold!
Yea, my soul was filled with joy as exceeding as was my pains.

21 Yea, I say unto you, my son,
that there can be nothing so exquisite and so bitter as was my pains.
Yea, and again I say unto you, my son,
that on the other hand
there can be nothing so exquisite and sweet as was my joy.

22 Yea, and methought I saw, even as our father Lehi saw,
God sitting upon his throne,
surrounded with numberless concourses of angels
in the attitude of singing and praising their God.
Yea, and my soul did long to be there.

23 But behold, my limbs did receive their strength again,
and I stood upon my feet and did manifest unto the people
that I had been born of God.

24 Yea, and from that time even until now I have labored without ceasing
that I might bring souls unto repentance,
that I might bring them to taste of the exceeding joy of which I did taste,
that they might also be born of God and be filled with the Holy Ghost.

25 Yea, and now behold, O my son,
the Lord doth give me exceeding great joy in the fruits of my labors;

26 for because of the word which he hath imparted unto me,
    behold, many hath been born of God
    and hath tasted as I have tasted
    and hath seen eye to eye as I have seen.
    Therefore they do know of these things of which I have spoken as I do know;
    and the knowledge which I have is of God.

27 And I have been supported under trials and troubles of every kind,
    yea, and in all manner of afflictions.
    Yea, God hath delivered me from prisons and from bonds and from death.
    Yea, and I do put my trust in him and he will still deliver me.

28 And I know that he will raise me up at the last day to dwell with him in glory.
    Yea, and I will praise him forever.
    For he hath brought our fathers out of Egypt,
    and he hath swallowed up the Egyptians in the Red Sea,
    and he led them by his power into the promised land;
    yea, and he hath delivered them out of bondage and captivity from time to time.

29 Yea, and he hath also brought our fathers out of the land of Jerusalem,
    and he hath also by his everlasting power delivered them
    out of bondage and captivity from time to time, even down to the present day.
    And I have always retained in remembrance their captivity;
    yea, and ye also had ought to
    retain in remembrance, as I have done, their captivity.

30 But behold, my son, this is not all.
    For ye had ought to know as I do know
    that inasmuch as ye shall keep the commandments of God
    ye shall prosper in the land;
    and ye had ought to know also
    that inasmuch as ye will not keep the commandments of God,
    ye shall be cut off from his presence.
    Now this is according to his word.

37 | 1 And now my son Helaman,
        I command you that ye take the records
        which have been entrusted with me.

    2 And I also command you
       that ye shall keep a record of this people,
       according as I have done,
       upon the plates of Nephi
       and keep all these things sacred which I have kept,
       even as I have kept them
       —for it is for a wise purpose that they are kept—

    3 and these plates of brass, which contain these engravings,

which have the records of the holy scriptures upon them,
which have the genealogy of our forefathers, even from the beginning.

4   And behold, it hath been prophesied by our fathers
that they should be kept and handed down from one generation to another,
and be kept and preserved by the hand of the Lord
until they should go forth unto every nation, kindred, tongue, and people,
that they shall know of the mysteries contained thereon.

5   And now behold, if they are kept, they must retain their brightness.
Yea, and they will retain their brightness —
yea, and also shall all the plates which do contain that which is holy writ.

6   Now ye may suppose that this is foolishness in me.
But behold, I say unto you
that by small and simple things are great things brought to pass.
And small means in many instances doth confound the wise.

7   And the Lord God doth work by means
to bring about his great and eternal purposes.
And by very small means the Lord doth confound the wise
and bringeth about the salvation of many souls.

8   And now it hath hitherto been wisdom in God
that these things should be preserved.
For behold, they have enlarged the memory of this people,
yea, and convinced many of the error of their ways
and brought them to the knowledge of their God,
unto the salvation of their souls.

9   Yea, I say unto you:
Were it not for these things that these records do contain,
which are on these plates,
Ammon and his brethren could not have convinced
so many thousands of the Lamanites of the incorrect tradition of their fathers.
Yea, these records and their words brought them unto repentance;
that is, they brought them to the knowledge of the Lord their God
and to rejoice in Jesus Christ their Redeemer.

10   And who knoweth but what they will be the means
of bringing many thousands of them
—yea, and also many thousands of our stiffnecked brethren, the Nephites,
which are now hardening their hearts in sins and iniquities—
to the knowledge of their Redeemer.

11   Now these mysteries are not yet fully made known unto me;
therefore I shall forbear.

12   And it may suffice if I only say
they are preserved for a wise purpose,

which purpose is known unto God.
For he doth counsel in wisdom over all his works,
and his paths are straight,
and his course is one eternal round.

13 O remember, remember, my son Helaman,
how strict is the commandments of God!
And he saith:
If ye will keep my commandments, ye shall prosper in the land.
But if ye keep not his commandments, ye shall be cut off from his presence.

14 And now remember, my son,
that God hath entrusted you with these things which are sacred,
which he hath kept sacred,
and also which he will keep and preserve for a wise purpose in him,
that he may shew forth his power unto future generations.

15 And now behold, I tell you by the spirit of prophecy
that if ye transgress the commandments of God,
behold, these things which are sacred
shall be taken away from you by the power of God;
and ye shall be delivered up unto Satan,
that he may sift you as chaff before the wind.

16 But if ye keep the commandments of God
and do with these things which are sacred
according to that which the Lord doth command you
—for you must appeal unto the Lord
for all things whatsoever ye must do with them—
behold, no power of earth or hell can take them from you,
for God is powerful to the fulfilling of all his words.

17 For he will fulfill all his promises which he shall make unto you,
for he hath fulfilled his promise which he hath made unto our fathers.

18 For he promised unto them
that he would preserve these things for a wise purpose in him,
that he might shew forth his power unto future generations.

19 And now behold, one purpose hath he fulfilled,
even to the restoration of many thousands of the Lamanites
to the knowledge of the truth.
And he hath shewn forth his power in them.
And he will also still shew forth his power in them unto future generations.
Therefore they shall be preserved.

20 Therefore I command you, my son Helaman,
that ye be diligent in fulfilling all my words

and that ye be diligent in keeping the commandments of God
as they are written.

21 And now I will speak unto you concerning those twenty four plates,
that ye keep them,
that the mysteries and the works of darkness and their secret works
—or the secret works of those people which have been destroyed—
may be made manifest unto this people
—yea, all their murders and robbings and their plunderings
and all their wickedness and abominations may be made manifest unto this people—
yea, and that ye preserve these directors.
22 For behold, the Lord saw that his people began to work in darkness
—yea, work secret murders and abominations—
therefore the Lord said
if they did not repent,
they should be destroyed from off the face of the earth.
23 And the Lord said:
I will prepare unto my servant Gazelem
a stone which shall shine forth in darkness unto light,
that I may discover unto my people which serve me—
that I may discover unto them the works of their brethren,
yea, their secret works, their works of darkness,
and their wickedness and abominations.

24 And now my son, these directors were prepared
that the word of God might be fulfilled which he spake, saying:
25 I will bring forth out of darkness unto light
all their secret works and their abominations.
And except they repent, I will destroy them from off the face of the earth.
And I will bring to light all their secrets and abominations
unto every nation which shall hereafter possess the land.
26 And now my son, we see that they did not repent;
therefore they have been destroyed.
And thus far the word of God hath been fulfilled;
yea, their secret abominations have been brought out of darkness
and made known unto us.

27 And now my son, I command you
that ye retain all their oaths and their covenants
and their agreements in their secret abominations;
yea, and all their signs and their wonders ye shall retain from this people,
that they know them not,
lest peradventure they should fall into darkness also and be destroyed.
28 For behold, there is a curse upon all this land,

that destruction shall come upon all those workers of darkness,
according to the power of God,
when they are fully ripe.
Therefore I desire that this people might not be destroyed.

29 Therefore ye shall keep
these secret plans of their oaths and their covenants
from this people.
And only their wickedness and their murders and their abominations
shall ye make known unto them.
And ye shall teach them
to abhor such wickedness and abominations and murders.

And ye shall also teach them that those people were destroyed
on account of their wickedness and abominations and their murders.

30 For behold, they murdered all the prophets of the Lord
which came among them to declare unto them concerning their iniquities.
And the blood of those which they murdered did cry unto the Lord their God
for vengeance upon those which were their murderers.
And thus the judgments of God did come
upon them workers of darkness and secret combinations.

31 Yea, and cursed be the land forever and ever
unto those workers of darkness and secret combinations, even unto destruction,
except they repent before they are fully ripe.

32 And now my son, remember the words which I have spoken unto you.
Trust not those secret plans unto this people,
but teach them an everlasting hatred against sin and iniquity.

33 Preach unto them repentance and faith on the Lord Jesus Christ.
Teach them to humble themselves and to be meek and lowly in heart.
Teach them to withstand every temptation of the devil,
with their faith on the Lord Jesus Christ.

34 Teach them to never be weary of good works,
but to be meek and lowly in heart,
for such shall find rest to their souls.

35 O remember, my son, and learn wisdom in thy youth;
yea, learn in thy youth to keep the commandments of God.

36 Yea, and cry unto God for all thy support.
Yea, let all thy doings be unto the Lord.
And whithersoever thou goest,
let it be in the Lord.
Yea, let all thy thoughts be directed unto the Lord.
Yea, let the affections of thy heart be placed upon the Lord forever.

37 Counsel the Lord in all thy doings,

and he will direct thee for good.
Yea, when thou liest down at night,
lie down unto the Lord,
that he may watch over you in your sleep.
And when thou risest in the morning,
let thy heart be full of thanks unto God.
And if ye always do these things,
ye shall be lifted up at the last day.

38 And now my son, I have somewhat to say
concerning the thing which our fathers call a ball or director
—or our fathers called it Liahona,
which is being interpreted a compass—
and the Lord prepared it.

39 And behold, there cannot any man work
after the manner of so curious a workmanship.
And behold, it was prepared to shew unto our fathers
the course which they should travel in the wilderness.

40 And it did work for them according to their faith in God.
Therefore if they had faith to believe
that God could cause that those spindles should point the way they should go,
behold, it was done.
Therefore they had this miracle
—and also many other miracles—
wrought by the power of God day by day.

41 Nevertheless, because those miracles were worked by small means
—nevertheless it did shew unto them marvelous works—
they were slothful and forgat to exercise their faith and diligence.
And then those marvelous works ceased,
and they did not progress in their journey.

42 Therefore they tarried in the wilderness,
or did not travel a direct course,
and were afflicted with hunger and thirst because of their transgression.

43 And now my son, I would that ye should understand
that these things are not without a shadow.
For as our fathers were slothful to give heed to this compass
—now these things were temporal—
they did not prosper;
even so it is with things which are spiritual.

44 For behold, it is as easy to give heed to the word of Christ,
which will point to you a straight course to eternal bliss,
as it was for our fathers to give heed to this compass,
which would point unto them a straight course to the promised land.

45 And now I say:
Is there not a type in this thing?
For just assuredly as this director did bring our fathers
by following its course to the promised land,
shall the word of Christ, if we follow its course, carry us
beyond this vale of sorrow into a far better land of promise.

46 O my son, do not let us be slothful because of the easiness of the way,
for so was it with our fathers.
For so was it prepared for them
that if they would look, they might live.
Even so it is with us:
the way is prepared;
and if we will look, we may live forever.

47 And now my son, see that ye take care of these sacred things.
Yea, see that ye look to God and live.
Go unto this people and declare the word,
and be sober.
My son, farewell.

The commandments of Alma to his son Shiblon.

38 | 1 My son, give ear to my words,
for I say unto you,
even as I said unto Helaman,
that inasmuch as ye shall keep the commandments of God,
ye shall prosper in the land;
and inasmuch as ye will not keep the commandments of God,
ye shall be cut off from his presence.

2 And now my son, I trust that I shall have great joy in you
because of your steadiness and your faithfulness unto God;
for as you have commenced in your youth to look to the Lord your God,
even so I hope that you will continue in keeping his commandments,
for blessed is he that endureth to the end.

3 I say unto you, my son, that I have had great joy in thee already
because of thy faithfulness and thy diligence and thy patience
and thy long-suffering among the people of the Zoramites.

4 For I knew that thou wast in bonds;
yea, and I also knew that thou wast stoned for the word's sake.
And thou didst bear all these things with patience

because the Lord was with thee.
And now thou knowest that the Lord did deliver thee.

5 And now my son Shiblon, I would that ye should remember
that as much as ye shall put your trust in God,
even so much ye shall be delivered out of your trials
and your troubles and your afflictions,
and ye shall be lifted up at the last day.

6 Now my son, I would not that ye should think
that I know these things of myself,
but it is the Spirit of God which is in me
which maketh these things known unto me.
For if I had not been born of God,
I should not have known these things.
7 But behold, the Lord in his great mercy sent his angel to declare unto me
that I must stop the work of destruction among his people.
Yea, I have seen an angel face to face,
and he spake with me.
And his voice was as thunder,
and it shook the whole earth.
8 And it came to pass that I was three days and three nights
in the most bitter pain and anguish of soul.
And never until I did cry out unto the Lord Jesus Christ for mercy
did I receive a remission of my sins.
But behold, I did cry unto him and I did find peace to my soul.

9 And now my son, I have told you this that ye might learn wisdom,
that ye may learn of me,
that there is no other way nor means whereby man can be saved,
only in and through Christ.
Behold, he is the life and the light of the world.
Behold, he is the word of truth and righteousness.

10 And now as ye have begun to teach the word,
even so I would that ye should continue to teach.
And I would that ye should be diligent and temperate in all things.
11 See that ye are not lifted up unto pride;
yea, see that ye do not boast in your own wisdom nor of your much strength.
12 Use boldness, but not overbearance.
And also see that ye bridle all your passions,
that ye may be filled with love.
See that ye refrain from idleness.
13 Do not pray as the Zoramites do,

for ye have seen that they pray to be heard of men
and to be praised for their wisdom.

14 Do not say:
O God, I thank thee that we are better than our brethren.
But rather say:
O Lord, forgive my unworthiness
and remember my brethren in mercy.
Yea, acknowledge your unworthiness before God at all times.

15 And may the Lord bless your soul
and receive you at the last day into his kingdom to sit down in peace.

Now go, my son, and teach the word unto this people;
be sober.
My son, farewell.

The commandments of Alma to his son Corianton.

39 | 1 And now my son, I have somewhat more to say unto thee
than what I said unto thy brother.
For behold, have ye not observed the steadiness of thy brother,
his faithfulness and his diligence in keeping the commandments of God?
Behold, has he not set a good example for thee?

2 For thou didst not give so much heed unto my words
as did thy brother among the people of the Zoramites.
Now this is what I have against thee:
thou didst go on unto boasting in thy strength and thy wisdom.

3 And this is not all, my son.
Thou didst do that which was grievous unto me,
for thou didst forsake the ministry
and did go over into the land of Siron among the borders of the Lamanites
after the harlot Isabel.

4 Yea, she did steal away the hearts of many,
but this was no excuse for thee, my son.
Thou shouldst have tended to the ministry wherewith thou wast entrusted.

5 Know ye not, my son, that these things
are an abomination in the sight of the Lord?
Yea, most abominable above all sins
save it be the shedding of innocent blood or denying the Holy Ghost.

6 For behold, if ye deny the Holy Ghost when it once hath had place in you
—and ye know that ye deny it—

behold, this is a sin which is unpardonable.
Yea, and whosoever murdereth against the light and knowledge of God,
it is not easy for him to obtain forgiveness.
Yea, I say unto you, my son,
that it is not easy for him to obtain a forgiveness.

7 And now my son, I would to God that ye had not been guilty of so great a crime.
I would not dwell upon your crimes to harrow up your soul
if it were not for your good.

8 But behold, ye cannot hide your crimes from God.
And except ye repent,
they will stand as a testimony against you at the last day.

9 Now my son, I would that ye should repent and forsake your sins
and go no more after the lusts of your eyes,
but cross yourself in all these things.
For except ye do this, ye can in no wise inherit the kingdom of God.
O remember, and take it upon you and cross yourself in these things.

10 And I command you to take it upon you
to counsel your elder brothers in your undertakings
—for behold, thou art in thy youth
and ye stand in need to be nourished by your brothers—
and give heed to their counsel.

11 Suffer not yourself to be led away by any vain or foolish thing.
Suffer not that the devil lead away your heart again after those wicked harlots.
Behold, O my son, how great iniquity ye brought upon the Zoramites!
For when they saw your conduct,
they would not believe in my words.

12 And now the Spirit of the Lord doth say unto me:
Command thy children to do good,
lest they lead away the hearts of many people to destruction.
Therefore I command you, my son, in the fear of God
that ye refrain from your iniquities,

13 that ye turn to the Lord with all your mind, might, and strength,
that ye lead away the hearts of no more to do wickedly,
but rather return unto them and acknowledge your faults
and repair that wrong which ye have done.

14 Seek not after riches nor the vain things of this world;
for behold, you cannot carry them with you.

15 And now my son, I would say somewhat unto you
concerning the coming of Christ.
Behold, I say unto you

that it is him that surely shall come to take away the sins of the world.
Yea, he cometh to declare glad tidings of salvation unto his people.

16 And now my son, this was the ministry unto which ye were called,
to declare these glad tidings unto this people,
to prepare their minds—
or rather that salvation might come unto them,
that they may prepare the minds of their children
to hear the word at the time of his coming.

17 And now I will ease your mind somewhat on this subject.
Behold, you marvel why these things should be known so long beforehand.
Behold, I say unto you:
Is not a soul at this time as precious unto God
as a soul will be at the time of his coming?

18 Is it not as necessary that the plan of redemption should be made known
unto this people as well as unto their children?

19 Is it not as easy at this time
for the Lord to send his angel to declare those glad tidings
unto us as unto our children
or as after the time of his coming?

40 | 1 Now my son, here is somewhat more I would say unto thee,
for I perceive that thy mind is worried concerning the resurrection of the dead.

2 Behold, I say unto you that there is no resurrection
—or I would say in other words
that this mortal does not put on immortality,
this corruption does not put on incorruption—
until after the coming of Christ.

3 Behold, he bringeth to pass the resurrection of the dead.
But behold, my son, the resurrection is not yet.

Now I unfold unto you a mystery.
Nevertheless there are many mysteries which are kept,
that no one knoweth them save God himself.
But I shew unto you one thing
which I have inquired diligently of God that I might know—
that is concerning the resurrection.

4 Behold, there is a time appointed that all shall come forth from the dead.
Now when this time cometh, no one knows;
but God knoweth the time which is appointed.

5 Now whether there shall be one time or a second time or a third time
that men shall come forth from the dead,
it mattereth not,
for God knoweth all these things.

And it sufficeth me to know that this is the case,
that there is a time appointed when all shall rise from the dead.

6 And now there must needs be a space
betwixt the time of death and the time of the resurrection.

7 And now I would inquire what becometh of the souls of men
from this time of death to the time appointed for the resurrection.

8 Now whether there is more than one time appointed for men to rise,
it mattereth not.
For all do not die at once,
and this mattereth not.
All is as one day with God,
and time only is measured unto man.

9 Therefore there is a time appointed unto men that they shall rise from the dead;
and there is a space between the time of death and the resurrection.

And now concerning this space of time,
what becometh of the souls of men is the thing
which I have inquired diligently of the Lord to know;
and this is the thing of which I do know.

10 And when the time cometh when all shall rise,
then shall they know that God knoweth all the times
which are appointed unto man.

11 Now concerning the state of the soul between death and the resurrection,
behold, it hath been made known unto me by an angel
that the spirits of all men, as soon as they are departed from this mortal body,
yea, the spirits of all men, whether they be good or evil,
are taken home to that God who gave them life.

12 And then shall it come to pass that
the spirits of those which are righteous are received into a state of happiness,
which is called paradise, a state of rest, a state of peace,
where they shall rest from all their troubles and from all care and sorrow etc.

13 And then shall it come to pass that
the spirits of the wicked, yea, which are evil
—for behold, they have no part nor portion of the Spirit of the Lord,
for behold, they chose evil works rather than good;
therefore the spirit of the devil did enter into them
and take possession of their house—
and these shall be cast out into outer darkness.
There shall be weeping and wailing and gnashing of teeth—
and this because of their own iniquity,
being led captive by the will of the devil.

14 Now this is the state of the souls of the wicked—

yea, in darkness and a state of awful fearful looking for
of the fiery indignation of the wrath of God upon them.
Thus they remain in this state,
as well as the righteous in paradise,
until the time of their resurrection.

15 Now there are some that have understood
that this state of happiness
and this state of misery of the soul before the resurrection
was a first resurrection.
Yea, I admit it may be termed a resurrection,
the raising the spirit or the soul and their consignation to happiness or misery,
according to the words which have been spoken.

16 And behold, again it hath been spoken that there is a first resurrection
—a resurrection of all those which have been or which are or which shall be,
down to the resurrection of Christ—
from the dead.

17 Now we do not suppose
that this first resurrection which is spoken of in this manner
can be the resurrection of the souls
and their consignation to happiness or misery.
Ye cannot suppose that this is what it meaneth.

18 Behold, I say unto you: Nay.
But it meaneth the reuniting of the soul with the body
of those from the days of Adam down to the resurrection of Christ.

19 Now whether the souls and the bodies of those of which have been spoken
shall all be reunited at once,
the wicked as well as the righteous,
I do not say.
Let it suffice that I say that they all come forth,
or in other words, that their resurrection cometh to pass
before the resurrection of those which die after the resurrection of Christ.

20 Now my son, I do not say
that their resurrection cometh at the resurrection of Christ.
But behold, I give it as my opinion
that the souls and the bodies are reunited of the righteous
at the resurrection of Christ and his ascension into heaven.

21 But whether it be at his resurrection or after, I do not say.
But this much I say,
that there is a space between death and the resurrection of the body
and a state of the soul in happiness or in misery
until the time which is appointed of God
that the dead shall come forth and be reunited, both soul and body,

and be brought to stand before God
and be judged according to their works.

22 Yea, this bringeth about the restoration of those things
of which have been spoken by the mouths of the prophets.

23 The soul shall be restored to the body and the body to the soul.
Yea, and every limb and joint shall be restored to its body
—yea, even a hair of their heads shall not be lost—
but all things shall be restored to its proper and perfect frame.

24 And now my son, this is the restoration
of which has been spoken by the mouths of the prophets.

25 And then shall the righteous shine forth in the kingdom of God.

26 But behold, an awful death cometh upon the wicked,
for they die as to things pertaining to things of righteousness;
for they are unclean,
and no unclean thing can inherit the kingdom of God.
But they are cast out and consigned to partake of the fruits of their labors
—or their works which have been evil—
and they drink the dregs of a bitter cup.

41 | 1 And now my son, I have somewhat to say
concerning the restoration of which has been spoken.
For behold, some have wrested the scriptures
and have gone far astray because of this thing.
And I perceive that thy mind hath been worried also concerning this thing.
But behold, I will explain it unto thee.

2 I say unto thee, my son,
that the plan of restoration is requisite with the justice of God,
for it is requisite that all things should be restored to their proper order.
Behold, it is requisite and just,
according to the power and resurrection of Christ,
that the soul of man should be restored to its body
and that every part of the body should be restored to itself.

3 And it is also requisite with the justice of God
that men should be judged according to their works—
and if their works were good in this life
and the desires of their hearts were good,
that they should also at the last day be restored unto that which is good.

4 And if his works are evil,
they shall be restored unto him for evil.
Therefore all things shall be restored to its proper order,
every thing to its natural frame
—mortality raised to immortality,

corruption to incorruption—
raised to endless happiness to inherit the kingdom of God,
or to endless misery to inherit the kingdom of the devil,
the one on one hand, the other on the other,

5 the one restored to happiness according to his desires of happiness
   —or to good according to his desires of good—
   and the other to evil according to his desires of evil.
   For as he has desired to do evil all the day long,
   even so shall he have his reward of evil when the night cometh.

6 And so it is on the other hand:
   if he hath repented of his sins
   and desired righteousness until the end of his days,
   even so shall he be rewarded unto righteousness.

7 These are they that are redeemed of the Lord.
   Yea, these are they that are taken out—
   that are delivered from that endless night of darkness;
   and thus they stand or fall.
   For behold, they are their own judges,
   whether to do good or do evil.

8 Now the decrees of God are unalterable.
   Therefore the way is prepared
   that whosoever will
   may walk therein and be saved.

9 And now behold, my son, do not risk one more offense against your God
   upon those points of doctrine which ye hath hitherto risked to commit sin.

10 Do not suppose because that it hath been spoken concerning restoration
   that ye shall be restored from sin to happiness.
   Behold, I say unto you:
   Wickedness never was happiness.

11 And now my son, all men that are in a state of nature
   —or I would say, in a carnal state—
   are in the gall of bitterness and in the bonds of iniquity.
   They are without God in the world,
   and they have gone contrary to the nature of God.
   Therefore they are in a state contrary to the nature of happiness.

12 And now behold, is the meaning of the word restoration
   to take a thing of a natural state and place it in an unnatural state,
   or to place it in a state opposite to its nature?

13 O my son, this is not the case.
   But the meaning of the word restoration is to bring back again evil for evil
   or carnal for carnal or devilish for devilish,

good for that which is good,
righteous for that which is righteous,
just for that which is just,
merciful for that which is merciful.

14 Therefore my son, see that ye are merciful unto your brethren.
Deal justly, judge righteously, and do good continually.
And if ye do all these things, then shall ye receive your reward.
Yea, ye shall have mercy restored unto you again;
ye shall have justice restored unto you again;
ye shall have a righteous judgment restored unto you again;
and ye shall have good rewarded unto you again.

15 For that which ye doth send out shall return unto you again and be restored.
Therefore the word restoration more fully condemneth the sinner
and justifieth him not at all.

42 | 1 And now my son, I perceive there is somewhat more
which doth worry your mind, which ye cannot understand,
which is concerning the justice of God in the punishment of the sinner.
For ye do try to suppose that it is injustice
that the sinner should be consigned to a state of misery.

2 Now behold, my son, I will explain this thing unto thee.
For behold, after the Lord God sent
our first parents forth from the garden of Eden
to till the ground from whence he was taken
—yea, he drove out the man—
and he placed at the east end of the garden of Eden cherubims
and a flaming sword which turned every way to keep the tree of life—

3 now we see that the man had became as God, knowing good and evil,
and lest he should put forth his hand
and take also of the tree of life and eat and live forever,
that the Lord God placed cherubims and the flaming sword
that he should not partake of the fruit.

4 And thus we see that there was a time granted unto man to repent,
yea, a probationary time, a time to repent and serve God.

5 For behold, if Adam had put forth his hand immediately
and partook of the tree of life,
he would have lived forever, according to the word of God,
having no space for repentance.
Yea, and also the word of God would have been void,
and the great plan of salvation would have been frustrated.

6 But behold, it was appointed unto man to die.
Therefore as they were cut off from the tree of life,

therefore they should be cut off from the face of the earth.
And man became lost forever;
yea, they became fallen man.

7 And now we see by this that our first parents were cut off,
both temporally and spiritually, from the presence of the Lord.
And thus we see they became subjects to follow after their own will.

8 Now behold, it was not expedient
that man should be reclaimed from this temporal death,
for that would destroy the great plan of happiness.

9 Therefore as the soul could never die
and the fall had brought upon all mankind
a spiritual death as well as a temporal
—that is, they were cut off from the presence of the Lord—
therefore it was expedient
that mankind should be reclaimed from this spiritual death.

10 Therefore as they had become carnal, sensual, and devilish by nature,
this probationary state became a state for them to prepare;
it became a preparatory state.

11 And now remember, my son,
if it were not for the plan of redemption—laying it aside—
as soon as they were dead,
their souls were miserable,
being cut off from the presence of the Lord.

12 And now there was no means to reclaim men from this fallen state,
which man had brought upon himself because of his own disobedience.

13 Therefore according to justice
the plan of redemption could not be brought about,
only on conditions of repentance of men in this probationary state,
yea, this preparatory state.
For except it were for these conditions,
mercy could not take effect except it should destroy the work of justice.
Now the work of justice could not be destroyed.
If so, God would cease to be God.

14 And thus we see that all mankind were fallen,
and they were in the grasp of justice,
yea, the justice of God which consigned them forever
to be cut off from his presence.

15 And now the plan of mercy could not be brought about
except an atonement should be made.
Therefore God himself atoneth for the sins of the world,
to bring about the plan of mercy,

to appease the demands of justice,
that God might be a perfect just God and a merciful God also.

16 Now repentance could not come unto men
except there were a punishment,
which also was as eternal as the life of the soul,
should be affixed opposite to the plan of happiness,
which was as eternal also as the life of the soul.

17 Now how could a man repent except he should sin?
How could he sin if there was no law?
How could there be a law save there was a punishment?

18 Now there was a punishment affixed and a just law given,
which brought remorse of conscience unto man.

19 Now if there was no law given if a man murdered he should die,
would he be afraid he should die if he should murder?

20 And also if there was no law given against sin,
men would not be afraid to sin.

21 And if there was no law given if men sinned,
what could justice do, or mercy either?
For they would have no claim upon the creature.

22 But there is a law given and a punishment affixed and repentance granted,
which repentance mercy claimeth.
Otherwise justice claimeth the creature and executeth the law,
and the law inflicteth the punishment.
If not so, the works of justice would be destroyed;
and God would cease to be God.

23 But God ceaseth not to be God;
and mercy claimeth the penitent,
and mercy cometh because of the atonement,
and the atonement bringeth to pass the resurrection of the dead,
and the resurrection of the dead bringeth back men into the presence of God.
And thus they are restored into his presence,
to be judged according to their works, according to the law and justice.

24 For behold, justice exerciseth all his demands;
and also mercy claimeth all which is her own.
And thus none but the truly penitent are saved.

25 What? Do ye suppose that mercy can rob justice?
I say unto you:
Nay, not one whit.
If so, God would cease to be God.

26 And thus God bringeth about his great and eternal purposes,
which was prepared from the foundation of the world.

And thus cometh about the salvation and the redemption of men,
and also their destruction and misery.

27 Therefore, O my son, whosoever will come
may come and partake of the waters of life freely.
And whosoever will not come,
the same is not compelled to come.
But in the last day it shall be restored unto him according to his deeds.

28 If he hath desired to do evil and hath not repented in his days,
behold, evil shall be done unto him according to the restoration of God.

29 And now my son, I desire that ye should let these things trouble you no more.
And only let your sins trouble you with that trouble
which shall bring you down unto repentance.

30 O my son, I desire that ye should deny the justice of God no more.
Do not endeavor to excuse yourself in the least point because of your sins
by denying the justice of God.
But do you let the justice of God and his mercy
and his long-suffering have full sway in your heart,
but let it bring you down to the dust in humility.

31 And now my son, ye are called of God to preach the word unto this people.
And now my son, go thy way;
declare the word with truth and soberness,
that thou mayest bring souls unto repentance,
that the great plan of mercy may have claim upon them.
And may God grant unto you, yea, even according to my words.
Amen.

43 | 1 And now it came to pass that
the sons of Alma did go forth among the people to declare the word unto them.
And Alma also himself could not rest, and he also went forth.

2 Now we shall say no more concerning their preaching
except that they preached the word and the truth
according to the spirit of prophecy and revelation,
and they preached after the holy order of God by which they were called.

3 And now I return to an account of the wars
between the Nephites and the Lamanites
in the eighteenth year of the reign of the judges.

4 For behold, it came to pass that the Zoramites became Lamanites.
Therefore in the commencement of the eighteenth year

the people of the Nephites saw that the Lamanites were coming upon them.
Therefore they made preparations for war;
yea, they gathered together their armies in the land of Jershon.

5 And it came to pass that the Lamanites came with their thousands.
And they came into the land of Antionum,
which was the land of the Zoramites;
and a man by the name of Zerahemnah was their leader.

6 And now as the Amlicites were of a more wicked and a murderous disposition
than the Lamanites were, in and of themselves,
therefore Zerahemnah appointed chief captains over the Lamanites,
and they were all of the Amlicites and the Zoramites.

7 Now this he done that he might preserve their hatred towards the Nephites,
that he might bring them into subjection to the accomplishment of his designs.

8 For behold, his designs were to stir up
the Lamanites to anger against the Nephites;
and this he done that he might usurp great power over them,
and also that he might gain power over the Nephites
by bringing them into bondage etc.

9 And now the design of the Nephites were to support their lands and their houses
and their wives and their children,
that they might preserve them from the hands of their enemies,
and also that they might preserve their rights and their privileges,
yea, and also their liberty,
that they might worship God according to their desires.

10 For they knew that if they should fall into the hands of the Lamanites
that whosoever should worship God in spirit and in truth,
the true and the living God,
the Lamanites would destroy.

11 Yea, and they also knew the extreme hatred of the Lamanites
towards their brethren which were the people of Anti-Nephi-Lehi,
which were called the people of Ammon.
And they would not take up arms;
yea, they had entered into a covenant and they would not break it.
Therefore if they should fall into the hands of the Lamanites,
they would be destroyed.

12 And the Nephites would not suffer that they should be destroyed;
therefore they gave them lands for their inheritance.

13 And the people of Ammon did give unto the Nephites
a large portion of their substance to support their armies.

And thus the Nephites were compelled alone to withstand against the Lamanites,
which were a compound of Laman and Lemuel and the sons of Ishmael

and all those which had dissented from the Nephites,
which were Amlicites and Zoramites and the descendants of the priests of Noah.

14 Now those dissenters were as numerous nearly as were the Nephites.
And thus the Nephites were obliged to contend with their brethren,
even unto bloodshed.

15 And it came to pass as the armies of the Lamanites
had gathered together in the land of Antionum,
behold, the armies of the Nephites were prepared
to meet them in the land of Jershon.

16 Now the leader of the Nephites,
or the man which had been appointed to be the chief captain over the Nephites
—now the chief captain took the command of all the armies of the Nephites—
and his name was Moroni.

17 And Moroni took all the command and the governments of their wars;
and he was only twenty and five years old
when he was appointed chief commander over the armies of the Nephites.

18 And it came to pass that he met the Lamanites in the borders of Jershon.
And his people were armed with swords
and with scimitars and all manner of weapons of war.

19 And it came to pass that
when the armies of the Lamanites saw
that the people of Nephi—
or that Moroni had prepared his people with breastplates and with armshields,
yea, and also shields to defend their heads,
and also they were dressed with thick clothing—

20 now the army of Zerahemnah was not prepared with any such thing;
they had only their swords and their scimitars,
their bows and their arrows,
their stones and their slings,
but they were naked save it were a skin which was girded about their loins;
yea, all were naked save it were the Zoramites and the Amlicites;

21 but they were not armed with breastplates nor shields—
therefore they were exceeding fraid of the armies of the Nephites
because of their armor,
notwithstanding their number being so much greater than the Nephites.

22 Behold, now it came to pass that
they durst not come against the Nephites in the borders of Jershon.
Therefore they departed out of the land of Antionum into the wilderness
and took their journey round about in the wilderness,
away by the head of the river Sidon,
that they might come into the land of Manti and take possession of the land,

for they did not suppose
that the armies of Moroni would know whither they had gone.

23 But it came to pass as soon as they had departed into the wilderness,
Moroni sent spies into the wilderness to watch their camp.
And Moroni also knowing of the prophecies of Alma
sent certain men unto him,
desiring him that he should inquire of the Lord
whither the armies of the Nephites should go
to defend themselves against the Lamanites.
24 And it came to pass that the word of the Lord came unto Alma.
And Alma informed the messengers of Moroni
that the armies of the Lamanites were marching round about in the wilderness,
that they might come over into the land of Manti,
that they might commence an attackt upon the more weak part of the people.
And those messengers went and delivered the message unto Moroni.

25 Now Moroni leaving a part of his army in the land of Jershon
—lest by any means a part of the Lamanites should come into that land
and take possession of the city—
and Moroni took the remainder part of his army
and marched over into the land of Manti.
26 And he caused that all the people in that quarter of the land
should gather themselves together to battle against the Lamanites,
to defend their lands and their country, their rights and their liberties.
Therefore they were prepared against the time of the coming of the Lamanites.
27 And it came to pass that Moroni caused
that his army should be secreted in the valley
which was near the bank of the river Sidon,
which was on the west of the river Sidon in the wilderness.
28 And Moroni placed spies round about
that he might know when the camp of the Lamanites should come.

29 And now as Moroni knew the intention of the Lamanites,
that it was their intention to destroy their brethren
or to subject them and bring them into bondage,
that they might establish a kingdom unto themselves over all the land,
30 and he also knowing that it was the only desire of the Nephites
to preserve their lands and their liberty and their church,
therefore he thought it no sin that he should defend them by stratagem;
therefore he found by his spies which course the Lamanites were to take.
31 Therefore he divided his army and brought a part over into the valley
and concealed them on the east and on the south of the hill Riplah.

32 And the remainder he concealed in the west valley,
     on the west of the river Sidon,
     and so down into the borders of the land Manti.
33 And thus having placed his army according to his desire,
     he was prepared to meet them.

34 And it came to pass that the Lamanites came up on the north of the hill,
     where a part of the army of Moroni was concealed.
35 And it came to pass that as the Lamanites had passed the hill Riplah
     and came into the valley and began to cross the river Sidon,
     the army which was concealed on the south of the hill,
     which was led by a man whose name was Lehi—
     and he led his army forth
     and encircled the Lamanites about on the east in their rear.
36 And it came to pass that the Lamanites,
     when they saw the Nephites coming upon them in their rear,
     they turned them about and began to contend with the army of Lehi.
37 And the work of death commenced on both sides,
     but it was more dreadful on the part of the Lamanites.
     For their nakedness was exposed to the heavy blows of the Nephites,
     with their swords and their scimitars,
     which brought death almost at every stroke;
38 while on the other hand
     there was now and then a man fell among the Nephites
     by their wounds and the loss of blood,
     they being shielded from the more vital parts of the body—
     or the more vital parts of the body being shielded
     from the strokes of the Lamanites
     by their breastplates and their armshields and their headplates.
     And thus the Nephites did carry on the work of death among the Lamanites.

39 And it came to pass that the Lamanites became frightened
     because of the great destruction among them,
     even until they began to flee towards the river Sidon.
40 And they were pursued by Lehi and his men.
     And they were driven by Lehi into the waters of Sidon,
     and they crossed the waters of Sidon.
     And Lehi retained his armies upon the bank of the river Sidon,
     that they should not cross.
41 And it came to pass that
     Moroni and his army met the army of the Lamanites in the valley,
     on the other side of the river Sidon.

And it came to pass that
Moroni and his army began to fall upon them and to slay them.

42 And it came to pass that
the Lamanites did flee again before them towards the land of Manti,
and they were met again by the armies of Moroni.

43 Now in this case the Lamanites did fight exceedingly.
Yea, never had the Lamanites been known
to have fought with such exceeding great strength and courage,
no, not even from the beginning.

44 And they were inspired by the Zoramites and the Amlicites,
which were their chief captains and leaders,
and by Zerahemnah,
who was their chief captain, or their chief leader and commander.
Yea, they did fight like dragons.
And many of the Nephites were slain by their hand;
yea, for they did smite in two many of their headplates,
and they did pierce many of their breastplates,
and they did smite off many of their arms.
And thus the Lamanites did smite in their fierce anger.

45 Nevertheless the Nephites were inspired by a better cause.
For they were not fighting for monarchy nor power,
but they were fighting for their homes and their liberties,
their wives and their children, and their all,
yea, for their rights of worship and their church.

46 And they were doing that which they felt
it was the duty which they owed to their God;
for the Lord had said unto them and also unto their fathers
that inasmuch as ye are not guilty of the first offense neither the second,
ye shall not suffer yourselves to be slain by the hands of your enemies.

47 And again the Lord hath said
that ye shall defend your families even unto bloodshed.
Therefore for this cause were the Nephites contending with the Lamanites,
to defend themselves and their families and their lands,
their country and their rights and their religion.

48 And it came to pass that
when the men of Moroni saw the fierceness and the anger of the Lamanites,
they were about to shrink and flee from them.
And Moroni perceiving their intent
sent forth and inspired their hearts with these thoughts,
yea, the thoughts of their lands, their liberty,

yea, their freedom from bondage.

49 And it came to pass that they turned upon the Lamanites
and they cried with one voice unto the Lord their God,
for their liberty and their freedom from bondage.

50 And they began to stand against the Lamanites with power.
And in that selfsame hour that they cried unto the Lord for their freedom,
the Lamanites began to flee before them;
and they fled even to the waters of Sidon.

51 Now the Lamanites were more numerous,
yea, by more than double the number of the Nephites.
Nevertheless they were driven,
insomuch that they were gathered together in one body in the valley,
upon the bank by the river Sidon.

52 Therefore the armies of Moroni encircled them about,
yea, even on both sides of the river;
for behold, on the east were the men of Lehi.

53 Therefore when Zerahemnah saw the men of Lehi on the east of the river Sidon
and the armies of Moroni on the west of the river Sidon,
that they were encircled about by the Nephites,
they were struck with terror.

54 Now Moroni, when he saw their terror,
he commanded his men that they should stop shedding their blood.

44 | 1 And it came to pass that they did stop and withdrew a pace from them;
and Moroni said unto Zerahemnah:
Behold, Zerahemnah, that we do not desire to be men of blood.
Ye know that ye are in our hands;
yet we do not desire to slay you.

2 Behold, we have not come out to battle against you
that we might shed your blood for power.
Neither do we desire to bring any one to the yoke of bondage.
But this is the very cause for which ye have come against us;
yea, and ye are angry with us because of our religion.

3 But now ye behold that the Lord is with us.
And ye behold that he hath delivered you into our hands.
And now I would that ye should understand
that this is done unto us because of our religion and our faith in Christ.
And now ye see that ye cannot destroy this our faith.

4 Now ye see that this is the true faith of God.
Yea, ye see that God will support and keep and preserve us
so long as we are faithful unto him and unto our faith and our religion.

And never will the Lord suffer that we shall be destroyed
except we should fall into transgression and deny our faith.

5 And now Zerahemnah, I command you
in the name of that all-powerful God who hath strengthened our arms
that we have gained power over you by our faith,
by our religion and by our rights of worship and by our church
and by the sacred support which we owe to our wives and our children
and by that liberty which binds us to our lands and our country,
yea, and also by the maintenance of the sacred word of God
to which we owe all our happiness,
and by all that is most dear unto us
6 —yea, and this is not all—
I command you by all the desires which ye have for life
that ye deliver up your weapons of war unto us
and we will seek not your blood,
but we will spare your lives if ye will go your way
and come not again to war against us.
7 And now if ye do not this,
behold, ye are in our hands.
And I will command my men that they shall fall upon you
and inflict the wounds of death in your bodies,
that ye may become extinct.
And then we will see who shall have power over this people.
Yea, we will see who shall be brought into bondage.

8 And now it came to pass that when Zerahemnah had heard these sayings,
he came forth and delivered up his sword and his scimitar and his bow
into the hands of Moroni
and saith unto him:
Behold, here is our weapons of war;
we will deliver them up unto you.
And we will not suffer ourselves to take an oath unto you
which we know that we shall break, and also our children.
But take our weapons of war
and suffer that we may depart into the wilderness.
Otherwise we will retain our swords,
and we will perish or conquer.
9 Behold, we are not of your faith.
We do not believe that it is God that hath delivered us into your hands.
But we believe that it is your cunning that hath preserved you from our swords;
behold, it is your breastplates and your shields that hath preserved you.

10 And now when Zerahemnah had made an end of speaking these words,

Moroni returned the sword and the weapons of war which he had received
unto Zerahemnah, saying:
Behold, we will end the conflict.

11 Now I cannot retain the words which I have spoken.
Therefore as the Lord liveth, ye shall not depart
except ye depart with an oath
that ye will not return again against us to war.
Now as ye are in our hands,
we will spill your blood upon the ground,
or ye shall submit to the conditions which I have proposed.

12 And now when Moroni had said these words,
Zerahemnah retained his sword.
And he was angry with Moroni,
and he rushed forward that he might slay Moroni.
But as he raised his sword,
behold, one of Moroni's soldiers smote it, even to the earth,
and it brake by the hilt.
And he also smote Zerahemnah,
that he took off his scalp and it fell to the earth.
And Zerahemnah withdrew from before them into the midst of his soldiers.

13 And it came to pass that the soldier which stood by
which smote off the scalp of Zerahemnah
took up the scalp from off the ground by the hair
and laid it upon the point of his sword and stretched it forth unto them,
crying unto them with a loud voice, saying:

14 Even as this scalp hath fallen to the earth,
which is the scalp of your chief,
so shall ye fall to the earth
except ye will deliver up your weapons of war
and depart with a covenant of peace.

15 Now there were many, when they heard these words
and saw the scalp which was upon the sword,
they were struck with fear.
And many came forth
and threw down their weapons of war at the feet of Moroni
and entered into a covenant of peace.
And as many as entered into a covenant
they suffered to depart into the wilderness.

16 Now it came to pass that Zerahemnah was exceeding wroth.
And he did stir up the remainder of his soldiers to anger,
to contend more powerfully against the Nephites.

17 And now Moroni was angry
because of the stubbornness of the Lamanites.
Therefore he commanded his people
that they should fall upon them and slay them.
And it came to pass that they began to slay them.
Yea, and the Lamanites did contend with their swords and their mights.

18 But behold, their naked skins and their bare heads were exposed
to the sharp swords of the Nephites.
Yea, behold, they were pierced and smitten,
yea, and did fall exceeding fast before the swords of the Nephites.
And they began to be swept down,
even as the soldier of Moroni had prophesied.

19 Now Zerahemnah, when he saw that they were all about to be destroyed,
he cried mightily unto Moroni,
promising that he would covenant, and also his people, with them,
if they would spare the remainder of their lives,
that they never would come to war again against them.

20 And it came to pass that Moroni caused
that the work of death should cease again among the people.
And it came to pass that he took the weapons of war from the Lamanites.
And after they had entered into a covenant with him of peace,
they were suffered to depart into the wilderness.

21 Now the number of their dead were not numbered
because of the greatness of the number;
yea, the number of their dead were exceeding great,
both on the Nephites and on the Lamanites.

22 And it came to pass that they did cast their dead into the waters of Sidon;
and they have gone forth and are buried in the depths of the sea.

23 And the armies of the Nephites—or of Moroni—returned
and came to their houses and their lands.

24 And thus ended the eighteenth year
of the reign of the judges over the people of Nephi.
And thus ended the record of Alma,
which was wrote upon the plates of Nephi.

The account of the people of Nephi
and their wars and dissensions in the days of Helaman,
according to the record of Helaman, which he kept in his days.

45 | 1 Behold, now it came to pass that the people of Nephi were exceedingly rejoiced
because the Lord had again delivered them out of the hands of their enemies.
Therefore they gave thanks unto the Lord their God.
Yea, and they did fast much and pray much,
and they did worship God with exceeding great joy.

2 And it came to pass in the nineteenth year
of the reign of the judges over the people of Nephi
that Alma came unto his son Helaman and saith unto him:
Believest thou the words which I spake unto thee
concerning those records which have been kept?

3 And Helaman saith unto him:
Yea, I believe.

4 And Alma saith again:
Believest thou in Jesus Christ, which shall come?

5 And he saith:
Yea, I believe all the words which thou hast spoken.

6 And Alma saith unto him again:
Will ye keep my commandments?

7 And he said:
Yea, I will keep thy commandments with all my heart.

8 Then Alma saith unto him:
Blessed art thou,
and the Lord shall prosper thee in this land.

9 But behold, I have somewhat to prophesy unto thee.
But what I prophesy unto thee ye shall not make known;
yea, what I prophesy unto thee shall not be made known
even until the prophecy is fulfilled.
Therefore write the words which I shall say.

10 And these are the words:
Behold, I perceive that this very people, the Nephites,
according to the spirit of revelation which is in me,
in four hundred years from the time
that Jesus Christ shall manifest himself unto them,
shall dwindle in unbelief.

11 Yea, and then shall they see wars and pestilences,
yea, famine and bloodshed,
even until the people of Nephi shall become extinct.
12 Yea, and this because they shall dwindle in unbelief
and fall into the works of darkness
and lasciviousness and all manner of iniquities.
Yea, I say unto you that
because they shall sin against so great light and knowledge,
yea, I say unto you that from that day
even the fourth generation shall not all pass away
before this great iniquity shall come.

13 And when that great day cometh,
behold, the time very soon cometh
that those which are now—
or the seed of those which are now numbered among the people of Nephi
shall no more be numbered among the people of Nephi.
14 But whosoever remaineth and is not destroyed in that great and dreadful day
shall be numbered among the Lamanites
and shall become like unto them,
all save it be a few which shall be called the disciples of the Lord.
And them shall the Lamanites pursue,
even until they shall become extinct.
And now because of iniquity this prophecy shall be fulfilled.

15 And now it came to pass that
after Alma had said these things to Helaman,
he blessed him and also his other sons.
And he also blessed the earth for the righteous' sake.
16 And he said:
Thus saith the Lord God:
Cursed shall be the land, yea, this land,
unto every nation, kindred, tongue, and people,
unto destruction, which do wickedly, when they are fully ripe.
And as I have said, so shall it be.
For this is the cursing and the blessing of God upon the land,
for the Lord cannot look upon sin with the least degree of allowance.

17 And now when Alma had said these words, he blessed the church,
yea, all those which should stand fast in the faith from that time henceforth.
18 And when Alma had done this, he departed out of the land of Zarahemla
as if to go into the land of Melek.
And it came to pass that he was never heard of more.
As to his death or his burial, we know not of.

19 Behold, this we know, that he was a righteous man.
And the saying went abroad in the church
that he was taken up by the Spirit
or buried by the hand of the Lord, even as Moses.
But behold, the scripture saith the Lord took Moses unto himself.
And we suppose that he hath also received Alma in the spirit unto himself.
Therefore for this cause we know nothing concerning his death and burial.

20 And now it came to pass in the commencement of the nineteenth year
of the reign of the judges over the people of Nephi
that Helaman went forth among the people to declare the word unto them.
21 For behold, because of their wars with the Lamanites
and the many little dissensions and disturbances
which had been among the people,
it became expedient that the word of God should be declared among them,
yea, and that a regulation should be made throughout the church.
22 Therefore Helaman and his brethren went forth
to establish the church again in all the land,
yea, in every city throughout all the land
which was possessed by the people of Nephi.
And it came to pass that they did appoint priests and teachers
throughout all the land, over all the churches.

23 And now it came to pass that after Helaman and his brethren
had appointed priests and teachers over the churches
that there arose a dissension among them,
and they would not give heed to the words of Helaman and his brethren;
24 but they grew proud,
being lifted up in their hearts because of their exceeding great riches.
Therefore they grew rich in their own eyes
and would not give heed to their words to walk uprightly before God.
46 | 1 And it came to pass that
as many as would not hearken to the words of Helaman and his brethren
were gathered together against their brethren.
2 And now behold, they were exceeding wroth,
insomuch that they were determined to slay them.

3 Now the leader of those which were wroth against their brethren
was a large and a strong man,
and his name was Amalickiah.
4 And Amalickiah was desirous to be a king;
and those people which were wroth were also desirous
that he should be their king.

And they were the greater part of them the lower judges of the land,
and they were seeking for power.

5 And they had been led by the flatteries of Amalickiah
that if they would support him and establish him to be their king
that he would make them rulers over the people.

6 Thus they were led away by Amalickiah to dissensions,
notwithstanding the preaching of Helaman and his brethren,
yea, notwithstanding their exceeding great care over the church,
for they were high priests over the church.

7 And there were many in the church
which believed in the flattering words of Amalickiah;
therefore they dissented even from the church.
And thus were the affairs of the people of Nephi
exceeding precarious and dangerous,
notwithstanding their great victory which they had had over the Lamanites,
and their great rejoicings which they had had
because of their deliverance by the hand of the Lord.

8 Thus we see how quick the children of men doth forget the Lord their God,
yea, how quick to do iniquity and to be led away by the evil one.

9 Yea, and we also see the great wickedness
one very wicked man can cause to take place among the children of men.

10 Yea, we see that Amalickiah,
because he was a man of cunning devices and a man of many flattering words,
that he led away the hearts of many people to do wickedly,
yea, and to seek to destroy the church of God
and to destroy the foundation of liberty
which God had granted unto them,
or which blessing God had sent upon the face of the land
for the righteous' sake.

11 And now it came to pass that when Moroni,
which was the chief commander of the armies of the Nephites,
had heard of these dissensions,
he was angry with Amalickiah.

12 And it came to pass that he rent his coat;
and he took a piece thereof and wrote upon it:
In memory of our God, our religion and freedom, and our peace,
our wives and our children.
And he fastened it upon the end of a pole thereof.

13 And he fastened on his headplate and his breastplate and his shields
and girded on his armor about his loins.

And he took the pole which had on the end thereof his rent coat,
and he called it the title of liberty.
And he bowed himself to the earth,
and he prayed mightily unto his God
for the blessings of liberty to rest upon his brethren
so long as there should a band of Christians remain to possess the land.

14 For thus were all the true believers of Christ
which belonged to the church of God
called by those who did not belong to the church.

15 And those who did belong to the church were faithful.
Yea, all those who were true believers in Christ
took upon them gladly the name of Christ,
or Christians, as they were called,
because of their belief in Christ, which should come.

16 And therefore at this time Moroni prayed
that the cause of the Christians and the freedom of the land might be favored.

17 And it came to pass that when he had poured out his soul to God,
he gave all the land which was south of the land Desolation
—yea, and in fine all the land, both on the north and on the south—
a chosen land and the land of liberty.

18 And he saith:
Surely God shall not suffer that we who are despised
because we take upon us the name of Christ
shall be trodden down and destroyed
until we bring it upon us by our own transgressions.

19 And when Moroni had said these words,
he went forth among the people,
waving the rent of his garment in the air,
that all might see the writing which he had wrote upon the rent,
and crying with a loud voice, saying:

20 Behold, whosoever will maintain this title upon the land,
let them come forth in the strength of the Lord
and enter into a covenant
that they will maintain their rights and their religion,
that the Lord God may bless them.

21 And it came to pass that when Moroni had proclaimed these words,
behold, the people came running together
with their armors girded about their loins,
rending their garments in token, or as a covenant,
that they would not forsake the Lord their God.

Or in other words, if they should transgress the commandments of God
—or fall into transgression—
and be ashamed to take upon them the name of Christ,
the Lord should rend them, even as they had rent their garments.

22 Now this was the covenant which they made;
and they cast their garments at the feet of Moroni, saying:
We covenant with our God that we shall be destroyed,
even as our brethren in the land northward,
if we shall fall into transgression.
Yea, he may cast us at the feet of our enemies,
even as we have cast our garments at thy feet,
to be trodden under foot if we should fall into transgression.

23 Moroni saith unto them:
Behold, we are a remnant of the seed of Jacob.
Yea, we are a remnant of the seed of Joseph,
whose coat was rent by his brethren into many pieces.
Yea, and now behold, let us remember to keep the commandments of God,
or our garments shall be rent by our brethren
and we be cast into prisons or be sold or be slain.

24 Yea, let us preserve our liberty as a remnant of Joseph.

Yea, let us remember the words of Jacob before his death.
For behold, he saw that a part of the remnant of the coat of Joseph
was preserved and had not decayed.
And he saith:
Even as this remnant of garment of my son's hath been preserved,
so shall a remnant of the seed of my son
be preserved by the hand of God and be taken unto himself,
while the remainder of the seed of Joseph shall perish,
even as the remnant of his garment.

25 Now behold, this giveth my soul sorrow.
Nevertheless my soul hath joy in my son
because of that part of his seed which shall be taken unto God.

26 Now behold, this was the language of Jacob.

27 And now, who knoweth but what the remnant of the seed of Joseph
which shall perish as his garment
are those which have dissented from us;
yea, and even it shall be us if we do not stand fast in the faith of Christ.

28 And now it came to pass that
when Moroni had said these words,
he went forth, and also sent forth,
in all the parts of the land where there were dissensions

and gathered together all the people
which were desirous to maintain their liberty,
to stand against Amalickiah and those which had dissented,
which were called Amalickiahites.

29 And it came to pass that when Amalickiah saw
that the people of Moroni were more numerous than the Amalickiahites,
and he also saw that his people were doubtful
concerning the justice of the cause which they had undertaken,
therefore fearing that he should not gain the point,
he took those of his people which would
and departed into the land of Nephi.

30 Now Moroni thought it was not expedient
that the Lamanites should have any more strength.
Therefore he thought to cut off the people of Amalickiah,
or to take them and bring them back
and put Amalickiah to death.
Yea, for he knew that they would stir up the Lamanites to anger against them
and cause them to come down to battle against them.
And this he knew that Amalickiah would do
that he might obtain his purposes.

31 Therefore Moroni thought it was expedient
that he should take his armies,
which had gathered themselves together and armed themselves
and entered into a covenant to keep the peace.
And it came to pass that
he took his army and marched out with his tents into the wilderness
to cut off the course of Amalickiah in the wilderness.

32 And it came to pass that
he did according to his desires and marched forth into the wilderness
and headed the armies of Amalickiah.

33 And it came to pass that Amalickiah fled with a small number of his men,
and the remainder were delivered up into the hands of Moroni
and were taken back into the land of Zarahemla.

34 Now Moroni being a man
which was appointed by the chief judges and the voice of the people,
therefore he had power to do according to his will
with the armies of the Nephites,
to establish and to exercise authority over them.

35 And it came to pass that whomsoever of the Amalickiahites
that would not enter into a covenant to support the cause of freedom,
that they might maintain a free government,

he caused to be put to death.
And there was but few which denied the covenant of freedom.

36 And it came to pass also that he caused the title of liberty
to be hoisted upon every tower
which was in all the land which was possessed by the Nephites.
And thus Moroni planted the standard of liberty among the Nephites.

37 And they began to have peace again in the land.
And thus they did maintain peace in the land
until nearly the end of the nineteenth year of the reign of the judges.

38 And Helaman and the high priests did also maintain order in the church;
yea, even for the space of four years
did they have much peace and rejoicing in the church.

39 And it came to pass that there were many who died
firmly believing that their souls were redeemed by the Lord Jesus Christ.
Thus they went out of the world rejoicing.

40 And there were some who died with fevers,
which at some seasons of the year was very frequent in the land
—but not so much so with fevers
because of the excellent qualities of the many plants and roots
which God had prepared to remove the cause of diseases
which was subsequent to man by the nature of the climate—

41 but there were many who died with old age.
And those who died in the faith of Christ are happy in him,
as we must needs suppose.

47 | 1 Now we will return in our record to Amalickiah
and those which fled with him into the wilderness.
For behold, he had took those which were with him
and went up into the land of Nephi among the Lamanites
and did stir up the Lamanites to anger against the people of Nephi,
insomuch that the king of the Lamanites sent a proclamation
throughout all his land among all his people
that they should gather themselves together again
to go to battle against the Nephites.

2 And it came to pass that
when the proclamation had gone forth among them,
they were exceeding fraid.
Yea, they feared to displease the king;
and they also feared to go to battle against the Nephites
lest they should lose their lives.
And it came to pass that they would not

—or the more part of them would not—
obey the commandment of the king.

3 And now it came to pass that
the king was wroth because of their disobedience.
Therefore he gave Amalickiah the command of that part of his army
which was obedient unto his commands,
and commanded him that he should go forth and compel them to arms.

4 Now behold, this was the desires of Amalickiah;
for he being a very subtle man to do evil,
therefore he laid the plan in his heart to dethrone the king of the Lamanites.

5 And now he had gat the command of those parts of the Lamanites
which were in favor of the king;
and he sought to gain favor of those which were not obedient.

Therefore he went forward to the place which was called Oneidah,
for thither had all the Lamanites fled.
For they discovered the army coming;
and supposing that they were coming to destroy them,
therefore they fled to Oneidah, to the place of arms.

6 And they had appointed a man to be a king and a leader over them,
being fixed in their minds with a determined resolution
that they would not be subjected to go against the Nephites.

7 And it came to pass that they had gathered themselves together
upon the top of the mount which was called Antipas
in preparation to battle.

8 Now it was not Amalickiah's intention
to give them battle according to the commandments of the king.
But behold, it was his intention to gain favor with the armies of the Lamanites,
that he might place himself at their head
and dethrone the king and take possession of the kingdom.

9 And behold, it came to pass that
he caused his army to pitch their tents
in the valley which was near the mount Antipas.

10 And it came to pass that when it was night,
he sent a secret embassy into the mount Antipas,
desiring that the leader of those which were upon the mount,
whose name was Lehonti,
that he should come down to the foot of the mount,
for he desired to speak with him.

11 And it came to pass that when Lehonti received the message,
he durst not go down to the foot of the mount.
And it came to pass that Amalickiah sent again the second time,

desiring him to come down.
And it came to pass that Lehonti would not.
And he sent again the third time.

12 And it came to pass that when Amalickiah found
that he could not get Lehonti to come down off from the mount,
he went up into the mount, nearly to Lehonti's camp.
And he sent again the fourth time his message unto Lehonti,
desiring that he would come down
and that he would bring his guards with him.

13 And it came to pass that when Lehonti had come down
with his guards to Amalickiah
that Amalickiah desired him to come down with his army in the nighttime
and surround those men in their camps
over whom the king had gave him command,
and that he would deliver them up into Lehonti's hands
if he would make him, Amalickiah, the second leader over the whole army.

14 And it came to pass that Lehonti came down with his men
and surrounded the men of Amalickiah,
so that before they awoke at the dawn of the day,
they were surrounded by the armies of Lehonti.

15 And it came to pass that when they saw that they were surrounded,
they pled with Amalickiah
that he would suffer them to fall in with their brethren,
that they might not be destroyed.
Now this was the very thing which Amalickiah desired.

16 And it came to pass that he delivered his men,
contrary to the commands of the king.
Now this was the thing that Amalickiah desired,
that he might accomplish his designs in dethroning the king.

17 Now it was the custom among the Lamanites,
if their chief leader was killed,
to appoint the second leader to be their chief leader.

18 And it came to pass that Amalickiah caused
that one of his servants should administer poison by degrees to Lehonti,
that he died.

19 Now when Lehonti was dead,
the Lamanites appointed Amalickiah
to be their leader and their chief commander.

20 And it came to pass that Amalickiah marched with his armies,
for he had gained his desires,

to the land of Nephi, to the city of Nephi, which was the chief city.

21 And the king came out to meet him with his guards,
for he supposed that Amalickiah had fulfilled his commands
and that Amalickiah had gathered together so great an army
for to go against the Nephites to battle.

22 But behold, as the king came out to meet him,
Amalickiah caused that his servants should go forth to meet the king.
And they went forth and bowed themselves before the king,
as if to reverence him because of his greatness.

23 And it came to pass that the king put forth his hand to raise them,
as was the custom with the Lamanites—and a token of peace—
which custom they had taken from the Nephites.

24 And it came to pass that when he had raised the first from the ground,
behold, he stabbed the king to the heart and he fell to the earth.

25 Now the servants of the king fled.
And the servants of Amalickiah raised a cry, saying:

26 Behold, the servants of the king have stabbed him to the heart,
and he has fell and they have fled.
Behold, come and see!

27 And it came to pass that Amalickiah commanded
that his armies should march forth and see what had happened to the king.
And when they had come to the spot and found the king lying in his gore,
Amalickiah pretended to be wroth and said:
Whosoever loved the king, let him go forth and pursue his servants,
that they may be slain.

28 And it came to pass that all they who loved the king,
when they heard these words,
came forth and pursued after the servants of the king.

29 Now when the servants of the king saw an army pursuing after them,
they were frightened again and fled into the wilderness
and came over into the land of Zarahemla and joined the people of Ammon.

30 And the army which pursued after them returned,
having pursued after them in vain.
And thus Amalickiah by his fraud gained the hearts of the people.

31 And it came to pass on the morrow
he entered the city Nephi with his armies and took possession of the city.

32 And now it came to pass that the queen,
when she had heard that the king was slain
—for Amalickiah had sent an embassy to the queen informing her
that the king had been slain by his servants,
that he had pursued them with his army,

but it was in vain and they had made their escape—

33 therefore when the queen had received this message,
she sent unto Amalickiah,
desiring him that he would spare the people of the city.
And she also desired him that he should come in unto her.
And she also desired him that he should bring witnesses with him
to testify concerning the death of the king.

34 And it came to pass that
Amalickiah took that same servant that slew the king,
and also they which were with him,
and went in unto the queen, unto the place where she sat.
And they all testified unto her that the king was slain by his own servants.
And they said also:
They have fled.
Does not this testify against them?
And thus they satisfied the queen concerning the death of the king.

35 And it came to pass that
Amalickiah sought the favor of the queen and took her unto him to wife.
And thus by his fraud and by the assistance of his cunning servants,
he obtained the kingdom.
Yea, he was acknowledged king throughout all the land
among all the people of the Lamanites,
which was composed of the Lamanites and the Lemuelites and the Ishmaelites,
and all the dissenters of the Nephites
from the reign of Nephi down to the present time.

36 Now these dissenters,
having the same instruction and the same information of the Nephites,
yea, having been instructed in the same knowledge of the Lord,
nevertheless it is strange to relate,
not long after their dissensions,
they became more hardened and impenitent
and more wild, wicked, and ferocious than the Lamanites,
drinking in with the traditions of the Lamanites,
giving way to indolence and all manner of lasciviousness,
yea, entirely forgetting the Lord their God.

48 | 1 And now it came to pass that
as soon as Amalickiah had obtained the kingdom,
he began to inspire the hearts of the Lamanites against the people of Nephi.
Yea, he did appoint men to speak
unto the Lamanites from their towers
against the Nephites.

2 And thus he did inspire their hearts against the Nephites,
insomuch that in the latter end of the nineteenth year of the reign of the judges,
he having accomplished his designs thus far,
yea, having been made king over the Lamanites,
he sought also to reign over all the land,
yea, and all the people which were in the land,
the Nephites as well as the Lamanites.

3 Therefore he had accomplished his design,
for he had hardened the hearts of the Lamanites and blinded their minds
and stirred them up to anger,
insomuch that he had gathered together a numerous host
to go to battle against the Nephites.

4 For he was determined because of the greatness of the number of his people
to overpower the Nephites and to bring them into bondage.

5 And thus he did appoint chief captains of the Zoramites,
they being the most acquainted with the strength of the Nephites
and their places of resort and the weakest parts of their cities;
therefore he appointed them to be chief captains over his armies.

6 And it came to pass that they took their camp
and moved forth towards the land of Zarahemla in the wilderness.

7 Now it came to pass that
while Amalickiah had thus been obtaining power by fraud and deceit,
Moroni, on the other hand, had been a preparing the minds of the people
to be faithful unto the Lord their God.

8 Yea, he had been strengthening the armies of the Nephites
and erecting small forts or places of resort,
throwing up banks of earth round about to encircle his armies,
and also building walls of stone to encircle them about,
round about their cities and the borders of their lands,
yea, all round about the land.

9 And in their weakest fortifications he did place the greater number of men.
And thus he did fortify and strengthen the land
which was possessed by the Nephites.

10 And thus he was preparing to support their liberty,
their lands, their wives and their children, and their peace,
and that they might live unto the Lord their God,
and that they might maintain
that which was called by their enemies the cause of Christians.

11 And Moroni was a strong and a mighty man.
He was a man of a perfect understanding;
yea, a man that did not delight in bloodshed,

a man whose soul did joy in the liberty
and the freedom of his country and his brethren from bondage and slavery,
12 yea, a man whose heart did swell with thanksgiving to his God
for the many privileges and blessings which he bestowed upon his people,
a man who did labor exceedingly for the welfare and safety of his people.
13 Yea, and he was a man who was firm in the faith of Christ.
And he had sworn with an oath to defend his people,
his rights and his country and his religion,
even to the loss of his blood.

14 Now the Nephites were taught to defend themselves against their enemies,
even to the shedding of blood even if it were necessary.
Yea, and they were also taught never to give an offense,
yea, and never to raise the sword
except it were against an enemy,
except it were to preserve their lives.
15 And this was their faith,
that by so doing God would prosper them in the land;
or in other words, if they were faithful in keeping the commandments of God,
that he would prosper them in the land
—yea, warn them to flee or to prepare for war, according to their danger—
16 and also that God would make it known unto them
whither they should go to defend themselves against their enemies,
and by so doing the Lord would deliver them.

And this was the faith of Moroni.
And his heart did glory in it—
not in the shedding of blood,
but in doing good, in preserving his people,
yea, in keeping the commandments of God,
yea, and resisting iniquity.
17 Yea, verily verily I say unto you:
If all men had been and were and ever would be like unto Moroni,
behold, the very powers of hell would have been shaken forever.
Yea, the devil would never have no power over the hearts of the children of men.
18 Behold, he was a man like unto Ammon the son of Mosiah,
yea, and even the other sons of Mosiah,
yea, and also Alma and his sons,
for they were all men of God.

19 Now behold, Helaman and his brethren
were not less serviceable unto the people than was Moroni;
for they did preach the word of God,
and they did baptize unto repentance all men

whosoever would hearken unto their words.

20 And thus they went forth;
and the people did humble themselves because of their words,
insomuch that they were highly favored of the Lord.
And thus they were free from wars and contentions among themselves,
yea, even for the space of four years.

21 But as I have said, in the latter end of the nineteenth year,
notwithstanding their peace amongst themselves,
they were compelled reluctantly to contend with their brethren the Lamanites.
22 Yea, and in fine, their wars never did cease for the space of many years
with the Lamanites,
notwithstanding their much reluctance.
23 Now they were sorry to take up arms against the Lamanites
because they did not delight in the shedding of blood.
Yea, and this was not all.
They were sorry to be the means of sending so many of their brethren
out of this world into an eternal world unprepared to meet their God.
24 Nevertheless they could not suffer to lay down their lives,
that their wives and their children should be massacreed
by the barbarous cruelty of those who was once their brethren,
yea, and had dissented from their church
and had left them and had gone to destroy them by joining the Lamanites.
25 Yea, they could not bear
that their brethren should rejoice over the blood of the Nephites,
so long as there were any who should keep the commandments of God;
for the promises of the Lord were
if they should keep his commandments,
they should prosper in the land.

49 | 1 And now it came to pass in the eleventh month of the nineteenth year,
on the tenth day of the month,
the armies of the Lamanites were seen approaching
towards the land of Ammonihah.
2 And behold, the city had been rebuilt,
and Moroni had stationed an army by the borders of the city.
And they had cast up dirt round about
to shield them from the arrows and the stones of the Lamanites.
For behold, they fought with stones and with arrows.
3 Behold, I said that the city of Ammonihah had been rebuilt.
I say unto you, yea, that it was in part rebuilt.
And because the Lamanites had destroyed it once,
because of the iniquity of the people,

they supposed that it would again become an easy prey for them.

4 But behold, how great was their disappointment!
For behold, the Nephites had dug up a ridge of earth round about them
which was so high that the Lamanites could not cast
their stones and their arrows at them that they might take effect,
neither could they come upon them
save it was by their place of entrance.

5 Now at this time the chief captains of the Lamanites were astonished exceedingly
because of the wisdom of the Nephites in repairing their places of security.

6 Now the leaders of the Lamanites had supposed
because of the greatness of their numbers—
yea, they supposed that they should be privileged
to come upon them as they had hitherto done;
yea, and they had also prepared themselves with shields and with breastplates;
and they had also prepared themselves with garments of skins,
yea, very thick garments to cover their nakedness—

7 and being thus prepared,
they supposed that they should easily overpower
and subject their brethren to the yoke of bondage,
or slay and massacre them according to their pleasure.

8 But behold, to their uttermost astonishment,
they were prepared for them in a manner
which never had been known among all the children of Lehi;
now they were prepared for the Lamanites,
to battle after the manner of the instructions of Moroni.

9 And it came to pass that the Lamanites, or the Amalickiahites,
were exceedingly astonished at their manner of preparation for war.

10 Now if king Amalickiah had came down out of the land of Nephi
at the head of his army,
perhaps he would have caused
the Lamanites to have attackted the Nephites at the city of Ammonihah;
for behold, he did care not for the blood of his people.

11 But behold, Amalickiah did not come down himself to battle.
And behold, his chief captains durst not attackt
the Nephites at the city of Ammonihah,
for Moroni had altered the management of affairs among the Nephites,
insomuch that the Lamanites were disappointed in their places of retreat
and they could not come upon them.

12 Therefore they retreated into the wilderness
and took their camp and marched towards the land of Noah,
supposing that to be the next best place for them to come against the Nephites.

13 For they knew not that Moroni had fortified —
    or had built forts of security for every city in all the land round about.
    Therefore they marched forward to the land of Noah with a firm determination.
    Yea, their chief captains came forward and took an oath
    that they would destroy the people of that city.

14 But behold, to their astonishment,
    the city of Noah, which had hitherto been a weak place,
    had now by the means of Moroni became strong,
    yea, even to exceed the strength of the city Ammonihah.

15 And now behold, this was wisdom in Moroni.
    For he had supposed that they would be frightened at the city Ammonihah;
    and as the city of Noah had hitherto been the weakest part of the land,
    therefore they would march thither to battle.
    And thus it was according to his desires.

16 And behold, Moroni had appointed Lehi
    to be chief captain over the men of that city.
    And it was that same Lehi which fought with the Lamanites
    in the valley on the east of the river Sidon.

17 And now behold, it came to pass that
    when the Lamanites had found that Lehi commanded the city,
    they were again disappointed,
    for they feared Lehi exceedingly.
    Nevertheless their chief captains had sworn with an oath to attackt the city;
    therefore they brought up their armies.

18 Now behold, the Lamanites could not get into their forts of security
    by any other way save by the entrance,
    because of the highness of the bank which had been thrown up
    and the depth of the ditch which had been dug round about,
    save it were by the entrance.

19 And thus were the Nephites prepared to destroy all such
    as should attempt to climb up to enter the fort by any other way
    by casting over stones and arrows at them.

20 Thus they were prepared,
    yea, a body of their most strong men with their swords and their slings
    to smite down all who should attempt
    to come into their place of security by the place of entrance.
    And thus were they prepared to defend themselves against the Lamanites.

21 And it came to pass that
    the captains of the Lamanites brought up their armies
    before the place of entrance
    and began to contend with the Nephites,

to get into their place of security.
But behold, they were driven back from time to time,
insomuch that they were slain with an immense slaughter.

22 Now when they found
that they could not obtain power over the Nephites by the pass,
they began to dig down their banks of earth
that they might obtain a pass to their armies,
that they might have an equal chance to fight.
But behold, in these attempts they were swept off
by the stones and the arrows which were thrown at them.
And instead of filling up their ditches by pulling down the banks of earth,
they were filled up in a measure with their dead and wounded bodies.

23 Thus the Nephites had all power over their enemies.

And thus the Lamanites did attempt to destroy the Nephites
until their chief captains were all slain
—yea, and more than a thousand of the Lamanites were slain—
while on the other hand
there was not a single soul of the Nephites which were slain.

24 There were about fifty which were wounded
which had been exposed to the arrows of the Lamanites through the pass.
But they were shielded by their shields
and their breastplates and their headplates,
insomuch that their wounds were upon their legs,
many of which were very severe.

25 And it came to pass that when the Lamanites saw
that their chief captains were all slain,
they fled into the wilderness.
And it came to pass that they returned to the land of Nephi
to inform their king Amalickiah, who was a Nephite by birth,
concerning their great loss.

26 And it came to pass that he was exceeding angry with his people
because he had not obtained his desires over the Nephites;
he had not subjected them to the yoke of bondage.

27 Yea, he was exceeding wroth,
and he did curse God, and also Moroni,
and swearing with an oath that he would drink his blood—
and this because Moroni had kept the commandments of God
in preparing for the safety of his people.

28 And it came to pass that on the other hand
the people of Nephi did thank the Lord their God
because of his miraculous power in delivering them

from the hands of their enemies.

29 And thus ended the nineteenth year
of the reign of the judges over the people of Nephi.

30 Yea, and there was continual peace among them
and exceeding great prosperity in the church
because of their heed and diligence which they gave unto the word of God,
which was declared unto them
by Helaman and Shiblon and Corianton and Ammon and his brethren etc.,
yea, and by all those which had been ordained by the holy order of God,
being baptized unto repentance
and sent forth to preach among the people etc.

50 | 1 And now it came to pass that
Moroni did not stop making preparations for war
or to defend themselves against the Lamanites,
for he caused that his armies should commence
in the commencement of the twentieth year of the reign of the judges
that they should commence in digging up heaps of earth
round about all the cities throughout all the land
which was possessed by the Nephites.

2 And upon the top of those ridges of earth
he caused that there should be timbers,
yea, works of timbers built up to the heighth of a man,
round about the cities.

3 And he caused that upon those works of timbers
that there should be a frame of pickets built upon the timbers round about;
and they were strong and high.

4 And he caused towers to be erected that overlooked those works of pickets;
and he caused places of security to be built upon those towers,
that the stones and the arrows of the Lamanites could not hurt them.

5 And they were prepared that they could cast stones from the top thereof,
according to their pleasure and their strength,
and slay him which should attempt to approach near the walls of the city.

6 Thus Moroni did prepare strong holds against the coming of their enemies
round about every city in all the land.

7 And it came to pass that Moroni caused
that his armies should go forth into the east wilderness.
Yea, and they went forth and drave all the Lamanites
which were in the east wilderness
into their own lands, which were south of the land of Zarahemla.

8 And the land of Nephi did run in a straight course from the east sea to the west.

9 And it came to pass that when Moroni had driven all the Lamanites out
of the east wilderness, which was north of the lands of their own possessions,
he caused that the inhabitants
which were in the land of Zarahemla and in the land round about
should go forth into the east wilderness,
even to the borders by the seashore,
and possess the land.

10 And he also placed armies on the south in the borders of their possessions
and caused them to erect fortifications
that they might secure their armies and their people
from the hands of their enemies.

11 And thus he cut off all the strong holds of the Lamanites
in the east wilderness, yea, and also on the west,
fortifying the line between the Nephites and the Lamanites,
between the land of Zarahemla and the land of Nephi,
from the west sea running by the head of the river Sidon,
the Nephites possessing all the land northward,
yea, even all the land which was northward of the land Bountiful,
according to their pleasure.

12 Thus Moroni with his armies
—which did increase daily because of the assurance of protection
which his works did bring forth unto them—
therefore they did seek to cut off the strength and the power of the Lamanites
from off the lands of their possessions,
that they should have no power upon the lands of their possessions.

13 And it came to pass that the Nephites began the foundation of a city,
and they called the name of the city Moroni.
And it was by the east sea;
and it was on the south by the line of the possessions of the Lamanites.

14 And they also began a foundation for a city
between the city of Moroni and the city of Aaron,
joining the borders of Aaron and Moroni,
and they called the name of the city, or the land, Nephihah.

15 And they also began in that same year to build many cities on the north,
one in a particular manner which they called Lehi,
which was in the north by the borders of the seashore.

16 And thus ended the twentieth year.

17 And in these prosperous circumstances were the people of Nephi
in the commencement of the twenty and first year
of the reign of the judges over the people of Nephi.

18 And they did prosper exceedingly,
   and they became exceeding rich.
   Yea, and they did multiply and wax strong in the land.
19 And thus we see how merciful and just are all the dealings of the Lord,
   to the fulfilling of all his words unto the children of men.
   Yea, we can behold that his words are verified, even at this time,
   which he spake unto Lehi, saying:
20 Blessed art thou and thy children.
   And they shall be blessed!
   And inasmuch as they shall keep my commandments,
   they shall prosper in the land.
   But remember, inasmuch as they will not keep my commandments,
   they shall be cut off from the presence of the Lord.

21 And we see that these promises have been verified to the people of Nephi;
   for it has been their quarrelings and their contentions,
   yea, their murderings and their plunderings,
   their idolatry and their whoredoms and their abominations
   which were among themselves,
   which brought upon them their wars and their destructions.
22 And those who were faithful in keeping the commandments of the Lord
   were delivered at all times,
   whilst thousands of their wicked brethren have been consigned
   to bondage or to perish by the sword
   or to dwindle in unbelief and mingle with the Lamanites.
23 But behold, there never was a happier time among the people of Nephi
   since the days of Nephi than in the days of Moroni,
   yea, even at this time, in the twenty and first year of the reign of the judges.

24 And it came to pass that the twenty and second year
   of the reign of the judges also ended in peace,
   yea, and also the twenty and third year.
25 And it came to pass that in the commencement
   of the twenty and fourth year of the reign of the judges,
   there would also have been peace among the people of Nephi
   had it not been for a contention which took place among them
   concerning the land of Lehi and the land of Morionton,
   which joined upon the borders of Lehi,
   both of which were on the borders by the seashore.
26 For behold, the people which possessed the land of Morionton
   did claim a part of the land of Lehi.
   Therefore there began to be a warm contention between them,
   insomuch that the people of Morionton took up arms against their brethren;

and they were determined by the sword to slay them.

27 But behold, the people which possessed the land of Lehi
fled to the camp of Moroni
and appealed unto him for assistance;
for behold, they were not in the wrong.

28 And it came to pass that when the people of Morionton,
which were led by a man whose name was Morionton,
found that the people of Lehi had fled to the camp of Moroni,
they were exceeding fearful
lest the army of Moroni should come upon them and destroy them.

29 Therefore Morionton put it into their hearts
that they should flee to the land which was northward,
which was covered with large bodies of water,
and take possession of the land which was northward.

30 And behold, they would have carried this plan into an effect
—which would have been a cause to have been lamented—
but behold, Morionton being a man of much passion,
therefore he was angry with one of his maidservants,
and he fell upon her and beat her much.

31 And it came to pass that she fled and came over to the camp of Moroni
and told Moroni all things concerning the matter
and also concerning their intentions to flee into the land northward.

32 Now behold, the people which were in the land of Bountiful
—or rather Moroni feared
that they would hearken to the words of Morionton and unite with his people,
and thus he would obtain possession of those parts of the land,
which would lay a foundation for serious consequences
among the people of Nephi,
yea, which consequences would lead to the overthrow of their liberty—

33 therefore Moroni sent an army with their camp
to head the people of Morionton,
to stop their flight into the land northward.

34 And it came to pass that they did not head them
until they had came to the borders of the land Desolation.
And there they did head them by the narrow pass
which led by the sea into the land northward,
yea, by the sea on the west and on the east.

35 And it came to pass that the army which was sent by Moroni,
which was led by a man whose name was Teancum,
did meet the people of Morionton.
And so stubborn were the people of Morionton,

being inspired by his wickedness and his flattering words,
that a battle commenced between them,
in the which Teancum did slay Morionton and defeat his army
and took them prisoners and returned to the camp of Moroni.
And thus ended the twenty and fourth year
of the reign of the judges over the people of Nephi.

36 And thus was the people of Morionton brought back.
And upon their covenanting to keep the peace,
they were restored to the land of Morionton.
And a union took place between them and the people of Lehi,
and they were also restored to their lands.

37 And it came to pass that in that same year
that the people of Nephi had peace restored unto them
that Nephihah the second chief judge died,
having filled the judgment seat with perfect uprightness before God.

38 Nevertheless he had refused Alma
to take possession of those records and those things
which were esteemed by Alma and his fathers to be most sacred.
Therefore Alma had conferred them upon his son Helaman.

39 Behold, it came to pass that the son of Nephihah was appointed
to fill the judgment seat in the stead of his father.
Yea, he was appointed chief judge and governor over the people,
with an oath and sacred ordinance to judge righteously,
and to keep the peace and the freedom of the people,
and to grant unto them their sacred privileges to worship the Lord their God,
yea, to support and maintain the cause of God all his days,
and to bring the wicked to justice according to their crime.

40 Now behold, his name was Parhoron.
And Parhoron did fill the seat of his father
and did commence his reign in the end of the twenty and fourth year
over the people of Nephi.

51 | 1 And now it came to pass
in the commencement of the twenty and fifth year
of the reign of the judges over the people of Nephi,
they having established peace
between the people of Lehi and the people of Morionton
concerning their lands,
and having commenced the twenty and fifth year in peace,

2 nevertheless they did not long maintain an entire peace in the land.

For there began to be a contention among the people
concerning the chief judge Parhoron;
for behold, there were a part of the people
which desired that a few particular points of the law should be altered.

3 But behold, Parhoron would not alter nor suffer the law to be altered.
Therefore he did not hearken to those
who had sent in their voices with their petitions
concerning the altering of the law.

4 Therefore those which were desirous that the law should be altered
were angry with him
and desired that he should no longer be chief judge over the land.
Therefore there arose a warm dispute concerning the matter,
but not unto bloodshed.

5 And it came to pass that those who were desirous
that Parhoron should be dethroned from the judgment seat
were called kingmen,
for they were desirous that the law should be altered in a manner
to overthrow the free government and to establish a king over the land.

6 And those who were desirous
that Parhoron should remain chief judge over the land
took upon them the name of freemen.
And thus was the division among them,
for the freemen had sworn or covenanted
to maintain their rights and the privileges of their religion by a free government.

7 And it came to pass that this matter of their contention
was settled by the voice of the people.
And it came to pass that the voice of the people came in the favor of the freemen;
and Parhoron retained the judgment seat,
which caused much rejoicing among the brethren of Parhoron
and also among the people of liberty,
which also put the kingmen to silence,
that they durst not oppose
but were obliged to maintain the cause of freedom.

8 Now those which were in favor of kings were those of high birth;
and they sought to be kings.
And they were supported by those
which sought power and authority over the people.

9 But behold, this was a critical time
for such contentions to be among the people of Nephi.
For behold, Amalickiah had again stirred up
the hearts of the people of the Lamanites against the people of the Nephites;

and he was gathering together soldiers from all parts of his land
and arming them and preparing for war with all diligence,
for he had sworn to drink the blood of Moroni.

10 But behold, we shall see that this promise which he made was rash.
Nevertheless he did prepare himself and his armies
to come to battle against the Nephites.

11 Now his armies were not so great as they had hitherto been
because of the many thousands which had been slain
by the hand of the Nephites.
But notwithstanding their great loss,
Amalickiah had gathered together a wonderful great army,
insomuch that he feared not to come down to the land of Zarahemla.

12 Yea, even Amalickiah did himself come down at the head of the Lamanites.
And it was in the twenty and fifth year of the reign of the judges;
and it was at the same time that they had began
to settle the affairs of their contentions concerning the chief judge Parhoron.

13 And it came to pass that when the men which were called kingmen
had heard that the Lamanites were coming down to battle against them,
they were glad in their hearts.
And they refused to take up arms,
for they were so wroth with the chief judge
and also with the people of liberty
that they would not take up arms to defend their country.

14 And it came to pass that when Moroni saw this
and also saw that the Lamanites were coming into the borders of the land,
he was exceeding wroth because of the stubbornness of those people
of whom he had labored with so much diligence to preserve.
Yea, he was exceeding wroth;
his soul was filled with anger against them.

15 And it came to pass that he sent a petition
with the voice of the people unto the governor of the land,
desiring that he should heed it
and give him, Moroni, power to compel those dissenters
to defend their country or to put them to death.

16 For it was his first care to put an end
to such contentions and dissensions among the people.
For behold, this had been hitherto a cause of all their destructions.
And it came to pass that it was granted according to the voice of the people.

17 And it came to pass that Moroni commanded
that his army should go against those kingmen,

to pull down their pride and their nobility
and level them with the earth,
or they should take up arms and support the cause of liberty.

18 And it came to pass that the armies did march forth against them,
and they did pull down their pride and their nobility,
insomuch that as they did lift their weapons of war
to fight against the men of Moroni,
they were hewn down and leveled to the earth.

19 And it came to pass that there were four thousand of those dissenters
which were hewn down by the sword.
And those of their leaders which were not slain in battle
were taken and cast into prison,
for there was no time for their trials at this period.

20 And the remainder of those dissenters,
rather than to be smote down to the earth by the sword,
yielded to the standard of liberty
and were compelled to hoist the title of liberty
upon their towers and in their cities
and to take up arms in defense of their country.

21 And thus Moroni put an end to those kingmen,
that there were not any known by the appellation of kingmen.
And thus he put an end to the stubbornness and the pride of those people
which professed the blood of nobility;
but they were brought down to humble themselves like unto their brethren
and to fight valiantly for their freedom from bondage.

22 Behold, it came to pass that while Moroni was thus breaking down
the wars and contentions among his own people
and subjecting them to peace and civilization
and making regulations to prepare for war against the Lamanites,
behold, the Lamanites had came into the land of Moroni,
which was in the borders by the seashore.

23 And it came to pass that
the Nephites were not sufficiently strong in the city of Moroni;
therefore Amalickiah did drive them, slaying many.
And it came to pass that Amalickiah took possession of the city,
yea, possession of all their fortifications.

24 And those which fled out of the city of Moroni came to the city of Nephihah.
And also the people of the city of Lehi gathered themselves together
and made preparations and were ready to receive the Lamanites to battle.

25 But it came to pass that Amalickiah would not suffer the Lamanites
to go against the city of Nephihah to battle,

but he kept them down by the seashore,
leaving men in every city to maintain and defend it.

26 And thus he went on, taking possession of many cities:
the city of Moroni and the city of Lehi and the city of Morionton
and the city of Omner and the city of Gid and the city of Mulek,
all of which were on the east borders by the seashore.

27 And thus had the Lamanites obtained by the cunning of Amalickiah
so many cities, by their numberless hosts,
all of which were strongly fortified
after the manner of the fortifications of Moroni,
all of which afforded strong holds for the Lamanites.

28 And it came to pass that they marched to the borders of the land Bountiful,
driving the Nephites before them and slaying many.

29 But it came to pass that they were met by Teancum,
who had slain Morionton and had headed his people in his flight.

30 And it came to pass that he headed Amalickiah also,
as he was marching forth with his numerous army
that he might take possession of the land Bountiful and also the land northward.

31 But behold, he met with a disappointment
of being repulsed by Teancum and his men,
for they were great warriors.
For every man of Teancum did exceed the Lamanites
in their strength and in their skill of war,
insomuch that they did gain advantage over the Lamanites.

32 And it came to pass that they did harass them,
insomuch that they did slay them even until it was dark.
And it came to pass that
Teancum and his men did pitch their tents in the borders of the land Bountiful;
and Amalickiah did pitch his tents in the borders on the beach by the seashore.
And after this manner were they driven.

33 And it came to pass that when the night had come,
Teancum and his servant stole forth and went out by night
and went into the camp of Amalickiah.
And behold, sleep had overpowered them
because of their much fatigue,
which was caused by the labors and heat of the day.

34 And it came to pass that Teancum stole privily into the tent of the king
and put a javelin to his heart.
And he did cause the death of the king immediately
that he did not awake his servants.

35 And he returned again privily to his own camp;

and behold, his men were asleep.
And he awoke them and told them all the things that he had done.

36 And he caused that his armies should stand in readiness
lest the Lamanites had awoke and should come upon them.

37 And thus ended the twenty and fifth year
of the reign of the judges over the people of Nephi.
And thus ended the days of Amalickiah.

52 | 1 And now it came to pass in the twenty and sixth year
of the reign of the judges over the people of Nephi,
behold, when the Lamanites awoke on the first morning of the first month,
behold, they found Amalickiah was dead in his own tent.
And they also saw that Teancum was ready to give them battle on that day.

2 And now when the Lamanites saw this, they were affrighted;
and they abandoned their design in marching into the land northward
and retreated with all their army into the city of Mulek
and sought protection in their fortifications.

3 And it came to pass that
the brother of Amalickiah was appointed king over the people;
and his name was Ammoron.
Thus king Ammoron, the brother of king Amalickiah,
was appointed to reign in his stead.

4 And it came to pass that
he did command that his people should maintain those cities
which they had taken by the shedding of blood,
for they had not taken any cities save they had lost much blood.

5 And now Teancum saw that the Lamanites were determined
to maintain those cities which they had taken
and those parts of the land which they had obtained possession of.
And also seeing the enormity of their number,
Teancum thought it was not expedient
that he should attempt to attackt them in their forts.

6 But he kept his men round about,
as if making preparations for war.
Yea, and truly he was preparing to defend himself against them
by casting up walls round about and preparing places of resort.

7 And it came to pass that he kept thus preparing for war
until Moroni had sent a large number of men to strengthen his army.

8 And Moroni also sent orders unto him
that he should retain all the prisoners which fell into his hands,

for as the Lamanites had taken many prisoners,
that he should retain all the prisoners of the Lamanites
as a ransom for those which the Lamanites had taken.

9 And he also sent orders unto him that he should fortify the land Bountiful
and secure the narrow pass which led into the land northward,
lest the Lamanites should obtain that point
and should have power to harass them on every side.

10 And Moroni also sent unto him, desiring him
that he would be faithful in maintaining that quarter of the land
and that he would seek every opportunity
to scourge the Lamanites in that quarter as much as was in his power,
that perhaps he might take again by stratagem or some other way
those cities which had been taken out of their hands,
and that he also would fortify and strengthen the cities round about
which had not fallen into the hands of the Lamanites.

11 And he also said unto him:
I would come unto you,
but behold, the Lamanites are upon us
in the borders of the land by the west sea.
And behold, I go against them;
therefore I cannot come unto you.

12 Now the king Ammoron had departed out of the land of Zarahemla
and had made known unto the queen concerning the death of his brother
and had gathered together a large number of men
and had marched forth against the Nephites on the borders by the west sea.

13 And thus he was endeavoring to harass the Nephites
and to draw away a part of their forces to that part of the land,
while he had commanded those which he had left
to possess the cities which he had taken
that they should also harass the Nephites on the borders by the east sea
and should take possession of their lands
as much as it were in their power,
according to the power of their armies.

14 And thus were the Nephites in those dangerous circumstances
in the ending of the twenty and sixth year
of the reign of the judges over the people of Nephi.

15 But behold, it came to pass
in the twentieth and seventh year of the reign of the judges
that Teancum by the command of Moroni
—who had established armies
to protect the south and the west borders of the land

    and had began his march towards the land of Bountiful,
    that he might assist Teancum with his men
    in retaking the cities which they had lost—

16 and it came to pass that Teancum had received orders
    to make an attackt upon the city of Mulek and retake it if it were possible.

17 And it came to pass that Teancum made preparations
    to make an attackt upon the city of Mulek
    and march forth with his army against the Lamanites.
    But he saw that it was impossible that he could overpower them
    while they were in their fortifications.
    Therefore he abandoned his designs
    and returned again to the city Bountiful
    to wait for the coming of Moroni,
    that he might receive strength to his army.

18 And it came to pass that
    Moroni did arrive with his army to the land of Bountiful
    in the latter end of the twenty and seventh year
    of the reign of the judges over the people of Nephi.

19 And in the commencement of the twenty and eighth year,
    Moroni and Teancum and many of the chief captains held a council of war,
    what they should do to cause the Lamanites to come out against them to battle,
    or that they might by some means flatter them out of their strong holds,
    that they might gain advantage over them and take again the city of Mulek.

20 And it came to pass that they sent embassies to the army of the Lamanites
    which protected the city of Mulek,
    to their leader, whose name was Jacob,
    desiring him that he would come out with his armies
    to meet them upon the plains between the two cities.
    But behold, Jacob, which was a Zoramite, would not come out
    with his army to meet them upon the plains.

21 And it came to pass that
    Moroni having no hopes of meeting them upon fair grounds,
    therefore he resolved upon a plan
    that he might decoy the Lamanites out of their strong holds.

22 Therefore he caused that Teancum should take a small number of men
    and march down near the seashore;
    and Moroni and his army by night marched
    into the wilderness on the west of the city Mulek.
    And thus on the morrow,
    when the guards of the Lamanites had discovered Teancum,
    they ran and told it unto Jacob, their leader.

23 And it came to pass that
the armies of the Lamanites did march forth against Teancum,
supposing by their numbers to overpower Teancum
because of the smallness of his numbers.
And as Teancum saw the armies of the Lamanites coming out against him,
he began a retreat down by the seashore, northward.

24 And it came to pass that when the Lamanites saw that he began to flee,
they took courage and pursued them with vigor.

And while Teancum was thus leading away the Lamanites,
which were pursuing them in vain,
behold, Moroni commanded that a part of his army which were with him
should march forth into the city and take possession of it.

25 And thus they did and slew all those who had been left to protect the city,
yea, all those who would not yield up their weapons of war.

26 And thus Moroni had obtained a possession of the city Mulek
with a part of his army
while he marched with the remainder to meet the Lamanites
when they should return from the pursuit of Teancum.

27 And it came to pass that the Lamanites did pursue Teancum
until they came near the city Bountiful,
and then they were met by Lehi and a small army
which had been left to protect the city Bountiful.

28 And now behold, when the chief captains of the Lamanites had beheld Lehi
with his army coming against them,
they fled in much confusion,
lest perhaps they should not obtain the city Mulek
before Lehi should overtake them;
for they were wearied because of their march,
and the men of Lehi were fresh.

29 Now the Lamanites did not know
that Moroni had been in their rear with his army,
and all they feared was Lehi and his men.

30 Now Lehi was not desirous to overtake them
till they should meet Moroni and his army.

31 And it came to pass that before the Lamanites had retreated far,
they were surrounded by the Nephites,
by the men of Moroni on one hand and the men of Lehi on the other,
all of whom were fresh and full of strength;
but the Lamanites were wearied because of their long march.

32 And Moroni commanded his men that they should fall upon them

until they had given up their weapons of war.

33 And it came to pass that Jacob being their leader,
   being also a Zoramite and having an unconquerable spirit,
   he led the Lamanites forth to battle with exceeding fury against Moroni;

34 Moroni being in their course of march,
   therefore Jacob was determined to slay them
   and cut his way through to the city of Mulek.
   But behold, Moroni and his men were more powerful;
   therefore they did not give way before the Lamanites.

35 And it came to pass that they fought on both hands with exceeding fury,
   and there were many slain on both sides;
   yea, and Moroni was wounded and Jacob was killed.

36 And Lehi pressed upon their rear with such fury with his strong men
   that the Lamanites in the rear delivered up their weapons of war.
   And the remainder of them, being much confused,
   knew not whither to go or to strike.

37 Moroni seeing their confusion, he said unto them:
   If ye will bring forth your weapons of war and deliver them up,
   behold, we will forbear shedding your blood.

38 And it came to pass that when the Lamanites had heard these words,
   their chief captains—all those which were not slain—came forth
   and threw down their weapons of war at the feet of Moroni
   and also commanded their men that they should do the same.

39 But behold, there were many that would not.
   And those who would not deliver up their swords were taken and bound;
   and their weapons of war were taken from them;
   and they were compelled to march with their brethren
   forth into the land Bountiful.

40 And now the number of prisoners which were taken
   exceeded more than the number of those which had been slain,
   yea, more than those which had been slain on both sides.

53 | 1 And it came to pass that they did set guards over the prisoners of the Lamanites
   and did compel them to go forth and bury their dead,
   yea, and also the dead of the Nephites which were slain.
   And Moroni placed men over them to guard them
   whilst they should perform their labors.

2 And Moroni went to the city of Mulek with Lehi
   and took command of the city and gave it unto Lehi.
   Now behold, this Lehi was a man who had been with Moroni
   in the more part of all his battles;
   and he was a man like unto Moroni.

And they rejoiced in each other's safety;
yea, they were beloved by each other
and also beloved by all the people of Nephi.

3 And it came to pass that
after the Lamanites had finished burying their dead
and also the dead of the Nephites,
they were marched back into the land Bountiful.
And Teancum by the orders of Moroni caused
that they should commence in laboring,
in digging a ditch round about the land, or the city Bountiful.
4 And he caused that they should build a breastwork of timbers
upon the inner bank of the ditch;
and they cast up dirt out of the ditch against the breastwork of timbers.
And thus they did cause the Lamanites to labor
until they had encircled the city of Bountiful round about
with a strong wall of timbers and earth to an exceeding heighth.
5 And this city became an exceeding strong hold ever after.
And in this city they did guard the prisoners of the Lamanites,
yea, even within a wall which they had caused them to build with their own hands.
Now Moroni was compelled to cause the Lamanites to labor
because it were easy to guard them while at their labor;
and he desired all his forces when he should make an attackt upon the Lamanites.

6 And it came to pass that Moroni had thus gained a victory
over one of the greatest of the armies of the Lamanites
and had obtained possession of the city Mulek,
which was one of the strongest holds of the Lamanites in the land of the Nephites.
And thus he had also built a strong hold to retain his prisoners.
7 And it came to pass that
he did no more attempt a battle with the Lamanites in that year,
but he did employ his men in preparing for war,
yea, and in making fortifications to guard against the Lamanites,
yea, and also delivering their women and their children
from famine and affliction,
and providing food for their armies.

8 And now it came to pass that the armies of the Lamanites on the west sea south,
while in the absence of Moroni,
on account of some intrigue amongst the Nephites,
which caused dissensions amongst them,
had gained some ground over the Nephites,
yea, insomuch that they had obtained possession

of a number of their cities in that part of the land.

9 And thus because of iniquity amongst themselves,
yea, because of dissensions and intrigue among themselves,
they were placed in the most dangerous circumstances.

10 And now behold, I have somewhat to say concerning the people of Ammon,
which in the beginning were Lamanites;
but by Ammon and his brethren
—or rather by the power and word of God—
they had been converted unto the Lord.
And they had been brought down into the land of Zarahemla
and had ever since been protected by the Nephites.

11 And because of their oath
they had been kept from taking up arms against their brethren,
for they had taken an oath that they never would shed blood more.
And according to their oath they would have perished
—yea, they would have suffered themselves
to have fallen into the hands of their brethren—
had it not been for the pity and the exceeding love
which Ammon and his brethren had had for them.

12 And for this cause they were brought down into the land of Zarahemla,
and they ever had been protected by the Nephites.

13 But it came to pass that
when they saw the danger and the many afflictions and tribulations
which the Nephites bare for them,
they were moved with compassion
and were desirous to take up arms in the defense of their country.

14 But behold, as they were about to take their weapons of war,
they were overpowered by the persuasions of Helaman and his brethren.
For they were about to break the oath which they had made,

15 and Helaman feared lest by so doing they should lose their souls.
Therefore all those which had entered into this covenant
were compelled to behold their brethren wade through their afflictions
in their dangerous circumstances at this time.

16 But behold, it came to pass they had many sons
which had not entered into a covenant
that they would not take their weapons of war
to defend themselves against their enemies.
Therefore they did assemble themselves together at this time,
as many as were able to take up arms,
and they called themselves Nephites.

17 And they entered into a covenant

to fight for the liberty of the Nephites,
yea, to protect the land,
unto the laying down of their lives;
yea, even they covenanted that they never would give up their liberty,
but they would fight in all cases
to protect the Nephites and themselves from bondage.

18 Now behold, there were two thousand of those young men
which entered into this covenant
and took their weapons of war to defend their country.

19 And now behold, as they never had hitherto
been a disadvantage to the Nephites,
they became now at this period of time also a great support;
for they took their weapons of war,
and they would that Helaman should be their leader.

20 And they were all young men,
and they were exceeding valiant for courage and also for strength and activity.
But behold, this was not all.
They were men which were true at all times
in whatsoever thing they were entrusted.

21 Yea, they were men of truth and soberness,
for they had been taught to keep the commandments of God
and to walk uprightly before him.

22 And now it came to pass that Helaman did march
at the head of his two thousand stripling soldiers
to the support of the people
in the borders of the land on the south by the west sea.

23 And thus ended the twenty and eighth year
of the reign of the judges over the people of Nephi etc.

54 | 1 And now it came to pass
in the commencement of the twenty and ninth year of the judges
that Ammoron sent unto Moroni, desiring that he would exchange prisoners.

2 And it came to pass that Moroni felt to rejoice exceedingly at this request,
for he desired the provisions
which was imparted for the support of the Lamanite prisoners
for the support of his own people;
and he also desired his own people
for the strengthening of his army.

3 Now the Lamanites had taken many women and children;
and there was not a woman nor a child among all the prisoners of Moroni,

or the prisoners which Moroni had taken.
Therefore Moroni resolved upon a stratagem to obtain
as many prisoners of the Nephites from the Lamanites as it were possible.

4 Therefore he wrote an epistle and sent it by the servant of Ammoron,
the same who had brought an epistle to Moroni.

Now these are the words which he wrote unto Ammoron, saying:

5 Behold, Ammoron, I have wrote unto you somewhat
concerning this war which ye have waged against my people,
or rather which thy brother hath waged against them,
and which ye are still determined to carry on after his death.

6 Behold, I would tell you something concerning the justice of God
and the sword of his almighty wrath, which doth hang over you
except ye repent and withdraw your armies into your own lands,
or the lands of your possessions, which is the land of Nephi.

7 Yea, I would tell you these things
if ye were capable of hearkening unto them.
Yea, I would tell you concerning that awful hell
that awaits to receive such murderers as thou and thy brother hath been
except ye repent and withdraw your murderous purposes
and return with your armies to your own lands.

8 But as ye have once rejected these things
and have fought against the people of the Lord,
even so I may expect you will do it again.

9 And now behold, we are prepared to receive you;
yea, and except you withdraw your purposes,
behold, ye will pull down
the wrath of that God whom you have rejected
upon you,
yea, even to your utter destruction.

10 But as the Lord liveth,
our armies shall come upon you except ye withdraw,
and ye shall soon be visited with death.
For we will retain our cities and our lands,
yea, and we will maintain our religion and the cause of our God.

11 But behold, it supposeth me that I talk to you concerning these things in vain,
or it supposeth me that thou art a child of hell.
Therefore I will close my epistle by telling you
that I will not exchange prisoners save it be on conditions
that ye will deliver up a man and his wife and his children for one prisoner.
If this be the case that ye will do it, I will exchange.

12 And behold, if ye do not this,
I will come against you with my armies,
yea, even I will arm my women and my children;
and I will come against you,
and I will follow you even into your own land,
which is the land of our first inheritance.
Yea, and it shall be blood for blood, yea, life for life.
And I will give you battle,
even until you are destroyed from off the face of the earth.

13 Behold, I am in my anger—and also my people.
Ye have sought to murder us,
and we have only sought to defend our lives.
But behold, if ye seek to destroy us more,
we will seek to destroy you.
Yea, and we will seek our lands,
the lands of our first inheritance.

14 Now I close my epistle.
I am Moroni;
I am a leader of the people of the Nephites.

15 Now it came to pass that Ammoron, when he had received this epistle,
he was angry, and he wrote another epistle unto Moroni.
And these are the words which he wrote, saying:

16 I am Ammoron the king of the Lamanites.
I am the brother of Amalickiah, whom ye have murdered.
Behold, I will avenge his blood upon you.
Yea, and I will come upon you with my armies,
for I fear not your threatenings.

17 For behold, your fathers did wrong their brethren,
insomuch that they did rob them of their right to the government
when it rightfully belonged unto them.

18 And now behold, if ye will lay down your arms
and subject yourselves to be governed by those
to whom the government doth rightly belong,
then will I cause that my people shall lay down their weapons
and shall be at war no more.

19 Behold, ye have breathed out many threatenings against me and my people.
But behold, we fear not your threatenings.

20 Nevertheless I will grant to exchange prisoners according to your request gladly,
that I may preserve my food for my men of war.
And we will wage a war which shall be eternal,

either to the subjecting the Nephites to our authority
or to their eternal extinction.

21 And as concerning that God whom ye say we have rejected,
behold, we know not such a being, neither do ye.
But if it so be that there is such a being,
we know not but that he hath made us as well as you.

22 And if it so be that there is a devil and a hell,
behold, will he not send you there
to dwell with my brother, which ye have murdered,
which ye have hinted that he hath gone to such a place?
But behold, these things matter not.

23 I am Ammoron and a descendant of Zoram,
whom your fathers pressed and brought out of Jerusalem.

24 And behold, I am now a bold Lamanite.
Behold, this war hath been waged to avenge their wrongs
and to maintain and to obtain their rights to the government.
And I close my epistle to Moroni.

55 | 1 Now it came to pass that when Moroni had received this epistle,
he was more angry
because he knew that Ammoron had a perfect knowledge of his fraud.
Yea, he knew that Ammoron knew that it was not a just cause
that had caused him to wage a war against the people of Nephi.

2 And he said:
Behold, I will not exchange prisoners with Ammoron
save he will withdraw his purpose, as I have stated in my epistle,
for I will not grant unto him
that he shall have any more power than what he hath gat.

3 Behold, I know the place where the Lamanites doth guard my people
which they have taken prisoners.
And as Ammoron would not grant unto me mine epistle,
behold, I will give unto him according to my words;
yea, I will seek death among them until they shall sue for peace.

4 And now it came to pass that when Moroni had said these words,
he caused that a search should be made among his men
that perhaps he might find a man
which was a descendant of Laman's among them.

5 And it came to pass that they found one, whose name was Laman,
and he was one of the servants of the king which was murdered by Amalickiah.

6 Now Moroni caused that Laman and a small number of his men
should go forth unto the guards which were over the Nephites.

7 Now the Nephites were guarded in the city of Gid;
therefore Moroni caused that Laman and a small number of men
which was appointed to go with him
should go to the city of Gid.

8 And it came to pass that when it was evening,
Laman went to the guards which were over the Nephites.
And behold, they saw him a coming and they hailed him,
but he saith unto them:
Fear not!
Behold, I am a Lamanite.
Behold, we have escaped from the Nephites and they sleepeth.
And behold, we have took of their wine and brought with us.

9 Now when the Lamanites heard these words,
they received him with joy.
And they said unto him:
Give us of your wine that we may drink.
We are glad that ye have thus taken wine with you,
for we are weary.

10 But Laman saith unto them:
Let us keep of our wine till we go against the Nephites to battle.
But this saying only made them more desirous to drink of the wine.

11 For, said they, we are weary;
therefore let us take of the wine.
And by and by we shall receive wine for our rations,
which will strengthen us to go against the Nephites.

12 And Laman saith unto them:
You may do according to your desires.

13 And it came to pass that they did take of the wine freely,
and it was pleasant to their taste;
therefore they took of it more freely.
And it was strong, having been prepared in its strength.

14 And it came to pass they did drink and were merry,
and by and by they were all drunken.

15 And now when Laman and his men saw
that they were all drunken and were in a deep sleep,
they returned to Moroni and told him all the things that had happened.

16 And now this was according to the design of Moroni.
And Moroni had prepared his men with weapons of war;
and he went to the city Gid
while the Lamanites were in a deep sleep and drunken,
and cast in the weapons of war in unto the prisoners,

insomuch that they were all armed,

17 yea, even to their women and all those of their children,
as many as were able to use a weapon of war.

When Moroni had armed all those prisoners—
and all those things were done in a profound silence;

18 but had they awoke the Lamanites
—behold, they were drunken—
and the Nephites could have slain them;

19 but behold, this was not the desire of Moroni;
he did not delight in murder or bloodshed,
but he delighted in the saving his people from destruction;
and for this cause that he might not bring upon him injustice,
he would not fall upon the Lamanites and destroy them in their drunkenness;

20 but he had obtained his desire,
for he had armed those prisoners of the Nephites
which were within the walls of the city
and had gave them power to gain possession
of those parts which were within the walls—

21 and then he caused his men which were with him
to withdraw a pace from them and surround the armies of the Lamanites.

22 Now behold, this was done in the nighttime,
so that when the Lamanites awoke in the morning,
they beheld that they were surrounded by the Nephites without
and that their prisoners were armed within.

23 And thus they saw that the Nephites had power over them.
And in these circumstances they found that it were not expedient
that they should fight with the Nephites.
Therefore their chief captains demanded their weapons of war;
and they brought them forth
and cast them at the feet of the Nephites,
pleading for mercy.

24 Now behold, this was the desire of Moroni.
He took them prisoners of war and took possession of the city
and caused that all the prisoners should be liberated, which were Nephites.
And they did join the army of Moroni and were a great strength to his army.

25 And it came to pass that
he did cause the Lamanites which he had taken prisoners
that they should commence a labor
in strengthening the fortifications round about the city Gid.

26 And it came to pass that
when he had fortified the city Gid according to his desires,

he caused that his prisoners should be taken to the city Bountiful.
And he also guarded that city with an exceeding strong force.

27 And it came to pass that they did,
notwithstanding all the intrigues of the Lamanites,
keep and protect all the prisoners which they had taken
and also maintain all the ground and the advantage which they had retaken.

28 And it came to pass that the Nephites began again to be victorious
and to reclaim their rights and their privileges.

29 Many times did the Lamanites attempt to encircle them about by night,
but in these attempts they did lose many prisoners.

30 And many times did they attempt to administer of their wine to the Nephites,
that they might destroy them with poison or with drunkenness.

31 But behold, the Nephites were not slow
to remember the Lord their God in this their times of affliction.
They could not be taken in their snares.
Yea, they would not take of their wine;
yea, they would not take of wine
save they had firstly given to some of the Lamanite prisoners.

32 And they were thus cautious
that no poison should be administered among them.
For if their wine would poison a Lamanite,
it would also poison a Nephite.
And thus they did try all their liquors.

33 And now it came to pass that it was expedient
for Moroni to make preparations to attackt the city Morionton.
For behold, the Lamanites had by their labors fortified the city Morionton
until it had become an exceeding strong hold.

34 And they were continually bringing new forces into that city,
and also new supplies of provisions.

35 And thus ended the twenty and ninth year
of the reign of the judges over the people of Nephi.

56 | 1 And now it came to pass
in the commencement of the thirtieth year of the reign of the judges
in the second day on the first month
Moroni received an epistle from Helaman
stating the affairs of the people in that quarter of the land.

2 And these are the words which he wrote, saying:
My dearly beloved brother Moroni,
as well in the Lord as in the tribulations of our warfare,

behold, my beloved brother, I have somewhat to tell you
concerning our warfare in this part of the land.

3 Behold, two thousand of the sons of those men
which Ammon brought down out of the land of Nephi—
now ye have known that these were a descendant of Laman,
which was the eldest son of our father Lehi—

4 now I need not rehearse unto you concerning their traditions or their unbelief,
for thou knowest concerning all these things—

5 therefore it sufficeth me that I tell you
that two thousand of these young men hath taken their weapons of war
and would that I should be their leader;
and we have come forth to defend our country.

6 And now ye also know concerning the covenant which their fathers made,
that they would not take up their weapons of war
against their brethren to shed blood.

7 But in the twenty and sixth year,
when they saw our afflictions and our tribulations for them,
they were about to break the covenant which they had made
and take up their weapons of war in our defense.

8 But I would not suffer them
that they should break this covenant which they had made,
supposing that God would strengthen us,
insomuch that we should not suffer more
because of the fulfilling the oath which they had taken.

9 But behold, here is one thing in which we may have great joy.
For behold, in the twenty and sixth year
I Helaman did march at the head of these two thousand young men
to the city of Judea to assist Antipus,
whom ye had appointed a leader over the people of that part of the land.

10 And I did join my two thousand sons
—for they are worthy to be called sons—
to the army of Antipus,
in the which strength Antipus did rejoice exceedingly.
For behold, his army had been reduced by the Lamanites
because of the enormity of their forces,
having slain a vast number of our men,
for which cause we have to mourn.

11 Nevertheless we may console ourselves in this point,
that they have died in the cause of their country and of their God;
yea, and they are happy.

12 And the Lamanites had also retained many prisoners,
all of whom are chief captains,

for none other have they spared alive.
And we suppose that they are now at this time in the land of Nephi;
it is so if they are not slain.

13 And now these are the cities
which the Lamanites have obtained possession of
by the shedding the blood of so many of our valiant men:

14 the land of Manti, or the city of Manti,
and the city of Zeezrom and the city of Cumeni and the city of Antiparah.

15 And these are the cities which they possessed when I arrived at the city of Judea.

And I found Antipus and his men toiling with their mights to fortify the city.

16 Yea, and they were depressed in body as well as in spirit,
for they had fought valiantly by day and toiled by night to maintain their cities.
And thus they had suffered great afflictions of every kind.

17 And now they were determined to conquer in this place or die.
Therefore you may well suppose
that the little force which I brought with me
—yea, those sons of mine—
gave them great hopes and much joy.

18 And now it came to pass that when the Lamanites saw
that Antipus had received a greater strength to his army,
they were compelled by the orders of Ammoron
to not come against the city of Judea or against us to battle.

19 And thus were we favored of the Lord.
For had they come upon us in this our weakness,
they might have perhaps destroyed our little army;
but thus were we favored.

20 They were commanded by Ammoron
to maintain those cities which they had taken.
And thus ended the twenty and sixth year.

And in the commencement of the twenty and seventh year
we had prepared our city and ourselves for defense.

21 Now we were desirous that the Lamanites should come upon us,
for we were not desirous to make an attackt upon them in their strong holds.

22 And it came to pass that we kept spies out round about
to watch the movements of the Lamanites,
that they might not pass us by night or by day
to make an attackt upon our other cities, which were on the northward.

23 For we knew in those cities they were not sufficiently strong to meet them.
Therefore we were desirous, if they should pass by us,
to fall upon them in their rear;

and thus bringing them up in the rear
at the same time they were met in the front,
we supposed that we could overpower them.
But behold, we were disappointed in this our desire.

24 They durst not pass by us with their whole army,
neither durst they with a part,
lest they should not be sufficiently strong and they should fall.

25 Neither durst they march down against the city of Zarahemla,
neither durst they cross the head of Sidon over to the city of Nephihah.

26 And thus with their forces they were determined
to maintain those cities which they had taken.

27 And now it came to pass in the second month of this year
there was brought unto us many provisions
from the fathers of those my two thousand sons.

28 And also there was sent two thousand men unto us from the land of Zarahemla.
And thus we were prepared with ten thousand men
and provisions for them, and also for their wives and their children.

29 And the Lamanites thus seeing our forces increase daily
and provisions arrive for our support,
they began to be fearful and began to sally forth,
if it were possible, to put an end to our receiving provisions and strength.

30 Now when we saw that the Lamanites began to grow uneasy on this wise,
we were desirous to bring a stratagem into an effect upon them.
Therefore Antipus ordered that I should march forth
with my little sons to a neighboring city
as if we were carrying provisions to a neighboring city.

31 And we were to march near the city Antiparah
as if we were going to the city beyond on the borders by the seashore.

32 And it came to pass that we did march forth
as if with our provisions to go to that city.

33 And it came to pass that Antipus did march forth with a part of his army,
leaving the remainder to maintain the city.
But he did not march forth
until I had gone forth with my little army and came near the city Antiparah.

34 And now in the city Antiparah were stationed
the strongest army of the Lamanites,
yea, the most numerous.

35 And it came to pass that when they had been informed by their spies,
they came forth with their army and marched against us.

36 And it came to pass that we did flee before them northward.
And thus we did lead away the most powerful army of the Lamanites,

37 yea, even to a considerable distance,
   insomuch that when they saw
   the army of Antipus pursuing them with their mights,
   they did not turn to the right nor to the left
   but pursued their march in a straight course after us,
   and as we supposed that it was their intent to slay us
   before Antipus should overtake them —
   and this that they might not be surrounded by our people.

38 And now Antipus beholding our danger
   did speed the march of his army.
   But behold, it was night;
   therefore they did not overtake us, neither did Antipus overtake them.
   Therefore we did camp for the night.

39 And it came to pass that before the dawn of the morning,
   behold, the Lamanites were pursuing us.
   Now we were not sufficiently strong to contend with them;
   yea, I would not suffer that my little sons should fall into their hands.
   Therefore we did continue our march;
   and we took our march into the wilderness.

40 Now they durst not turn to the right nor to the left
   lest they should be surrounded,
   neither would I turn to the right or to the left lest they should overtake me.
   And we could not stand against them but be slain
   and they would make their escape.
   And thus we did flee all that day into the wilderness, even until it was dark.

41 And it came to pass that again when the light of the morning came,
   we saw the Lamanites upon us;
   and we did flee before them.

42 But it came to pass that they did not pursue us far before they halted.
   And it was in the morning of the third day on the seventh month.

43 And now whether they were overtaken by Antipus, we knew not.
   But I said unto my men:
   Behold, we know not but they have halted
   for the purpose that we should come against them,
   that they may catch us in their snare.

44 Therefore what say ye, my sons?
   Will ye go against them to battle?

45 And now I say unto you, my beloved brother Moroni,
   that never had I seen so great courage, nay, not amongst all the Nephites.

46 For as I had ever called them my sons
   — for they were all of them very young —

even so they said unto me:
Father, behold, our God is with us,
and he will not suffer that we shall fall;
then let us go forth.
We would not slay our brethren if they would let us alone.
Therefore let us go lest they should overpower the army of Antipus.

47 Now they never had fought, yet they did not fear death.
And they did think more upon the liberty of their fathers
than they did upon their lives.
Yea, they had been taught by their mothers
that if they did not doubt that God would deliver them.

48 And they rehearsed unto me the words of their mothers, saying:
We do not doubt; our mothers knew.

49 And it came to pass that I did return with my two thousand
against these Lamanites which had pursued us.
And now behold, the armies of Antipus had overtaken them,
and a terrible battle had commenced.

50 The army of Antipus being weary
because of their long march in so short a space of time
were about to fall into the hands of the Lamanites.
And had I not returned with my two thousand,
they would have obtained their purpose.

51 For Antipus had fallen by the sword, and many of his leaders,
because of their weariness which was occasioned by the speed of their march.
Therefore the men of Antipus
being confused because of the fall of their leaders
began to give way before the Lamanites.

52 And it came to pass that the Lamanites took courage and began to pursue them.
And thus were the Lamanites pursuing them with great vigor
when Helaman came upon their rear with his two thousand
and began to slay them exceedingly,
insomuch that the whole army of the Lamanites halted and turned upon Helaman.

53 Now when the people of Antipus saw that the Lamanites had turned them about,
they gathered together their men and came again upon the rear of the Lamanites.

54 And now it came to pass that we the people of Nephi
—the people of Antipus and I with my two thousand—
did surround the Lamanites and did slay them,
yea, insomuch that they were compelled to deliver up their weapons of war
and also themselves as prisoners of war.

55 And now it came to pass that when they had surrendered themselves up unto us,
behold, I numbered those young men which had fought with me,

fearing lest there were many of them slain.

56 But behold, to my great joy there had not one soul of them fallen to the earth.
Yea, and they had fought as if with the strength of God;
yea, never was men known to have fought with such miraculous strength.
And with such mighty power did they fall upon the Lamanites
that they did frighten them;
and for this cause did the Lamanites deliver themselves up as prisoners of war.

57 And as we had no place for our prisoners,
that we could guard them to keep them from the armies of the Lamanites,
therefore we sent them to the land of Zarahemla,
and a part of those men which were not slain of Antipus with them.
And the remainder I took and joined them to my stripling Ammonites
and took our march back to the city of Judea.

57 | 1 And now it came to pass that I received an epistle from Ammoron the king
stating that if I would deliver up those prisoners of war which we had taken
that he would deliver up the city of Antiparah unto us.

2 But I sent an epistle unto the king that we were sure
that our forces were sufficient to take the city of Antiparah by our force,
and by delivering up the prisoners for that city
we should suppose ourselves unwise,
and that we would only deliver up our prisoners on exchange.

3 And as Ammoron refused mine epistle
—for he would not exchange prisoners—
therefore we began to make preparations to go against the city of Antiparah.

4 But the people of Antiparah did leave the city
and fled to their other cities which they had possession of, to fortify them.
And thus the city of Antiparah fell into our hands.

5 And thus ended the twenty and eighth year of the reign of the judges.

6 And it came to pass that in the commencement of the twenty and ninth year
we received a supply of provisions
and also an addition to our army
from the land of Zarahemla and from the land round about
to the number of six thousand men,
besides sixty of the sons of the Ammonites
which had come to join their brethren, my little band of two thousand.
And now behold, we were strong;
yea, and we had also a plenty of provisions brought unto us.

7 And it came to pass that it was our desire to wage a battle
with the army which was placed to protect the city Cumeni.

8 And now behold, I will shew unto you that we soon accomplished our desire.

Yea, with our strong force—or with a part of our strong force—
we did surround by night the city Cumeni
a little before they were to receive a supply of provisions.

9 And it came to pass that we did camp round about the city for many nights,
but we did sleep upon our swords and keep guards
that the Lamanites could not come upon us by night and slay us,
which they attempted many times.
But as many times as they attempted this, their blood was spilt.

10 At length their provisions did arrive,
and they were about to enter the city by night.
And we, instead of being Lamanites, were Nephites;
therefore we did take them and their provisions.

11 And notwithstanding the Lamanites being cut off
from their support after this manner,
they were still determined to maintain the city.
Therefore it became expedient
that we should take those provisions and send them to Judea
and our prisoners to the land of Zarahemla.

12 And it came to pass that not many days had passed away
before the Lamanites began to lose all hopes of succor;
therefore they yielded up the city into our hands.
And thus we had accomplished our designs in obtaining the city Cumeni.

13 But it came to pass that our prisoners were so numerous
that notwithstanding the enormity of our number,
we were obliged to employ all our force
to keep them or put them to death.

14 For behold, they would break out in great numbers
and would fight with stones and with clubs,
or whatsoever thing they could get into their hands,
insomuch that we did slay upwards of two thousand of them
after they had surrendered themselves prisoners of war.

15 Therefore it became expedient for us
that we should put an end to their lives
or guard them sword in hand down to the land of Zarahemla.
And also our provisions were not any more than sufficient for our own people,
notwithstanding that which we had taken from the Lamanites.

16 And now in those critical circumstances
it became a very serious matter to determine concerning those prisoners of war.
Nevertheless we did resolve to send them down to the land of Zarahemla.
Therefore we selected a part of our men and gave them charge over our prisoners
to go down to the land of Zarahemla.

17 But it came to pass that on the morrow they did return.
And now behold, we did not inquire of them concerning the prisoners;
for behold, the Lamanites were upon us,
and they returned in season to save us from falling into their hands.
For behold, Ammoron had sent to their support a new supply of provision
and also a numerous army of men.

18 And it came to pass that those men which we sent with the prisoners
did arrive in season to check them as they were about to overpower us.

19 But behold, my little band of two thousand and sixty fought most desperately.
Yea, they were firm before the Lamanites
and did administer death unto all those who opposed them.

20 And as the remainder of our army were about to give way before the Lamanites,
behold, these two thousand and sixty were firm and undaunted.

21 Yea, and they did obey and observe to perform
every word of command with exactness.
Yea, and even according to their faith it was done unto them.
And I did remember the words which they said unto me
that their mothers had taught them.

22 And now behold, it was these my sons
and those men which had been selected to convey the prisoners
to whom we owe this great victory,
for it was they who did beat the Lamanites.
Therefore they were driven back to the city of Manti.

23 And we retained our city Cumeni
and were not all destroyed by the sword;
nevertheless we had suffered great loss.

24 And it came to pass that after the Lamanites had fled,
I immediately gave orders that my men which had been wounded
should be taken from among the dead
and caused that their wounds should be dressed.

25 And it came to pass that
there were two hundred out of my two thousand and sixty
which had fainted because of the loss of blood.
Nevertheless, according to the goodness of God
and to our great astonishment and also the joy of our whole army,
there was not one soul of them which did perish.
Yea, and neither was there one soul among them
which had not received many wounds.

26 And now their preservation was astonishing to our whole army,
yea, that they should be spared,
while there was a thousand of our brethren which were slain.

And we do justly ascribe it to the miraculous power of God
because of their exceeding faith in that which they had been taught to believe,
that there was a just God,
and whosoever did not doubt,
that they should be preserved by his marvelous power.

27 Now this was the faith of these of which I have spoken.
They are young and their minds are firm;
and they do put their trust in God continually.

28 And now it came to pass that after we had thus taken care of our wounded men
and had buried our dead and also the dead of the Lamanites, which were many,
behold, we did inquire of Gid concerning the prisoners
which they had started to go down to the land of Zarahemla with.

29 Now Gid was the chief captain over the band
which was appointed to guard them down to that land.

30 And now these are the words which Gid said unto me:
Behold, we did start to go down to the land of Zarahemla with our prisoners.
And it came to pass that we did meet the spies of our armies,
which had been sent out to watch the camp of the Lamanites.

31 And they cried unto us, saying:
Behold, the armies of the Lamanites are a marching
towards the city of Cumeni.
And behold, they will fall upon them, yea, and will destroy our people.

32 And it came to pass that our prisoners did hear their cries,
which caused them to take courage,
and they did raise up in rebellion against us.

33 And it came to pass because of their rebellion
we did cause that our swords should come upon them.
And it came to pass that they did in a body run upon our swords,
in the which the greater number of them were slain.
And the remainder of them brake through and fled from us.

34 And behold, when they had fled and we could not overtake them,
we took our march with speed towards the city Cumeni.
And behold, we did arrive in time
that we might assist our brethren in preserving the city.

35 And behold, we are again delivered out of the hands of our enemies.
And blessed is the name of our God;
for behold, it is he that hath delivered us,
yea, that hath done this great thing for us.

36 Now it came to pass that when I Helaman had heard these words of Gid,
I was filled with exceeding joy
because of the goodness of God in preserving us, that we might not all perish.

Yea, and I trust that the souls of them which has been slain
have entered into the rest of their God.

58 | 1 And behold, now it came to pass that
our next object was to obtain the city of Manti.
But behold, there was no way
that we could lead them out of the city by our small bands.
For behold, they remembered that which we had hitherto done.
Therefore we could not decoy them away from their strong holds.

2 And they were so exceeding more numerous than was our army
that we durst not go forth and attackt them in their strong holds.

3 Yea, and it became expedient
that we should employ our men to the maintaining those parts of the land
of the which we had retained of our possessions.
Therefore it became expedient that we should wait,
that we might receive more strength from the land of Zarahemla
and also a new supply of provisions.

4 And it came to pass that
I thus did send an embassy to the great governor of our land
to acquaint him concerning the affairs of our people.
And it came to pass that we did wait
to receive provisions and strength from the land of Zarahemla.

5 But behold, this did not profit us but little,
for the Lamanites were also receiving great strength from day to day
and also many provisions.
And thus were our circumstances at this period of time.

6 And the Lamanites were sallying forth against us from time to time,
resolving by stratagem to destroy us.
Nevertheless we could not come to battle with them
because of their retreats and their strong holds.

7 And it came to pass that we did wait in these difficult circumstances
for the space of many months,
even until we were about to perish for the want of food.

8 But it came to pass that we did receive food
which was guarded to us with an army of two thousand men to our assistance.
And this is all the assistance which we did receive
to defend ourselves and our country
from falling into the hands of our enemies,
yea, to contend with an enemy which was innumerable.

9 And now the cause of these our embarrassments,
or the cause why they did not send more strength unto us, we knew not.

Therefore we were grieved and also filled with fear,
lest by any means the judgments of God should come upon our land,
to our overthrow and utter destruction.

10 Therefore we did pour out our souls in prayer to God
that he would strengthen us and deliver us out of the hands of our enemies,
yea, and also give us strength,
that we might retain our cities and our lands and our possessions
for the support of our people.

11 Yea, and it came to pass that
the Lord our God did visit us with assurances
that he would deliver us,
yea, insomuch that he did speak peace to our souls
and did grant unto us great faith
and did cause us that we should hope for our deliverance in him.

12 And we did take courage with our small force which we had received
and were fixed with a determination to conquer our enemies
and to maintain our lands and our possessions
and our wives and our children and the cause of our liberty.

13 And thus we did go forth with all our might against the Lamanites
which were in the city of Manti.
And we did pitch our tents by the wilderness side, which was near to the city.

14 And it came to pass on the morrow
that when the Lamanites saw that we were in the borders
by the wilderness which was near the city
that they sent out their spies round about us
that they might discover the number and the strength of our army.

15 And it came to pass that when they saw
that we were not strong according to our numbers,
and fearing that we should cut them off from their support
except they should come out to battle against us and kill us,
and also supposing that they could easily destroy us with their numerous hosts,
therefore they began to make preparations to come out against us to battle.

16 And when we saw that they were making preparations to come out against us,
behold, I caused that Gid with a small number of men
should secrete himself in the wilderness
and also that Teomner should with a small number of men
secrete himself also in the wilderness.

17 Now Gid and his men was on the right and the other on the left.
And when they had thus secreted themselves,
behold, I remained with the remainder of my army in that same place

where we had first pitched our tents,
against the time that the Lamanites should come out to battle.

18 And it came to pass that
the Lamanites did come out with their numerous army against us.
And when they had come and were about to fall upon us with the sword,
I caused that my men—those which were with me—
should retreat into the wilderness.

19 And it came to pass that the Lamanites did follow after us with great speed,
for they were exceedingly desirous to overtake us that they might slay us.
Therefore they did follow us into the wilderness.
And we did pass by in the midst of Gid and Teomner,
insomuch that they were not discovered by the Lamanites.

20 And it came to pass that when the Lamanites had passed by,
or when the army had passed by,
Gid and Teomner did rise up from their secret places
and did cut off the spies of the Lamanites,
that they should not return to the city.

21 And it came to pass that when they had cut them off,
they ran to the city and fell upon the guards which were left to guard the city,
insomuch that they did destroy them and did take possession of the city.

22 Now this was done because the Lamanites did suffer
their whole army, save a few guards only,
to be led away into the wilderness.

23 And it came to pass that
Gid and Teomner by this means had obtained possession of their strong hold.

And it came to pass that we took our course,
after having traveled much in the wilderness,
towards the land of Zarahemla.

24 And when the Lamanites saw that they were marching
towards the land of Zarahemla,
they were exceeding fraid
lest there was a plan laid to lead them on to destruction.
Therefore they began to retreat into the wilderness again,
yea, even back by the same way which they had come.

25 And behold, it was night and they did pitch their tents.
For the chief captains of the Lamanites had supposed
that the Nephites were weary because of their march;
and supposing that they had driven their whole army,
therefore they took no thought concerning the city of Manti.

26 Now it came to pass that when it was night
that I caused that my men should not sleep

but that they should march forward by another way towards the land of Manti.

27 And because of this our march in the nighttime,
behold, on the morrow we were beyond the Lamanites,
insomuch that we did arrive before them to the city of Manti.

28 And thus it came to pass that by this stratagem
we did take possession of the city of Manti without the shedding of blood.

29 And it came to pass that
when the armies of the Lamanites did arrive near the city
and saw that we were prepared to meet them,
they were astonished exceedingly and struck with great fear,
insomuch that they did flee into the wilderness.

30 Yea, and it came to pass that
the armies of the Lamanites did flee out of all this quarter of the land.
But behold, they have carried with them
many women and children out of the land.

31 And those cities which had been taken by the Lamanites,
all of them are at this period of time in our possession.
And our fathers and our women and our children are returning to their homes,
all save it be those which have been taken prisoners
and carried off by the Lamanites.

32 But behold, our armies are small
to maintain so great a number of cities and so great possessions.

33 But behold, we trust that it is our God
who hath given us victory over those lands,
insomuch that we have obtained those cities and those lands which were our own.

34 Now we do not know the cause
that the government does not grant us more strength,
neither does those men which came up unto us know
why we have not received greater strength.

35 Behold, we do not know but what ye are unsuccessful
and ye have drawn away the forces into that quarter of the land.
If so, we do not desire to murmur.

36 And if it is not so,
behold, we fear that there is some faction in the government,
that they do not send more men to our assistance.
For we know that they are more numerous than that which they have sent.

37 But behold, it mattereth not.
We trust God will deliver us, notwithstanding the weakness of our armies,
yea, and deliver us out of the hands of our enemies.

38 Behold, this is the twenty and ninth year, in the latter end,
and we are in the possession of our lands

and the Lamanites have fled to the land of Nephi.

39 And those sons of the people of Ammon, of which I have so highly spoken,
   are with me in the city of Manti.
   And the Lord hath supported them,
   yea, and kept them from falling by the sword,
   insomuch that even one soul hath not been slain.

40 But behold, they have received many wounds.
   Nevertheless they stand fast in that liberty wherewith God hath made them free.
   And they are strict to remember the Lord their God from day to day.
   Yea, they do observe to keep his statutes
   and his judgments and his commandments continually.
   And their faith is strong in the prophecies concerning that which is to come.

41 And now my beloved brother Moroni,
   that the Lord our God,
   who hath redeemed us and made us free,
   may keep you continually in his presence,
   yea, and that he may favor this people,
   even that ye may have success in obtaining the possession
   of all that which the Lamanites hath taken from us,
   which was for our support.
   And now behold, I close mine epistle.
   I am Helaman the son of Alma.

59 | 1 Now it came to pass in the thirtieth year
       of the reign of the judges over the people of Nephi,
       after Moroni had received and had read Helaman's epistle,
       he was exceedingly rejoiced because of the welfare,
       yea, the exceeding success which Helaman had had
       in obtaining those lands which were lost.

2 Yea, and he did make it known unto all his people
   in all the land round about in that part where he was,
   that they might rejoice also.

3 And it came to pass that he immediately sent an epistle to Parhoron,
   desiring that he should cause men to be gathered together
   to strengthen Helaman, or the armies of Helaman,
   insomuch that he might with ease maintain that part of the land
   which he had been so miraculously prospered in retaining.

4 And it came to pass
   when Moroni had sent this epistle to the land of Zarahemla,
   he began again to lay a plan

that he might obtain the remainder of those possessions and cities
which the Lamanites had taken from them.

5 And it came to pass that while Moroni was thus making preparations
to go against the Lamanites to battle,
behold, the people of Nephihah, which were gathered together
from the city of Moroni and the city of Lehi and the city of Morionton,
were attackted by the Lamanites;

6 yea, even those which had been compelled to flee
from the land of Manti and from the land round about
had came over and joined the Lamanites in this part of the land.

7 And thus being exceeding numerous,
yea, and receiving strength from day to day by the command of Ammoron,
they came forth against the people of Nephihah;
and they did begin to slay them with an exceeding great slaughter.

8 And their armies were so numerous
that the remainder of the people of Nephihah were obliged to flee before them;
and they came over and joined the army of Moroni.

9 And now as Moroni had supposed
that there should be men sent to the city of Nephihah
to the assistance of the people to maintain that city
—and knowing that it was easier to keep the city
from falling into the hands of the Lamanites,
he supposed that they would easily maintain that city—

10 therefore he retained all his force
to maintain those places which he had recovered.

11 And now when Moroni saw that the city of Nephihah was lost,
he was exceeding sorrowful
and began to doubt because of the wickedness of the people
whether they should not fall into the hands of their brethren.

12 Now this was the case with all his chief captains.
They doubted and marveled also because of the wickedness of the people—
and this because of the success of the Lamanites over them.

13 And it came to pass that Moroni was angry with the government
because of their indifference concerning the freedom of their country.

60 | 1 And it came to pass that he wrote again
to the governor of the land, which was Parhoron.
And these are the words which he wrote, saying:
Behold, I direct mine epistle to Parhoron in the city of Zarahemla,
which is the chief judge and the governor over the land,
and also to all those who hath been chosen by this people
to govern and manage the affairs of this war.

2 For behold, I have somewhat to say unto them by the way of condemnation.
For behold, ye yourselves know
that ye have been appointed to gather together men
and arm them with swords and with scimitars
and all manner of weapons of war of every kind
and send forth against the Lamanites
in whatsoever parts they should come into our land.

3 And now behold, I say unto you
that myself and also my men, and also Helaman and his men,
have suffered exceeding great sufferings,
yea, even hunger, thirst, and fatigue, and all manner of afflictions of every kind.

4 But behold, were this all we had suffered,
we would not murmur nor complain.

5 But behold, great has been the slaughter among our people
—yea, thousands have fallen by the sword—
while it might have otherwise been
if ye had rendered unto our armies sufficient strength and succor for them.
Yea, great has been your neglect towards us.

6 And now behold, we desire to know the cause of this exceeding great neglect.
Yea, we desire to know the cause of your thoughtless state.

7 Can you think to sit upon your thrones in a state of thoughtless stupor
while your enemies are spreading the work of death around you,
yea, while they are murdering thousands of your brethren—

8 yea, even they which have looked up to you for protection,
yea, have placed you in a situation that ye might have succored them?
Yea, ye might have sent armies unto them to have strengthened them
and have saved thousands of them from falling by the sword.

9 But behold, this is not all.
Ye have withheld your provisions from them,
insomuch that many have fought and bled out their lives
because of their great desires which they had for the welfare of this people.
Yea, and this they have done when they were about to perish with hunger
because of your exceeding great neglect towards them.

10 And now my beloved brethren
—for ye had ought to be beloved—
yea, and ye had ought to have stirred yourselves more diligently
for the welfare and the freedom of this people.
But behold, ye have neglected them,
insomuch that the blood of thousands
shall come upon your heads for vengeance.
Yea, for known unto God were all their cries and all their sufferings.

11 Behold, could ye suppose that ye could sit upon your thrones,
and because of the exceeding goodness of God
ye could do nothing and he would deliver you?
Behold, if ye have supposed this, ye have supposed in vain.

12 Do ye suppose that because so many of your brethren have been killed,
it is because of their wickedness?
I say unto you:
If ye have supposed this, ye have supposed in vain.
For I say unto you:
There are many which have fallen by the sword;
and behold, it is to your condemnation.

13 For the Lord suffereth the righteous to be slain
that his justice and judgment may come upon the wicked.
Therefore ye need not suppose
that the righteous are lost because they are slain;
but behold, they do enter into the rest of the Lord their God.

14 And now behold, I say unto you:
I fear exceedingly that the judgments of God will come upon this people
because of their exceeding slothfulness,
yea, even the slothfulness of our government
and their exceeding great neglect towards their brethren,
yea, towards those which have been slain.

15 For were it not for the wickedness which first commenced at our head,
we could have withstood our enemies,
that they could have gained no power over us.

16 Yea, had it not been for the war which broke out among ourselves
— yea, were it not for those kingmen
which caused so much bloodshed among ourselves;
yea, at the time we were contending among ourselves,
if we had united our strength as we hitherto have done;
yea, had it not been for the desire of power and authority
which those kingmen had over us,
had they been true to the cause of our freedom
and united with us and gone forth against our enemies
instead of taking up their swords against us,
which was the cause of so much bloodshed among ourselves—
yea, if we had gone forth against them in the strength of the Lord,
we should have dispersed our enemies,
for it would have been done according to the fulfilling of his word.

17 But behold, now the Lamanites are coming upon us;
and they are murdering our people with the sword,
yea, our women and our children

—taking possession of our lands—
and also carrying them away captive,
causing them that they should suffer all manner of afflictions—
and this because of the great wickedness of those
who are seeking for power and authority,
yea, even those kingmen.

18 But why should I say much concerning this matter?
For we know not but what ye yourselves are a seeking for authority.
We know not but what ye are also traitors to your country.

19 Or is it that ye have neglected us
because ye are in the heart of our country
and ye are surrounded by security,
that ye do not cause food to be sent unto us
and also men to strengthen our armies?

20 Have ye forgat the commandments of the Lord your God?
Yea, have ye forgat the captivity of our fathers?
Have ye forgat the many times
we have been delivered out of the hands of our enemies?

21 Or do ye suppose that the Lord will still deliver us
while we sit upon our thrones and do not make use of the means
which the Lord hath provided for us?

22 Yea, will ye sit in idleness while ye are surrounded with thousands of those
—yea, and tens of thousands—which do also sit in idleness
while there are thousands round about in the borders of the land
which are falling by the sword, yea, wounded and bleeding?

23 Do ye suppose that God will look upon you as guiltless
while ye sit still and behold these things?
Behold, I say unto you: Nay.

Now I would that ye should remember that God hath said
that the inward vessel shall be cleansed first,
and then shall the outer vessel be cleansed also.

24 And now except ye do repent of that which ye have done
and begin to be up and doing and send forth food and men
unto us and also unto Helaman,
that he may support those parts of our country which he hath retained,
and that we may also recover the remainder of our possessions in these parts,
behold, it will be expedient that we contend no more with the Lamanites
until we have first cleansed our inward vessel,
yea, even the great head of our government.

25 And except ye grant mine epistle
and come out and shew unto me a true spirit of freedom

and strive to strengthen and fortify our armies
and grant unto them food for their support,
behold, I will leave a part of my freemen to maintain this part of our land.
And I will leave the strength and the blessings of God upon them,
that none other power can operate against them

26 —and this because of their exceeding faith
and their patience in their tribulations—

27 and I will come unto you.
And if there be any among you that hath a desire for freedom,
yea, if there be even a spark of freedom remaining,
behold, I will stir up insurrections among you,
even until those who hath desires to usurp power and authority
shall become extinct.

28 Yea, behold, I do not fear your power nor your authority,
but it is my God whom I fear.
And it is according to his commandments
that I do take my sword to defend the cause of my country.
And it is because of your iniquity that we have suffered so much loss.

29 Behold, it is time—yea, the time is now at hand—
that except ye do bestir yourselves
in the defense of your country and your little ones,
the sword of justice doth hang over you;
yea, and it shall fall upon you and visit you,
even to your utter destruction.

30 Behold, I wait for assistance from you.
And except ye do administer unto our relief,
behold, I come unto you, even into the land of Zarahemla,
and smite you with the sword,
insomuch that ye can have no more power
to impede the progress of this people in the cause of our freedom.

31 For behold, the Lord will not suffer
that ye shall live and wax strong in your iniquities to destroy his righteous people.

32 Behold, can you suppose that the Lord will spare you
and come out in judgment against the Lamanites
when it is the tradition of their fathers that hath caused their hatred
—yea, and it hath been redoubled by those which have dissented from us—
while your iniquity is for the cause of your love of glory
and the vain things of the world?

33 Ye know that ye do transgress the laws of God;
and ye do know that ye do trample them under your feet.

Behold, the Lord saith unto me:

If those whom ye have appointed your governors
do not repent of their sins and iniquities,
ye shall go up to battle against them.

34 And now behold, I Moroni am constrained,
according to the covenant which I have made,
to keep the commandments of my God.
Therefore I would that ye should adhere to the word of God
and send speedily unto me of your provisions and of your men,
and also to Helaman.

35 And behold, if ye will not do this,
I come unto you speedily.
For behold, God will not suffer that we should perish with hunger.
Therefore he will give unto us of your food,
even if it must be by the sword.
Now see that ye fulfill the word of God.

36 Behold, I am Moroni your chief captain.
I seek not for power but to pull it down.
I seek not for honor of the world
but for the glory of my God and the freedom and welfare of my country.
And thus I close mine epistle.

61 | 1 Behold, now it came to pass that
soon after Moroni had sent his epistle unto the chief governor,
he received an epistle from Parhoron the chief governor.
And these are the words which he received:

2 I Parhoron, which art the chief governor of this land,
do send these words unto Moroni, the chief captain over the army.
Behold, I say unto you Moroni
that I do not joy in your great afflictions;
yea, it grieves my soul.

3 But behold, there are those who do joy in your afflictions,
yea, insomuch that they have risen up in rebellion against me
and also those of my people which are freemen;
yea, and those which have risen up are exceeding numerous.

4 And it is those who have sought to take away the judgment seat from me
that have been the cause of this great iniquity.
For they have used great flattery;
and they have led away the hearts of many people,
which will be the cause of sore affliction among us.
They have withheld our provisions and have daunted our freemen
that they have not come unto you.

5 And behold, they have driven me out before them.
And I have fled to the land of Gideon
with as many men as it were possible that I could get.

6 And behold, I have sent a proclamation throughout this part of the land.
And behold, they are flocking to us daily, to their arms,
in the defense of their country and their freedom,
and to avenge our wrongs.

7 And they have come unto us,
insomuch that those which have rose up in rebellion against us
are set at defiance,
yea, insomuch that they do fear us
and durst not come out against us to battle.

8 They have got possession of the land, or the city of Zarahemla.
They have appointed a king over them;
and he hath written unto the king of the Lamanites,
in the which he hath joined an alliance with him,
in the which alliance he hath agreed to maintain the city of Zarahemla,
which maintenance he supposeth will enable
the Lamanites to conquer the remainder of the land,
and he shall be placed king over this people
when they shall be conquered under the Lamanites.

9 And now in your epistle ye hath censured me,
but it mattereth not.
I am not angry, but do rejoice in the greatness of your heart.
I Parhoron do not seek for power, save only to retain my judgment seat
that I may preserve the rights and the liberty of my people.
My soul standeth fast in that liberty in the which God hath made us free.

10 And now behold, we will resist wickedness, even unto bloodshed.
We would not shed the blood of the Lamanites
if they would stay in their own land.

11 We would not shed the blood of our brethren
if they would not rise up in rebellion and take the sword against us.

12 We would subject ourselves to the yoke of bondage
if it were requisite with the justice of God,
or if he should command us so to do.

13 But behold, he doth not command us
that we shall subject ourselves to our enemies,
but that we should put our trust in him and he will deliver us.

14 Therefore my beloved brother Moroni, let us resist evil.
And whatsoever evil we cannot resist with our words
—yea, such as rebellions and dissensions—

let us resist them with our swords,
that we may retain our freedom,
that we may rejoice in the great privilege of our church
and in the cause of our Redeemer and our God.

15 Therefore come unto me speedily with a few of your men
and leave the remainder in the charge of Lehi and Teancum.
Give unto them power to conduct the war in that part of the land
according to the Spirit of God,
which is also the spirit of freedom which is in them.

16 Behold, I have sent a few provisions unto them,
that they may not perish until ye can come unto me.

17 Gather together whatsoever force ye can upon your march hither;
and we will go speedily against those dissenters
in the strength of our God, according to the faith which is in us.

18 And we will take possession of the city of Zarahemla
that we may obtain more food to send forth unto Lehi and Teancum.
Yea, we will go forth against them in the strength of the Lord,
and we will put an end to this great iniquity.

19 And now Moroni, I do joy in receiving your epistle.
For I was somewhat worried concerning what we should do,
whether it should be just in us to go against our brethren.

20 But ye have said:
Except they repent,
the Lord hath commanded you
that ye should go against them.

21 See that ye strengthen Lehi and Teancum in the Lord.
Tell them to fear not,
for God will deliver them,
yea, and also all those who stand fast in that liberty
wherewith God hath made them free.
And now I close mine epistle to my beloved brother Moroni.

62 | 1 And now it came to pass that when Moroni had received this epistle,
his heart did take courage and was filled with exceeding great joy
because of the faithfulness of Parhoron,
that he was not also a traitor to the freedom and cause of his country.

2 But he did also mourn exceedingly
because of the iniquity of those
who had driven Parhoron from the judgment seat,

yea, in fine, because of those who had rebelled
against their country and also their God.

3 And it came to pass that Moroni took a small number of men,
according to the desire of Parhoron,
and gave Lehi and Teancum command over the remainder of his army
and took his march towards the land of Gideon.

4 And he did raise the standard of liberty
in whatsoever place he did enter
and gained whatsoever force he could
in all his march towards the land of Gideon.

5 And it came to pass that thousands did flock unto his standard
and did take up their swords in the defense of their freedom,
that they might not come into bondage.

6 And thus when Moroni had gathered together
whatsoever men he could in all his march,
he came to the land of Gideon.
And uniting his forces with that of Parhoron's,
they became exceeding strong,
even stronger than the men of Pachus,
which was the king of those dissenters
which had driven out the freemen out of the land of Zarahemla
and had taken possession of the land.

7 And it came to pass that Moroni and Parhoron went down
with their armies into the land of Zarahemla
and went forth against the city
and did meet the men of Pachus,
insomuch that they did come to battle.

8 And behold, Pachus was slain and his men were taken prisoners;
and Parhoron was restored to his judgment seat.

9 And the men of Pachus received their trial according to the law,
and also those kingmen which had been taken and cast into prison.
And they were executed according to the law;
yea, those men of Pachus and those kingmen
—whosoever would not take up arms in the defense of their country
but would fight against it—
were put to death.

10 And thus it became expedient
that this law should be strictly observed for the safety of their country.
Yea, and whosoever was found a denying their freedom
was speedily executed according to the law.

11 And thus ended the thirtieth year

of the reign of the judges over the people of Nephi,
Moroni and Parhoron having restored peace
to the land of Zarahemla among their own people,
having inflicted death upon all those who were not true to the cause of freedom.

12 And it came to pass in the commencement of the thirty and first year
of the reign of the judges over the people of Nephi,
Moroni immediately caused that provisions should be sent,
and also an army of six thousand men should be sent unto Helaman
to assist him in preserving that part of the land.

13 And he also caused that an army of six thousand men
with a sufficient quantity of food
should be sent to the armies of Lehi and Teancum.
And it came to pass that this was done to fortify the land against the Lamanites.

14 And it came to pass that Moroni and Parhoron,
leaving a large body of men in the land of Zarahemla,
took their march with a large body of men towards the land of Nephihah,
being determined to overthrow the Lamanites in that city.

15 And it came to pass that as they were marching towards the land,
they took a large body of men of the Lamanites and slew many of them
and took their provisions and their weapons of war.

16 And it came to pass after they had took them,
they caused them to enter into a covenant
that they would no more take up their weapons of war against the Nephites.

17 And when they had entered into this covenant,
they sent them to dwell with the people of Ammon.
And they were in number about four thousand which had not been slain.

18 And it came to pass that when they had sent them away,
they pursued their march towards the land of Nephihah.
And it came to pass that when they had come to the city Nephihah,
they did pitch their tents in the plains of Nephihah,
which is near the city Nephihah.

19 Now Moroni was desirous
that the Lamanites should come out to battle against them upon the plains.
But the Lamanites knowing of their exceeding great courage
and beholding the greatness of their numbers,
therefore they durst not come out against them;
therefore they did not come to battle in that day.

20 And when the night came Moroni went forth in the darkness of the night
and came up on the top of the wall
to spy out in what part of the city the Lamanites did camp with their army.

21 And it came to pass that they were on the east by the entrance,
    and they were all asleep.
    And now Moroni returned to his army
    and caused that they should prepare in haste strong cords and ladders
    to be let down from the top of the wall into the inner part of the wall.

22 And it came to pass that Moroni caused
    that his men should march forth
    and come up upon the top of the wall
    and let themselves down into that part of the city,
    yea, even on the west, where the Lamanites did not camp with their armies.

23 And it came to pass that they were all let down into the city by night
    by the means of their strong cords and their ladders.
    Thus when the morning came, they were all within the walls of the city.

24 And now when the Lamanites awoke
    and saw that the armies of Moroni were within the walls,
    they were affrightened exceedingly,
    insomuch that they did flee out by the pass.

25 And now when Moroni saw that they were fleeing before him,
    he did cause that his men should march forth against them,
    and they slew many and surrounded many others and took them prisoners.
    And the remainder of them fled into the land of Moroni,
    which was in the borders by the seashore.

26 Thus had Moroni and Parhoron obtained the possession of the city of Nephihah
    without the loss of one soul;
    and there were many of the Lamanites which were slain.

27 Now it came to pass that as many of the Lamanites that were prisoners
    were desirous to join the people of Ammon and become a free people—

28 and it came to pass that as many as were desirous,
    unto them it was granted according to their desires.

29 Therefore all the prisoners of the Lamanites
    did join the people of Ammon and did begin to labor exceedingly,
    tilling the ground, raising all manner of grain and flocks and herds of every kind.
    And thus were the Nephites relieved from a great burthen,
    yea, insomuch that they were relieved from all the prisoners of the Lamanites.

30 Now it came to pass that Moroni,
    after he had obtained possession of the city of Nephihah,
    having taken many prisoners,
    which did reduce the armies of the Lamanites exceedingly,
    and having retained many of the Nephites which had been taken prisoners,
    which did strengthen the army of Moroni exceedingly,

therefore Moroni went forth from the land of Nephihah to the land of Lehi.

31 And it came to pass that when the Lamanites saw
that Moroni was a coming against them,
they were again frightened and fled before the army of Moroni.

32 And it came to pass that Moroni and his army did pursue them from city to city
until they were met by Lehi and Teancum.
And the Lamanites fled from Lehi and Teancum,
even down upon the borders by the seashore,
until they came to the land of Moroni.

33 And the armies of the Lamanites were all gathered together,
insomuch that they were all in one body in the land of Moroni.
Now Ammoron the king of the Lamanites was also with them.

34 And it came to pass that Moroni and Lehi and Teancum did encamp
with their armies round about in the borders of the land of Moroni,
insomuch that the Lamanites were encircled about
in the borders by the wilderness on the south
and in the borders by the wilderness on the east.

35 And thus they did encamp for the night.
For behold, the Nephites and the Lamanites also were weary
because of the greatness of the march;
therefore they did not resolve upon any stratagem in the nighttime—
save it were Teancum,
for he was exceeding angry with Ammoron,
insomuch that he considered that Ammoron and Amalickiah his brother
had been the cause of this great and lasting war
between them and the Lamanites,
which had been the cause of so much war and bloodshed,
yea, and so much famine.

36 And it came to pass that
Teancum in his anger did go forth into the camp of the Lamanites
and did let himself down over the walls of the city.
And he went forth with a cord from place to place,
insomuch that he did find the king;
and he did cast a javelin at him, which did pierce him near the heart.
But behold, the king did awake his servants before he died,
insomuch that they did pursue Teancum and slew him.

37 Now it came to pass that
when Lehi and Moroni knew that Teancum was dead,
they were exceeding sorrowful.
For behold, he had been a man which had fought valiantly for his country
—yea, a true friend to liberty—

and he had suffered very many exceeding sore afflictions.
But behold, he was dead and had gone the way of all the earth.

38 Now it came to pass that
Moroni marched forth on the morrow and came upon the Lamanites,
insomuch that they did slay them with a great slaughter
and they did drive them out of the land.
And they did flee,
even that they did not return at that time against the Nephites.

39 And thus ended the thirty and first year
of the reign of the judges over the people of Nephi.

And thus they had had wars and bloodsheds and famine and affliction
for the space of many years.

40 And there had been murders and contentions and dissensions
and all manner of iniquity among the people of Nephi.
Nevertheless, for the righteous' sake
—yea, because of the prayers of the righteous—
they were spared.

41 But behold, because of the exceeding great length of the war
between the Nephites and the Lamanites,
many had become hardened because of the exceeding great length of the war;
and many were softened because of their afflictions,
insomuch that they did humble themselves before God,
even in the depths of humility.

42 And it came to pass that after Moroni had fortified those parts of the land
which were most exposed to the Lamanites
until they were sufficiently strong,
he returned to the city of Zarahemla.
And also Helaman returned to the place of his inheritance.
And there was once more peace established among the people of Nephi.

43 And Moroni yielded up the command of his armies
into the hands of his son, whose name was Moronihah.
And he retired to his own house,
that he might spend the remainder of his days in peace.

44 And Parhoron did return to his judgment seat.

And Helaman did take upon him again
to preach unto the people the word of God.
For because of so many wars and contentions
it had become expedient
that a regulation should be made again in the church.

45 Therefore Helaman and his brethren went forth

and did declare the word of God with much power
unto the convincing of many people of their wickedness,
which did cause them to repent of their sins
and to be baptized unto the Lord their God.

46 And it came to pass that
they did establish again the church of God throughout all the land.
47 Yea, and regulations were made concerning the law;
and their judges and their chief judges were chosen.
48 And the people of Nephi began to prosper again in the land
and began to multiply and to wax exceeding strong again in the land,
and they began to grow exceeding rich.
49 But notwithstanding their riches or their strength or their prosperity,
they were not lifted up in the pride of their eyes.
Neither were they slow to remember the Lord their God,
but they did humble themselves exceedingly before him.
50 Yea, they did remember how great things the Lord had done for them,
that he had delivered them from death and from bonds and from prisons
and from all manner of afflictions,
and he had delivered them out of the hands of their enemies.
51 And they did pray unto the Lord their God continually,
insomuch that the Lord did bless them according to his word,
so that they did wax strong and prosper in the land.
52 And it came to pass that all these things were done,
and Helaman died in the thirty and fifth year
of the reign of the judges over the people of Nephi.

63 | 1 And it came to pass in the commencement of the thirty and sixth year
of the reign of the judges over the people of Nephi
that Shiblon took possession of those sacred things
which had been delivered unto Helaman by Alma.
2 And he was a just man,
and he did walk uprightly before God;
and he did observe to do good continually,
to keep the commandments of the Lord his God,
and also did his brother.
3 And it came to pass that Moroni died also.
And thus ended the thirty and sixth year of the reign of the judges.

4 And it came to pass that
in the thirtieth and seventh year of the reign of the judges
there was a large company of men

—even to the amount of five thousand and four hundred men,
with their wives and their children—
departed out of the land of Zarahemla into the land which was northward.

5 And it came to pass that Hagoth,
he being an exceeding curious man,
therefore he went forth and built him an exceeding large ship
on the borders of the land Bountiful by the land Desolation
and launched it forth into the west sea
by the narrow neck which led into the land northward.

6 And behold, there were many of the Nephites which did enter therein
and did sail forth with much provisions
and also many women and children;
and they took their course northward.
And thus ended the thirty and seventh year.

7 And in the thirty and eighth year this man built other ships.
And the first ship did also return;
and many more people did enter into it,
and they also took much provisions
and set out again to the land northward.

8 And it came to pass that they never were heard of more.
And we suppose that they are drowned up in the depths of the sea.
And it came to pass that one other ship also did sail forth,
and whither she did go we know not.

9 And it came to pass that in this year
there were many people which went forth into the land northward.
And thus ended the thirty and eighth year.

10 And it came to pass
in the thirty and ninth year of the reign of the judges
Shiblon died also.
And Corianton had gone forth to the land northward in a ship,
to carry forth provisions unto those people which had gone forth into that land.

11 Therefore it became expedient
for Shiblon to confer those sacred things before his death
upon the son of Helaman, who was called Helaman,
being called after the name of his father.

12 Now behold, all those engravings which were in the possession of Helaman
were written and sent forth among the children of men throughout all the land,
save it were those parts
which had been commanded by Alma should not go forth.

13 Nevertheless these things were to be kept sacred
and handed down from one generation to another.

Therefore in this year they had been conferred upon Helaman
before the death of Shiblon.

14 And it came to pass also in this year
that there were some dissenters which had gone forth unto the Lamanites;
and they were stirred up again to anger against the Nephites.

15 And also in this same year they came down with a numerous army
to war against the people of Moronihah, or against the army of Moronihah,
in the which they were beaten
and driven back again to their own lands,
suffering great loss.

16 And thus ended the thirty and ninth year
of the reign of the judges over the people of Nephi.

17 And thus ended the account of Alma
and Helaman his son
and also Shiblon, which was his son.

THE BOOK OF HELAMAN

An account of the Nephites,
their wars and contentions and their dissensions,
and also the prophecies of many holy prophets before the coming of Christ,
according to the record of Helaman, which was the son of Helaman,
and also according to the records of his sons,
even down to the coming of Christ.

And also many of the Lamanites are converted;
an account of their conversion.

An account of the righteousness of the Lamanites
and the wickedness and abominations of the Nephites,
according to the record of Helaman and his sons,
even down to the coming of Christ,
which is called the book of Helaman etc.

1 | 1 And now behold, it came to pass in the commencement of the fortieth year
of the reign of the judges over the people of Nephi,
there began to be a serious difficulty among the people of the Nephites.

2 For behold, Parhoron had died and gone the way of all the earth.

Therefore there began to be a serious contention
concerning who should have the judgment seat
among the brethren which were the sons of Parhoron.

3 Now these are their names which did contend for the judgment seat,
which did also cause the people to contend:
Parhoron, Paanchi, and Pacumeni.

4 Now these are not all the sons of Parhoron—for he had many—
but these are they which did contend for the judgment seat.
Therefore they did cause three divisions among the people.

5 Nevertheless it came to pass that
Parhoron was appointed by the voice of the people
to be a chief judge and a governor over the people of Nephi.

6 And it came to pass that Pacumeni,
when he saw that he could not obtain the judgment seat,
he did unite with the voice of the people.

7 But behold, Paanchi and that part of the people
that were desirous that he should be their governor
was exceeding wroth.
Therefore he was about to flatter away those people
to rise up in rebellion against their brethren.

8 And it came to pass as he was about to do this,
behold, he was taken
and was tried according to the voice of the people
and condemned unto death,
for he had raised up in rebellion
and sought to destroy the liberty of the people.

9 Now when those people
which were desirous that he should be their governor
saw that he was condemned unto death,
therefore they were angry;
and behold, they sent forth one Kishcumen,
even to the judgment seat of Parhoron,
and murdered Parhoron as he sat upon the judgment seat.

10 And he was pursued by the servants of Parhoron.
But behold, so speedy was the flight of Kishcumen
that no man could overtake him.

11 And he went unto those that sent him;
and they all entered into a covenant
—yea, swearing by their everlasting Maker—
that they would tell no man that Kishcumen had murdered Parhoron.

12 Therefore Kishcumen was not known among the people of Nephi,
for he was in disguise at the time that he murdered Parhoron.
And Kishcumen and his band, which had covenanted with him,
did mingle themselves among the people
in a manner that they all could not be found—
but as many as were found were condemned unto death.

13 And now behold, Pacumeni was appointed according to the voice of the people
to be a chief judge and a governor over the people
to reign in the stead of his brother Parhoron;
and it was according to his right.
And all this was done in the fortieth year of the reign of the judges,
and it had an end.

14 And it came to pass in the forty and first year of the reign of the judges
that the Lamanites had gathered together an innumerable army of men
and armed them with swords and with scimitars
and with bows and with arrows
and with headplates and with breastplates
and with all manner of shields of every kind.

15 And they came down again that they might pitch battle against the Nephites.
And they were led by a man whose name was Coriantumr,
and he was a descendant of Zarahemla;
and he was a dissenter from among the Nephites,
and he was a large and a mighty man.

16 Therefore the king of the Lamanites,
whose name was Tubaloth, who was the son of Ammoron
—now Tubaloth supposing that Coriantumr,
he being a mighty man,
could stand against the Nephites
insomuch with his strength and also with his great wisdom
that by sending him forth he should gain power over the Nephites—

17 therefore he did stir them up to anger,
and he did gather together his armies,
and he did appoint Coriantumr to be their leader
and did cause that they should march down to the land of Zarahemla
to battle against the Nephites.

18 And it came to pass that
because of so much contention and so much difficulty in the government
that they had not kept sufficient guards in the land of Zarahemla,
for they had supposed that the Lamanites durst not come
into the heart of their lands and attackt that great city Zarahemla.

19 But it came to pass that Coriantumr did march forth
at the head of his numerous host and came upon the inhabitants of the city.
And their march was with such exceeding great speed
that there was no time for the Nephites to gather together their armies.

20 Therefore Coriantumr did cut down the watch by the entrance of the city
and did march forth with his whole army into the city.
And they did slay every one who did oppose them,
insomuch that they did take possession of the whole city.

21 And it came to pass that Pacumeni, which was the chief judge,
did flee before Coriantumr, even to the walls of the city.
And it came to pass that Coriantumr did smite him against the wall,
insomuch that he died;
and thus ended the days of Pacumeni.

22 And now when Coriantumr saw
that he was in possession of the city of Zarahemla
and saw that the Nephites had fled before them and were slain
and were taken and were cast into prison
and that he had obtained the possession of the strongest hold in all the land,
his heart took courage,
insomuch that he was about to go forth against all the land.

23 And now he did not tarry in the land of Zarahemla,
but he did march forth with a large army, even towards the city of Bountiful.
For it was his determination to go forth and cut his way through with the sword,
that he might obtain the north parts of the land.

24 And supposing that their greatest strength was in the center of the land,
therefore he did march forth,
giving them no time to assemble themselves together save it were in small bodies.
And in this manner they did fall upon them and cut them down to the earth.

25 But behold, this march of Coriantumr's through the center of the land
gave Moronihah great advantage over them,
notwithstanding the greatness of the number of the Nephites which were slain.

26 For behold, Moronihah had supposed
that the Lamanites durst not come into the center of the land,
but that they would attackt the cities round about in the borders,
as they had hitherto done.
Therefore Moronihah had caused
that their strong armies should maintain those parts round about by the borders.

27 But behold, the Lamanites were not frightened according to his desire,
but they had come into the center of the land
and had taken the capital city, which was the city of Zarahemla,
and were marching through the most capital parts of the land,

slaying the people with a great slaughter,
both men, women, and children,
taking possession of many cities and of many strong holds.

28 But when Moronihah had discovered this,
he immediately sent forth Lehi with an army round about to head them
before they should come to the land Bountiful.

29 And thus he did head them before they came to the land Bountiful
and gave unto them battle,
insomuch that they began to retreat back towards the land of Zarahemla.

30 And it came to pass that Moronihah did head them in their retreat
and did give unto them battle,
insomuch that it became an exceeding bloody battle;
yea, many were slain.
And among the number which were slain Coriantumr was also found.

31 And now behold, the Lamanites could not retreat neither way,
neither on the north nor on the south nor on the east nor on the west,
for they were surrounded on every hand by the Nephites.

32 And thus had Coriantumr plunged the Lamanites into the midst of the Nephites,
insomuch that they were in the power of the Nephites;
and he himself was slain,
and the Lamanites did yield themselves up into the hands of the Nephites.

33 And it came to pass that
Moronihah took possession of the city of Zarahemla again
and caused that the Lamanites which had been taken prisoners
should depart out of the land in peace.

34 And thus ended the forty and first year of the reign of the judges.

2 | 1 And it came to pass in the forty and second year of the reign of the judges,
after Moronihah had established again the peace
between the Nephites and the Lamanites,
behold, there was no one to fill the judgment seat.
Therefore there began to be a contention again among the people
concerning who should fill the judgment seat.

2 And it came to pass that Helaman, which was the son of Helaman,
was appointed to fill the judgment seat by the voice of the people.

3 But behold, Kishcumen, who had murdered Parhoron,
did lay wait to destroy Helaman also.
And he was upheld by his band,
which had entered into a covenant
that no one should know his wickedness.

4 For there was one Gaddianton who was exceeding expert

in many words and also in his craft
to carry on the secret work of murder and of robbery;
therefore he became the leader of the band of Kishcumen.

5 Therefore he did flatter them, and also Kishcumen,
that if they would place him in the judgment seat,
he would grant unto those which belonged to his band
that they should be placed in power and authority among the people.
Therefore Kishcumen sought to destroy Helaman.

6 And it came to pass as he went forth
towards the judgment seat to destroy Helaman,
behold, one of the servants of Helaman,
having been out by night
and having obtained through disguise a knowledge of those plans
which had been laid by this band to destroy Helaman—

7 and it came to pass that he met Kishcumen,
and he gave unto him a sign.
Therefore Kishcumen made known unto him the object of his desire,
desiring that he would conduct him to the judgment seat
that he might murder Helaman.

8 And it came to pass that
when the servant of Helaman had known all the heart of Kishcumen
and how that it was his object to murder
and also that it was the object of all those which belonged to his band
to murder and to rob and to gain power
—and this was their secret plan and their combination—
the servant of Helaman saith unto Kishcumen:
Let us go forth unto the judgment seat.

9 Now this did please Kishcumen exceedingly,
for he did suppose that he should accomplish his design.
But behold, the servant of Helaman,
as they were going forth unto the judgment seat,
did stab Kishcumen, even to the heart,
that he fell dead without a groan.
And he ran and told Helaman all the things
which he had seen and heard and done.

10 And it came to pass that Helaman did send forth
to take this band of robbers and secret murderers,
that they might be executed according to the law.

11 But behold, when Gaddianton had found that Kishcumen did not return,
he feared lest that he should be destroyed.
Therefore he caused that his band should follow him,

and they took their flight out of the land by a secret way into the wilderness.
And thus when Helaman sent forth to take them,
they could nowhere be found.

12 And more of this Gaddianton shall be spoken hereafter.
And thus ended the forty and second year
of the reign of the judges over the people of Nephi.

13 And behold, in the end of this book
ye shall see that this Gaddianton did prove the overthrow,
yea, almost the entire destruction of the people of Nephi.

14 Behold, I do not mean the end of the book of Helaman,
but I mean the end of the book of Nephi,
from which I have taken all the account which I have written.

3 | 1 And now it came to pass in the forty and third year of the reign of the judges,
there was no contention among the people of Nephi
save it were a little pride which was in the church,
which did cause some little dissension among the people,
which affairs were settled in the ending of the forty and third year.

2 And there was no contention among the people in the forty and fourth year,
neither was there much contention in the forty and fifth year.

3 And it came to pass in the forty and sixth year
there were much contentions and many dissensions,
in the which there were an exceeding great many
which departed out of the land of Zarahemla
and went forth unto the land northward to inherit the land.

4 And they did travel to an exceeding great distance,
insomuch that they came to large bodies of water and many rivers;

5 yea, and even they did spread forth into all parts of the land
in whatsoever parts it had not been rendered desolate and without timber
because of the many inhabitants which had before inherited the land.

6 And now no part of the land was desolate save it were for timber etc.
But because of the greatness of the destruction of the people
which had before inhabited the land,
it was called desolate.

7 And there being but little timber upon the face of the land,
nevertheless the people which went forth
became exceeding expert in the working of cement;
therefore they did build houses of cement in the which they did dwell.

8 And it came to pass that they did multiply and spread
and did go forth from the land southward to the land northward

and did spread insomuch that they began to cover the face of the whole earth,
from the sea south to the sea north, from the sea west to the sea east.

9 And the people which were in the land northward
did dwell in tents and in houses of cement.

And they did suffer whatsoever tree should spring up upon the face of the land,
that it should grow up,
that in time they might have timber to build their houses,
yea, their cities and their temples and their synagogues and their sanctuaries
and all manner of their buildings.

10 And it came to pass as timber was exceeding scarce in the land northward,
they did send forth much by the way of shipping.

11 And thus they did enable the people in the land northward
that they might build many cities, both of wood and of cement.

12 And it came to pass that
there were many of the people of Ammon,
which were Lamanites by birth,
did also go forth into this land.

13 And now there are many records kept
of the proceedings of this people, by many of this people,
which are particular and very large concerning them.

14 But behold, a hundredth part of the proceedings of this people
—yea, the account of the Lamanites and of the Nephites
and their wars and contentions and dissensions
and their preaching and their prophecies
and their shipping and their building of ships
and their building of temples and of synagogues and of sanctuaries
and their righteousness and their wickedness
and their murders and their robbings and their plunderings
and all manner of abominations and whoredoms—
cannot be contained in this work.

15 But behold, there are many books and many records of every kind,
and they have been kept chiefly by the Nephites.

16 And they have been handed down
from one generation to another by the Nephites,
even until they have fallen into transgression
and have been murdered, plundered, and hunted
and driven forth and slain
and scattered upon the face of the earth
and mixed with the Lamanites
until they are no more called the Nephites,

becoming wicked and wild and ferocious,
yea, even becoming Lamanites.

17 And now I return again to mine account.
Therefore what I have spoken had passed;
after there had been great contentions and disturbances
and wars and dissensions among the people of Nephi,
18 the forty and sixth year of the reign of the judges ended.
19 And it came to pass that there was still great contentions in the land,
yea, even in the forty and seventh year,
and also in the forty and eighth year.
20 Nevertheless Helaman did fill the judgment seat with justice and equity.
Yea, he did observe to keep the statutes and the judgments
and the commandments of God,
and he did do that which was right in the sight of God continually,
and he did walk after the ways of his father,
insomuch that he did prosper in the land.

21 And it came to pass that he had two sons.
He gave unto the eldest the name of Nephi
and unto the youngest the name of Lehi.
And they began to grow up unto the Lord.
22 And it came to pass that the wars and contentions began to cease
in a small degree among the people of the Nephites
in the latter end of the forty and eighth year
of the reign of the judges over the people of Nephi.

23 And it came to pass in the forty and ninth year of the reign of the judges,
there was continual peace established in the land,
all save it were the secret combinations
which Gaddianton the robber had established
in the more settled parts of the land,
which at that time were not known
unto those which were at the head of government;
therefore they were not destroyed out of the land.

24 And it came to pass that in this same year
there was exceeding great prosperity in the church,
insomuch that there were thousands who did join themselves unto the church
and were baptized unto repentance.
25 And so great was the prosperity of the church
and so many the blessings which were poured out upon the people
that even the high priests and the teachers
were themselves astonished beyond measure.

26 And it came to pass that the work of the Lord did prosper
unto the baptizing and uniting to the church of God many souls,
yea, even tens of thousands.

27 Thus we may see that the Lord is merciful unto all
who will in the sincerity of their hearts call upon his holy name.

28 Yea, thus we see that the gate of heaven is open unto all,
even to those who will believe on the name of Jesus Christ,
which is the Son of God.

29 Yea, we see that whosoever will lay hold upon the word of God,
which is quick and powerful,
which shall divide asunder
all the cunning and the snares and the wiles of the devil
and lead the man of Christ in a straight and narrow course
across that everlasting gulf of misery,
which is prepared to engulf the wicked,

30 and land their souls—yea, their immortal souls—
at the right hand of God in the kingdom of heaven,
to sit down with Abraham and Isaac and with Jacob
and with all our holy fathers,
to go no more out.

31 And in this year there were continual rejoicing
in the land of Zarahemla and in all the regions round about,
even in all the land which was possessed by the Nephites.

32 And it came to pass that there was peace and exceeding great joy
in the remainder of the forty and ninth year.
Yea, and also there was continual peace and great joy
in the fiftieth year of the reign of the judges.

33 And in the fifty and first year of the reign of the judges,
there was peace also,
save it were the pride which began to enter into the church—
not into the church of God,
but into the hearts of the people
who professed to belong to the church of God.

34 And they were lifted up in pride,
even to the persecution of many of their brethren.

Now this was a great evil
which did cause the more humble part of the people
to suffer great persecutions and to wade through much affliction.

35 Nevertheless they did fast and pray oft
and did wax stronger and stronger in their humility
and firmer and firmer in the faith of Christ

unto the filling their souls with joy and consolation,
yea, even to the purifying and the sanctification of their hearts,
which sanctification cometh because of their yielding their hearts unto God.

36 And it came to pass that the fifty and second year ended in peace also,
save it were the exceeding great pride
which had got into the hearts of the people
— and it was because of their exceeding great riches
and their prosperity in the land —
and it did grow upon them from day to day.

37 And it came to pass in the fifty and third year of the reign of the judges,
Helaman died, and his eldest son Nephi began to reign in his stead.
And it came to pass that he did fill the judgment seat with justice and equity.
Yea, he did keep the commandments of God
and did walk in the ways of his father.

4 | 1 And it came to pass in the fifty and fourth year
there were many dissensions in the church.
And there was also a contention among the people,
insomuch that there was much bloodshed.

2 And the rebellious part were slain and driven out of the land,
and they did go unto the king of the Lamanites.

3 And it came to pass that they did endeavor
to stir up the Lamanites to war against the Nephites;
but behold, the Lamanites were exceeding fraid,
insomuch that they would not hearken to the words of those dissenters.

4 But it came to pass in the fifty and sixth year of the reign of the judges,
there were dissenters which went up from the Nephites unto the Lamanites;
and they succeeded with those others
in stirring them up to anger against the Nephites;
and they were all that year preparing for war.

5 And in the fifty and seventh year
they did come down against the Nephites to battle,
and they did commence the work of death;
yea, insomuch that in the fifty and eighth year of the reign of the judges,
they succeeded in obtaining possession of the land of Zarahemla,
yea, and also all the lands, even unto the land which was near the land Bountiful.

6 And the Nephites and the armies of Moronihah were driven,
even into the land of Bountiful.

7 And there they did fortify against the Lamanites,
from the west sea even unto the east,
it being a day's journey for a Nephite on the line
which they had fortified and stationed their armies

to defend their north country.

8 And thus those dissenters of the Nephites,
with the help of a numerous army of the Lamanites,
had obtained all the possession of the Nephites
which was in the land southward.
And all this was done in the fifty and eighth and ninth years
of the reign of the judges.

9 And it came to pass in the sixtieth year of the reign of the judges,
Moronihah did succeed with his armies in obtaining many parts of the land.
Yea, they retained many cities which had fallen into the hands of the Lamanites.

10 And it came to pass in the sixty and first year of the reign of the judges,
they succeeded in retaining even the half of all their possessions.

11 Now this great loss of the Nephites
and the great slaughter which was among them
would not have happened had it not been
for their wickedness and their abomination which was among them.
Yea, and it was among those also
which professed to belong to the church of God.

12 And it was because of the pride of their hearts,
because of their exceeding riches;
yea, it was because of their oppression to the poor,
withholding their food from the hungry,
withholding their clothing from the naked,
and smiting their humble brethren upon the cheeks,
making a mock of that which was sacred,
denying the spirit of prophecy and of revelation,
murdering, plundering, lying, stealing, committing adultery,
raising up in great contentions,
and dissenting away into the land of Nephi among the Lamanites.

13 And because of this their great wickedness
and their boastings in their own strength,
they were left in their own strength.
Therefore they did not prosper,
but were afflicted and smitten and driven before the Lamanites
until they had lost possession of almost all their lands.

14 But behold, Moronihah did preach many things unto the people
because of their iniquity.
And also Nephi and Lehi, which were the sons of Helaman,
did preach many things unto the people,
yea, and did prophesy many things unto them concerning their iniquities
and what should come unto them if they did not repent of their sins.

15 And it came to pass that they did repent;
    and inasmuch as they did repent, they did begin to prosper.
16 For when Moronihah saw that they did repent,
    he did venture to lead them forth from place to place and from city to city,
    even until they had retained the one half of their property
    and the one half of all their lands.
17 And thus ended the sixty and first year of the reign of the judges.

18 And it came to pass in the sixty and second year of the reign of the judges
    that Moronihah could obtain no more possessions over the Lamanites.
19 Therefore they did abandon their design to obtain the remainder of their lands,
    for so numerous was the Lamanites
    that it became impossible for the Nephites to obtain more power over them.
    Therefore Moronihah did employ all his armies
    in maintaining those parts which he had taken.

20 And it came to pass because of the greatness of the number of the Lamanites,
    the Nephites were in great fear lest they should be overpowered
    and trodden down and slain and destroyed.
21 Yea, they began to remember the prophecies of Alma
    and also the words of Mosiah.
    And they saw that they had been a stiffnecked people
    and that they had set at naught the commandments of God
22 and that they had altered and trampled under their feet the laws of Mosiah
    —or that which the Lord commanded him to give unto the people—
    and thus seeing that their laws had become corrupted
    and that they had become a wicked people,
    insomuch that they were wicked even like unto the Lamanites.
23 And because of their iniquity the church had began to dwindle.
    And they began to disbelieve in the spirit of prophecy
    and in the spirit of revelation.
    And the judgments of God did stare them in the face.
24 And they saw they had become weak like unto their brethren the Lamanites
    and that the Spirit of the Lord did no more preserve them.
    Yea, it had withdrawn from them
    because the Spirit of the Lord doth not dwell in unholy temples.
25 Therefore the Lord did cease to preserve them
    by his miraculous and matchless power,
    for they had fallen into a state of unbelief and awful wickedness.
    And they saw that the Lamanites were more exceeding numerous than they;
    and except they should cleave unto the Lord their God,
    they must unavoidably perish.
26 For behold, they saw that the strength of the Lamanites
    was as great as their strength, even man for man.

And thus had they fallen into this great transgression;
yea, thus had they become weak because of their transgression
in the space of not many years.

5 | 1 And it came to pass that in this same year,
behold, Nephi delivered up the judgment seat
to a man whose name was Cezoram.

2 For as their laws and their governments
were established by the voice of the people
and they which chose evil were more numerous
than they which chose good,
therefore they were ripening for destruction,
for the laws had become corrupted.

3 Yea, and this was not all.
They were a stiffnecked people,
insomuch that they could not be governed by the law nor justice
save it were to their destruction.

4 And it came to pass that Nephi had become weary because of their iniquity;
and he yielded up the judgment seat and took it upon him
to preach the word of God all the remainder of his days,
and his brother Lehi also all the remainder of his days.

5 For they remembered the words which their father Helaman spake unto them.
And these are the words which he spake:

6 Behold, my sons, I desire
that ye should remember to keep the commandments of God.
And I would that ye should declare unto the people these words.
Behold, I have given unto you the names of our first parents
which came out of the land of Jerusalem.
And this I have done
that when you remember your names
that ye may remember them.
And when ye remember them,
ye may remember their works.
And when ye remember their works,
ye may know how that it is said, and also written, that they were good.

7 Therefore my sons, I would that ye should do that which is good,
that it may be said of you, and also written,
even as it has been said and written of them.

8 And now my sons, behold, I have somewhat more to desire of you,
which desire is that ye may not do these things that ye may boast,
but that ye may do these things to lay up for yourselves a treasure in heaven
—yea, which is eternal and which fadeth not away—

yea, that ye may have that precious gift of eternal life
which we have reason to suppose hath been given to our fathers.

9 O remember, remember, my sons,
the words which king Benjamin spake unto his people.
Yea, remember that there is no other way nor means whereby man can be saved,
only through the atoning blood of Jesus Christ, which shall come.
Yea, remember that he cometh to redeem the world.

10 And remember also the words
which Amulek spake unto Zeezrom in the city of Ammonihah,
for he said unto him that the Lord surely should come to redeem his people,
but that he should not come to redeem them in their sins
but to redeem them from their sins.

11 And he hath power given unto him from the Father
to redeem them from their sins because of repentance.
Therefore he hath sent his angels
to declare the tidings of the conditions of repentance,
which bringeth unto the power of the Redeemer,
unto the salvation of their souls.

12 And now my sons, remember, remember
that it is upon the rock of our Redeemer,
which is Christ the Son of God,
that ye must build your foundation,
that when the devil shall send forth his mighty winds
—yea, his shafts in the whirlwind—
yea, when all his hail and his mighty storm shall beat upon you,
it shall have no power over you
to drag you down to the gulf of misery and endless woe
because of the rock upon which ye are built,
which is a sure foundation,
a foundation whereon if men buildeth they cannot fall.

13 And it came to pass that these were the words which Helaman taught to his sons.
Yea, he did teach them many things which are not written,
and also many things which are written;

14 and they did remember his words.
And therefore they went forth, keeping the commandments of God,
to teach the word of God among all the people of Nephi,
beginning at the city Bountiful,

15 and from thenceforth to the city of Gid,
and from the city of Gid to the city of Mulek,

16 and even from one city to another
until they had gone forth among all the people of Nephi

which were in the land southward,
and from thence into the land of Zarahemla among the Lamanites.

17 And it came to pass that they did preach with great power,
insomuch that they did confound many of those dissenters
which had gone over from the Nephites,
insomuch that they came forth and did confess their sins
and were baptized unto repentance
and immediately returned to the Nephites
to endeavor to repair unto them the wrongs which they had done.

18 And it came to pass that Nephi and Lehi did preach unto the Lamanites
with such great power and authority,
for they had power and authority given unto them that they might speak.
And they also had what they should speak given unto them.

19 Therefore they did speak unto the great astonishment of the Lamanites,
to the convincing them,
insomuch that there were eight thousand of the Lamanites
which were in the land of Zarahemla and round about
baptized unto repentance
and were convinced of the wickedness of the traditions of their fathers.

20 And it came to pass that
Nephi and Lehi did proceed from thence to go to the land of Nephi.

21 And it came to pass that
they were taken by an army of the Lamanites and cast into prison,
yea, even in that same prison
in which Ammon and his brethren were cast by the servants of Limhi.

22 And after they had been cast into prison many days without food,
behold, they went forth into the prison to take them,
that they might slay them.

23 And it came to pass that
Nephi and Lehi were encircled about as if by fire,
even insomuch that they durst not lay their hands upon them
for fear lest they should be burned.
Nevertheless Nephi and Lehi were not burned;
and they were as standing in the midst of fire and were not burned.

24 And when they saw
that they were encircled about with a pillar of fire
and that it burned them not,
their hearts did take courage;

25 for they saw that the Lamanites durst not lay their hands upon them,
neither durst they come near unto them,
but stood as if they were struck dumb with amazement.

26 And it came to pass that Nephi and Lehi did stand forth
and began to speak unto them, saying:
Fear not!
For behold, it is God that hath shown unto you this marvelous thing,
in the which is shewn unto you
that ye cannot lay your hands on us to slay us.

27 And behold, when they had said these words,
the earth shook exceedingly.
And the walls of the prison did shake
as if they were about to tumble to the earth;
but behold, they did not fall.
And behold, they that were in the prison
were Lamanites and Nephites which were dissenters.

28 And it came to pass that they were overshadowed with a cloud of darkness,
and an awful solemn fear came upon them.

29 And it came to pass that there came a voice
as if it were above the cloud of darkness, saying:
Repent ye, repent ye,
and seek no more to destroy my servants,
which I have sent unto you to declare good tidings.

30 And it came to pass when they heard this voice
and beheld that it was not a voice of thunder,
neither was it a voice of a great tumultuous noise,
but behold, it was a still voice of perfect mildness
as if it had been a whisper,
and it did pierce even to the very soul—

31 and notwithstanding the mildness of the voice,
behold, the earth shook exceedingly.
And the walls of the prison trembled again
as if it were about to tumble to the earth.
And behold, the cloud of darkness
which had overshadowed them did not disperse.

32 And behold, the voice came again, saying:
Repent ye, repent ye,
for the kingdom of heaven is at hand;
and seek no more to destroy my servants.
And it came to pass that the earth shook again and the walls trembled.

33 And also again the third time the voice came
and did speak unto them marvelous words which cannot be uttered by man.
And the walls did tremble again;

and the earth shook as if it were about to divide asunder.

34 And it came to pass that the Lamanites could not flee
because of the cloud of darkness which did overshadow them;
yea, and also they were immovable
because of the fear which did come upon them.

35 Now there was one among them
who was a Nephite by birth
who had once belonged to the church of God but had dissented from them.

36 And it came to pass that he turned him about;
and behold, he saw through the cloud of darkness the faces of Nephi and Lehi.
And behold, they did shine exceedingly, even as the face of angels.
And he beheld that they did lift their eyes to heaven
and they were in the attitude as if talking or lifting their voices
to some being which they beheld.

37 And it came to pass that this man did cry unto the multitude,
that they might turn and look.
And behold, there was power given unto them
that they did turn and look;
and they did behold the faces of Nephi and Lehi.

38 And they said unto the man:
Behold, what doth all these things mean?
And who is it with whom these men do converse?

39 Now the man's name was Aminadab.
And Aminadab saith unto them:
They do converse with the angels of God.

40 And it came to pass that the Lamanites said unto him:
What shall we do that this cloud of darkness
may be removed from overshadowing us?

41 And Aminadab saith unto them:
You must repent and cry unto the voice,
even until ye shall have faith in Christ,
which was taught unto you by Alma and Amulek and by Zeezrom.
And when ye shall do this,
the cloud of darkness shall be removed from overshadowing you.

42 And it came to pass that they all did begin
to cry unto the voice of him which had shook the earth.
Yea, they did cry even until the cloud of darkness was dispersed.

43 And it came to pass that when they cast their eyes about
and saw that the cloud of darkness was dispersed from overshadowing them,
and behold, they saw that they were encircled about

—yea, every soul—by a pillar of fire.

44 And Nephi and Lehi was in the midst of them.
Yea, they were encircled about;
yea, they were as if in the midst of a flaming fire.
Yet it did harm them not,
neither did it take hold upon the walls of the prison.
And they were filled with that joy which is unspeakable and full of glory.

45 And behold, the Holy Spirit of God did come down from heaven
and did enter into their hearts.
And they were filled as if with fire,
and they could speak forth marvelous words.

46 And it came to pass that there came a voice unto them,
yea, a pleasant voice, as if it were a whisper, saying:

47 Peace, peace be unto you
because of your faith in my Well Beloved,
which was from the foundation of the world.

48 And now when they heard this,
they cast up their eyes as if to behold from whence the voice came.
And behold, they saw the heavens open,
and angels came down out of heaven and ministered unto them.

49 And there were about three hundred souls which saw and heard these things.
And they were bid to go forth and marvel not,
neither should they doubt.

50 And it came to pass that they did go forth and did minister unto the people,
declaring throughout all the regions round about
all the things which they had heard and seen,
insomuch that the more part of the Lamanites were convinced of them
because of the greatness of the evidences which they had received.

51 And as many as were convinced did lay down their weapons of war,
and also their hatred and the tradition of their fathers.

52 And it came to pass that
they did yield up unto the Nephites the lands of their possession.

6 | 1 And it came to pass that when the sixty and second year
of the reign of the judges had ended,
all these things had happened;
and the Lamanites had become the more part of them a righteous people,
insomuch that their righteousness did exceed that of the Nephites
because of their firmness and their steadiness in the faith.

2 For behold, there were many of the Nephites
which had become hardened and impenitent and grossly wicked,

insomuch that they did reject the word of God
and all the preaching and the prophesying which did come among them.

3 Nevertheless the people of the church did have great joy
because of the conversion of the Lamanites,
yea, because of the church of God which had been established among them.
And they did fellowship one with another
and did rejoice one with another and did have great joy.

4 And it came to pass that
many of the Lamanites did come down into the land of Zarahemla
and did declare unto the people of the Nephites the manner of their conversion
and did exhort them to faith and repentance.

5 Yea, and many did preach with exceeding great power and authority,
unto the bringing down many of them into the depths of humility,
to be the humble followers of God and the Lamb.

6 And it came to pass that many of the Lamanites did go into the land northward.
And also Nephi and Lehi went into the land northward
to preach unto the people.
And thus ended the sixty and third year.

7 And behold, there was peace in all the land,
insomuch that the Nephites did go into whatsoever part of the land they would,
whether among the Nephites or the Lamanites.

8 And it came to pass that the Lamanites did also go whithersoever they would,
whether it were among the Lamanites or among the Nephites.
And thus they did have free intercourse one with another,
for to buy and to sell and to get gain according to their desire.

9 And it came to pass that they became exceeding rich,
both the Lamanites and the Nephites.
And they did have an exceeding plenty of gold and of silver
and of all manner of precious metals,
both in the land south and in the land north.

10 Now the land south was called Lehi;
and the land north was called Muloch,
which was after the son of Zedekiah.
For the Lord did bring Muloch into the land north
and Lehi into the land south.

11 And behold, there was all manner of gold in both these lands,
and of silver and of precious ore of every kind.
And there was also curious workmen
which did work all kinds of ore and did refine it.
And thus they did become rich.

12 They did raise grain in abundance, both in the north and in the south.

And they did flourish exceedingly, both in the north and in the south.
And they did multiply and wax exceeding strong in the land;
and they did raise many flocks and herds, yea, many fatlings.

13 Behold, their women did toil and spin
and did make all manner of cloth,
of fine twined linen and cloth of every kind,
to clothe their nakedness.
And thus the sixty and fourth year did pass away in peace.

14 And in the sixty and fifth year they did also have great joy and peace,
yea, much preaching and many prophecies concerning that which was to come.
And thus passed away the sixty and fifth year.

15 And it came to pass that in the sixty and sixth year of the reign of the judges,
behold, Cezoram was murdered by an unknown hand
as he sat upon the judgment seat.
And it came to pass that in the same year
that his son, which had been appointed by the people in his stead,
was also murdered.
And thus ended the sixty and sixth year.

16 And in the commencement of the sixty and seventh year,
the people began to grow exceeding wicked again.

17 For behold, the Lord had blessed them so long with the riches of the world
that they had not been stirred up to anger, to wars nor to bloodsheds.
Therefore they began to set their hearts upon their riches.
Yea, they began to seek to get gain
that they might be lifted up one above another.
Therefore they began to commit secret murders and to rob and to plunder
that they might get gain.

18 And now behold, those murderers and plunderers were a band
which had been formed by Kishcumen and Gaddianton.

And now it had came to pass that
there were many, even among the Nephites, of Gaddianton's band.
But behold, they were more numerous
among the more wicked part of the Lamanites.
And they were called Gaddianton's robbers and murderers.

19 And it was they which did murder the chief judge Cezoram and his son
while in the judgment seat.
And behold, they were not found.

20 And now it came to pass that
when the Lamanites found that there were robbers among them,
they were exceeding sorrowful.
And they did use every means, whatsoever was in their power,

to destroy them off the face of the earth.

21 But behold, Satan did stir up the hearts of the more parts of the Nephites,
insomuch that they did unite with those bands of robbers
and did enter into their covenants and their oaths,
that they would protect and preserve one another
in whatsoever difficult circumstances they should be placed in,
that they should not suffer for their murders
and their plunderings and their stealings.

22 And it came to pass that they did have their signs,
yea, their secret signs and their secret words—
and this that they might distinguish a brother
who had entered into the covenant,
that whatsoever wickedness his brother should do,
he should not be injured by his brother,
nor by those who did belong to his band who had taken this covenant.

23 And thus they might murder and plunder and steal
and commit whoredoms and all manner of wickedness
contrary to the laws of their country and also the laws of their God.

24 And whosoever of those which belonged to their band
should reveal unto the world of their wickedness and their abominations
should be tried, not according to the laws of their country,
but according to the laws of their wickedness,
which had been given by Gaddianton and Kishcumen.

25 Now behold, it is these secret oaths and covenants
which Alma commanded his son should not go forth unto the world
lest they should be a means of bringing down the people unto destruction.

26 Now behold, those secret oaths and covenants
did not come forth unto Gaddianton
from the records which were delivered unto Helaman;
but behold, they were put into the heart of Gaddianton
by that same being who did entice our first parents
to partake of the forbidden fruit—

27 yea, that same being who did plot with Cain
that if he would murder his brother Abel,
it should not be known unto the world.
And he did plot with Cain and his followers from that time forth.

28 And also it is that same being who put it into the hearts of the people
to build a tower sufficiently high that they might get to heaven.
And it was that same being
which led on the people which came from that tower into this land
which spread the works of darkness and abominations
over all the face of the land

until he dragged the people down
to an entire destruction and to an everlasting hell.

29 Yea, it is that same being who put it into the heart of Gaddianton
to still carry on the work of darkness and of secret murder.
And he hath brought it forth from the beginning of man,
even down to this time.

30 And behold, it is he which is the author of all sin.
And behold, he doth carry on his works of darkness and secret murder
and doth hand down their plots and their oaths
and their covenants and their plans of awful wickedness
from generation to generation,
according as he can get hold upon the hearts of the children of men.

31 And now behold, he had got great hold upon the hearts of the Nephites,
yea, insomuch that they had become exceeding wicked.
Yea, the more part of them had turned out of the way of righteousness
and did trample under their feet the commandments of God
and did turn unto their own ways
and did build up unto themselves idols of their gold and their silver.

32 And it came to pass that all these iniquities did come unto them
in the space of not many years,
insomuch that a more part of it had come unto them
in the sixty and seventh year of the reign of the judges over the people of Nephi.

33 And they did grow in their iniquities in the sixty and eighth year also,
to the great sorrow and lamentation of the righteous.

34 And thus we see that the Nephites did begin to dwindle in unbelief
and grow in wickedness and abominations,
while the Lamanites began to grow exceedingly in the knowledge of their God.
Yea, they did begin to keep his statutes and commandments
and to walk in truth and uprightness before him.

35 And thus we see that the Spirit of the Lord began to withdraw from the Nephites
because of the wickedness and the hardness of their hearts.

36 And thus we see that the Lord began to pour out his Spirit upon the Lamanites
because of their easiness and willingness to believe in his word.

37 And it came to pass that the Lamanites did hunt
the band of robbers of Gaddianton.
And they did preach the word of God among the more wicked part of them,
insomuch that this band of robbers was utterly destroyed
from among the Lamanites.

38 And it came to pass, on the other hand,
that the Nephites did build them up and support them,
beginning at the more wicked part of them,

until they had overspread all the land of the Nephites
and had seduced the more part of the righteous
until they had come down to believe in their works
and partake of their spoils
and to join with them in their secret murders and combinations.

39 And thus they did obtain the sole management of the government,
insomuch that they did trample under their feet and smite and rend
and turn their backs upon the poor and the meek and humble followers of God.

40 And thus we see that they were in an awful state
and ripening for an everlasting destruction.

41 And it came to pass that thus ended the sixty and eighth year
of the reign of the judges over the people of Nephi.

The Prophecy of Nephi
the son of Helaman

God threatens the people of Nephi
that he will visit them in his anger to their utter destruction
except they repent of their wickedness.

God smiteth the people of Nephi with pestilence;
they repent and turn unto him.

Samuel, a Lamanite, prophesies unto the Nephites.

7 | 1 Behold, now it came to pass in the sixty and ninth year
of the reign of the judges over the people of the Nephites
that Nephi the son of Helaman returned
to the land of Zarahemla from the land northward.

2 For he had been forth among the people
which was in the land northward
and did preach the word of God unto them
and did prophesy many things unto them.

3 And they did reject all his words,
insomuch that he could not stay among them
but returned again unto the land of his nativity.

4 And seeing the people in a state of such awful wickedness
and those Gaddianton robbers filling the judgment seats,
having usurped the power and authority of the land,
laying aside the commandments of God

and not in the least aright before him,
doing no justice unto the children of men,
5 condemning the righteous because of their righteousness,
letting the guilty and the wicked go unpunished because of their money—
and moreover, to be held in office at the head of government,
to rule and to do according to their wills,
that they might get gain and glory of the world
and moreover that they might the more easy commit adultery
and steal and kill and do according to their own wills
6 —now this great iniquity had come upon the Nephites
in the space of not many years—
and when Nephi saw it,
his heart was swollen with sorrow within his breast.

And he did exclaim in the agony of his soul:
7 O that I could have had my days in the days
when my father Nephi first came out of the land of Jerusalem,
that I could have joyed with him in the promised land.
Then were his people easy to be entreated,
firm to keep the commandments of God,
and slow to be led to do iniquity.
And they were quick to hearken unto the words of the Lord.
8 Yea, if my days could have been in them days,
then would my soul have had joy in the righteousness of my brethren.
9 But behold, I am consigned that these are my days
and that my soul shall be filled with sorrow
because of this the wickedness of my brethren.

10 And behold, now it came to pass that it was upon a tower
which was in the garden of Nephi, which was by the highway
which led to the chief market which was in the city of Zarahemla.
Therefore as Nephi had bowed himself upon the tower which was in his garden
—which tower was also near unto the garden gate which was by the highway—
11 and it came to pass that there was certain men passing by
and saw Nephi as he was a pouring out his soul unto God upon the tower;
and they ran and told the people what they had seen.
And the people came together in multitudes
that they might know the cause of so great mourning
for the wickedness of the people.

12 And now when Nephi arose,
he beheld the multitudes of people which had gathered together.
13 And it came to pass that he opened his mouth and said unto them:

Behold, why have ye gathered yourselves together?
That I may tell you of your iniquities?

14 Yea, because I have got upon my tower
that I might pour out my soul unto my God
because of the exceeding sorrow of my heart,
which is because of your iniquities?

15 And because of my mourning and lamentation
ye have gathered yourselves together and do marvel?
Yea, and ye have great need to marvel!
Yea, ye had ought to marvel because ye are given away
that the devil hath got so great hold upon your hearts.

16 Yea, how could ye have given away to the enticing of him
who art seeking to hurl away your souls
down to everlasting misery and endless woe?

17 O repent ye, repent ye!
Why will ye die?
Turn ye, turn ye unto the Lord your God!
Why hath he forsaken you?

18 It is because you have hardened your hearts.
Yea, ye will not hearken unto the voice of the good shepherd.
Yea, ye have provoked him to anger against you.

19 And behold, instead of gathering you,
except ye will repent,
behold, he shall scatter you forth
that ye shall become meat for dogs and wild beasts.

20 O how could you have forgotten your God
in the very day that he hath delivered you?

21 But behold, it is to get gain, to be praised of men,
yea, and that ye might get gold and silver.
And ye have set your hearts upon the riches and the vain things of this world,
for the which ye do murder and plunder and steal
and bear false witness against your neighbor
and do all manner of iniquity.

22 And for this cause
woe shall come unto you except ye shall repent.
For if ye will not repent,
behold, this great city
—and also all those great cities which are round about
which are in the land of our possession—
shall be taken away,
that ye shall have no place in them.

For behold, the Lord will not grant unto you strength,
as he hath hitherto done,
to withstand against your enemies.

23 For behold, thus saith the Lord:
I will not shew unto the wicked of my strength,
to one more than the other,
save it be unto those who repenteth of their sins and hearken unto my words.

Now therefore I would that ye should behold, my brethren,
that it shall be better for the Lamanites than for you except ye shall repent.

24 For behold, they are more righteous than you,
for they have not sinned against that great knowledge which ye have received.
Therefore the Lord will be merciful unto them.
Yea, he will lengthen out their days and increase their seed,
even when thou shalt be utterly destroyed except thou shalt repent.

25 Yea, woe be unto you because of that great abomination
which hath come among you;
and ye have united yourselves unto it,
yea, to that secret band which was established by Gaddianton.

26 Yea, woe shall come unto you because of that pride
which ye have suffered to enter your hearts,
which hath lifted you up beyond that which is good
because of your exceeding great riches.

27 Yea, woe be unto you because of your wickedness and abominations.

28 And except ye repent, ye shall perish;
yea, even your lands shall be taken from you,
and ye shall be destroyed from off the face of the earth.

29 Behold, now I do not say that these things shall be, of myself,
because it is not of myself that I know these things.
But behold, I know that these things are true
because the Lord God hath made them known unto me;
therefore I testify that they shall be.

8 | 1 And now it came to pass that when Nephi had said these words,
behold, there were men which were judges
which also belonged to the secret band of Gaddianton,
and they were angry,
and they cried out against him, saying unto the people:
Why do ye not seize upon this man and bring him forth,
that he may be condemned according to the crime which he hath done?

2 Why seest thou this man and hearest him
revile against this people and against our law?

3 For behold, Nephi had spoken unto them

concerning the corruptness of their law.

Yea, many things did Nephi speak which cannot be written.

And nothing did he speak which were contrary to the commandments of God.

4 And those judges were angry with him
because he spake plain unto them concerning their secret works of darkness.
Nevertheless they durst not lay their own hands upon him,
for they feared the people lest they should cry out against them.

5 Therefore they did cry unto the people, saying:
Why do ye suffer this man to revile against us?
For behold, he doth condemn all this people, even unto destruction—
yea, and also that these our great cities shall be taken from us,
that we shall have no place in them.

6 And now we know that this is impossible.
For behold, we are powerful and our cities great;
therefore our enemies can have no power over us.

7 And it came to pass that
thus they did stir up the people to anger against Nephi
and raised contentions among them.
For there were some which did cry out:
Let this man alone, for he is a good man;
and those things which he saith will surely come to pass except we repent.

8 Yea, behold, all the judgments will come upon us
which he hath testified unto us,
for we know that he hath testified aright unto us concerning our iniquities;
and behold, they are many.
And he knoweth as well all things which shall befall us
as he knoweth of our iniquities.

9 Yea, and behold, if he had not been a prophet,
he could not have testified concerning those things.

10 And it came to pass that those people
which sought to destroy Nephi
were compelled because of their fear
that they did not lay their hands on him.
Therefore he began again to speak unto them,
seeing that he had gained favor in the eyes of some,
insomuch that the remainder of them did fear.

11 Therefore he was constrained to speak more unto them, saying:
Behold, my brethren, have ye not read
that God gave power unto one man, even Moses,
to smite upon the waters of the Red Sea
and they departed hither and thither,

insomuch that the Israelites, which were our fathers,
came through upon dry ground;
and the waters closed upon the armies of the Egyptians and swallowed them up.

12 And now behold, if God gave unto this man such power,
then why should ye dispute among yourselves
and say that he hath given unto me no power
whereby I may know concerning the judgments
that shall come upon you except ye repent?
13 But behold, ye not only deny my words,
but ye also deny all the words which hath been spoken by our fathers,
and also the words which was spoken by this man Moses,
which had such great power given unto him—
yea, the words which he hath spoken concerning the coming of the Messiah.
14 Yea, did he not bear record that the Son of God should come?
And as he lifted up the brazen serpent in the wilderness,
even so should he be lifted up which should come.
15 And as many as should look upon that serpent should live,
even so as many as should look upon the Son of God with faith,
having a contrite spirit, might live,
even unto that life which is eternal.

16 And now behold, Moses did not only testify of these things,
but also all the holy prophets from his day even to the days of Abraham.
17 Yea, and behold, Abraham saw of his coming
and was filled with gladness and did rejoice.
18 Yea, and behold, I say unto you that Abraham not only knew of these things,
but there were many before the days of Abraham
which were called by the order of God,
yea, even after the order of his Son—
and this that it should be shewn unto the people
a great many thousand years before his coming
that even redemption should come unto them.

19 And now I would that ye should know
that ever since the days of Abraham
there hath been many prophets that hath testified these things.
Yea, behold, the prophet Zenos did testify boldly,
for the which he was slain—
20 and behold, also Zenoch and also Ezaias and also Isaiah and Jeremiah,
Jeremiah being that same prophet
which testified of the destruction of Jerusalem
—and now we know that Jerusalem was destroyed
according to the words of Jeremiah—

O then why not the Son of God come according to his prophecy?

21 And now will ye dispute that Jerusalem was not destroyed?
Will ye say that the sons of Zedekiah were not slain,
all except it were Muloch?
Yea, and do ye not behold that the seed of Zedekiah are with us
and they were driven out of the land of Jerusalem?

But behold, this is not all.

22 Our father Lehi was driven out of Jerusalem
because he testified of these things.
Nephi also testified of these things,
and also almost all of our fathers, even down to this time.
Yea, they have testified of the coming of Christ
and have looked forward
and have rejoiced in his day, which is to come.

23 And behold, he is God;
and he is with them,
and he did manifest himself unto them,
that they were redeemed by him.
And they gave unto him glory because of that which is to come.

24 And now seeing ye know these things
and cannot deny them except ye shall lie,
therefore in this ye have sinned,
for ye have rejected all these things,
notwithstanding so many evidences which ye have received.
Yea, even ye have received all things
—both things in heaven and all things which are in earth—
as a witness that they are true.

25 But behold, ye have rejected the truth
and rebelled against your holy God.
And even at this time,
instead of laying up for yourselves treasures in heaven
—where nothing doth corrupt
and where nothing can come which is unclean—
ye are heaping up for yourselves wrath against the day of judgment.

26 Yea, even at this time ye are ripening
because of your murders and your fornication and wickedness
for everlasting destruction.
Yea, and except ye repent,
it will come unto you soon.

27 Yea, behold, it is now even at your doors.
Yea, go ye in unto the judgment seat and search;

and behold, your judge is murdered,
and he lieth in his blood.
And he hath been murdered by his brother,
who seeketh to sit in the judgment seat.
28 And behold, they both belong to your secret band
whose author is Gaddianton and the evil one,
which seeketh to destroy the souls of men.

9 | 1 Behold, now it came to pass that
when Nephi had spoken these words,
certain men which were among them ran to the judgment seat;
yea, even there were five which went.
And they said among themselves as they went:
2 Behold, now we will know of a surety
whether this man be a prophet
and God hath commanded him
to prophesy such marvelous things unto us.
Behold, we do not believe that he hath;
yea, we do not believe that he is a prophet.
Nevertheless, if this thing
which he hath said concerning the chief judge be true,
that he be dead,
then will we believe
that the other words which he hath spoken is true.

3 And it came to pass that they ran in their might
and came in unto the judgment seat;
and behold, the chief judge had fallen to the earth
and did lie in his blood.
4 And now behold, when they saw this,
they were astonished exceedingly,
insomuch that they fell to the earth,
for they had not believed the words
which Nephi had spoken concerning the chief judge.
5 But now when they saw, they believed;
and fear came upon them
lest all the judgments which Nephi had spoken should come upon the people.
Therefore they did quake and had fallen to the earth.

6 Now immediately when the judge had been murdered,
he being stabbed by his brother by a garb of secrecy
—and he fled—
and the servants ran and told the people,

raising the cry of murder among them.

7   And behold, the people did gather themselves together
    unto the place of the judgment seat.
    And behold, to their astonishment they saw those five men
    which had fallen to the earth.

8   And now behold, the people knew nothing concerning the multitude
    which had gathered together at the garden of Nephi.
    Therefore they said among themselves:
    These men are they which have murdered the judge;
    and God hath smitten them that they could not flee from us.

9   And it came to pass that they laid hold on them
    and bound them and cast them into prison.
    And there was a proclamation sent abroad
    that the judge was slain
    and that the murderers had been taken and was cast into prison.

10 And it came to pass that on the morrow
    the people did assemble themselves together to mourn and to fast
    at the burial of the great and chief judge, which had been slain.

11 And thus were also those judges
    which were at the garden of Nephi and heard his words
    were also gathered together at the burial.

12 And it came to pass that they inquired among the people, saying:
    Where are the five which was sent to inquire concerning the chief judge,
    whether he was dead?
    And they answered and said:
    Concerning this five which ye say ye have sent, we know not.
    But there are five which are the murderers,
    whom we have cast into prison.

13 And it came to pass that
    the judges desired that they should be brought;
    and they were brought.
    And behold, they were the five which were sent.
    And behold, the judges inquired of them to know concerning the matter.
    And they told them all that they had done, saying:

14 We ran and came to the place of the judgment seat.
    And when we saw all things even as Nephi had testified,
    we were astonished, insomuch that we fell to the earth.
    And when we were recovered from our astonishment,
    behold, they cast us into prison.

15 Now as for the murder of this man,

we know not who hath done it.
And only this much we know:
we ran and came according as ye desired;
and behold, he was dead according to the words of Nephi.

16 And now it came to pass that
the judges did expound the matter unto the people
and did cry out against Nephi, saying:
Behold, we know that this Nephi must have agreed
with some one to slay the judge;
and then he might declare it unto us,
that he might convert us unto his faith,
that he might raise himself to be a great man,
chosen of God and a prophet.
17 And now behold, we will detect this man,
and he shall confess his fault
and make known unto us the true murderer of this judge.

18 And it came to pass that the five were liberated on the day of the burial.
Nevertheless they did rebuke the judges
in the words which they had spoken against Nephi
and did contend with them one by one,
insomuch that they did confound them.
19 Nevertheless they caused that Nephi should be taken and bound
and brought before the multitude.
And they began to question him in divers ways that they might cross him,
that they might accuse him to death,
20 saying unto him:
Thou art confederate!
Who is this man that hath done this murder?
Now tell us and acknowledge thy fault!
—saying—
Behold, here is money!
And also we will grant unto thee thy life
if thou wilt tell us and acknowledge the agreement
which thou hast made with him.

21 But Nephi saith unto them:
O ye fools, ye uncircumcised of heart,
ye blind and ye stiffnecked people,
do ye know how long the Lord your God will suffer you
that ye shall go on in this your ways of sin?
22 O ye had ought to begin to howl and mourn

because of the great destruction
at this time which doth await you
except ye shall repent.

23 Behold, ye say that I have agreed with a man
that he should murder Seezoram, our chief judge.
But behold, I say unto you
that this is because I have testified unto you
that ye might know concerning this thing,
yea, even for a witness unto you
that I did know of the wickedness and abominations which is among you.

24 And because I have done this,
ye say that I have agreed with a man that he should do this thing.
Yea, because I shewed unto you this sign,
ye are angry with me and seek to destroy my life.

25 And now behold, I will shew unto you another sign;
and see if ye will in this thing seek to destroy me.

26 Behold, I say unto you:
Go to the house of Seantum, which is the brother of Seezoram,
and say unto him:

27 Hath Nephi the pretended prophet,
which doth prophesy so much evil concerning this people,
agreed with thee in the which ye have murdered Seezoram,
which is your brother?

28 And behold, he shall say unto you: Nay.

29 And ye shall say unto him:
Have ye murdered your brother?

30 And he shall stand with fear and wist not what to say.
And behold, he shall deny unto you;
and he shall make as if he were astonished.
Nevertheless he shall declare unto you that he is innocent.

31 But behold, ye shall examine him,
and ye shall find blood upon the skirts of his cloak.

32 And when ye have seen this, ye shall say:
From whence cometh this blood?
Do we not know that it is the blood of your brother?

33 And then shall he tremble and shall look pale,
even as if death had come upon him.

34 And then shall ye say:
Because of this fear and this paleness which hath come upon your face,
behold, we know that thou art guilty.

35 And then shall greater fear come upon him;
and then shall he confess unto you

and deny no more that he hath done this murder.

36 And then shall he say unto you
that I Nephi knew nothing concerning the matter
save it were given unto me by the power of God.
And then shall ye know that I am an honest man
and that I am sent unto you from God.

37 And it came to pass that they went
and did even according as Nephi had said unto them.
And behold, the words which he had said were true;
for according to the words he did deny,
and also according to the words he did confess.

38 And he was brought to prove that he himself was the very murderer,
insomuch that the five were set at liberty, and also was Nephi.

39 And there were some of the Nephites which believed on the words of Nephi.
And there were some also which believed because of the testimony of the five,
for they had been converted while they were in prison.

40 And now there were some among the people
which said that Nephi was a prophet.

41 And there were others which said:
Behold, he is a god;
for except he was a god,
he could not know of all things.
For behold, he hath told us the thoughts of our hearts,
and also hath told us things—
and even he hath brought unto our knowledge
the true murderer of our chief judge.

10 | 1 And it came to pass that there arose a division among the people,
insomuch that they divided hither and thither and went their ways,
leaving Nephi alone as he was standing in the midst of them.

2 And it came to pass that Nephi went his way towards his own house,
pondering upon the things which the Lord had shewn unto him.

3 And it came to pass as he was thus pondering,
being much cast down because of the wickedness of the people of the Nephites,
their secret works of darkness
and their murderings and their plunderings
and all manner of iniquities—
and it came to pass as he was thus pondering in his heart,
behold, a voice came unto him, saying:

4 Blessed art thou Nephi for those things which thou hast done.
For I have beheld how thou hast with unwearyingness
declared the word which I have given unto thee
unto this people.

And thou hast not feared them and hast not sought thine own life,
but hath sought my will and to keep my commandments.

5 And now because thou hast done this with such unwearyingness,
behold, I will bless thee forever.
And I will make thee mighty in word and in deed, in faith and in works,
yea, even that all things shall be done unto thee according to thy word,
for thou shalt not ask that which is contrary to my will.

6 Behold, thou art Nephi and I am God.
Behold, I declare it unto thee in the presence of mine angels
that ye shall have power over this people
and shall smite the earth with famine and with pestilence and destruction
according to the wickedness of this people.

7 Behold, I give unto you power
that whatsoever ye shall seal on earth shall be sealed in heaven,
and whatsoever ye shall loose on earth shall be loosed in heaven;
and thus shall ye have power among this people.

8 And thus if ye shall say unto this temple:
It shall be rent in twain!
—and it shall be done.

9 And if ye shall say unto this mountain:
Be thou cast down and become smooth!
—and it shall be done.

10 And behold, if ye shall say
that God shall smite this people,
it shall come to pass.

11 And now behold, I command you
that ye shall go and declare unto this people
that thus saith the Lord God, who is the Almighty:
Except ye repent, ye shall be smitten, even unto destruction.

12 And behold, now it came to pass that
when the Lord had spoken these words unto Nephi,
he did stop and did not go unto his own house,
but did return unto the multitudes
which were scattered about upon the face of the land
and began to declare unto them the word of the Lord
which had been spoken unto him
concerning their destruction if they did not repent.

13 Now behold, notwithstanding that great miracle which Nephi had done
in telling them concerning the death of the chief judge,
they did harden their hearts
and did not hearken unto the words of the Lord.

14 Therefore Nephi did declare unto them the word of the Lord, saying:
Except ye repent, thus saith the Lord, ye shall be smitten, even unto destruction.

15 And it came to pass that when Nephi had declared unto them the word,
behold, they did still harden their hearts
and would not hearken unto his words.
Therefore they did revile against him
and did seek to lay their hands upon him
that they might cast him into prison.

16 But behold, the power of God was with him;
and they could not take him to cast him into prison,
for he was taken by the Spirit and conveyed away out of the midst of them.

17 And it came to pass that
thus he did go forth in the Spirit from multitude to multitude
declaring the word of God,
even until he had declared it unto them all,
or sent it forth among all the people.

18 And it came to pass that they would not hearken unto his words.
And there began to be contentions,
insomuch that they were divided against themselves
and began to slay one another with the sword.

19 And thus ended the seventy and first year
of the reign of the judges over the people of Nephi.

11 | 1 And now it came to pass
in the seventy and second year of the reign of the judges
that the contentions did increase,
insomuch that there were wars throughout all the land
among all the people of Nephi.

2 And it was this secret band of robbers
which did carry on this work of destruction and wickedness.
And this war did last all that year;
and in the seventy and third year it did also last.

3 And it came to pass that in this year Nephi did cry unto the Lord, saying:

4 O Lord, do not suffer that this people shall be destroyed by the sword.
But O Lord, rather let there be a famine in the land
to stir them up in remembrance of the Lord their God;
and perhaps they will repent and turn unto thee.

5 And so it was done according to the words of Nephi,
and there was a great famine upon the land among all the people of Nephi.
And thus in the seventy and fourth year the famine did continue;

and the work of destruction did cease by the sword
but became sore by famine.

6 And this work of destruction did also continue in the seventy and fifth year,
for the earth was smitten
that it was dry and did not yield forth grain in the season of grain.
And the whole earth was smitten,
even among the Lamanites as well as among the Nephites,
so that they were smitten
that they did perish by thousands in the more wicked parts of the land.

7 And it came to pass that the people saw
that they were about to perish by famine.
And they began to remember the Lord their God,
and they began to remember the words of Nephi.

8 And the people began to plead with their chief judges and their leaders
that they would say unto Nephi:
Behold, we know that thou art a man of God.
And therefore cry unto the Lord our God
that he turn away from us this famine, lest all the words
which thou hast spoken concerning our destruction be fulfilled.

9 And it came to pass that the judges did say unto Nephi
according to the words which had been desired.

And it came to pass that when Nephi saw
that the people had repented and did humble themselves in sackcloth,
he cried again unto the Lord, saying:

10 O Lord, behold, this people repenteth.
And they have swept away the band of Gaddianton from amongst them,
insomuch that they have become extinct;
and they have concealed their secret plans in the earth.

11 Now, O Lord, because of this their humility,
wilt thou turn away thine anger
and let thine anger be appeased in the destruction of those wicked men
whom thou hast already destroyed?

12 O Lord, wilt thou turn away thine anger—yea, thy fierce anger—
and cause that this famine may cease in this land?

13 O Lord, wilt thou hearken unto me
and cause that it may be done according to my words
and send forth rain upon the face of the earth,
that she may bring forth her fruit and her grain in the season of grain?

14 O Lord, thou didst hearken unto my words when I said:
Let there be a famine that the pestilence of the sword might cease.

And I know that thou wilt even at this time hearken unto my words,
for thou saidst that if this people repent, I will spare them.

15 Yea, O Lord, and thou seest that they have repented
because of the famine and the pestilence and destruction
which has come unto them.

16 And now, O Lord, wilt thou turn away thine anger
and try again if they will serve thee?
And if so, O Lord, thou canst bless them
according to thy word which thou hast said.

17 And it came to pass that in the seventy and sixth year
the Lord did turn away his anger from the people
and caused that rain should fall upon the earth,
insomuch that it did bring forth her fruit in the season of her fruit.
And it came to pass that it did bring forth her grain in the season of her grain.

18 And behold, the people did rejoice and glorify God,
and the whole face of the land was filled with rejoicing.
And they did no more seek to destroy Nephi,
but they did esteem him as a great prophet and a man of God,
having great power and authority given unto him from God.

19 And behold, Lehi his brother was not a whit behind him
as to things pertaining to righteousness.

20 And thus it did come to pass that
the people of Nephi began to prosper again in the land
and began to build up their waste places
and began to multiply and spread,
even until they did cover the whole face of the land,
both on the northward and on the southward,
from the sea west to the sea east.

21 And it came to pass that the seventy and sixth year did end in peace;
and the seventy and seventh year began in peace.
And the church did spread throughout the face of all the land.
And the more part of the people,
both the Nephites and the Lamanites,
did belong to the church.
And they did have exceeding great peace in the land.
And thus ended the seventy and seventh year.

22 And also they had peace in the seventy and eighth year,
save it were a few contentions concerning the points of doctrine
which had been laid down by the prophets.

23 And in the seventy and ninth year there began to be much strife.

But it came to pass that Nephi and Lehi and many of their brethren,
which knew concerning the true points of doctrine,
having many revelations daily,
therefore they did preach unto the people,
insomuch that they did put an end to their strife in that same year.

24 And it came to pass that in the eightieth year
of the reign of the judges over the people of Nephi,
there were a certain number of the dissenters from the people of Nephi
which had some years before gone over unto the Lamanites
and took upon themselves the name of Lamanites
—and also a certain number which were real descendants of the Lamanites,
being stirred up to anger by them, or by those dissenters—
therefore they commenced a war with their brethren.

25 And they did commit murder and plunder;
and then they would retreat back into the mountains
and into the wilderness and secret places,
hiding themselves that they could not be discovered,
receiving daily an addition to their numbers,
inasmuch as there were dissenters that went forth unto them.

26 And thus in time—yea, even in the space of not many years—
they became an exceeding great band of robbers.
And they did search out all the secret plans of Gaddianton,
and thus they became robbers of Gaddianton.

27 Now behold, these robbers did make great havoc,
yea, even great destruction among the people of Nephi
and also among the people of the Lamanites.

28 And it came to pass that it was expedient
that there should be a stop put to this work of destruction.
Therefore they sent an army of strong men
into the wilderness and upon the mountains
to search out this band of robbers and to destroy them.

29 But behold, it came to pass that in that same year
they were driven back, even into their own lands.
And thus ended the eightieth year
of the reign of the judges over the people of Nephi.

30 And it came to pass in the commencement of the eighty and first year
they did go forth again against this band of robbers and did destroy many.
And they were also visited with much destruction;

31 and they were again obliged to return
out of the wilderness and out of the mountains unto their own lands
because of the exceeding greatness of the numbers of those robbers

which infested the mountains and the wilderness.

32 And it came to pass that thus ended this year.
And the robbers did still increase and wax strong,
insomuch that they did defy the whole armies of the Nephites
and also of the Lamanites.
And they did cause great fear to come unto the people
upon all the face of the land.

33 Yea, for they did visit many parts of the land
and did do great destruction unto them,
yea, did kill many and did carry away others captive into the wilderness,
yea, and more especially their women and their children.

34 Now this great evil which came unto the people because of their iniquity
did stir them up again in remembrance of the Lord their God.

35 And thus ended the eighty and first year of the reign of the judges.

36 And in the eighty and second year
they began again to forget the Lord their God.
And in the eighty and third year
they began to wax strong in iniquity.
And in the eighty and fourth year they did not mend their ways.

37 And it came to pass in the eighty and fifth year
they did wax stronger and stronger in their pride and in their wickedness.
And thus they were ripening again for destruction.

38 And thus ended the eighty and fifth year.

12 | 1 And thus we can behold how false
and also the unsteadiness of the hearts of the children of men.
Yea, we can see that the Lord in his great infinite goodness
doth bless and prosper those who put their trust in him.

2 Yea, and we may see at the very time when he doth prosper his people
—yea, in the increase of their fields, their flocks and their herds,
and in gold and in silver
and in all manner of precious things of every kind—
and art sparing their lives
and delivering them out of the hands of their enemies,
softening the hearts of their enemies,
that they should not declare wars against them,
yea, and in fine, doing all things for the welfare and happiness of his people,
yea, then is the time that they do harden their hearts
and do forget the Lord their God
and do trample under their feet the Holy One—
yea, and this because of their ease and their exceeding great prosperity.

3 And thus we see that

except the Lord doth chasten his people with many afflictions,
yea, except he doth visit them with death and with terror
and with famine and with all manner of pestilences,
they will not remember him.

4 O how foolish and how vain and how evil and devilish,
and how quick to do iniquity and how slow to do good,
are the children of men;
yea, how quick to hearken unto the words of the evil one
and to set their hearts upon the vain things of the world;

5 yea, how quick to be lifted up in pride;
yea, how quick to boast and do all manner of that which is iniquity;
and how slow are they to remember the Lord their God
and to give ear unto his counsels;
yea, how slow to walk in wisdom's paths.

6 Behold, they do not desire that the Lord their God, who hath created them,
should rule and reign over them.
Notwithstanding his great goodness and his mercy towards them,
they do set at naught his counsels
and they will not that he should be their guide.

7 O how great is the nothingness of the children of men;
yea, even they are less than the dust of the earth.

8 For behold, the dust of the earth moveth hither and thither,
to the dividing asunder at the command of our great and everlasting God.

9 Yea, behold, at his voice doth the hills and the mountains tremble and quake.

10 And by the power of his voice they are broken up and become smooth,
yea, even like unto a valley.

11 Yea, by the power of his voice doth the whole earth shake;

12 yea, by the power of his voice doth the foundations rock,
even to the very center.

13 Yea, and if he saith unto the earth: Move!
—and it is moved.

14 Yea, if he say unto the earth:
Thou shalt go back, that it lengthen out the day for many hours
—and it is done.

15 And thus according to his word the earth goeth back,
and it appeareth unto man that the sun standeth still.
Yea, and behold, this is so;
for sure it is the earth that moveth and not the sun.

16 And behold also, if he saith unto the waters of the great deep:
Be thou dried up!

—and it is done.

17 Behold, if he saith unto this mountain:
Be thou raised up and come over and fall upon that city that it be buried up!
—and behold, it is done.

18 And behold, if a man hideth up a treasure in the earth and the Lord shall say:
Let it be accursed because of the iniquity of him that hath hid it up!
—behold, it shall be accursed.

19 And if the Lord shall say:
Be thou accursed that no man shall find thee
from this time henceforth and forever!
—and behold, no man getteth it henceforth and forever.

20 And behold, if the Lord shall say unto a man:
Because of thine iniquities thou shalt be accursed forever
—and it shall be done.

21 And if the Lord shall say:
Because of thine iniquities thou shalt be cut off from my presence
—and he will cause that it shall be so.

22 And woe unto whom he shall say this;
for it shall be unto him that will do iniquity,
and he cannot be saved.

Therefore for this cause, that men might be saved,
hath repentance been declared.

23 Therefore blessed are they who will repent
and hearken unto the voice of the Lord their God,
for these are they that shall be saved.

24 And may God grant in his great fullness
that men might be brought unto repentance and good works,
that they might be restored unto grace for grace according to their works.

25 And I would that all men might be saved.
But we read that in that great and last day
there are some which shall be cast out,
yea, which shall be cast off from the presence of the Lord,

26 yea, which shall be consigned to a state of endless misery,
fulfilling the words which saith:
They that have done good shall have everlasting life;
and they that have done evil shall have everlasting damnation.
And thus it is.
Amen.

The prophecy of Samuel the Lamanite to the Nephites.

13 | 1 And now it came to pass in the eighty and sixth year
the Nephites did still remain in wickedness—yea, in great wickedness—
while the Lamanites did observe strictly to keep the commandments of God
according to the law of Moses.

2 And it came to pass that in this year
there was one Samuel, a Lamanite, came into the land of Zarahemla
and began to preach unto the people.
And it came to pass that he did preach many days repentance unto the people.
And they did cast him out,
and he was about to return to his own land.

3 But behold, the voice of the Lord came unto him,
that he should return again
and prophesy unto the people
whatsoever things should come into his heart.

4 And it came to pass that they would not suffer
that he should enter into the city.
Therefore he went and got upon the wall thereof
and stretched forth his hand and cried with a loud voice
and prophesied unto the people whatsoever things the Lord put into his heart.

5 And he said unto them:
Behold, I Samuel, a Lamanite, do speak the words of the Lord
which he doth put into my heart.
And behold, he hath put it into my heart to say unto this people
that the sword of justice hangeth over this people;
and four hundred years passeth not away
save the sword of justice falleth upon this people.

6 Yea, heavy destruction awaiteth this people.
And it surely cometh unto this people;
and nothing can save this people
save it be repentance and faith on the Lord Jesus Christ,
which surely shall come into the world
and shall suffer many things
and shall be slain for his people.

7 And behold, an angel of the Lord hath declared it unto me;
and he did bring glad tidings to my soul.
And behold, I was sent unto you to declare it unto you also,
that ye might have glad tidings.

But behold, ye would not receive me.

8 Therefore thus saith the Lord:
Because of the hardness of the hearts of the people of the Nephites,
except they repent,
I will take away my word from them
and I will withdraw my Spirit from them.
And I will suffer them no longer,
and I will turn the hearts of their brethren against them.

9 And four hundred years shall not pass away
before I will cause that they shall be smitten.
Yea, I will visit them with the sword and with famine and with pestilence;

10 yea, I will visit them in my fierce anger.
And there shall be those of the fourth generation
which shall live, of your enemies,
to behold your utter destruction.
And this shall surely come except ye repent, saith the Lord.
And those of the fourth generation shall visit your destruction.

11 But if ye will repent and return unto the Lord your God,
I will turn away mine anger, saith the Lord.
Yea, thus saith the Lord:
Blessed are they who will repent and turn unto me,
but woe unto him that repenteth not.

12 Yea, woe unto this great city of Zarahemla!
For behold, it is because of they which are righteous that it is saved.
Yea, woe unto this great city!
For I perceive, saith the Lord, that there are many,
yea, even the more part of this great city,
that will harden their hearts against me, saith the Lord.

13 But blessed are they who will repent,
for them will I spare.
But behold, if it were not for the righteous which are in this great city,
behold, I would cause that fire should come down out of heaven and destroy it.

14 But behold, it is for the righteous' sake that it is spared.

But behold, the time cometh, saith the Lord,
that when ye shall cast out the righteous from among you,
then shall ye be ripe for destruction.
Yea, woe be unto this great city
because of the wickedness and abominations which is in her.

15 Yea, and woe be unto the city of Gideon
for the wickedness and abominations which is in her.

16 Yea, and woe be unto all the cities
which are in the land round about which is possessed by the Nephites
because of the wickedness and the abominations which is in them.

17 And behold, a curse shall come upon the land, saith the Lord of Hosts,
because of the people's sake which is upon the land,
yea, because of their wickedness and their abominations.

18 And it shall come to pass, saith the Lord of Hosts,
yea, our great and true God,
that whoso shall hide up treasures in the earth
shall find them again no more because of the great curse of the land,
save he be a righteous man and shall hide it up unto the Lord.

19 For I will, saith the Lord, that they shall hide up their treasures unto me.
And cursed be they who hideth not up their treasures unto me,
for none hideth up their treasures unto me save it be the righteous.
And he that hideth not up his treasure unto me,
cursed is he and also the treasure;
and none shall redeem it because of the curse of the land.

20 And the day shall come that they shall hide up their treasures
because they have set their hearts upon riches.
And because they have set their hearts upon their riches
and will hide up their treasures when they shall flee before their enemies,
because they will not hide them up unto me,
cursed be they and also their treasures.
And in that day shall they be smitten, saith the Lord.

21 Behold, ye the people of this great city,
and hearken unto my words.
Yea, hearken unto the words which the Lord saith.
For behold, he saith that ye are cursed because of your riches;
and also are your riches cursed
because ye have set your hearts upon them
and hath not hearkened unto the words of him who gave them unto you.

22 Ye do not remember the Lord your God
in the things which he hath blessed you.
But ye do always remember your riches,
not to thank the Lord your God for them.
Yea, your heart is not drawn out unto the Lord,
but they do swell with great pride unto boasting
and unto great swelling, envyings, strifes, malice, persecutions, and murders,
and all manner of iniquities.

23 For this cause hath the Lord God caused

that a curse should come upon the land and also upon your riches—
and this because of your iniquities.

24 Yea, woe unto this people because of this time which has arriven
that ye do cast out the prophets and do mock them
and cast stones at them and do slay them
and do do all manner of iniquity unto them,
even as they did of old time.

25 And now when ye talk, ye say:
If our days had been in the days of our fathers of old,
we would not have slain the prophets;
we would not have stoned them and cast them out.

26 Behold, ye are worse than they.
For as the Lord liveth,
if a prophet come among you
and declareth unto you the word of the Lord,
which testifieth of your sins and iniquities,
ye are angry with him and cast him out
and seek all manner of ways to destroy him.
Yea, you will say that he is a false prophet
and that he is a sinner and of the devil
because he testifieth that your deeds are evil.

27 But behold, if a man shall come among you and shall say:
Do this and there is no iniquity!
Do that and ye shall not suffer!
Yea, he will say:
Walk after the pride of your own hearts;
yea, walk after the pride of your eyes
and do whatsoever your heart desireth.
And if a man shall come among you and say this,
ye will receive him.
And ye will say that he is a prophet;

28 yea, ye will lift him up.
And ye will give unto him of your substance;
ye will give unto him of your gold and of your silver;
and ye will clothe him with costly apparel.
And because he speaketh flattering words unto you
and he saith that all is well,
and then ye will not find no fault with him.

29 O ye wicked and ye perverse generation,
ye hardened and ye stiffnecked people,

how long will ye suppose that the Lord will suffer you?
Yea, how long will ye suffer yourselves to be led by foolish and blind guides?
Yea, how long will ye choose darkness rather than light?

30 Yea, behold, the anger of the Lord is already kindled against you.
Behold, he hath cursed the land because of your iniquity.

31 And behold, the time cometh that he curseth your riches,
that it becometh slippery, that ye cannot hold them;
and in the days of your poverty ye cannot retain them.

32 And in the days of your poverty ye shall cry unto the Lord,
and in vain shall ye cry;
for your desolation is already come upon you,
and your destruction is made sure.

And then shall ye weep and howl in that day, saith the Lord of Hosts,
and then shall ye lament and say:

33 O that I had repented
and had not killed the prophets and stoned them and cast them out.
Yea, in that day shall ye say:
O that we had remembered the Lord our God
in the day that he gave us our riches,
and then they would not have become slippery,
that we should lose them.
For behold, our riches are gone from us.

34 Behold, we layeth a tool here and on the morrow it is gone.
And behold, our swords are taken from us
in the day we have sought them for battle.

35 Yea, we have hid up our treasures,
and they have slipped away from us because of the curse of the land.

36 O that we had repented in the day that the word of the Lord came unto us.
For behold, the land is cursed;
and all things are become slippery and we cannot hold them.

37 Behold, we are surrounded by demons;
yea, we are encircled about by the angels of him
who hath sought to destroy our souls.
Behold, our iniquities are great.
O Lord, canst thou not turn away thine anger from us?
And this shall be your language in them days.

38 But behold, your days of probation is past.
Ye have procrastinated the day of your salvation
until it is everlastingly too late and your destruction is made sure.
Yea, for ye have sought all the days of your lives
for that which ye could not obtain.

And ye have sought for happiness in doing iniquity,
which thing is contrary to the nature of that righteousness
which is in our great and eternal Head.

39 O ye people of the land,
that ye would hear my words!
And I pray that the anger of the Lord be turned away from you
and that ye would repent and be saved.

14 | 1 And now it came to pass that
Samuel the Lamanite did prophesy a great many more things
which cannot be written.

2 And behold, he saith unto them:
Behold, I give unto you a sign.
For five years more cometh,
and behold, then cometh the Son of God
to redeem all those who shall believe on his name.

3 And behold, this will I give unto you for a sign at the time of his coming.
For behold, there shall be great lights in heaven,
insomuch that in the night before he cometh
there shall be no darkness,
insomuch that it shall appear unto man as if it was day.

4 Therefore there shall be one day and a night and a day,
as if it were one day and there were no night.
And this shall be unto you for a sign,
for ye shall know of the rising of the sun and also of its sitting.
Therefore they shall know of a surety that there shall be two days and a night;
nevertheless the night shall not be darkened.
And it shall be the night before he is born.

5 And behold, there shall be a new star arise,
such an one as ye never have beheld;
and this also shall be a sign unto you.

6 And behold, this is not all.
There shall be many signs and wonders in heaven.

7 And it shall come to pass that ye shall all be amazed and wonder,
insomuch that ye shall fall to the earth.

8 And it shall come to pass that whosoever shall believe on the Son of God,
the same shall have everlasting life.

9 And behold, thus hath the Lord commanded me by his angel
that I should come and tell this thing unto you.
Yea, he hath commanded that I should prophesy these things unto you;
yea, he hath said unto me:

Cry unto this people:
Repent and prepare the way of the Lord.

10 And now because I am a Lamanite
and hath spoken unto you the words which the Lord hath commanded me
and because it was hard against you,
ye are angry with me and do seek to destroy me
and have cast me out from among you.

11 And ye shall hear my words,
for for this intent I have come up upon the walls of this city,
that ye might hear and know of the judgments of God
which doth await you because of your iniquities,
and also that ye might know the conditions of repentance,

12 and also that ye might know of the coming of Jesus Christ the Son of God,
the Father of heaven and of earth,
the Creator of all things from the beginning,
and that ye might know of the signs of his coming,
to the intent that ye might believe on his name.

13 And if ye believe on his name,
ye will repent of all your sins,
that thereby ye may have a remission of them through his merits.

14 And behold, again another sign I give unto you, yea, a sign of his death.

15 For behold, he surely must die, that salvation may come.
Yea, it behooveth him and becometh expedient
that he dieth to bring to pass the resurrection of the dead,
that thereby men may be brought into the presence of the Lord.

16 Yea, behold, this death bringeth to pass the resurrection
and redeemeth all mankind from the first death, that spiritual death.
For all mankind,
by the fall of Adam being cut off from the presence of the Lord,
are considered as dead,
both as to things temporal and to things spiritual.

17 But behold, the resurrection of Christ redeemeth mankind,
yea, even all mankind,
and bringeth them back into the presence of the Lord.

18 Yea, and it bringeth to pass the conditions of repentance,
that whosoever repenteth, the same is not hewn down and cast into the fire.
But whosoever repenteth not is hewn down and cast into the fire.
And there cometh upon them again a spiritual death,
yea, a second death,
for they are cut off again as to things pertaining to righteousness.

19 Therefore repent ye, repent ye,
    lest by knowing these things and not doing them,
    ye shall suffer yourselves to come under condemnation
    and ye are brought down unto this second death.

20 But behold, as I said unto you concerning another sign, a sign of his death,
    behold, in that day that he shall suffer death,
    the sun shall be darkened and refuse to give his light unto you,
    and also the moon and the stars;
    and there shall be no light upon the face of this land,
    even from the time that he shall suffer death,
    for the space of three days,
    to the time that he shall rise again from the dead.

21 Yea, at the time that he shall yield up the ghost,
    there shall be thunderings and lightnings for the space of many hours.
    And the earth shall shake and tremble.
    And the rocks which is upon the face of the earth,
    which is both above the earth and beneath,
    which ye know at this time is solid
    — or the more part of it is one solid mass —
    shall be broken up.

22 Yea, they shall be rent in twain
    and shall ever after be found in seams and in cracks
    and in broken fragments upon the face of the whole earth,
    yea, both above the earth and beneath.

23 And behold, there shall be great tempests.
    And there shall be many mountains laid low like unto a valley.
    And there shall be many places which are now called valleys
    which shall become mountains whose heighth thereof is great.

24 And many highways shall be broken up;
    and many cities shall become desolate.

25 And many graves shall be opened
    and shall yield up many of their dead;
    and many saints shall appear unto many.

26 And behold, thus hath the angel spoken unto me.
    For he said unto me that there should be thunderings and lightnings
    for the space of many hours.

27 And he said unto me that
    while the thunder and the lightning lasted, and the tempest,
    that these things should be
    and that darkness should cover the face of the whole earth

for the space of three days.

28 And the angel said unto me
that many shall see greater things than these,
to the intent that they might believe —
that these signs and these wonders should come to pass
upon all the face of this land,
to the intent that there should be no cause
for unbelief among the children of men —

29 and this to the intent that whosoever will believe might be saved
and that whosoever will not believe,
a righteous judgment might come upon them;
and also if they are condemned,
they bring upon themselves their own condemnation.

30 And now remember, remember, my brethren,
that whosoever perisheth perisheth unto himself
and whosoever doeth iniquity doeth it unto himself.
For behold, ye are free;
ye are permitted to act for yourselves.
For behold, God hath given unto you a knowledge,
and he hath made you free.

31 He hath given unto you that ye might know good from evil.
And he hath given unto you that ye might choose life or death.
And ye can do good and be restored unto that which is good,
or have that which is good restored unto you;
or ye can do evil and have that which is evil restored unto you.

15 | 1 And now my beloved brethren,
behold, I declare unto you
that except ye shall repent,
your houses shall be left unto you desolate.

2 Yea, except ye repent,
your women shall have great cause to mourn
in the day that they shall give suck.
For ye shall attempt to flee and there shall be no place for refuge.
Yea, and woe unto them which are with child,
for they shall be heavy and cannot flee.
Therefore they shall be trodden down and shall be left to perish.

3 Yea, woe unto this people which are called the people of Nephi
except they shall repent when they shall see all those signs and wonders
which shall be shewed unto them.
For behold, they have been a chosen people of the Lord.
Yea, the people of Nephi hath he loved.

lest by any means those things which had been spoken might not come to pass.

8 But behold, they did watch steadfastly for that day and that night and that day
which should be as one day, as if there were no night,
that they might know that their faith had not been vain.

9 Now it came to pass that there was a day set apart by the unbelievers
that all those who believed in those traditions should be put to death
except the sign should come to pass
which had been given by Samuel the prophet.

10 Now it came to pass that
when Nephi the son of Nephi saw this wickedness of his people,
his heart was exceeding sorrowful.

11 And it came to pass that he went out
and bowed himself down upon the earth
and cried mightily to his God in behalf of his people,
yea, those which were about to be destroyed
because of their faith in the tradition of their fathers.

12 And it came to pass that he cried mightily unto the Lord all that day.
And behold, the voice of the Lord came unto him, saying:

13 Lift up your head and be of good cheer.
For behold, the time is at hand,
and on this night shall the sign be given.
And on the morrow come I into the world,
to shew unto the world that I will fulfill all that
which I have caused to be spoken by the mouth of my holy prophets.

14 Behold, I come unto my own
to fulfill all things which I have made known unto the children of men
from the foundation of the world,
and to do the will both of the Father and of the Son—
of the Father because of me, and of the Son because of my flesh.
And behold, the time is at hand,
and this night shall the sign be given.

15 And it came to pass that the words which came unto Nephi was fulfilled,
according as they had been spoken.
For behold, at the going down of the sun there was no darkness.
And the people began to be astonished
because there was no darkness when the night came.

16 And there were many which had not believed the words of the prophets
fell to the earth and became as if they were dead,
for they knew that the great plan of destruction
which they had laid for those who believed in the words of the prophets
had been frustrated,

for the sign which had been given was already at hand.

17 And they began to know that the Son of God must shortly appear.
Yea, and in fine, all the people upon the face of the whole earth,
from the west to the east,
both in the land north and in the land south,
were so exceedingly astonished that they fell to the earth.

18 For they knew that the prophets had testified of these things for many years
and that the sign which had been given was already at hand.
And they began to fear because of their iniquity and their unbelief.

19 And it came to pass that there was no darkness in all that night,
but it was as light as though it was midday.
And it came to pass that the sun did rise in the morning again,
according to its proper order.
And they knew that it was the day that the Lord should be born,
because of the sign which had been given.

20 And it had come to pass—yea, all things—
every whit according to the words of the prophets.

21 And it came to pass also that a new star did appear, according to the word.

22 And it came to pass that from this time forth
there began to be lyings sent forth among the people by Satan,
to harden their hearts,
to the intent that they might not believe
in those signs and wonders which they had seen.
But notwithstanding these lyings and deceivings,
the more part of the people did believe and were converted unto the Lord.

23 And it came to pass that
Nephi went forth among the people, and also many others,
baptizing unto repentance, in the which there were a great remission of sins.
And thus the people began again to have peace in the land.

24 And there were no contentions
save it were a few that began to preach
—endeavoring to prove by the scriptures—
that it was no more expedient to observe the law of Moses.
Now in this thing they did err, having not understood the scriptures.

25 But it came to pass that they soon became converted
and were convinced of the error which they were in,
for it was made known unto them that the law was not yet fulfilled
and that it must be fulfilled in every whit.
Yea, the word came unto them that it must be fulfilled—
yea, that one jot nor tittle should not pass away till it should all be fulfilled.
Therefore in this same year were they brought to a knowledge of their error

and did confess their faults.

26 And thus the ninety and second year did pass away,
   bringing glad tidings unto the people
   because of the signs which did come to pass
   according to the words of the prophecy of all the holy prophets.

27 And it came to pass that the ninety and third year did also pass away in peace
   save it were for the Gaddianton robbers, which dwelt upon the mountains,
   which did infest the land.
   For so strong were their holds and their secret places
   that the people could not overpower them;
   therefore they did commit many murders
   and did do much slaughter among the people.

28 And it came to pass that in the ninety and fourth year
   they began to increase in a great degree
   because there were many dissenters of the Nephites which did flee unto them,
   which did cause much sorrow unto those Nephites
   which did remain in the land.

29 And there was also a cause of much sorrow among the Lamanites;
   for behold, they had many children
   which did grow up and began to wax strong in years,
   that they became for themselves,
   and were led away by some which were Zoramites
   by their lyings and their flattering words to join those Gaddianton robbers.

30 And thus were the Lamanites afflicted also
   and began to decrease as to their faith and righteousness
   because of the wickedness of the rising generation.

2 | 1 And it came to pass that thus passed away the ninety and fifth year also.
   And the people began to forget those signs and wonders which they had heard
   and began to be less and less astonished at a sign or a wonder from heaven,
   insomuch that they began to be hard in their hearts and blind in their minds
   and began to disbelieve all which they had heard and seen,

2 imagining up some vain thing in their hearts,
   that it was wrought by men and by the power of the devil
   to lead away and deceive the hearts of the people.
   And thus did Satan get possession of the hearts of the people again,
   insomuch that he did blind their eyes
   and lead them away to believe
   that the doctrine of Christ was a foolish and a vain thing.

3 And it came to pass that
   the people began to wax strong in wickedness and abominations.
   And they did not believe that there should be any more signs or wonders given.

And Satan did go about leading away the hearts of the people, tempting them
and causing them that they should do great wickedness in the land.

4 And thus did pass away the ninety and sixth year,
and also the ninety and seventh year,
and also the ninety and eighth year,
and also the ninety and ninth year.

5 And also an hundred years had passed away
since the days of Mosiah, which was king over the people of the Nephites.

6 And six hundred and nine years had passed away since Lehi left Jerusalem.

7 And nine years had passed away from the time
which the sign was given which was spoken of by the prophets
that Christ should come into the world.

8 Now the Nephites began to reckon their time
from this period which the sign was given, or from the coming of Christ;
therefore nine years had passed away.

9 And Nephi, which was the father of Nephi,
which had the charge of the records,
did not return to the land of Zarahemla
and could nowhere be found in all the land.

10 And it came to pass that the people did still remain in wickedness,
notwithstanding the much preaching and prophesying
which was sent among them.
And thus passed away the tenth year also;
and the eleventh year also passed away in iniquity.

11 And it came to pass in the thirteenth year
there began to be wars and contentions throughout all the land,
for the Gaddianton robbers had become so numerous
and did slay so many of the people and did lay waste so many cities
and did spread so much death and carnage throughout the land
that it became expedient that all the people,
both the Nephites and the Lamanites,
should take up arms against them.

12 Therefore all the Lamanites which had become converted unto the Lord
did unite with their brethren the Nephites
and were compelled for the safety of their lives
and their women and their children
to take up arms against those Gaddianton robbers,
yea, and also to maintain their rights and the privileges of their church
and of their worship and their freedom and their liberty.

13 And it came to pass that before this thirteenth year had passed away,
the Nephites were threatened with utter destruction

because of this war, which had become exceeding sore.

14 And it came to pass that
those Lamanites which had united with the Nephites
were numbered among the Nephites.

15 And their curse was taken from them,
and their skin became white like unto the Nephites.

16 And their young men and their daughters became exceeding fair;
and they were numbered among the Nephites and were called Nephites.
And thus ended the thirteenth year.

17 And it came to pass in the commencement of the fourteenth year
the war between the robbers and the people of Nephi did continue
and did become exceeding sore.
Nevertheless the people of Nephi did gain some advantage of the robbers,
insomuch that they did drive them back out of their lands
into the mountains and into their secret places.

18 And thus ended the fourteenth year.
And in the fifteenth year they did come forth again against the people of Nephi.
And because of the wickedness of the people of Nephi
and their many contentions and dissensions,
the Gaddianton robbers did gain many advantages over them.

19 And thus ended the fifteenth year.
And thus were the people in a state of many afflictions;
and the sword of destruction did hang over them,
insomuch that they were about to be smitten down by it—
and this because of their iniquity.

3 | 1 And now it came to pass that
in the sixteenth year from the coming of Christ
Lachoneus the governor of the land received an epistle
from the leader and the governor of this band of robbers.
And these are the words which were written, saying:

2 Lachoneus, most noble and chief governor of the land,
behold, I write this epistle unto you
and do give unto you exceeding great praise
because of your firmness, and also the firmness of your people,
in maintaining that which ye suppose to be your right and liberty.
Yea, ye do stand well as if ye were supported by the hand of a god
in the defense of your liberty and your property and your country,
or that which ye do call so.

3 And it seemeth a pity unto me, most noble Lachoneus,
that ye should be so foolish and vain as to suppose

that ye can stand against so many brave men which are at my command,
which do now at this time stand in their arms
and do await with great anxiety for the word:
Go down upon the Nephites and destroy them!

4 And I knowing of their unconquerable spirit,
having proved them in the field of battle,
and knowing of their everlasting hatred towards you
because of the many wrongs which ye have done unto them
—therefore if they should come down against you,
they would visit you with utter destruction—

5 therefore I have wrote this epistle,
sealing it with mine own hand,
feeling for your welfare
because of your firmness in that which ye believe to be right
and your noble spirit in the field of battle.

6 Therefore I write unto you,
desiring that ye would yield up unto this my people
your cities, your lands, and your possessions,
rather than that they should visit you with the sword
and that destruction should come upon you.

7 Or in other words, yield yourselves up unto us and unite with us
and become acquainted with our secret works and become our brethren,
that ye may be like unto us, not our slaves,
but our brethren and partners of all our substance.

8 And behold, I swear unto you:
If ye will do this with an oath, ye shall not be destroyed.
But if ye will not do this, I swear unto you with an oath
that on the morrow month I will command
that my armies shall come down against you,
and they shall not stay their hand and shall spare not,
but shall slay you and shall let fall the sword upon you,
yea, even until ye shall become extinct.

9 And behold, I am Giddianhi
and am the governor of this the secret society of Gaddianton,
which society and the works thereof I know to be good.
And they are of ancient date,
and they have been handed down unto us.

10 And I write this epistle unto you Lachoneus;
and I hope that ye will deliver up your lands and your possessions
without the shedding of blood,
that this my people may recover their rights and government,

which have dissented away from you because of your wickedness
in retaining from them their rights of government.
And except ye do this, I will avenge their wrongs.
I am Giddianhi.

11   And now it came to pass when Lachoneus received this epistle,
he was exceedingly astonished because of the boldness of Giddianhi
in demanding the possession of the land of the Nephites,
and also of threatening the people,
and avenging the wrongs of those that had received no wrong
save it were they had wronged themselves
by dissenting away unto those wicked and abominable robbers.

12   And now behold, this Lachoneus, the governor, was a just man
and could not be frightened by the demands and the threatenings of a robber.
Therefore he did not hearken to the epistle of Giddianhi,
the governor of the robbers,
but he did cause that his people should cry unto the Lord
for strength against the time that the robbers should come down against them.

13   Yea, he sent a proclamation among all the people
that they should gather together their women and their children,
their flocks and their herds and all their substance
—save it were their land—unto one place.

14   And he caused that fortifications should be built round about them,
and the strength thereof should be exceeding great.
And he caused that there should be armies
both of the Nephites and of the Lamanites
—or of all them which were numbered among the Nephites—
should be placed as guards round about to watch them
and to guard them from the robbers day and night.

15   Yea, he said unto them:
As the Lord liveth,
except ye repent of all your iniquities and cry unto the Lord
that they would in no wise be delivered
out of the hands of those Gaddianton robbers.

16   And so great and marvelous were the words and prophecies of Lachoneus
that they did cause fear to come upon all the people.
And they did exert themselves in their might
to do according to the words of Lachoneus.

17   And it came to pass that
Lachoneus did appoint chief captains over all the armies of the Nephites
to command them at the time
that the robbers should come down out of the wilderness against them.

18 Now the chiefest among all the chief captains
and the great commander of all the armies of the Nephites was appointed,
and his name was Gidgiddoni.

19 Now it was the custom among all the Nephites
to appoint for their chief captains—save it were in their times of wickedness—
some one that had the spirit of revelation and also of prophecy.
Therefore this Gidgiddoni was a great prophet among them,
and also was the chief judge.

20 Now the people said unto Gidgiddoni: Pray unto the Lord
and let us go up upon the mountains and into the wilderness,
that we may fall upon the robbers and destroy them in their own lands.

21 But Gidgiddoni saith unto them:
The Lord forbid!
For if we should go up against them,
the Lord would deliver us into their hands.
Therefore we will prepare ourselves in the center of our lands;
and we will gather all our armies together.
And we will not go against them,
but we will wait till they shall come against us.
Therefore, as the Lord liveth,
if we do this, he will deliver them into our hands.

22 And it came to pass in the seventeenth year, in the latter end of the year,
the proclamation of Lachoneus had gone forth
throughout all the face of the land.
And they had taken their horses and their chariots
and their cattle and all their flocks and their herds
and their grain and all their substance
and did march forth by thousands and by tens of thousands
until they had all gone forth to the place which had been appointed
that they should gather themselves together
to defend themselves against their enemies.

23 And the land which was appointed was the land of Zarahemla
and the land which was between the land of Zarahemla and the land Bountiful,
yea, to the line which was betwixt the land Bountiful and the land Desolation.

24 And there were a great many thousand people which were called Nephites
which did gather themselves together in this land.
Now Lachoneus did cause
that they should gather themselves together in the land southward
because of the great curse which was upon the land northward.

25 And they did fortify themselves against their enemies;
and they did dwell in one land and in one body.

And they did fear the words which had been spoken by Lachoneus,
insomuch that they did repent of all their sins.
And they did put up their prayers unto the Lord their God
that he would deliver them
in the time that their enemies should come down against them to battle.

26 And they were exceeding sorrowful because of their enemy.
And Gidgiddoni did cause that they should make weapons of war of every kind,
that they should be strong with armor and with shields and with bucklers,
after the manner of his instructions.

4 | 1 And it came to pass that in the latter end of the eighteenth year
those armies of robbers had prepared for battle
and began to come down and to sally forth from the hills
and out of the mountains and the wilderness
and their strong holds and their secret places
and began to take possession of the lands,
both which was in the land south and which was in the land north,
and began to take possession of all the lands
which had been deserted by the Nephites
and the cities which had been left desolate.

2 But behold, there was no wild beasts nor game in those lands
which had been deserted by the Nephites;
and there was no game for the robbers save it were in the wilderness.

3 And the robbers could not exist
—save it were in the wilderness—
for the want of food;
for the Nephites had left their lands desolate
and had gathered their flocks and their herds and all their substance,
and they were in one body.

4 Therefore there were no chance for the robbers to plunder and to obtain food
save it were to come up in open battle against the Nephites.
And the Nephites being in one body
and having so great a number
and having reserved for themselves provisions
and horses and cattle and flocks of every kind
that they might subsist for the space of seven years,
in the which time they did hope
to destroy the robbers from off the face of the land—
and thus the eighteenth year did pass away.

5 And it came to pass that in the nineteenth year
Giddianhi found that it was expedient
that he should go up to battle against the Nephites,

for there was no way that they could subsist
save it were to plunder and rob and murder.

6 And they durst not spread themselves upon the face of the land
insomuch that they could raise grain,
lest the Nephites should come upon them and slay them.
Therefore Giddianhi gave commandment unto his armies
that in this year they should go up to battle against the Nephites.

7 And it came to pass that they did come up to battle,
and it was in the sixth month.
And behold, great and terrible was the day that they did come up to battle.
And they were girded about after the manner of robbers;
and they had a lambskin about their loins.
And they were dyed in blood,
and their heads were shorn,
and they had headplates upon them.
And great and terrible was the appearance of the armies of Giddianhi
because of their armor and because of their being dyed in blood.

8 And it came to pass that the armies of the Nephites,
when they saw the appearance of the army of Giddianhi,
had all fallen to the earth and did lift their cries to the Lord their God
that he would spare them and deliver them out of the hands of their enemies.

9 And it came to pass that when the armies of Giddianhi saw this,
they began to shout with a loud voice because of their joy.
For they had supposed that the Nephites had fallen with fear
because of the terror of their armies.

10 But in this thing they were disappointed;
for the Nephites did not fear them,
but they did fear their God and did supplicate him for protection.
Therefore when the armies of Giddianhi did rush upon them,
they were prepared to meet them;
yea, in the strength of the Lord they did receive them.

11 And the battle commenced in this the sixth month.
And great and terrible was the battle thereof;
yea, great and terrible was the slaughter thereof,
insomuch that there never was known so great a slaughter
among all the people of Lehi since he left Jerusalem.

12 And notwithstanding the threatenings and the oaths
which Giddianhi had made,
behold, the Nephites did beat them,
insomuch that they did fall back from before them.

13 And it came to pass that Gidgiddoni commanded

that his armies should pursue them as far as to the borders of the wilderness
and that they should not spare any that should fall into their hands by the way.
And thus they did pursue them and did slay them
to the borders of the wilderness,
even until they had fulfilled the commandment of Gidgiddoni.

14 And it came to pass that Giddianhi,
who had stood and fought with boldness,
was pursued as he fled.
And being weary because of his much fighting,
he was overtaken and slain.
And thus was the end of Giddianhi the robber.

15 And it came to pass that
the armies of the Nephites did return again to their place of security.

And it came to pass that this nineteenth year did pass away
and the robbers did not come again to battle,
neither did they come again in the twentieth year.

16 But in the twenty and first year they did not come up to battle
but they came up on all sides to lay siege round about the people of Nephi.
For they did suppose that
if they should cut off the people of Nephi from their lands
and should hem them in on every side,
and if they should cut them off from all their outward privileges,
that they could cause them to yield themselves up according to their wishes.

17 Now they had appointed unto themselves another leader,
whose name was Zemnarihah.
Therefore it was Zemnarihah that did cause that this siege should take place.

18 But behold, this was an advantage unto the Nephites.
For it was impossible for the robbers to lay siege sufficiently long
to have any effect upon the Nephites
because of their much provision which they had laid up in store,

19 and because of the scantiness of provisions among the robbers;
for behold, they had nothing save it were meat for their subsistence,
which meat they did obtain in the wilderness.

20 And it came to pass that the wild game became scarce in the wilderness,
insomuch that the robbers were about to perish with hunger.

21 And the Nephites were continually marching out by day and by night
and falling upon their armies
and cutting them off by thousands and by tens of thousands.

22 And thus it became the desire of the people of Zemnarihah
to withdraw from their design
because of the great destruction which came upon them by night and by day.

23 And it came to pass that Zemnarihah did give command unto his people
   that they should withdraw themselves from the siege
   and to march into the farthermost parts of the land northward.

24 And now Gidgiddoni being aware of their design
   and knowing of their weakness because of the want of food
   and the great slaughter which had been made among them,
   therefore he did send out his armies in the nighttime
   and did cut off the way of their retreat
   and did place his armies in the way of their retreat.

25 And this did they do in the nighttime
   and gat on their march beyond the robbers,
   so that on the morrow, when the robbers began their march,
   they were met by the armies of the Nephites,
   both in their front and in their rear.

26 And the robbers which were on the south
   were also cut off in their places of retreat.
   And all these things were done by command of Gidgiddoni.

27 And there were many thousands
   which did yield themselves up prisoners unto the Nephites,
   and the remainder of them were slain.

28 And their leader Zemnarihah was taken and hanged upon a tree,
   yea, even upon the top thereof until he was dead.
   And when they had hanged him until he was dead,
   they did fall the tree to the earth
   and did cry with a loud voice, saying:

29 May the Lord preserve his people in righteousness and in holiness of heart,
   that they may cause to be fell to the earth all who shall seek to slay them
   because of power and secret combinations,
   even as this man hath been fell to the earth.

30 And they did rejoice and cry again with one voice, saying:
   May the God of Abraham and the God of Isaac and the God of Jacob
   protect this people in righteousness,
   so long as they shall call on the name of their God for protection.

31 And it came to pass that they did break forth, all as one,
   in singing and praising their God
   for the great thing which he had done for them
   in preserving them from falling into the hands of their enemies.

32 Yea, they did cry:
   Hosanna to the Most High God!
   And they did cry:
   Blessed be the name of the Lord God Almighty, the Most High God!

33 And their hearts were swollen with joy
   unto the gushing out of many tears
   because of the great goodness of God
   in delivering them out of the hands of their enemies.
   And they knew it was because of their repentance and their humility
   that they had been delivered from an everlasting destruction.

5 | 1 And now behold, there was not a living soul
   among all the people of the Nephites
   which did doubt in the least thing
   in the words of all the holy prophets which had been spoken.
   For they knew that it must needs be that they must be fulfilled.

2 And they knew that it must be expedient that Christ had come
   because of the many signs which had been given,
   according to the words of the prophets.
   And because of the things which had come to pass already,
   they knew it must needs be that all things should come to pass
   according to that which had been spoken.

3 Therefore they did forsake all their sins
   and their abominations and their whoredoms
   and did serve God with all diligence day and night.

4 And now it came to pass that when they had taken all the robbers prisoners,
   insomuch that none did escape which were not slain,
   they did cast their prisoners into prison
   and did cause the word of God to be preached unto them.
   And as many as would repent of their sins
   and enter into a covenant that they would murder no more
   were set at liberty.

5 But as many as there were who did not enter into a covenant
   and who did still continue to have those secret murders in their hearts
   —yea, as many as were found breathing out threatenings against their brethren—
   were condemned and punished according to the law.

6 And thus they did put an end
   to all those wicked and secret and abominable combinations
   in the which there were so much wickedness and so many murders committed.

7 And thus had the twenty and second year passed away,
   and the twenty and third year also,
   and the twenty and fourth, and the twenty and fifth.

   And thus had twenty and five years passed away;

8 and there had many things transpired
   which in the eyes of some would be great and marvelous.
   Nevertheless they cannot all be written in this book.

Yea, this book cannot contain even a hundredth part of what was done
among so many people in the space of twenty and five years.

9 But behold, there are records
which do contain all the proceedings of this people.
And a more short but a true account was given by Nephi.

10 Therefore I have made my record of these things
according to the record of Nephi,
which were engraven on the plates which were called the plates of Nephi.

11 And behold, I do make the record on plates
which I have made with mine own hands.

12 And behold, I am called Mormon, being called after the land of Mormon,
the land in the which Alma did establish the church among this people,
yea, the first church which was established among them
after their transgression.

13 Behold, I am a disciple of Jesus Christ the Son of God.
I have been called of him to declare his word among his people,
that they might have everlasting life.

14 And it hath become expedient
that I, according to the will of God
—that the prayers of those which have gone hence,
which were the holy ones,
should be fulfilled according to their faith—
should make a record of these things which have been done,

15 yea, a small record of that which hath taken place
from the time that Lehi left Jerusalem even down until the present time.

16 Therefore I do make my record from the accounts
which hath been given by those which were before me
until the commencement of my day.

17 And then do I make a record of the things
which I have seen with mine own eyes.

18 And I know the record which I make to be a just and a true record.
Nevertheless there are many things
which according to our language we are not able to write.

19 And now I make an end of my saying which is of myself
and proceed to give my account of the things which hath been before me.

20 I am Mormon and a pure descendant of Lehi.
I have reason to bless my God and my Savior Jesus Christ,
that he brought our fathers out of the land of Jerusalem
—and no one knew it save it were himself
and those which he brought out of that land—
and that he hath given me and my people

so much knowledge unto the salvation of our souls.

21 Surely he hath blessed the house of Jacob
and hath been merciful unto the seed of Joseph.

22 And inasmuch as the children of Lehi hath kept his commandments,
he hath blessed them and prospered them according to his word.

23 Yea, and surely shall he again bring a remnant of the seed of Joseph
to the knowledge of the Lord their God.

24 And as surely as the Lord liveth
will he gather in from the four quarters of the earth
all the remnant of the seed of Jacob,
which are scattered abroad upon all the face of the earth.

25 And as he hath covenanted with all the house of Jacob,
even so shall the covenant
wherewith he hath covenanted with the house of Jacob
be fulfilled in his own due time,
unto the restoring all the house of Jacob unto the knowledge of the covenant
that he hath covenanted with them.

26 And then shall they know their Redeemer,
which is Jesus Christ the Son of God;
and then shall they be gathered in from the four quarters of the earth
unto their own lands from whence they have been dispersed.
Yea, as the Lord liveth, so shall it be.
Amen.

6 | 1 And now it came to pass that
the people of the Nephites did all return to their own lands
in the twenty and sixth year,
every man with his family, his flocks and his herds, his horses and his cattle,
and all things whatsoever did belong unto them.

2 And it came to pass that they had not eaten up all their provisions,
therefore they did take with them
all that they had not devoured of all their grain of every kind,
and their gold and their silver and all their precious things;
and they did return to their own lands and their possessions,
both on the north and on the south,
both on the land northward and on the land southward.

3 And they granted unto those robbers
which had entered into a covenant to keep the peace of the land,
which were desirous to remain Lamanites,
lands according to their numbers,
that they might have with their labors wherewith to subsist upon.

And thus they did establish peace in all the land;

4 and they began again to prosper and to wax great.

And the twenty and sixth and seventh years passed away.
And there was great order in the land,
and they had formed their laws according to equity and justice.

5 And now there was nothing in all the land
to hinder the people from prospering continually
except they should fall into transgression.

6 And now it was Gidgiddoni and the judge Lachoneus
and those which had been appointed leaders
which had established this great peace in the land.

7 And it came to pass that there were many cities built anew,
and there were many old cities repaired.

8 And there were many highways cast up
and many roads made which led from city to city
and from land to land and from place to place.

9 And thus passed away the twenty and eighth year;
and the people had continual peace.

10 But it came to pass in the twenty and ninth year
there began to be some disputings among the people.
And some were lifted up unto pride and boastings
because of their exceeding great riches,
yea, even unto great persecutions.

11 For there were many merchants in the land,
and also many lawyers and many officers.

12 And the people began to be distinguished by ranks
according to their riches and their chance for learning.
Yea, some were ignorant because of their poverty;
and others did receive great learning because of their riches.

13 Some were lifted up in pride;
and others were exceeding humble.
Some did return railing for railing,
while others would receive railing and persecution and all manner of afflictions
and would not turn and revile again,
but were humble and penitent before God.

14 And thus there became a great unequality in all the land,
insomuch that the church began to be broken up,
yea, insomuch that in the thirtieth year the church was broken up in all the land
save it were among a few of the Lamanites
which were converted unto the true faith;
and they would not depart from it,

for they were firm and steadfast and immovable,
willing with all diligence to keep the commandments of the Lord.

15 Now the cause of this iniquity of the people was this:
Satan had great power unto the stirring up of the people
to do all manner of iniquity
and to the puffing them up with pride, tempting them to seek
for power and authority and riches and the vain things of the world.
16 And thus Satan did lead away the hearts of the people
to do all manner of iniquity.
Therefore they had not enjoyed peace but a few years.

17 And thus in the commencement of the thirtieth year
—the people having been delivered up for the space of a long time
to be carried about by the temptations of the devil
whithersoever he desired to carry them
and to do whatsoever iniquity he desired they should—
and thus in the commencement of this the thirtieth year,
they were in a state of awful wickedness.
18 Now they did not sin ignorantly;
for they knew the will of God concerning them,
for it had been taught unto them.
Therefore they did willfully rebel against God.

19 And now it was in the days of Lachoneus the son of Lachoneus
—for Lachoneus did fill the seat of his father
and did govern the people that year—
20 and there began to be men inspired from heaven and sent forth,
standing among the people in all the land,
preaching and testifying boldly of the sins and iniquities of the people,
and testifying unto them concerning the redemption
which the Lord would make for his people
—or in other words, the resurrection of Christ—
and they did testify boldly of his death and sufferings.
21 Now there were many of the people which were exceeding angry
because of those which testified of these things.
And those which were angry were chiefly the chief judges
and they which had been high priests and lawyers;
yea, all they which were lawyers were angry
with those which testified of these things.
22 Now there was no lawyer nor judge nor high priest
that could have power to condemn any one to death
save their condemnation was signed by the governor of the land.
23 Now there were many of those

which testified of the things pertaining to Christ,
which testified boldly,
which were taken and put to death secretly by the judges,
that the knowledge of their death came not unto the governor of the land
until after their death.

24 Now behold, this was contrary to the laws of the land,
that any man should be put to death
except they had power from the governor of the land.

25 Therefore a complaint came up unto the land of Zarahemla
to the governor of the land against these judges
which had condemned the prophets of the Lord unto death
not according to the law.

26 Now it came to pass that they were taken
and brought up before the judge
to be judged of their crime which they had done,
according to the law which had been given by the people.

27 Now it came to pass that
those judges had many friends and kindreds;
and the remainder—yea, even almost all the lawyers and the high priests—
did gather themselves together and unite with the kindreds of those judges
which were to be tried according to the law.

28 And they did enter into a covenant one with another,
yea, even into that covenant which was given by them of old,
which covenant was given and administered by the devil,
to combine against all righteousness.

29 Therefore they did combine against the people of the Lord
and enter into a covenant to destroy them
and to deliver those which were guilty of murder from the grasp of justice,
which was about to be administered according to the law.

30 And they did set at defiance the law and the rights of their country.
And they did covenant one with another to destroy the governor
and to establish a king over the land,
that the land should no more be at liberty but should be subject unto kings.

7 | 1 Now behold, I will shew unto you
that they did not establish a king over the land.
But in this same year—yea, the thirtieth year—
they did destroy upon the judgment seat,
yea, did murder the chief judge of the land.

2 And the people were divided one against another.
And they did separate one from another into tribes,
every man according to his family and his kindred and friends.

And thus they did destroy the government of the land.

3 And every tribe did appoint a chief or a leader over them;
and thus there became tribes and leaders of tribes.

4 Now behold, there was no man among them
save he had much family and many kindreds and friends;
therefore their tribes became exceeding great.

5 Now all this was done, and there was no wars as yet among them.
And all this iniquity had come upon the people
because they did yield themselves unto the power of Satan.

6 And the regulations of the government was destroyed
because of the secret combination of the friends and the kindreds of them
which murdered the prophets.

7 And they did cause a great contention in the land,
insomuch that the more righteous part of the people—
although they were nearly all become wicked;
yea, there were but few righteous men among them—

8 and thus six years had not passed away
since the more part of the people had turned from their righteousness
like the dog to his vomit,
or like the sow to her wallowing in the mire.

9 Now this secret combination
which had brought so great iniquity upon the people
did gather themselves together
and did place at their head a man whom they did call Jacob;

10 and they did call him their king.
Therefore he became a king over this wicked band.
And he was one of the chiefest
which had given his voice against the prophets which testified of Jesus.

11 And it came to pass that they were not so strong in numbers
as the tribes of the people which were united together,
save it were their leaders did establish their laws,
every one according to his tribe;
nevertheless they were enemies.
Notwithstanding they were not a righteous people,
yet they were united in the hatred of those
who had entered into a covenant to destroy the government.

12 Therefore Jacob seeing that their enemies were more numerous than they,
he being the king of the band,
therefore he commanded his people
that they should take their flight into the northernmost part of the land
and there build up unto themselves a kingdom

until they were joined by dissenters
—for he flattered them that there would be many dissenters—
and they become sufficiently strong to contend with the tribes of the people;
and they did so.

13 And so speedy was their march that it could not be impeded
until they had gone forth out of the reach of the people.
And thus ended the thirtieth year;
and thus were the affairs of the people of Nephi.

14 And it came to pass in the thirty and first year
that they were divided into tribes,
every man according to his family, kindred, and friends.
Nevertheless they had come to an agreement
that they would not go to war one with another.
But they were not united as to their laws and their manner of government,
for they were established according to the minds of them
which was their chiefs and their leaders.
But they did establish very strict laws,
that one tribe should not trespass against another,
insomuch that in some degree they had peace in the land.
Nevertheless their hearts were turned from the Lord their God;
and they did stone the prophets and did cast them out from among them.

15 And it came to pass that
Nephi, having been visited by angels and also by the voice of the Lord,
therefore having seen angels and being eyewitness,
and having had power given unto him
that he might know concerning the ministry of Christ,
and also being eyewitness to their quick return from righteousness
unto their wickedness and abominations,

16 therefore being grieved for the hardness of their hearts
and the blindness of their minds,
went forth among them in that same year
and began to testify boldly
repentance and remission of sins through faith on the Lord Jesus Christ.

17 And he did minister many things unto them.
And all of them cannot be written,
and a part of them would not suffice;
therefore they are not written in this book.
And Nephi did minister with power and with great authority.

18 And it came to pass that they were angry with him,
even because he had greater power than they.
For it were not possible that they could disbelieve his words,

for so great was his faith on the Lord Jesus Christ
that angels did minister unto him daily.

19 And in the name of Jesus did he cast out devils and unclean spirits;
and even his brother did he raise from the dead
after he had been stoned and suffered death by the people.

20 And the people saw it and did witness of it
and were angry with him because of his power.
And he did also do many more miracles in the sight of the people,
in the name of Jesus.

21 And it came to pass that the thirty and first year did pass away.
And there were but few which were converted unto the Lord.
But as many as were converted did truly signify unto the people
that they had been visited by the power and Spirit of God
which was in Jesus Christ, in whom they believed.

22 And as many as had devils cast out from them
and were healed of their sicknesses and their infirmities
did truly manifest unto the people
that they had been wrought upon by the Spirit of God and had been healed.
And they did shew forth signs also and did do some miracles among the people.

23 And it came to pass that thus passed away the thirty and second year also.

And Nephi did cry unto the people
in the commencement of the thirty and third year;
and he did preach unto them repentance and remission of sins.

24 Now I would have you to remember also
that there were none which were brought unto repentance
who were not baptized with water.

25 Therefore there were ordained of Nephi men unto this ministry,
that all such as should come unto them should be baptized with water—
and this as a witness and a testimony before God and unto the people
that they had repented and received a remission of their sins.

26 And there were many in the commencement of this year
that were baptized unto repentance.
And thus the more part of the year did pass away.

8 | 1 And now it came to pass that according to our record—
and we know our record to be true,
for behold, it was a just man which did keep the record;
for he truly did many miracles in the name of Jesus,
and there was not any man which could do a miracle in the name of Jesus
save he were cleansed every whit from his iniquity—

2 and now it came to pass,
   if there was no mistake made by this man in the reckoning of our time,
   the thirty and third year had passed away.

3 And the people began to look with great earnestness for the sign
   which had been given by the prophet Samuel the Lamanite,
   yea, for the time that there should be darkness
   for the space of three days over the face of the land.

4 And there began to be great doubtings and disputations among the people,
   notwithstanding so many signs had been given.

5 And it came to pass in the thirty and fourth year,
   in the first month, in the fourth day of the month,
   there arose a great storm,
   such an one as never had been known in all the land.

6 And there was also a great and terrible tempest;
   and there was terrible thunder,
   insomuch that it did shake the whole earth
   as if it was about to divide asunder.

7 And there was exceeding sharp lightnings
   such as never had been known in all the land.

8 And the city of Zarahemla did take fire.

9 And the city of Moroni did sink into the depths of the sea
   and the inhabitants thereof were drowned.

10 And the earth was carried up upon the city of Moronihah,
   that in the place of the city thereof there became a great mountain.

11 And there was a great and terrible destruction in the land southward.

12 But behold, there was a more great and terrible destruction
   in the land northward;
   for behold, the whole face of the land was changed
   because of the tempests and the whirlwinds
   and the thunderings and the lightnings
   and the exceeding great quaking of the whole earth.

13 And the highways were broken up,
   and the level roads were spoiled,
   and many smooth places became rough.

14 And many great and notable cities were sunk,
   and many were burned,
   and many were shook till the buildings thereof had fallen to the earth
   and the inhabitants thereof were slain
   and the places were left desolate.

15 And there were some cities which remained,
   but the damage thereof was exceeding great;

and there were many in them which were slain.

16 And there were some which were carried away in the whirlwind;
and whither they went no man knoweth,
save they know that they were carried away.

17 And thus the face of the whole earth became deformed
because of the tempests and the thunderings and the lightnings
and the quaking of the earth.

18 And behold, the rocks were rent in twain;
yea, they were broken up upon the face of the whole earth,
insomuch that they were found in broken fragments
and in seams and in cracks upon all the face of the land.

19 And it came to pass that when the thunderings and the lightnings
and the storm and the tempest and the quakings of the earth did cease—
for behold, they did last for about the space of three hours;
and it was said by some that the time was greater;
nevertheless all these great and terrible things were done
in about the space of three hours—
and then behold, there was darkness upon the face of the land.

20 And it came to pass that there was thick darkness upon the face of all the land,
insomuch that the inhabitants thereof which had not fallen
could feel the vapor of darkness.

21 And there could be no light because of the darkness,
neither candles, neither torches;
neither could there be fire kindled with their fine and exceeding dry wood,
so that there could not be any light at all.

22 And there was not any light seen,
neither fire nor glimmer,
neither the sun nor the moon nor the stars,
for so great were the mists of darkness
which were upon the face of the land.

23 And it came to pass that it did last for the space of three days
that there was no light seen.
And there was great mourning and howling and weeping
among all the people continually;
yea, great were the groanings of the people
because of the darkness and the great destruction
which had come upon them.

24 And in one place they were heard to cry, saying:
O that we had repented before this great and terrible day,
and then would our brethren have been spared

and they would not have been burned in that great city Zarahemla.

25 And in another place they were heard to cry and mourn, saying:
O that we had repented before this great and terrible day
and had not killed and stoned the prophets and cast them out,
then would our mothers and our fair daughters
and our children have been spared
and not have been buried up in that great city Moronihah.
And thus were the howlings of the people great and terrible.

9 | 1 And it came to pass that there was a voice heard
among all the inhabitants of the earth upon all the face of this land, crying:

2 Woe woe woe unto this people!
Woe unto the inhabitants of the whole earth except they shall repent,
for the devil laugheth and his angels rejoice
because of the slain of the fair sons and daughters of my people.
And it is because of their iniquity and abominations that they are fallen.

3 Behold, that great city Zarahemla have I burned with fire
and the inhabitants thereof.

4 And behold, that great city Moroni have I caused
to be sunk in the depths of the sea
and the inhabitants thereof to be drowned.

5 And behold, that great city Moronihah have I covered with earth
and the inhabitants thereof,
to hide their iniquities and their abominations from before my face,
that the blood of the prophets and of the saints
shall not come up any more unto me against them.

6 And behold, the city of Gilgal have I caused to be sunk
and the inhabitants thereof to be buried up in the depths of the earth —

7 yea, and the city of Onihah and the inhabitants thereof,
and the city of Mocum and the inhabitants thereof,
and the city of Jerusalem and the inhabitants thereof;
and waters have I caused to come up in the stead thereof,
to hide their wickedness and abominations from before my face,
that the blood of the prophets and the saints
shall not come up any more unto me against them.

8 And behold, the city of Gadiandi and the city of Gadiomnah
and the city of Jacob and the city of Gimgimno,
all these have I caused to be sunk
and made hills and valleys in the places thereof;
and the inhabitants thereof have I buried up in the depths of the earth,
to hide their wickedness and abominations from before my face,

that the blood of the prophets and the saints
should not come up any more unto me against them.

9 And behold, that great city Jacob-Ugath,
which was inhabited by the people of the king Jacob,
have I caused to be burned with fire
because of their sins and their wickedness,
which was above all the wickedness of the whole earth
because of their secret murders and combinations,
for it was they that did destroy the peace of my people
and the government of the land.
Therefore I did cause them to be burned,
to destroy them from before my face,
that the blood of the prophets and the saints
should not come up unto me any more against them.

10 And behold, the city of Laman and the city of Josh
and the city of Gad and the city of Kishcumen
have I caused to be burned with fire,
and the inhabitants thereof,
because of their wickedness in casting out the prophets
and stoning them which I did send to declare unto them
concerning their wickedness and their abominations.

11 And because they did cast them all out,
that there were none righteous among them,
I did send down fire and destroy them,
that their wickedness and abominations might be hid from before my face,
that the blood of the prophets and the saints which I sent among them
might not cry unto me from the ground against them.

12 And many great destructions have I caused
to come upon this land and upon this people
because of their wickedness and their abominations.

13 O all ye that are spared because ye were more righteous than they,
will ye not now return unto me and repent of your sins and be converted,
that I may heal you?

14 Yea, verily I say unto you:
If ye will come unto me, ye shall have eternal life.
Behold, mine arm of mercy is extended towards you.
And whosoever will come, him will I receive.
And blessed are they which cometh unto me.

15 Behold, I am Jesus Christ the Son of God.
I created the heavens and the earth and all things that in them is.

I was with the Father from the beginning.
I am in the Father and the Father in me;
and in me hath the Father glorified his name.

16 I came unto my own, and my own received me not;
and the scriptures concerning my coming are fulfilled.

17 And as many as have received me,
to them have I given to become the sons of God.
And even so will I to as many as shall believe on my name.
For behold, by me redemption cometh,
and in me is the law of Moses fulfilled.

18 I am the light and the life of the world.
I am Alpha and Omega, the beginning and the end.

19 And ye shall offer up unto me no more the shedding of blood;
yea, your sacrifices and your burnt offerings shall be done away,
for I will accept none of your sacrifices and your burnt offerings.

20 And ye shall offer for a sacrifice unto me a broken heart and a contrite spirit.
And whoso cometh unto me with a broken heart and a contrite spirit,
him will I baptize with fire and with the Holy Ghost,
even as the Lamanites
because of their faith in me at the time of their conversion
were baptized with fire and with the Holy Ghost —
and they knew it not.

21 Behold, I have come into the world
to bring redemption unto the world,
to save the world from sin.

22 Therefore whoso repenteth and cometh unto me as a little child,
him will I receive,
for of such is the kingdom of God.
Behold, for such I have laid down my life and have taken it up again.
Therefore repent and come unto me, ye ends of the earth, and be saved.

10 | 1 And now behold, it came to pass that
all the people of the land did hear these sayings and did witness of it.
And after these sayings
there was silence in the land for the space of many hours,

2 for so great was the astonishment of the people
that they did cease lamenting and howling
for the loss of their kindreds which had been slain.
Therefore there was silence in all the land for the space of many hours.

3 And it came to pass that
there came a voice again unto the people

—and all the people did hear and did witness of it—
saying:

4 O ye people of these great cities which have fallen,
which are a descendant of Jacob
—yea, which are of the house of Israel—
O ye people of the house of Israel,
how oft have I gathered you
as a hen gathereth her chickens under her wings
and have nourished you!

5 And again, how oft would I have gathered you
as a hen gathereth her chickens under her wings!
Yea, O ye people of the house of Israel which have fallen
—yea, O ye people of the house of Israel,
ye that dwell at Jerusalem as ye that have fallen—
yea, how oft would I have gathered you
as a hen gathereth her chickens
and ye would not!

6 O ye house of Israel whom I have spared,
how oft will I gather you
as a hen gathereth her chickens under her wings
if ye will repent and return unto me with full purpose of heart!

7 But if not, O house of Israel, the places of your dwellings shall become desolate
until the time of the fulfilling of the covenant to your fathers.

8 And now it came to pass that after the people had heard these words,
behold, they began to weep and howl again
because of the loss of their kindreds and friends.

9 And it came to pass that thus did the three days pass away.
And it was in the morning,
and the darkness dispersed from off the face of the land
and the earth did cease to tremble
and the rocks did cease to rend
and the dreadful groanings did cease
and all the tumultuous noises did pass away.

10 And the earth did cleave together again, that it stood.
And the mourning and the weeping and the wailing
of the people which were spared alive did cease.
And their mourning was turned into joy
and their lamentations into the praise and the thanksgiving
unto the Lord Jesus Christ their Redeemer.

11 And thus far were the scriptures fulfilled
which had been spoken by the prophets.

12 And it was the more righteous part of the people which were saved.
And it was they which received the prophets and stoned them not;
and it was they which had not shed the blood of the saints which were spared.

13 And they were spared and were not sunk and buried up in the earth,
and they were not drowned in the depths of the sea,
and they were not burned by fire,
neither were they fallen upon and crushed to death;
and they were not carried away in the whirlwind,
neither were they overpowered by the vapors of smoke and of darkness.

14 And now whoso readeth, let him understand;
he that hath the scriptures, let him search them
and see and behold if all these deaths and destructions
by fire and by smoke and by tempests and by whirlwinds
and by the opening of the earth to receive them
and all these things is not unto the fulfilling
of the prophecies of many of the holy prophets.

15 Behold, I say unto you:
Yea, many have testified of these things at the coming of Christ
and were slain because they testified of these things

16 —yea, the prophet Zenos did testify of these things,
and also Zenoch spake concerning these things—
because they testified particular concerning us,
which is the remnant of their seed.

17 Behold, our father Jacob also testified
concerning a remnant of the seed of Joseph.
And behold, are not we a remnant of the seed of Joseph?
And these things which testifies of us,
are they not written upon the plates of brass
which our father Lehi brought out of Jerusalem?

18 And it came to pass that in the ending of the thirty and fourth year,
behold, I will shew unto you that the people of Nephi which were spared,
and also they which had been called Lamanites which had been spared,
did have great favors shewn unto them
and great blessings poured out upon their heads,
insomuch that soon after the ascension of Christ into heaven
he did truly manifest himself unto them,

19 shewing his body unto them and ministering unto them.
And an account of his ministry shall be given hereafter.
Therefore for this time I make an end of my sayings.

Jesus Christ sheweth himself unto the people of Nephi
as the multitude were gathered together in the land Bountiful
and did minister unto them.

And on this wise did he shew himself unto them.

11 | 1 And now it came to pass that
there were a great multitude gathered together of the people of Nephi
round about the temple which was in the land Bountiful.
And they were marveling and wondering one with another
and were shewing one to another
the great and marvelous change which had taken place.

2 And they were also conversing about this Jesus Christ
of which the sign had been given concerning his death.

3 And it came to pass that while they were thus conversing one with another,
they heard a voice as if it came out of heaven.
And they cast their eyes round about,
for they understood not the voice which they heard.
And it was not a harsh voice, neither was it a loud voice.
Nevertheless—and notwithstanding it being a small voice—
it did pierce them that did hear to the center,
insomuch that there were no part of their frame that it did not cause to quake.
Yea, it did pierce them to the very soul and did cause their hearts to burn.

4 And it came to pass that again they heard the voice,
and they understood it not.

5 And again the third time they did hear the voice
and did open their ears to hear it.
And their eyes were towards the sound thereof,
and they did look steadfastly towards heaven from whence the sound came.

6 And behold, the third time they did understand the voice which they heard,
and it saith unto them:

7 Behold my Beloved Son, in whom I am well pleased,
in whom I have glorified my name.
Hear ye him!

8 And it came to pass as they understood,
they cast their eyes up again towards heaven.
And behold, they saw a man descending out of heaven,
and he was clothed in a white robe.
And he came down and stood in the midst of them,
and the eyes of the whole multitude was turned upon him.

And they durst not open their mouths, even one to another,
and wist not what it meant,
for they thought it was an angel that had appeared unto them.

9 And it came to pass that he stretched forth his hand
and spake unto the people, saying:

10 Behold, I am Jesus Christ
—of which the prophets testified—
that should come into the world.

11 And behold, I am the light and the life of the world.
And I have drank out of that bitter cup which the Father hath given me
and have glorified the Father in taking upon me the sins of the world,
in the which I have suffered the will of the Father
in all things from the beginning.

12 And it came to pass that when Jesus had spake these words,
the whole multitude fell to the earth,
for they remembered that it had been prophesied among them
that Christ should shew himself unto them after his ascension into heaven.

13 And it came to pass that the Lord spake unto them, saying:

14 Arise and come forth unto me,
that ye may thrust your hands into my side,
and also that ye may feel the prints of the nails in my hands and in my feet,
that ye may know that I am the God of Israel and the God of the whole earth
and have been slain for the sins of the world.

15 And it came to pass that the multitude went forth
and thrust their hands into his side
and did feel the prints of the nails in his hands and in his feet.
And this they did do, going forth one by one
until they had all gone forth
and did see with their eyes and did feel with their hands
and did know of a surety
and did bear record that it was he
—of whom it was written by the prophets—
that should come.

16 And it came to pass that
when they had all gone forth and had witnessed for themselves,
they did cry out with one accord, saying:

17 Hosanna! Blessed be the name of the Most High God!
And they did fall down at the feet of Jesus and did worship him.

18 And it came to pass that he spake unto Nephi
—for Nephi was among the multitude—

and commanded him that he should come forth.

19 And Nephi arose and went forth and bowed himself before the Lord,
and he did kiss his feet.

20 And the Lord commanded him that he should arise;
and he arose and stood before him.

21 And the Lord said unto him:
I give unto you power that ye shall baptize this people
when I am again ascended into heaven.

22 And again the Lord called others and said unto them likewise;
and he gave unto them power to baptize.

And he saith unto them:
On this wise shall ye baptize,
and there shall be no disputations among you.

23 Verily I say unto you
that whoso repenteth of his sins through your words
and desireth to be baptized in my name,
on this wise shall ye baptize them.
Behold, ye shall go down and stand in the water,
and in my name shall ye baptize them.

24 And now behold, these are the words which ye shall say,
calling them by name, saying:

25 Having authority given me of Jesus Christ,
I baptize you in the name of the Father and of the Son and of the Holy Ghost.
Amen.

26 And then shall ye immerse them in the water
and come forth again out of the water.

27 And after this manner shall ye baptize in my name.
For behold, verily I say unto you
that the Father and the Son and the Holy Ghost are one;
and I am in the Father and the Father in me,
and the Father and I are one.

28 And according as I have commanded you, thus shall ye baptize.
And there shall be no disputations among you
as there hath hitherto been,
neither shall there be disputations among you
concerning the points of my doctrine
as there hath hitherto been.

29 For verily verily I say unto you:
He that hath the spirit of contention is not of me,
but is of the devil, which is the father of contention.
And he stirreth up the hearts of men

to contend with anger one with another.

30 Behold, this is not my doctrine,
   to stir up the hearts of men with anger one against another.
   But this is my doctrine,
   that such things should be done away.

31 Behold, verily verily I say unto you:
   I will declare unto you my doctrine.

32 And this is my doctrine,
   and it is the doctrine which the Father hath given unto me.
   And I bear record of the Father,
   and the Father beareth record of me,
   and the Holy Ghost beareth record of the Father and me.
   And I bear record that the Father commandeth all men everywhere
   to repent and believe in me.

33 And whoso believeth in me and is baptized, the same shall be saved.
   And they are they which shall inherit the kingdom of God.

34 And whoso believeth not in me and is not baptized shall be damned.

35 Verily verily I say unto you that this is my doctrine,
   and I bear record of it from the Father.
   And whoso believeth in me believeth in the Father also.
   And unto him will the Father bear record of me,
   for he will visit him with fire and with the Holy Ghost.

36 And thus will the Father bear record of me.
   And the Holy Ghost will bear record unto him of the Father and me,
   for the Father and I and the Holy Ghost are one.

37 And again I say unto you:
   Ye must repent and become as a little child and be baptized in my name,
   or ye can in no wise receive these things.

38 And again I say unto you:
   Ye must repent and be baptized in my name and become as a little child,
   or ye can in no wise inherit the kingdom of God.

39 Verily verily I say unto you that this is my doctrine.
   And whoso buildeth upon this buildeth upon my rock;
   and the gates of hell shall not prevail against them.

40 And whoso shall declare more or less than this
   and establisheth it for my doctrine,
   the same cometh of evil and is not built upon my rock,
   but he buildeth upon a sandy foundation;
   and the gates of hell standeth open to receive such
   when the floods come and the winds beat upon them.

41 Therefore go forth unto this people

and declare the words which I have spoken
unto the ends of the earth.

12 | 1   And it came to pass that when Jesus had spake these words
unto Nephi and to those which had been called
— now the number of them which had been called
and received power and authority to baptize were twelve —
and behold, he stretched forth his hand unto the multitude
and cried unto them, saying:
Blessed are ye if ye shall give heed unto the words of these twelve
which I have chosen from among you
to minister unto you and to be your servants.
And unto them I have given power
that they may baptize you with water.
And after that ye are baptized with water,
behold, I will baptize you with fire and with the Holy Ghost.
Therefore blessed are ye if ye shall believe in me and be baptized
after that ye have seen me and know that I am.

2   And again, more blessed are they which shall believe in your words
because that ye shall testify that ye have seen me
and that ye know that I am.
Yea, blessed are they which shall believe in your words
and come down into the depths of humility and be baptized,
for they shall be visited with fire and with the Holy Ghost
and shall receive a remission of their sins.

3   Yea, blessed are the poor in spirit which cometh unto me,
for theirs is the kingdom of heaven.

4   And again, blessed are all they that mourn,
for they shall be comforted.

5   And blessed are the meek,
for they shall inherit the earth.

6   And blessed are all they which do hunger and thirst after righteousness,
for they shall be filled with the Holy Ghost.

7   And blessed are the merciful,
for they shall obtain mercy.

8   And blessed are all the pure in heart,
for they shall see God.

9   And blessed are all the peacemakers,
for they shall be called the children of God.

10   And blessed are all they which are persecuted for my name's sake,
for theirs is the kingdom of heaven.

11 And blessed are ye when men shall revile you and persecute
and shall say all manner of evil against you falsely, for my sake,

12 for ye shall have great joy and be exceeding glad,
for great shall be your reward in heaven;
for so persecuted they the prophets which were before you.

13 Verily verily I say unto you:
I give unto you to be the salt of the earth.
But if the salt shall lose its savor,
wherewith shall the earth be salted?
The salt shall be thenceforth good for nothing
but to be cast out and to be trodden under foot of men.

14 Verily verily I say unto you:
I give unto you to be the light of this people.
A city that is set on a hill cannot be hid.

15 Behold, do men light a candle and put it under a bushel?
Nay, but on a candlestick,
and it giveth light to all that are in the house.

16 Therefore let your light so shine before this people,
that they may see your good works
and glorify your Father which is in heaven.

17 Think not that I am come to destroy the law or the prophets.
I am not come to destroy but to fulfill.

18 For verily I say unto you:
One jot nor one tittle hath not passed away from the law,
but in me it hath all been fulfilled.

19 And behold, I have given unto you
the law and the commandments of my Father,
that ye shall believe in me
and that ye shall repent of your sins
and come unto me with a broken heart and a contrite spirit.

Behold, ye have the commandments before you, and the law is fulfilled.

20 Therefore come unto me and be ye saved,
for verily I say unto you
that except ye shall keep my commandments,
which I have commanded you at this time,
ye shall in no case enter into the kingdom of heaven.

21 Ye have heard that it hath been said by them of old time
—and it is also written before you—
that thou shalt not kill.

And whosoever shall kill shall be in danger of the judgment of God.

22 But I say unto you
   that whosoever is angry with his brother shall be in danger of his judgment.
   And whosoever shall say to his brother, Raca, shall be in danger of the council;
   and whosoever shall say, thou fool, shall be in danger of hell fire.

23 Therefore if ye shall come unto me or shall desire to come unto me
   and rememberest that thy brother hath aught against thee,

24 go thy way unto thy brother and first be reconciled to thy brother
   and then come unto me with full purpose of heart and I will receive you.

25 Agree with thine adversary quickly
   while thou art in the way with him,
   lest at any time he shall get thee
   and thou shalt be cast into prison.

26 Verily I say unto thee:
   Thou shalt by no means come out thence
   until thou hast paid the uttermost senine.
   And while ye are in prison, can ye pay even one senine?
   Verily verily I say unto you: Nay.

27 Behold, it is written by them of old time
   that thou shalt not commit adultery.

28 But I say unto you
   that whosoever looketh on a woman to lust after her
   hath committed adultery already in his heart.

29 Behold, I give unto you a commandment
   that ye suffer none of these things to enter into your heart.

30 For it is better that ye should deny yourselves of these things,
   wherein ye will take up your cross,
   than that ye should be cast into hell.

31 It hath been written that whosoever shall put away his wife,
   let him give her a writing of divorcement.

32 Verily verily I say unto you
   that whosoever shall put away his wife,
   saving for the cause of fornication,
   causeth her to commit adultery;
   and whoso shall marry her who is divorced committeth adultery.

33 And again it is written:
   Thou shalt not forswear thyself
   but shalt perform unto the Lord thine oaths.

34 But verily verily I say unto you:

Swear not at all,
neither by heaven—for it is God's throne—
35 nor by the earth—for it is his footstool—
36 neither shalt thou swear by thy head,
because thou canst not make one hair black or white.
37 But let your communication be, yea yea, nay nay;
for whatsoever cometh of more than these are evil.

38 And behold, it is written:
An eye for an eye and a tooth for a tooth.
39 But I say unto you that ye shall not resist evil,
but whosoever shall smite thee on thy right cheek,
turn to him the other also.
40 And if any man will sue thee at the law and take away thy coat,
let him have thy cloak also.
41 And whosoever shall compel thee to go a mile,
go with him twain.
42 Give to him that asketh thee,
and from him that would borrow of thee turn thou not away.

43 And behold, it is written also
that thou shalt love thy neighbor and hate thine enemy.
44 But behold, I say unto you:
Love your enemies!
Bless them that curse you!
Do good to them that hate you,
and pray for them which despitefully use you and persecute you,
45 that ye may be the children of your Father which is in heaven,
for he maketh his sun to rise on the evil and on the good.

46 Therefore those things which were of old time
which were under the law,
in me are all fulfilled.
47 Old things are done away,
and all things have become new.
48 Therefore I would that ye should be perfect,
even as I or your Father which is in heaven is perfect.

13 | 1 Verily verily I say that I would that ye should do alms unto the poor.
But take heed that ye do not your alms before men, to be seen of them.
Otherwise ye have no reward of your Father which is in heaven.
2 Therefore when ye shall do your alms,
do not sound a trumpet before you,
as will hypocrites do in the synagogues and in the streets,

that they may have glory of men.
Verily I say unto you:
They have their reward.

3 But when thou doest alms,
let not thy left hand know what thy right hand doeth,

4 that thine alms may be in secret;
and thy Father, which seeth in secret, himself shall reward thee openly.

5 And when thou prayest, thou shalt not do as the hypocrites.
For they love to pray standing in the synagogues
and in the corners of the streets,
that they may be seen of men.
Verily I say unto you:
They have their reward.

6 But thou, when thou prayest, enter into thy closet.
And when thou hast shut thy door,
pray to thy Father, which is in secret;
and thy Father, which seeth in secret, shall reward thee openly.

7 But when ye pray, use not vain repetitions as the heathen,
for they think that they shall be heard for their much speaking.

8 Be not ye therefore like unto them,
for your Father knoweth what things ye have need of before ye ask him.

9 After this manner therefore pray ye:
Our Father which art in heaven,
hallowed be thy name.

10 Thy will be done in earth as it is in heaven.

11 And forgive us our debts as we forgive our debtors.

12 And lead us not into temptation but deliver us from evil,

13 for thine is the kingdom and the power and the glory forever.
Amen.

14 For if ye forgive men their trespasses,
your heavenly Father will also forgive you.

15 But if ye forgive not men their trespasses,
neither will your Father forgive your trespasses.

16 Moreover, when ye fast,
be not as the hypocrites of a sad countenance,
for they disfigure their faces that they may appear unto men to fast.
Verily I say unto you:
They have their reward.

17 But thou, when thou fastest,
anoint thy head and wash thy face,

18 that thou appear not unto men to fast
   but unto thy Father, which is in secret;
   and thy Father, which seeth in secret, shall reward thee openly.

19 Lay not up for yourselves treasures upon earth,
   where moth and rust doth corrupt
   and thieves break through and steal.
20 But lay up for yourselves treasures in heaven,
   where neither moth nor rust doth corrupt,
   and where thieves do not break through nor steal.
21 For where your treasure is, there will your heart be also.

22 The light of the body is the eye.
   If therefore thine eye be single,
   thy whole body shall be full of light.
23 But if thine eye be evil,
   thy whole body shall be full of darkness.
   If therefore the light that is in thee be darkness,
   how great is that darkness!

24 No man can serve two masters;
   for either he will hate the one and love the other,
   or else he will hold to the one and despise the other.
   Ye cannot serve God and mammon.

25 And now it came to pass that when Jesus had spoken these words,
   he looked upon the twelve whom he had chosen and saith unto them:
   Remember the words which I have spoken,
   for behold, ye are they which I have chosen to minister unto this people.
   Therefore I say unto you:
   Take no thought for your life,
   what ye shall eat or what ye shall drink,
   nor yet for your body, what ye shall put on.
   Is not the life more than meat and the body than raiment?

26 Behold the fowls of the air, for they sow not,
   neither do they reap nor gather into barns,
   yet your heavenly Father feedeth them.
   Are ye not much better than they?
27 Which of you, by taking thought, can add one cubit unto his stature?
28 And why take ye thought for raiment?
   Consider the lilies of the field, how they grow.
   They toil not, neither do they spin.

29 And yet I say unto you
    that even Solomon in all his glory was not arrayed like one of these.
30 Wherefore if God so clothe the grass of the field
    —which today is and tomorrow is cast into the oven—
    even so will he clothe you, if ye are not of little faith.

31 Therefore take no thought, saying:
    What shall we eat or what shall we drink
    or wherewithal shall we be clothed?
32 For your heavenly Father knoweth that ye have need of all these things.
33 But seek ye first the kingdom of God and his righteousness,
    and all these things shall be added unto you.
34 Take therefore no thought for the morrow,
    for the morrow shall take thought for the things of itself.
    Sufficient is the day unto the evil thereof.

14 | 1 And now it came to pass that
    when Jesus had spoken these words,
    he turned again to the multitude
    and did open his mouth unto them again, saying:
    Verily verily I say unto you:
    Judge not that ye be not judged.
2   For with what judgment ye judge, ye shall be judged.
    And with what measure ye mete, it shall be measured to you again.

3   And why beholdest thou the mote that is in thy brother's eye,
    but considerest not the beam that is in thine own eye?
4   Or how wilt thou say to thy brother:
    Let me pull out the mote out of thine eye—
    and behold, a beam is in thine own eye?
5   Thou hypocrite, first cast out the beam out of thine own eye,
    and then shalt thou see clearly to cast out the mote out of thy brother's eye.

6   Give not that which is holy unto the dogs,
    neither cast ye your pearls before swine
    lest they trample them under their feet and turn again and rend you.

7   Ask and it shall be given unto you;
    seek and ye shall find;
    knock and it shall be opened unto you.
8   For every one that asketh receiveth;
    and he that seeketh findeth;
    and to him that knocketh it shall be opened.
9   Or what man is there of you
    whom if his son ask bread, will he give him a stone?

10 Or if he ask a fish, will he give him a serpent?

11 If ye then, being evil, know how to give good gifts unto your children,
how much more shall your Father which is in heaven
give good things to them that ask him?

12 Therefore all things whatsoever ye would that men should do to you,
do ye even so to them,
for this is the law and the prophets.

13 Enter ye in at the strait gate,
for wide is the gate and broad is the way that leadeth to destruction.
And many there be which go in thereat,

14 because strait is the gate and narrow is the way which leadeth unto life,
and few there be that find it.

15 Beware of false prophets which come to you in sheep's clothing,
but inwardly they are ravening wolves.

16 Ye shall know them by their fruits.
Do men gather grapes of thorns or figs of thistles?

17 Even so every good tree bringeth forth good fruit,
but a corrupt tree bringeth forth evil fruit.

18 A good tree cannot bring forth evil fruit
neither a corrupt tree bring forth good fruit.

19 Every tree that bringeth not forth good fruit
is hewn down and cast into the fire.

20 Wherefore by their fruits ye shall know them.

21 Not every one that saith unto me, Lord Lord,
shall enter into the kingdom of heaven,
but he that doeth the will of my Father which is in heaven.

22 Many will say to me in that day:
Lord Lord, have we not prophesied in thy name
and in thy name have cast out devils
and in thy name done many wonderful works?

23 And then will I profess unto them:
I never knew you.
Depart from me, ye that work iniquity.

24 Therefore whoso heareth these sayings of mine and doeth them,
I will liken him unto a wise man which built his house upon a rock.

25 And the rain descended and the floods came,
and the winds blew and beat upon that house.
And it fell not, for it was founded upon a rock.

26 And every one that heareth these sayings of mine and doeth them not

shall be likened unto a foolish man which built his house upon the sand.

27 And the rain descended and the floods came,
and the winds blew and beat upon that house.
And it fell, and great was the fall of it.

⌐—⌐

15 | 1 And now it came to pass that when Jesus had ended these sayings,
he cast his eyes round about on the multitude and saith unto them:
Behold, ye have heard the things
which I have taught before I ascended to my Father.
Therefore whoso remembereth these sayings of mine and doeth them,
him will I raise up at the last day.

2 And it came to pass that when Jesus had said these words,
he perceived that there were some among them
which marveled and wondered what he would concerning the law of Moses,
for they understood not the saying
that old things had passed away
and that all things had become new.

3 And he saith unto them:
Marvel not that I said unto you that old things had passed away
and that all things had become new.

4 Behold, I say unto you that the law is fulfilled that was given unto Moses.

5 Behold, I am he that gave the law,
and I am he which covenanted with my people Israel.
Therefore the law in me is fulfilled,
for I have come to fulfill the law.
Therefore it hath an end.

6 Behold, I do not destroy the prophets,
for as many as have not been fulfilled in me
—verily I say unto you—shall all be fulfilled.

7 And because I said unto you that old things hath passed away,
I do not destroy that which hath been spoken
concerning things which is to come.

8 For behold, the covenant which I have made with my people is not all fulfilled,
but the law which was given unto Moses hath an end in me.

9 Behold, I am the law and the light.
Look unto me and endure to the end, and ye shall live;
for unto him that endureth to the end will I give eternal life.

10 Behold, I have given unto you the commandments.
Therefore keep my commandments;

and this is the law and the prophets,
for they truly testified of me.

11 And now it came to pass that when Jesus had spoken these words,
he said unto those twelve whom he had chosen:
12 Ye are my disciples,
and ye are a light unto this people,
which are a remnant of the house of Joseph.
13 And behold, this is the land of your inheritance,
and the Father hath given it unto you.
14 And not at any time hath the Father given me commandment
that I should tell it unto your brethren at Jerusalem.
15 Neither at any time hath the Father given me commandment
that I should tell unto them concerning the other tribes of the house of Israel,
which the Father hath led away out of the land.
16 This much did the Father command me that I should tell unto them,
17 that other sheep I have which are not of this fold;
them also I must bring, and they shall hear my voice;
and there shall be one fold and one shepherd.

18 And now because of stiffneckedness and unbelief
they understood not my word.
Therefore I was commanded to say no more
of the Father concerning this thing unto them.
19 But verily I say unto you that the Father hath commanded me
—and I tell it unto you—
that ye were separated from among them because of their iniquity.
Therefore it is because of their iniquity that they know not of you.

20 And verily I say unto you again
that the other tribes hath the Father separated from them.
And it is because of their iniquity that they know not of them.
21 And verily I say unto you that ye are they of which I said:
Other sheep I have which are not of this fold;
them also I must bring, and they shall hear my voice;
and there shall be one fold and one shepherd.
22 And they understood me not,
for they supposed it had been the Gentiles.
For they understood not
that the Gentiles should be converted through their preaching.
23 And they understood me not
that I said they shall hear my voice.
And they understood me not
that the Gentiles should not at any time hear my voice,

that I should not manifest myself unto them
save it were by the Holy Ghost.

24 But behold, ye have both heard my voice and seen me,
and ye are my sheep,
and ye are numbered among them which the Father hath given me.

16 | 1 And verily verily I say unto you
that I have other sheep which are not of this land,
neither of the land of Jerusalem,
neither in any parts of that land round about whither I have been to minister.

2 For they of which I speak are they which have not as yet heard my voice,
neither have I at any time manifested myself unto them.

3 But I have received a commandment of the Father that I shall go unto them
and that they shall hear my voice and shall be numbered among my sheep,
that there may be one fold and one shepherd.
Therefore I go to shew myself unto them.

4 And I command you that ye shall write these sayings after that I am gone,
that if it so be that my people at Jerusalem
—they which have seen me and been with me in my ministry—
do not ask the Father in my name
that they may receive a knowledge of you by the Holy Ghost,
and also of the other tribes which they know not of,
that these sayings which ye shall write shall be kept
and shall be manifested unto the Gentiles,
that through the fullness of the Gentiles
the remnant of their seed,
which shall be scattered forth upon the face of the earth
because of their unbelief,
may be brought in—
or may be brought to a knowledge of me, their Redeemer.

5 And then will I gather them in from the four quarters of the earth;
and then will I fulfill the covenant
which the Father hath made unto all the people of the house of Israel.

6 And blessed are the Gentiles because of their belief in me,
in and of the Holy Ghost, which witness unto them of me and of the Father.

7 Behold, because of their belief in me, saith the Father,
and because of the unbelief of you, O house of Israel,
in the latter day shall the truth come unto the Gentiles,
that the fullness of these things shall be made known unto them.

8 But woe, saith the Father, unto the unbelieving of the Gentiles,
for notwithstanding that they have come forth upon the face of this land
and have scattered my people which are of the house of Israel

—and my people which are of the house of Israel
have been cast out from among them
and have been trodden under feet by them—

9 and because of the mercies of the Father unto the Gentiles
and also the judgments of the Father
upon my people which are of the house of Israel,
verily verily I say unto you
that after all this and I have caused my people which are of the house of Israel
to be smitten and to be afflicted and to be slain
and to be cast out from among them and to become hated by them
and to become a hiss and a byword among them—

10 and thus commandeth the Father that I should say unto you:
At that day when the Gentiles shall sin against my gospel
and shall reject the fullness of my gospel
and shall be lifted up in the pride of their hearts
above all nations and above all the people of the whole earth
and shall be filled with all manner of lyings and of deceits and of mischiefs
and all manner of hypocrisy and murders and priestcrafts and whoredoms
and of secret abominations—
and if they shall do all these things and shall reject the fullness of my gospel,
behold, saith the Father, I will bring
the fullness of my gospel from among them.

11 And then will I remember my covenant
which I have made unto my people, O house of Israel,
and I will bring my gospel unto them.

12 And I will shew unto thee, O house of Israel,
that the Gentiles shall not have power over you,
but I will remember my covenant unto you, O house of Israel,
and ye shall come unto the knowledge of the fullness of my gospel.

13 But if the Gentiles will repent and return unto me, saith the Father,
behold, they shall be numbered among my people, O house of Israel.

14 And I will not suffer my people, which are of the house of Israel,
to go through among them and tread them down, saith the Father.

15 But if they will not return unto me and hearken unto my voice,
I will suffer them—yea, I will suffer my people, O house of Israel—
that they shall go through among them and shall tread them down.
And they shall be as salt that hath lost his savor,
which is thenceforth good for nothing but to be cast out
and to be trodden under foot of my people, O house of Israel.

16 Verily verily I say unto you:
Thus hath the Father commanded me

that I should give unto this people this land for their inheritance.

17 And when the words of the prophet Isaiah shall be fulfilled which saith:

18 Thy watchmen shall lift up the voice;
with the voice together shall they sing.
For they shall see eye to eye when the Lord shall bring again Zion.

19 Break forth into joy!
Sing together, ye waste places of Jerusalem!
For the Lord hath comforted his people;
he hath redeemed Jerusalem.

20 The Lord hath made bare his holy arm in the eyes of all the nations,
and all the ends of the earth shall see the salvation of God—

17 | 1 Behold, now it came to pass that
when Jesus had spoken these words,
he looked round about again on the multitude,
and he saith unto them:
Behold, my time is at hand.

2 I perceive that ye are weak,
that ye cannot understand all my words
which I am commanded of the Father to speak unto you,
at this time.

3 Therefore go ye unto your homes
and ponder upon the things which I have said
and ask of the Father in my name
that ye may understand and prepare your minds for the morrow,
and I come unto you again.

4 But now I go unto the Father,
and also to shew myself unto the lost tribes of Israel—
for they are not lost unto the Father,
for he knoweth whither he hath taken them.

5 And it came to pass that when Jesus had thus spoken,
he cast his eyes round about again on the multitude,
and behold, they were in tears
and did look steadfastly upon him,
as if they would ask him to tarry a little longer with them.

6 And he saith unto them:
Behold, my bowels is filled with compassion towards you.

7 Have ye any that are sick among you?
Bring them hither.
Have ye any that are lame or blind or halt or maimed or leprous

or that are withered or that are deaf or that are afflicted in any manner?
Bring them hither and I will heal them,
for I have compassion upon you;
my bowels is filled with mercy.

8 For I perceive that ye desire
that I should shew unto you what I have done unto your brethren at Jerusalem,
for I see that your faith is sufficient that I should heal you.

9 And it came to pass that when he had thus spoken,
all the multitude with one accord did go forth
with their sick and their afflicted and their lame
and with their blind and with their dumb
and with all they that were afflicted in any manner;
and he did heal them every one as they were brought forth unto him.

10 And they did all—both they which had been healed and they which were whole—
bow down at his feet and did worship him.
And as many as could come for the multitude did kiss his feet,
insomuch that they did bathe his feet with their tears.

11 And it came to pass that he commanded
that their little children should be brought.

12 So they brought their little children
and sat them down upon the ground round about him,
and Jesus stood in the midst;
and the multitude gave way till they had all been brought unto him.

13 And it came to pass that
when they had all been brought—and Jesus stood in the midst—
he commanded the multitude that they should kneel down upon the ground.

14 And it came to pass that when they had knelt upon the ground,
Jesus groaned within himself and saith:
Father, I am troubled
because of the wickedness of the people of the house of Israel.

15 And when he had said these words,
he himself also knelt upon the earth.
And behold, he prayed unto the Father,
and the things which he prayed cannot be written.
And the multitude did bear record which heard him;

16 and after this manner do they bear record:
The eye hath never seen, neither hath the ear heard before
so great and marvelous things as we saw and heard Jesus speak unto the Father.

17 And no tongue cannot speak, neither can there be written by any man,
neither can the hearts of men conceive so great and marvelous things
as we both saw and heard Jesus speak.

And no one can conceive of the joy
which filled our souls at the time we heard him pray for us unto the Father.

18 And it came to pass that
when Jesus had made an end of praying unto the Father, he arose.
But so great was the joy of the multitude that they were overcome.

19 And it came to pass that Jesus spake unto them and bade them arise;

20 and they arose from the earth.
And he saith unto them:
Blessed are ye because of your faith.
And now behold, my joy is full.

21 And when he had said these words, he wept;
and the multitude bare record of it.
And he took their little children, one by one, and blessed them
and prayed unto the Father for them.

22 And when he had done this, he wept again.

23 And he spake unto the multitude and saith unto them:
Behold your little ones.

24 And as they looked to behold,
they cast their eyes towards heaven;
and they saw the heavens open,
and they saw angels descending out of heaven
as it were in the midst of fire.
And they came down and encircled those little ones about
—and they were encircled about with fire—
and the angels did minister unto them.

25 And the multitude did see and hear and bear record.
And they know that their record is true,
for they all of them did see and hear, every man for himself.
And they were in number about two thousand and five hundred souls,
and they did consist of men, women, and children.

18 | 1 And it came to pass that Jesus commanded his disciples
that they should bring forth some bread and wine unto him.

2 And while they were gone for bread and wine,
he commanded the multitude
that they should sit themselves down upon the earth.

3 And when the disciples had come with bread and wine,
he took of the bread and brake and blessed it,
and he gave unto the disciples
and commanded that they should eat.

4 And when they had eat and were filled,
he commanded that they should give unto the multitude.

5 And when the multitude had eaten and were filled,
   he saith unto the disciples:
   Behold, there shall one be ordained among you,
   and to him will I give power that he shall break bread and bless it
   and give it unto the people of my church,
   unto all they which shall believe and be baptized in my name.
6 And this shall ye always observe to do, even as I have done,
   even as I have broken bread and blessed it and gave it unto you.
7 And this shall ye do in remembrance of my body, which I have shewn unto you.
   And it shall be a testimony unto the Father,
   that ye do always remember me.
   And if ye do always remember me,
   ye shall have my Spirit to be with you.

8 And it came to pass that when he had said these words,
   he commanded his disciples
   that they should take of the wine of the cup and drink of it,
   and that they should also give unto the multitude that they might drink of it.
9 And it came to pass that they did so and did drink of it and were filled.
   And they gave unto the multitude and they did drink and they were filled.
10 And when the disciples had done this, Jesus saith unto them:
   Blessed are ye for this thing which ye have done,
   for this is fulfilling my commandments.
   And this doth witness unto the Father
   that ye are willing to do that which I have commanded you.
11 And this shall ye always do unto those
   who repent and are baptized in my name.
   And ye shall do it in remembrance of my blood, which I have shed for you,
   that ye may witness unto the Father that ye do always remember me.
   And if ye do always remember me, ye shall have my Spirit to be with you.

12 And I give unto you a commandment that ye shall do these things.
   And if ye shall always do these things, blessed are ye,
   for ye are built upon my rock.
13 But whoso among you shall do more or less than these
   are not built upon my rock but are built upon a sandy foundation.
   And when the rain descends and the floods come
   and the winds blow and beat upon them,
   they shall fall;
   and the gates of hell is already open to receive them.
14 Therefore blessed are ye if ye shall keep my commandments,
   which the Father hath commanded me that I should give unto you.
15 Verily verily I say unto you:

Ye must watch and pray always lest ye be tempted by the devil
and ye are led away captive by him.

16 And as I have prayed among you,
even so shall ye pray in my church,
among my people which do repent and are baptized in my name.
Behold, I am the light;
I have set an example before you.

17 And it came to pass that when Jesus had spake these words unto his disciples,
he turned again unto the multitude and saith unto them:

18 Behold, verily verily I say unto you:
Ye must watch and pray always lest ye enter into temptation,
for Satan desireth to have you,
that he may sift you as wheat.

19 Therefore ye must always pray unto the Father in my name.

20 And whatsoever ye shall ask the Father in my name which is right,
believing that ye shall receive,
and behold, it shall be given unto you.

21 Pray in your families unto the Father always in my name,
that your wives and your children may be blessed.

22 And behold, ye shall meet together oft.
And ye shall not forbid any man from coming unto you
when ye shall meet together,
but suffer them that they may come unto you and forbid them not;

23 but ye shall pray for them and shall not cast them out.
And if it so be that they come unto you oft,
ye shall pray for them unto the Father in my name.

24 Therefore hold up your light,
that it may shine unto the world.
Behold, I am the light which ye shall hold up,
that which ye have seen me do.
Behold, ye see that I have prayed unto the Father,
and ye all have witnessed.

25 And ye see that I have commanded that none of you should go away,
but rather have commanded that ye should come unto me,
that ye might feel and see;
even so shall ye do unto the world.
And whosoever breaketh this commandment
suffereth himself to be led into temptation.

26 And now it came to pass that when Jesus had spoken these words,
he turned his eyes again upon the disciples whom he had chosen

and saith unto them:

27 Behold, verily verily I say unto you:
I give unto you another commandment;
and then I must go unto my Father,
that I may fulfill other commandments which he hath given me.

28 And now behold, this is the commandment which I give unto you,
that ye shall not suffer any one knowingly
to partake of my flesh and blood unworthily when ye shall minister it.

29 For whoso eateth and drinketh my flesh and blood unworthily
eateth and drinketh damnation to his soul.
Therefore if ye know that a man is unworthy
to eat and drink of my flesh and blood,
ye shall forbid him.

30 Nevertheless ye shall not cast him out from among you,
but ye shall minister unto him
and shall pray for him unto the Father in my name.
And if it so be that he repenteth and is baptized in my name,
then shall ye receive him
and shall minister unto him of my flesh and blood.

31 But if he repenteth not,
he shall not be numbered among my people,
that he may not destroy my people.
For behold, I know my sheep and they are numbered.

32 Nevertheless ye shall not cast him out of your synagogues,
or your places of worship,
for unto such shall ye continue to minister.
For ye know not but what they will return and repent
and come unto me with full purpose of heart
and I shall heal them,
and ye shall be the means of bringing salvation unto them.

33 Therefore keep these sayings which I have commanded you,
that ye come not under condemnation.
For woe unto him whom the Father condemneth.

34 And I give you these commandments
because of the disputations which hath been among you beforetimes.
And blessed are ye if ye have no disputations among you.

35 And now I go unto the Father
because it is expedient that I should go unto the Father for your sakes.

36 And it came to pass that when Jesus had made an end of these sayings,
he touched with his hand the disciples whom he had chosen, one by one,
even until he had touched them all

and spake unto them as he touched them.

37 And the multitude heard not the words which he spake;
therefore they did not bear record.
But the disciples bare record
that he gave them power to give the Holy Ghost.
And I will shew unto you hereafter that this record is true.

38 And it came to pass that when Jesus had touched them all,
there came a cloud and overshadowed the multitude,
that they could not see Jesus.

39 And while they were overshadowed,
he departed from them and ascended into heaven.
And the disciples saw and did bear record
that he ascended again into heaven.

19 | 1 And now it came to pass that
when Jesus had ascended into heaven,
the multitude did disperse;
and every man did take his wife and his children
and did return to his own home.

2 And it was noised abroad among the people immediately,
before it was yet dark,
that the multitude had seen Jesus
and that he had ministered unto them
and that he would also shew himself on the morrow unto the multitude.

3 Yea, and even all the night it was noised abroad concerning Jesus.
And insomuch did they send forth unto the people
that there were many — yea, an exceeding great number —
did labor exceedingly all that night
that they might be on the morrow in the place
where Jesus should shew himself unto the multitude.

4 And it came to pass that on the morrow
when the multitude was gathered together,
behold, Nephi and his brother
— whom he had raised from the dead, whose name was Timothy —
and also his son, whose name was Jonas,
and also Mathoni and Mathonihah, his brother,
and Kumen and Kumenonhi and Jeremiah and Shemnon
and Jonas and Zedekiah and Isaiah
— now these were the names of the disciples whom Jesus had chosen —
and it came to pass that they went forth

and stood in the midst of the multitude.

5 And behold, the multitude was so great
that they did cause that they should be separated into twelve bodies.

6 And the twelve did teach the multitude.
And behold, they did cause
that the multitude should kneel down upon the face of the earth
and should pray unto the Father in the name of Jesus.

7 And the disciples did pray unto the Father also in the name of Jesus.
And it came to pass that they arose and ministered unto the people.

8 And when they had ministered
them same words which Jesus had spoken,
nothing varying from the words which Jesus had spoken,
behold, they knelt again and prayed to the Father in the name of Jesus.

9 And they did pray for that which they most desired;
and they desired that the Holy Ghost should be given unto them.

10 And when they had thus prayed,
they went down unto the water's edge;
and the multitude followed them.

11 And it came to pass that Nephi went down into the water and was baptized.

12 And he came up out of the water and began to baptize,
and he baptized all they whom Jesus had chosen.

13 And it came to pass when they were all baptized
and had come up out of the water,
the Holy Ghost did fall upon them;
and they were filled with the Holy Ghost and with fire.

14 And behold, they were encircled about as if it were fire;
and it came down from heaven.
And the multitude did witness it and do bear record.
And angels did come down out of heaven and did minister unto them.

15 And it came to pass that while the angels were ministering unto the disciples,
behold, Jesus came and stood in the midst and ministered unto them.

16 And it came to pass that he spake unto the multitude
and commanded them that they should kneel down again upon the earth,
and also that his disciples should kneel down upon the earth.

17 And it came to pass that when they had all knelt down upon the earth,
he commanded his disciples that they should pray.

18 And behold, they began to pray;
and they did pray unto Jesus, calling him their Lord and their God.

19 And it came to pass that Jesus departed out of the midst of them
and went a little way off from them
and bowed himself to the earth, and he saith:

20 Father, I thank thee that thou hast given the Holy Ghost
  unto these whom I have chosen.
  And it is because of their belief in me
  that I have chosen them out of the world.

21 Father, I pray thee that thou wilt give the Holy Ghost
  unto all them that shall believe in their words.

22 Father, thou hast given them the Holy Ghost because they believe in me.
  And thou seest that they believe in me
  because thou hearest them, and they pray unto me;
  and they pray unto me because I am with them.

23 And now Father, I pray unto thee for them,
  and also for all they which shall believe on their words,
  that they may believe in me,
  that I may be in them as thou Father art in me,
  that we may be one.

24 And it came to pass that
  when Jesus had thus prayed unto the Father,
  he came unto his disciples,
  and behold, they did still continue without ceasing to pray unto him.
  And they did not multiply many words,
  for it was given unto them what they should pray;
  and they were filled with desire.

25 And it came to pass that Jesus blessed them as they did pray unto him.
  And his countenance did smile upon them,
  and the light of his countenance did shine upon them.
  And behold, they were as white as the countenance
  and also the garments of Jesus.
  And behold, the whiteness thereof did exceed all whiteness;
  yea, even there could be nothing upon earth so white as the whiteness thereof.

26 And Jesus saith unto them: Pray on.
  Never the less they did not cease to pray.

27 And he turned from them again and went a little way off
  and bowed himself to the earth,
  and he prayed again unto the Father, saying:

28 Father, I thank thee that thou hast purified these
  which I have chosen because of their faith.
  And I pray for them and also for them which shall believe on their words,
  that they may be purified in me through faith on their words,
  even as they are purified in me.

29 Father, I pray not for the world but for them
  which thou hast given unto me out of the world because of their faith,

that they may be purified in me,
that I may be in them as thou Father art in me,
that we may be one,
that I may be glorified in them.

30 And it came to pass that when Jesus had spake these words,
he came again unto his disciples,
and behold, they did pray steadfastly without ceasing unto him.
And he did smile upon them again.
And behold, they were white, even as Jesus.

31 And it came to pass that he went again a little way off
and prayed unto the Father.

32 And tongue cannot speak the words which he prayed,
neither can be written by man the words which he prayed.

33 And the multitude did hear and do bear record.
And their hearts were open,
and they did understand in their hearts the words which he prayed.

34 Nevertheless, so great and marvelous were the words which he prayed
that they cannot be written, neither can they be uttered by man.

35 And it came to pass that when Jesus had made an end of praying,
he came again to the disciples and saith unto them:
So great faith have I never seen among all the Jews.
Wherefore I could not shew unto them
so great miracles because of their unbelief.

36 Verily I say unto you:
There are none of them that have seen so great things as ye have seen,
neither have they heard so great things as ye have heard.

20 | 1 And it came to pass that he commanded the multitude
that they should cease to pray, and also his disciples.
And he commanded them that they should not cease to pray in their hearts.

2 And he commanded them that they should arise and stand up upon their feet.
And they arose up and stood upon their feet.

3 And it came to pass that he brake bread again
and blessed it and gave to the disciples to eat.

4 And when they had eat,
he commanded them that they should break bread
and give unto the multitude.

5 And when they had given unto the multitude,
he also gave them wine to drink
and commanded them that they should give unto the multitude.

6 Now there had been no bread neither wine

brought by the disciples, neither by the multitude.

7 But he truly gave unto them bread to eat, and also wine to drink.

8 And he saith unto them:
He that eateth this bread eateth of my body to their soul.
And he that drinketh of this wine drinketh of my blood to their soul.
And their soul shall never hunger nor thirst but shall be filled.

9 Now when the multitude had all eat and drank,
behold, they were filled with the Spirit.
And they did cry out with one voice
and gave glory to Jesus, whom they both saw and heard.

10 And it came to pass that when they had all given glory unto Jesus,
he saith unto them:
Behold, now I finish the commandment
which the Father hath commanded me concerning this people,
which are a remnant of the house of Israel.

11 Ye remember that I spake unto you
and said that when the words of Isaiah should be fulfilled—
behold, they are written;
ye have them before you.
Therefore search them.

12 And verily verily I say unto you
that when they shall be fulfilled,
then is the fulfilling of the covenant
which the Father hath made unto his people, O house of Israel.

13 And then shall the remnants
which shall be scattered abroad upon the face of the earth
be gathered in from the east and from the west
and from the south and from the north.
And they shall be brought to the knowledge
of the Lord their God who hath redeemed them.

14 And the Father hath commanded me
that I should give unto you this land for your inheritance.

15 And I say unto you that if the Gentiles do not repent
after the blessings which they shall receive,
after that they have scattered my people,

16 then shall ye which are a remnant of the house of Jacob go forth among them.
And ye shall be in the midst of them, which shall be many,
and ye shall be among them as a lion among the beasts of the forest.
And as a young lion among the flocks of sheep
who, if he goeth through, both treadeth down and teareth in pieces,
and none can deliver.

17 Thy hand shall be lifted up upon thine adversaries,
and all thine enemies shall be cut off.

18 And I will gather my people together
as a man gathereth his sheaves into the floor,

19 for I will make my people with whom the Father hath covenanted.
Yea, I will make thy horn iron,
and I will make thy hoofs brass;
and thou shalt beat in pieces many people.
And I will consecrate their gain unto the Lord
and their substance unto the Lord of the whole earth.
And behold, I am he which doeth it.

20 And it shall come to pass, saith the Father,
that the sword of my justice shall hang over them at that day.
And except they repent, it shall fall upon them, saith the Father,
yea, even upon all the nations of the Gentiles.

21 And it shall come to pass that I will establish my people, O house of Israel.

22 And behold, this people will I establish in this land
unto the fulfilling of the covenant which I made with your father Jacob;
and it shall be a New Jerusalem.
And the powers of heaven shall be in the midst of this people;
yea, even I will be in the midst of you.

23 Behold, I am he of whom Moses spake, saying:
A prophet shall the Lord your God raise up
unto you, of your brethren, like unto me.
Him shall ye hear in all things whatsoever he shall say unto you.
And it shall come to pass that every soul which will not hear that prophet
shall be cut off from among the people.

24 Verily I say unto you:
Yea, and all the prophets from Samuel and those that follow after,
as many as have spoken, have testified of me.

25 And behold, ye are the children of the prophets,
and ye are of the house of Israel,
and ye are of the covenant which the Father made with your fathers,
saying unto Abraham:
And in thy seed shall all the kindreds of the earth be blessed.

26 The Father having raised me up unto you first
and sent me to bless you
in turning away every one of you from his iniquities—
and this because ye are the children of the covenant.

27 And after that ye were blessed,
then fulfilleth the Father the covenant
which he made with Abraham, saying:
In thy seed shall all the kindreds of the earth be blessed—
unto the pouring out of the Holy Ghost through me upon the Gentiles,
which blessing upon the Gentiles shall make them mighty above all,
unto the scattering of my people, O house of Israel.

28 And they shall be a scourge unto the people of this land.

Nevertheless, when they shall have received the fullness of my gospel,
then if they shall harden their hearts against me,
I will return their iniquities upon their own heads, saith the Father,

29 and I will remember the covenant which I have made with my people.
And I have covenanted with them
that I would gather them together in mine own due time,
that I would give unto them again the land of their fathers for their inheritance,
which is the land of Jerusalem,
which is the promised land unto them forever, saith the Father.

30 And it shall come to pass that the time cometh
when the fullness of my gospel shall be preached unto them.

31 And they shall believe in me,
that I am Jesus Christ the Son of God,
and shall pray unto the Father in my name.

32 Then shall their watchmen lift up their voice;
and with the voice together shall they sing,
for they shall see eye to eye.

33 Then will the Father gather them together again
and give unto them Jerusalem for the land of their inheritance.

34 Then shall they break forth into joy.
Sing together, ye waste places of Jerusalem!
For the Father hath comforted his people;
he hath redeemed Jerusalem.

35 The Father hath made bare his holy arm in the eyes of all the nations,
and all the ends of the earth shall see the salvation of the Father.
And the Father and I are one.

36 And then shall be brought to pass that which is written:
Awake, awake again and put on thy strength, O Zion!
Put on thy beautiful garments, O Jerusalem the holy city!
For henceforth there shall no more come into thee
the uncircumcised and the unclean.

37 Shake thyself from the dust! Arise!

Sit down, O Jerusalem!
Loose thyself from the bands of thy neck, O captive daughter of Zion!
38 For thus saith the Lord:
Ye have sold yourselves for naught;
and ye shall be redeemed without money.

39 Verily verily I say unto you
that my people shall know my name.
Yea, in that day they shall know that I am he that doth speak.
40 And then shall they say:
How beautiful upon the mountains are the feet of him
that bringeth good tidings unto them,
that publisheth peace,
that bringeth good tidings unto them of good,
that publisheth salvation,
that saith unto Zion:
Thy God reigneth!

41 And then shall a cry go forth:
Depart ye, depart ye!
Go ye out from thence!
Touch not that which is unclean!
Go ye out of the midst of her!
Be ye clean that bear the vessels of the Lord!
42 For ye shall not go out with haste nor go by flight;
for the Lord will go before you,
and the God of Israel shall be your rearward.
43 Behold, my servant shall deal prudently.
He shall be exalted and extolled and be very high.
44 As many were astonished at thee
—his visage was so marred, more than any man,
and his form more than the sons of men—
45 so shall he sprinkle many nations.
The kings shall shut their mouths at him;
for that which had not been told them shall they see,
and that which they had not heard shall they consider.

46 Verily verily I say unto you:
All these things shall surely come,
even as the Father hath commanded me.
And then shall this covenant
which the Father hath covenanted with his people
be fulfilled.

And then shall Jerusalem be inhabited again with my people,
and it shall be the land of their inheritance.

21 | 1 And verily I say unto you:
I give unto you a sign that ye may know the time
when these things shall be about to take place,
that I shall gather in from their long dispersion my people, O house of Israel,
and shall establish again among them my Zion.

2 And behold, this is the thing which I will give unto you for a sign.
For verily I say unto you
that when these things which I declare unto you
—and which I shall declare unto you hereafter of myself
and by the power of the Holy Ghost,
which shall be given unto you of the Father—
shall be made known unto the Gentiles,
that they may know concerning this people
which are a remnant of the house of Jacob
and concerning this my people which shall be scattered by them—

3 verily verily I say unto you:
When these things shall be made known unto them of the Father
and shall come forth of the Father from them unto you—

4 for it is wisdom in the Father
that they should be established in this land
and be set up as a free people by the power of the Father,
that these things might come forth from them unto a remnant of your seed,
that the covenant of the Father may be fulfilled
which he hath covenanted with his people, O house of Israel—

5 therefore when these works,
and the works which shall be wrought among you hereafter,
shall come forth from the Gentiles unto your seed,
which shall dwindle in unbelief because of iniquity—

6 for thus it behooveth the Father
that it should come forth from the Gentiles,
that he may shew forth his power unto the Gentiles,
for this cause that the Gentiles—if they will not harden their hearts—
that they may repent and come unto me and be baptized in my name
and know of the true points of my doctrine,
that they may be numbered among my people, O house of Israel.

7 And when these things come to pass,
that thy seed shall begin to know these things,
it shall be a sign unto them
that they may know that the work of the Father hath already commenced

unto the fulfilling of the covenant which he hath made unto the people
which are of the house of Israel.

8 And when that day shall come,
it shall come to pass that kings shall shut their mouths;
for that which had not been told them shall they see,
and that which they had not heard shall they consider.

9 For in that day, for my sake, shall the Father work a work
which shall be a great and a marvelous work among them.
And there shall be many among them which will not believe it,
although a man shall declare it unto them.

10 But behold, the life of my servant shall be in my hand;
therefore they shall not hurt him,
although he shall be marred because of them.
Yet I will heal him,
for I will shew unto them that my wisdom is greater
than the cunning of the devil.

11 Therefore it shall come to pass that
whosoever will not believe in my words—which am Jesus Christ—
which the Father shall cause him to bring forth unto the Gentiles
and shall give unto him power that he shall bring them forth unto the Gentiles,
it shall be done, even as Moses said:
They shall be cut off from among my people which are of the covenant.

12 And my people which are a remnant of Jacob shall be among the Gentiles,
yea, in the midst of them as a lion among the beasts of the forest,
as a young lion among the flocks of sheep
who, if he go through, both treadeth down and teareth in pieces,
and none can deliver.

13 Their hand shall be lifted up upon their adversaries,
and all their enemies shall be cut off.

14 Yea, woe be unto the Gentiles except they repent.
For it shall come to pass in that day, saith the Father,
that I will cut off thy horses out of the midst of thee,
and I will destroy thy chariots.

15 And I will cut off the cities of thy land
and throw down all thy strong holds.

16 And I will cut off witchcrafts out of thy hand,
and thou shalt have no more soothsayers.

17 Thy graven images I will also cut off,
and thy standing images out of the midst of thee.
And thou shalt no more worship the works of thy hands.

18 And I will pluck up thy groves out of the midst of thee;
so will I destroy thy cities.

19 And it shall come to pass that all lyings and deceivings
and envyings and strifes and priestcrafts and whoredoms shall be done away.

20 For it shall come to pass, saith the Father,
that at that day whosoever will not repent and come unto my Beloved Son,
them will I cut off from among my people, O house of Israel.

21 And I will execute vengeance and fury upon them,
even as upon the heathen, such as they have not heard.

22 But if they will repent and hearken unto my words
and harden not their hearts,
I will establish my church among them.
And they shall come in unto the covenant
and be numbered among this the remnant of Jacob,
unto whom I have given this land for their inheritance.

23 And they shall assist my people, the remnant of Jacob,
and also as many of the house of Israel as shall come,
that they may build a city which shall be called the New Jerusalem.

24 And then shall they assist my people
that they may be gathered in
which are scattered upon all the face of the land,
in unto the New Jerusalem.

25 And then shall the powers of heaven come down among them,
and I also will be in the midst.

26 And then shall the work of the Father commence at that day,
even when this gospel shall be preached among the remnant of this people.

Verily I say unto you:
At that day shall the work of the Father commence
among all the dispersed of my people,
yea, even the tribes which have been lost,
which the Father hath led away out of Jerusalem.

27 Yea, the work shall commence
among all the dispersed of my people
with the Father to prepare the way
whereby they may come unto me,
that they may call on the Father in my name.

28 Yea, and then shall the work commence with the Father
among all nations in preparing the way

whereby his people may be gathered home to the land of their inheritance.

29 And they shall go out from all nations.
And they shall not go out in haste nor go by flight,
for I will go before them, saith the Father,
and I will be their rearward.

22 | 1 And then shall that which is written come to pass:
Sing, O barren,
thou that didst not bear.
Break forth into singing and cry aloud,
thou that didst not travail with child.
For more are the children of the desolate
than the children of the married wife, saith the Lord.

2 Enlarge the place of thy tent,
and let them stretch forth the curtains of thy habitations.
Spare not! Lengthen thy cords and strengthen thy stakes!

3 For thou shalt break forth on the right hand and on the left.
And thy seed shall inherit the Gentiles
and make the desolate cities to be inhabited.

4 Fear not, for thou shalt not be ashamed,
neither be thou confounded,
for thou shalt not be put to shame;
for thou shalt forget the shame of thy youth
and shalt not remember the reproach of thy widowhood any more.

5 For thy maker, thy husband, the Lord of Hosts is his name.
And thy Redeemer, the Holy One of Israel,
the God of the whole earth shall he be called.

6 For the Lord hath called thee
as a woman forsaken and grieved in spirit,
and a wife of youth,
when thou wast refused, saith thy God.

7 For a small moment have I forsaken thee,
but with great mercies will I gather thee.

8 In a little wrath I hid my face from thee for a moment,
but with everlasting kindness will I have mercy on thee,
saith the Lord thy Redeemer.

9 For this, the waters of Noah unto me.
For as I have sworn that the waters of Noah should no more go over the earth,
so have I sworn that I would not be wroth with thee.

10 For the mountains shall depart and the hills be removed,
but my kindness shall not depart from thee.

Neither shall the covenant of my peace be removed,
saith the Lord that hath mercy on thee.

11 O thou afflicted, tossed with tempest and not comforted!

Behold, I will lay thy stones with fair colors
and lay thy foundations with sapphires.

12 And I will make thy windows of agates
and thy gates of carbuncles
and all thy borders of pleasant stones.

13 And all thy children shall be taught of the Lord,
and great shall be the peace of thy children.

14 In righteousness shalt thou be established.
Thou shalt be far from oppression, for thou shalt not fear,
and from terror, for it shall not come near thee.

15 Behold, they shall surely gather together against thee, not by me.
Whosoever shall gather together against thee shall fall for thy sake.

16 Behold, I have created the smith that bloweth the coals in the fire
and that bringeth forth an instrument for his work.
And I have created the waster to destroy.

17 No weapon that is formed against thee shall prosper.
And every tongue that shall rise against thee in judgment,
thou shalt condemn.
This is the heritage of the servants of the Lord;
and their righteousness is of me, saith the Lord.

23 | 1 And now behold, I say unto you
that ye had ought to search these things.
Yea, a commandment I give unto you
that ye search these things diligently,
for great is the words of Isaiah.

2 For surely he spake as touching all things
concerning my people which are of the house of Israel.
Therefore it must needs be that he must speak also to the Gentiles.

3 And all things that he spake hath been and shall be,
even according to the words which he spake.

4 Therefore give heed to my words.
Write the things which I have told you.
And according to the time and the will of the Father,
they shall go forth unto the Gentiles.

5 And whosoever will hearken unto my words
and repenteth and is baptized,

the same shall be saved.
Search the prophets, for many there be that testify of these things.

6 And now it came to pass that
when Jesus had said these words,
he saith unto them again —
after he had expounded all the scriptures unto them
which they had received,
he saith unto them:
Behold, other scriptures I would that ye should write that ye have not.

7 And it came to pass that he saith unto Nephi:
Bring forth the record which ye have kept.

8 And when Nephi had brought forth the records
and laid them before him,
and he cast his eyes upon them and saith:

9 Verily I say unto you:
I commanded my servant Samuel the Lamanite
that he should testify unto this people
that at the day that the Father should glorify his name in me
that there were many saints which should arise from the dead
and should appear unto many and should minister unto them.
And he saith unto them:
Were it not so?

10 And his disciples answered him and said:
Yea, Lord, Samuel did prophesy according to thy words,
and they were all fulfilled.

11 And Jesus saith unto them:
How be it that ye have not written this thing?
— that many saints did arise and appear unto many
and did minister unto them.

12 And it came to pass that Nephi remembered
that this thing had not been written.

13 And it came to pass that Jesus commanded that it should be written.
Therefore it was written according as he commanded.

14 And now it came to pass that
when Jesus had expounded all the scriptures in one which they had written,
he commanded them that they should teach the things
which he had expounded unto them.

24 | 1 And it came to pass that he commanded them
that they should write the words which the Father had given unto Malachi

which he should tell unto them.
And it came to pass that after they were written, he expounded them.

And these are the words which he did tell unto them, saying:
Thus said the Father unto Malachi:
Behold, I will send my messenger,
and he shall prepare the way before me.
And the Lord whom ye seek shall suddenly come to his temple,
even the messenger of the covenant whom ye delight in.
Behold, he shall come, saith the Lord of Hosts.

2 But who may abide the day of his coming?
And who shall stand when he appeareth?
For he is like a refiner's fire and like fullers' soap.

3 And he shall sit as a refiner and purifier of silver.
And he shall purify the sons of Levi and purge them as gold and silver,
that they may offer unto the Lord an offering in righteousness.

4 Then shall the offering of Judah and Jerusalem be pleasant unto the Lord
as in the days of old and as in former years.

5 And I will come near to you to judgment.
And I will be a swift witness against the sorcerers
and against the adulterers and against false swearers
and against those that oppress the hireling in his wages,
the widow and the fatherless,
and that turn aside the stranger and fear not me,
saith the Lord of Hosts.

6 For I am the Lord; I change not.
Therefore ye sons of Jacob are not consumed.

7 Even from the days of your fathers,
ye are gone away from mine ordinances and have not kept them.
Return unto me, and I will return unto you, saith the Lord of Hosts.
But ye said: Wherein shall we return?

8 Will a man rob God? Yet ye have robbed me!
But ye say: Wherein have we robbed thee?
In tithes and offerings!

9 Ye are cursed with a curse,
for ye have robbed me, even this whole nation.

10 Bring ye all the tithes into the storehouse,
that there may be meat in my house.
And prove me now herewith, saith the Lord of Hosts,
if I will not open you the windows of heaven
and pour you out a blessing
that there shall not be room enough to receive it.

11 And I will rebuke the devourer for your sakes,
   and he shall not destroy the fruits of your ground;
   neither shall your vine cast her fruit before the time in the field,
   saith the Lord of Hosts.

12 And all nations shall call you blessed,
   for ye shall be a delightsome land,
   saith the Lord of Hosts.

13 Your words have been stout against me, saith the Lord.
   Yet ye say: What have we spoken against thee?

14 Ye have said: It is vain to serve God.
   And what doth it profit that we have kept his ordinance
   and that we have walked mournfully before the Lord of Hosts?

15 And now, we call the proud happy.
   Yea, they that work wickedness are set up;
   yea, them that tempt God are even delivered.

16 Then they that feared the Lord spake often one to another,
   and the Lord hearkened and heard.
   And a book of remembrance was written before him
   for them that feared the Lord
   and that thought upon his name.

17 And they shall be mine, saith the Lord of Hosts,
   in that day when I make up my jewels.
   And I will spare them as a man spareth his own son that serveth him.

18 Then shall ye return and discern between the righteous and the wicked,
   between him that serveth God and him that serveth him not.

25 | 1 For behold, the day cometh that shall burn as an oven.
   And all the proud—yea, and all that do wickedly—shall be stubble.
   And the day that cometh shall burn them up, saith the Lord of Hosts,
   that it shall leave them neither root nor branch.

2 But unto you that fear my name
   shall the Sun of righteousness arise with healing in his wings.
   And ye shall go forth and grow up as calves of the stall.

3 And ye shall tread down the wicked,
   for they shall be ashes under the soles of your feet
   in the day that I shall do this, saith the Lord of Hosts.

4 Remember ye the law of Moses my servant,
   which I commanded unto him in Horeb for all Israel
   with the statutes and judgments.

5 Behold, I will send you Elijah the prophet
   before the coming of the great and dreadful day of the Lord.

6 And he shall turn the heart of the fathers to the children
and the heart of the children to their fathers,
lest I come and smite the earth with a curse.

26 | 1 And now it came to pass that when Jesus had told these things,
he expounded them unto the multitude.
And he did expound all things unto them, both great and small.
2 And he saith:
These scriptures which ye had not with you,
the Father commanded that I should give unto you.
For it was wisdom in him that they should be given unto future generations.
3 And he did expound all things, even from the beginning
until the time that he should come in his glory
—yea, even all things which should come upon the face of the earth—
even until the elements should melt with fervent heat
and the earth should be wrapped together as a scroll
and the heavens and the earth should pass away,
4 and even unto the great and last day
when all people and all kindreds and all nations and tongues
shall stand before God to be judged of their works,
whether they be good or whether they be evil—
5 if they be good, to the resurrection of everlasting life;
and if they be evil, to the resurrection of damnation
—being on a parallel, the one on the one hand and the other on the other hand—
according to the mercy and the justice and the holiness which is in Christ,
which was before the world began.

6 And now there cannot be written in this book
even an hundredth part of the things
which Jesus did truly teach unto the people.
7 But behold, the plates of Nephi do contain
the more part of the things which he taught the people.
8 And these things have I written
which are a lesser part of the things which he taught the people.
And I have wrote them to the intent
that they may be brought again unto this people from the Gentiles,
according to the words which Jesus hath spoken.
9 And when they shall have received this
—which is expedient that they should have first, to try their faith—
and if it should so be that they shall believe these things,
then shall the greater things be made manifest unto them.

10 And if it so be that they will not believe these things,
then shall the greater things be withheld from them, unto their condemnation.

11 Behold, I were about to write them all
which were engraven upon the plates of Nephi,
but the Lord forbid it, saying:
I will try the faith of my people.

12 Therefore I Mormon do write the things
which have been commanded me of the Lord.

And now I Mormon make an end of my sayings
and proceed to write the things which have been commanded me.

13 Therefore I would that ye should behold
that the Lord truly did teach the people for the space of three days.
And after that, he did shew himself unto them oft
and did break bread oft and bless it and give it unto them.

14 And it came to pass that he did teach and minister
unto the children of the multitude, of whom hath been spoken,
and he did loose their tongues.
And they did speak unto their fathers great and marvelous things—
even greater than he had revealed unto the people
and loosed their tongues that they could utter.

15 And it came to pass that after he had ascended into heaven
—the second time that he shewed himself unto them—
and gone unto the Father,
after having healed all their sick and their lame
and opened the eyes of the blind and unstopped the ears of the deaf
—and even had done all manner of cures among them—
and raised a man from the dead
and had shewn forth his power unto them
and had ascended unto the Father,

16 behold, it came to pass on the morrow
that the multitude gathered themselves together.
And they both saw and heard these children,
yea, even babes did open their mouths and utter marvelous things.
And the things which they did utter were forbidden,
that there should not any man write them.

17 And it came to pass that the disciples whom Jesus had chosen
began from that time forth to baptize and to teach
as many as did come unto them.
And as many as were baptized in the name of Jesus
were filled with the Holy Ghost.

18 And many of them saw and heard unspeakable things
      which are not lawful to be written.

19 And they taught and did minister one to another;
      and they had all things common among them,
      every man dealing justly one with another.

20 And it came to pass that they did do all things
      even as Jesus had commanded them.

21 And they which were baptized in the name of Jesus
      were called the church of Christ.

27 | 1 And it came to pass that as the disciples of Jesus were journeying
      and were preaching the things which they had both heard and seen
      and were baptizing in the name of Jesus,
      it came to pass that the disciples were gathered together
      and were united in mighty prayer and fasting.

2 And Jesus again shewed himself unto them,
      for they were praying unto the Father in his name.
      And Jesus came and stood in the midst of them
      and saith unto them:
      What will ye that I shall give unto you?

3 And they saith unto him:
      Lord, we will that thou wouldst tell us the name
      whereby we shall call this church,
      for there are disputations among the people concerning this matter.

4 And the Lord said unto them:
      Verily verily I say unto you:
      Why is it that the people should murmur and dispute because of this thing?

5 Have they not read the scriptures which saith:
      Ye must take upon you the name of Christ,
      which is my name.
      For by this name shall ye be called at the last day.

6 And whoso taketh upon him my name and endureth to the end,
      the same shall be saved at the last day.

7 Therefore whatsoever ye shall do,
      ye shall do it in my name.
      Therefore ye shall call the church in my name.
      And ye shall call upon the Father in my name,
      that he will bless the church for my sake.

8 And how be it my church save it be called in my name?
      For if a church be called in Moses' name, then it be Moses' church.
      Or if it be called in the name of a man, then it be the church of a man.

But if it be called in my name, then it is my church,
if it so be that they are built upon my gospel.

9 Verily I say unto you that ye are built upon my gospel;
therefore ye shall call whatsoever things ye do call, in my name.
Therefore if ye call upon the Father for the church,
if it be in my name, the Father will hear you.

10 And if it so be that the church is built upon my gospel,
then will the Father shew forth his own works in it.

11 But if it be not built upon my gospel
and is built upon the works of men or upon the works of the devil,
verily I say unto you:
They have joy in their works for a season;
and by and by the end cometh,
and they are hewn down and cast into the fire
from whence there is no return.

12 For their works do follow them,
for it is because of their works that they are hewn down.
Therefore remember the things that I have told you.

13 Behold, I have given unto you my gospel.
And this is the gospel which I have given unto you,
that I came into the world to do the will of my Father,
because my Father sent me.

14 And my Father sent me that I might be lifted up upon the cross
—and after that I had been lifted up upon the cross,
I might draw all men unto me—
that as I have been lifted up by men,
even so should men be lifted up by the Father
to stand before me to be judged of their works,
whether they be good or whether they be evil.

15 And for this cause have I been lifted up.
Therefore, according to the power of the Father,
I will draw all men unto me
that they may be judged according to their works.

16 And it shall come to pass that whoso repenteth
and is baptized in my name shall be filled.
And if he endureth to the end,
behold, him will I hold guiltless before my Father
at that day when I shall stand to judge the world.

17 And he that endureth not unto the end,
the same is he that is also hewn down and cast into the fire

from whence they can no more return
because of the justice of the Father.

18 And this is the word which he hath given unto the children of men.
And for this cause he fulfilleth the words which he hath given;
and he lieth not but fulfilleth all his words.

19 And no unclean thing can enter into his kingdom.
Therefore nothing entereth into his rest
save it be those who have washed their garments in my blood
because of their faith and the repentance of all their sins
and their faithfulness unto the end.

20 Now this is the commandment:
repent, all ye ends of the earth,
and come unto me and be baptized in my name,
that ye may be sanctified by the reception of the Holy Ghost,
that ye may stand spotless before me at the last day.

21 Verily verily I say unto you: This is my gospel.
And ye know the things that ye must do in my church.
For the works which ye have seen me do, that shall ye also do;
for that which ye have seen me do, even that shall ye do.

22 Therefore if ye do these things, blessed are ye,
for ye shall be lifted up at the last day.

23 Write the things which ye have seen and heard,
save it be those which are forbidden.

24 Write the works of this people which shall be,
even as hath been written of that which hath been.

25 For behold, out of the books
which have been written and which shall be written
shall this people be judged,
for by them shall their works be known unto men.

26 And behold, all things are written by the Father.
Therefore out of the books which shall be written shall the world be judged.

27 And know ye that ye shall be judges of this people,
according to the judgment which I shall give unto you, which shall be just.
Therefore what manner of men had ye ought to be?
Verily I say unto you: Even as I am.

28 And now I go unto the Father.
And verily I say unto you:
Whatsoever things ye shall ask the Father in my name,

it shall be given unto you.

29 Therefore ask and ye shall receive;
knock and it shall be opened unto you.
For he that asketh receiveth;
and unto him that knocketh it shall be opened.

30 And now behold, my joy is great, even unto fullness,
because of you and also this generation.
Yea, and even the Father rejoiceth, and also all the holy angels,
because of you and this generation,
for none of them are lost.

31 Behold, I would that ye should understand,
for I mean them which are now alive of this generation.
And none of them are lost,
and in them I have fullness of joy.

32 But behold, it sorroweth me
because of the fourth generation from this generation,
for they are led away captive by him,
even as was the son of perdition.
For they will sell me for silver and for gold
and for that which moth doth corrupt
and which thieves can break through and steal.
And in that day will I visit them,
even in turning their works upon their own heads.

33 And it came to pass that when Jesus had ended these sayings,
he saith unto his disciples:
Enter ye in at the strait gate.
For strait is the gate and narrow is the way that leads to life,
and few there be that find it.
But wide is the gate and broad the way which leads to death,
and many there be that traveleth therein
until the night cometh wherein no man can work.

28 | 1 And it came to pass when Jesus had said these words,
he spake unto his disciples one by one, saying unto them:
What is it that ye desire of me after that I am gone to the Father?

2 And they all spake, save it were three, saying:
We desire that after we have lived unto the age of man
that our ministry wherein thou hast called us may have an end,
that we may speedily come unto thee in thy kingdom.

3 And he saith unto them:

Blessed are ye because ye desire this thing of me.
Therefore after that ye are seventy and two years old,
ye shall come unto me in my kingdom,
and with me ye shall find rest.

4 And when he had spake unto them,
he turned himself unto the three and said unto them:
What will ye that I should do unto you when I am gone unto the Father?
5 And they sorrowed in their hearts,
for they durst not speak unto him the thing which they desired.
6 And he saith unto them:
Behold, I know your thoughts.
And ye have desired the thing
which John my beloved,
which was with me in my ministry before that I was lifted up by the Jews,
desired of me.
7 Therefore more blessed are ye;
for ye shall never taste of death,
but ye shall live to behold all the doings of the Father unto the children of men,
even until all things shall be fulfilled according to the will of the Father
when I shall come in my glory with the powers of heaven.
8 And ye shall never endure the pains of death.
But when I shall come in my glory,
ye shall be changed in the twinkling of an eye from mortality to immortality.
And then shall ye be blessed in the kingdom of my Father.
9 And again, ye shall not have pain while ye shall dwell in the flesh,
neither sorrow, save it be for the sins of the world.

And all this will I do because of the thing which ye have desired of me,
for ye have desired that ye might bring the souls of men unto me
while the world shall stand.
10 And for this cause ye shall have fullness of joy;
and ye shall sit down in the kingdom of my Father.
Yea, your joy shall be full, even as the Father hath given me fullness of joy.
And ye shall be even as I am,
and I am even as the Father;
and the Father and I are one.
11 And the Holy Ghost beareth record of the Father and me.
And the Father giveth the Holy Ghost unto the children of men because of me.

12 And it came to pass that when Jesus had spake these words,
he touched every one of them with his finger

save it were the three which were to tarry;
and then he departed.

13 And behold, the heavens were opened,
and they were caught up into heaven
and saw and heard unspeakable things.

14 And it was forbidden them that they should utter,
neither was it given unto them power
that they could utter the things which they saw and heard.

15 And whether they were in the body or out of the body, they could not tell.
For it did seem unto them like a transfiguration of them,
that they were changed from this body of flesh into an immortal state,
that they could behold the things of God.

16 But it came to pass that they did again minister upon the face of the earth.
Nevertheless they did not minister of the things which they had heard and seen
because of the commandment which was given them in heaven.

17 And now whether they were mortal or immortal
from the day of their transfiguration,
I know not.

18 But this much I know,
according to the record which hath been given,
they did go forth upon the face of the land
and did minister unto all the people,
uniting as many to the church as would believe in their preaching,
baptizing them;
and as many as were baptized did receive the Holy Ghost.

19 And they were cast into prison by them who did not belong to the church.
And the prisons could not hold them,
for they were rent in twain.

20 And they were cast down into the earth,
but they did smite the earth with the word of God,
insomuch that by his power they were delivered out of the depths of the earth.
And therefore they could not dig pits sufficiently to hold them.

21 And thrice they were cast into a furnace and received no harm.

22 And twice were they cast into a den of wild beasts,
and behold, they did play with the beasts
as a child with a suckling lamb
and received no harm.

23 And it came to pass that thus they did go forth among all the people of Nephi
and did preach the gospel of Christ unto all people upon the face of the land,
and they were converted unto the Lord
and were united unto the church of Christ.

And thus the people of that generation were blessed
according to the word of Jesus.

24 And now I Mormon make an end of speaking
concerning these things for a time.
25 Behold, I were about to write the names of those
who were never to taste of death,
but the Lord forbade.
Therefore I write them not,
for they are hid from the world.
26 But behold, I have seen them,
and they have ministered unto me.
27 And behold, they will be among the Gentiles,
and the Gentiles knoweth them not.
28 They will also be among the Jews,
and the Jews shall know them not.
29 And it shall come to pass, when the Lord seeth fit in his wisdom,
that they shall minister unto all the scattered tribes of Israel
and unto all nations, kindreds, tongues, and people
and shall bring out of them unto Jesus many souls,
that their desire may be fulfilled,
and also because of the convincing power of God which is in them.
30 And they are as the angels of God.
And if they shall pray unto the Father in the name of Jesus,
they can shew themselves unto whatsoever man it seemeth them good.
31 Therefore great and marvelous works shall be wrought by them
before the great and coming day
when all people must surely stand before the judgment seat of Christ.
32 Yea, even among the Gentiles shall there be
a great and marvelous work wrought by them before that judgment day.

33 And if ye had all the scriptures
which gives an account of all the marvelous works of Christ,
ye would, according to the words of Christ,
know that these things must surely come.
34 And woe be unto him
that will not hearken unto the words of Jesus
and also to them which he hath chosen and sent among them.
For whoso receiveth not the words of Jesus
and the words of them which he hath sent
receiveth not him,
and therefore he will not receive them at the last day.

35 And it would be better for them if they had not been born.
    For do ye suppose that ye can get rid of the justice of an offended God
    who hath been trampled under feet of men,
    that thereby salvation might come?

36 And now behold, as I spake concerning them whom the Lord had chosen
    —yea, even three which were caught up into the heavens—
    that I knew not whether they were changed from mortality to immortality—

37 but behold, since I wrote, I have inquired of the Lord;
    and he hath made it manifest unto me
    that there must needs be a change wrought upon their bodies,
    or else it needs be that they must taste of death.

38 Therefore that they might not taste of death,
    there was a change wrought upon their bodies
    that they might not suffer pain nor sorrow,
    save it were for the sins of the world.

39 Now this change was not equal
    to that which should take place at the last day,
    but there was a change wrought upon them,
    insomuch that Satan could have no power over them,
    that he could not tempt them.
    And they were sanctified in the flesh, that they were holy
    and that the powers of the earth could not hold them.

40 And in this state they were to remain until the judgment day of Christ.
    And at that day they were to receive a greater change
    and to be received into the kingdom of the Father,
    to go no more out but to dwell with God eternally in the heavens.

29 | 1 And now behold, I say unto you
    that when the Lord shall see fit in his wisdom
    that these sayings shall come unto the Gentiles according to his word,
    then ye may know that the covenant
    which the Father hath made with the children of Israel
    concerning their restoration to the lands of their inheritance
    is already beginning to be fulfilled.

2 And ye may know that the words of the Lord
    which have been spoken by the holy prophets shall all be fulfilled.
    And ye need not say
    that the Lord delays his coming unto the children of Israel.

3 And ye need not imagine in your hearts
    that the words which have been spoken are vain;

for behold, the Lord will remember his covenant
which he hath made unto his people of the house of Israel.

4 And when ye shall see these sayings coming forth among you,
then ye need not any longer spurn at the doings of the Lord,
for the sword of his justice is in his right hand.
And behold, at that day, if ye shall spurn at his doings,
he will cause it that it shall soon overtake you.
5 Woe unto him that spurneth at the doings of the Lord.
Yea, woe unto him that shall deny the Christ and his works.
6 Yea, woe unto him that shall deny the revelations of the Lord and that shall say:
The Lord no longer worketh by revelation or by prophecy
or by gifts or by tongues or by healings or by the power of the Holy Ghost.
7 Yea, and woe unto him that shall say at that day
that there can be no miracle wrought by Jesus Christ,
for to get gain;
for he that doeth this shall become like unto the son of perdition,
for whom there was no mercy, according to the words of Christ.
8 Yea, and ye need not any longer hiss nor spurn
nor make game of the Jews nor of any of the remnant of the house of Israel,
for behold, the Lord remembereth his covenant unto them;
and he will do unto them according to that which he hath sworn.
9 Therefore ye need not suppose
that ye can turn the right hand of the Lord unto the left,
that he may not execute judgment unto the fulfilling of the covenant
which he hath made unto the house of Israel.

30 | 1 Hearken, O ye Gentiles,
and hear the words of Jesus Christ, the Son of the living God,
which he hath commanded me that I should speak concerning you.
For behold, he commandeth me that I should write, saying:
2 Turn, all ye Gentiles, from your wicked ways
and repent of your evil doings, of your lyings and deceivings,
and of your whoredoms, and of your secret abominations and your idolatries,
and of your murders and your priestcrafts and your envyings and your strifes,
and from all your wickedness and abominations,
and come unto me and be baptized in my name,
that ye may receive a remission of your sins
and be filled with the Holy Ghost,
that ye may be numbered with my people
which are of the house of Israel.

The Book of Nephi,

which is the son of Nephi,
one of the disciples of Jesus Christ

An account of the people of Nephi according to his record.

1 | 1 And it came to pass that the thirty and fourth year passed away,
and also the thirty and fifth,
and behold, the disciples of Jesus had formed a church of Christ
in all the lands round about.
And as many as did come unto them and did truly repent of their sins
were baptized in the name of Jesus;
and they did also receive the Holy Ghost.

2 And it came to pass in the thirty and sixth year
the people were all converted unto the Lord
upon all the face of the land,
both Nephites and Lamanites.
And there was no contentions and disputations among them.
And every man did deal justly one with another.

3 And they had all things common among them;
therefore there were not rich and poor, bond and free,
but they were all made free and partakers of the heavenly gift.

4 And it came to pass that the thirty and seventh year passed away also,
and there still continued to be peace in the land.

5 And there were great and marvelous works wrought by the disciples of Jesus,
insomuch that they did heal the sick and raise the dead
and cause the lame to walk
and the blind to receive their sight and the deaf to hear.
And all manner of miracles did they work among the children of men;
and in nothing did they work miracles save it were in the name of Jesus.

6 And thus did the thirty and eighth year pass away,
and also the thirty and ninth,
and the forty and first,
and the forty and second,
yea, even until forty and nine years had passed away,
and also the fifty and first,

and the fifty and second,
yea, and even until fifty and nine years had passed away.

7 And the Lord did prosper them exceedingly in the land,
yea, insomuch that they did build cities again
where there had been cities burned;

8 yea, even that great city Zarahemla did they cause to be built again.

9 But there were many cities which had been sunk
and waters came up in the stead thereof;
therefore these cities could not be renewed.

10 And now behold, it came to pass that
the people of Nephi did wax strong and did multiply exceeding fast
and became an exceeding fair and delightsome people.

11 And they were married and given in marriage,
and were blessed according to the multitude of the promises
which the Lord had made unto them.

12 And they did not walk any more
after the performances and ordinances of the law of Moses,
but they did walk after the commandments
which they had received from their Lord and their God,
continuing in fasting and prayer and in meeting together oft,
both to pray and to hear the word of the Lord.

13 And it came to pass that there was no contention
among all the people in all the land,
but there were mighty miracles wrought among the disciples of Jesus.

14 And it came to pass that the seventy and first year passed away,
and also the seventy and second year,
yea, and in fine, until the seventy and ninth year had passed away;
yea, even an hundred years had passed away.
And the disciples of Jesus whom he had chosen
had all gone to the paradise of God,
save it were the three which should tarry;
and there were other disciples ordained in their stead
and also many of that generation which had passed away.

15 And it came to pass that there was no contention in the land
because of the love of God which did dwell in the hearts of the people.

16 And there were no envyings nor strifes nor tumults nor whoredoms
nor lyings nor murders nor no manner of lasciviousness.
And surely there could not be a happier people
among all the people which had been created by the hand of God.

17 There were no robbers nor no murderers,
neither were there Lamanites nor no manner of ites,

but they were in one,
the children of Christ and heirs to the kingdom of God.

18 And how blessed were they!
For the Lord did bless them in all their doings;
yea, even they were blessed and prospered
until an hundred and ten years had passed away.
And the first generation from Christ had passed away,
and there was no contention in all the land.

19 And it came to pass that Nephi,
he that kept this last record
—and he kept it upon the plates of Nephi—
died, and his son Amos kept it in his stead.
And he kept it upon the plates of Nephi also;

20 and he kept it eighty and four years.
And there was still peace in the land
save it were a small part of the people which had revolted from the church
and took upon them the name of Lamanites;
therefore there began to be Lamanites again in the land.

21 And it came to pass that Amos died also.
And it was an hundred and ninety and four years from the coming of Christ,
and his son Amos kept the record in his stead.
And he also kept it upon the plates of Nephi;
and it was also written in the book of Nephi, which is this book.

22 And it came to pass that two hundred years had passed away;
and the second generation had all passed away save it were a few.

23 And now I Mormon would that ye should know
that the people had multiplied,
insomuch that they were spread upon all the face of the land,
and that they had become exceeding rich because of their prosperity in Christ.

24 And now in this two hundred and first year
there began to be among them those which were lifted up in pride,
such as the wearing of costly apparel and all manner of fine pearls
and of the fine things of the world.

25 And from that time forth they did have their goods and their substance
no more common among them.

26 And they began to be divided into classes.
And they began to build up churches unto themselves to get gain
and began to deny the true church of Christ.

27 And it came to pass that when two hundred and ten years had passed away,
there were many churches in the land.

Yea, there were churches which professed to know the Christ;
and yet they did deny the more parts of his gospel,
insomuch that they did receive all manner of wickedness
and did administer that which was sacred unto him
to whom it had been forbidden because of unworthiness.

28 And this church did multiply exceedingly because of iniquity
and because of the power of Satan, which did get hold upon their hearts.

29 And again, there was another church which denied the Christ.
And they did persecute the true church of Christ
because of their humility and their belief in Christ.
And they did despise them because of the many miracles
which were wrought among them.

30 Therefore they did exercise power and authority
over the disciples of Jesus which did tarry with them.
And they did cast them into prison;
but by the power of the word of God which was in them,
the prisons were rent in twain;
and they went forth doing mighty miracles among them.

31 Nevertheless—and notwithstanding all these miracles—
the people did harden their hearts
and did seek to kill them,
even as the Jews at Jerusalem sought to kill Jesus,
according to his word.

32 And they did cast them into furnaces of fire,
and they came forth receiving no harm.

33 And they also cast them into dens of wild beasts,
and they did play with the wild beasts, even as a child with a lamb;
and they did come forth from among them, receiving no harm.

34 Nevertheless the people did harden their hearts,
for they were led by many priests and false prophets
to build up many churches and to do all manner of iniquity.
And they did smite upon the people of Jesus,
but the people of Jesus did not smite again.
And thus they did dwindle in unbelief and wickedness from year to year,
even until two hundred and thirty years had passed away.

35 And now it came to pass in this year
—yea, in the two hundred and thirty and first year—
there were a great division among the people.

36 And it came to pass that in this year
there arose a people which was called the Nephites,

and they were true believers in Christ.
And among them there were they which was called by the Lamanites
Jacobites and Josephites and Zoramites.

37 Therefore the true believers in Christ and the true worshippers of Christ,
among whom were the three disciples of Jesus which should tarry,
were called Nephites and Jacobites and Josephites and Zoramites.

38 And it came to pass that they which rejected the gospel
were called Lamanites and Lemuelites and Ishmaelites.
And they did not dwindle in unbelief,
but they did willfully rebel against the gospel of Christ.
And they did teach their children that they should not believe,
even as their fathers from the beginning did dwindle.

39 And it was because of the wickedness and abominations of their fathers,
even as it was in the beginning.
And they were taught to hate the children of God,
even as the Lamanites were taught
to hate the children of Nephi from the beginning.

40 And it came to pass that
two hundred and forty and four years had passed away,
and thus were the affairs of the people.
And the more wicked part of the people did wax strong
and became exceeding more numerous than were the people of God.

41 And they did still continue to build up churches unto themselves
and adorn them with all manner of precious things.
And thus did two hundred and fifty years pass away,
and also two hundred and sixty years.

42 And it came to pass that
the wicked part of the people began again
to build up the secret oaths and combinations of Gaddianton.

43 And also the people which were called the people of Nephi began
to be proud in their hearts because of their exceeding riches
and became vain like unto their brethren the Lamanites.

44 And from this time the disciples began to sorrow for the sins of the world.

45 And it came to pass that when three hundred years had passed away,
both the people of Nephi and the Lamanites had become exceeding wicked,
one like unto another.

46 And it came to pass that
the robbers of Gaddianton did spread over all the face of the land.
And there were none that were righteous,
save it were the disciples of Jesus.

And gold and silver did they lay up in store in abundance
and did traffic in all manner of traffic.

47 And it came to pass that after three hundred and five years had passed away
—and the people did still remain in wickedness—
and Amos died, and his brother Ammaron did keep the record in his stead.

48 And it came to pass that when three hundred and twenty years had passed away,
Ammaron being constrained by the Holy Ghost
did hide up the records which were sacred,
yea, even all the sacred records which had been handed down
from generation to generation, which were sacred,
even until the three hundred and twentieth year from the coming of Christ.

49 And he did hide them up unto the Lord,
that they might come again unto the remnant of the house of Jacob,
according to the prophecies and the promises of the Lord.
And thus is the end of the record of Ammaron.

THE BOOK OF MORMON

1 | 1 And now I Mormon make a record of the things
which I have both seen and heard
and call it the book of Mormon.

2 And about the time that Ammaron hid up the records unto the Lord,
he came unto me, I being about ten years of age
—and I began to be learned somewhat
after the manner of the learning of my people—
and Ammaron saith unto me:
I perceive that thou art a sober child and art quick to observe.

3 Therefore, when ye are about twenty and four years old,
I would that ye should remember the things
that ye have observed concerning this people;
and when ye are of that age,
go to the land of Antum unto a hill which shall be called Shim;
and there have I deposited unto the Lord
all the sacred engravings concerning this people.

4 And behold, ye shall take the plates of Nephi unto yourself,
and the remainder shall ye leave in the place where they are.
And ye shall engrave upon the plates of Nephi all the things

that ye have observed concerning this people.

5 And I Mormon being a descendant of Nephi
—and my father's name was Mormon—
and I remembered the things which Ammaron commanded me.

6 And it came to pass that I being eleven years old
was carried by my father into the land southward,
even to the land of Zarahemla,

7 the whole face of the land having become covered with buildings;
and the people were as numerous almost as it were the sand of the sea.

8 And it came to pass in this year there began to be a war between the Nephites,
which consisted of the Nephites and the Jacobites
and the Josephites and the Zoramites—
and this war was between the Nephites and the Lamanites
and the Lemuelites and the Ishmaelites.

9 Now the Lamanites and the Lemuelites and the Ishmaelites
were called Lamanites;
and the two parties were Nephites and Lamanites.

10 And it came to pass that the war began to be among them
in the borders of Zarahemla by the waters of Sidon.

11 And it came to pass that the Nephites had gathered together
a great number of men, even to exceed the number of thirty thousand.
And it came to pass that they did have in this same year a number of battles,
in the which the Nephites did beat the Lamanites and did slay many of them.

12 And it came to pass that the Lamanites withdrew their design,
and there was peace settled in the land.
And peace did remain for the space of about four years,
that there were no bloodshed.

13 But wickedness did prevail upon the face of the whole land,
insomuch that the Lord did take away his beloved disciples;
and the work of miracles and of healing did cease
because of the iniquity of the people.

14 And there were no gifts from the Lord.
And the Holy Ghost did not come upon any
because of their wickedness and unbelief.

15 And I being fifteen years of age
and being somewhat of a sober mind,
therefore I was visited of the Lord
and tasted and knew of the goodness of Jesus.

16 And I did endeavor to preach unto this people,
but my mouth was shut.
And I were forbidden that I should preach unto them,

for behold, they had willfully rebelled against their God.
And the beloved disciples were taken away out of the land
because of their iniquity.

17 But I did remain among them,
but I were forbidden that I should preach unto them
because of the hardness of their hearts.
And because of the hardness of their hearts
the land was cursed for their sake.

18 And these Gaddianton robbers,
which were among the Lamanites,
did infest the land,
insomuch that the inhabitants thereof began
to hide up their treasures in the earth;
and they became slippery
because the Lord had cursed the land,
that they could not hold them nor retain them again.

19 And it came to pass that there were sorceries and witchcrafts and magics;
and the power of the evil one was wrought upon all the face of the land,
even unto the fulfilling of all the words of Abinadi
and also Samuel the Lamanite.

2 | 1 And it came to pass that in that same year
there began to be a war again between the Nephites and the Lamanites.
And notwithstanding I being young was large in stature;
therefore the people of Nephi appointed me
that I should be their leader, or the leader of their armies.

2 Therefore it came to pass that in my sixteenth year
I did go forth at the head of an army of the Nephites against the Lamanites.
Therefore three hundred and twenty and six years had passed away.

3 And it came to pass that in the three hundred and twenty and seventh year
the Lamanites did come upon us with exceeding great power,
insomuch that they did frighten my armies;
therefore they would not fight,
and they began to retreat towards the north countries.

4 And it came to pass that we did come to the city of Angolah;
and we did take possession of the city
and make preparations to defend ourselves against the Lamanites.
And it came to pass that we did fortify the city with our mights.
But notwithstanding all our fortifications, the Lamanites did come upon us
and did drive us out of the city.

5 And they did also drive us forth out of the land of David.

6 And we marched forth and came to the land of Joshua,
which was in the borders west by the seashore.

7 And it came to pass that we did gather in our people as fast as it were possible,
that we might get them together in one body.

8 But behold, the land was filled with robbers and with Lamanites.
And notwithstanding the great destruction which hung over my people,
they did not repent of their evil doings.
Therefore there was blood and carnage
spread throughout all the face of the land,
both on the part of the Nephites and also on the part of the Lamanites.
And it was one complete revolution throughout all the face of the land.

9 And now the Lamanites had a king,
and his name was Aaron.
And he came against us with an army of forty and four thousand.
And behold, I withstood him with forty and two thousand.
And it came to pass that I beat him with my army, that he fled before me.
And behold, all this was done,
and three hundred and thirty years had passed away.

10 And it came to pass that the Nephites began to repent of their iniquity
and began to cry, even as had been prophesied by Samuel the prophet.
For behold, no man could keep that which was his own
for the thieves and the robbers and the murderers
and the magic art and the witchcraft which was in the land.

11 Thus there began to be a mourning and a lamentation in all the land
because of these things,
and more especially among the people of Nephi.

12 And it came to pass that when I Mormon saw their lamentation
and their mourning and their sorrowing before the Lord,
my heart did begin to rejoice within me,
knowing the mercies and the long-suffering of the Lord,
therefore supposing that he would be merciful unto them,
that they would again become a righteous people.

13 But behold, this my joy was vain;
for their sorrowing was not unto repentance because of the goodness of God,
but it was rather the sorrowing of the damned
because the Lord would not always suffer them to take happiness in sin.

14 And they did not come unto Jesus with broken hearts and contrite spirits,
but they did curse God and wish to die.
Nevertheless they would struggle with the sword for their lives.

15 And it came to pass that my sorrow did return unto me again.

And I saw that the day of grace was past with them,
both temporally and spiritually,
for I saw thousands of them hewn down
in open rebellion against their God
and heaped up as dung upon the face of the land.
And thus three hundred and forty and four years had passed away.

16 And it came to pass that in the three hundred and forty and fifth year
the Nephites did begin to flee before the Lamanites.
And they were pursued until they came even to the land of Jashon
before it were possible to stop them in their retreat.

17 And now the city of Jashon was near the land
where Ammaron had deposited the records unto the Lord,
that they might not be destroyed.
And behold, I had gone according to the words of Ammaron
and taken the plates of Nephi and did make a record,
according to the words of Ammaron.

18 And upon the plates of Nephi I did make a full account
of all the wickedness and abominations;
but upon these plates I did forbear to make a full account
of their wickedness and abominations.
For behold, a continual scene of wickedness and abominations
has been before mine eyes
ever since I have been sufficient to behold the ways of man.

19 And woe is me because of their wickedness,
for my heart has been filled with sorrow
because of their wickedness, all my days.
Nevertheless I know that I shall be lifted up at the last day.

20 And it came to pass that in this year
the people of Nephi again were hunted and driven.
And it came to pass that we were driven forth
until we had come northward to the land which was called Shem.

21 And it came to pass that we did fortify the city of Shem;
and we did gather in our people as much as it were possible,
that perhaps we might save them from destruction.

22 And it came to pass in the three hundred and forty and sixth year
they began to come upon us again.

23 And it came to pass that I did speak unto my people
and did urge them with great energy
that they would stand boldly before the Lamanites
and fight for their wives and their children
and their houses and their homes.

24 And my words did arouse them somewhat to vigor,
insomuch that they did not flee from before the Lamanites
but did stand with boldness against them.

25 And it came to pass that we did contend with an army of thirty thousand
against an army of fifty thousand.
And it came to pass that we did stand before them with such firmness
that they did flee from before us.

26 And it came to pass that when they had fled,
we did pursue them with our armies
and did meet them again and did beat them.
Nevertheless the strength of the Lord was not with us.
Yea, we were left to ourselves,
that the Spirit of the Lord did not abide in us.
Therefore we had become weak like unto our brethren.

27 And my heart did sorrow because of this the great calamity of my people,
because of their wickedness and their abominations.
But behold, we did go forth against the Lamanites
and the robbers of Gaddianton
until we had again taken possession of the lands of our inheritance.

28 And the three hundred and forty and ninth year had passed away.

And in the three hundred and fiftieth year
we made a treaty with the Lamanites and the robbers of Gaddianton,
in the which we did get the lands of our inheritance divided.

29 And the Lamanites did give unto us the land northward,
yea, even to the narrow passage which led into the land southward.
And we did give unto the Lamanites all the land southward.

3 | 1 And it came to pass that the Lamanites did not come to battle again
until ten years more had passed away.
And behold, I had employed my people the Nephites
in preparing their lands and their arms against the time of battle.

2 And it came to pass that the Lord did say unto me:
Cry unto this people: Repent ye and come unto me
and be ye baptized and build up again my church,
and ye shall be spared.

3 And I did cry unto this people, but it was in vain.
And they did not realize that it was the Lord
that had spared them and granted unto them a chance for repentance.
And behold, they did harden their hearts against the Lord their God.

4 And it came to pass that after this tenth year had passed away,
making in the whole three hundred and sixty years

from the coming of Christ,
and the king of the Lamanites sent an epistle unto me
which gave unto me to know
that they were preparing to come again to battle against us.

5 And it came to pass that I did cause my people
that they should gather themselves together at the land Desolation
to a city which was in the borders by the narrow pass
which led into the land southward.

6 And there we did place our armies,
that we might stop the armies of the Lamanites,
that they might not get possession of any of our lands.
Therefore we did fortify against them with all our force.

7 And it came to pass that in the three hundred and sixty and first year
the Lamanites did come down to the city of Desolation to battle against us.
And it came to pass that in that year we did beat them,
insomuch that they did return to their own lands again.

8 And in the three hundred and sixty and second year
they did come down again to battle.
And we did beat them again
and did slay a great number of them,
and their dead was cast into the sea.

9 And now because of this great thing
which my people the Nephites had done,
they began to boast in their own strength
and began to swear before the heavens
that they would avenge themselves of the blood of their brethren
which had been slain by their enemies.

10 And they did swear by the heavens and also by the throne of God
that they would go up to battle against their enemies
and would cut them off from the face of the land.

11 And it came to pass that I Mormon did utterly refuse from this time forth
to be a commander and a leader of this people
because of their wickedness and abomination.

12 Behold, I had led them
—notwithstanding their wickedness, I had led them many times to battle—
and I had loved them
according to the love of God which was in me
with all my heart.
And my soul had been poured out in prayer unto my God
all the day long for them.
Nevertheless it was without faith

because of the hardness of their hearts.

13 And thrice have I delivered them out of the hands of their enemies,
and they have repented not of their sins.

14 And when they had sworn by all
that had been forbidden them by our Lord and Savior Jesus Christ
that they would go up unto their enemies to battle
and avenge themselves of the blood of their brethren,
behold, the voice of the Lord came unto me, saying:

15 Vengeance is mine, and I will repay.
And because this people repented not after that I had delivered them,
behold, they shall be cut off from the face of the earth.

16 And it came to pass that I utterly refused to go up against mine enemies.
And I did even as the Lord had commanded me,
and I did stand as an idle witness
to manifest unto the world the things which I saw and heard,
according to the manifestations of the Spirit,
which had testified of things to come.

17 Therefore I write unto you Gentiles,
and also unto you house of Israel,
when the work shall commence,
that ye shall be about to prepare to return to the land of your inheritance.

18 Yea, behold, I write unto all the ends of the earth,
yea, unto you twelve tribes of Israel,
which shall be judged according to your works by the twelve
whom Jesus chose to be his disciples in the land of Jerusalem.

19 And I write also unto the remnant of this people,
which shall also be judged by the twelve whom Jesus chose in this land;
and they shall be judged by the other twelve
whom Jesus chose in the land of Jerusalem.

20 And these things do the Spirit manifest unto me.

Therefore I write unto you all;
and for this cause I write unto you,
that ye may know that ye must all stand before the judgment seat of Christ,
yea, every soul which belongeth to the whole human family of Adam
—and ye must stand to be judged of your works,
whether they be good or evil—

21 and also that ye may believe the gospel of Jesus Christ,
which ye shall have among you,
and also that the Jews, the covenant people of the Lord,
shall have other witness besides that which they saw and heard,
that Jesus, whom they slew, was the very Christ and the very God.

22 And I would that I could persuade all ye ends of the earth
to repent and prepare to stand before the judgment seat of Christ.

4 | 1 And now it came to pass that in the three hundred and sixty and third year
the Nephites did go up with their armies to battle against the Lamanites
out of the land of Desolation.

2 And it came to pass that
the armies of the Nephites were driven back again to the land of Desolation.
And while they were yet weary,
a fresh army of the Lamanites did come upon them.
And they had a sore battle,
insomuch that the Lamanites did take possession of the city Desolation
and did slay many of the Nephites and did take many prisoners.

3 And the remainder did flee and join the inhabitants of the city Teancum.
Now the city Teancum lay in the borders by the seashore,
and it was also near the city Desolation.

4 And it was because that the armies of the Nephites went up unto the Lamanites
that they began to be smitten;
for were it not for that,
the Lamanites could have had no power over them.

5 But behold, the judgments of God will overtake the wicked.
And it is by the wicked that the wicked are punished.
For it is the wicked
that stirreth up the hearts of the children of men unto bloodshed.

6 And it came to pass that the Lamanites did make preparations
to come against the city Teancum.

7 And it came to pass in the three hundred and sixty and fourth year
the Lamanites did come against the city Teancum,
that they might take possession of the city Teancum also.

8 And it came to pass that they were repulsed and driven back by the Nephites.
And when the Nephites saw that they had driven the Lamanites,
they did again boast of their own strength.
And they went forth in their own might
and took possession again of the city Desolation.

9 And now all these things had been done;
and there had been thousands slain on both sides,
both the Nephites and the Lamanites.

10 And it came to pass that
the three hundred and sixty and sixth year had passed away,
and the Lamanites came again upon the Nephites to battle.

And yet the Nephites repented not of the evil which they had done,
but persisted in their wickedness continually.

11 And it is impossible for the tongue to describe—
or for man to write a perfect description
of the horrible scene of the blood and carnage
which was among the people, both of the Nephites and of the Lamanites.
And every heart was hardened,
so that they delighted in the shedding of blood continually.

12 And there never had been so great wickedness among all the children of Lehi,
nor even among all the house of Israel,
according to the words of the Lord,
as were among this people.

13 And it came to pass that
the Lamanites did take possession of the city Desolation—
and this because their number did exceed the number of the Nephites.

14 And they did also march forward against the city Teancum
and did drive the inhabitants forth out of her
and did take many prisoners of women and of children
and did offer them up as sacrifices unto their idol gods.

15 And it came to pass that in the three hundred and sixty and seventh year,
the Nephites being angry
because the Lamanites had sacrificed their women and their children,
that they did go against the Lamanites with exceeding great anger,
insomuch that they did beat again the Lamanites
and drive them out of their lands.

16 And the Lamanites did not come again against the Nephites
until the three hundred and seventy and fifth year.

17 And in this year they did come down against the Nephites with all their powers,
and they were not numbered because of the greatness of their number.

18 And from this time forth did the Nephites gain no power over the Lamanites,
but began to be swept off by them even as a dew before the sun.

19 And it came to pass that the Lamanites did come down
against the city Desolation.
And there was an exceeding sore battle fought in the land Desolation,
in the which they did beat the Nephites.

20 And they fled again from before them, and they came to the city Boaz.
And there they did stand against the Lamanites with exceeding boldness,
insomuch that the Lamanites did not beat them
until they had come again the second time.

21 And when they had come the second time,
the Nephites were driven and slaughtered with an exceeding great slaughter;

their women and their children were again sacrificed unto idols.

22 And it came to pass that the Nephites did again flee from before them,
taking all the inhabitants with them, both in towns and villages.

23 And now I Mormon
seeing that the Lamanites were about to overthrow the land,
therefore I did go to the hill Shim
and did take up all the records which Ammaron had hid up unto the Lord.

5 | 1 And it came to pass that I did go forth among the Nephites
and did repent of the oath which I had made,
that I would no more assist them.
And they gave me command again of their armies,
for they looked upon me
as though I could deliver them from their afflictions.

2 But behold, I was without hopes,
for I knew the judgments of the Lord which should come upon them;
for they repented not of their iniquities
but did struggle for their lives
without calling upon that Being who had created them.

3 And it came to pass that the Lamanites did come against us
as we had fled to the city of Jordan.
But behold, they were driven back,
that they did not take the city at that time.

4 And it came to pass that they came against us again,
and we did maintain the city.
And there were also other cities which were maintained by the Nephites,
which strong holds did cut them off
that they could not get into the country which lay before us
to destroy the inhabitants of our land.

5 But it came to pass that whatsoever lands we had passed by
and the inhabitants thereof were not gathered in
were destroyed by the Lamanites;
and their towns and villages and cities were burned with fire.
And thus three hundred and seventy and nine years passed away.

6 And it came to pass that in the three hundred and eightieth year
the Lamanites did come again against us to battle.
And we did stand against them boldly.
But it was all in vain,
for so great were their numbers
that they did tread the people of the Nephites under their feet.

7 And it came to pass that we did again take to flight.
And they whose flight were swifter than the Lamanites did escape;

and they whose flight did not exceed the Lamanites
were swept down and destroyed.

8 And now behold, I Mormon do not desire to harrow up the souls of men
in casting before them such an awful scene of blood and carnage
as was laid before mine eyes.
But I knowing that these things must surely be made known
and that all things which are hid must be revealed upon the housetops

9 and also that a knowledge of these things
must come unto the remnant of these people and also unto the Gentiles,
which the Lord hath said should scatter this people
—and this people should be counted as naught among them—
therefore I write a small abridgment,
daring not to give a full account of the things which I have seen
because of the commandment which I have received—
and also that ye might not have too great sorrow
because of the wickedness of this people.

10 And now behold, this I speak unto their seed
and also to the Gentiles which hath care for the house of Israel,
that realize and know from whence their blessings come.

11 For I know that such will sorrow for the calamity of the house of Israel;
yea, they will sorrow for the destruction of this people.
They will sorrow that this people had not repented,
that they might have been clasped in the arms of Jesus.

12 Now these things are written unto the remnant of the house of Jacob.
And they are written after this manner
because it is known of God
that wickedness will not bring them forth unto them.
And they are to be hid up unto the Lord,
that they may come forth in his own due time.

13 And this is the commandment which I have received.
And behold, they shall come forth according to the commandment of the Lord
when he shall see fit in his wisdom.

14 And behold, they shall go unto the unbelieving of the Jews.
And for this intent shall they go,
that they may be persuaded that Jesus is the Christ,
the Son of the living God,
that the Father may bring about through his Most Beloved
his great and eternal purpose
in the restoring the Jews or all the house of Israel
to the land of their inheritance,
which the Lord their God hath given them,

unto the fulfilling of his covenant,

15 and also that the seed of this people may more fully believe his gospel,
which shall go forth unto them from the Gentiles.

For this people shall be scattered
and shall become a dark, a filthy, and a loathsome people,
beyond the description of that which ever hath been amongst us,
yea, even that which hath been among the Lamanites —
and this because of their unbelief and idolatry.

16 For behold, the Spirit of the Lord hath already ceased to strive with their fathers.
And they are without Christ and God in the world,
and they are driven about as chaff before the wind.

17 They were once a delightsome people.
And they had Christ for their shepherd;
yea, they were led even by God the Father.

18 But now behold, they are led about by Satan,
even as chaff is driven before the wind,
or as a vessel is tossed about upon the waves without sail or anchor
or without any thing wherewith to steer her;
and even as she is, so are they.

19 And behold, the Lord hath reserved their blessing
which they might have received in the land
for the Gentiles which shall possess the land.

20 But behold, it shall come to pass
that they shall be driven and scattered by the Gentiles.
And after that they have been driven and scattered by the Gentiles,
behold, then will the Lord remember the covenant
which he made unto Abraham and unto all the house of Israel.

21 And also the Lord will remember the prayers of the righteous
which hath been put up unto him for them.

22 And then, O ye Gentiles, how can ye stand before the power of God
except ye shall repent and turn from your evil ways?

23 Know ye not that ye are in the hands of God?
Know ye not that he hath all power
and at his great command the earth shall be rolled together as a scroll?

24 Therefore repent ye and humble yourselves before him
lest he shall come out in justice against you,
lest a remnant of the seed of Jacob shall go forth among you as a lion
and tear you in pieces,
and there is none to deliver.

6 | 1 And now I finish my record
concerning the destruction of my people the Nephites.
And it came to pass that we did march forth before the Lamanites.

2 And I Mormon wrote an epistle unto the king of the Lamanites
and desired of him that he would grant unto us
that we might gather together our people unto the land of Cumorah
by a hill which was called Cumorah,
and there we would give them battle.

3 And it came to pass that
the king of the Lamanites did grant unto me the thing which I desired.

4 And it came to pass that we did march forth to the land of Cumorah,
and we did pitch our tents round about the hill Cumorah.
And it was in a land of many waters, rivers, and fountains.
And here we had hope to gain advantage over the Lamanites.

5 And when three hundred and eighty and four years had passed away,
we had gathered in all the remainder of our people unto the land Cumorah.

6 And it came to pass that
when we had gathered in all our people in one to the land of Cumorah,
behold, I Mormon began to be old.
And knowing it to be the last struggle of my people
and having been commanded of the Lord
that I should not suffer that the records
which had been handed down by our fathers, which were sacred,
to fall into the hands of the Lamanites
—for the Lamanites would destroy them—
therefore I made this record out of the plates of Nephi
and hid up in the hill Cumorah all the records
which had been entrusted to me by the hand of the Lord,
save it were these few plates which I gave unto my son Moroni.

7 And it came to pass that my people with their wives and their children
did now behold the armies of the Lamanites a marching towards them.
And with that awful fear of death which fills the breasts of all the wicked
did they await to receive them.

8 And it came to pass that they came to battle against us,
and every soul was filled with terror
because of the greatness of their numbers.

9 And it came to pass that they did fall upon my people
with the sword and with the bow and with the arrow and with the ax
and with all manner of weapons of war.

10 And it came to pass that my men were hewn down,
yea, or even my ten thousand which were with me,

and I fell wounded in the midst.
And they passed by me,
that they did not put an end to my life.

11 And when they had gone through and hewn down all my people
save it were twenty and four of us
—among whom was my son Moroni—
and we having survived the dead of our people
did behold on the morrow,
when the Lamanites had returned unto their camps,
from the top of the hill Cumorah
the ten thousand of my people which were hewn down,
being led in the front by me.

12 And we also beheld the ten thousand of my people
which were led by my son Moroni.

13 And behold, the ten thousand of Gidgiddonah had fallen,
and he also in the midst.

14 And Lamah had fallen with his ten thousand,
and Gilgal had fallen with his ten thousand,
and Limhah had fallen with his ten thousand,
and Joneum had fallen with his ten thousand;
and Cumenihah and Moronihah and Antionum
and Shiblom and Shem and Josh
had fallen with their ten thousand each.

15 And it came to pass that there were ten more
which did fall by the sword with their ten thousand each,
yea, even all my people
—save it were those twenty and four which were with me
and also a few which had escaped into the south countries
and a few which had dissented over unto the Lamanites—
had fallen.
And their flesh and bones and blood lay upon the face of the earth,
being left by the hands of those who slew them
to molder upon the land and to crumble and to return to their mother earth.

16 And my soul was rent with anguish
because of the slain of my people,
and I cried:

17 O ye fair ones,
how could ye have departed from the ways of the Lord!
O ye fair ones,
how could ye have rejected that Jesus
who stood with open arms to receive you!

18 Behold, if ye had not done this,
   ye would not have fallen.
   But behold, ye are fallen,
   and I mourn your loss.

19 O ye fair sons and daughters,
   ye fathers and mothers,
   ye husbands and wives,
   ye fair ones,
   how is it that ye could have fallen!

20 But behold, ye are gone,
   and my sorrows cannot bring your return.

21 And the day soon cometh that your mortal must put on immortality.
   And these bodies which are now moldering in corruption
   must soon become incorruptible bodies.
   And then ye must stand before the judgment seat of Christ
   to be judged according to your works.
   And if it so be that ye are righteous,
   then are ye blessed with your fathers which have gone before you.

22 O that ye had repented
   before that this great destruction had come upon you!
   But behold, ye are gone.
   And the Father—yea, the Eternal Father of heaven—knoweth your state,
   and he doeth with you according to his justice and mercy.

7 | 1 And now behold, I would speak somewhat
   unto the remnant of this people which are spared,
   if it so be that God may give unto them my words,
   that they may know of the things of their fathers.
   Yea, I speak unto you, ye remnant of the house of Israel.
   And this is the words which I speak:

2 Know ye that ye are of the house of Israel.

3 Know ye that ye must come unto repentance or ye cannot be saved.

4 Know ye that ye must lay down your weapons of war
   and delight no more in the shedding of blood
   and take them not again, save it be that God shall command you.

5 Know ye that ye must come to the knowledge of your fathers
   and repent of all your sins and iniquities
   and believe in Jesus Christ,
   that he is the Son of God
   and that he was slain by the Jews,
   and by the power of the Father he hath risen again,
   whereby he hath gained the victory over the grave.

And also in him is the sting of death swallowed up.

6 And he bringeth to pass the resurrection of the dead,
whereby man must be raised to stand before his judgment seat.

7 And he hath brought to pass the redemption of the world,
whereby he that is found guiltless before him at the judgment day
hath it given unto them to dwell in the presence of God in his kingdom,
to sing ceaseless praises with the choirs above
unto the Father and unto the Son and unto the Holy Ghost,
which is one God,
in a state of happiness which hath no end.

8 Therefore repent and be baptized in the name of Jesus
and lay hold upon the gospel of Christ,
which shall be set before you,
not only in this record but also in the record
which shall come unto the Gentiles from the Jews,
which record shall come from the Gentiles unto you.

9 For behold, this is written for the intent that ye may believe that.
And if ye believe that,
ye will believe this also.
And if ye believe this,
ye will know concerning your fathers and also the marvelous works
which were wrought by the power of God among them.

10 And ye will also know that ye are a remnant of the seed of Jacob.
Therefore ye are numbered among the people of the first covenant.
And if it so be that ye believe in Christ and are baptized
—first with water, then with fire and with the Holy Ghost,
following the example of our Savior,
according to that which he hath commanded us—
it shall be well with you in the day of judgment.
Amen.

8 | 1 Behold, I Moroni do finish the record of my father Mormon.
Behold, I have but few things to write,
which things I have been commanded of my father.

2 And now it came to pass that
after the great and tremendious battle at Cumorah,
behold, the Nephites which had escaped into the country southward
were hunted by the Lamanites until they were all destroyed.

3 And my father also was killed by them.
And I, even I, remaineth alone

to write the sad tale of the destruction of my people.
But behold, they are gone,
and I fulfill the commandment of my father.
And whether they will slay me, I know not.

4 Therefore I will write and hide up the records in the earth.
And whither I go, it mattereth not.

5 Behold, my father hath made this record,
and he hath written the intent thereof.
And behold, I would write it also
if I had room upon the plates,
but I have not.
And ore I have none,
for I am alone.
My father hath been slain in battle,
and all my kinsfolks.
And I have not friends nor whither to go.
And how long that the Lord will suffer that I may live, I know not.

6 Behold, four hundred years have passed away
since the coming of our Lord and Savior.

7 And behold, the Lamanites have hunted my people the Nephites down
from city to city and from place to place,
even until they are no more.
And great has been their fall;
yea, great and marvelous is the destruction of my people the Nephites.

8 And behold, it is the hand of the Lord which hath done it.

And behold also, the Lamanites are at war one with another;
and the whole face of this land
is one continual round of murder and bloodshed,
and no one knoweth the end of the war.

9 And now behold, I say no more concerning them,
for there are none save it be Lamanites and robbers
that do exist upon the face of the land.

10 And there are none that do know the true God,
save it be the disciples of Jesus which did tarry in the land
until the wickedness of the people were so great
that the Lord would not suffer them to remain with the people.
And whither they be upon the face of the land no man knoweth.

11 But behold, my father and I have seen them,
and they have ministered unto us.

12 And whoso receiveth this record and shall not condemn it
because of the imperfections which are in it,

the same shall know of greater things than these.
Behold, I am Moroni.
And were it possible,
I would make all things known unto you.

13 Behold, I make an end of speaking concerning this people.
I am the son of Mormon,
and my father was a descendant of Nephi.
14 And I am the same which hideth up this record unto the Lord.
The plates thereof are of no worth
because of the commandment of the Lord,
for he truly saith that no one shall have them to get gain.
But the record thereof is of great worth.
And whoso shall bring it to light,
him will the Lord bless.
15 For none can have power to bring it to light
save it be given him of God,
for God will that it shall be done with an eye singled to his glory
or the welfare of the ancient and long dispersed covenant people of the Lord.
16 And blessed be him that shall bring this thing to light,
for it shall be brought out of darkness unto light,
according to the word of God.
Yea, it shall be brought out of the earth.
And it shall shine forth out of darkness
and come unto the knowledge of the people.
And it shall be done by the power of God.

17 And if there be faults,
they be the faults of a man;
but behold, we know no fault.
Nevertheless God knoweth all things.
Therefore he that condemneth,
let him be aware lest he shall be in danger of hell fire.
18 And he that saith:
Shew unto me or ye shall be smitten!
—let him be aware lest he commandeth
that which is forbidden of the Lord.
19 For behold, the same that judgeth rashly shall be judged rashly again,
for according to his works shall his wages be.
Therefore he that smiteth shall be smitten again of the Lord.
20 Behold what the scripture saith:
Man shall not smite, neither shall he judge;

for judgment is mine, saith the Lord,
and vengeance is mine also, and I will repay.

21 And he that shall breathe out wrath and strifes against the work of the Lord
and against the covenant people of the Lord, which is the house of Israel,
and shall say:
We will destroy the work of the Lord,
and the Lord will not remember his covenant
which he hath made unto the house of Israel—
the same is in danger to be hewn down and cast into the fire.

22 For the eternal purposes of the Lord shall roll on
until all his promises shall be fulfilled.

23 Search the prophecies of Isaiah.
Behold, I cannot write them.
Yea, behold, I say unto you
that those saints which have gone before me
which have possessed this land
shall cry—yea, even from the dust will they cry unto the Lord;
and as the Lord liveth,
he will remember the covenant which he hath made with them.

24 And he knoweth their prayers,
that they were in the behalf of their brethren.
And he knoweth their faith,
for in his name could they remove mountains;
and in his name could they cause the earth to shake;
and by the power of his word did they cause prisons to tumble to the earth.
Yea, even the fiery furnace could not harm them,
neither wild beasts nor poisonous serpents,
because of the power of his word.

25 And behold, their prayers were also in behalf of him
that the Lord should suffer to bring these things forth.

26 And no one need not say:
They shall not come.
For they surely shall,
for the Lord hath spoken it;
for out of the earth shall they come by the hand of the Lord,
and none can stay it.

And it shall come in a day
when it shall be said that miracles are done away.
And it shall come even as if one should speak from the dead.

27 And it shall come in a day
when the blood of saints shall cry unto the Lord

because of secret combinations and the works of darkness.

28 Yea, it shall come in a day
when the power of God shall be denied
and churches become defiled
and shall be lifted up in the pride of their hearts,
yea, even in a day when leaders of churches and teachers
shall be lifted up in the pride of their hearts,
even to the envying of them who belong to their churches.

29 Yea, it shall come in a day
when there shall be heard of fires and tempests
and vapors of smoke in foreign lands.

30 And there shall also be heard of wars and rumors of wars
and earthquakes in divers places.

31 Yea, it shall come in a day
when there shall be great pollutions upon the face of the earth:
there shall be murders and robbing and lying and deceivings and whoredoms
and all manner of abominations,
when there shall be many which will say:
Do this or do that, and it mattereth not,
for the Lord will uphold such at the last day.
But woe unto such, for they are in the gall of bitterness
and in the bonds of iniquity.

32 Yea, it shall come in a day
when there shall be churches built up that shall say:
Come unto me, and for your money you shall be forgiven of your sins.

33 O ye wicked and perverse and stiffnecked people,
why have ye built up churches unto yourselves to get gain?
Why have ye transfigured the holy word of God
that ye might bring damnation upon your souls?
Behold, look ye unto the revelations of God,
for behold, the time cometh at that day
when all these things must be fulfilled.

34 Behold, the Lord hath shewn unto me great and marvelous things
concerning that which must shortly come,
at that day when these things shall come forth among you.

35 Behold, I speak unto you as if ye were present
—and yet ye are not—
but behold, Jesus Christ hath shewn you unto me,
and I know your doing.

36 And I know that ye do walk in the pride of your hearts.
And there are none, save a few only,

which do not lift themselves up in the pride of their hearts
unto the wearing of very fine apparel,
unto envying and strifes and malice and persecutions
and all manner of iniquity.
And your churches — yea, even every one — have become polluted
because of the pride of your hearts.

37 For behold, ye do love money and your substance and your fine apparel
and the adorning of your churches
more than ye love the poor and the needy, the sick and the afflicted.

38 O ye pollutions, ye hypocrites,
ye teachers which sell yourselves for that which will canker,
why have ye polluted the holy church of God?
Why are ye ashamed to take upon you the name of Christ?
Why do ye not think that greater is the value of an endless happiness
than that misery which never dies?
Because of the praise of the world?

39 Why do ye adorn yourselves with that which hath no life,
and yet suffer the hungry and the needy and the naked
and the sick and the afflicted to pass by you and notice them not?

40 Yea, why do ye build up your secret abominations to get gain
and cause that widows should mourn before the Lord,
and also orphans to mourn before the Lord,
and also the blood of their fathers and their husbands
to cry unto the Lord from the ground for vengeance upon your heads?

41 Behold, the sword of vengeance hangeth over you;
and the time soon cometh that he avengeth the blood of the saints upon you,
for he will not suffer their cries any longer.

9 | 1 And now I speak also concerning those who do not believe in Christ.

2 Behold, will ye believe in the day of your visitation?
Behold, when the Lord shall come
— yea, even that great day
when the earth shall be rolled together as a scroll
and the elements shall melt with fervent heat —
yea, in that great day when ye shall be brought
to stand before the Lamb of God,
then will ye say that there is no God?

3 Then will ye longer deny the Christ?
Or can ye behold the Lamb of God?
Do ye suppose that ye shall dwell with him
under a consciousness of your guilt?
Do ye suppose that ye could be happy to dwell with that holy Being

when your souls are racked with a consciousness of your guilt,
that ye have ever abused his laws?

4 Behold, I say unto you
that ye would be more miserable to dwell with a holy and a just God
under a consciousness of your filthiness before him
than ye would to dwell with the damned souls in hell.

5 For behold, when ye shall be brought to see your nakedness before God
and also the glory of God and the holiness of Jesus Christ,
it will kindle a flame of unquenchable fire upon you.

6 O then, ye unbelieving, turn ye unto the Lord.
Cry mightily unto the Father in the name of Jesus,
that perhaps ye may be found spotless, pure, fair, and white
—having been cleansed by the blood of the Lamb—
at that great and last day.

7 And again I speak unto you who deny the revelations of God
and say that they are done away,
that there is no revelations nor prophecies nor gifts nor healing
nor speaking with tongues and the interpretation of tongues;

8 behold, I say unto you:
He that denieth these things knoweth not the gospel of Christ.
Yea, they have not read the scriptures;
if so, they do not understand them.

9 For do we not read that God is the same yesterday, today, and forever,
and in him there is no variableness, neither shadow of changing?

10 And now if ye have imagined up unto yourselves a god
which doth vary and in him there is shadow of changing,
then have ye imagined up unto yourselves a god
which is not a God of miracles.

11 But behold, I will shew unto you a God of miracles,
even the God of Abraham and the God of Isaac and the God of Jacob.
And it is that same God
which created the heavens and the earth and all things that in them is.

12 Behold, he created Adam;
and by Adam came the fall of man;
and because of the fall of man came Jesus Christ,
even the Father and the Son;
and because of Jesus Christ came the redemption of man;

13 and because of the redemption of man which came by Jesus Christ
they are brought back into the presence of the Lord.
Yea, this is wherein all men are redeemed,
because the death of Christ bringeth to pass the resurrection,

which bringeth to pass a redemption from an endless sleep,
from which sleep all men shall be awoke by the power of God
when the trump shall sound.
And they shall come forth, both small and great,
and all shall stand before his bar,
being redeemed and loosed from this eternal band of death,
which death is a temporal death.

14 And then cometh the judgment of the Holy One upon them.
And then cometh the time
that he that is filthy shall be filthy still,
and he that is righteous shall be righteous still;
he that is happy shall be happy still,
and he that is unhappy shall be unhappy still.

15 And now, O all ye that have imagined up unto yourselves
a god which can do no miracles,
I would ask of you:
Have all these things passed of which I have spoken?
Has the end come yet?
Behold, I say unto you: Nay.
And God has not ceased to be a God of miracles.

16 Behold, are not the things that God hath wrought marvelous in our eyes?
Yea, and who can comprehend the marvelous works of God?

17 Who shall say that it was not a miracle
that by his word the heaven and the earth should be
and by the power of his word man was created of the dust of the earth
and by the power of his word hath miracles been wrought?

18 And who shall say that Jesus Christ did not do many mighty miracles?
And there was many mighty miracles wrought by the hands of the apostles.

19 And if there was miracles wrought,
then why has God ceased to be a God of miracles
and yet be an unchangeable Being?
And behold, I say unto you:
He changeth not;
if so, he would cease to be God.
And he ceaseth not to be God and is a God of miracles.

20 And the reason why he ceaseth to do miracles among the children of men
is because that they dwindle in unbelief
and depart from the right way
and know not the God in whom they should trust.

21 Behold, I say unto you
that whoso believeth in Christ, doubting nothing,

whatsoever he shall ask the Father in the name of Christ,
it shall be granted them.
And this promise is unto all, even unto the ends of the earth.

22 For behold, thus saith Jesus Christ the Son of God
unto his disciples which should tarry,
yea, and also to all his disciples,
in the hearing of the multitude:
Go ye into all the world and preach the gospel to every creature.

23 And he that believeth and is baptized shall be saved,
but he that believeth not shall be damned.

24 And these signs shall follow them that believe:
in my name shall they cast out devils;
they shall speak with new tongues;
they shall take up serpents;
and if they drink any deadly thing, it shall not hurt them;
they shall lay hands on the sick and they shall recover.

25 And whosoever shall believe in my name, doubting nothing,
unto him will I confirm all my words, even unto the ends of the earth.

26 And now behold, who can stand against the works of the Lord?
Who can deny his sayings?
Who will rise up against the almighty power of the Lord?
Who will despise the works of the Lord?
Who will despise the children of Christ?
Behold, all ye that are despisers of the works of the Lord—
for ye shall wonder and perish.

27 O then despise not and wonder not,
but hearken unto the words of the Lord
and ask the Father in the name of Jesus
for what things soever ye shall stand in need.
Doubt not, but be believing.
And begin as in times of old
and come unto the Lord with all your heart
and work out your own salvation with fear and trembling before him.

28 Be wise in the days of your probation.
Strip yourselves of all uncleanness.
Ask not that ye may consume it on your lusts,
but ask with a firmness unshaken,
that ye will yield to no temptation,
but that ye will serve the true and living God.

29 See that ye are not baptized unworthily.
See that ye partake not of the sacrament of Christ unworthily.

But see that ye do all things in worthiness
and do it in the name of Jesus Christ, the Son of the living God.
And if ye do this and endure to the end,
ye will in no wise be cast out.

30 Behold, I speak unto you as though I spake from the dead,
for I know that ye shall have my words.

31 Condemn me not because of mine imperfection,
neither my father because of his imperfection,
neither them which have written before him,
but rather give thanks unto God
that he hath made manifest unto you our imperfections,
that ye may learn to be more wise than that which we have been.

32 And now behold, we have written this record,
according to our knowledge,
in the characters which are called among us the reformed Egyptian,
being handed down and altered by us according to our manner of speech.

33 And if our plates had been sufficiently large,
we should have written in the Hebrew;
but the Hebrew hath been altered by us also.
And if we could have written in the Hebrew,
behold, ye would have had none imperfection in our record.

34 But the Lord knoweth the things which we have written
and also that none other people knoweth our language.
And because that none other people knoweth our language,
therefore he hath prepared means for the interpretation thereof.

35 And these things are written
that we may rid our garments of the blood of our brethren,
which have dwindled in unbelief.

36 And behold, these things which we have desired concerning our brethren,
yea, even their restoration to the knowledge of Christ,
is according to the prayers of all the saints which have dwelt in the land.

37 And may the Lord Jesus Christ grant
that their prayers may be answered according to their faith;
and may God the Father remember the covenant
which he hath made with the house of Israel;
and may he bless them forever
through faith on the name of Jesus Christ.
Amen.

The Book of Ether

1 | 1 And now I Moroni proceed to give an account
of those ancient inhabitants which were destroyed by the hand of the Lord
upon the face of this north country.

2 And I take mine account from the twenty and four plates
which were found by the people of Limhi,
which is called the book of Ether.

3 And as I suppose that the first part of this record
—which speaketh concerning the creation of the world and also of Adam,
and an account from that time even to the great tower,
and whatsoever things transpired among the children of men until that time—
is had among the Jews,

4 therefore I do not write those things
which transpired from the days of Adam until that time.
But they are had upon the plates;
and whoso findeth them,
the same will have power that he may get the full account.

5 But behold, I give not the full account,
but a part of the account I give,
from the tower down until they were destroyed.

6 And on this wise do I give the account.
He that wrote this record was Ether,
and he was a descendant of Coriantor.

7 And Coriantor was the son of Moron,

8 and Moron was the son of Ethem,

9 and Ethem was the son of Ahah,

10 and Ahah was the son of Seth,

11 and Seth was the son of Shiblon,

12 and Shiblon was the son of Com,

13 and Com was the son of Coriantum,

14 and Coriantum was the son of Amnigaddah,

15 and Amnigaddah was the son of Aaron.

16 And Aaron was a descendant of Heth,
who was the son of Hearthom.

17 And Hearthom was the son of Lib,

18 and Lib was the son of Kish,

19 and Kish was the son of Corom,

20 and Corom was the son of Levi,

21 and Levi was the son of Kim,

22 and Kim was the son of Morianton.

23 And Morianton was a descendant of Riplakish,

24 and Riplakish was the son of Shez,

25 and Shez was the son of Heth,

26 and Heth was the son of Com,

27 and Com was the son of Coriantum,

28 and Coriantum was the son of Emer,

29 and Emer was the son of Omer,

30 and Omer was the son of Shule,

31 and Shule was the son of Kib,

32 and Kib was the son of Orihah,
which was the son of Jared,

33 which Jared came forth
with his brother and their families,
with some others and their families,
from the great tower
at the time the Lord confounded the language of the people
and sware in his wrath
that they should be scattered upon all the face of the earth;
and according to the word of the Lord the people were scattered.

34 And the brother of Jared being a large and a mighty man
and being a man highly favored of the Lord,
therefore Jared his brother said unto him:
Cry unto the Lord
that he will not confound us that we may not understand our words.

35 And it came to pass that the brother of Jared did cry unto the Lord,
and the Lord had compassion upon Jared.
Therefore he did not confound the language of Jared,
and Jared and his brother were not confounded.

36 Then Jared said unto his brother:
Cry again unto the Lord,
and it may be that he will turn away his anger from them which are our friends,
that he confound not their language.

37 And it came to pass that the brother of Jared did cry unto the Lord,
and the Lord had compassion upon their friends and their families also,
that they were not confounded.

38 And it came to pass that Jared spake again unto his brother, saying:
Go and inquire of the Lord whether he will drive us out of the land.
And if he will drive us out of the land, cry unto him:

Whither shall we go?
And who knoweth but the Lord will carry us forth into a land
which is choice above all the earth.
And if it so be, let us be faithful unto the Lord,
that we may receive it for our inheritance.

39 And it came to pass that the brother of Jared did cry unto the Lord,
according to that which had been spoken by the mouth of Jared.

40 And it came to pass that the Lord did hear the brother of Jared
and had compassion upon him and said unto him:

41 Go to and gather together thy flocks, both male and female, of every kind,
and also of the seed of the earth, of every kind,
and thy family, and also Jared thy brother and his family,
and also thy friends and their families,
and the friends of Jared and their families.

42 And when thou hast done this,
thou shalt go at the head of them down into the valley which is northward.
And there will I meet thee,
and I will go before thee into a land
which is choice above all the land of the earth.

43 And there will I bless thee and thy seed
and raise up unto me of thy seed,
and the seed of thy brother and they which shall go with thee,
a great nation.
And there shall be none greater than the nation
which I will raise up unto me of thy seed
upon all the face of the earth.
And this I will do unto thee
because of this long time which ye have cried unto me.

2 | 1 And it came to pass that Jared and his brother and their families,
and also the friends of Jared and his brother and their families,
went down into the valley which was northward
—and the name of the valley was Nimrod,
being called after the mighty hunter—
with their flocks which they had gathered together,
male and female, of every kind.

2 And they did also lay snares and catch fowls of the air.
And they did also prepare a vessel,
in the which they did carry with them the fish of the waters.

3 And they did also carry with them deseret,
which by interpretation is a honey bee.
And thus they did carry with them swarms of bees

and all manner of that which was upon the face of the land,
seeds of every kind.

4 And it came to pass that when they had came down into the valley of Nimrod,
the Lord came down and talked with the brother of Jared.
And he was in a cloud and the brother of Jared saw him not.

5 And it came to pass that the Lord commanded them
that they should go forth into the wilderness,
yea, into that quarter where there never had man been.
And it came to pass that the Lord did go before them
and did talk with them as he stood in a cloud
and gave directions whither they should travel.

6 And it came to pass that they did travel in the wilderness
and did build barges, in the which they did cross many waters,
being directed continually by the hand of the Lord.

7 And the Lord would not suffer
that they should stop beyond the sea in the wilderness,
but he would that they should come forth, even unto the land of promise,
which was choice above all other lands,
which the Lord God had preserved for a righteous people.

8 And he had sworn in his wrath unto the brother of Jared
that whoso should possess this land of promise,
from that time henceforth and forever,
should serve him, the true and only God,
or they should be swept off
when the fullness of his wrath should come upon them.

9 And now we can behold the decrees of God concerning this land,
that it is a land of promise,
and whatsoever nation shall possess it shall serve God
or they shall be swept off
when the fullness of his wrath shall come upon them.
And the fullness of his wrath cometh upon them
when they are ripened in iniquity.

10 For behold, this is a land which is choice above all other lands.
Wherefore he that doth possess it shall serve God or shall be swept off,
for it is the everlasting decrees of God.
And it is not until the fullness of iniquity among the children of the land
that they are swept off.

11 And this cometh unto you, O ye Gentiles,
that ye may know the decrees of God,
that ye may repent and not continue in your iniquities
until the fullness be come,

that ye may not bring down the fullness of the wrath of God upon you
as the inhabitants of the land hath hitherto done.

12 Behold, this is a choice land;
and whatsoever nation shall possess it
shall be free from bondage and from captivity
and from all other nations under heaven
if they will but serve the God of the land, which is Jesus Christ,
which hath been manifested by the things which we have written.

13 And now I proceed with my record.
For behold, it came to pass that the Lord did bring Jared and his brethren forth,
even to that great sea which divideth the lands.
And as they came to the sea, they pitched their tents;
and they called the name of the place Moriancumer.
And they dwelt in tents upon the seashore for the space of four years.

14 And it came to pass at the end of the four years
that the Lord came again unto the brother of Jared
and stood in a cloud and talked with him.
And for the space of three hours did the Lord talk with the brother of Jared
and chastened him because he remembered not
to call upon the name of the Lord.

15 And the brother of Jared repented him of the evil which he had done
and did call upon the name of the Lord
for his brethren which were with him.
And the Lord said unto him:
I will forgive thee and thy brethren of their sins,
but thou shalt not sin any more.
For ye shall remember that my Spirit will not always strive with man.
Wherefore if ye will sin until ye are fully ripe,
ye shall be cut off from the presence of the Lord.
And this is my thoughts upon the land
which I shall give you for your inheritance,
for it shall be a land choice above all other lands.

16 And the Lord said: Go to work
and build after the manner of barges which ye have hitherto built.
And it came to pass that
the brother of Jared did go to work and also his brethren
and built barges after the manner which they had built,
according to the instructions of the Lord.
And they were small and they were light upon the water,
even like unto the lightness of a fowl upon the water.

17 And they were built after a manner that they were exceeding tight,

even that they would hold water like unto a dish;
and the bottom thereof was tight like unto a dish,
and the sides thereof was tight like unto a dish,
and the ends thereof were peaked,
and the top thereof was tight like unto a dish,
and the length thereof was the length of a tree,
and the door thereof—when it was shut—was tight like unto a dish.

18 And it came to pass that the brother of Jared cried unto the Lord, saying:
O Lord, I have performed the work which thou hast commanded me,
and I have made the barges according as thou hast directed me.

19 And behold, O Lord, in them there is no light.
Whither shall we steer?
And also we shall perish,
for in them we cannot breathe
save it is the air which is in them;
therefore we shall perish.

20 And the Lord said unto the brother of Jared:
Behold, thou shalt make a hole in the top thereof
and also in the bottom thereof.
And when thou shalt suffer for air,
thou shalt unstop the hole thereof and receive air.
And if it so be that the water come in upon thee,
behold, ye shall stop the hole thereof,
that ye may not perish in the flood.

21 And it came to pass that the brother of Jared did so,
according as the Lord had commanded.

22 And he cried again unto the Lord, saying:
O Lord, behold, I have done even as thou hast commanded me,
and I have prepared the vessels for my people.
And behold, there is no light in them.
Behold, O Lord, wilt thou suffer that we shall cross this great water in darkness?

23 And the Lord said unto the brother of Jared:
What will ye that I should do that ye may have light in your vessels?
For behold, ye cannot have windows,
for they will be dashed in pieces.
Neither shall ye take fire with you,
for ye shall not go by the light of fire.

24 For behold, ye shall be as a whale in the midst of the sea,
for the mountain waves shall dash upon you.
Nevertheless I will bring you up again out of the depths of the sea;

for the winds have gone forth out of my mouth,
and also the rains and the floods have I sent forth.
25 And behold, I prepare you against these things;
for how be it, ye cannot cross this great deep
save I prepare you against the waves of the sea
and the winds which have gone forth
and the floods which shall come.
Therefore what will ye that I should prepare for you
that ye may have light when ye are swallowed up in the depths of the sea?

3 | 1 And it came to pass that the brother of Jared
—now the number of the vessels which had been prepared was eight—
therefore the brother of Jared went forth unto the mount,
which they called the mount Shelem because of its exceeding heighth,
and did molten out of a rock sixteen small stones;
and they were white and clear, even as transparent glass.
And he did carry them in his hands up on the top of the mount
and cried again unto the Lord, saying:
2 O Lord, thou hast said that we must be encompassed about by the floods.
Now behold, O Lord, and do not be angry with thy servant
because of his weakness before thee,
for we know that thou art holy and dwellest in the heavens
and that we are unworthy before thee;
because of the fall our natures have become evil continually.
Nevertheless, O Lord, thou hast given us a commandment
that we must call upon thee,
that from thee we may receive according to our desires.
3 Behold, O Lord, thou hast smitten us because of our iniquity
and hath driven us forth,
and for this many years we have been in the wilderness;
nevertheless thou hast been merciful unto us.

O Lord, look upon me in pity
and turn away thine anger from this thy people
and suffer not that they shall go forth across this raging deep in darkness,
but behold these things which I have molten out of the rock.
4 And I know, O Lord, that thou hast all power
and can do whatsoever thou wilt for the benefit of man.
Therefore touch these stones, O Lord, with thy finger
and prepare them that they may shine forth in darkness;
and they shall shine forth unto us in the vessels which we have prepared,
that we may have light while we shall cross the sea.
5 Behold, O Lord, thou canst do this.

We know that thou art able to shew forth great power
which looks small unto the understanding of men.

6 And it came to pass that when the brother of Jared had said these words,
   behold, the Lord stretched forth his hand
   and touched the stones one by one with his finger.
   And the veil was taken from off the eyes of the brother of Jared,
   and he saw the finger of the Lord.
   And it was as the finger of a man, like unto flesh and blood;
   and the brother of Jared fell down before the Lord,
   for he was struck with fear.

7 And the Lord saw that the brother of Jared had fallen to the earth,
   and the Lord said unto him: Arise.
   Why hast thou fallen?
8 And he saith unto the Lord:
   I saw the finger of the Lord;
   and I feared lest he should smite me,
   for I knew not that the Lord had flesh and blood.
9 And the Lord said unto him:
   Because of thy faith thou hast seen
   that I shall take upon me flesh and blood.
   And never has man come before me with such exceeding faith as thou hast;
   for were it not so, ye could not have seen my finger.
   Sawest thou more than this?
10 And he answered: Nay, Lord.
   Shew thyself unto me.
11 And the Lord said unto him:
   Believest thou the words which I shall speak?
12 And he answered: Yea, Lord.
   I know that thou speakest the truth,
   for thou art a God of truth and canst not lie.

13 And when he had said these words,
   behold, the Lord shewed himself unto him and said:
   Because thou knowest these things, ye are redeemed from the fall.
   Therefore ye are brought back into my presence;
   therefore I shew myself unto you.
14 Behold, I am he which was prepared
   from the foundation of the world
   to redeem my people.
   Behold, I am Jesus Christ.
   I am the Father and the Son.

In me shall all mankind have life—and that eternally—
even they which shall believe on my name;
and they shall become my sons and my daughters.

15 And never hath I shewed myself unto man, whom I have created,
for never hath man believed in me as thou hast.
Seest thou that ye are created after mine own image?
Yea, even all men were created in the beginning after mine own image.

16 Behold, this body which ye now behold is the body of my spirit.
And man have I created after the body of my spirit.
And even as I appear unto thee to be in the spirit
will I appear unto my people in the flesh.

17 And now as I Moroni said
I could not make a full account of these things which are written,
therefore it sufficeth me to say
that Jesus shewed himself unto this man in the spirit,
even after the manner and in the likeness of the same body
even as he shewed himself unto the Nephites.

18 And he ministered unto him
even as he ministered unto the Nephites—
and all this because that this man knew that he was God
because of the many great works which the Lord had shewed unto him.

19 And because of the knowledge of this man,
he could not be kept from beholding within the veil.
And he saw the finger of Jesus,
which when he saw, he fell with fear,
for he knew that it was the finger of the Lord.
And he had faith no longer,
for he knew, nothing doubting.

20 Wherefore having this perfect knowledge of God,
he could not be kept from within the veil.
Therefore he saw Jesus, and he did minister unto him.

21 And it came to pass that the Lord said unto the brother of Jared:
Behold, thou shalt not suffer these things which ye have seen and heard
to go forth unto the world
until the time cometh that I shall glorify my name in the flesh.
Wherefore ye shall treasure up the things which ye have seen and heard
and shew it to no man.

22 And behold, when ye shall come unto me,
ye shall write them and shall seal them up,
that no one can interpret them;
for ye shall write them in a language that they cannot be read.

23 And behold, these two stones will I give unto thee;
and ye shall seal them up also with the things which ye shall write.

24 For behold, the language which ye shall write I have confounded.
Wherefore I will cause in mine own due time
that these stones shall magnify to the eyes of men
these things which ye shall write.

25 And when the Lord had said these words,
the Lord shewed unto the brother of Jared
all the inhabitants of the earth which had been
and also all that would be.
And the Lord withheld them not from his sight,
even unto the ends of the earth.

26 For the Lord had said unto him in times before
that if he would believe in him that he could shew unto him all things,
it should be shewn unto him.
Therefore the Lord could not withhold any thing from him,
for he knew that the Lord could shew him all things.

27 And the Lord said unto him:
Write these things and seal them up,
and I will shew them in mine own due time unto the children of men.

28 And it came to pass that the Lord commanded him
that he should seal up the two stones which he had received
and shew them not until the Lord should shew them unto the children of men.

4 | 1 And the Lord commanded the brother of Jared
to go down out of the mount from the presence of the Lord
and write the things which he had seen.
And they were forbidden to come unto the children of men
until after that he should be lifted up upon the cross.
And for this cause did king Benjamin keep them,
that they should not come unto the world
until after Christ should shew himself unto his people.

2 And after that Christ truly had shewed himself unto his people,
he commanded that they should be made manifest.

3 And now after that they have all dwindled in unbelief
and there is none save it be the Lamanites
—and they have rejected the gospel of Christ—
therefore I am commanded that I should hide them up again in the earth.

4 Behold, I have written upon these plates
the very things which the brother of Jared saw.
And there never was greater things made manifest

than that which was made manifest unto the brother of Jared.

5 Wherefore the Lord hath commanded me to write them
and I have wrote them.
And he commanded me that I should seal them up.
And he also hath commanded that I should seal up the interpretation thereof;
wherefore I have sealed up the interpreters
according to the commandment of the Lord.

6 For the Lord saith unto me:
They shall not go forth unto the Gentiles
until the day that they shall repent of their iniquity
and become clean before the Lord.

7 And in that day that they shall exercise faith in me, saith the Lord,
even as the brother of Jared did,
that they may become sanctified in me,
then will I manifest unto them the things which the brother of Jared saw,
even to the unfolding unto them all my revelations,
saith Jesus Christ the Son of God,
the Father of the heavens and of the earth and all things that in them is.

8 And he that will contend against the word of the Lord, let him be accursed.
And he that shall deny these things, let him be accursed.
For unto them will I shew no greater things, saith Jesus Christ,
for I am he which speaketh.

9 And at my command the heavens are opened and are shut.
And at my word the earth shall shake.
And at my command the inhabitants thereof shall pass away,
even so as by fire.

10 And he that believeth not my words believeth not my disciples.
And if it so be that I do not speak, judge ye;
for ye shall know that it is I that speaketh,
at the last day.

11 But he that believeth these things which I have spoken,
him will I visit with the manifestations of my Spirit.
And he shall know and bear record;
for because of my Spirit he shall know that these things are true,
for it persuadeth men to do good.

12 And whatsoever thing persuadeth men to do good is of me,
for good cometh of none save it be of me.
I am the same that leadeth men to all good.

He that will not believe my words will not believe me, that I am.
And he that will not believe me will not believe the Father, which sent me.
For behold, I am the Father.

I am the light and the life and the truth of the world.

13 Come unto me, O ye Gentiles,
and I will shew unto you the greater things,
the knowledge which is hid up because of unbelief.

14 Come unto me, O ye house of Israel,
and it shall be made manifest unto you
how great things the Father hath laid up for you
from the foundation of the world;
and it hath not come unto you,
because of unbelief.

15 Behold, when ye shall rend that veil of unbelief
which doth cause you to remain in your awful state of wickedness
and hardness of heart and blindness of mind,
then shall the great and marvelous things
which have been hid up from the foundation of the world from you
—yea, when ye shall call upon the Father in my name
with a broken heart and a contrite spirit—
then shall ye know that the Father hath remembered the covenant
which he made unto your fathers, O house of Israel.

16 And then shall my revelations
which I have caused to be written by my servant John
be unfolded in the eyes of all the people.

Remember, when ye see these things,
ye shall know that the time is at hand
that they shall be made manifest in very deed.

17 Therefore when ye shall receive this record,
ye may know that the work of the Father has commenced
upon all the face of the land.

18 Therefore repent, all ye ends of the earth,
and come unto me and believe in my gospel
and be baptized in my name.
For he that believeth and is baptized shall be saved,
but he that believeth not shall be damned.
And signs shall follow them that believe in my name.

19 And blessed is he that is found faithful unto my name at the last day,
for they shall be lifted up to dwell in the kingdom
prepared for them from the foundation of the world.
And behold, it is I that hath spoken it.
Amen.

5 | 1 And now I Moroni have written the words
which was commanded me,
according to my memory.
And I have told you the things which I have sealed up.
Therefore touch them not, in order that ye may translate;
for that thing is forbidden you except by and by it shall be wisdom in God.

2 And behold, ye may be privileged
that ye may shew the plates unto those
who shall assist to bring forth this work.

3 And unto three shall they be shewn by the power of God;
wherefore they shall know of a surety that these things are true.

4 And in the mouth of three witnesses shall these things be established;
and the testimony of three and this work
— in the which shall be shewn forth the power of God and also his word,
of which the Father and the Son and the Holy Ghost beareth record —
and all this shall stand as a testimony against the world at the last day.

5 And if it so be that they repent and come unto the Father in the name of Jesus,
they shall be received into the kingdom of God.

6 And now if I have no authority for these things, judge ye;
for ye shall know that I have authority when ye shall see me,
and we shall stand before God at the last day.
Amen.

6 | 1 And now I Moroni proceed to give the record of Jared and his brother.

2 For it came to pass after that the Lord had prepared the stones
which the brother of Jared had carried up into the mount,
the brother of Jared came down out of the mount;
and he did put forth the stones into the vessels which were prepared,
one in each end thereof.
And behold, they did give light unto the vessels thereof.

3 And thus the Lord caused stones to shine in darkness,
to give light unto men, women, and children,
that they might not cross the great waters in darkness.

4 And it came to pass that when they had prepared all manner of food,
that thereby they might subsist upon the water
— and also food for their flocks and herds
and whatsoever beast or animal or fowl that they should carry with them —
and it came to pass that when they had done all these things,
they got aboard of their vessels or barges and set forth into the sea,
commending themselves unto the Lord their God.

5 And it came to pass that the Lord God caused
that there should a furious wind blow
upon the face of the waters towards the promised land;
and thus they were tossed upon the waves of the sea before the wind.

6 And it came to pass that they were many times buried in the depths of the sea
because of the mountain waves which broke upon them,
and also the great and terrible tempests
which were caused by the fierceness of the wind.

7 And it came to pass that when they were buried in the deep,
there was no water that could hurt them,
their vessels being tight like unto a dish;
and also they were tight like unto the ark of Noah.
Therefore when they were encompassed about by many waters,
they did cry unto the Lord,
and he did bring them forth again upon the top of the waters.

8 And it came to pass that the wind did never cease
to blow towards the promised land while they were upon the waters;
and thus they were driven forth before the wind.

9 And they did sing praises unto the Lord;
yea, the brother of Jared did sing praises unto the Lord,
and he did thank and praise the Lord all the day long.
And when the night came, they did not cease to praise the Lord.

10 And thus they were driven forth;
and no monster of the sea could break them,
neither whale that could mar them.
And they did have light continually,
whether it was above the water or under the water.

11 And thus they were driven forth
three hundred and forty and four days upon the water;

12 and they did land upon the shore of the promised land.
And when they had set their feet upon the shores of the promised land,
they bowed themselves down upon the face of the land
and did humble themselves before the Lord
and did shed tears of joy before the Lord
because of the multitude of his tender mercies over them.

13 And it came to pass that they went forth upon the face of the land
and began to till the earth.

14 And Jared had four sons,
and they were called Jacom and Gilgah and Mahah and Orihah.

15 And the brother of Jared also begat sons and daughters.

16 And the friends of Jared and his brother
were in number about twenty and two souls.
And they also begat sons and daughters before they came to the promised land;
and therefore they began to be many.

17 And they were taught to walk humbly before the Lord;
and they were also taught from on high.

18 And it came to pass that they began to spread upon the face of the land
and to multiply and to till the earth,
and they did wax strong in the land.

19 And the brother of Jared began to be old
and saw that he must soon go down to the grave;
wherefore he saith unto Jared:
Let us gather together our people that we may number them,
that we may know of them what they will desire of us
before we go down to our graves.

20 And accordingly the people were gathered together.
Now the number of the sons and the daughters of the brother of Jared
were twenty and two souls;
and the number of the sons and daughters of Jared were twelve,
he having four sons.

21 And it came to pass that they did number their people.
And after that they had numbered them,
they did desire of them the things
which they would that they should do
before they went down to their graves.

22 And it came to pass that the people desired of them
that they should anoint one of their sons to be a king over them

23 —and now behold, this was grievous unto them—
but the brother of Jared said unto them:
Surely this thing leadeth into captivity.

24 But Jared said unto his brother:
Suffer them that they may have a king.
And therefore he said unto them:
Choose ye out from among our sons a king, even whom ye will.

25 And it came to pass that
they chose even the first born of the brother of Jared,
and his name was Pagag.
And it came to pass that he refused and would not be their king.
And the people would that his father should constrain him,
but his father would not.

And he commanded them
that they should constrain no man to be their king.

26 And it came to pass that they chose all the brothers of Pagag,
and they would not.

27 And it came to pass that neither would the sons of Jared,
even all save it were one;
and Orihah, he was anointed to be king over the people.

28 And he began to reign, and the people began to prosper;
and they became exceeding rich.

29 And it came to pass that Jared died and his brother also.

30 And it came to pass that Orihah did walk humbly before the Lord
and did remember how great things the Lord had done for his father,
and also taught his people how great things the Lord had done for their fathers.

7 | 1 And it came to pass that Orihah did execute judgment upon the land
in righteousness all his days,
whose days were exceeding many.

2 And he begat sons and daughters;
yea, he begat thirty and one,
among whom were twenty and three sons.

3 And it came to pass that he also begat Kib in his old age.
And it came to pass that Kib reigned in his stead;
and Kib begat Corihor.

4 And when Corihor was thirty and two years old,
he rebelled against his father and went over and dwelt in the land of Nehor;
and he begat sons and daughters.
And they became exceeding fair;
wherefore Corihor drew away many people after him.

5 And when he had gathered together an army,
he came up unto the land of Moron, where the king dwelt,
and took him captive, which brought to pass
the saying of the brother of Jared
that they would be brought into captivity.

6 Now the land of Moron, where the king dwelt, was near the land
which is called Desolation by the Nephites.

7 And it came to pass that Kib dwelt in captivity,
and his people under Corihor his son,
until he became exceeding old.
Nevertheless Kib begat Shule in his old age,
while he was yet in captivity.

8 And it came to pass that Shule was angry with his brother.
And Shule waxed strong

and became mighty as to the strength of a man;
and he was also mighty in judgment.

9 Wherefore he came to the hill Ephraim,
and he did molten out of the hill and made swords out of steel
for those which he had drew away with him.
And after that he had armed them with swords,
he returned to the city Nehor
and gave battle unto his brother Corihor,
by which means he obtained the kingdom
and restored it unto his father Kib.

10 And now because of the thing which Shule had done,
his father bestowed upon him the kingdom;
therefore he began to reign in the stead of his father.

11 And it came to pass that he did execute judgment in righteousness.
And he did spread his kingdom upon all the face of the land,
for the people had become exceeding numerous.

12 And it came to pass that Shule also begat many sons and daughters.

13 And Corihor repented of the many evils which he had done;
wherefore Shule gave him power in his kingdom.

14 And it came to pass that Corihor had many sons and daughters.
And among the sons of Corihor there was one whose name was Noah.

15 And it came to pass that
Noah rebelled against Shule the king and also his father Corihor
and drew away Cohor his brother
and also all his brethren and many of the people.

16 And he gave battle unto Shule the king,
in the which he did obtain the land of their first inheritance;
and he became a king over that part of the land.

17 And it came to pass that he gave battle again unto Shule the king;
and he took Shule the king and carried him away captive into Moron.

18 And it came to pass as he was about to put him to death,
the sons of Shule crept into the house of Noah by night and slew him
and broke down the door of the prison and brought out their father
and placed him upon his throne in his own kingdom.

19 Wherefore the son of Noah did build up his kingdom in his stead.
Nevertheless they did not gain power any more over Shule the king.
And the people which were under the reign of Shule the king
did prosper exceedingly and wax great.

20 And the country was divided and there was two kingdoms:
the kingdom of Shule and the kingdom of Cohor the son of Noah.

21 And Cohor the son of Noah caused
   that his people should give battle unto Shule,
   in the which Shule did beat them and did slay Cohor.
22 And now Cohor had a son which was called Nimrod;
   and Nimrod gave up the kingdom of Cohor unto Shule,
   and he did gain favor in the eyes of Shule;
   wherefore Shule did bestow great favors upon him,
   in the which he did do in the kingdom of Shule according to his desires.

23 And also in the reign of Shule there came prophets among the people,
   which were sent from the Lord,
   prophesying that the wickedness and idolatry of the people
   was bringing a curse upon the land,
   in the which they should be destroyed if they did not repent.
24 And it came to pass that
   the people did revile against the prophets and did mock them.
   And it came to pass that king Shule did execute judgment
   against all those who did revile against the prophets.
25 And he did execute a law throughout all the land
   which gave power unto the prophets
   that they should go whithersoever they would.
   And by this cause the people were brought unto repentance.
26 And because the people did repent of their iniquities and idolatries,
   the Lord did spare them;
   and they began to prosper again in the land.

   And it came to pass that Shule begat sons and daughters in his old age.
27 And there was no more wars in the days of Shule.
   And he remembered the great things that the Lord had done for his fathers
   in bringing them across the great deep into the promised land;
   wherefore he did execute judgment in righteousness all his days.
8 | 1 And it came to pass that he begat Omer,
   and Omer reigned in his stead.
   And Omer begat Jared;
   and Jared begat sons and daughters.

2 And Jared rebelled against his father
   and came and dwelt in the land of Heth.
   And it came to pass that he did flatter much people
   because of his cunning words
   until he had gained the half of the kingdom.
3 And when he had gained the half of the kingdom,
   he gave battle unto his father;

and he did carry away his father into captivity
and did make him serve in captivity.

4 And now in the days of the reign of Omer
he was in captivity the half of his days.
And it came to pass that he begat sons and daughters,
among whom were Esrom and Coriantumr.
5 And they were exceeding angry because of the doings of Jared their brother,
insomuch that they did raise an army and gave battle unto Jared.
And it came to pass that they did give battle unto him by night.
6 And it came to pass that when they had slew the army of Jared,
they were about to slay him also;
and he pled with them that they would not slay him
and he would give up the kingdom unto his father.
And it came to pass that they did grant unto him his life.

7 And now Jared became exceeding sorrowful because of the loss of the kingdom,
for he had set his heart upon the kingdom and upon the glory of the world.
8 Now the daughter of Jared being exceeding expert,
and seeing the sorrow of her father,
thought to devise a plan
whereby she could redeem the kingdom unto her father.
9 Now the daughter of Jared was exceeding fair.
And it came to pass that she did talk with her father and saith unto him:
Whereby hath my father so much sorrow?
Hath he not read the record which our fathers brought across the great deep?
Behold, is there not an account concerning them of old,
that they by their secret plans did obtain kingdoms and great glory?
10 And now therefore let my father send for Akish the son of Kimnor.
And behold, I am fair and I will dance before him.
And I will please him, that he will desire me to wife.
Wherefore if he shall desire of thee
that ye shall give unto him me to wife,
then shall ye say:
I will give her
if ye will bring unto me the head of my father the king.

11 And now Omer was a friend to Akish.
Wherefore when Jared had sent for Akish,
the daughter of Jared danced before him,
that she pleased him,
insomuch that he desired her to wife.
And it came to pass that he said unto Jared:
Give her unto me to wife.

12 And Jared said unto him: I will give her unto you
      if ye will bring unto me the head of my father the king.

13 And it came to pass that
      Akish gathered in unto the house of Jared all his kinsfolks
      and saith unto them:
      Will ye swear unto me that ye will be faithful unto me
      in the thing which I shall desire of you?
14 And it came to pass that they all sware unto him by the God of heaven
      and also by the heavens and also by the earth and by their heads
      that whoso should vary from the assistance which Akish desired
      should lose his head;
      and whoso should divulge whatsoever thing Akish made known unto them,
      the same should lose his life.

15 And it came to pass that thus they did agree with Akish.
      And Akish did administer unto them the oaths
      which was given by them of old, who also sought power,
      which had been handed down even from Cain,
      who was a murderer from the beginning.
16 And they were kept up by the power of the devil,
      to administer these oaths unto the people, to keep them in darkness,
      to help such as sought power to gain power
      and to murder and to plunder and to lie
      and to commit all manner of wickedness and whoredoms.
17 And it was the daughter of Jared
      which put it into his heart to search up these things of old;
      and Jared put it into the heart of Akish.
      Wherefore Akish administered it unto his kindreds and friends,
      leading them away by fair promises to do whatsoever thing he desired.
18 And it came to pass that they formed a secret combination,
      even as they of old,
      which combination is most abominable and wicked
      above all in the sight of God.
19 For the Lord worketh not in secret combinations,
      neither doth he will that man should shed blood;
      but in all things hath forbidden it from the beginning of man.

20 And now I Moroni do not write the manner of their oaths and combinations,
      for it hath been made known unto me that they are had among all people;
      and they are had among the Lamanites.
21 And they have caused the destruction of this people
      of which I am now speaking,
      and also the destruction of the people of Nephi.

22 And whatsoever nation shall uphold such secret combinations,
    to get power and gain,
    until they shall spread over the nation,
    behold, they shall be destroyed;
    for the Lord will not suffer
    that the blood of his saints which shall be shed by them
    shall always cry unto him from the ground for vengeance upon them
    and yet he avengeth them not.

23 Wherefore, O ye Gentiles,
    it is wisdom in God that these things should be shewn unto you,
    that thereby ye may repent of your sins
    and suffer not that these murderous combinations shall get above you,
    which are built up to get power and gain,
    and the work—yea, even the work of destruction—come upon you;
    yea, even the sword of the justice of the Eternal God shall fall upon you,
    to your overthrow and destruction,
    if ye shall suffer these things to be.

24 Wherefore the Lord commandeth you,
    when ye shall see these things come among you,
    that ye shall awake to a sense of your awful situation
    because of this secret combination which shall be among you;
    for woe be unto it because of the blood of them which have been slain,
    for they cry from the dust for vengeance upon it,
    and also upon those who build it up.

25 For it cometh to pass that whoso buildeth it up
    seeketh to overthrow the freedom of all lands, nations, and countries.
    And it bringeth to pass the destruction of all people,
    for it is built up by the devil, which is the father of all lies,
    even that same liar which beguiled our first parents,
    yea, even that same liar
    which hath caused man to commit murder from the beginning,
    which hath hardened the hearts of men
    that they have murdered the prophets
    and stoned them and cast them out from the beginning.

26 Wherefore I Moroni am commanded to write these things,
    that evil may be done away
    and that the time may come
    that Satan may have no power upon the hearts of the children of men,
    but that they may be persuaded to do good continually,
    that they may come unto the fountain of all righteousness and be saved.

9 | 1 And now I Moroni proceed with my record.
Therefore, behold, it came to pass that
because of the secret combinations of Akish and his friends,
behold, they did overthrow the kingdom of Omer.

2 Nevertheless the Lord was merciful unto Omer,
and also to his sons and to his daughters
which were not—or which did not seek his destruction.

3 And the Lord warned Omer in a dream that he should depart out of the land.
Wherefore Omer departed out of the land with his family
and traveled many days and came over and passed by the hill of Shim
and came over by the place where the Nephites were destroyed,
and from thence eastward
and came to a place which was called Ablom,
by the seashore.
And there he pitched his tent,
and also his sons and his daughters and all his household,
save it were Jared and his family.

4 And it came to pass that
Jared was anointed king over the people by the hand of wickedness,
and he gave unto Akish his daughter to wife.

5 And it came to pass that Akish sought the life of his father-in-law,
and he applied unto those whom he had sworn by the oath of the ancients.
And they obtained the head of his father-in-law
as he sat upon his throne giving audience to his people.

6 For so great had been the spreading of this wicked and secret society
that it had corrupted the hearts of all the people.
Therefore Jared was murdered upon his throne,
and Akish reigned in his stead.

7 And it came to pass that Akish began to be jealous of his son.
Therefore he shut him up in prison
and kept him upon a little or no food
until he had suffered death.

8 And now the brother of him that suffered death
—and his name was Nimrah—
and he was angry with his father
because of that which his father had done unto his brother.

9 And it came to pass that Nimrah gathered together a small number of men
and fled out of the land
and came over and dwelt with Omer.

10 And it came to pass that Akish begat other sons;
and they won the hearts of the people,

notwithstanding they had sworn unto him
to do all manner of iniquity according to that which he desired.

11 Now the people of Akish were desirous for gain,
even as Akish was desirous for power.
Wherefore the sons of Akish did offer them money,
by the which means they drew away the more part of the people after them.

12 And there began to be a war between the sons of Akish and Akish,
which lasted for the space of many years,
yea, unto the destruction of nearly all the people of the kingdom,
yea, even all save it were thirty souls
and they which fled with the house of Omer.

13 Wherefore Omer was restored again to the land of his inheritance.

14 And it came to pass that Omer began to be old.
Nevertheless in his old age he begat Emer;
and he anointed Emer to be king to reign in his stead.

15 And after that he had anointed Emer to be king,
he saw peace in the land for the space of two years, and he died,
having seen exceeding many days which were full of sorrow.
And it came to pass that Emer did reign in his stead
and did fill the steps of his father.

16 And the Lord began again to take the curse from off the land.
And the house of Emer did prosper exceedingly under the reign of Emer.
And in the space of sixty and two years they had become exceeding strong,
insomuch that they became exceeding rich,

17 having all manner of fruit and of grain
and of silks and of fine linen
and of gold and of silver and of precious things

18 and also all manner of cattle, of oxen and cows,
and of sheep and of swine and of goats,
and also many other kind of animals which were useful for the food of man;

19 and they also had horses and asses;
and there were elephants and cureloms and cumoms,
all of which were useful unto man,
and more especially the elephants and cureloms and cumoms.

20 And thus the Lord did pour out his blessings upon this land,
which was choice above all other lands.
And he commanded that whoso should possess the land
should possess it unto the Lord,
or they should be destroyed when they were ripened in iniquity.
For upon such, saith the Lord, I will pour out the fullness of my wrath.

21 And Emer did execute judgment in righteousness all his days,
and he begat many sons and daughters;

and he begat Coriantum,
and he anointed Coriantum to reign in his stead.

22 And after that he had anointed Coriantum to reign in his stead,
he lived four years, and he saw peace in the land.
Yea, and he even saw the Sun of righteousness
and did rejoice and glory in his day;
and he died in peace.

23 And it came to pass that Coriantum did walk in the steps of his father
and did build many mighty cities
and did administer that which was good unto his people in all his days.
And it came to pass that he had no children even until he was exceeding old.

24 And it came to pass that his wife died,
being an hundred and two years old.
And it came to pass that Coriantum took to wife in his old age a young maid
and begat sons and daughters;
wherefore he lived until he was an hundred and forty and two years old.

25 And it came to pass that he begat Com,
and Com reigned in his stead.
And he reigned forty and nine years,
and he begat Heth;
and he also begat other sons and daughters.

26 And the people had spread again over all the face of the land.
And there began again to be an exceeding great wickedness
upon the face of the land;
and Heth began to embrace the secret plans again of old,
to destroy his father.

27 And it came to pass that he did dethrone his father,
for he slew him with his own sword;
and he did reign in his stead.

28 And there came prophets in the land again,
crying repentance unto them,
that they must prepare the way of the Lord
or there should come a curse upon the face of the land;
yea, even there should be a great famine,
in the which they should be destroyed if they did not repent.

29 But the people believed not the words of the prophets,
but they cast them out.
And some of them they cast into pits and left them to perish.
And it came to pass that they done all these things
according to the commandment of the king Heth.

30 And it came to pass that there began to be a great dearth upon the land.

And the inhabitants began to be destroyed exceeding fast because of the dearth,
for there was no rain upon the face of the earth.

31 And there came forth poisonous serpents also upon the face of the land
and did poison many people.
And it came to pass that their flocks began to flee before the poisonous serpents
towards the land southward, which was called by the Nephites Zarahemla.

32 And it came to pass that there were many of them which did perish by the way;
nevertheless there were some which fled into the land southward.

33 And it came to pass that the Lord did cause the serpents
that they should pursue them no more,
but that they should hedge up the way, that the people could not pass,
that whoso should attempt to pass might fall by the poisonous serpents.

34 And it came to pass that the people did follow the course of the beasts
and did devour the carcasses of them which fell by the way
until they had devoured them all.

Now when the people saw that they must perish,
they began to repent of their iniquities and cry unto the Lord.

35 And it came to pass that
when they had humbled themselves sufficiently before the Lord,
the Lord did send rain upon the face of the earth.
And the people began to revive again;
and there began to be fruit in the north countries
and in all the countries around about.
And the Lord did shew forth his power unto them
in preserving them from famine.

10 | 1 And it came to pass that Shez, which was a descendant of Heth
—for Heth had perished by the famine and all his household, save it were Shez—
wherefore Shez began to build up again a broken people.

2 And it came to pass that Shez did remember the destruction of his fathers,
and he did build up a righteous kingdom;
for he remembered what the Lord had done
in bringing Jared and his brother across the deep.
And he did walk in the ways of the Lord,
and he begat sons and daughters.

3 And his eldest son, whose name was Shez, did rebel against him.
Nevertheless Shez was smitten by the hand of a robber
because of his exceeding riches,
which brought peace again unto his father.

4 And it came to pass that
his father did build up many cities upon the face of the land.
And the people began again to spread over all the face of the land.
And Shez did live to an exceeding old age,

and he begat Riplakish;
and he died,
and Riplakish reigned in his stead.

5 And it came to pass that Riplakish did not do that
which was right in the sight of the Lord,
for he did have many wives and concubines
and did lay that upon men's shoulders which was grievous to be borne.
Yea, he did tax them with heavy taxes,
and with the taxes he did build many spacious buildings.
6 And he did erect him an exceeding beautiful throne.
And he did build many prisons.
And whoso would not be subject unto taxes he did cast into prison.
And whoso were not able to pay taxes he did cast into prison.
And he did cause that they should labor continually for their support.
And whoso refused to labor he did cause to be put to death.
7 Wherefore he did obtain all his fine work;
yea, even his fine gold he did cause to be refined in prison,
and all manner of fine workmanship he did cause to be wrought in prison.

And it came to pass that
he did afflict the people with his whoredoms and abominations.
8 And when he had reigned for the space of forty and two years,
the people did raise up in rebellion against him.
And there began to be war again in the land,
insomuch that Riplakish was killed
and his descendants were driven out of the land.
9 And it came to pass after the space of many years
Morianton, he being a descendant of Riplakish,
gathered together an army of outcasts
and went forth and gave battle unto the people,
and he gained power over many cities.
And the war became exceeding sore and did last for the space of many years,
and he did gain power over all the land
and did establish himself king over all the land.
10 And after that he had established himself king,
he did ease the burden of the people,
in the which he did gain favor in the eyes of the people;
and they did anoint him to be their king.
11 And he did do justice unto the people,
but not unto himself because of his many whoredoms;
wherefore he was cut off from the presence of the Lord.

12 And it came to pass that Morianton built up many cities.

And the people became exceeding rich under his reign,
both in buildings and in gold and in silver
and in raising grain and in flocks and herds
and such things which had been restored unto them.

13 And Morianton did live to an exceeding great age,
and then he begat Kim.
And Kim did reign in the stead of his father,
and he did reign eight years and his father died.

And it came to pass that Kim did not reign in righteousness;
wherefore he was not favored of the Lord.

14 And his brother did raise up in rebellion against him,
in the which he did bring him into captivity.
And he did remain in captivity all his days,
and he begat sons and daughters in captivity.
And in his old age he begat Levi,
and he died.

15 And it came to pass that Levi did serve in captivity,
after the death of his father,
for the space of forty and two years.
And he did make war against the king of the land,
in the which he did obtain unto himself the kingdom.

16 And after that he had obtained unto himself the kingdom,
he did that which was right in the sight of the Lord.
And the people did prosper in the land.
And he did live to a good old age and begat sons and daughters;
and he also begat Corom, whom he anointed king in his stead.

17 And it came to pass that Corom did that
which was good in the sight of the Lord all his days;
and he begat many sons and daughters.
And after that he had seen many days, he did pass away,
even like unto the rest of the earth,
and Kish reigned in his stead.

18 And it came to pass that Kish passed away also,
and Lib reigned in his stead.

19 And it came to pass that
Lib also did that which was good in the sight of the Lord.

And in the days of Lib the poisonous serpents were destroyed.
Wherefore they did go into the land southward
to hunt food for the people of the land,
for the land was covered with animals of the forest;
and Lib also himself became a great hunter.

20 And they built a great city by the narrow neck of land,
   by the place where the sea divides the land.
21 And they did preserve the land southward for a wilderness to get game.
   And the whole face of the land northward was covered with inhabitants.
22 And they were exceeding industrious,
   and they did buy and sell and traffic one with another that they might get gain.
23 And they did work in all manner of ore,
   and they did make gold and silver and iron and brass and all manner of metals;
   and they did dig it out of the earth.
   Wherefore they did cast up mighty heaps of earth for to get ore,
   of gold and of silver and of iron and of copper.
   And they did work all manner of fine work.
24 And they did have silks and fine twined linen;
   and they did work all manner of cloth
   that they might clothe themselves from their nakedness.
25 And they did make all manner of tools to till the earth,
   both to plow and to sow,
   to reap and to hoe, and also to thrash.
26 And they did make all manner of tools,
   in the which they did work their beasts.
27 And they did make all manner of weapons of war.
   And they did work all manner of work of exceeding curious workmanship.
28 And never could be a people more blessed than were they
   and more prospered by the hand of the Lord.
   And they were in a land that was choice above all lands,
   for the Lord had spoken it.

29 And it came to pass that Lib did live many years
   and begat sons and daughters;
   and he also begat Hearthom.
30 And it came to pass that Hearthom reigned in the stead of his father.
   And when Hearthom had reigned twenty and four years,
   behold, the kingdom was taken away from him.
   And he served many years in captivity,
   yea, even all the remainder of his days.
31 And he begat Heth;
   and Heth lived in captivity all his days,
   and Heth begat Aaron;
   and Aaron dwelt in captivity all his days,
   and he begat Amnigaddah;
   and Amnigaddah also dwelt in captivity all his days,
   and he begat Coriantum;

and Coriantum dwelt in captivity all his days,
and he begat Com.

32 And it came to pass that Com drew away the half of the kingdom;
and he reigned over the half of the kingdom forty and two years.
And he went to battle against the king Amgid;
and they fought for the space of many years,
in the which Com gained power over Amgid
and obtained power over the remainder of the kingdom.

33 And in the days of Com there began to be robbers in the land,
and they adopted the old plans
and administered oaths after the manner of the ancients
and sought again to destroy the kingdom.

34 Now Com did fight against them much;
nevertheless he did not prevail against them.

11 | 1 And there came also in the days of Com many prophets
and prophesied of the destruction of that great people
except they should repent and turn unto the Lord
and forsake their murders and wickedness.

2 And it came to pass that the prophets were rejected by the people;
and they fled unto Com for protection,
for the people sought to destroy them.

3 And they prophesied unto Com many things;
and he was blessed in all the remainder of his days.

4 And he lived to a good old age and begat Shiblon;
and Shiblon reigned in his stead.

And the brother of Shiblon rebelled against him,
and there began to be an exceeding great war in all the land.

5 And it came to pass that the brother of Shiblon did cause
that all the prophets which prophesied of the destruction of the people
should be put to death.

6 And there was great calamity in all the land,
for they had testified that a great curse should come upon the land,
and also upon the people,
and that there should be a great destruction among them,
such an one as never had been upon the face of the earth;
and their bones should become as heaps of earth upon the face of the land
except they should repent of their wickedness.

7 And they hearkened not unto the voice of the Lord
because of their wicked combinations;
wherefore there began to be wars and contentions in all the land,

and also many famines and pestilences,
insomuch that there was a great destruction,
such an one as never had been known upon the face of the earth.
And all this came to pass in the days of Shiblon.

8   And the people began to repent of their iniquity;
and inasmuch as they did, the Lord did have mercy on them.

9   And it came to pass that Shiblon was slain;
and Seth was brought into captivity,
and he did dwell in captivity all his days.

10 And it came to pass that Ahah his son did obtain the kingdom,
and he did reign over the people all his days.
And he did do all manner of iniquity in his days,
in the which he did cause the shedding of much blood;
and few were his days.

11 And Ethem being a descendant of Ahah did obtain the kingdom;
and he also did do that which was wicked in his days.

12 And it came to pass in the days of Ethem
there came many prophets and prophesied again unto the people;
yea, they did prophesy that the Lord would utterly destroy them
from off the face of the earth
except they repented of their iniquities.

13 And it came to pass that the people hardened their hearts
and would not hearken unto their words.
And the prophets mourned and withdrew from among the people.

14 And it came to pass that
Ethem did execute judgment in wickedness all his days;
and he begat Moron.
And it came to pass that Moron did reign in his stead,
and Moron did do that which was wicked before the Lord.

15 And it came to pass that there arose a rebellion among the people
because of that secret combination which was built up to get power and gain.
And there arose a mighty man among them in iniquity
and gave battle unto Moron,
in the which he did overthrow the half of the kingdom;
and he did maintain the half of the kingdom for many years.

16 And it came to pass that Moron did overthrow him
and did obtain the kingdom again.

17 And it came to pass that there arose another mighty man,
and he was a descendant of the brother of Jared.

18 And it came to pass that he did overthrow Moron and obtain the kingdom;

wherefore Moron dwelt in captivity all the remainder of his days,
and he begat Coriantor.

19 And it came to pass that Coriantor dwelt in captivity all his days.

20 And in the days of Coriantor there also came many prophets
and prophesied of great and marvelous things
and cried repentance unto the people
—and except they should repent,
the Lord God would execute judgment against them to their utter destruction—

21 and that the Lord God would send or bring forth
another people to possess the land,
by his power, after the manner which he brought their fathers.

22 And they did reject all the words of the prophets
because of their secret society and wicked abominations.

23 And it came to pass that Coriantor begat Ether;
and he died, having dwelt in captivity all his days.

12 | 1 And it came to pass that the days of Ether was in the days of Coriantumr;
and Coriantumr was king over all the land.

2 And Ether was a prophet of the Lord;
wherefore Ether came forth in the days of Coriantumr
and began to prophesy unto the people,
for he could not be constrained
because of the Spirit of the Lord which was in him.

3 For he did cry from the morning even until the going down of the sun,
exhorting the people to believe in God unto repentance
lest they should be destroyed,
saying unto them that by faith all things are fulfilled.

4 Wherefore whoso believeth in God might with surety hope for a better world,
yea, even a place at the right hand of God,
which hope cometh of faith
and maketh an anchor to the souls of men,
which would make them sure and steadfast,
always abounding in good works,
being led to glorify God.

5 And it came to pass that
Ether did prophesy great and marvelous things unto the people,
which they did not believe because they saw them not.

6 And now I Moroni would speak somewhat concerning these things.
I would shew unto the world
that faith is things which are hoped for and not seen.

Wherefore dispute not because ye see not,
for ye receive no witness not until after the trial of your faith.

7 For it was by faith that Christ shewed himself unto our fathers
after that he had risen from the dead.
And he shewed not himself unto them until after they had faith in him.
Wherefore it must needs be that some had faith in him,
for he shewed himself not unto the world but because of the faith of men:

8 he has shewn himself unto the world
and glorified the name of the Father
and prepared a way that thereby others might be partakers of the heavenly gift,
that they might hope for those things which they have not seen.

9 Wherefore ye may also have hope and be partakers of the gift
if ye will but have faith.

10 Behold, it was by faith
that they of old were called after the holy order of God.

11 Wherefore by faith was the law of Moses given.
But in the gift of his Son hath God prepared a more excellent way;
and it is by faith that it hath been fulfilled.

12 For if there be no faith among the children of men,
God can do no miracle among them;
wherefore he shewed not himself until after their faith.

13 Behold, it was the faith of Alma and Amulek
that caused the prison to tumble to the earth.

14 Behold, it was the faith of Nephi and Lehi
that wrought the change upon the Lamanites,
that they were baptized with fire and with the Holy Ghost.

15 Behold, it was the faith of Ammon and his brethren
which wrought so great a miracle among the Lamanites.

16 Yea, and even all they which wrought miracles wrought them by faith,
even those which were before Christ,
and also them which were after.

17 And it was by faith that the three disciples obtained a promise
that they should not taste of death;
and they obtained not the promise until after their faith.

18 And neither at any time hath any wrought miracles until after their faith;
wherefore they first believed in the Son of God.

19 And there were many whose faith was so exceeding strong,
even before Christ came,
which could not be kept from within the veil
but truly saw with their eyes the things

which they had beheld with an eye of faith,
and they were glad.

20 And behold, we have seen in this record
that one of these was the brother of Jared;
for so great was his faith in God
that when God put forth his finger,
he could not hide it from the sight of the brother of Jared
because of his word which he had spoken unto him,
which word he had obtained by faith.

21 And after that the brother of Jared had beheld the finger of the Lord
because of the promise which the brother of Jared had obtained by faith,
the Lord could not withhold any thing from his sight;
wherefore he shewed him all things,
for he could no longer be kept without the veil.

22 And it is by faith that my fathers have obtained the promise
that these things should come unto their brethren through the Gentiles.
Therefore the Lord hath commanded me,
yea, even Jesus Christ.

23 And I said unto him:
Lord, the Gentiles will mock at these things
because of our weakness in writing;
for Lord, thou hast made us mighty in word by faith,
where unto thou hast not made us mighty in writing.
For thou hast made all this people
that they could speak much because of the Holy Ghost
which thou hast given them.

24 And thou hast made us that we could write but little
because of the awkwardness of our hands.
Behold, thou hast not made us mighty in writing
like unto the brother of Jared,
for thou madest him that the things which he wrote were mighty,
even as thou art,
unto the overpowering of man to read them.

25 Thou hast also made our words powerful and great,
even that we cannot write them.
Wherefore when we write,
we behold our weakness and stumble because of the placing of our words.
And I fear lest the Gentiles shall mock at our words.

26 And when I had said this,
the Lord spake unto me, saying:
Fools mock, but they shall mourn.

And my grace is sufficient for the meek,
that they shall take no advantage of your weakness.
27 And if men come unto me, I will shew unto them their weakness.
I give unto men weakness that they may be humble.
And my grace is sufficient for all men that humble themselves before me.
For if they humble themselves before me and have faith in me,
then will I make weak things become strong unto them.
28 Behold, I will shew unto the Gentiles their weakness.
And I will shew unto them
that faith, hope, and charity bringeth unto me,
the fountain of all righteousness.

29 And I Moroni having heard these words was comforted and said:
O Lord, thy righteous will be done,
for I know that thou workest unto the children of men according to their faith.
30 For the brother of Jared said unto the mountain Zerin: Remove!
—and it was removed.
And if he had not had faith,
it would not have moved.
Wherefore thou workest after that men have faith.
31 For thus did thou manifest thyself unto thy disciples;
for after that they had faith and did speak in thy name,
thou didst shew thyself unto them in great power.

32 And I also remember that thou hast said
that thou hast prepared a house for man,
yea, even among the mansions of thy Father,
in the which man might have a more excellent hope.
Wherefore man must hope or he cannot receive an inheritance
in the place which thou hast prepared.
33 And again I remember that thou hast said
that thou hast loved the world,
even unto the laying down of thy life for the world,
that thou mightest take it again,
to prepare a place for the children of men.
34 And now I know
that this love which thou hast had for the children of men is charity.
Wherefore except men shall have charity,
they cannot inherit that place
which thou hast prepared in the mansions of thy Father.
35 Wherefore I know by this thing which thou hast said
that if the Gentiles have not charity because of our weakness
that thou wilt prove them and take away their talent,

yea, even that which they have received,
and give unto them which shall have more abundantly.

36 And it came to pass that I prayed unto the Lord
that he would give unto the Gentiles grace,
that they might have charity.

37 And it came to pass that the Lord said unto me:
If they have not charity, it mattereth not unto thee.
Thou hast been faithful;
wherefore thy garments shall be made clean.
And because thou hast seen thy weakness,
thou shalt be made strong,
even unto the sitting down in the place
which I have prepared in the mansions of my Father.

38 And now I Moroni bid farewell unto the Gentiles,
yea, and also unto my brethren, whom I love,
until we shall meet before the judgment seat of Christ,
where all men shall know that my garments are not spotted with your blood.

39 And then shall ye know that I have seen Jesus
and that he hath talked with me face to face
and that he told me in plain humility,
even as a man telleth another
in mine own language concerning these things.

40 And only a few have I written because of my weakness in writing.

41 And now I would commend you to seek this Jesus
of whom the prophets and apostles have written,
that the grace of God the Father and also the Lord Jesus Christ
and the Holy Ghost, which beareth record of them,
may be and abide in you forever.
Amen.

13 | 1 And now I Moroni proceed to finish my record
concerning the destruction of the people of which I have been writing.

2 For behold, they rejected all the words of Ether,
for he truly told them of all things from the beginning of man,
and how that after the waters had receded from off the face of this land,
it became a choice land above all other lands, a chosen land of the Lord
—wherefore the Lord would have that all men should serve him
which dwelt upon the face thereof—

3 and that it was the place of the New Jerusalem,

which should come down out of heaven,
and the holy sanctuary of the Lord.

4 Behold, Ether saw the days of Christ.
And he spake concerning a New Jerusalem upon this land.
5 And he spake also concerning the house of Israel
and the Jerusalem from whence Lehi should come—
after that it should be destroyed,
it should be built up again an holy city unto the Lord;
wherefore it could not be a New Jerusalem, for it had been in a time of old,
but it should be built up again and become a holy city of the Lord;
and it should be built up unto the house of Israel—
6 and that a New Jerusalem should be built up upon this land
unto the remnant of the seed of Joseph,
for the which things there has been a type.
7 For as Joseph brought his father down into the land of Egypt,
even so he died there;
wherefore the Lord brought a remnant of the seed of Joseph
out of the land of Jerusalem,
that he might be merciful unto the seed of Joseph,
that they should perish not,
even as he was merciful unto the father of Joseph,
that he should perish not.

8 Wherefore the remnant of the house of Joseph shall be built up upon this land,
and it shall be a land of their inheritance.
And they shall build up a holy city unto the Lord like unto the Jerusalem of old.
And they shall no more be confounded until the end come,
when the earth shall pass away.
9 And there shall be a new heaven and a new earth;
and they shall be like unto the old,
save the old have passed away and all things have become new.
10 And then cometh the New Jerusalem;
and blessed are they which dwell therein,
for it is they whose garments are white through the blood of the Lamb;
and they are they which are numbered
among the remnant of the seed of Joseph,
which were of the house of Israel.
11 And then also cometh the Jerusalem of old;
and the inhabitants thereof, blessed are they,
for they have been washed in the blood of the Lamb;
and they are they which were scattered and gathered in
from the four quarters of the earth and from the north countries
and are partakers of the fulfilling of the covenant

which God made with their father Abraham.

12 And when these things come
bringeth to pass the scripture which saith:
There are they which were first which shall be last;
and there are they which were last which shall be first.

13 And I was about to write more, but I am forbidden;
but great and marvelous were the prophecies of Ether.
But they esteemed him as naught and cast him out.
And he hid himself in the cavity of a rock by day,
and by night he went forth,
viewing the things which should come upon the people.

14 And as he dwelt in the cavity of a rock,
he made the remainder of this record,
viewing the destructions which came upon the people,
by night.

15 And it came to pass that in that same year
which he was cast out from among the people,
there began to be a great war among the people,
for there were many which rose up who were mighty men
and sought to destroy Coriantumr
by their secret plans of wickedness, of which hath been spoken.

16 And now Coriantumr having studied himself
in all the arts of war and all the cunning of the world,
wherefore he gave battle unto them which sought to destroy him.

17 But he repented not, neither his fair sons nor daughters,
neither the fair sons and daughters of Cohor,
neither the fair sons and daughters of Corihor.
And in fine, there was none of the fair sons and daughters
upon the face of the whole earth
which repented of their sins.

18 Wherefore it came to pass that
in the first year that Ether dwelt in the cavity of a rock,
there was many people which was slain by the sword
by those secret combinations fighting against Coriantumr
that they might obtain the kingdom.

19 And it came to pass that the sons of Coriantumr fought much and bled much.

20 And in the second year the word of the Lord came to Ether
that he should go and prophesy unto Coriantumr
that if he would repent and all his household,
the Lord would give unto him his kingdom and spare the people.

21 Otherwise, they should be destroyed,

and all his household, save it were himself.
And he should only live to see the fulfilling of the prophecies
which had been spoken concerning another people
receiving the land for their inheritance,
and Coriantumr should receive a burial by them,
and every soul should be destroyed save it were Coriantumr.

22 And it came to pass that Coriantumr repented not,
neither his household neither the people;
and the wars did cease not.
And they sought to kill Ether,
but he fled from before them and hid again in the cavity of the rock.

23 And it came to pass that there arose up Shared,
and he also gave battle unto Coriantumr;
and he did beat him,
insomuch that in the third year he did bring him into captivity.

24 And the sons of Coriantumr in the fourth year did beat Shared
and did obtain the kingdom again unto their father.

25 Now there began to be a war upon all the face of the land,
every man with his band fighting for that which he desired.

26 And there was robbers,
and in fine, all manner of wickedness upon all the face of the land.

27 And it came to pass that Coriantumr was exceeding angry with Shared,
and he went against him with his armies to battle.
And they did meet in great anger;
and they did meet in the valley of Gilgal,
and the battle became exceeding sore.

28 And it came to pass that Shared fought against him for the space of three days.
And it came to pass that Coriantumr beat him and did pursue him
until he came to the plains of Heshlon.

29 And it came to pass that Shared gave him battle again upon the plains.
And behold, he did beat Coriantumr
and drove him back again to the valley of Gilgal.

30 And Coriantumr gave Shared battle again in the valley of Gilgal,
in the which he beat Shared and slew him.

31 And Shared wounded Coriantumr in his thigh,
that he did not go to battle again for the space of two years,
in the which time all the people upon all the face of the land
were a shedding blood
and there was none to constrain them.

14 | 1 And now there began to be a great curse upon the land
because of the iniquity of the people,

in the which if a man should lay his tool or his sword upon the shelf,
or upon the place whither he would keep it,
and behold, upon the morrow he could not find it,
so great was the curse upon the land.

2 Wherefore every man did cleave
unto that which was his own
with his hands
and would not borrow, neither would he lend.
And every man kept the hilt of his sword thereof in his right hand,
in the defense of his property
and his own life and they of his wife and children.

3 And now after the space of two years and after the death of Shared,
behold, there arose the brother of Shared,
and he gave battle unto Coriantumr,
in the which Coriantumr did beat him
and did pursue him to the wilderness of Akish.

4 And it came to pass that
the brother of Shared did give battle unto him in the wilderness of Akish,
and the battle became exceeding sore;
and many thousands fell by the sword.

5 And it came to pass that Coriantumr did lay siege to the wilderness.
And the brother of Shared did march forth out of the wilderness by night
and slew a part of the army of Coriantumr
as they were drunken.

6 And he came forth to the land of Moron
and placed himself upon the throne of Coriantumr.

7 And it came to pass that
Coriantumr dwelt with his army in the wilderness for the space of two years,
in the which he did receive great strength to his army.

8 Now the brother of Shared, whose name was Gilead,
also received great strength to his army because of secret combinations.

9 And it came to pass that his high priest murdered him as he sat upon his throne.

10 And it came to pass that one of the secret combinations
murdered him in a secret pass and obtained unto himself the kingdom,
and his name was Lib.
And Lib was a man of great stature,
more than any other man among all the people.

11 And it came to pass that in the first year of Lib,
Coriantumr came up unto the land of Moron and gave battle unto Lib.

12 And it came to pass that he fought with Lib,
in the which Lib did smite upon his arm, that he was wounded.

Nevertheless the army of Coriantumr did press forward upon Lib,
that he fled to the borders by the seashore.

13 And it came to pass that Coriantumr pursued him;
and Lib gave battle unto him upon the seashore.

14 And it came to pass that Lib did smite the army of Coriantumr,
that they fled again to the wilderness of Akish.

15 And it came to pass that Lib did pursue him
until he came to the plains of Agosh.
And Coriantumr had taken all the people with him as he fled before Lib,
in that quarter of the land whither he fled.

16 And when he had came to the plains of Agosh, he gave battle unto Lib;
and he smote upon him until he died.
Nevertheless the brother of Lib did come against Coriantumr
in the stead thereof;
and the battle became exceeding sore,
in the which Coriantumr fled again before the army of the brother of Lib.

17 Now the name of the brother of Lib was called Shiz.
And it came to pass that Shiz pursued after Coriantumr;
and he did overthrow many cities,
and he did slay both men, women, and children,
and he did burn the cities thereof.

18 And there went a fear of Shiz throughout all the land;
yea, a cry went forth throughout the land:
Who can stand before the army of Shiz?
Behold, he sweepeth the earth before him!

19 And it came to pass that the people began to flock together in armies
throughout all the face of the land.

20 And they were divided;
and a part of them fled to the army of Shiz,
and a part of them fled to the army of Coriantumr.

21 And so great and lasting had been the war
and so long had been the scene of bloodshed and carnage
that the whole face of the land was covered with the bodies of the dead.

22 And so swift and speedy was the war
that there was none left to bury the dead,
but they did march forth from the shedding of blood to the shedding of blood,
leaving the bodies of both men, women, and children
strewed upon the face of the land,
to become a prey to the worms of the flesh.

23 And the scent thereof went forth upon the face of the land,
even upon all the face of the land.

Wherefore the people became troubled by day and by night
because of the scent thereof.

24 Nevertheless Shiz did not cease to pursue Coriantumr,
for he had sworn to avenge himself upon Coriantumr
of the blood of his brother, which had been slain,
and the word of the Lord which came to Ether
that Coriantumr should not fall by the sword.

25 And thus we see that the Lord did visit them in the fullness of his wrath.
And their wickedness and abominations had prepared a way
for their everlasting destruction.

26 And it came to pass that Shiz did pursue Coriantumr eastward,
even to the borders by the seashore.
And there he gave battle unto Shiz for the space of three days.

27 And so terrible was the destruction among the armies of Shiz
that the people began to be frightened
and began to flee before the armies of Coriantumr.
And they fled to the land of Corihor
and swept off the inhabitants before them,
all they that would not join them.

28 And they pitched their tents in the valley of Corihor;
and Coriantumr pitched his tents in the valley of Shurr
— now the valley of Shurr was near the hill Comron —
wherefore Coriantumr did gather his armies together upon the hill Comron
and did sound a trumpet unto the armies of Shiz to invite them forth to battle.

29 And it came to pass that they came forth but were driven again.
And they came the second time, and they were driven again the second time.
And it came to pass that they came again the third time,
and the battle became exceeding sore.

30 And it came to pass that Shiz smote upon Coriantumr,
that he gave him many deep wounds.
And Coriantumr having lost his blood fainted
and was carried away, as though he were dead.

31 Now the loss of men, women, and children on both sides were so great
that Shiz commanded his people
that they should not pursue the armies of Coriantumr;
wherefore they returned to their camp.

15 | 1 And it came to pass that when Coriantumr had recovered of his wounds,
he began to remember the words which Ether had spoken unto him.

2 He saw that there had been slain by the sword
already nearly two millions of his people.
And he began to sorrow in his heart;

yea, there had been slain two millions of mighty men,
and also their wives and their children.

3 He began to repent of the evil which he had done.
He began to remember the words
which had been spoken by the mouth of all the prophets;
and he saw them that they were fulfilled thus far, every whit.
And his soul mourned and refused to be comforted.

4 And it came to pass that he wrote an epistle unto Shiz,
desiring him that he would spare the people
and he would give up the kingdom for the sake of the lives of the people.

5 And it came to pass that when Shiz had received his epistle,
he wrote an epistle unto Coriantumr
that if he would give himself up that he might slay him with his own sword
that he would spare the lives of the people.

6 And it came to pass that the people repented not of their iniquity.
And the people of Coriantumr were stirred up to anger
against the people of Shiz,
and the people of Shiz were stirred up to anger
against the people of Coriantumr;
wherefore the people of Shiz did give battle unto the people of Coriantumr.

7 And when Coriantumr saw that he was about to fall,
he fled again before the people of Shiz.

8 And it came to pass that he came to the waters of Ripliancum,
which by interpretation is large or to exceed all;
wherefore when they came to these waters, they pitched their tents;
and Shiz also pitched his tents near unto them.
And therefore on the morrow they did come to battle.

9 And it came to pass that they fought an exceeding sore battle,
in the which Coriantumr was wounded again;
and he fainted with the loss of blood.

10 And it came to pass that
the armies of Coriantumr did press upon the armies of Shiz,
that they beat them, that they caused them to flee before them.
And they did flee southward
and did pitch their tents in a place which was called Ogath.

11 And it came to pass that
the army of Coriantumr did pitch their tents by the hill Ramah,
and it was that same hill
where my father Mormon did hide up the records unto the Lord
which were sacred.

12 And it came to pass that they did gather together
all the people upon all the face of the land

which had not been slain,
save it were Ether.

13 And it came to pass that Ether did behold all the doings of the people.
And he beheld that the people which were for Coriantumr
were gathered together to the army of Coriantumr,
and the people which were for Shiz
were gathered together to the army of Shiz.

14 Wherefore they were for the space of four years gathering together the people,
that they might get all which were upon the face of the land
and that they might receive all the strength
which it were possible that they could receive.

15 And it came to pass that when they were all gathered together,
every one to the army which he would,
with their wives and their children
—both men, women, and children being armed with weapons of war,
having shields and breastplates and headplates,
and being clothed after the manner of war—
and they did march forth one against another to battle;
and they fought all that day and conquered not.

16 And it came to pass that when it was night,
they were weary and retired to their camps.
And after that they had retired to their camps,
they took up a howling and a lamentation
for the loss of the slain of their people.
And so great were their cries, their howlings and lamentations
that it did rend the air exceedingly.

17 And it came to pass that on the morrow they did go again to battle.
And great and terrible was that day;
nevertheless they conquered not.
And when the night came, again they did rend the air
with their cries and their howlings and their mournings
for the loss of the slain of their people.

18 And it came to pass that Coriantumr wrote again an epistle unto Shiz,
desiring that he would not come again to battle,
but that he would take the kingdom and spare the lives of the people.

19 But behold, the Spirit of the Lord had ceased striving with them.
And Satan had full power over the hearts of the people,
for they were given up unto the hardness of their hearts
and the blindness of their minds,
that they might be destroyed;
wherefore they went again to battle.

20 And it came to pass that they fought all that day.
    And when the night came, they slept upon their swords.
21 And on the morrow they fought even until the night came.
22 And when the night came,
    they were drunken with anger,
    even as a man which is drunken with wine.
    And they slept again upon their swords.

23 And on the morrow they fought again.
    And when the night came, they had all fallen by the sword
    save it were fifty and two of the people of Coriantumr
    and sixty and nine of the people of Shiz.
24 And it came to pass that they slept upon their swords that night.
    And on the morrow they fought again;
    and they contended in their mights
    with their swords and with their shields all that day.
25 And when the night came, there was thirty and two of the people of Shiz
    and twenty and seven of the people of Coriantumr.

26 And it came to pass that they ate and slept
    and prepared for death on the morrow.
    And they were large and mighty men as to the strength of men.
27 And it came to pass that they fought for the space of three hours,
    and they fainted with the loss of blood.
28 And it came to pass that
    when the men of Coriantumr had received sufficient strength
    that they could walk,
    they were about to flee for their lives.
    But behold, Shiz arose, and also his men,
    and he swore in his wrath that he would slay Coriantumr
    or he would perish by the sword;
29 wherefore he did pursue them.

    And on the morrow he did overtake them,
    and they fought again with the sword.
    And it came to pass that when they had all fallen by the sword,
    save it were Coriantumr and Shiz,
    behold, Shiz had fainted with loss of blood.
30 And it came to pass that when Coriantumr had leaned upon his sword,
    that he rested a little,
    and he smote off the head of Shiz.
31 And it came to pass that after he had smote off the head of Shiz
    that Shiz raised upon his hands and fell.
    And after that he had struggled for breath, he died.

32 And it came to pass that Coriantumr fell to the earth
and became as if he had no life.

33 And the Lord spake unto Ether
and said unto him:
Go forth.
And he went forth
and beheld that the words of the Lord had all been fulfilled.
And he finished his record
—and the hundredth part I have not written—
and he hid them in a manner that the people of Limhi did find them.

34 Now the last words which are written by Ether are these:
Whether the Lord will that I be translated
or that I suffer the will of the Lord in the flesh,
it mattereth not if it so be that I am saved in the kingdom of God.
Amen.

The Book of Moroni

1 | 1 Now I Moroni after having made an end of abridging
the account of the people of Jared,
I had supposed to not have written more,
but I have not as yet perished.
And I make not myself known to the Lamanites
lest they should destroy me.

2 For behold, their wars are exceeding fierce among themselves.
And because of their hatred
they put to death every Nephite that will not deny the Christ.

3 And I Moroni will not deny the Christ;
wherefore I wander whithersoever I can for the safety of mine own life.

4 Wherefore I write a few more things,
contrary to that which I had supposed,
for I had supposed not to have written any more.
But I write a few more things,
that perhaps they may be of worth
unto my brethren the Lamanites in some future day,
according to the will of the Lord.

2 | 1 The words of Christ which he spake unto his disciples,
the twelve whom he had chosen,
as he laid his hands upon them.

   2 And he called them by name, saying:
Ye shall call on the Father in my name in mighty prayer.
And after that ye have done this,
ye shall have power
that on him whom ye shall lay your hands
ye shall give the Holy Ghost.
And in my name shall ye give it,
for thus do mine apostles.

   3 Now Christ spake these words unto them at the time of his first appearing.
And the multitude heard it not, but the disciples heard it.
And on as many as they laid their hands fell the Holy Ghost.

3 | 1 The manner which the disciples,
which were called the elders of the church,
ordained priests and teachers.

   2 After they had prayed unto the Father in the name of Christ,
they laid their hands upon them and said:

   3 In the name of Jesus Christ,
I ordain you to be a priest
— or if he be a teacher,
I ordain you to be a teacher —
to preach repentance and remission of sins through Jesus Christ
by the endurance of faith on his name to the end.
Amen.

   4 And after this manner did they ordain priests and teachers,
according to the gifts and callings of God unto men.
And they ordained them by the power of the Holy Ghost which was in them.

4 | 1 The manner of their elders and priests administering
the flesh and blood of Christ unto the church.
And they administered it according to the commandments of Christ;
wherefore we know that the manner to be true.
And the elder or priest did minister it;

   2 and they did kneel down with the church
and pray to the Father in the name of Christ, saying:

3 O God the Eternal Father,
we ask thee in the name of thy Son Jesus Christ
to bless and sanctify this bread
to the souls of all those who partake of it,
that they may eat in remembrance of the body of thy Son,
and witness unto thee, O God the Eternal Father,
that they are willing to take upon them the name of thy Son
and always remember him
and keep his commandments which he hath given them,
that they may always have his Spirit to be with them.
Amen.

5 | 1 The manner of administering the wine.
Behold, they took the cup and said:

2 O God the Eternal Father,
we ask thee in the name of thy Son Jesus Christ
to bless and sanctify this wine
to the souls of all those who drink of it,
that they may do it in remembrance of the blood of thy Son,
which was shed for them,
that they may witness unto thee, O God the Eternal Father,
that they do always remember him,
that they may have his Spirit to be with them.
Amen.

6 | 1 And now I speak concerning baptism.
Behold, elders, priests, and teachers were baptized;
and they were not baptized
save they brought forth fruit meet that they were worthy of it.

2 Neither did they receive any unto baptism
save they came forth with a broken heart and a contrite spirit
and witnessed unto the church
that they truly repented of all their sins.

3 And none were received unto baptism
save they took upon them the name of Christ,
having a determination to serve him unto the end.

4 And after that they had been received unto baptism
and were wrought upon and cleansed by the power of the Holy Ghost,
they were numbered among the people of the church of Christ
and their names were taken,

that they might be remembered
and nourished by the good word of God,
to keep them in the right way,
to keep them continually watchful unto prayer,
relying alone upon the merits of Christ,
who was the author and the finisher of their faith.

5 And the church did meet together oft
to fast and to pray and to speak one with another
concerning the welfare of their souls.
6 And they did meet together oft
to partake of bread and wine in remembrance of the Lord Jesus.

7 And they were strict to observe
that there should be no iniquity among them.
And whoso was found to commit iniquity
—and three witnesses of the church did condemn them before the elders—
and if they repented not and confessed not,
their names were blotted out
and they were not numbered among the people of Christ.
8 But as oft as they repented
and sought forgiveness, with real intent,
they were forgiven.

9 And their meetings were conducted by the church
after the manner of the workings of the Spirit
and by the power of the Holy Ghost,
for as the power of the Holy Ghost led them
whether to preach or exhort or to pray or to supplicate or to sing,
even so it was done.

7 | 1 And now I Moroni write a few of the words of my father Mormon
which he spake concerning faith, hope, and charity,
for after this manner did he speak unto the people
as he taught them in the synagogue
which they had built for the place of worship.

2 And now I Mormon speak unto you, my beloved brethren.
And it is by the grace of God the Father and our Lord Jesus Christ
and his holy will, because of the gift of his calling unto me,
that I am permitted to speak unto you at this time.
3 Wherefore I would speak unto you that are of the church,
that are the peaceable followers of Christ,

and that have obtained a sufficient hope
by which ye can enter into the rest of the Lord,
from this time henceforth until ye shall rest with him in heaven.

4 And now my brethren, I judge these things of you
because of your peaceable walk with the children of men.
5 For I remember the word of God which saith:
By their works ye shall know them.
For if their works be good, then they are good also.
6 For behold, God hath said:
A man being evil cannot do that which is good.
For if he offereth a gift or prayeth unto God,
except he shall do it with real intent,
it profiteth him nothing;
7 for behold, it is not counted unto him for righteousness.
8 For behold, if a man being evil giveth a gift,
he doeth it grudgingly;
wherefore it is counted unto him the same
as if he had retained the gift.
Wherefore he is counted evil before God.
9 And likewise also is it counted evil unto a man
if he shall pray and not with real intent of heart.
Yea, and it profiteth him nothing,
for God receiveth none such.

10 Wherefore a man being evil cannot do that which is good,
neither will he give a good gift.
11 For behold, a bitter fountain cannot bring forth good water,
neither can a good fountain bring forth bitter water.
Wherefore a man being the servant of the devil cannot follow Christ;
and if he follow Christ, he cannot be a servant of the devil.
12 Wherefore all things which are good cometh of God;
and that which is evil cometh of the devil.
For the devil is an enemy unto God and fighteth against him continually
and inviteth and enticeth to sin and to do that which is evil continually.
13 But behold, that which is of God inviteth and enticeth to do good continually.
Wherefore every thing
which inviteth and enticeth to do good
and to love God and to serve him
is inspired of God.

14 Wherefore take heed, my beloved brethren,
that ye do not judge that which is evil to be of God,

or that which is good and of God to be of the devil.

15 For behold, my brethren, it is given unto you to judge,
that ye may know good from evil.
And the way to judge is as plain,
that ye may know with a perfect knowledge,
as the daylight is from the dark night.

16 For behold, the Spirit of Christ is given to every man
that they may know good from evil.

Wherefore I shew unto you the way to judge.
For every thing which inviteth to do good and persuadeth to believe in Christ
is sent forth by the power and gift of Christ.
Wherefore ye may know with a perfect knowledge it is of God.

17 But whatsoever thing persuadeth men to do evil
and believe not in Christ and deny him and serve not God,
then ye may know with a perfect knowledge it is of the devil.
For after this manner doth the devil work,
for he persuadeth no man to do good—no, not one—
neither doth his angels,
neither doth they which subject themselves unto him.

18 And now my brethren,
seeing that ye know the light by which ye may judge,
which light is the light of Christ,
see that ye do not judge wrongfully;
for with that same judgment which ye judge,
ye shall also be judged.

19 Wherefore I beseech of you, brethren,
that ye should search diligently in the light of Christ
that ye may know good from evil.
And if ye will lay hold upon every good thing and condemn it not,
ye certainly will be a child of Christ.

20 And now my brethren,
how is it possible that ye can lay hold upon every good thing?

21 And now I come to that faith of which I said I would speak.
And I will tell you the way whereby ye may lay hold on every good thing.

22 For behold, God knowing all things,
being from everlasting to everlasting,
behold, he sent angels to minister unto the children of men,
to make manifest concerning the coming of Christ;
and in Christ there should come every good thing.

23 And God also declared unto prophets by his own mouth
that Christ should come.

24 And behold, there were divers ways
that he did manifest things unto the children of men which were good;
and all things which are good cometh of Christ.
Otherwise, men were fallen and there could no good thing come unto them.

25 Wherefore by the ministering of angels
and by every word which proceeded forth out of the mouth of God,
men began to exercise faith in Christ.
And thus by faith they did lay hold upon every good thing;
and thus it was until the coming of Christ.

26 And after that he came, men also were saved by faith in his name,
and by faith they became the sons of God.
And assuredly as Christ liveth, he spake these words unto our fathers, saying:
Whatsoever thing ye shall ask the Father in my name which is good,
in faith believing that ye shall receive,
behold, it shall be done unto you.

27 Wherefore, my beloved brethren, hath miracles ceased
because that Christ hath ascended into heaven
and hath sit down on the right hand of God,
to claim of the Father his rights of mercy
which he hath upon the children of men?

28 For he hath answered the ends of the law,
and he claimeth all those that hath faith in him.
And they that have faith in him will cleave unto every good thing.
Wherefore he advocateth the cause of the children of men,
and he dwelleth eternally in the heavens.

29 And because that he hath done this, my beloved brethren,
hath miracles ceased?
Behold, I say unto you: Nay.
Neither hath angels ceased to minister unto the children of men.

30 For behold, they are subject unto him,
to minister according to the word of his command,
shewing themselves unto them of strong faith
and a firm mind in every form of godliness.

31 And the office of their ministry is to call men unto repentance
and to fulfill and to do the work of the covenants of the Father
which he hath made unto the children of men,
to prepare the way among the children of men
by declaring the word of Christ unto the chosen vessels of the Lord,
that they may bear testimony of him.

32 And by so doing the Lord God prepareth the way

that the residue of men may have faith in Christ,
that the Holy Ghost may have place in their hearts
according to the power thereof.
And after this manner bringeth to pass the Father the covenants
which he hath made unto the children of men.

33 And Christ hath said:
If ye will have faith in me,
ye shall have power to do whatsoever thing is expedient in me.

34 And he hath said:
Repent, all ye ends of the earth, and come unto me
and be baptized in my name and have faith in me,
that ye may be saved.

35 And now my beloved brethren,
if this be the case that these things are true
which I have spoken unto you
—and God will shew unto you
with power and great glory at the last day
that they are true—
and if they are true,
hath the day of miracles ceased?

36 Or hath angels ceased to appear unto the children of men?
Or hath he withheld the power of the Holy Ghost from them?
Or will he so long as time shall last or the earth shall stand
or there shall be one man upon the face thereof to be saved?

37 Behold, I say unto you: Nay.
For it is by faith that miracles are wrought.
And it is by faith that angels appear and minister unto men.

Wherefore if these things have ceased,
woe be unto the children of men,
for it is because of unbelief;
and all is vain,

38 for no man can be saved,
according to the words of Christ,
save they shall have faith in his name.
Wherefore if these things have ceased,
then has faith ceased also;
and awful is the state of man,
for they are as though there had been no redemption made.

39 But behold, my beloved brethren, I judge better things of you.
For I judge that ye have faith in Christ because of your meekness;

for if ye have not faith in him,
then ye are not fit to be numbered among the people of his church.

40 And again, my beloved brethren, I would speak unto you concerning hope.
How is it that ye can attain unto faith save ye shall have hope?

41 And what is it that ye shall hope for?
Behold, I say unto you that ye shall have hope
through the atonement of Christ and the power of his resurrection,
to be raised unto life eternal—
and this because of your faith in him, according to the promise.

42 Wherefore if a man have faith, he must needs have hope;
for without faith there cannot be any hope.

43 And again, behold, I say unto you that he cannot have faith and hope
save he shall be meek and lowly of heart.

44 If so, his faith and hope is vain,
for none is acceptable before God
save the meek and lowly of heart.

And if a man be meek and lowly in heart
and confesses by the power of the Holy Ghost
that Jesus is the Christ,
he must needs have charity.
For if he have not charity, he is nothing;
wherefore he must needs have charity.

45 And charity suffereth long
and is kind and envieth not
and is not puffed up,
seeketh not her own,
is not easily provoked,
thinketh no evil,
and rejoiceth not in iniquity
but rejoiceth in the truth,
beareth all things,
believeth all things,
hopeth all things,
endureth all things.

46 Wherefore, my beloved brethren,
if ye have not charity, ye are nothing;
for charity never faileth.
Wherefore cleave unto charity,
which is the greatest of all.
For all things must fail;

47 but charity is the pure love of Christ,
and it endureth forever.
And whoso is found possessed of it at the last day,
it shall be well with them.

48 Wherefore, my beloved brethren,
pray unto the Father with all the energy of heart
that ye may be filled with this love
which he hath bestowed upon all
who are true followers of his Son Jesus Christ,
that ye may become the sons of God,
that when he shall appear, we shall be like him
—for we shall see him as he is—
that we may have this hope,
that we may be purified even as he is pure.
Amen.

8 | 1 An epistle of my father Mormon, written to me Moroni;
and it was written unto me soon after my calling to the ministry.
And on this wise did he write unto me, saying:

2 My beloved son Moroni, I rejoice exceedingly
that your Lord Jesus Christ hath been mindful of you
and hath called you to his ministry and to his holy work.

3 I am mindful of you always in my prayers,
continually praying unto God the Father in the name of his Holy Child Jesus
that he through his infinite goodness and grace will keep you
through the endurance of faith on his name to the end.

4 And now my son, I speak unto you
concerning that which grieveth me exceedingly,
for it grieveth me that there should disputations rise among you.

5 For if I have learned the truth,
there has been disputations among you
concerning the baptism of your little children.

6 And now my son, I desire that ye should labor diligently
that this gross error should be removed from among you,
for for this intent I have written this epistle.

7 For immediately after I had learned these things of you,
I inquired of the Lord concerning the matter.
And the word of the Lord came to me by the power of the Holy Ghost, saying:

8 Listen to the words of Christ your Redeemer, your Lord and your God.

Behold, I came into the world
not to call the righteous but sinners to repentance.
The whole need no physician, but they that are sick.
Wherefore little children are whole,
for they are not capable of committing sin.
Wherefore the curse of Adam is taken from them in me,
that it hath no power over them.
And the law of circumcision is done away in me.

9 And after this manner did the Holy Ghost manifest the word of God unto me.

Wherefore, my beloved son,
I know that it is solemn mockery before God
that ye should baptize little children.

10 Behold, I say unto you that this thing shall ye teach:
repentance and baptism unto they
which are accountable and capable of committing sin.
Yea, teach parents that they must repent and be baptized
and humble themselves as their little children,
and they shall all be saved with their little children.

11 And their little children need no repentance, neither baptism.
Behold, baptism is unto repentance,
to the fulfilling the commandments unto the remission of sins.

12 But little children are alive in Christ,
even from the foundation of the world.
If not so, God is a partial God,
and also a changeable God and a respecter to persons.
For how many little children have died without baptism!

13 Wherefore if little children could not be saved without baptism,
these must have gone to an endless hell.

14 Behold, I say unto you
that he that supposeth that little children needeth baptism
is in the gall of bitterness and in the bonds of iniquity,
for he hath neither faith, hope, nor charity.
Wherefore should he be cut off while in the thought,
he must go down to hell.

15 For awful is the wickedness to suppose
that God saveth one child because of baptism
and the other must perish because he hath no baptism.

16 Woe be unto him that shall pervert the ways of the Lord after this manner,
for they shall perish except they repent.

Behold, I speak with boldness, having authority from God.
And I fear not what man can do,

for perfect love casteth out all fear.

17 And I am filled with charity, which is everlasting love.
Wherefore all children are alike unto me;
wherefore I love little children with a perfect love,
and they are all alike and partakers of salvation.

18 For I know that God is not a partial God, neither a changeable being,
but he is unchangeable from all eternity to all eternity.

19 Little children cannot repent.
Wherefore it is awful wickedness
to deny the pure mercies of God unto them,
for they are all alive in him because of his mercy.

20 And he that saith that little children needeth baptism
denieth the mercies of Christ
and setteth at naught the atonement of him
and the power of his redemption.

21 Woe unto such,
for they are in danger of death, hell, and an endless torment.

I speak it boldly;
God hath commanded me.
Listen unto them and give heed,
or they stand against you at the judgment seat of Christ.

22 For behold that all little children are alive in Christ,
and also all they that are without the law,
for the power of redemption cometh on all they that have no law.
Wherefore he that is not condemned
—or he that is under no condemnation—cannot repent,
and unto such baptism availeth nothing;

23 but it is mockery before God,
denying the mercies of Christ and the power of his Holy Spirit
and putting trust in dead works.

24 Behold, my son, this thing had not ought to be.
For repentance is unto them that are under condemnation
and under the curse of a broken law.

25 And the firstfruits of repentance is baptism.
And baptism cometh by faith unto the fulfilling the commandments;
and the fulfilling the commandments bringeth remission of sins;

26 and the remission of sins bringeth meekness and lowliness of heart.
And because of meekness and lowliness of heart
cometh the visitation of the Holy Ghost,
which Comforter filleth with hope and perfect love,
which love endureth by diligence unto prayer

until the end shall come,
when all the saints shall dwell with God.

27 Behold, my son, I will write unto you again
if I go not out soon against the Lamanites.
Behold, the pride of this nation — or the people of the Nephites —
hath proved their destruction except they should repent.

28 Pray for them, my son, that repentance may come unto them.
But behold, I fear lest the Spirit hath ceased striving with them.
And in this part of the land they are also seeking
to put down all power and authority which cometh from God,
and they are denying the Holy Ghost.

29 And after rejecting so great a knowledge, my son, they must perish soon,
unto the fulfilling of the prophecies which was spoken by the prophets
as well as the words of our Savior himself.

30 Farewell, my son, until I shall write unto you
or shall meet you again.
Amen.

The second epistle of Mormon to his son Moroni.

9 | 1 My beloved son, I write unto you again,
that ye may know that I am yet alive,
but I write somewhat that which is grievous.

2 For behold, I have had a sore battle with the Lamanites,
in the which we did not conquer.
And Archeantus has fallen by the sword,
and also Luram and Emron;
yea, and we have lost a great number of our choice men.

3 And now behold, my son,
I fear lest the Lamanites shall destroy this people,
for they do not repent.
And Satan stirreth them up continually to anger one with another.

4 Behold, I am laboring with them continually.
And when I speak the word of God with sharpness,
they tremble and anger against me.
And when I use no sharpness,
they harden their hearts against it.
Wherefore I fear lest the Spirit of the Lord hath ceased striving with them.

5 For so exceedingly do they anger

that it seemeth me that they have no fear of death.
And they have lost their love one towards another;
and they thirst after blood and revenge continually.

6 And now my beloved son,
notwithstanding their hardness, let us labor diligently.
For if we should cease to labor,
we should be brought under condemnation.
For we have a labor to perform whilst in this tabernacle of clay,
that we may conquer the enemy of all righteousness
and rest our souls in the kingdom of God.

7 And now I write somewhat concerning the sufferings of this people.
For according to the knowledge which I have received from Amoron,
behold, the Lamanites have many prisoners
which they took from the tower of Sherrizah,
and there were men, women, and children.
8 And the husbands and fathers of those women and children they have slain.
And they feed the women upon the flesh of their husbands,
and the children upon the flesh of their fathers.
And no water, save a little, do they give unto them.

9 And notwithstanding this great abomination of the Lamanites,
it doth not exceed that of our people in Moriantum.
For behold, many of the daughters of the Lamanites have they taken prisoners.
And after depriving them of that
which was most dear and precious above all things
—which is chastity and virtue—
10 and after that they had done this thing,
they did murder them in a most cruel manner,
torturing their bodies even unto death.
And after that they have done this,
they devour their flesh like unto wild beasts
because of the hardness of their hearts;
and they do it for a token of bravery.

11 O my beloved son,
how can a people like this,
that are without civilization
12 —and only a few years have passed away
and they were a civil and a delightsome people—
13 but O my son,
how can a people like this,
whose delight is in so much abomination,

14 how can we expect
  that God will stay his hand in judgment against us?
15 Behold, my heart cries:
  Woe unto this people!
  Come out in judgment, O God,
  and hide their sins and wickedness and abominations
  from before thy face!

16 And again, my son,
  there are many widows and their daughters which remain in Sherrizah.
  And that part of the provisions which the Lamanites did not carry away,
  behold, the army of Zenephi has carried away
  and left them to wander whithersoever they can for food.
  And many old women do faint by the way and die.
17 And the army which is with me is weak.
  And the armies of the Lamanites are betwixt Sherrizah and me.
  And as many as have fled to the army of Aaron
  have fallen victims to their awful brutality.

18 O the depravity of my people!
  They are without order and without mercy.
  Behold, I am but a man, and I have but the strength of a man.
  And I cannot any longer enforce my commands.
19 And they have become strong in their perversion.
  And they are alike brutal,
  sparing none, neither old nor young.
  And they delight in every thing save that which is good.
  And the sufferings of our women and our children
  upon all the face of this land
  doth exceed every thing.
  Yea, tongue cannot tell,
  neither can it be written.

20 And now my son, I dwell no longer upon this horrible scene.
  Behold, thou knowest the wickedness of this people.
  Thou knowest that they are without principle and past feeling,
  and their wickedness doth exceed that of the Lamanites.
21 Behold, my son, I cannot recommend them unto God
  lest he should smite me.
22 But behold, my son, I recommend thee unto God.
  And I trust in Christ that thou wilt be saved.
  And I pray unto God that he would spare thy life
  to witness the return of his people unto him or their utter destruction;

for I know that they must perish except they repent and return unto him.

23 And if they perish, it will be like unto the Jaredites,
   because of the willfulness of their hearts,
   seeking for blood and revenge.

24 And if it so be that they perish,
   we know that many of our brethren have dissented over unto the Lamanites,
   and many more will also dissent over unto them.
   Wherefore write somewhat a few things
   if thou art spared and I should perish and not see thee.
   But I trust that I may see thee soon,
   for I have sacred records that I would deliver up unto thee.

25 My son, be faithful in Christ.
   And may not the things which I have written grieve thee,
   to weigh thee down unto death;
   but may Christ lift thee up.
   And may his sufferings and death and the shewing his body unto our fathers
   and his mercy and long-suffering
   and the hope of his glory and of eternal life
   rest in your mind forever.

26 And may the grace of God the Father,
   whose throne is high in the heavens,
   and our Lord Jesus Christ,
   who sitteth on the right hand of his power
   until all things shall become subject unto him,
   be and abide with you forever.
   Amen.

10 | 1 Now I Moroni write somewhat as seemeth me good.
   And I write unto my brethren the Lamanites.
   And I would that they should know
   that more than four hundred and twenty years has passed away
   since the sign was given of the coming of Christ.

2 And I seal up these records
   after that I have spoken a few words by way of exhortation unto you.

3 Behold, I would exhort you
   that when ye shall read these things,
   if it be wisdom in God that ye should read them,
   that ye would remember
   how merciful the Lord hath been unto the children of men

from the creation of Adam even down until the time
that ye shall receive these things
and ponder it in your hearts.

4 And when ye shall receive these things,
I would exhort you
that ye would ask God the Eternal Father,
in the name of Christ,
if these things are not true.
And if ye shall ask with a sincere heart,
with real intent, having faith in Christ,
and he will manifest the truth of it unto you
by the power of the Holy Ghost.

5 And by the power of the Holy Ghost
ye may know the truth of all things.

6 And whatsoever thing is good is just and true.
Wherefore nothing that is good denieth the Christ,
but acknowledgeth that he is.

7 And ye may know that he is
by the power of the Holy Ghost.
Wherefore I would exhort you that ye deny not the power of God,
for he worketh by power according to the faith of the children of men,
the same today and tomorrow and forever.

8 And again I exhort you, my brethren,
that ye deny not the gifts of God,
for they are many and they come from the same God.
And there are different ways that these gifts are administered,
but it is the same God which worketh all in all.
And they are given by the manifestations of the Spirit of God
unto men to profit them.

9 For behold, to one is given by the Spirit of God
that he may teach the word of wisdom,

10 and to another that he may teach the word of knowledge by the same Spirit,

11 and to another exceeding great faith,
and to another the gifts of healing by the same Spirit,

12 and again, to another that he may work mighty miracles,

13 and again, to another that he may prophesy concerning all things,

14 and again, to another the beholding of angels and ministering spirits,

15 and again, to another all kinds of tongues,

16 and again, to another the interpretation of languages
and of divers kinds of tongues.

17 And all these gifts comes by the Spirit of Christ,

and they come unto every man severally according as he will.

18 And I would exhort you, my beloved brethren,
   that ye remember that every good gift cometh of Christ.

19 And I would exhort you, my beloved brethren,
   that ye remember that he is the same yesterday, today, and forever,
   and that all these gifts of which I have spoken, which are spiritual,
   never will be done away even as long as the world shall stand,
   only according to the unbelief of the children of men.

20 Wherefore there must be faith;
   and if there must be faith, there must also be hope;
   and if there must be hope, there must also be charity.

21 And except ye have charity,
   ye can in no wise be saved in the kingdom of God;
   neither can ye be saved in the kingdom of God if ye have not faith;
   neither can ye if ye have no hope.

22 And if ye have no hope, ye must needs be in despair;
   and despair cometh because of iniquity.

23 And Christ truly said unto our fathers:
   If ye have faith, ye can do all things which is expedient unto me.

24 And now I speak unto all the ends of the earth
   that if the day cometh
   that the power and gifts of God shall be done away among you,
   it shall be because of unbelief.

25 And woe be unto the children of men if this be the case,
   for there shall be none that doeth good among you—no, not one—
   for if there be one among you that doeth good,
   he shall work by the power and gifts of God.

26 And woe unto them which shall do these things away and die,
   for they die in their sins
   and they cannot be saved in the kingdom of God.
   And I speak it according to the words of Christ, and I lie not.

27 And I exhort you to remember these things,
   for the time speedily cometh that ye shall know that I lie not,
   for ye shall see me at the bar of God.
   And the Lord God will say unto you:
   Did I not declare my words unto you,
   which was written by this man like as one crying from the dead,
   yea, even as one speaking out of the dust?

28 I declare these things unto the fulfilling of the prophecies.

And behold, they shall proceed forth
out of the mouth of the everlasting God,
and his word shall hiss forth from generation to generation.

29   And God shall shew unto you
that that which I have written is true.

30   And again I would exhort you
that ye would come unto Christ
and lay hold upon every good gift,
and touch not the evil gift nor the unclean thing.

31   And awake and arise from the dust, O Jerusalem!
Yea, and put on thy beautiful garments, O daughter of Zion,
and strengthen thy stakes and enlarge thy borders forever,
that thou mayest no more be confounded,
that the covenants of the Eternal Father
which he hath made unto thee, O house of Israel,
may be fulfilled.

32   Yea, come unto Christ and be perfected in him,
and deny yourselves of all ungodliness.
And if ye shall deny yourselves of all ungodliness
and love God with all your might, mind, and strength,
then is his grace sufficient for you,
that by his grace ye may be perfect in Christ.
And if by the grace of God ye are perfect in Christ,
ye can in no wise deny the power of God.

33   And again, if ye by the grace of God are perfect in Christ
and deny not his power,
then are ye sanctified in Christ by the grace of God
through the shedding of the blood of Christ,
which is in the covenant of the Father,
unto the remission of your sins,
that ye become holy, without spot.

34   And now I bid unto all farewell.
I soon go to rest in the paradise of God
until my spirit and body shall again reunite
and I am brought forth triumphant through the air
to meet you before the pleading bar of the great Jehovah,
the Eternal Judge of both quick and dead.
Amen.

The Testimony of Three Witnesses

Be it known unto all nations, kindreds, tongues, and people
unto whom this work shall come
that we through the grace of God the Father and our Lord Jesus Christ
have seen the plates which contain this record,
which is a record of the people of Nephi,
and also of the Lamanites, his brethren,
and also of the people of Jared,
which came from the tower of which hath been spoken.

And we also know
that they have been translated by the gift and power of God,
for his voice hath declared it unto us;
wherefore we know of a surety that the work is true.
And we also testify that we have seen the engravings
which are upon the plates;
and they have been shewn unto us
by the power of God and not of man.
And we declare with words of soberness
that an angel of God came down from heaven,
and he brought and laid before our eyes
that we beheld and saw the plates and the engravings thereon.
And we know that it is by the grace of God the Father and our Lord Jesus Christ
that we beheld and bare record that these things are true;
and it is marvelous in our eyes.
Nevertheless the voice of the Lord commanded us
that we should bear record of it;
wherefore to be obedient unto the commandments of God,
we bear testimony of these things.

And we know that if we are faithful in Christ,
we shall rid our garments of the blood of all men
and be found spotless before the judgment seat of Christ
and shall dwell with him eternally in the heavens.
And the honor be to the Father and to the Son and to the Holy Ghost,
which is one God.
Amen.

Oliver Cowdery
David Whitmer
Martin Harris

And also the Testimony of Eight Witnesses

Be it known unto all nations, kindreds, tongues, and people
unto whom this work shall come
that Joseph Smith, Junior, the translator of this work,
has shewn unto us the plates of which hath been spoken,
which have the appearance of gold.
And as many of the leaves as the said Smith has translated,
we did handle with our hands.
And we also saw the engravings thereon,
all of which has the appearance of ancient work
and of curious workmanship.
And this we bear record with words of soberness
that the said Smith has shewn unto us,
for we have seen and hefted and know of a surety
that the said Smith has got the plates of which we have spoken.

And we give our names unto the world,
to witness unto the world that which we have seen.
And we lie not,
God bearing witness of it.

Christian Whitmer
Jacob Whitmer
Peter Whitmer, Junior
John Whitmer
Hiram Page
Joseph Smith, Senior
Hyrum Smith
Samuel H. Smith

APPENDIX

Significant Textual Changes

In this appendix, I list the significant textual changes that have occurred in the history of the Book of Mormon text. For the most part, I exclude the numerous cases of grammatical emendation that the text has undergone throughout its textual history. The evidence for each of the following changes in the text is discussed in volume 4 of the critical text, *Analysis of Textual Variants of the Book of Mormon,* published in six parts by the Foundation for Ancient Research and Mormon Studies at Brigham Young University (first edition, 2004–2009; second edition, 2017).

The sources for determining the original text and the history of the Book of Mormon text consist of two manuscripts and twenty printed editions.

MANUSCRIPTS

𝒪   the original manuscript, 1828–29; only 28 percent of the canonical text is extant in 𝒪; written down by Oliver Cowdery and other scribes from dictation by Joseph Smith

𝒫   the printer's manuscript, August 1829 – January 1830; a handwritten copy of the original manuscript; grammatical emendations were later added by Joseph Smith in his editing for the 1837 edition; the manuscript is fully extant except for only a few lines of text at the bottom of the first leaf

EDITIONS

1830   the first edition, published in Palmyra, New York; printed by E. B. Grandin, with typesetting by John Gilbert; set for the most part from the printer's manuscript (for one sixth of the text, from Helaman 13:17 through Mormon 9:37, the 1830 edition was set from the original manuscript)

1837   the second edition, published in Kirtland, Ohio; printed by the LDS Church; shows Joseph Smith's major editing towards standard English

1840   the third edition, published in Nauvoo, Illinois; typeset, stereotyped, and printed in Cincinnati, Ohio, by Shepard and Stearns, with the first impression released in Cincinnati; shows minor editing by Joseph Smith (including a few restored phrases from the original manuscript); various impressions printed in Nauvoo from the stereotyped plates (up through 1842), with a new title page for the last impression

1841   the first British edition, published in Liverpool, England; printed by J. Tompkins for Brigham Young, Heber C. Kimball, and Parley P. Pratt; this edition is basically a resetting of the 1837 edition, although poorly executed

1849   the second British edition, published in Liverpool, England; printed by Richard James for Orson Pratt; set from a copy of the 1841 edition, but with minor editing by Pratt (including his correction of most of the 1841 typos)

1852   the third British edition, published in Liverpool, England; typeset by William Bowden for Franklin D. Richards, with printing from stereotyped plates; the 1849 edition served as the copytext; the paragraphs, deriving from the original paragraphs in the 1830 edition, were numbered; the second impression from the stereotyped plates (also in 1852) includes a considerable number of changes based on the 1840 Nauvoo edition; the stereotyped plates were later taken to Utah and used to print additional issues of this edition (up through 1877)

1858W   a private edition published in New York City by James O. Wright (also issued in 1860 with a new introduction by Zadoc Brook); the text was set from the 1840 Nauvoo edition; the 1858 edition was used by RLDS Church members until their first edition was published in 1874

1874R   the first RLDS edition, published in Plano, Illinois (later issued from Lamoni, Iowa); this edition was typeset, it would appear, from both the 1840 Nauvoo edition and the 1858 Wright edition; the numbered paragraphs of the 1852 LDS edition were added to this edition

1879   a major LDS edition published in Liverpool, England; typeset by William Budge for Orson Pratt; shows minor editing by Pratt; the copytext was the corrected 1852 edition; two sets of stereotyped plates were produced, of which one set remained in England and the other was taken to Utah; for this edition Pratt divided up the original chapters and assigned the verse numbers that have continued in the LDS text; this edition was used as the copytext for most LDS editions from 1888 through 1906

1888   a large-print LDS edition published in Salt Lake City, Utah, by the *Juvenile Instructor*

1892R   the second RLDS edition, published in Lamoni, Iowa; a large-print edition, in double columns; this edition is basically a resetting of the 1874 RLDS edition

1902   an LDS missionary edition published in Kansas City, Missouri; printed by Burd and Fletcher; this edition served as the copytext for the 1905 LDS missionary edition

1905   an LDS missionary edition published in Chicago, Illinois; prepared by German Ellsworth and printed by Henry C. Etten; for the third impression of this edition (in 1907), Ellsworth made some additional changes in the plates

1906   an LDS large-print edition published in Salt Lake City, Utah, by *The Deseret News*

1907   an LDS vest-pocket edition published in Salt Lake City, Utah, by the Deseret Sunday School Union

1908R   the third RLDS edition, a major edition published in Lamoni, Iowa; although this edition used the 1892 RLDS edition as its copytext, there are numerous corrections based on the printer's manuscript

1911   an LDS large-print edition published in Chicago, Illinois; prepared by German Ellsworth and printed by Henry C. Etten (the date 1911 is uncertain); the copytext for this edition by Ellsworth was his 1905 edition (but as corrected by him for the third impression of that edition, in 1907)

1920   a major LDS edition published in Salt Lake City, Utah; printed in Hammond, Indiana, by W. B. Conkey; double columns and chapter summaries are introduced into the LDS text; shows considerable grammatical editing, plus some restoration of readings from earlier editions; the copytext for this edition was the 1911 LDS edition

1953R   the current RLDS edition, published in Independence, Missouri; a minor revision of the 1908 RLDS edition

1981   another major LDS edition, published in Salt Lake City, Utah; a revision of the 1920 LDS edition, with some restoration of original readings from the two manuscripts and the 1840 edition; the current LDS edition (2013) is a revision of the 1981 edition, with only six minor textual changes

For seven early copies of the title page, see pages 16–17 of *Analysis of Textual Variants*. They are referred to as "title page copies" in the following list of textual changes.

In this appendix, for each case of textual variation I provide the surrounding words and use bolding to show the textual variants under consideration. The surrounding words, set in regular type, are given as they are here in *The Earliest Text*. In other words, in referring to a particular case of variation, the relevant variants are set in bold and I ignore all other variants that the surrounding words might have had. For a given case of variation, the variants are arranged in chronological order, and the symbol ▶ indicates which variant has been accepted as the original reading. The abbreviation *conj* stands for a conjectural emendation.

The spelling for each citation is regularized, even for the textual variant itself unless the spelling plays a role in the change. If a variant involves the deletion of a long phrase or clause, this may be represented as NULL. Punctuation and capitalization are generally ignored, but within a citation a phrasal break is represented by the symbol / while a sentential break is represented by the symbol //.

For each case of variation, the readings of the two manuscripts (𝓞 and 𝓟) and the first edition (1830) are consistently listed except in cases where 𝓞 is lacking. This means that if 𝓞 is not listed for a particular case of variation, then 𝓞 is not extant in that case. Any given edition after 1830 will generally not be listed unless that edition introduced a change into the text or restored an earlier reading. This means that if a given edition after 1830 follows the reading of its copytext (the edition it was typeset from), then it will not be listed. If a different Book of Mormon passage is listed along with the textual sources, it means that for an explanation the reader will need to consult under that passage in volume 4 of the critical text.

Occasionally a textual variant involves only punctuation. Originally the manuscripts lacked punctuation, so in those cases we still list the manuscript readings but mark them as NA, meaning non-applicable.

Sometimes a variant reading is also found in the King James Bible; in that case, the biblical passage is specified. If the variant reading is a paraphrase of a King James reading, then a tilde is placed before the biblical specification, as in 1 Nephi 10:10 where the original reading is a paraphrase of John 1:29; thus the variant "the Lamb of God which should take away the sin of the world" is followed by ~John 1:29.

Sometimes we need to refer in the listing to the initial state versus the corrected state in a textual source. In general, we make the following distinction:

α*   initial text in source α
α^c   corrected text in source α

Here α can be either a manuscript or an edition. In the manuscripts, the superscript *c* is used to refer to a change made by the initial scribe. If the change was made by a different person, additional specification is added to the symbol 𝓞 or 𝓟. For known correctors, we use their initials in lowercase:

oc   Oliver Cowdery, the chief scribe for both manuscripts
jw   John Whitmer, a scribe in the original manuscript
jg   John Gilbert, the typesetter for the 1830 edition
js   Joseph Smith, who marked in 𝓟 many of his corrections for the 1837 edition

Thus we can have 𝒪oc, 𝒪jw, 𝒫oc, 𝒫jg, and 𝒫js. If the correction in a printed edition occurred in a later year, the year of that correction (if known) will be added in square brackets, such as 1905ᶜ [1907] and 1981ᶜ [1982].

There are two textual traditions, the LDS and the RLDS. The LDS textual tradition starts with the 1841 British edition and goes through to the 1981 edition. In listing the textual sources, one can easily identify these editions in the LDS textual tradition as those appearing after 1841 that have no extra letter assigned to their date, such as 1852, 1879, and 1920. It should be noted that the 1841 British edition was set from the 1837 Kirtland edition, not from the 1840 Nauvoo edition. On the other hand, the 1840 edition served as the textual source for the first edition in the RLDS textual tradition, namely, the 1858 Wright edition. Although the 1858 edition was published by James Wright and not by the RLDS Church, it was used by the RLDS until they published their first edition (in 1874). The RLDS textual tradition therefore includes the 1858 Wright edition (identified as 1858w) and four actual RLDS editions, each of which is followed by the symbol R (such as 1874R and 1908R).

In the following charts, I provide the stemmas that show the relationships between the manuscripts and editions of the Book of Mormon. For each edition after 1830, one can determine its copytext by referring to the edition found immediately above it in the stemma. The 1830 edition had two copytexts: 𝒫 for five sixths of the text, 𝒪 for one sixth of the text (from Helaman 13:17 through Mormon 9:37). Strangely, the first RLDS edition (1874) seems to have had two copytexts, used alternatively (the 1840 edition and the 1858 Wright edition). Sometimes earlier editions or the manuscripts were consulted in producing an edition. If this resulted in a textual change, that later edition will be included in the list of textual sources for that change.

STEMMAS FOR THE MANUSCRIPTS

NORMAL STEMMA
(1 Nephi – Helaman 13:16; Ether – Moroni)

𝒪
|
𝒫
|
1830

EXCEPTIONAL STEMMA
(Helaman 13:17 – Mormon 9:37)

𝒪

𝒫   1830

STEMMA FOR THE PRINTED EDITIONS

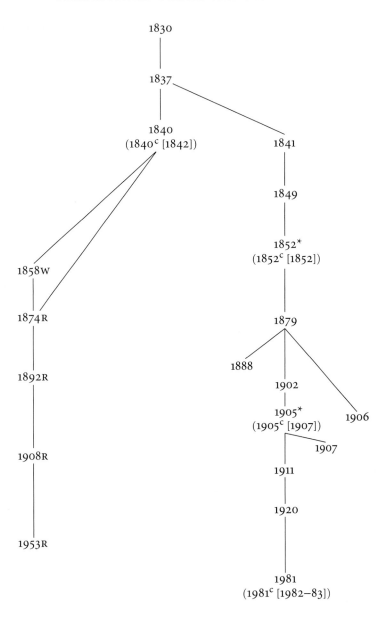

1830

1837

1840
(1840^c [1842])

1841

1849

1852*
(1852^c [1852])

1858W

1874R

1879

1888

1892R

1902

1905*
(1905^c [1907])

1906

1907

1908R

1911

1920

1953R

1981
(1981^c [1982–83])

RLDS Textual Tradition

LDS Textual Tradition

EXTRACANONICAL TEXT

half title
> NULL (𝔓, 1830, 1852ᶜ, 1892R, 1906, 1920)
> ► **The** Book of Mormon (1840, 1849, 1908R, 1981*)
> Book of Mormon (1879)
> **The** Book of Mormon / **Another Testament of Jesus Christ** (1981ᶜ [1982])

attribution
> by Joseph Smith **Junior / author and proprietor** (𝔓, title page copies, 1830)
> ► **translated** by Joseph Smith **Junior** (1837, 1858w)
> **translated** by Joseph Smith (1840ᶜ [1842])

CANONICAL TEXT

title page
> NA An account written . . . upon plates taken from the plates of Nephi (𝔓)
> An account written . . . upon **plates taken from the plates** of Nephi (4 title page copies, 1830)
> ► An account written . . . upon **plates / taken from the plates** of Nephi (2 title page copies; conj)

title page
> ► written and sealed and hid **up** unto the Lord (title page copies)
> written and sealed **up** and hid **up** unto the Lord (𝔓, 1830)
> written and sealed **up** and hid unto the Lord (1908R)

title page
> ► sealed **up** by the hand of Moroni and hid up unto the Lord (title page copies)
> sealed by the hand of Moroni and hid up unto the Lord (𝔓, 1830)

title page
> ► to come forth in due time by **the** way of Gentile (𝔓, title page copies, 1830)
> to come forth in due time by way of **the** Gentile (1920)

title page
> ► **how** great things the Lord hath done (𝔓, title page copies, 1830)
> **what** great things the Lord hath done (1837)

title page
> ► if there **be fault / it be the mistake** of men (𝔓, title page copies, 1830)
> if there **are faults / they are the mistakes** of men (1837)

end of title page
> ► NULL (𝔓, title page copies, 1830, 1879, 1908R)
> **Moroni** (1840, 1852ᶜ)

1 Nephi title
> ► The Book of Nephi (𝔓*)
> The **First** Book of Nephi (𝔓ᶜ, 1830)

1 Nephi preface
> they **call** the place Bountiful (𝔓, 1830, 1852ᶜ, 1908R)
> ► they **call the name of** the place Bountiful (1840, 1981)
> they **called** the place Bountiful (1841)

1 Nephi 1:9
> ► he saw **one** descending out of the midst of heaven (𝔓, 1830)
> he saw **One** descending out of the midst of heaven (1981)

1 Nephi 2:5
▶ in the borders which **was nearer** the Red Sea (𝒪, 𝒫*, 1830)
in the borders which **were nearer** the Red Sea (𝒫js, 1908R)
in the borders which **are nearer** the Red Sea (1837, 1852ᶜ)
in the borders which **are near** the Red Sea (1841)

1 Nephi 2:5
▶ which consisted of my mother Sariah and my elder **brethren** (𝒪, 𝒫*)
which consisted of my mother Sariah and my elder **brothers** (𝒫ᶜ, 1830)

1 Nephi 2:6
▶ he pitched his tent in a valley **beside** a river of water (𝒪, 𝒫*, 1830)
he pitched his tent in a valley **by the side of** a river of water (𝒫js, 1837)

1 Nephi 2:10
▶ and he also spake unto Lemuel **saying** (𝒪)
and he also spake unto Lemuel (𝒫, 1830)

1 Nephi 3:3
▶ and also a genealogy of **my** forefathers (𝒪, 𝒫*, 1830, 1840, 1981)
and also a genealogy of **thy** forefathers (𝒫js, 1837, 1908R)

1 Nephi 3:10
when we had **come** up to the land of Jerusalem (𝒪*, 𝒫, 1830)
▶ when we had **gone** up to the land of Jerusalem (𝒪ᶜ, 1981)

1 Nephi 3:16
▶ because of the **commandment** (𝒪*)
because of the **commandment of the Lord** (𝒪oc)
because of the **commandments of the Lord** (𝒫, 1830)

1 Nephi 3:17
▶ for he **knowing** that Jerusalem must be destroyed (𝒪, 𝒫, 1830, 1908R)
for he **knew** that Jerusalem must be destroyed (1840, 1852ᶜ)

1 Nephi 4:21
▶ and he **supposing** me to be his master Laban (𝒪, 𝒫*)
and he **supposed** me to be his master Laban (𝒫ᶜ, 1830)

1 Nephi 4:33
if he would go down **in** the wilderness with us (𝒪, 𝒫, 1830)
▶ if he would go down **into** the wilderness with us (conj)

1 Nephi 4:34
▶ and shall we not be diligent in keeping the **commandment** of the Lord (𝒪)
and shall we not be diligent in keeping the **commandments** of the Lord (𝒫, 1830)

1 Nephi 4:35
▶ that he would go down into the wilderness unto **our** father (𝒪, 𝒫ᶜ, 1830, 1908R, 1981)
that he would go down into the wilderness unto **my** father (𝒫*, 1837)

1 Nephi 7:1
▶ the Lord spake unto him again (𝒪)
the Lord spake unto him again **saying** (𝒫, 1830)

1 Nephi 7:1
that his sons should take daughters to wife that might raise up seed (𝒪)
▶ that his sons should take daughters to wife that **they** might raise up seed (𝒫, 1830)

1 Nephi 7:2
> ▸ that I Nephi and my brethren should again return **into** the land of Jerusalem (Ⓞ, ℗)
> that I Nephi and my brethren should again return **unto** the land of Jerusalem (1830)

1 Nephi 7:5
> Ishmael and also his **hole** (Ⓞ*)
> Ishmael and also his **hole hole** (Ⓞᶜ)
> Ishmael and also his **household** (℗, 1830)
> ▸ Ishmael and also his **whole household** (conj)

1 Nephi 7:11
> ▸ ye have forgotten **how** great things the Lord hath done (Ⓞ, ℗*, 1830)
> ye have forgotten **what** great things the Lord hath done (℗js, 1837)

1 Nephi 7:17
> ▸ according to my faith which is in **me** (Ⓞ*)
> according to my faith which is in **thee** (Ⓞoc, ℗, 1830)

1 Nephi 7:22
> and they did **give thanks** and **offer** burnt offerings unto him (Ⓞ*)
> and they did **offer sacrifice** and **offer** burnt offerings unto him (Ⓞᶜ)
> ▸ and they did **offer sacrifice** and burnt offerings unto him (℗, 1830)

1 Nephi 8:4
> ▸ methought I saw a dark and dreary wilderness (Ⓞ, ℗*, 1830)
> methought I saw **in my dream** a dark and dreary wilderness (℗js, 1837)

1 Nephi 8:12
> ▸ it was **desirous** above all other fruit (Ⓞ, ℗*, 1830)
> it was **desirable** above all other fruit (℗js, 1837)

1 Nephi 8:18
> ▸ they would not come unto me **and partake of the fruit** (Ⓞ, 1840, 1920)
> they would not come unto me (℗, 1830)

1 Nephi 8:20
> and I also beheld a **strait** and narrow path (Ⓞ, ℗, 1981)
> ▸ and I also beheld a **straight** and narrow path (1830)

1 Nephi 8:26
> ▸ I also cast my eyes around about and **beheld** . . . a great and spacious building (Ⓞ, 1830)
> I also cast my eyes around about and **behold** . . . a great and spacious building (℗)

1 Nephi 8:27
> ▸ those which had came **up** and were partaking of the fruit (Ⓞ)
> those which had came **at** and were partaking of the fruit (℗, 1830)

1 Nephi 8:31
> ▸ and he also saw other multitudes **pressing** their way (Ⓞ)
> and he also saw other multitudes **feeling** their way (℗, 1830)

1 Nephi 8:34
> ▸ **thus is** the words of my father (Ⓞ*)
> **thus are** the words of my father (Ⓞjw)
> **these are** the words of my father (℗, 1830)

1 Nephi 10:3
> ▸ to possess again **their land of** inheritance (Ⓞ)
> to possess again **the land of their** inheritance (℗, 1830)

1 Nephi 10:9
- ► and he also **spake that** he should baptize with water (Ο, Ρ*, 1830)
  and he also **said** he should baptize with water (Ρjs, 1837)

1 Nephi 10:10
- ► the Lamb of God which should take away the **sin** of the world (Ο, Ρ*; ~John 1:29)
  the Lamb of God which should take away the **sins** of the world (Ρᶜ, 1830)

1 Nephi 10:18
- ► and the way is prepared **for all men** (Ο, 1840, 1852ᶜ)
  and the way is prepared (Ρ, 1830, 1908ᴿ)

1 Nephi 10:19
- ► as well in **this time** as in times of old (Ο, Ρ, 1908ᴿ)
  as well in **these times** as in times of old (1830)

1 Nephi 11:1
- ► into an exceeding high mountain / **a mountain** which I never had before seen (Ο)
  into an exceeding high mountain which I never had before seen (Ρ, 1830)

1 Nephi 11:6
- ► the Son of the Most High (Ο*)
  the Son of the Most High **God** (Οoc, Ρ, 1830)

1 Nephi 11:9
- ► the tree which is **most** precious above all (Ο)
  the tree which is precious above all (Ρ, 1830)

1 Nephi 11:18
- ► the mother of God (Ο, Ρ*, 1830)
  the mother **of the Son** of God (Ρjs, 1837)

1 Nephi 11:21
- ► the Lamb of God yea even the Eternal Father (Ο, Ρ, 1830)
  the Lamb of God yea even **the Son of** the Eternal Father (1837)

1 Nephi 11:32
- ► the everlasting God was judged of the world (Ο, Ρ, 1830)
  the Son of the everlasting God was judged of the world (1837)

1 Nephi 11:32
- ► and I saw and **bare** record (Ο)
  and I saw and **bear** record (Ρ, 1830)

1 Nephi 11:36
- ► I saw and **bare** record (Ο, 1852)
  I saw and **bear** record (Ρ, 1830, 1879)

1 Nephi 11:36
- ► and the fall thereof was exceeding great (Ο*)
  and it fell and the fall thereof was exceeding great (Οjw, Ρ, 1830)

1 Nephi 12:4
- ► and I saw the earth **that it rent** the rocks (Ο*)
  and I saw the earth **rent** the rocks (Οᶜ)
  and I saw the earth **and the rocks that they rent** (Οoc, Ρ, 1830)

1 Nephi 12:5
- ► I saw **the** multitudes which had **not** fallen (Ο)
  I saw multitudes which had fallen (Ρ, 1830)
  I saw multitudes which had **not** fallen (1981)

1 Nephi 12:7
    ► and I also saw and **bare** record (Ο)
    and I also saw and **bear** record (𝒫, 1830)

1 Nephi 12:17
    ► that they perish and are lost (Ο, 1852)
    that they **may** perish and are lost (𝒫, 1830)

1 Nephi 12:18
    ► yea even the **sword** of the justice of the Eternal God (Ο)
    yea even the **word** of the justice of the Eternal God (𝒫, 1830)

1 Nephi 12:18
    ► and **Jesus Christ** which is the Lamb of God (Ο, 𝒫*, 1830)
    and **Mosiah** which is the Lamb of God (𝒫js)
    and **the Messiah** which is the Lamb of God (1837)

1 Nephi 13:4
    ► I saw among the nations of the Gentiles the **formation** of a great church (Ο, 1981)
    I saw among the nations of the Gentiles the **foundation** of a great church (𝒫, 1830)

1 Nephi 13:5
    ► behold the **formation** of a church which is most abominable (Ο, 1981)
    behold the **foundation** of a church which is most abominable (𝒫, 1830)

1 Nephi 13:6
    ► I saw the devil that he was the **founder** of it (Ο, 𝒫*, 1830, 1981)
    I saw the devil that he was the **foundation** of it (𝒫js, 1837)

1 Nephi 13:12
    I looked and beheld a man among the Gentiles which **where** separated (Ο)
    I looked and beheld a man among the Gentiles which **was** separated (𝒫, 1830)
    ► I looked and beheld a man among the Gentiles which **were** separated (conj)

1 Nephi 13:15
    ► they did prosper and obtain the land **for** their inheritance (Ο, 𝒫, 1837)
    they did prosper and obtain the land **of** their inheritance (1830)

1 Nephi 13:22
    ► and I saith (Ο)
    and I saith **unto him** (𝒫, 1830)

1 Nephi 13:24
    ► it contained the **fullness** (Ο, 1981)
    it contained the **plainness** (𝒫, 1830)

1 Nephi 13:24
    of the gospel of the **Land** (Ο)
    of the gospel of the **Lord** (𝒫, 1830)
    ► of the gospel of the **Lamb** (conj)

1 Nephi 13:24
    ► of whom the twelve apostles **bare** record (Ο)
    of whom the twelve apostles **bear** record (𝒫, 1830)

1 Nephi 13:24
    ► and they **bare** record according to the truth (Ο)
    and they **bear** record according to the truth (𝒫, 1830)

1 Nephi 13:26
> ▸ thou seest the **formation** of **that** great and abominable church (𝓞, 1981)
> thou seest the **foundation** of **a** great and abominable church (𝓟, 1830)

1 Nephi 13:26
> ▸ which is **the** most abominable **of** all other churches (𝓞)
> which is **the** most abominable **above** all other churches (𝓟, 1830)
> which is most abominable **above** all other churches (1837)

1 Nephi 13:28
> ▸ there are many plain and **most** precious things taken away (𝓞)
> there are many plain and precious things taken away (𝓟, 1830)

1 Nephi 13:32
> in that **state of awful woundedness** (𝓞, 𝓟ᶜ, 1830)
> in that **awful state of woundedness** (𝓟*)
> in that **awful state of blindness** (𝓟js, 1837)
> ▸ in that **state of awful wickedness** (conj)

1 Nephi 13:34
> ▸ I will be merciful unto the Gentiles in that day / **saith the Lamb** (𝓞, 𝓟*, 1830)
> I will be merciful unto the Gentiles in that day (𝓟js, 1837)

1 Nephi 13:39
> ▸ from the Gentiles unto them . . . and also **to** the Jews (𝓟*, 1830)
> from the Gentiles unto them . . . and also the Jews (𝓟js, 1837)

1 Nephi 13:40
> ▸ the Lamb of God is the Eternal Father (𝓟*, 1830)
> the Lamb of God is **the Son of** the Eternal Father (𝓟js, 1837)

1 Nephi 14:7
> ▸ unto their being brought down into captivity and also **unto** destruction (𝓟, 1830)
> unto their being brought down into captivity and also **into** destruction (1849)

1 Nephi 14:9
> ▸ whose **founder** is the devil (𝓟, 1908R, 1981)
> whose **foundation** is the devil (1830)

1 Nephi 14:13
> ▸ the great mother of abominations did gather together **in** multitudes (𝓞, 𝓟, 1908R)
> the great mother of abominations did gather together multitudes (1830)

1 Nephi 14:15
> ▸ the wrath of God was poured out upon **that** great and abominable church (𝓞, 1981)
> the wrath of God was poured out upon **the** great and abominable church (𝓟, 1830)

1 Nephi 14:17
> ▸ whose **founder** is the devil (𝓟*, 1830, 1981)
> whose **foundation** is the devil (𝓟js, 1837)

1 Nephi 14:27
> ▸ and I Nephi heard and **bare** record (𝓞)
> and I Nephi heard and **bear** record (𝓟, 1830)

1 Nephi 14:28
> ▸ the remainder of the things which I saw (𝓞)
> the remainder of the things which I saw **and heard** (𝓟, 1830)

1 Nephi 15:5
> ▸ because of the **destruction** of my people (☉, 1953R, 1981)
> because of the **destructions** of my people (𝒫, 1830)

1 Nephi 15:11
> ▸ do ye not remember the **thing** which the Lord hath said (☉, 𝒫ᶜ)
> do ye not remember the **things** which the Lord hath said (𝒫*, 1830)

1 Nephi 15:12
> ▸ the Spirit of the Lord which was in our **father** (☉, 1981)
> the Spirit of the Lord which was in our **fathers** (𝒫, 1830)

1 Nephi 15:16
> ▸ they shall be **numbered** again among the house of Israel (☉)
> they shall be **remembered** again among the house of Israel (𝒫, 1830)

1 Nephi 15:20
> ▸ I did speak **so many** words unto my brethren that they were pacified (☉)
> I did speak **many** words unto my brethren that they were pacified (𝒫, 1830)

1 Nephi 15:21
> what meaneth **the thing** which our father saw (☉, 𝒫*, 1830)
> what meaneth **this thing** which our father saw (𝒫js, 1837)
> ▸ what meaneth **the things** which our father saw (conj)

1 Nephi 15:28
> ▸ an awful gulf which **separateth** the wicked from the tree of life (☉, 𝒫, 1830)
> an awful gulf which **separated** the wicked from the tree of life (1852)

1 Nephi 15:35
> and the devil is the **prepriator** of it (☉)
> and the devil is the **preparator** of it (𝒫*, 1830, 1981)
> and the devil is the **father** of it (𝒫js1)
> and the devil is the **foundation** of it (𝒫js2, 1837)
> ▸ and the devil is the **proprietor** of it (conj)

1 Nephi 15:35
> the final state of the **souls of man** (☉)
> the final state of the **souls of men** (𝒫, 1830)
> ▸ the final state of the **soul of man** (conj)

1 Nephi 15:36
> ▸ the wicked are **separated** from the righteous (☉)
> the wicked are **rejected** from the righteous (𝒫, 1830)

1 Nephi 15:36
> ▸ whose fruit is most precious and most desirable **of** all other fruits (☉)
> whose fruit is most precious and most desirable **above** all other fruits (𝒫, 1830)

1 Nephi 16:7
> and also Zoram took the **elder** daughter of Ishmael to wife (☉, 𝒫)
> ▸ and also Zoram took the **eldest** daughter of Ishmael to wife (1830)

1 Nephi 16:24
> ▸ for they had humbled themselves because of my **words** (☉, 1981)
> for they had humbled themselves because of my **word** (𝒫, 1830)

1 Nephi 17:2
> ▸ they began to bear their journeyings without **murmuring** (☉)
> they began to bear their journeyings without **murmurings** (𝒫, 1830)

1 Nephi 17:3
- ▶ he doth nourish them and strengthen them and provide **ways and means** (⊙)
- he doth nourish them and strengthen them and provide **means** (𝒫, 1830)

1 Nephi 17:3
- ▶ wherefore he did provide **ways and means** for us (⊙)
- wherefore he did provide **means** for us (𝒫, 1830)

1 Nephi 17:22
- ▶ for they **keep** the statutes and the judgments of the Lord (⊙, 𝒫)
- for they **kept** the statutes and the judgments of the Lord (1830)

1 Nephi 17:41
- ▶ he sent **flying fiery** serpents among them (⊙)
- he sent **fiery flying** serpents among them (𝒫, 1830)

1 Nephi 17:47
- ▶ insomuch **as if** my frame **had** no strength (⊙, 𝒫*, 1830)
- insomuch **that** my frame **has** no strength (𝒫js, 1837)

1 Nephi 17:48
- whoso shall lay their hands upon me shall wither even as a dried **weed** (⊙, 𝒫)
- ▶ whoso shall lay their hands upon me shall wither even as a dried **reed** (1830)

1 Nephi 17:53
- and they shall not wither before thee but I will **shock** them (⊙, 𝒫, 1830)
- ▶ and they shall not wither before thee but I will **shake** them (conj)

1 Nephi 18:7
- ▶ the **elder** was called Jacob and the younger Joseph (⊙, 1911)
- the **eldest** was called Jacob and the younger Joseph (𝒫, 1830)

1 Nephi 18:18
- ▶ they were near to be cast **with sorrow** into **a** watery grave (⊙, 1840, 1920)
- they were near to be cast into **a** watery grave (𝒫, 1830)
- they were near to be cast into **the** watery grave (1837)

1 Nephi 19:2
- ▶ the record of my father and the genealogy of his **forefathers** (⊙, 𝒫, 1840)
- the record of my father and the genealogy of his **fathers** (1830)

1 Nephi 19:2
- ▶ engraven upon those **first** plates of which I have spoken (⊙, 1981)
- engraven upon those plates of which I have spoken (𝒫, 1830)

1 Nephi 19:4
- ▶ this have I done and commanded my people **that** they should do (⊙, 𝒫, 1830)
- this have I done and commanded my people **what** they should do (1837)

1 Nephi 19:13
- ▶ they shall be scourged by all people / **saith the prophet** (⊙, 𝒫*, 1830)
- they shall be scourged by all people (𝒫js, 1837)

1 Nephi 19:20
- for **had** not the Lord been merciful to shew unto me concerning them
  even as he had prophets of old (⊙, 𝒫*, 1830)
- for **had** not the Lord been merciful to shew unto me concerning them
  even as he had prophets of old / **I should have perished also** (𝒫js, 1837)
- ▶ for **hath** not the Lord been merciful to shew unto me concerning them
  even as he had prophets of old (conj)

1 Nephi 19:23
- ▸ which were in the **books** of Moses (𝓞*)
  which were in the **book** of Moses (𝓟*)
  which were **written** in the **books** of Moses (𝓞ᶜ)
  which were **written** in the **book** of Moses (𝓟ᶜ, 1830)
  which were **written** in the **books** of Moses (1981)

1 Nephi 20:1
- ▸ out of the waters of Judah (𝓞, 𝓟, 1830, 1908ʀ; Isaiah 48:1)
  out of the waters of Judah **or out of the waters of baptism** (1840, 1920)

1 Nephi 20:6
- ▸ thou hast **heard and seen** all this (𝓞; ~Isaiah 48:6)
  thou hast **seen and heard** all this (𝓟, 1830)

1 Nephi 20:8
- ▸ and wast called a transgressor from **the** womb (𝓞, 1830, 𝓟js, 1837; Isaiah 48:8)
  and wast called a transgressor from **thy** womb (𝓟*)

1 Nephi 20:11
- ▸ for **how should I** suffer my name to be polluted (𝓞*; ~Isaiah 48:11)
  for **I will not** suffer my name to be polluted (𝓞ᶜ, 𝓟, 1830)

1 Nephi 21:20
- ▸ after thou hast lost the **other** (𝓞, 𝓟*, 1830; Isaiah 49:20)
  after thou hast lost the **first** (𝓟js, 1837)

1 Nephi 22:2
- ▸ behold they were **made** manifest unto the prophet (𝓞, 𝓟, 1830, 1908ʀ)
  behold they were manifest unto the prophet (1837)

1 Nephi 22:8
- ▸ wherefore it is likened unto **the** being **nursed** by the Gentiles (𝓞)
  wherefore it is likened unto **the** being **nourished** by the Gentiles (𝓟, 1830)
  wherefore it is likened unto **their** being **nourished** by the Gentiles (1840, 1852ᶜ)

1 Nephi 22:12
- ▸ they shall be gathered together to the lands of their **first** inheritance (𝓞)
  they shall be gathered together to the lands of their inheritance (𝓟, 1830)

2 Nephi title
- ▸ The Book of Nephi (𝓞*, 𝓟*)
  The **Second** Book of Nephi (𝓞ᶜ, 𝓟ᶜ, 1830)

2 Nephi 1:1
- ▸ **and rehearsed unto them** how great things the Lord had done for them (𝓞, 1981)
  how great things the Lord had done for them (𝓟, 1830)

2 Nephi 1:5
- ▸ the Lord hath **consecrated** this land unto me (𝓞)
  the Lord hath **covenanted** this land unto me (𝓟, 1830)

2 Nephi 1:6
- ▸ there shall **be** none come into this land (𝓞, 𝓟*, 1830)
  there shall none come into this land (𝓟js, 1837)

2 Nephi 1:20
- ▸ but inasmuch as ye will not keep **his** commandments ye shall be cut off from **his** presence (𝓞*)
  but inasmuch as ye will not keep **my** commandments ye shall be cut off from **my** presence (𝓞ᶜ, 𝓟, 1830)

2 Nephi 1:26
 ▸ which he could not **constrain** (⊙, 𝒫*, 1830)
 which he could not **restrain** (𝒫js, 1837)

2 Nephi 2:11
 neither **holiness** nor misery / neither good nor bad (𝒫, 1830)
 ▸ neither **happiness** nor misery / neither good nor bad (conj)

2 Nephi 2:27
 ▸ through the great **Mediator** of all men (𝒫, 1981)
 through the great **mediation** of all men (1830)

2 Nephi 3:12
 wherefore the fruit of **my** loins shall write (𝒫, 1830)
 ▸ wherefore the fruit of **thy** loins shall write (1837)

2 Nephi 3:14
 for this promise . . . of the fruit of **thy** loins shall be fulfilled (𝒫, 1830)
 ▸ for this promise . . . of the fruit of **my** loins shall be fulfilled (1849)

2 Nephi 3:17
 ▸ I will make **one** a spokesman for him (𝒫)
 I will make a spokesman for him (1830)

2 Nephi 3:18
 I will raise up unto the fruit of thy loins (𝒫, 1830)
 ▸ I will raise up **one** unto the fruit of thy loins (conj)

2 Nephi 3:20
 their cry shall go (𝒫, 1830)
 ▸ their cry shall go **forth** (conj)

2 Nephi 4:5
 ▸ if ye are brought up in the **right** way **that** ye should go (𝒫*, 1830)
 if ye are brought up in the way ye should go (𝒫js, 1837; ~Proverbs 22:6)

2 Nephi 4:12
 ▸ after Lehi had **spake** unto all his household (𝒫*, 1830)
 my Father after Lehi had **spake** unto all his household (𝒫js)
 after **my father** Lehi had **spoken** unto all his household (1837)

2 Nephi 4:14
 ▸ for I Nephi was constrained to speak unto them according to **the** word (𝒫*, 1830)
 for I Nephi was constrained to speak unto them according to **his** word (𝒫js, 1837)

2 Nephi 4:26
 ▸ if the Lord . . . hath visited **me** in so much mercy (𝒫, 1908R)
 if the Lord . . . hath visited **men** in so much mercy (1830)

2 Nephi 7:5
 ▸ the Lord God hath **opened** mine ear (⊙, 1840, 1852ᶜ; Isaiah 50:5)
 the Lord God hath **appointed** mine ear (𝒫, 1830, 1908R)

2 Nephi 8:4
 for a light **thing of** the people (𝒫*, 1830)
 for a light **for** the people (𝒫js, 1837)
 ▸ for a light **of** the people (conj; Isaiah 51:4)

2 Nephi 9:13
 and the grave deliver up the **body** of the righteous (𝒫, 1830)
 ▸ and the grave deliver up the **bodies** of the righteous (1953R)

2 Nephi 9:16
> ▸ and their torment is a lake of fire and brimstone (𝓟*, 1830)
> and their torment is **as** a lake of fire and brimstone (𝓟js, 1837)

2 Nephi 9:29
> ▸ if **it so be that** they hearken unto the counsels of God (𝓟*, 1830)
> if they hearken unto the counsels of God (𝓟js, 1837)

2 Nephi 9:41
> ▸ remember that his paths are **righteousness** (𝓟, 1830, 1908R)
> remember that his paths are **righteous** (1837)

2 Nephi 10:3
> ▸ and they shall crucify him / for it behooveth our God (𝓟*)
> and they shall crucify him / for **thus** it behooveth our God (𝓟jg, 1830)

2 Nephi 12:9
> and the mean **men** boweth down and the great man humbleth himself **not** (𝓟*)
> and the mean **man** boweth down and the great man humbleth himself **not** (1830)
> and the mean **men** boweth **not** down and the great man humbleth himself **not** (𝓟js)
> and the mean **man** boweth **not** down and the great man humbleth himself **not** (1837)
> ▸ and the mean **man** boweth down and the great man humbleth himself (conj; Isaiah 2:9)

2 Nephi 13:24
> ▸ and it shall **all** come to pass (𝓟)
> and it shall come to pass (1830; Isaiah 3:24)

2 Nephi 20:2
> ▸ to turn **aside** the needy from judgment (𝓟, 1830, 1908R; Isaiah 10:2)
> to turn **away** the needy from judgment (1837)

2 Nephi 20:10
> as my hand hath **founded** the kingdoms of the idols (𝓟, 1830)
> ▸ as my hand hath **found** the kingdoms of the idols (conj; Isaiah 10:10)

2 Nephi 20:13
> and I have **moved** the borders of the people (𝓟, 1830)
> ▸ and I have **removed** the borders of the people (conj; ~Isaiah 10:13)

2 Nephi 20:29
> **Ramath** is afraid (𝓟, 1830)
> ▸ **Ramah** is afraid (conj; Isaiah 10:29)

2 Nephi 23:10
> ▸ the sun shall be darkened in **his** going forth (𝓟, 1908R, 1981; Isaiah 13:10)
> the sun shall be darkened in **her** going forth (1830)

2 Nephi 24:19
> the **remnant** of those that are slain (𝓟, 1830)
> ▸ the **raiment** of those that are slain (conj; Isaiah 14:19)

2 Nephi 24:25
> ▸ that I will **break** the Assyrian in my land (𝓞; Isaiah 14:25)
> that I will **bring** the Assyrian in my land (𝓟, 1830)

2 Nephi 26:9
> but the **Son** of righteousness shall appear unto them (𝓟, 1830)
> ▸ but the **Sun** of righteousness shall appear unto them (conj)

2 Nephi 26:15
- ▶ and after that they shall have been brought down low **in** the dust (𝒫, 1837)
- and after that they shall have been brought down low **into** the dust (1830)

2 Nephi 26:22
- ▶ for he is the **founder** of all these things (𝒫*, 1830, 1981)
- for he is the **foundation** of all these things (𝒫js, 1837)

2 Nephi 26:22
- ▶ yea the **founder** of murder and works of darkness (𝒫*, 1830, 1981)
- yea the **foundation** of murder and works of darkness (𝒫js, 1837)

2 Nephi 28:12
- ▶ and because of false teachers and false **doctrines** (𝒫*)
- and because of false teachers and false **doctrine** (𝒫ᶜ, 1830)

2 Nephi 28:23
- they are grasped with death and hell **and death and hell** and the devil (𝒫, 1830)
- ▶ they are grasped with death and hell and the devil (conj)

2 Nephi 29:4
- do they remember the **travels** and the labors and the pains of the Jews (𝒫, 1830)
- ▶ do they remember the **travails** and the labors and the pains of the Jews (1981)

2 Nephi 29:7
- yea even **upon** all the nations of the earth (𝒫, 1830)
- ▶ yea even **unto** all the nations of the earth (conj)

2 Nephi 30:6
- ▶ save they shall be a **white** and a delightsome people (𝒫, 1830, 1908R)
- save they shall be a **pure** and a delightsome people (1840, 1981)

2 Nephi 30:18
- ▶ I **must** make an end of my sayings (𝒫, 1830, 1908R)
- I make an end of my sayings (1840, 1981)

2 Nephi 31:4
- ▶ which should take away the **sin** of the world (𝒫, 1908R; ~John 1:29)
- which should take away the **sins** of the world (1830)

2 Nephi 31:9
- ▶ it sheweth unto the children of men the **straitness** of the path (𝒫, 1981)
- it sheweth unto the children of men the **straightness** of the path (1830)

2 Nephi 31:18
- and then are ye in this **strait** and narrow path (𝒫, 1953R, 1981)
- ▶ and then are ye in this **straight** and narrow path (1830)

2 Nephi 31:19
- after that ye have got into this **strait** and narrow path (𝒫, 1953R, 1981)
- ▶ after that ye have got into this **straight** and narrow path (1830)

2 Nephi 33:4
- ▶ will **he make** strong unto them (𝒫, 1908R)
- will **be made** strong unto them (1830)

2 Nephi 33:4
- ▶ and persuadeth **men** to believe in him (𝒫, 1830)
- and persuadeth **them** to believe in him (1837)

2 Nephi 33:9
> ▸ and walk in the **strait** path which leads to life (𝔓, 1981)
>
> and walk in the **straight** path which leads to life (1830)

Jacob 1:11
> ▸ let them be of **whatsoever** name they would (𝔓)
>
> let them be of **whatever** name they would (1830)

Jacob 3:5
> the **commandments** of the Lord which **was** given unto our **father** (𝔓*)
>
> ▸ the **commandment** of the Lord which **was** given unto our **father** (𝔓ᶜ, 1981)
>
> the **commandment** of the Lord which **was** given unto our **fathers** (1830)
>
> the **commandments** of the Lord which **was** given unto our **fathers** (1908R)
>
> the **commandments** of the Lord which **were** given unto our **fathers** (1953R)

Jacob 4:1
> and I cannot write but little of my words (𝔓*, 1858w)
>
> ▸ and I cannot write but **a** little of my words (𝔓ᶜ, 1830)

Jacob 4:11
> ▸ wherefore beloved / be reconciled unto him (𝔓*)
>
> wherefore beloved **brethren** / be reconciled unto him (𝔓jg, 1830)

Jacob 4:11
> having faith and obtained a good hope of glory in him (𝔓, 1830)
>
> ▸ having faith and **having** obtained a good hope of glory in him (conj)

Jacob 5:1
> the words of the prophet Zenos which spake unto the house of Israel (𝔓, 1830)
>
> ▸ the words of the prophet Zenos which **he** spake unto the house of Israel (1879)

Jacob 5:8
> I take away many of these young and tender branches (𝔓, 1830)
>
> ▸ I **will** take away many of these young and tender branches (conj)

Jacob 5:13
> and these will I place in the nithermost **part** of my vineyard (𝔓, 1830)
>
> ▸ and these will I place in the nithermost **parts** of my vineyard (conj)

Jacob 5:19
> ▸ come let us go to the nithermost **parts** of the vineyard (𝔓, 1908R)
>
> come let us go to the nithermost **part** of the vineyard (1830)

Jacob 5:20
> whither the master had hid the natural branches (𝔓*, 1837)
>
> ▸ whither the master **of the vineyard** had hid the natural branches (𝔓ᶜ, 1830, 1908R)

Jacob 5:21
> ▸ it was the poorest spot in all the land of **thy** vineyard (𝔓, 1830, 1908R, 1981)
>
> it was the poorest spot in all the land of **the** vineyard (1840, 1852ᶜ)

Jacob 5:29
> come let us go down **in** the vineyard (𝔓)
>
> ▸ come let us go down **into** the vineyard (1830)

Jacob 5:37
> thou **beheldest** that it beginneth to perish (𝔓)
>
> ▸ thou **beholdest** that it beginneth to perish (1830)

Jacob 5:45
    a part thereof brought forth good fruit and **the** part thereof brought forth wild fruit (𝓟)
    a part thereof brought forth good fruit and **a** part thereof brought forth wild fruit (1830)
    ► a part thereof brought forth good fruit and **the other** part thereof brought forth wild fruit (conj)

Jacob 5:46
    ► and these I had **hope** to preserve (𝓟*, 1830, 1837*)
    and these I had **hoped** to preserve (𝓟js, 1837ᶜ)

Jacob 5:47
    ► and I have digged it (𝓞, 𝓟*, 1830)
    and I have digged **about** it (𝓟js, 1837)

Jacob 5:72
    ► the servants did go **to it** and labor with their mights (𝓟*, 1830)
    the servants did go and labor with their mights (𝓟js, 1837)

Jacob 5:74
    and the Lord had preserved unto himself (𝓟, 1830)
    ► and **the good** the Lord had preserved unto himself (conj)

Jacob 5:74
    that the trees had **become** again the natural fruit (𝓟, 1830)
    ► that the trees had **brought** again the natural fruit (conj)

Jacob 5:75
    ye have been diligent . . . and **hath** brought unto me again the natural fruit (𝓟*, 1830)
    ye have been diligent . . . and **have** brought unto me again the natural fruit (𝓟js, 1837)
    ► ye have been diligent . . . and **it hath** brought unto me again the natural fruit (conj)

Jacob 6:13
    until I shall meet you before the **pleasing** bar of God (𝓟, 1830)
    ► until I shall meet you before the **pleading** bar of God (conj)

Jacob 7:1
    some years had passed away there came a man (𝓞*, 𝓟*)
    after some years had passed away there came a man (𝓞ᶜ, 𝓟ᶜ, 1830)
    ► some years had passed away **and** there came a man (conj)

Jacob 7:19
   ɴᴀ I greatly fear lest my case shall be awful but I confess unto God (𝓟)
    I greatly fear lest my case **shall be awful // but I confess** unto God (1830)
    ► I greatly fear lest my case **shall be awful but I confess** unto God (conj)

Jacob 7:25
    ► the people of Nephi did fortify against them with their **arms** (𝓞, 𝓟, 1981)
    the people of Nephi did fortify against them with their **armies** (1830)

Jacob 7:26
    ► born in tribulation in a **wild** wilderness (𝓞, 𝓟)
    born in tribulation in a wilderness (1830)

Enos 1:3
    and the words which I had often heard my father speak (𝓟, 1830)
    ► and **I remembered** the words which I had often heard my father speak (conj)

Enos 1:3
    ► **and the words of my father** sunk deep into my heart (𝓟*, 1830)
    and sunk deep into my heart (𝓟js)
    sunk deep into my heart (1837)

Enos 1:8
- ▸ because of thy faith in Christ whom thou hast **not** heard nor seen (𝓟*, 1830)
  because of thy faith in Christ whom thou hast **never before** heard nor seen (𝓟js, 1837)

Enos 1:8
- ▸ wherefore go to **it** (𝓟*, 1830)
  wherefore go to (𝓟js, 1837)

Enos 1:14
- ▸ our **strugglings** were vain in restoring them to the true faith (𝓟, 1837)
  our **struggles** were vain in restoring them to the true faith (1830)

Enos 1:20
- ▸ and I **bear** record (𝓟, 1837)
  and I **bare** record (1830)

Enos 1:20
  with a short skin **girted** about their loins (𝓟, 1908R)
- ▸ with a short skin **girded** about their loins (1830)
  with a short skin **girdle** about their loins (1837)

The Words of Mormon 1:5
  wherefore I **chosed** these things (𝓟*)
  wherefore I **chose** these things (𝓟ᶜ, 1830, 1920)
- ▸ wherefore I **choose** these things (1852)

The Words of Mormon 1:16
- ▸ and false **preachers and teachers** among the people (𝓟, 1830, 1920)
  and false **teachers and preachers** among the people (1852)

Mosiah 2:4
- ▸ that **thereby** they might rejoice (𝓟, 1908R)
  that they might rejoice (1830)

Mosiah 2:15
- ▸ I can answer a **clear** conscience before God this day (𝓟*, 1830)
  I can answer a **clean** conscience before God this day (𝓟ᶜ)

Mosiah 3:9
- ▸ they shall consider him **as** a man (𝓟)
  they shall consider him a man (1830)

Mosiah 3:19
- ▸ **but if** he yieldeth to the enticings of the Holy Spirit (𝓟, 1830)
  unless he yieldeth to the enticings of the Holy Spirit (1920)

Mosiah 4:5
  and your **worthlessness** and fallen state (𝓟*, 1840)
- ▸ and your **worthless** and fallen state (𝓟ᶜ, 1830, 1908R)

Mosiah 4:14
  and fight and quarrel one with another and **save** the devil (𝓟*)
- ▸ and fight and quarrel one with another and **serve** the devil (𝓟ᶜ, 1830)

Mosiah 4:30
- ▸ and observe **to keep** the commandments of God (𝓟, 1830, 1908R)
  and observe the commandments of God (1837)

Mosiah 5:2
  which hath wrought a mighty **chance** in us (𝓟*)
- ▸ which hath wrought a mighty **change** in us (𝓟ᶜ, 1830)

Mosiah 6:2

there was not one soul **save** it were little children (𝓟*)
▶ there was not one soul **except** it were little children (𝓟^c, 1830)

Mosiah 7:20

▶ it is because of our iniquities and abominations that has brought us into bondage (𝓟, 1830)
it is because of our iniquities and abominations that **he** has brought us into bondage (1905^c [1907])

Mosiah 8:17

a seer can know of things which **has past** (𝓟*, 1830)
a seer can know of things which **have past** (𝓟js, 1837)
a seer can know of things which **are past** (1920)
▶ a seer can know of things which **has passed** (conj)

Mosiah 9:2

▶ until the **greatest** number of our army was destroyed (𝓟, 1830)
until the **greater** number of our army was destroyed (1920)

Mosiah 9:14

▶ and to take **of** their flocks (𝓟, 1830, 1908R)
and to take **off** their flocks (1837)

Mosiah 10:5

the women should spin and toil and work **and work** all manner of fine linen (𝓟, 1830)
▶ the women should spin and toil and work all manner of fine linen (conj)

Mosiah 11:12

▶ a very high tower / **even** so high that he could . . . overlook the land (𝓟, 1830, 1841, 1858w)
a very high tower / **ever** so high that he could . . . overlook the land (1837)

Mosiah 11:23

except this people repent and turn the Lord their God (𝓟*)
except this people repent and turn **unto** the Lord their God (𝓟^c, 1830)
▶ except this people repent and turn **to** the Lord their God (conj)

Mosiah 12:1

▶ and began **again** to prophesy among them (𝓟, 1830, 1908R)
and began to prophesy among them (1837)

Mosiah 15:9

having broken the bands of death / taken upon himself their iniquity (𝓟, 1830)
▶ having broken the bands of death / **having** taken upon himself their iniquity (conj)

Mosiah 15:24

▶ and **there** are those who have part in the first resurrection (𝓟, 1830)
and **these** are those who have part in the first resurrection (1837)

Mosiah 16:7

▶ if Christ had not risen from the dead or broken the bands of death (𝓟*)
if Christ had not risen from the dead or **have** broken the bands of death (𝓟^c, 1830)

Mosiah 17:7

we have found an **acquisition** against thee (𝓟)
▶ we have found an **accusation** against thee (1830)

Mosiah 17:10

yea and I will suffer even **until** death (𝓟, 1830)
▶ yea and I will suffer even **unto** death (conj)

Mosiah 17:13
> ▸ they took him **and bound him** (𝔓, 1830, 1906, 1905ᶜ [1907], 1907, 1908ʀ)
> they took him (1837)

Mosiah 17:13
> and **scourged** his skin with fagots / yea even unto death (𝔓, 1830)
> ▸ and **scorched** his skin with fagots / yea even unto death (conj)

Mosiah 17:15
> ▸ many shall suffer **the pains that I do suffer** (𝔓, 1830, 1908ʀ, 1981)
> many shall suffer (1837)

Mosiah 18:27
> ▸ and **he** that hath but little / but little should be required (𝔓, 1830)
> and **of him** that hath but little / but little should be required (1920)

Mosiah 18:33
> ▸ Alma was **a** stirring up the people to **a** rebellion against him (𝔓*)
> Alma was stirring up the people to **a** rebellion against him (𝔓jg, 1830)
> Alma was stirring up the people to rebellion against him (1837)

Mosiah 19:7
> ▸ for the Lamanites are upon us and they will destroy **them** (𝔓, 1830)
> for the Lamanites are upon us and they will destroy **us** (1906, 1905ᶜ [1907], 1907)

Mosiah 19:15
> ▸ that they would deliver up **the** king Noah into the hands of the Lamanites (𝔓, 1830)
> that they would deliver up king Noah into the hands of the Lamanites (1837)

Mosiah 19:24
> after they had ended the **ceremony** that they returned to the land of Nephi (𝔓, 1830)
> ▸ after they had ended the **sermon** that they returned to the land of Nephi (conj)

Mosiah 21:18
> the people of Limhi kept together . . . **and secure** their grain and their flocks (𝔓, 1830)
> the people of Limhi kept together . . . **and secured** their grain and their flocks (1849)
> ▸ the people of Limhi kept together . . . **to secure** their grain and their flocks (conj)

Mosiah 21:21
> ▸ and carried off **of** their grain (𝔓, 1830)
> and carried off their grain (1837)

Mosiah 21:28
> ▸ king **Benjamin** had a gift from God (𝔓, 1830)
> king **Mosiah** had a gift from God (1837)

Mosiah 21:29
> ▸ because so many of **his** brethren had been slain (𝔓*, 1830)
> because so many of **their** brethren had been slain (𝔓js, 1837)

Mosiah 22:7
> ▸ we will pass through the secret pass on the left of **their** camp (𝔓, 1908ʀ, 1981)
> we will pass through the secret pass on the left of **the** camp (1830)

Mosiah 22:13
> ▸ they arrived in the land of Zarahemla and joined **his** people (𝔓, 1830)
> they arrived in the land of Zarahemla and joined **Mosiah's** people (1920)

Mosiah 23:20
> ▸ and they built a city which they called **the city of** Helam (𝔓, 1837)
> and they built a city which they called Helam (1830)

Mosiah 23:26
> ► and gathered themselves together **into** the city of Helam (𝓟, 1830)
> and gathered themselves together **in** the city of Helam (1852)

Mosiah 24:13
> ► and I will covenant with **this** my people (𝓟, 1908R)
> and I will covenant with my people (1830)

Mosiah 24:20
> ► and they called **the name of** the valley Alma (𝓟)
> and they called the valley Alma (1830)

Mosiah 25:2
> ► which was a descendant of **Muloch** (𝓟)
> which was a descendant of **Mulok** (1830)
> which was a descendant of **Mulek** (1879)

Mosiah 25:5
> ► until **the time** they returned again (𝓟, 1830)
> until they returned again (1837)

Mosiah 25:6
> and he also read the account of Alma and his brethren and all their afflictions
> from the time they left the land of Zarahemla until the time they returned again (𝓟, 1830)
> ► and he also read the account of Alma and his brethren and all their afflictions
> **and he also read the account of Ammon and his brethren and all their afflictions**
> from the time they left the land of Zarahemla until the time they returned again (conj)

Mosiah 26:9
> ► Alma did know concerning them / **for** there were many witnesses (𝓟*)
> Alma did **not** know concerning them / **for** there were many witnesses (𝓟oc, 1830)
> Alma did **not** know concerning them / **but** there were many witnesses (1920)

Mosiah 26:23
> ► it is I that granteth unto him that believeth **in** the end a place (𝓟, 1830, 1908R)
> it is I that granteth unto him that believeth **unto** the end a place (1840, 1852ᶜ)

Mosiah 27:14
> ► the Lord hath heard **the prayers of his people and also** the prayers of his servant Alma (𝓟, 1830, 1908R)
> the Lord hath heard the prayers of his servant Alma (1840)

Mosiah 27:28
> ► after **wading** through much tribulation (𝓟, 1908R, 1981)
> after **wandering** through much tribulation (1830)

Mosiah 27:29
> my soul was **wrecked** with eternal torment (𝓟, 1830)
> ► my soul was **racked** with eternal torment (1879)

Mosiah 27:30
> but now that they may foresee that he will come (𝓟, 1830, 1879, 1908R)
> but now that they may foresee **and** that he will come (1837)
> ► but now **I know** that they may foresee that he will come (conj)

Mosiah 28:4
> ► **and** suffering much fearing that they should be cast off forever (𝓟, 1830)
> suffering much **and** fearing that they should be cast off forever (1920)

Mosiah 28:17
> ► and even from that time until the creation of Adam (𝓟, 1830)
> and even from that time **back** until the creation of Adam (1920)

Mosiah 29:1
> ▸ he sent out **through** all the land among all the people (𝓟, 1908R)
> he sent out **throughout** all the land among all the people (1830)

Mosiah 29:15
> ▸ **according to the crime which he hath committed** / according to the law (𝓟*, 1830)
> **according to the crime which he has committed** / according to the law (𝓟js, 1908R, 1981)
> according to the law (1837)

Mosiah 29:19
> they must unavoidably **remain** in bondage until now (𝓟*, 1849)
> they must unavoidably **remained** in bondage until now (𝓟oc, 1830, 1908R)
> they must unavoidably **have remained** in bondage until now (1858W, 1953R)
> ▸ they must **have** unavoidably **remained** in bondage until now (conj)

Mosiah 29:42
> ▸ Alma was appointed to be the chief judge (𝓟, 1830, 1908R)
> Alma was appointed to be the **first** chief judge (1837)

Mosiah 29:46
> being sixty and three years (𝓟)
> ▸ being sixty and three years **old** (1830)

Alma 1:10
> ▸ according to the **crime** which he had committed (𝓟, 1830)
> according to the **crimes** which he had committed (1852)

Alma 1:24
> their names were blotted out / that they were **remembered** no more among the people of God (𝓟, 1830)
> ▸ their names were blotted out / that they were **numbered** no more among the people of God (conj)

Alma 1:32
> ▸ **persecuting** lying thieving robbing (𝓟, 1908R, 1981)
> lying thieving robbing (1830)

Alma 1:33
> ▸ they **became** more still and durst not commit any wickedness (𝓟, 1830)
> they **become** more still and durst not commit any wickedness (1840)

Alma 2:15
> ▸ the Amlicites came **up** upon the hill Amnihu (𝓟, 1830)
> the Amlicites came upon the hill Amnihu (1837)

Alma 2:18
> ▸ they slew the Amlicites with **a** great slaughter (𝓟, 1830)
> they slew the Amlicites with great slaughter (1905, 1907)

Alma 2:30
> ▸ to save and **protect** this people (𝓟, 1908R)
> to save and **preserve** this people (1830)

Alma 3:5
> save it were skin which was girded about their loins (𝓟, 1830)
> ▸ save it were **a** skin which was girded about their loins (conj)

Alma 3:27
> ▸ and thus **ended** the fifth year (𝓟, 1888, 1908R)
> and thus **endeth** the fifth year (1830)

Alma 4:5
▸ and thus **ended** the seventh year (𝒫, 1830, 1906, 1908R, 1981)
and thus **endeth** the seventh year (1837)

Alma 5:1
▸ Alma began to **declare** the word of God unto the people (𝒫)
Alma began to **deliver** the word of God unto the people (1830)

Alma 5:11
▸ did he not speak the **word** of God and my father Alma **believed** them (𝒫*)
did he not speak the **word** of God and my father Alma **believe** them (𝒫jg, 1830)
did he not speak the **words** of God and my father Alma **believe** them (𝒫js, 1837)

Alma 5:25
▸ **or also** ye cannot suppose that such **an one** can have place in the kingdom (𝒫*, 1830)
ye cannot suppose that such can have place in the kingdom (𝒫js, 1837)

Alma 5:35
and ye shall not be **put** down and cast into the fire (𝒫)
and ye shall not be **hewn** down and cast into the fire (1830)
▸ and ye shall not be **cut** down and cast into the fire (conj)

Alma 5:45
▸ do ye suppose that I know **not** of these things myself (𝒫*, 1830)
do ye **not** suppose that I know of these things myself (𝒫js, 1837)

Alma 5:48
the Son **of** the Only Begotten of the Father (𝒫*, 1830)
▸ the Son / the Only Begotten of the Father (𝒫js, 1837)

Alma 7:9
▸ repent ye **repent ye** and prepare the way of the Lord (𝒫, 1908R)
repent ye and prepare the way of the Lord (1830)

Alma 7:10
▸ he shall be born of Mary at Jerusalem which is the land of our forefathers (𝒫, 1830, 1920)
he shall be born of Mary at Jerusalem which is **in** the land of our forefathers (1905)

Alma 7:12
how to **suffer** his people according to their infirmities (𝒫, 1830)
▸ how to **succor** his people according to their infirmities (1837)

Alma 7:27
▸ according to your faith and good **works** (𝒫, 1830, 1858w)
according to your faith and good **words** (1840)

Alma 8:23
▸ I am Alma and am the high priest over the **churches** of God (𝒫)
I am Alma and am the high priest over the **church** of God (1830)

Alma 9:19
▸ he would rather suffer that the Lamanites might destroy all **this** people (𝒫, 1830)
he would rather suffer that the Lamanites might destroy all **his** people (1852)

Alma 9:22
▸ and they having **been** waxed strong in battle (𝒫, 1830)
and they having waxed strong in battle (1920)

Alma 9:25
▸ repent ye **repent ye** for the kingdom of heaven is nigh at hand (𝒫, 1908R)
repent ye for the kingdom of heaven is nigh at hand (1830)

Alma 9:28

> ► **every man** shall reap a reward of **their** works (𝒫*, 1830)
> **every man** shall reap a reward of **his** works (𝒫js1)
> **all men** shall reap a reward of **his** works (𝒫js2)
> **all men** shall reap a reward of **their** works (1837)

Alma 10:2

> ► I am the son of **Gidanah** (𝒫)
> I am the son of **Giddonah** (1830, 1908R)
> I am the son of **Giddonan** (1892R)

Alma 10:5

> ► for I have seen much of his mysteries and his **miraculous** power (𝒫, 1908R)
> for I have seen much of his mysteries and his **marvelous** power (1830)

Alma 10:6

> ► which is in the tenth year of the reign of **our** judges (𝒫, 1830)
> which is in the tenth year of the reign of **the** judges (1837)

Alma 10:19

> that the voice of this people should **cause** iniquity (𝒫*)
> ► that the voice of this people should **choose** iniquity (𝒫jg, 1830)

Alma 10:20

> ► well doth he cry unto **this** people (𝒫, 1830, 1920)
> well doth he cry unto **his** people (1852)

Alma 10:28

> ► the people cried out against him (𝒫*)
> the people cried out against him **saying** (𝒫oc, 1830)

Alma 11:2

> ► and the **evidences** which are brought against him (𝒪, 𝒫oc, 1830)
> and the **witnesses** which are brought against him (𝒫*)

Alma 11:2

> ► the man is compelled to pay that which he oweth or be **striped** (𝒫, 1830, 1908R)
> the man is compelled to pay that which he oweth or be **stripped** (1840, 1879)

Alma 11:6

> ► an **ezrum** of silver (𝒫)
> an **ezrom** of silver (1830)

Alma 11:16

> a **shiblum** is a half of a shiblon (𝒪*, 1830)
> a **shillum** is a half of a shiblon (𝒪c1)
> ► a **shilum** is a half of a shiblon (𝒪c2, 𝒫)

Alma 11:18

> ► an antion of gold is equal to three **shiblons** (𝒫, 1840, 1920; Alma 11:19)
> an antion of gold is equal to three **shublons** (1830)

Alma 11:21

> and **this** Zeezrom began to question Amulek (𝒫, 1830)
> ► and **thus** Zeezrom began to question Amulek (conj)

Alma 11:22

> ► yea **I will** if it be according to the Spirit of the Lord (𝒫, 1908R)
> yea if it be according to the Spirit of the Lord (1830)

Alma 11:36

▸ thou sayest that I **speak** as though I had authority (𝓞, 𝓟oc)
thou sayest that I **spake** as though I had authority (𝓟*, 1830)

Alma 11:44

▸ but **all things** shall be restored to its perfect frame (𝓞, 𝓟, 1830)
but **every thing** shall be restored to its perfect frame (1920)

Alma 11:44

and shall be brought and be **reigned** before the bar of Christ (𝓟*)
and shall be brought and be **arraigned** before the bar of Christ (𝓟jg, 1830, 1874R)
and shall be brought and be **arranged** before the bar of Christ (1858w)
▸ and **all** shall be brought and be **raigned** before the bar of Christ (conj)

Alma 12:14

for our **works** will condemn us / yea all our **work** will condemn us (𝓟*)
for our **words** will condemn us / yea all our **work** will condemn us (𝓟ᶜ, 1830)
for our **words** will condemn us / yea all our **works** will condemn us (1837)
▸ for our **works** will condemn us / yea all our **works** will condemn us (conj)

Alma 13:6

▸ and thus being called by **this** holy calling (𝓟, 1830)
and thus being called by **his** holy calling (1953R)

Alma 13:9

after the order of the Son **of** the Only Begotten of the Father (𝓟*, 1830)
▸ after the order of the Son / the Only Begotten of the Father (𝓟js, 1837)

Alma 13:10

▸ as I said concerning the holy order **or** this high priesthood (𝓟, 1981)
as I said concerning the holy order **of** this high priesthood (1830)

Alma 13:20

the scriptures are before you // if ye will **arrest** them (𝓟*, 1830)
▸ the scriptures are before you // if ye will **wrest** them (𝓟js, 1837)

Alma 14:28

▸ and every soul **which was within** the walls thereof . . . **were** slain (𝓟*, 1830)
and every soul **who was within** the walls thereof . . . **were** slain (𝓟js, 1837)
and every soul **who were in** the walls thereof . . . **were** slain (1852)
and every soul **within** the walls thereof . . . **were** slain (1906, 1907)
and every soul **within** the walls thereof . . . **was** slain (1905ᶜ [1907])

Alma 15:3

▸ they had been slain **by the cause** of his iniquity (𝓟, 1830)
they had been slain **because** of his iniquity (1920)

Alma 16:5

to know **whether** the Lord would that they should go (𝓟*, 1830, 1837)
▸ to know **whither** the Lord would that they should go (𝓟js, 1981)

Alma 17:1

▸ he met the sons of Mosiah (𝓟, 1908R)
he met **with** the sons of Mosiah (1830)

Alma 17:6

▸ in the first year **of the reign** of the judges (𝓟, 1830)
in the first year of the judges (1849)

Alma 17:8
> ▸ to preach the word unto the Lamanites (℘*)
> to preach the word **of God** unto the Lamanites (℘ᶜ, 1830)

Alma 17:9
> ▸ and they fasted much **and prayed much** (℘, 1830, 1908R, 1920)
> and they fasted much (1837)

Alma 17:18
> or rather he did **minister** unto them (℘*, ℘jg, 1858w)
> ▸ or rather he did **administer** unto them (℘ᶜ, 1830)

Alma 17:26
> to the place of water which was called the **water** of Sebus (℘, 1830)
> ▸ to the place of water which was called the **waters** of Sebus (conj)

Alma 17:31
> ▸ and thus we will **reserve** the flocks unto the king (℘, 1830)
> and thus we will **preserve** the flocks unto the king (1849)
> and thus we will **restore** the flocks unto the king (conj)

Alma 17:34
> ▸ and they were **not** in number a **very** few (℘*, 1830)
> and they were in number **not** a few (℘js, 1837)

Alma 17:38
> but he slew none save it were their leader (℘*, 1830)
> but he slew none save it were their leader **with this sword** (℘js1)
> but he slew none save it were their leader **with his sword** (℘js2, 1837)
> ▸ but he slew none **with the sword** save it were their leader (conj)

Alma 18:25
> ▸ and he answered unto him (℘)
> and he answered **and said** unto him (1830)

Alma 18:37
> and all their sufferings with hunger and thirst and their **travel** (℘, 1830)
> ▸ and all their sufferings with hunger and thirst and their **travail** (1981)

Alma 19:1
> they were about to take his body and lay it **in** a sepulchre (℘*, 1830)
> ▸ they were about to take his body and lay it **into** a sepulchre (℘ᶜ)

Alma 19:6
> ▸ yea this light had infused **such** joy into his soul (℘, 1830, 1908R)
> yea this light had infused **much** joy into his soul (1840)

Alma 19:6
> and the light of everlasting **light** was lit up in his soul (Ο, ℘*, 1830, 1837)
> ▸ and the light of everlasting **life** was lit up in his soul (℘js, 1852)

Alma 19:30
> ▸ and when she had said this / she **clapped** her hands (℘, 1908R)
> and when she had said this / she **clasped** her hands (1830)

Alma 20:4
> ▸ who told thee that **thy** brethren were in prison (℘, 1840, 1852)
> who told thee that **my** brethren were in prison (1830)

Alma 21:3

▸ that they should wax **stronger** in wickedness (𝓟, 1830)
that they should wax **strong** in wickedness (1837)

Alma 22:1

▸ we will return to the account of Aaron and his **other** brethren (𝓟, 1908R)
we will return to the account of Aaron and his brethren (1830)

Alma 22:23

▸ this was done in the presence of the queen and many of **his** servants (𝓞, 𝓟*)
this was done in the presence of the queen and many of **the** servants (𝓟ᶜ, 1830)

Alma 22:28

▸ the more idle part of the Lamanites lived in the wilderness and **lived** in tents (𝓟*)
the more idle part of the Lamanites lived in the wilderness and **dwelt** in tents (𝓟ᶜ, 1830)

Alma 22:32

on the line Bountiful and the land Desolation (𝓞, 𝓟, 1830)
▸ on the line **between the land** Bountiful and the land Desolation (conj)

Alma 23:3

▸ therefore he sent **this** proclamation throughout the land (𝓞, 𝓟, 1830)
therefore he sent **his** proclamation throughout the land (1849)

Alma 23:12

▸ and in the city of **Shimnilom** (𝓟, 1830, 1920)
and in the city of **Shimnilon** (1852, 1953R)

Alma 23:16

▸ the king and those **people which** were converted (𝓞, 𝓟, 1830)
the king and those **who** were converted (1837)

Alma 23:17

▸ they called their **name** Anti-Nephi-Lehies (𝓞, 𝓟, 1830)
they called their **names** Anti-Nephi-Lehies (1852)

Alma 24:1

the **Amelicites** and the Amulonites (𝓞)
the **Amalekites** and the Amulonites (𝓟, 1830)
▸ the **Amlicites** and the Amulonites (conj; Alma 2:11–12)

Alma 24:5

they came forth to the land of **Medeon** (𝓞*)
they came forth to the land of **Midion** (𝓟*)
they came forth to the land of **Midian** (𝓞ᶜ, 𝓟ᶜ, 1830)
▸ they came forth to the land of **Middoni** (conj)

Alma 24:18

and **this** they did / it being in their view a testimony to God (𝓞*, 𝓟*, 1830, 𝓟js2, 1837)
▸ and **thus** they did / it being in their view a testimony to God (𝓞ᶜ, 𝓟js1)

Alma 24:20

▸ for the purpose of **dethroning** the king (𝓞)
for the purpose of **destroying** the king (𝓟, 1830)

Alma 24:24

▸ for they repented of the **thing** which they had done (𝓟)
for they repented of the **things** which they had done (1830)

Alma 24:29
  ▸ or which were **after** the order of Nehor (Ｏ)
    or which were **of** the order of Nehor (𝓟, 1830)

Alma 24:30
  ▸ and thus their **state** becometh worse (𝓟, 1837)
    and thus their **estate** becometh worse (1830)

Alma 26:14
  ▸ and has loosed **these** our brethren from the chains of hell (Ｏ)
    and has loosed our brethren from the chains of hell (𝓟, 1830)

Alma 27:24
  ▸ and we will guard them from their enemies **by** our armies (Ｏ, 𝓟)
    and we will guard them from their enemies **with** our armies (1830)

Alma 27:25
  ▸ into the wilderness **where** they had pitched their tents (𝓟, 1830, 1908R, 1920)
    into the wilderness **whence** they had pitched their tents (1837)

Alma 27:25
  ▸ and Alma also related unto them his **conversion** (𝓟, 1830, 1852*, 1879)
    and Alma also related unto them his **conversation** (1841, 1852ᶜ)
    and Alma also related unto them his **convertion** (1849)

Alma 27:27
  ▸ and they were **numbered** among the people of Nephi (Ｏ)
    and they were among the people of Nephi (𝓟, 1830)

Alma 28:1
  ▸ and a church also established in the land (Ｏ)
    and a church also established in the land **of Jershon** (𝓟, 1830)

Alma 28:2
    and thus a tremendious battle (Ｏ, 𝓟*, 1830)
  ▸ and thus **there was** a tremendious battle (𝓟js, 1837)

Alma 28:5
  ▸ the cry of mourning was heard among **every one** of them (Ｏ, 𝓟, 1830)
    the cry of mourning was heard among **all** of them (1920)

Alma 28:7
  ▸ and thus **ended** the fifteenth year (Ｏ, 𝓟, 1830, 1888, 1906, 1908R)
    and thus **endeth** the fifteenth year (1837)

Alma 28:7
  ▸ of the reign of the judges **over** the people of Nephi (Ｏ, 𝓟, 1830)
    of the reign of the judges **of** the people of Nephi (1874R)

Alma 28:8
  ▸ their journeyings **into** the land of Nephi (𝓟)
    their journeyings **in** the land of Nephi (1830)

Alma 29:2
  ▸ that there might **be no** more sorrow (𝓟, 1908R)
    that there might **not be no** more sorrow (1830)
    that there might **not be** more sorrow (1837)

Alma 29:4
  ▸ **yea decreeth unto them decrees which are unalterable** (Ｏ, 𝓟, 1830, 1908R, 1981)
    NULL (1837)

Alma 29:5
> ► **or** he that knoweth not good from evil is blameless (𝓞, 𝓟, 1830)
> he that knoweth not good from evil is blameless (1920)

Alma 29:8
> the Lord doth counsel in wisdom (𝓟*, 1830, 1953R)
> ► the Lord doth counsel in **his** wisdom (𝓟ᶜ, 1908R)

Alma 29:11
> and **I then** did establish his church (𝓞*)
> and **by then** did establish his church (𝓞ᶜ)
> and **by this** did establish his church (𝓟, 1830)
> ► and **by them** did establish his church (conj)

Alma 30:5
> ► in **the commencement of** the seventeenth year (𝓞, 1981)
> in the seventeenth year (𝓟, 1830)

Alma 30:7
> ► it was strictly contrary to the **commandments** of God (𝓞)
> it was strictly contrary to the **commands** of God (𝓟, 1830)

Alma 30:24
> **there** are in bondage (𝓞*, 𝓟*)
> ► **these** are in bondage (𝓞ᶜ)
> **they** are in bondage (𝓟ᶜ, 1830)

Alma 30:30
> ► yea he went on to **blasphemy** (𝓟)
> yea he went on to **blaspheme** (1830)

Alma 30:31
> for the sake of glutting **by** the labors of the people (𝓞*)
> ► for the sake of glutting **in** the labors of the people (𝓞ᶜ, 𝓟, 1830)
> for the sake of glutting **on** the labors of the people (1920)

Alma 30:35
> believest thou that we deceive this people that causeth such joy in their hearts (𝓞*, 𝓟, 1830)
> ► believest thou that we deceive this people **and** that causeth such joy in their hearts (𝓞ᶜ)

Alma 30:39
> ► **if** ye deny again that there is a God and also deny the Christ (𝓟*, 1830)
> **will** ye deny again that there is a God and also deny the Christ (𝓟js, 1837)

Alma 30:51
> art thou convinced of the power of **gd** (𝓞*)
> ► art thou convinced of the power of **God** (𝓞ᶜ, 1840, 1852)
> art thou convinced of the power of **a God** (𝓟, 1830)

Alma 30:52
> ► and I **always** knew that there was a God (𝓞, 1981)
> and I **also** knew that there was a God (𝓟, 1830)

Alma 31:5
> ► as the preaching of the word **had had** a **greater** tendency (𝓞, 𝓟, 1908R)
> as the preaching of the word **had** a **great** tendency (1830)

Alma 31:8
> ► they **had** the word of God preached unto them (𝓞, 𝓟, 1830)
> they **had had** the word of God preached unto them (1920)

Alma 31:13
- ► a place **of** standing (𝒪, 𝒫, 1830)
  a place **for** standing (1837)

Alma 31:22
- ► and that he **had not led** them away (𝒪)
  and that he **did not lead** them away (𝒫, 1830)

Alma 31:23
- ► now **when** the people had all offered up thanks (𝒪)
  now **after** the people had all offered up thanks (𝒫, 1830)

Alma 31:23
- ► the people had all offered up thanks after **their** manner (𝒫)
  the people had all offered up thanks after **this** manner (1830)

Alma 31:30
- ► that such wickedness and **infidelity** shall be among this people (𝒪, 1981)
  that such wickedness and **iniquity** shall be among this people (𝒫, 1830)

Alma 31:35
- ► and many of them are our **near** brethren (𝒪, 𝒫, 1830, 1908R)
  and many of them are our brethren (1837)

Alma 32:2
  they began to have success among the **poorer** class of people (𝒪*)
- ► they began to have success among the **poorer** class of **the** people (𝒪ᶜ)
  they began to have success among the **poor** class of people (𝒫, 1830)

Alma 32:5
- ► the one which was the **most** foremost among them (𝒪, 𝒫, 1830)
  the one which was the foremost among them (1920, 1953R)

Alma 32:5
- ► they have cast us out because of **this** our exceeding poverty (𝒪, 𝒫, 1830)
  they have cast us out because of our exceeding poverty (1837)

Alma 32:25
  let **them** be in whatsoever circumstances **he** might (𝒫)
  let **them** be in whatsoever circumstances **they** might (1830)
- ► let **him** be in whatsoever circumstances **he** might (conj)

Alma 32:30
- ► and now behold will not this strengthen your faith
  yea it will strengthen your faith
  for ye will say / I know that this is a good seed
  for behold it sprouteth and beginneth to grow (𝒪, 𝒫, 1908R, 1981)
  NULL (1830)

Alma 32:40
- ► and thus **it is** // if ye will not nourish the word (𝒪, 𝒫, 1908R)
  and thus if ye will not nourish the word (1830)

Alma 33:2
- ► if ye suppose that ye cannot worship **your** God (𝒪, 𝒫)
  if ye suppose that ye cannot worship God (1830)

Alma 33:15
  but **Zenock** also spake of these things (𝒪*, 𝒫, 1830; 1 Nephi 19:10)
- ► but **Zenoch** also spake of these things (𝒪ᶜ)

Alma 33:16
> ► because they will not understand **of** thy mercies (◯, 𝒫, 1830)
> because they will not understand thy mercies (1920)

Alma 33:21
> ► that ye might **behold** / would ye not behold quickly (◯)
> that ye might **be healed** / would ye not behold quickly (𝒫, 1830)

Alma 34:6
> ► and ye also **behold** that my brother hath proven unto you (◯)
> and ye also **beheld** that my brother hath proven unto you (𝒫, 1830)

Alma 34:9
> ► according to the great **plans** of the Eternal God (◯)
> according to the great **plan** of the Eternal God (𝒫, 1830)

Alma 34:12
> there **can** nothing . . . which will suffice (◯, 𝒫ᶜ, 1830)
> there **is** nothing . . . which will suffice (𝒫*)
> ► there **can be** nothing . . . which will suffice (𝒫js, 1837)

Alma 34:28
> ► and now behold my brethren (◯, 𝒫, 1908R)
> and now behold my **beloved** brethren (1830)

Alma 36:9
> ► if thou wilt of thyself be destroyed (◯, 𝒫, 1830, 1852ᶜ)
> if thou wilt **not** of thyself be destroyed (1852*, 1953R)

Alma 36:11
> ► if thou wilt be destroyed of thyself (◯, 𝒫, 1830, 1852ᶜ)
> if thou wilt **not** be destroyed of thyself (1852*, 1953R)

Alma 36:27
> ► God hath delivered me from **prisons** (◯, 𝒫)
> God hath delivered me from **prison** (1830)

Alma 37:10
> ► which are now hardening their hearts in **sins** and iniquities (𝒫, 1858w)
> which are now hardening their hearts in **sin** and iniquities (1830)

Alma 37:13
> ► but if ye keep not **his** commandments / ye shall be cut off from **his** presence (◯, 𝒫, 1830)
> but if ye keep not **my** commandments / ye shall be cut off from **my** presence (1953R)

Alma 37:18
> ► that he would **preserve** these things for a wise purpose in him (◯, 1981)
> that he would **reserve** these things for a wise purpose in him (𝒫, 1830)

Alma 37:21
> ► yea and that ye preserve these **directors** (𝒫, 1830)
> yea and that ye preserve these **interpreters** (1920)

Alma 37:24
> ► these **directors** were prepared that the word of God might be fulfilled (◯, 𝒫, 1830)
> these **interpreters** were prepared that the word of God might be fulfilled (1920)

Alma 37:27
> ► all their signs and their wonders ye shall **retain** from this people (◯, 𝒫, 1830)
> all their signs and their wonders ye shall **keep** from this people (1920)

Alma 37:36
> ► let **all** thy thoughts be directed unto the Lord (𝒪, 1981)
> let thy thoughts be directed unto the Lord (𝒫, 1830)

Alma 37:37
> ► counsel the Lord in all thy doings (𝒪, 𝒫, 1830)
> counsel **with** the Lord in all thy doings (1920)

Alma 37:37
> ► and if ye **always** do these things / ye shall be lifted up at the last day (𝒪, 𝒫)
> and if ye do these things / ye shall be lifted up at the last day (1830)

Alma 37:45
> ► for just **assuredly as** this director did bring our fathers (𝒫, 1830)
> for just **as surely as** this director did bring our fathers (1840, 1852)

Alma 38:1
> ► ye shall be **cut** off from his presence (𝒪, 𝒫, 1981)
> ye shall be **cast** off from his presence (1830)

Alma 38:4
> ► for I **knew** that thou wast in bonds (𝒪, 𝒫, 1830, 1908R)
> for I **know** that thou wast in bonds (1840, 1841)

Alma 38:4
> ► and I also **knew** that thou wast stoned for the word's sake (𝒪, 𝒫, 1830)
> and I also **know** that thou wast stoned for the word's sake (1920)

Alma 38:5
> ► even so much ye shall be delivered (𝒪, 𝒫, 1830)
> even so much **as** ye shall be delivered (1953R)

Alma 39:10
> ► take it upon you to counsel your elder brothers in your undertakings (𝒪, 𝒫, 1830)
> take it upon you to counsel **with** your elder brothers in your undertakings (1920)

Alma 39:13
> ► acknowledge your faults and **repair** that wrong which ye have done (𝒪)
> acknowledge your faults and **retain** that wrong which ye have done (𝒫, 1830)
> acknowledge your faults and that wrong which ye have done (1920)

Alma 40:5
> ► there is a time appointed **when** all shall rise from the dead (𝒪)
> there is a time appointed **that** all shall rise from the dead (𝒫, 1830)

Alma 40:13
> ► they **chose** evil works rather than good (𝒪, 𝒫, 1830, 1852)
> they **choose** evil works rather than good (1837)

Alma 40:14
> ► fearful looking for **of** the fiery indignation of the wrath of God (𝒪, 𝒫, 1830; ~Hebrews 10:27)
> fearful looking for the fiery indignation of the wrath of God (1841)

Alma 40:23
> ► even a hair of **their heads** shall not be lost (𝒪, 𝒫)
> even a hair of **the head** shall not be lost (1830)

Alma 40:26
> and they drink the **drugs** of a bitter cup (𝒪, 𝒫)
> ► and they drink the **dregs** of a bitter cup (1830)

Alma 41:1
> some have **arrested** the scriptures (ᴏ, ᴘ*, 1830)
> ► some have **wrested** the scriptures (ᴘjs, 1837)

Alma 41:5
> ► the one **restored** to happiness (ᴏ)
> the one **raised** to happiness (ᴘ, 1830)

Alma 42:2
> ► he **drove** out the man (ᴏ; Genesis 3:24)
> he **drew** out the man (ᴘ, 1830)

Alma 42:7
> ► and now **we** see by this that our first parents were cut off (ᴏ, ᴘ, 1830)
> and now **ye** see by this that our first parents were cut off (1911)

Alma 42:10
> ► it became a **preparatory** state (ᴏ, 1830)
> it became a **probationary** state (ᴘ)

Alma 42:16
> ɴᴀ a punishment which also was **as** eternal as the life of the soul should be affixed (ᴏ, ᴘ*)
> ► a punishment which also was **as** eternal as **the life of the soul** / **should be affixed** (ᴘjg)
> a punishment which also was **as** eternal as **the life of the soul should be** / **affixed** (1830)
> a punishment which also was eternal as **the life of the soul should be** / **affixed** (1841)

Alma 42:22
> ► there is a law given and a punishment affixed and repentance granted (ᴏ, ᴘ, 1830)
> there is a law given and a punishment affixed and **a** repentance granted (1841)

Alma 42:23
> ► and the resurrection of the dead **bringeth** back men (ᴏ, 1830)
> and the resurrection of the dead **bringing** back men (ᴘ)

Alma 43:6
> and they were all **the** Amlicites and **the** Zoramites (ᴏ, ᴘ, 1830, 1908ʀ)
> and they were all **the** Amlicites and Zoramites (1849, 1858w)
> and they were all Amlicites and Zoramites (1920)
> ► and they were all **of the** Amlicites and **the** Zoramites (conj)

Alma 43:14
> now those **desenters** were as numerous nearly as were the Nephites (ᴏ)
> now those **descendants** were as numerous nearly as were the Nephites (ᴘ, 1830)
> ► now those **dissenters** were as numerous nearly as were the Nephites (conj)

Alma 43:17
> ► when he was appointed chief **commander** over the armies of the Nephites (ᴏ, 1830)
> when he was appointed chief **captain** over the armies of the Nephites (ᴘ, 1837)

Alma 43:23
> ► **desiring him** that he should inquire of the Lord (ᴏ, 1830)
> that he should inquire of the Lord (ᴘ)

Alma 43:23
> ► inquire of the Lord **whither** the armies of the Nephites should go (ᴘ, 1830, 1908ʀ)
> inquire of the Lord **whether** the armies of the Nephites should go (1840)

Alma 43:24
> ► and Alma informed the **messengers** of Moroni (ᴘ, 1830)
> and Alma informed the **messenger** of Moroni (1874ʀ)

Alma 43:25
> ► now Moroni . . . took the **remainder** part of his army (𝔓, 1830)
> now Moroni . . . took the **remaining** part of his army (1920)

Alma 43:38
> ► now and then a man fell among the Nephites by their **wounds** (𝔒)
> now and then a man fell among the Nephites by their **swords** (𝔓, 1830)

Alma 43:41
> ► Moroni and his army met **the army of** the Lamanites (𝔒)
> Moroni and his army met the Lamanites (𝔓, 1830)

Alma 43:43
> ► never had the Lamanites been known to **have fought** with such . . . strength (𝔒, 𝔓*, 1830)
> never had the Lamanites been known to **fight** with such . . . strength (𝔓js, 1837)

Alma 43:45
> they were fighting . . . for their **rites** of worship and their church (𝔒, 𝔓, 1830)
> ► they were fighting . . . for their **rights** of worship and their church (conj)

Alma 44:5
> by our religion and by our **rites** of worship and by our church (𝔒, 𝔓, 1830)
> ► by our religion and by our **rights** of worship and by our church (conj)

Alma 44:8
> ► and we will not suffer ourselves to **take** an oath unto you (𝔓, 1830)
> and we will not suffer ourselves to **make** an oath unto you (conj)

Alma 44:11
> ► now I cannot **retain** the words which I have spoken (𝔒, 𝔓, 1830)
> now I cannot **recall** the words which I have spoken (1920)

Alma 44:11
> or ye shall submit to the conditions **to** which I have proposed (𝔒, 𝔓, 1830)
> ► or ye shall submit to the conditions which I have proposed (1920)

Alma 44:13
> **saying** unto them with a loud voice **saying** (𝔒, 𝔓*, 1830)
> **saying** unto them with a loud voice (𝔓js, 1837)
> ► **crying** unto them with a loud voice **saying** (conj)

Alma 44:19
> ► that they never would come to war **again** against them (𝔒, 𝔓, 1830)
> that they never would come to war against them (1892R)

Alma 45:19
> ► but behold the **scripture** saith the Lord took Moses unto himself (𝔓, 1830)
> but behold the **scriptures** saith the Lord took Moses unto himself (1879)

Alma 46:7
> because of their **delivery** by the **hands** of the Lord (𝔓)
> because of their **deliverance** by the **hands** of the Lord (1830)
> ► because of their **deliverance** by the **hand** of the Lord (1920)

Alma 46:10
> ► he was a man of cunning **devices** (𝔒, 𝔓, 1830)
> he was a man of cunning **device** (1841)

Alma 46:13
> ► so long as there should a band of Christians remain (𝔒, 𝔓, 1830)
> so long as there should **be** a band of Christians remain (1953R)

Alma 46:17

    ▸ he **gave** all the land which was south . . . a chosen land (𝒪, 𝒫, 1830)

    he **named** all the land which was south . . . a chosen land (1920)

Alma 46:19

    ▸ waving the rent of his garment in the air (𝒫, 1830)

    waving the rent **part** of his garment in the air (1906, 1905ᶜ [1907], 1907)

Alma 46:19

    ▸ the writing which he had wrote upon the rent (𝒫, 1830)

    the writing which he had wrote upon the rent **part** (1906, 1905ᶜ [1907], 1907)

Alma 46:23

    ▸ and we be cast into **prisons** (𝒪)

    and we be cast into **prison** (𝒫, 1830)

Alma 46:27

    the remnant of the seed of Joseph . . . are those which have **deserted** from us (𝒫*)

    the remnant of the seed of Joseph . . . are those which have **desented** from us (𝒫ᶜ)

    ▸ the remnant of the seed of Joseph . . . are those which have **dissented** from us (1830)

Alma 46:27

    ▸ it shall be **us** if we do not stand fast (𝒪, 𝒫, 1830)

    it shall be **ourselves** if we do not stand fast (1920)

Alma 46:30

    ▸ and cause them to come **down** to battle against them (𝒪)

    and cause them to come to battle against them (𝒫, 1830)

Alma 46:31

    ▸ he took his army and marched out **with his tents** into the wilderness (𝒪, 1981)

    he took his army and marched out into the wilderness (𝒫, 1830)

Alma 46:34

    ▸ he had power **to do** according to his will with the armies of the Nephites (𝒪)

    he had power according to his will with the armies of the Nephites (𝒫, 1830)

Alma 46:40

    ▸ to remove the cause of diseases **which was subsequent to man** (𝒪, 𝒫*, 1830)

    to remove the cause of diseases **which was subject** (𝒫js)

    to remove the cause of diseases **to which men was subject** (1837)

    to remove the cause of diseases **to which men were subject** (1840, 1849)

    to remove the cause of diseases **to which man was subject** (1908ʀ)

Alma 47:1

    and those which **were** with him into the wilderness (𝒪*)

    ▸ and those which **fled** with him into the wilderness (𝒪ᶜ)

    and those which **had fled** with him into the wilderness (𝒫, 1830)

Alma 47:1

    he had took those which **went** with him and went up (𝒪*, 𝒫, 1830)

    ▸ he had took those which **were** with him and went up (𝒪ᶜ)

Alma 47:1

    ▸ and went up **into** the land of Nephi (𝒫, 1830, 1908ʀ)

    and went up **in** the land of Nephi (1837)

Alma 47:2

    ▸ they would not . . . obey the **commandment** of the king (𝒪, 𝒫)

    they would not . . . obey the **commandments** of the king (1830)

Alma 47:5
> ▸ he went forward to the place which was called **Oneidah** (𝇋, 𝒫)
> he went forward to the place which was called **Onidah** (1830)

Alma 47:13
> ▸ if he would make him Amalickiah **the** second leader over the whole army (𝇋)
> if he would make him Amalickiah **a** second leader over the whole army (𝒫, 1830)

Alma 47:22
> and they went **up** and bowed themselves before the king (𝇋*)
> ▸ and they went **forth** and bowed themselves before the king (𝇋ᶜ)
> and they went and bowed themselves before the king (𝒫, 1830)

Alma 47:28
> **when** all they who loved the king / when they heard these words / came forth (𝒫, 1830)
> ▸ all they who loved the king / when they heard these words / came forth (1920)

Alma 47:29
> ▸ they were **frightened** again (𝇋, 𝒫, 1830, 1892R, 1920)
> they were **frighted** again (1837)

Alma 47:29
> ▸ and came over **into** the land of Zarahemla (𝒫, 1830, 1920)
> and came over **in** the land of Zarahemla (1837)

Alma 47:34
> ▸ and **also** they which were with him (𝇋, 𝒫, 1830)
> and **all** they which were with him (1837)

Alma 48:8
> ▸ throwing up banks of earth round about to **encircle** his armies (𝇋)
> throwing up banks of earth round about to **enclose** his armies (𝒫, 1830)

Alma 48:19
> ▸ Helaman and his brethren were **not** less serviceable (𝇋)
> Helaman and his brethren were **no** less serviceable (𝒫, 1830)

Alma 48:21
> ▸ in the latter end of the nineteenth **year** / notwithstanding their peace (𝇋)
> in the latter end of the nineteenth / **yea** notwithstanding their peace (𝒫, 1830)
> in the latter end of the nineteenth **year** / **yea** notwithstanding their peace (1849)

Alma 49:5
> the wisdom of the Nephites in **prepairing** their places of security (𝇋*, 𝒫)
> ▸ the wisdom of the Nephites in **repairing** their places of security (𝇋ᶜ)
> the wisdom of the Nephites in **preparing** their places of security (1830)

Alma 49:8
> ▸ which never had been known among **all** the children of Lehi (𝇋, 𝒫, 1830, 1908R)
> which never had been known among the children of Lehi (1837)

Alma 49:28
> ▸ because of his **miraculous** power (𝇋)
> because of his **matchless** power (𝒫, 1830)

Alma 50:1
> ▸ or to defend **themselves** (𝇋, 𝒫*, 1830)
> or to defend **his people** (𝒫js, 1837)

Alma 50:18

- ► they did multiply and **wax** strong in the land (𝒪, 𝒫, 1908R, 1981)
  they did multiply and **were** strong in the land (1830)

Alma 50:25

- ► and the land of **Morionton** (𝒪)
  and the land of **Morianton** (𝒫, 1830)

Alma 50:26

- ► the people of Morionton took **up** arms against their brethren (𝒫, 1830, 1908R)
  the people of Morionton took arms against their brethren (1840)

Alma 50:40

- ► his name was **Parhoron** (𝒪)
  his name was **Pahoran** (𝒫, 1830)

Alma 51:7

- ► among the brethren of Parhoron and also **among the people** of liberty (𝒪)
  among the brethren of Parhoron and also **many** of liberty (𝒫*)
  among the brethren of Parhoron and also **many the people** of liberty (𝒫ᶜ)
  among the brethren of Parhoron and also **many of the people** of liberty (𝒫jg, 1830)

Alma 51:10

- ► we shall see that **this** promise which he made was rash (𝒪)
  we shall see that **his** promise which he made was rash (𝒫, 1830)

Alma 51:15

  he sent a petition . . . desiring that he should **head** it (𝒪, 𝒫ᶜ)
- ► he sent a petition . . . desiring that he should **heed** it (𝒫*)
  he sent a petition . . . desiring that he should **read** it (𝒫jg, 1830)

Alma 51:26

  taking possession of many cities / the city of **Nephihah** (𝒪, 𝒫, 1830)
- ► taking possession of many cities / the city of **Moroni** (conj)

Alma 51:29

- ► who had slain Morionton and had headed **his** people in his flight (𝒪, 𝒫, 1830, 1908R)
  who had slain Morionton and had headed **the** people in his flight (1840)

Alma 51:30

- ► **as** he was marching forth with his numerous army (𝒪, 𝒫, 1830, 1908R, 1920)
  and he was marching forth with his numerous army (1837)

Alma 51:37

- ► and thus **ended** the twenty and fifth year (𝒪, 𝒫, 1830)
  and thus **endeth** the twenty and fifth year (1849)

Alma 51:37

- ► and thus **ended** the days of Amalickiah (𝒪, 𝒫, 1830)
  and thus **endeth** the days of Amalickiah (1849)

Alma 52:22

- ► Moroni and his army by night marched **into** the wilderness (𝒪, 𝒫, 1830, 1908R)
  Moroni and his army by night marched **in** the wilderness (1837)

Alma 52:23

- ► he began **a** retreat down by the seashore (𝒪)
  he began **to** retreat down by the seashore (𝒫, 1830)

Alma 52:36
> ▶ the remainder of them . . . knew not **whither** to go or to strike (Ⓞ, 1841, 1981)
> the remainder of them . . . knew not **where** to go or to strike (𝓟*)
> the remainder of them . . . knew not **whether** to go or to strike (𝓟ᶜ, 1830, 1879)

Alma 53:3
> ▶ that they should commence **in** laboring / in digging a ditch (𝓟*, 1830)
> that they should commence laboring in digging a ditch (𝓟js, 1837)

Alma 53:6
> one of the strongest holds of the Lamanites in the land of **Nephi** (Ⓞ, 𝓟, 1830)
> ▶ one of the strongest holds of the Lamanites in the land of **the Nephites** (conj)

Alma 53:10
> ▶ by the power and **word** of God they had been converted (Ⓞ, 𝓟, 1830)
> by the power and **work** of God they had been converted (1953R)

Alma 54:1
> ▶ in **the commencement of** the twenty and ninth year (Ⓞ, 1981)
> in the twenty and ninth year (𝓟, 1830)

Alma 54:6
> ▶ I would tell you **something** concerning the justice of God (Ⓞ, 𝓟, 1830)
> I would tell you **somewhat** concerning the justice of God (1849)

Alma 54:8
> ▶ as ye have **once** rejected these things (Ⓞ, 𝓟, 1908R, 1981)
> as ye have rejected these things (1830)

Alma 54:10
> ▶ for we will **retain** our cities and our lands (Ⓞ, 𝓟ᶜ, 1830)
> for we will **retake** our cities and our lands (𝓟*)

Alma 54:13
> ▶ and we have only sought to defend **our lives** (Ⓞ)
> and we have only sought to defend **ourselves** (𝓟, 1830)

Alma 54:13
> ▶ we will seek our **lands** / **the lands** of our first inheritance (Ⓞ)
> we will seek our **land** / **the lands** of our first inheritance (𝓟, 1830, 1908R)
> we will seek our **land** of our first inheritance (1837)
> we will seek our **land** / **the land** of our first inheritance (1920)

Alma 54:17
> ▶ when it **rightfully** belonged unto them (Ⓞ)
> when it **rightly** belonged unto them (𝓟, 1830)

Alma 54:24
> ▶ and behold I am **now** a bold Lamanite (Ⓞ)
> and behold **now** I am a bold Lamanite (𝓟, 1830)

Alma 55:7
> Moroni **caused that** Laman and a small number of men **which was appointed to** go with him (Ⓞ, 𝓟, 1830)
> Moroni **appointed** Laman and **caused that** a small number of men **should** go with him (1837)
> ▶ Moroni **caused that** Laman and a small number of men **which was appointed to** go with him **should go to the city of Gid** (conj)

Alma 55:16
> ▸ and he **went** to the city Gid (𝒪, 𝒫, 1830, 1981)
> and he **sent** to the city Gid (1837)

Alma 55:21
> ▸ he caused **his** men which were with him to withdraw a pace from them (𝒪, 𝒫)
> he caused **the** men which were with him to withdraw a pace from them (1830)

Alma 55:31
> yea they would not **partake** of their wine (𝒫, 1830)
> ▸ yea they would not **take** of their wine (conj)

Alma 55:31
> ▸ **yea they would not take of wine** (𝒪, 𝒫, 1830)
> NULL (1837)
> **yea they would not partake of wine** (1908R)

Alma 56:5
> ▸ therefore it **sufficeth** me (𝒪, 1840, 1852ᶜ)
> therefore it **supposeth** me (𝒫, 1830, 1908R)

Alma 56:10
> because **of the numerority of** their forces / **having** slain a vast number (𝒪, 𝒫, 1830)
> because their forces **had** slain a vast number (1837)
> ▸ because **of the enormity of** their forces / **having** slain a vast number (conj)

Alma 56:19
> ▸ but thus were we **favored** (𝒪)
> but thus were we **preserved** (𝒫, 1830)

Alma 56:37
> and as we **suppose that** it was their intent to slay us (𝒪, 𝒫)
> and as we **supposed** it was their intent to slay us (1830)
> and as we **suppose** it was their intent to slay us (1849, 1858w)
> ▸ and as we **supposed that** it was their intent to slay us (conj)

Alma 56:48
> ▸ our mothers knew (𝒪, 𝒫, 1908R)
> our mothers knew **it** (1830)

Alma 57:6
> ▸ we had also **a** plenty of provisions brought unto us (𝒪, 𝒫, 1830)
> we had also plenty of provisions brought unto us (1981)

Alma 57:12
> ▸ they yielded up the city **into** our hands (𝒪, 𝒫, 1830)
> they yielded up the city **unto** our hands (1920)

Alma 57:13
> ▸ notwithstanding the **enormity** of our **number** (𝒪)
> notwithstanding the **enumerority** of our **numbers** (𝒫*)
> notwithstanding the **enormity** of our **numbers** (𝒫ᶜ, 1830)

Alma 57:25
> ▸ to our great astonishment and also the **joy** of our whole army (𝒪, 𝒫, 1908R, 1981)
> to our great astonishment and also the **foes** of our whole army (1830)

Alma 58:2
> ▸ and they were so **exceeding** more numerous (𝒪, 𝒫, 1830)
> and they were so **much** more numerous (1837)

Alma 58:3
> ▸ those parts of the land of the which we had **retained** of our possessions (O, P, 1830)
> those parts of the land of the which we had **regained** of our possessions (1920)

Alma 58:4
> ▸ I thus did send an embassy to the **great** governor of our land (O)
> I thus did send an embassy to the governor of our land (P, 1830)

Alma 58:8
> ▸ which was guarded to us **with** an army of two thousand men (O)
> which was guarded to us **by** an army of two thousand men (P, 1830)

Alma 58:33
> but behold we trust **that** our God who hath given us victory (O, P, 1830)
> but behold we trust **in** our God who hath given us victory (1920)
> ▸ but behold we trust **that it is** our God who hath given us victory (conj)

Alma 58:36
> there is some **fraction** in the government (O)
> there is some **fartion** in the government (P*)
> there is some **farction** in the government (Pᶜ)
> ▸ there is some **faction** in the government (1830)

Alma 58:41
> ▸ **that** the Lord our God . . . **may** keep you continually (O, P, 1830)
> **may** the Lord our God . . . keep you continually (1920)

Alma 58:41
> ▸ yea and **that** he **may** favor this people (O, P, 1830)
> yea and **may** he favor this people (1920)

Alma 59:3
> ▸ which he had been so miraculously prospered in **retaining** (P, 1830)
> which he had been so miraculously prospered in **regaining** (1920)

Alma 59:8
> and they came **even** and joined the army of Moroni (O, P, 1830)
> ▸ and they came **over** and joined the army of Moroni (conj)

Alma 59:9
> ▸ it was easier to keep the city from falling into the hands of the Lamanites (O*, P*)
> it was easier to keep the city from falling into the hands of the Lamanites
> **than to retake it from them** (Oᶜ, Pᶜ, 1830)

Alma 60:12
> because of their wickedness (O, P, 1830, 1908R)
> ▸ **it is** because of their wickedness (1840, 1852ᶜ)

Alma 60:24
> those parts of our country which he hath **obtained** (P*)
> ▸ those parts of our country which he hath **retained** (Pᶜ, 1830)
> those parts of our country which he hath **regained** (1920)

Alma 60:30
> ▸ behold I come unto you / even **into** the land of Zarahemla (P, 1830, 1908R)
> behold I come unto you / even **in** the land of Zarahemla (1837)

Alma 61:8
> **in the which** maintenance he supposeth will enable the Lamanites to conquer (P, 1830)
> ▸ **which** maintenance he supposeth will enable the Lamanites to conquer (1837)

Alma 61:19

▸ I do joy in receiving your epistle (𝓟, 1830, 1908R)

I do **not** joy in receiving your epistle (1874R)

Alma 62:22

▸ and come **up** upon the top of the wall (𝓟)

and come upon the top of the wall (1830)

Alma 62:25

and slew many and surrounded many others (𝓟, 1830)

▸ and **they** slew many and surrounded many others (conj)

Alma 62:30

▸ and having **retained** many of the Nephites which had been taken prisoners (𝓟, 1830)

and having **regained** many of the Nephites which had been taken prisoners (1920)

Alma 62:36

the king did awake his **servant** before he died / insomuch that **they** did pursue Teancum (𝓟, 1830, 1908R)

the king did awake his **servant** before he died / insomuch that **he** did pursue Teancum (1840)

▸ the king did awake his **servants** before he died / insomuch that **they** did pursue Teancum (1981)

Alma 63:8

▸ and we suppose that they **are** drowned **up** in the depths of the sea (𝓞)

and we suppose that they **were** drowned **up** in the depths of the sea (𝓟, 1830)

and we suppose that they **were** drowned in the depths of the sea (1920)

Helaman 1:5

▸ Parhoron was appointed . . . to be **a** chief judge (𝓞, 𝓟, 1830)

Parhoron was appointed . . . to be chief judge (1837)

Helaman 1:9

▸ they sent forth one **Kishcumen** (𝓞)

they sent forth one **Kishkumen** (𝓟, 1830)

Helaman 1:29

and thus he did **and he did** head them (𝓟, 1830)

▸ and thus he did head them (conj)

Helaman 1:32

▸ and the Lamanites did yield themselves **up** into the hands of the Nephites (𝓞)

and the Lamanites did yield themselves into the hands of the Nephites (𝓟, 1830)

Helaman 2:6

▸ those plans which had been laid by **this** band (𝓞, 𝓟, 1830)

those plans which had been laid by **his** band (1874R)

Helaman 2:11

▸ when **Gaddianton** had found that Kishcumen did not return (𝓞; Helaman 2:4)

when **Gadianton** had found that Kishcumen did not return (𝓟, 1830)

Helaman 3:3

and it came to pass in the forty and sixth **yea** there were much contentions (𝓞, 𝓟*)

and it came to pass in the forty and sixth / **yea** there were much contentions (𝓟jg, 1830)

▸ and it came to pass in the forty and sixth **year** / there were much contentions (conj)

Helaman 3:5

▸ **in whatsoever** parts it had not been rendered desolate (𝓞, 𝓟ᶜ)

into whatsoever parts it had not been rendered desolate (𝓟*)

into whatever parts it had not been rendered desolate (1830)

Helaman 3:23
> ▸ which Gaddianton the **robber** had established (𝓟, 1837)
> which Gaddianton the **nobler** had established (1830)

Helaman 3:29
> ▸ whosoever will lay hold upon the word of God (𝓟, 1830)
> whosoever will **may** lay hold upon the word of God (1920)

Helaman 3:29
> and lead the man of Christ in a **strait** and narrow course (𝓟, 1953R, 1981)
> ▸ and lead the man of Christ in a **straight** and narrow course (1830)

Helaman 4:9
> ▸ yea they **retained** many cities (𝓟, 1830)
> yea they **regained** many cities (1920)

Helaman 4:10
> ▸ they succeeded in **retaining** even the half of all their possessions (𝓟, 1830)
> they succeeded in **regaining** even the half of all their possessions (1906, 1907, 1911)

Helaman 4:12
> and **desenting** away into the land of Nephi among the Lamanites (𝓟)
> and **deserting** away into the land of Nephi among the Lamanites (1830)
> ▸ and **dissenting** away into the land of Nephi among the Lamanites (conj)

Helaman 4:16
> ▸ even until they had **retained** the one half of their property (𝓟, 1830)
> even until they had **regained** the one half of their property (1907, 1911)

Helaman 4:22
> ▸ and **thus seeing** that their laws had become corrupted (𝓟, 1830)
> and **they saw** that their laws had become corrupted (1920)

Helaman 4:25
> ▸ the Lamanites were **more exceeding** numerous than they (𝓟, 1830)
> the Lamanites were **exceedingly more** numerous than they (1920)

Helaman 5:6
> ▸ and when ye remember them (𝓟, 1830)
> and when ye **may** remember them (1840)

Helaman 5:36
> ▸ they did lift their eyes to heaven (𝓟, 1830, 1908R)
> they did lift **up** their eyes to heaven (1840)

Helaman 6:20
> ▸ they did use every means / **whatsoever was** in their power (𝓟, 1830)
> they did use every means in their power (1837)

Helaman 6:21
> ▸ Satan did stir up the hearts of the more **parts** of the Nephites (𝓟, 1830)
> Satan did stir up the hearts of the more **part** of the Nephites (1840, 1920)

Helaman 7:10
> near unto the garden gate **which led by** the highway (𝓟, 1830)
> near unto the garden gate **by which led** the highway (1920)
> ▸ near unto the garden gate **which was by** the highway (conj)

Helaman 7:16
> ▸ how could ye have given **away** to the enticing of him (𝓟, 1830)
> how could ye have given **way** to the enticing of him (1905, 1907)

Helaman 8:11
▸ to smite upon the waters of the Red Sea and they **departed** hither and thither (𝒫)
to smite upon the waters of the Red Sea and they **parted** hither and thither (1830)

Helaman 8:19
even since the days of Abraham there hath been many prophets (𝒫, 1830)
▸ **ever** since the days of Abraham there hath been many prophets (conj)

Helaman 8:20
▸ and also **Ezaias** (𝒫, 1908R)
and also **Ezias** (1830)
and also **Esias** (1906)

Helaman 8:21
▸ will ye dispute that Jerusalem was **not** destroyed (𝒫)
will ye dispute that Jerusalem was destroyed (1830)

Helaman 9:14
▸ we ran and came to the place of the **judgment seat** (𝒫, 1908R, 1981)
we ran and came to the place of the **judgment** (1830)

Helaman 9:36
▸ then shall he say unto you that I Nephi **knew** nothing concerning the matter (𝒫, 1908R)
then shall he say unto you that I Nephi **know** nothing concerning the matter (1830)

Helaman 12:2
ɴᴀ and in all manner of precious things of every kind and art sparing their lives (𝒫)
and in all manner of precious things of **every kind and art / sparing** their lives (1830)
▸ and in all manner of precious things of **every kind / and art sparing** their lives (conj)

Helaman 13:3
▸ whatsoever things should come **into** his heart (𝒫, 1837)
whatsoever things should come **in** his heart (1830)

Helaman 13:18
save **it** be a righteous man and shall hide it up unto the Lord (𝒫)
▸ save **he** be a righteous man and shall hide it up unto the Lord (1830)

Helaman 13:22
▸ in the things which he hath blessed you (𝒫, 1830)
in the things **with** which he hath blessed you (1920)

Helaman 13:25
ye would not have slain the prophets // **ye** would not have stoned them (𝒫, 1830)
▸ **we** would not have slain the prophets // **we** would not have stoned them (1905, 1907, 1953R)

Helaman 14:5
▸ there shall **be** a new star arise (𝒫, 1840)
there shall a new star arise (1830)

Helaman 14:7
▸ ye shall **all** be amazed and wonder (𝒫, 1830, 1908R)
ye shall be amazed and wonder (1840)

Helaman 14:13
that thereby ye may have remission of them through his merits (𝒫)
▸ that thereby ye may have **a** remission of them through his merits (1830)

Helaman 14:16
▸ for all mankind . . . being cut off . . . **are** considered as dead (𝒫, 1830, 1879)
for all mankind . . . being cut off . . . **or** considered as dead (1837)

Helaman 15:8
>   and in the **things** wherewith they have been made free (𝒫, 1908R)
> ► and in the **thing** wherewith they have been made free (1830)

Helaman 15:13
> ► that they shall **again** be brought to the true knowledge (𝒪, 𝒫, 1830, 1908R, 1981)
>   that they shall be brought to the true knowledge (1837)

Helaman 16:3
>   now when they saw that they could not hit him (𝒫, 1908R, 1981)
> ► now when they saw **this** / that they could not hit him (1830)

Helaman 16:6
> ► they cried **out** unto their captains (𝒫, 1830)
>   they cried unto their captains (1852)

Helaman 16:7
> ► and did flee out of their **lands** (𝒪, 1830)
>   and did flee out of their **hands** (𝒫)

Helaman 16:11
> ► and **thus** were the conditions also in the eighty and eighth year (𝒫)
>   and **these** were the conditions also in the eighty and eighth year (1830)

Helaman 16:19
> ► as well as in the land **of** Jerusalem (𝒫, 1830)
>   as well as in the land **at** Jerusalem (1874R)

3 Nephi title
> ► **The** Book of Nephi (𝒫, 1830; 1 Nephi title)
>   **Three Nephi** / **The** Book of Nephi (1879)
>   **Third Nephi** / **The** Book of Nephi (1920)
>   **Third** Book of Nephi (1953R)

3 Nephi 1:15
>   for **he beheld** at the going down of the sun there was no darkness (𝒫)
> ► for **behold** at the going down of the sun there was no darkness (1830)

3 Nephi 1:16
> ► for the **sign** which had been given was already at hand (𝒫, 1830, 1908R, 1981)
>   for the **signal** which had been given was already at hand (1837)

3 Nephi 2:12
> ► and also to maintain their **rights** and the privileges of their church (𝒫*, 1830)
>   and also to maintain their **rites** and the privileges of their church (𝒫ᶜ, 1908R)

3 Nephi 2:18
> ► they did come forth **again** against the people of Nephi (𝒫, 1830, 1908R)
>   they did come forth against the people of Nephi (1837)

3 Nephi 3:11
> ► because of the boldness of Giddianhi **in** demanding the possession of the land (𝒫, 1908R)
>   because of the boldness of Giddianhi demanding the possession of the land (1830)

3 Nephi 3:18
> ► now the chiefest among all the **chief** captains (𝒫, 1908R, 1981)
>   now the chiefest among all the captains (1830)

3 Nephi 3:23
> ► **and the land which was between the land of Zarahemla** (𝒫, 1830, 1908R)
>   NULL (1837)
>   **and the land which was between the land Zarahemla** (1981)

3 Nephi 4:15
    neither did they come in the twentieth year (𝒫, 1908R)
    ► neither did they come **again** in the twentieth year (1830)

3 Nephi 4:16
    to yield themselves according to their wishes (𝒫)
    ► to yield themselves **up** according to their wishes (1830)

3 Nephi 5:1
    ► which did doubt in the least **thing in** the words of all the holy prophets (𝒫*, 1830)
    which did doubt in the least the words of all the holy prophets (𝒫js, 1837)

3 Nephi 5:22
    ► and **inasmuch** as the children of Lehi hath kept his commandments (𝒫)
    and **insomuch** as the children of Lehi hath kept his commandments (1830)

3 Nephi 6:3
    ► to keep the peace of the **land** (𝒫, 1908R, 1981)
    to keep the peace of the **band** (1830)

3 Nephi 6:14
    to keep the **commands** of the Lord (𝒫)
    ► to keep the **commandments** of the Lord (1830)

3 Nephi 6:15
    and to the **buffeting** them up with pride (𝒫)
    ► and to the **puffing** them up with pride (1830)

3 Nephi 6:25
    ► a complaint came **up** unto the land of Zarahemla (𝒫, 1830)
    a complaint came unto the land of Zarahemla (1892R)

3 Nephi 6:25
    ► which had condemned the prophets of the **Lord** (𝒫, 1837)
    which had condemned the prophets of the **land** (1830)

3 Nephi 7:3
    and thus **they** became tribes and leaders of tribes (𝒫, 1830)
    ► and thus **there** became tribes and leaders of tribes (conj)

3 Nephi 7:12
    ► until they were joined by dissenters . . . and they **become** sufficiently strong (𝒫, 1830)
    until they were joined by dissenters . . . and they **became** sufficiently strong (1906)

3 Nephi 8:9
    ► and the inhabitants **thereof** were drowned (𝒫, 1830, 1852ᶜ)
    and the inhabitants **therefore** were drowned (1841)

3 Nephi 8:15
    ► and there were many **in** them which were slain (𝒫, 1830, 1981ᶜ [1983])
    and there were many **of** them which were slain (1981*)

3 Nephi 9:5
    ► the blood of the prophets . . . shall not come **up** any more unto me (𝒫, 1830, 1908R)
    the blood of the prophets . . . shall not come any more unto me (1837)

3 Nephi 9:9
    Jacob-Ugath which was inhabited by the people of **the king of Jacob** (𝒫, 1830)
    Jacob-Ugath which was inhabited by the people of **king Jacob** (1920)
    ► Jacob-Ugath which was inhabited by the people of **the king Jacob** (conj)

3 Nephi 9:21
    behold I have come **unto** the world (𝓟, 1830)
    ► behold I have come **into** the world (conj)

3 Nephi 10:4
    ► **O ye people of the house of Israel** (𝓟, 1830, 1908R)
    NULL (1837)

3 Nephi 11 preface
    ► Jesus Christ **sheweth** himself unto the people of Nephi (𝓟, 1830)
    Jesus Christ **showeth** himself unto the people of Nephi (1888, 1906, 1907, 1911)
    Jesus Christ **did show** himself unto the people of Nephi (1920)

3 Nephi 11:8
    ► and behold they saw a **man** descending out of heaven (𝓟, 1830)
    and behold they saw a **Man** descending out of heaven (1920)

3 Nephi 12:36
    ► neither shalt thou swear by **thy** head (𝓟, 1908R, 1981; Matthew 5:36)
    neither shalt thou swear by **the** head (1830)

3 Nephi 12:42
    and **to** him that would borrow of thee turn thou not away (𝓟, 1830)
    ► and **from** him that would borrow of thee turn thou not away (1920; Matthew 5:42)

3 Nephi 13:10
    ► thy will be done **in** earth (𝓟*, 1830; Matthew 6:10)
    thy will be done **on** earth (𝓟js, 1837)

3 Nephi 14:13
    ► enter ye in at the **strait** gate (𝓟, 1907, 1911, 1953R; Matthew 7:13)
    enter ye in at the **straight** gate (1830)

3 Nephi 14:14
    ► because **strait** is the gate (𝓟, 1907, 1911, 1953R; Matthew 7:14)
    because **straight** is the gate (1830)

3 Nephi 16:10
    ► **and shall reject the fullness of my gospel** (𝓟, 1830, 1908R, 1981)
    NULL (1837)

3 Nephi 16:15
    ► but if they will not **return** unto me (𝓟*)
    but if they will not **turn** unto me (1830, 𝓟js, 1837)

3 Nephi 16:15
    and they shall be as salt that hath lost **its** savor (𝓟*, 𝓟js, 1837)
    ► and they shall be as salt that hath lost **his** savor (𝓟ᶜ, 1830; ~Matthew 5:13)

3 Nephi 16:17
    ► and **when** the words of the prophet Isaiah shall be fulfilled (𝓟, 1830)
    and **then** the words of the prophet Isaiah shall be fulfilled (1920)

3 Nephi 17:5
    ► he cast his eyes round about . . . and **behold** they were in tears (𝓟)
    he cast his eyes round about . . . and **beheld** they were in tears (1830)

3 Nephi 17:21
    and the multitude **bear** record of it (𝓟, 1830)
    ► and the multitude **bare** record of it (1920)

3 Nephi 18:13
> ▸ and the gates of hell is **already** open to receive them (𝒫, 1830, 1908R)
> and the gates of hell is **ready** / open to receive them (1837)

3 Nephi 18:16
> ▸ I have set an example **before** you (𝒫*)
> I have set an example **for** you (1830, 𝒫js, 1837)

3 Nephi 18:34
> ▸ because of the disputations which hath been among you **beforetimes** (𝒫*)
> because of the disputations which hath been among you **beforetime** (1830)
> because of the disputations which hath been among you (𝒫js, 1837)

3 Nephi 18:37
> but the disciples **bear** record that he gave them power (𝒫, 1830)
> ▸ but the disciples **bare** record that he gave them power (1920)

3 Nephi 19:14
> ▸ and the multitude did witness it and **do** bear record (𝒫, 1830)
> and the multitude did witness it and **did** bear record (1920)

3 Nephi 19:22
> thou hast given them the Holy Ghost because they **believed** in me (𝒫)
> ▸ thou hast given them the Holy Ghost because they **believe** in me (1830)

3 Nephi 19:25
> Jesus **beheld** them as they did pray unto him (𝒫, 1908R)
> ▸ Jesus **blessed** them as they did pray unto him (1830)

3 Nephi 19:26
> and Jesus saith unto them : pray on // **nevertheless** they did not cease to pray (𝒫, 1830)
> ▸ and Jesus saith unto them : pray on // **never the less** they did not cease to pray (conj)

3 Nephi 20:2
> that they should arise and stand upon their feet (𝒫*, 1874R)
> ▸ that they should arise and stand **up** upon their feet (𝒫oc, 1830)

3 Nephi 20:2
> ▸ and they arose **up** and stood upon their feet (𝒫, 1830)
> and they arose and stood **up** upon their feet (1906)

3 Nephi 20:45
> for that which had been told them shall they see (𝒫, 1830)
> ▸ for that which had **not** been told them shall they see (1879, 1953R; Isaiah 52:15)

3 Nephi 21:9
> and there shall be among **them which** will not believe it (𝒫*, 1830)
> and there shall be among **them who** will not believe it (𝒫js, 1849, 1908R)
> and there shall be among **who** will not believe it (1837)
> and there shall be among **them those who** will not believe it (1840, 1920)
> ▸ and there shall be **many** among **them which** will not believe it (conj)

3 Nephi 21:16
> ▸ and I will cut off witchcrafts out of thy **hand** (𝒫, 1830, 1908R; Micah 5:12)
> and I will cut off witchcrafts out of thy **land** (1840, 1920)

3 Nephi 22:4
> ▸ for thou shalt forget the shame of thy youth and shalt not remember the reproach
> of thy widowhood any more (𝒫, 1830, 1908R; Isaiah 54:4)
> for thou shalt forget the shame of thy youth and **shalt not remember the reproach
> of thy youth** and shalt not remember the reproach of thy widowhood any more (1837)

3 Nephi 22:10
> ► neither shall the covenant of my **peace** be removed (𝓟, 1908R, 1981; Isaiah 54:10)
> neither shall the covenant of my **people** be removed (1830)

3 Nephi 22:17
> and every tongue that shall **revile** against thee in judgment (𝓟, 1908R, 1981)
> ► and every tongue that shall **rise** against thee in judgment (1830; Isaiah 54:17)

3 Nephi 24:7
> ► but ye **said** / wherein shall we return (𝓟, 1830; Malachi 3:7)
> but ye **say** / wherein shall we return (1920)

3 Nephi 25:2
> the **Son** of righteousness (𝓟, 1830)
> ► the **Sun** of righteousness (conj; Malachi 4:2)

3 Nephi 25:2
> ► with **healing** in his wings (𝓟, 1837, 1908R; Malachi 4:2)
> with **healings** in his wings (1830, 1892R)

3 Nephi 25:2
> ► as calves **of** the stall (𝓟, 1908R; Malachi 4:2)
> as calves **in** the stall (1830)

3 Nephi 27:24
> write the **words** of this people (𝓟*, 1888)
> ► write the **works** of this people (𝓟oc, 1830)

3 Nephi 27:33
> ► enter ye in at the **strait** gate (𝓟, 1906, 1907, 1911, 1953R; Matthew 7:13)
> enter ye in at the **straight** gate (1830)

3 Nephi 27:33
> ► for **strait** is the gate and narrow is the way (𝓟, 1906, 1907, 1911, 1953R; Matthew 7:14)
> for **straight** is the gate and narrow is the way (1830)

3 Nephi 28:2
> ► and they all spake save it were three **saying** (𝓟, 1830, 1908R, 1920)
> and they all spake save it were three (1837)

3 Nephi 28:3
> ► blessed are ye because ye **desire** this thing of me (𝓟, 1908R)
> blessed are ye because ye **desired** this thing of me (1830)

3 Nephi 28:36
> ► concerning them whom the Lord **had** chosen (𝓟, 1830)
> concerning them whom the Lord **hath** chosen (1905, 1907)

3 Nephi 28:36
> I knew not whether they were **cleansed** from mortality to immortality (𝓟, 1830)
> ► I knew not whether they were **changed** from mortality to immortality (conj)

3 Nephi 29:2
> ► the words of the Lord . . . shall **all** be fulfilled (𝓟, 1830, 1908R)
> the words of the Lord . . . shall be fulfilled (1840)

4 Nephi title
> ► **The** Book of Nephi (𝓟, 1830; 1 Nephi title)
> **Four Nephi** / **The** Book of Nephi (1879)
> **Fourth Nephi** / **The** Book of Nephi (1920)
> **Fourth** Book of Nephi (1953R)

4 Nephi 1:3
> ► therefore **there** were not rich and poor (𝒫, 1830, 1920)
> therefore **they** were not rich and poor (1841, 1953R)

4 Nephi 1:7
> ► they did **build** cities again (𝒫, 1908R, 1920)
> they did **fill** cities again (1830)

4 Nephi 1:27
> yea there were churches which professed to know the Christ (𝒫, 1830)
> yea there were **many** churches which professed to know the Christ (1837)

4 Nephi 1:27
> and yet they did deny the more **part** of his gospel (𝒫, 1908R)
> ► and yet they did deny the more **parts** of his gospel (1830)

4 Nephi 1:43
> ► and **became** vain like unto their brethren (𝒫, 1892R)
> and **become** vain like unto their brethren (1830)

Mormon 2:4
> ► we did come to the city of **Angolah** (𝒫)
> we did come to the city of **Angelah** (1830)
> we did come to the city of **Angola** (1837)

Mormon 2:12
> ► and their **sorrowing** before the Lord (𝒫, 1830, 1908R)
> and their **sorrow** before the Lord (1837)

Mormon 2:15
> the day of grace was **passed** with them (𝒫, 1849)
> ► the day of grace was **past** with them (1830)

Mormon 4:14
> ► and did take many prisoners **of women and of children** (𝒫, 1830)
> and did take many prisoners **both women and children** (1837)

Mormon 5:2
> ► but behold I was without **hopes** (𝒫, 1830, 1908R)
> but behold I was without **hope** (1840, 1920)

Mormon 6:2
> the land of **Camorah** (𝒫*, 1830)
> ► the land of **Cumorah** (𝒫oc, 1837)

Mormon 6:14
> and **Jeneum** had fallen with his ten thousand (𝒫*, 1908R, 1981)
> ► and **Joneum** had fallen with his ten thousand (𝒫ᶜ)
> and **Joneam** had fallen with his ten thousand (1830)

Mormon 6:14
> ► and **Cumenihah** ... had fallen (𝒫, 1908R, 1981)
> and **Camenihah** ... had fallen (1830)

Mormon 6:15
> and a few which had **deserted** over unto the Lamanites (𝒫, 1908R, 1981)
> ► and a few which had **dissented** over unto the Lamanites (1830)

Mormon 8:6
  behold four hundred years have passed (𝓟, 1908R)
  ▶ behold four hundred years have passed **away** (1830)

Mormon 8:10
  ▶ and **whither** they be upon the face of the land no man knoweth (𝓟)
  and **whether** they be upon the face of the land no man knoweth (1830)

Mormon 8:15
  ▶ for God **will** that it shall be done with an eye singled to his glory (𝓟, 1830)
  for God **wills** that it shall be done with an eye singled to his glory (1920)

Mormon 8:15
  ▶ with an eye **singled** to his glory (𝓟*, 1830)
  with an eye **single** to his glory (𝓟js, 1837)

Mormon 8:17
  ▶ let him **be aware** lest he shall be in danger of hell fire (𝓟, 1830)
  let him **beware** lest he shall be in danger of hell fire (1874R)

Mormon 8:18
  ▶ let him **be aware** lest he commandeth that which is forbidden (𝓟)
  let him **beware** lest he commandeth that which is forbidden (1830)

Mormon 8:28
  leaders of churches and teachers in the pride of their hearts (𝓟, 1830)
  leaders of churches and teachers **shall rise** in the pride of their hearts (1905ᶜ [1907], 1907)
  ▶ leaders of churches and teachers **shall be lifted up** in the pride of their hearts (conj)

Mormon 8:28
  even to the envying of them who belong to their **church** (𝓟)
  ▶ even to the envying of them who belong to their **churches** (1830)

Mormon 9:3
  ▶ when your souls are racked with a consciousness of **your** guilt (𝓟, 1830, 1908R)
  when your souls are racked with a consciousness of guilt (1837)

Mormon 9:5
  it will kindle a flame of **anguishable** fire upon you (𝓟)
  ▶ it will kindle a flame of **unquenchable** fire upon you (1830)

Mormon 9:15
  have all these things **past** (𝓟, 1830)
  ▶ have all these things **passed** (1920)

Mormon 9:30
  ▶ for I know that ye shall **have** my words (𝓟, 1908R, 1981)
  for I know that ye shall **hear** my words (1830)

Mormon 9:34
  ▶ **and because that none other people knoweth our language** (𝓟, 1830, 1908R, 1981)
  NULL (1837)

Ether title
  ▶ **The** Book of Ether (𝓟, 1849)
  Book of Ether (1830)
  The Book of Ether / **The record of the Jaredites taken from the twenty-four plates
  found by the people of Limhi in the days of king Mosiah** (1920)

Ether 1:19
> ▸ and Kish was the son of **Corom** (𝓟, 1830, 1920)
> and Kish was the son of **Corum** (1837)

Ether 1:34
> and **being** a man highly favored of the Lord / **for** Jared his brother said (𝓟, 1830)
> and a man highly favored of the Lord // Jared his brother said (1920)
> ▸ and **being** a man highly favored of the Lord / **therefore** Jared his brother said (conj)

Ether 1:41
> ▸ and thy **family** . . . and also thy friends and their families (𝓟, 1908R)
> and thy **families** . . . and also thy friends and their families (1830)

Ether 1:43
> ▸ and **this** I will do unto thee (𝓟, 1908R)
> and **thus** I will do unto thee (1830)

Ether 2:11
> ▸ until the fullness **be** come (𝓟, 1830)
> until the fullness come (1837)

Ether 2:13
> and they dwelt in tents **and dwelt in tents** upon the seashore (𝓟, 1830)
> ▸ and they dwelt in tents upon the seashore (conj)

Ether 2:14
> ▸ and it came to pass at the end of **the** four years (𝓟, 1830)
> and it came to pass at the end of four years (1837)

Ether 2:15
> for it shall be a land **of** choice above all other lands (𝓟*)
> ▸ for it shall be a land choice above all other lands (𝓟jg, 1830)

Ether 2:25
> ▸ for **how be it** / ye cannot cross this great deep save I prepare you (𝓟)
> for **howbeit** / ye cannot cross this great deep save I prepare you (1830)
> for ye cannot cross this great deep save I prepare you (1920)

Ether 3:9
> for were it so / ye could not have seen my finger (𝓟, 1830)
> ▸ for were it **not** so / ye could not have seen my finger (1837)

Ether 3:14
> ▸ in me shall all mankind have **life** and that eternally (𝓟, 1908R, 1981)
> in me shall all mankind have **light** and that eternally (1830)

Ether 3:18
> and all this **that** this man **knew** that he was God (𝓟, 1830, 1908R)
> and all this **that** this man **might know** that he was God (1840, 1852)
> ▸ and all this **because that** this man **knew** that he was God (conj)

Ether 4:1
> ▸ and for this cause did king **Benjamin** keep them (𝓟, 1830)
> and for this cause did king **Mosiah** keep them (1849)
> and for this cause did king **Benjamin** [**Mosiah**?] keep them (1908R)
> and for this cause did king **Benjamin** {**Mosiah**?} keep them (1953R)

Ether 4:3
> ▸ and now after that they have **all** dwindled in unbelief (𝓟, 1830, 1908R)
> and now after that they have dwindled in unbelief (1840)

Ether 6:5
- that there should a furious wind blow (𝓟, 1830)

  that there should **be** a furious wind blow (1905)

Ether 8:18

  which combination is **a** most abominable and wicked above all (𝓟*, 1830)
- which combination is most abominable and wicked above all (𝓟js, 1837)

Ether 8:24

  or woe be unto it because of the blood of them which have been slain (𝓟, 1830)
- **for** woe be unto it because of the blood of them which have been slain (conj)

Ether 8:24
- and also upon those who **build** it up (𝓟, 1830)

  and also upon those who **built** it up (1920)

Ether 9:2
- **which were not or which** did not seek his destruction (𝓟*, 1830)

  who did not seek his destruction (𝓟js, 1837)

Ether 9:7
- and kept him upon **a** little or no food (𝓟, 1830)

  and kept him upon little or no food (1837)

Ether 9:22

  yea and he even saw the **Son** of righteousness (𝓟, 1830)
- yea and he even saw the **Sun** of righteousness (conj)

Ether 10:7
- fine workmanship he did cause to be wrought in **prison** (𝓟, 1830, 1908R)

  fine workmanship he did cause to be wrought in **prisons** (1840)

Ether 11:4

  and the brother of **Shiblom** rebelled against him (𝓞, 𝓟, 1830)
- and the brother of **Shiblon** rebelled against him (conj; Ether 1:11–12)

Ether 11:6
- that a **great** curse should come upon the land (𝓞, 𝓟, 1830, 1920)

  that a **greater** curse should come upon the land (1837)

Ether 12:2
- for he could not be **constrained** because of the Spirit of the Lord (𝓟, 1830)

  for he could not be **restrained** because of the Spirit of the Lord (1837)

Ether 12:4

  which hope cometh of faith / maketh an anchor to the souls of men (𝓟, 1830)
- which hope cometh of faith **and** maketh an anchor to the souls of men (conj)

Ether 12:6
- for ye receive no witness **not** until after the trial of your faith (𝓟)

  for ye receive no witness until after the trial of your faith (1830)

Ether 13:2
- all men should serve him which **dwelt** upon the face thereof (𝓟)

  all men should serve him which **dwelleth** upon the face thereof (1830)

  all men should serve him which **dwell** upon the face thereof (1837)

Ether 13:5
- and it should be built **up** unto the house of Israel (𝓟, 1830, 1908R)

  and it should be built unto the house of Israel (1841, 1858w)

Ether 13:8
- ▸ the remnant of the house of Joseph shall be built **up** upon this land (𝒫, 1908R)
  the remnant of the house of Joseph shall be built upon this land (1830)

Ether 13:18
- many people which was slain by the sword those secret combinations (𝒫*)
  many people which was slain by the sword **of** those secret combinations (𝒫jg, 1830)
- ▸ many people which was slain by the sword **by** those secret combinations (conj)

Ether 13:27
- ▸ and they did meet in the valley of Gilgal (𝒪, 𝒫, 1830, 1920)
  and they did meet **him** in the valley of Gilgal (1849)

Ether 13:31
- ▸ and there was none to **constrain** them (𝒫, 1830)
  and there was none to **restrain** them (1837)

Ether 14:1
- ▸ if a man should lay his tool or his sword upon **the** shelf (𝒫, 1830, 1908R)
  if a man should lay his tool or his sword upon **his** shelf (1837)

Ether 14:2
- his property and his own life and **they** of his **wives** and children (𝒫*, 1830)
  his property and his own life and of his **wives** and children (𝒫js, 1837, 1849)
  his property and his own life and of his **wives** and **his** children (1841)
- ▸ his property and his own life and **they** of his **wife** and children (conj)

Ether 14:12
- he fled to the borders **upon** the seashore (𝒫, 1830)
- ▸ he fled to the borders **by** the seashore (conj)

Ether 14:17
- and he did slay both women and children and he did burn the cities **thereof** (𝒫, 1830)
  and he did slay both women and children and he did burn the cities (1920)
- ▸ and he did slay both **men** women and children and he did burn the cities **thereof** (conj)

Ether 14:26
- ▸ even to the borders **by** the seashore (𝒫, 1830, 1981)
  even to the borders **of** the seashore (1837)

Ether 14:28
- ▸ now the valley of Shurr was near the hill **Comron** (𝒫)
  now the valley of Shurr was near the hill **Comnor** (1830)

Ether 15:31
- ▸ Shiz raised **upon** his hands (𝒫, 1830, 1908R)
  Shiz raised **up** his hands (1874R)
  Shiz raised **up on** his hands (1981)

Moroni 7:11
- ▸ a man being **the** servant of the devil cannot follow Christ (𝒫, 1830)
  a man being **a** servant of the devil cannot follow Christ (1837)

Moroni 7:16
- every thing which inviteth to do good and **to persuade** to believe in Christ (𝒫, 1830)
- ▸ every thing which inviteth to do good and **persuadeth** to believe in Christ (conj)

Moroni 7:25
- ▸ by every word which **proceeded** forth out of the mouth of God (𝒫, 1830)
  by every word which **proceedeth** forth out of the mouth of God (1888, 1908R; Matthew 4:4)

Moroni 7:26
> and by faith they **become** the sons of God (𝒫, 1830)
> ► and by faith they **became** the sons of God (1906)

Moroni 7:26
> ► and **assuredly as** Christ liveth (𝒫*, 1830)
> and **as sure as** Christ liveth (𝒫js, 1837)
> and **as surely as** Christ liveth (1981)

Moroni 7:44
> ► none is acceptable before God save the meek and lowly **of** heart (𝒫, 1830)
> none is acceptable before God save the meek and lowly **in** heart (1841)

Moroni 8:12
> ► and a respecter **to** persons (𝒫, 1830, 1849, 1908R)
> and a respecter **of** persons (1841, 1874R)

Moroni 9:24
> many of our brethren have **desented** over unto the Lamanites (𝒫)
> ► many of our brethren have **dissented** over unto the Lamanites (1830)
> many of our brethren have **deserted** over unto the Lamanites (1981)

Moroni 9:24
> and many more will also **desent** over unto them (𝒫)
> ► and many more will also **dissent** over unto them (1830)
> and many more will also **desert** over unto them (1981)

Moroni 10:34
> to meet you before the **pleasing** bar of the great Jehovah (𝒫, 1830)
> ► to meet you before the **pleading** bar of the great Jehovah (conj)

EXTRACANONICAL TEXT

three-witness statement
> ► a record of the people of Nephi and also of the Lamanites **his** brethren (𝒫, 1830)
> a record of the people of Nephi and also of the Lamanites **their** brethren (1837)

three-witness statement
> we beheld and **bear** record (𝒫, 1830, 1908R)
> ► we beheld and **bare** record (1874R)

eight-witness statement
> ► **And also** the testimony of eight witnesses (𝒫, 1830)
> The testimony of eight witnesses (1981)

eight-witness statement
> Joseph Smith Junior / the **author and proprietor** of this work (𝒫, 1830)
> ► Joseph Smith Junior / the **translator** of this work (1837)

A NOTE ON THE TYPE

The text for this book was set in Adobe Minion, a contemporary
typeface designed in 1990 by Robert Slimbach (b. 1956).
As the Principal Type Designer at Adobe Systems, he has created
many original typefaces including Adobe Jensen, Garamond Premier, Arno,
and Myriad (with Carol Twombly). In 1991 he received the Prix Charles Peignot
from the Association Typographique Internationale for excellence
in type design; in 2018 he received the Frederick W. Goudy Award
for Excellence in Typography from the Rochester Institute of Technology.

Slimbach modeled his new typeface after classical old-style types
from the late Renaissance period, and called his typeface Minion
after one of the names denoting a typeface size
in early printing; the word means "a beloved servant."

BOOK DESIGN AND TYPOGRAPHY
BY JONATHAN SALTZMAN